Microsoft® Office 365™
OFFICE 2016

BRIEF

Steven M. Freund

Mary Z. Last

Philip J. Pratt

Susan L. Sebok

Misty E. Vermaat

CENGAGE
Learning®

SHELLY CASHMAN SERIES®

Australia • Brazil • Japan • Korea • Mexico • Singapore • Spain • United Kingdom • United States

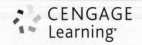
CENGAGE
Learning®

Microsoft® Office 2016: Brief
Steven M. Freund, Mary Z. Last, Philip J. Pratt, Susan L. Sebok, Misty E. Vermaat

SVP, GM Skills & Global Product Management: Dawn Gerrain

Product Director: Kathleen McMahon

Senior Product TeamManager: Lauren Murphy

Associate Product Managers: Reed Curry, William Guiliani, Melissa Stehler

Senior Director, Development: Marah Bellegarde

Product Development Manager: Leigh Hefferon

Managing Content Developer: Emma F. Newsom

Developmental Editors: Amanda Brodkin, Deb Kaufmann, Lyn Markowicz, Lisa Ruffolo, Karen Stevens

Product Assistant: Erica Chapman

Manuscript Quality Assurance: Jeffrey Schwartz, John Freitas, Serge Palladino, Susan Pedicini, Danielle Shaw, Susan Whalen

Senior Production Director: Wendy Troeger

Production Director: Patty Stephan

SeniorContent Project Manager: Matthew Hutchinson

Manufacturing Planner: Julio Esperas

Designer: Diana Graham

Vice President, Marketing: Brian Joyner

Marketing Director: Michele McTighe

Marketing Managers: Stephanie Albrecht

Cover image(s): karawan/Shutterstock.com; Mrs. Opossum/Shutterstock.com

Compositor: Lumina Datamatics, Inc.

Microsoft and the Office logo are either registered trademarks or trademarks of Microsoft Corporation in the United States and/ or other countries. Cengage Learning is an independent entity from the Microsoft Corporation, and not affiliated with Microsoft in any manner.

Mac users: If you're working through this book using a Mac, some of the steps may vary. Additional information for Mac users is included with the data files for this book.

The material in this book was written using Microsoft Office 2016 and was Quality Assurance tested before the publication date. As Microsoft continually updates Office 2016 and Office 365, your software experience may vary slightly from what is seen in the printed text.

Library of Congress Control Number: 2015957840

ISBN-13: 978-1-305-87005-5

ISBN-13: 978-1-305-87037-6 (spiral bound)

Cengage Learning
20 Channel Center Street
Boston, MA 02210
USA

Cengage Learning is a leading provider of customized learning solutions with employees residing in nearly 40 different countries and sales in more than 125 countries around the world. Find your local representative at **www.cengage.com**.

Cengage Learning products are represented in Canada by Nelson Education, Ltd.

To learn more about Cengage Learning, visit **www.cengage.com**

Purchase any of our products at your local college store or at our preferred online store **www.cengagebrain.com**

Printed in the United States of America
Print Number: 01   Print Year: 2016

Microsoft® Office 365™
OFFICE 2016

BRIEF

Contents

Productivity Apps for School and Work
Introduction to OneNote 2016	PA 2
Introduction to Sway	PA 6
Introduction to Office Mix	PA 10
Introduction to Microsoft Edge	PA 14

Microsoft **Office 2016 and Windows 10**

Office 2016 and Windows 10: Essential Concepts and Skills

Objectives	**OFF 1**
Roadmap	OFF 1
Introduction to the Windows 10 Operating System	**OFF 2**
Using a Touch Screen and a Mouse	OFF 3
Scrolling	OFF 4
Keyboard Shortcuts	OFF 5
Starting Windows	OFF 5
To Sign In to an Account	OFF 6
The Windows Desktop	OFF 7
Introduction to Microsoft Office 2016	**OFF 7**
Microsoft Office 2016 Apps	OFF 7
Microsoft Office 2016 Suites	OFF 8
Running and Using an App	**OFF 9**
Word	OFF 9
To Run an App Using the Start Menu and Create a Blank Document	OFF 9
To Maximize a Window	OFF 11
Word Document Window, Ribbon, and Elements Common to Office Apps	OFF 12
To Display a Different Tab on the Ribbon	OFF 16
To Collapse and Expand the Ribbon and Use Full Screen Mode	OFF 17
To Use a Shortcut Menu to Relocate the Quick Access Toolbar	OFF 19
To Customize the Quick Access Toolbar	OFF 20
To Enter Text in a Document	OFF 21
Document Properties	**OFF 22**
To Change Document Properties	OFF 22
Printing, Saving, and Organizing Files	**OFF 23**
Printing a Document	OFF 23
To Print a Document	OFF 23
Organizing Files and Folders	OFF 25
To Create a Folder	OFF 26

Folder Windows	OFF 27
To Create a Folder within a Folder	OFF 28
To Create the Remaining Folders	OFF 28
To Expand a Folder, Scroll through Folder Contents, and Collapse a Folder	OFF 29
To Switch from One App to Another	OFF 30
To Save a File in a Folder	OFF 31
Navigating in Dialog Boxes	OFF 34
To Minimize and Restore a Window	OFF 34
To Save a File on OneDrive	OFF 35
To Sign Out of a Microsoft Account	OFF 37
Screen Resolution	**OFF 38**
To Change the Screen Resolution	OFF 39
To Exit an Office App with One Document Open	OFF 41
To Copy a Folder to OneDrive	OFF 42
To Unlink a OneDrive Account	OFF 44
Additional Microsoft Office Apps	**OFF 45**
PowerPoint	OFF 46
To Run an App Using the Search Box	OFF 47
The PowerPoint Window and Ribbon	OFF 48
To Enter Content in a Title Slide	OFF 49
To Save a File in a Folder	OFF 49
To Create a New Office Document from the Backstage View	OFF 50
To Enter Content in a Title Slide of a Second PowerPoint Presentation	OFF 51
To Save a File in a Folder	OFF 51
To Close an Office File Using the Backstage View	OFF 52
To Open a Recent Office File Using the Backstage View	OFF 52
To Exit an Office App	OFF 53
Excel	OFF 53
To Create a New Blank Office Document from File Explorer	OFF 54
To Run an App from File Explorer and Open a File	OFF 55
Unique Features of Excel	OFF 56
To Enter a Worksheet Title	OFF 57
To Save an Existing Office File with the Same File Name	OFF 58
To Save a File with a New File Name	OFF 59
To Exit an Office App	OFF 59
Access	OFF 59
To Run an App	OFF 59

Unique Elements in Access OFF 60
To Create an Access Database OFF 61
To Close an Office File OFF 62
To Open an Existing Office File OFF 63
To Exit an Office App OFF 63
Other Office Apps **OFF 64**
Outlook OFF 64
Publisher OFF 65
OneNote OFF 66
Renaming, Moving, and Deleting Files **OFF 67**
To Rename a File OFF 68
To Move a File OFF 68
To Delete a File OFF 69
Microsoft Office and Windows Help **OFF 70**
To Open the Help Window
in an Office App OFF 70
Moving and Resizing Windows OFF 70
To Move a Window by Dragging OFF 70
To Resize a Window by Dragging OFF 71
Using Office Help OFF 72
To Obtain Help Using the Search Text Box OFF 72
Obtaining Help while Working in an
Office App OFF 73
To Obtain Help Using the Tell Me Box OFF 74
Using the Windows Search Box OFF 74
To Use the Windows Search Box OFF 74
Summary and Exercises **OFF 75**

Microsoft **Word 2016**

MODULE ONE
Creating, Formatting, and Editing a Word Document with a Picture

Objectives **WD 1**
Introduction **WD 1**
Project — Flyer with a Picture **WD 1**
To Run Word and Specify Settings WD 3
Entering Text **WD 3**
To Type Text WD 4
To Display Formatting Marks WD 5
To Insert a Blank Line WD 5
To Zoom Page Width WD 6
Wordwrap WD 7
To Wordwrap Text as You Type WD 7
Spelling and Grammar Check WD 8
To Check Spelling and Grammar as You Type WD 8
To Enter More Text WD 9
Navigating a Document WD 10
Formatting Paragraphs and Characters **WD 11**
Font, Font Sizes, and Themes WD 12
To Center a Paragraph WD 13
To Center Another Paragraph WD 13
Formatting Single versus Multiple Paragraphs
and Characters WD 14
To Select a Line WD 14
To Change the Font Size of Selected Text WD 15
To Change the Font of Selected Text WD 16
To Change the Case of Selected Text WD 17
To Apply a Text Effect to Selected Text WD 18
To Shade a Paragraph WD 19

To Select Multiple Lines WD 20
To Change the Font Size of Selected Text WD 20
To Bullet a List of Paragraphs WD 21
To Undo and Redo an Action WD 22
To Italicize Text WD 23
To Color Text WD 24
To Use the Mini Toolbar to Format Text WD 25
To Select a Group of Words WD 26
To Underline Text WD 27
To Bold Text WD 27
To Zoom One Page WD 28
To Change Theme Colors WD 29
To Zoom Page Width WD 30
Selecting Text WD 30
Inserting and Formatting a Picture
in a Word Document **WD 31**
To Center Another Paragraph WD 31
To Insert a Picture WD 31
To Zoom the Document WD 33
To Resize a Graphic WD 34
To Zoom 100% WD 35
To Apply a Picture Style WD 36
To Apply Picture Effects WD 37
Enhancing the Page **WD 38**
To Add a Page Border WD 39
To Zoom One Page WD 40
To Change Spacing before and
after Paragraphs WD 40
To Center Page Contents Vertically WD 41
To Save the Document and Exit Word WD 42
Correcting Errors and Revising a Document **WD 42**
Types of Changes Made to Documents WD 43
To Run Word, Open a Document, and
Specify Settings WD 43
To Insert Text in an Existing Document WD 43
To Delete Text WD 44
To Move Text WD 44
To Save and Print the Document WD 45
To Switch to Read Mode WD 46
To Switch to Print Layout View WD 46
Summary and Exercises **WD 47**

MODULE TWO
Creating a Research Paper with References and Sources

Objectives **WD 57**
Introduction **WD 57**
Project — Research Paper **WD 57**
MLA Documentation Style WD 58
Changing Document Settings **WD 60**
To Run Word and Specify Settings WD 60
Styles WD 60
To Modify a Style WD 61
Adjusting Line and Paragraph Spacing WD 62
To Change Line Spacing WD 62
To Remove Space after a Paragraph WD 63
To Update a Style to Match a Selection WD 64
Creating a Header **WD 64**
To Switch to the Header WD 65
To Right-Align a Paragraph WD 66
To Enter Text WD 66

To Insert a Page Number   WD 66
To Close the Header   WD 68
Typing the Research Paper Text   **WD 68**
To Enter Name and Course Information   WD 69
To Click and Type   WD 70
Keyboard Shortcuts   WD 71
To Format Text Using a Keyboard Shortcut   WD 71
To Display the Rulers   WD 72
To First-Line Indent Paragraphs   WD 72
To AutoCorrect as You Type   WD 74
To Use the AutoCorrect Options Button   WD 75
To Create an AutoCorrect Entry   WD 75
The AutoCorrect Dialog Box   WD 77
To Enter More Text   WD 77
Citations   WD 78
To Change the Bibliography Style   WD 78
To Insert a Citation and Create Its Source   WD 79
To Enter More Text   WD 81
Footnotes   WD 82
To Insert a Footnote Reference Mark   WD 82
To Enter Footnote Text   WD 83
To Insert a Citation Placeholder   WD 83
Footnote Text Style   WD 84
To Modify a Style Using a Shortcut Menu   WD 84
To Edit a Source   WD 86
To Edit a Citation   WD 88
Working with Footnotes and Endnotes   WD 89
To Enter More Text   WD 90
To Count Words   WD 90
Automatic Page Breaks   WD 91
To Enter More Text and Insert a Citation
    Placeholder   WD 91
To Hide and Show White Space   WD 92
To Edit a Source   WD 93
To Enter More Text   WD 94
Creating an Alphabetical Works Cited Page   **WD 95**
To Page Break Manually   WD 95
To Apply a Style   WD 96
To Center Text   WD 96
To Create a Bibliographical List   WD 96
Proofreading and Revising the
    Research Paper   **WD 98**
To Modify a Source   WD 99
To Update a Field   WD 99
To Go to a Page   WD 101
Copying, Cutting, and Pasting   WD 101
To Copy and Paste   WD 102
To Display the Paste Options Menu   WD 103
To Find Text   WD 103
To Replace Text   WD 104
Find and Replace Dialog Box   WD 105
To Find and Insert a Synonym   WD 105
To Check Spelling and Grammar at Once   WD 106
The Main and Custom Dictionaries   WD 107
To Look Up Information   WD 108
To Zoom Multiple Pages   WD 109
To Change Read Mode Color   WD 110
To Save and Print the Document and
    Exit Word   WD 111
Summary and Exercises   **WD 111**

Microsoft **PowerPoint 2016**

MODULE ONE
Creating and Editing a Presentation with Pictures

Objectives   **PPT 1**
Introduction   **PPT 1**
Project — Presentation with a Bulleted List
    and Pictures   **PPT 2**
Choosing a Document Theme and Variant   **PPT 3**
To Choose a Document Theme
    and Variant   PPT 3
Creating a Title Slide   **PPT 5**
To Enter the Presentation Title   PPT 6
Correcting a Mistake When Typing   PPT 7
Paragraphs   PPT 7
To Enter the Presentation
    Subtitle Paragraph   PPT 7
To Zoom a Slide   PPT 8
Formatting Characters in a Presentation   **PPT 9**
Fonts and Font Styles   PPT 9
To Select a Paragraph   PPT 9
To Italicize Text   PPT 10
To Increase Font Size   PPT 10
To Select a Word   PPT 11
To Change the Text Color   PPT 11
Adding a New Slide to a Presentation   **PPT 12**
To Add a New Text Slide with
    a Bulleted List   PPT 12
Creating a Text Slide with a Multilevel Bulleted List   **PPT 13**
To Enter a Slide Title   PPT 14
To Select a Text Placeholder   PPT 15
To Type a Multilevel Bulleted List   PPT 15
To Type the Remaining Text for Slide 2   PPT 17
To Select a Group of Words   PPT 17
To Bold Text   PPT 18
To Increase Font Size   PPT 18
Adding New Slides, Changing Slide Layouts,
    and Changing the Theme   **PPT 19**
To Add a New Slide and Enter
    a Slide Title and Headings   PPT 19
To Add a Slide with the Title Only Layout   PPT 21
To Enter a Slide Title   PPT 23
To Change the Theme   PPT 23
To Change the Variant   PPT 25
Powerpoint Views   **PPT 26**
To Move to Another Slide in Normal View   PPT 26
Inserting Pictures into Slides   **PPT 28**
To Insert a Picture into the Title Slide   PPT 28
To Insert a Picture into a Slide without a
    Content Placeholder   PPT 29
To Insert a Picture into a Content Placeholder   PPT 30
To Insert a Picture into a Slide without a
    Content Placeholder   PPT 31
Resizing Photos and Illustrations   **PPT 32**
To Proportionally Resize Pictures   PPT 32
To Nonproportionally Resize the
    Photograph on Slide 2   PPT 33

To Resize the Illustration on Slide 4 .... PPT 34
To Move Pictures .... PPT 35
To Rotate a Picture .... PPT 36
Ending a Slide Show with a Closing Slide .... **PPT 37**
To Duplicate a Slide .... PPT 38
To Arrange a Slide .... PPT 39
Making Changes to Slide Text Content .... **PPT 39**
Replacing Text in an Existing Slide .... PPT 40
Deleting Text .... PPT 40
To Delete Text in a Placeholder .... PPT 40
Adding a Transition .... **PPT 42**
To Add a Transition between Slides .... PPT 42
Document Properties .... PPT 44
Viewing the Presentation in Slide Show View .... **PPT 45**
To Start Slide Show View .... PPT 45
To Move Manually through Slides in
a Slide Show .... PPT 46
To Save and Print the Presentation .... PPT 47
Summary and Exercises .... **PPT 48**

MODULE TWO
**Enhancing a Presentation with
Pictures, Shapes, and WordArt**
Objectives .... PPT 57
Introduction .... PPT 57
Project — Presentation with Pictures,
Shapes, and Wordart .... PPT 57
Downloading a Theme and Editing Slides .... PPT 59
To Search for and Download an Online Theme .... PPT 59
To Delete a Slide .... PPT 60
To Create a Title Slide .... PPT 61
To Create the First Text Slide .... PPT 62
To Create the Second Text Slide .... PPT 63
Inserting and Formatting Pictures in a Presentation .... PPT 63
To Insert a Picture into a Slide
without a Content Placeholder .... PPT 63
To Change a Picture .... PPT 65
To Correct a Picture .... PPT 66
To Apply a Picture Style .... PPT 67
To Add a Picture Border .... PPT 68
To Change a Picture Border Color .... PPT 69
To Apply Picture Effects .... PPT 70
Inserting and Formatting a Shape .... **PPT 71**
To Add a Shape .... PPT 72
To Resize a Shape .... PPT 73
To Add Other Shapes .... PPT 74
To Apply a Shape Style .... PPT 75
To Apply Another Style .... PPT 77
To Add Text to a Shape .... PPT 78
To Change the Font .... PPT 78
To Format the Text .... PPT 79
Format Painter .... PPT 80
To Format Text Using the Format Painter .... PPT 80
To Copy and Paste a Shape .... PPT 81
Formatting Slide Backgrounds .... **PPT 83**
To Insert a Texture Fill .... PPT 84
To Format the Background Texture
Fill Transparency .... PPT 86
To Insert a Gradient Fill .... PPT 86
To Insert a Picture to Create a Background .... PPT 87
To Format the Background Picture
Fill Transparency .... PPT 88

Inserting and Formatting Wordart .... **PPT 88**
To Insert WordArt .... PPT 89
To Change the WordArt Shape .... PPT 90
To Apply a WordArt Text Fill .... PPT 91
To Change the Weight of the WordArt Outline .... PPT 92
To Change the Color of the
WordArt Outline .... PPT 93
Reviewing and Revising Individual Slides .... **PPT 94**
Replace Dialog Box .... PPT 94
To Find and Insert a Synonym .... PPT 94
To Add Notes .... PPT 95
To Find and Replace Text .... PPT 96
Checking Spelling .... PPT 97
To Check Spelling .... PPT 98
To Add a Transition between Slides .... PPT 100
To Print Speaker Notes .... PPT 101
To Save and Print the Presentation .... PPT 102
Summary and Exercises .... **PPT 103**

Microsoft **Excel 2016**

MODULE ONE
Creating a Worksheet and a Chart
Objectives .... EX 1
Introduction .... EX 1
Project — Personal Budget Worksheet
and a Chart .... EX 1
Selecting a Cell .... EX 4
Entering Text .... EX 4
To Enter the Worksheet Titles .... EX 5
AutoCorrect .... EX 7
To Enter Column Titles .... EX 7
To Enter Row Titles .... EX 9
Entering Numbers .... EX 9
To Enter Numbers .... EX 10
Calculating a Sum .... EX 12
To Sum a Column of Numbers .... EX 12
Using the Fill Handle to Copy a Cell to
Adjacent Cells .... EX 13
To Copy a Cell to Adjacent Cells in a Row .... EX 14
To Calculate Multiple Totals at the
Same Time .... EX 16
To Enter a Formula Using the Keyboard .... EX 18
To Copy a Cell to Adjacent Cells in a Row .... EX 19
Formatting the Worksheet .... EX 19
Font Style, Size, and Color .... EX 21
To Change a Cell Style .... EX 21
To Change the Font .... EX 22
To Apply Bold Style to a Cell .... EX 23
To Increase the Font Size of a Cell Entry .... EX 24
To Change the Font Color of a Cell Entry .... EX 25
To Center Cell Entries across Columns
by Merging Cells .... EX 26
To Format Rows Using Cell Styles .... EX 27
To Format Numbers in the Worksheet .... EX 29
To Adjust the Column Width .... EX 31
To Use the Name Box to Select a Cell .... EX 32
Other Ways to Select Cells .... EX 33
Adding a Pie Chart to the Worksheet .... EX 33
To Add a 3-D Pie Chart .... EX 35
To Apply a Style to a Chart .... EX 36

Changing the Sheet Tab Names	**EX 37**
To Move a Chart to a New Sheet	EX 38
To Change the Sheet Tab Name	EX 39
Document Properties	EX 40
Printing a Worksheet	**EX 41**
To Preview and Print a Worksheet in Landscape Orientation	EX 41
Autocalculate	**EX 43**
To Use the AutoCalculate Area to Determine a Maximum	EX 44
Correcting Errors	**EX 45**
Correcting Errors while Entering Data into a Cell	EX 45
Correcting Errors after Entering Data into a Cell	EX 45
Undoing the Last Cell Entry	EX 46
Clearing a Cell or Range of Cells	EX 47
Clearing the Entire Worksheet	EX 48
Summary and Exercises	**EX 49**

MODULE TWO
Formulas, Functions, and Formatting

Objectives	**EX 57**
Introduction	**EX 57**
Project — Worksheet with Formulas and Functions	**EX 58**
Entering the Titles and Numbers into the Worksheet	**EX 60**
To Enter the Worksheet Title and Subtitle	EX 61
To Enter the Column Titles	EX 61
To Enter the Salary Data	EX 62
Flash Fill	**EX 62**
To Use Flash Fill	EX 63
To Enter the Row Titles	EX 64
To Change the Sheet Tab Name and Color	EX 64
Entering Formulas	**EX 65**
To Enter a Formula Using the Keyboard	EX 65
Arithmetic Operations	EX 66
Order of Operations	EX 66
To Enter Formulas Using Point Mode	EX 67
To Copy Formulas Using the Fill Handle	EX 69
Option Buttons	**EX 70**
To Determine Totals Using the Sum Button	EX 70
To Determine the Total Tax Percentage	EX 71
Using the AVERAGE, MAX, and MIN Functions	**EX 72**
To Determine the Highest Number in a Range of Numbers Using the Insert Function Dialog Box	EX 72
To Determine the Lowest Number in a Range of Numbers Using the Sum Menu	EX 74
To Determine the Average of a Range of Numbers Using the Keyboard	EX 76
To Copy a Range of Cells across Columns to an Adjacent Range Using the Fill Handle	EX 77
Verifying Formulas Using Range Finder	**EX 78**
To Verify a Formula Using Range Finder	EX 78
Formatting the Worksheet	**EX 79**
To Change the Workbook Theme	EX 80
To Format the Worksheet Titles	EX 81
To Change the Background Color and Apply a Box Border to the Worksheet Title and Subtitle	EX 82
To Apply a Cell Style to the Column Headings and Format the Total Rows	EX 83
To Format Dates and Center Data in Cells	EX 84
To Apply an Accounting Number Format and Comma Style Format Using the Ribbon	EX 85
To Apply a Currency Style Format with a Floating Dollar Sign Using the Format Cells Dialog Box	EX 86
To Apply a Percent Style Format and Use the Increase Decimal Button	EX 87
Conditional Formatting	EX 87
To Apply Conditional Formatting	EX 88
Conditional Formatting Operators	EX 91
Changing Column Width and Row Height	EX 91
To Change Column Width	EX 91
To Change Row Height	EX 94
Checking Spelling	**EX 95**
To Check Spelling on the Worksheet	EX 96
Additional Spelling Checker Considerations	EX 97
Printing the Worksheet	**EX 97**
To Change the Worksheet's Margins, Header, and Orientation in Page Layout View	EX 98
To Print a Worksheet	EX 100
To Print a Section of the Worksheet	EX 101
Displaying and Printing the Formulas Version of the Worksheet	**EX 102**
To Display the Formulas in the Worksheet and Fit the Printout on One Page	EX 103
To Change the Print Scaling Option Back to 100%	EX 104
Summary and Exercises	**EX 105**

Microsoft Access 2016

MODULE ONE
Databases and Database Objects: An Introduction

Objectives	**AC 1**
Introduction	**AC 1**
Project — Database Creation	**AC 1**
Creating a Database	**AC 4**
To Create a Database	AC 4
To Create a Database Using a Template	AC 5
The Access Window	**AC 5**
Navigation Pane and Access Work Area	AC 6
Determining Tables and Fields	**AC 6**
Naming Tables and Fields	AC 6
Determining the Primary Key	AC 6
Determining Data Types for the Fields	AC 7
Creating a Table	**AC 8**
To Modify the Primary Key	AC 10
To Define the Remaining Fields in a Table	AC 11
Making Changes to the Structure	AC 12
To Save a Table	AC 13
To View the Table in Design View	AC 14
Checking the Structure in Design View	AC 14
To Change a Field Size in Design View	AC 15
To Close the Table	AC 16
To Add Records to a Table	AC 17
Making Changes to the Data	AC 20
To Add Records to a Table that Contains Data	AC 20
To Resize Columns in a Datasheet	AC 23
Previewing and Printing the Contents of a Table	**AC 24**
To Preview and Print the Contents of a Table	AC 25

Importing or Linking Data From Other
    Applications to Access **AC 27**
  To Import an Excel Worksheet AC 28
  Modifying the Table AC 31
  To Modify a Table in Design View AC 31
  Correcting Errors in the Structure AC 33
  To Close the Table AC 33
  To Resize Columns in a Datasheet AC 33
Additional Database Objects **AC 34**
  Creating Queries AC 34
  To Use the Simple Query Wizard to Create a Query AC 34
  Using Queries AC 36
  To Use a Criterion in a Query AC 37
  To Print the Results of a Query AC 38
  Creating Forms AC 39
  To Create a Form AC 39
  Using a Form AC 41
  Creating and Printing Reports AC 41
  To Create a Report AC 41
  Using Layout View in a Report AC 43
  To Modify Report Column Headings
    and Resize Columns AC 43
  To Add Totals to a Report AC 46
  To Print a Report AC 47
Database Properties **AC 47**
  To Change Database Properties AC 48
Special Database Operations **AC 48**
  Backup and Recovery AC 48
  Compacting and Repairing a Database AC 49
  Additional Operations AC 49
  To Exit Access AC 50
Database Design **AC 50**
  Database Requirements AC 51
  Database Design Process AC 52
  Identifying the Tables AC 53
  Determining the Primary Keys AC 53
  Determining Additional Fields AC 53
  Determining and Implementing
    Relationships between the Tables AC 54
  Assigning Data Types to the Fields AC 54
  Identifying and Removing Redundancy AC 54
Summary and Exercises **AC 56**

MODULE TWO
Querying a Database
Objectives **AC 65**
Introduction **AC 65**
Project — Querying a Database **AC 65**
Creating Queries **AC 67**
  To Create a Query in Design View AC 67
  To Add Fields to the Design Grid AC 69

  Determining Criteria AC 69
  Running the Query AC 69
  To Use Text Data in a Criterion AC 70
  Using Saved Queries AC 71
  Wildcards AC 72
  To Use a Wildcard AC 72
  To Use Criteria for a Field Not Included
    in the Results AC 74
  Creating a Parameter Query AC 75
  To Create and View a Parameter Query AC 76
  To Use a Parameter Query AC 77
  To Use a Number in a Criterion AC 78
  Comparison Operators AC 79
  To Use a Comparison Operator in a Criterion AC 79
  Using Compound Criteria AC 80
  To Use a Compound Criterion Involving AND AC 80
  To Use a Compound Criterion Involving OR AC 81
  Special Criteria AC 82
Sorting **AC 83**
  To Clear the Design Grid AC 83
  To Sort Data in a Query AC 84
  To Omit Duplicates AC 85
  To Sort on Multiple Keys AC 86
  To Create a Top-Values Query AC 88
Joining Tables **AC 89**
  To Join Tables AC 90
  To Change Join Properties AC 92
  To Create a Report from a Query AC 94
  To Print a Report AC 95
Creating a Form for a Query **AC 96**
  To Create a Form for a Query AC 96
  Using a Form AC 97
Exporting Data From Access to Other
    Applications **AC 97**
  To Export Data to Excel AC 98
  Text Files AC 100
Adding Criteria to a Join Query **AC 101**
  To Restrict the Records in a Join AC 102
Calculations **AC 102**
  To Use a Calculated Field in a Query AC 103
  To Change a Caption AC 104
  To Calculate Statistics AC 106
  To Use Criteria in Calculating Statistics AC 107
  To Use Grouping AC 108
Crosstab Queries **AC 108**
  To Create a Crosstab Query AC 109
Customizing the Navigation Pane **AC 111**
  To Customize the Navigation Pane AC 112
Summary and Exercises **AC 113**

Index **IND 1**

Productivity Apps for School and Work

Corinne Hoisington

Lochlan keeps track of his class notes, football plays, and internship meetings with OneNote.

Zoe is using the annotation features of Microsoft Edge to take and save web notes for her research paper.

Nori is creating a Sway site to highlight this year's activities for the Student Government Association.

Hunter is adding interactive videos and screen recordings to his PowerPoint resume.

© Rawpixel/Shutterstock.com

Being computer literate no longer means mastery of only Word, Excel, PowerPoint, Outlook, and Access. To become technology power users, Hunter, Nori, Zoe, and Lochlan are exploring Microsoft OneNote, Sway, Mix, and Edge in Office 2016 and Windows 10.

In this Module

Introduction to OneNote 2016 2
Introduction to Sway 6
Introduction to Office Mix 10
Introduction to Microsoft Edge.............. 14

Learn to use productivity apps!
Links to companion **Sways**, featuring **videos** with hands-on instructions, are located on www.cengagebrain.com.

Introduction to OneNote 2016

notebook | section tab | To Do tag | screen clipping | note | template | Microsoft OneNote Mobile app | sync | drawing canvas | inked handwriting | Ink to Text

As you glance around any classroom, you invariably see paper notebooks and notepads on each desk. Because deciphering and sharing handwritten notes can be a challenge, Microsoft OneNote 2016 replaces physical notebooks, binders, and paper notes with a searchable, digital notebook. OneNote captures your ideas and schoolwork on any device so you can stay organized, share notes, and work with others on projects. Whether you are a student taking class notes as shown in **Figure 1** or an employee taking notes in company meetings, OneNote is the one place to keep notes for all of your projects.

Figure 1: OneNote 2016 notebook

Each **notebook** is divided into sections, also called **section tabs**, by subject or topic.

Use **To Do tags**, icons that help you keep track of your assignments and other tasks.

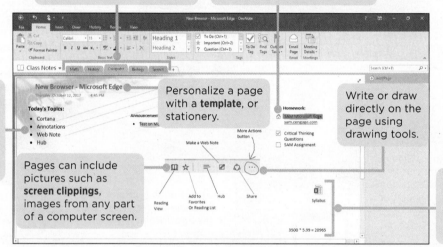

Type on a page to add a **note**, a small window that contains text or other types of information.

Personalize a page with a **template**, or stationery.

Write or draw directly on the page using drawing tools.

Pages can include pictures such as **screen clippings**, images from any part of a computer screen.

Attach files and enter equations so you have everything you need in one place.

Creating a OneNote Notebook

OneNote is divided into sections similar to those in a spiral-bound notebook. Each OneNote notebook contains sections, pages, and other notebooks. You can use One-Note for school, business, and personal projects. Store information for each type of project in different notebooks to keep your tasks separate, or use any other organization that suits you. OneNote is flexible enough to adapt to the way you want to work.

When you create a notebook, it contains a blank page with a plain white background by default, though you can use templates, or stationery, to apply designs in categories such as Academic, Business, Decorative, and Planners. Start typing or use the buttons on the Insert tab to insert notes, which are small resizable windows that can contain text, equations, tables, on-screen writing, images, audio and video recordings, to-do lists, file attachments, and file printouts. Add as many notes as you need to each page.

Syncing a Notebook to the Cloud

OneNote saves your notes every time you make a change in a notebook. To make sure you can access your notebooks with a laptop, tablet, or smartphone wherever you are, OneNote uses cloud-based storage, such as OneDrive or SharePoint. **Microsoft OneNote Mobile app**, a lightweight version of OneNote 2016 shown in **Figure 2**, is available for free in the Windows Store, Google Play for Android devices, and the AppStore for iOS devices.

If you have a Microsoft account, OneNote saves your notes on OneDrive automatically for all your mobile devices and computers, which is called **syncing**. For example, you can use OneNote to take notes on your laptop during class, and then open OneNote on your phone to study later. To use a notebook stored on your computer with your OneNote Mobile app, move the notebook to OneDrive. You can quickly share notebook content with other people using OneDrive.

Figure 2: Microsoft OneNote Mobile app

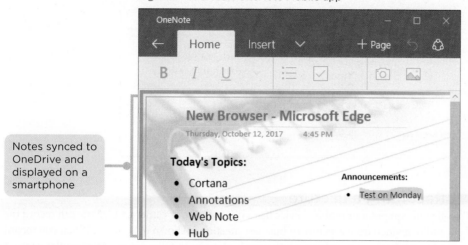

Notes synced to OneDrive and displayed on a smartphone

Taking Notes

Use OneNote pages to organize your notes by class and topic or lecture. Beyond simple typed notes, OneNote stores drawings, converts handwriting to searchable text and mathematical sketches to equations, and records audio and video.

OneNote includes drawing tools that let you sketch freehand drawings such as biological cell diagrams and financial supply-and-demand charts. As shown in **Figure 3**, the Draw tab on the ribbon provides these drawing tools along with shapes so you can insert diagrams and other illustrations to represent your ideas. When you draw on a page, OneNote creates a **drawing canvas**, which is a container for shapes and lines.

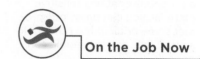

On the Job Now

OneNote is ideal for taking notes during meetings, whether you are recording minutes, documenting a discussion, sketching product diagrams, or listing follow-up items. Use a meeting template to add pages with content appropriate for meetings.

Figure 3: Tools on the Draw tab

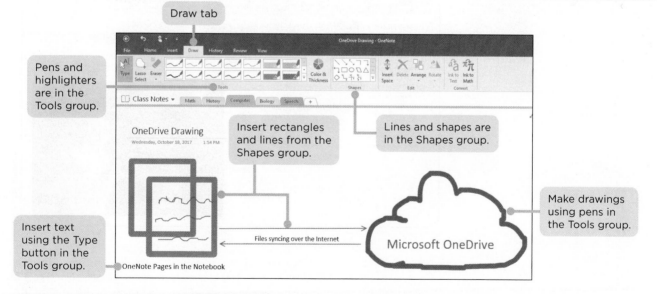

Draw tab

Pens and highlighters are in the Tools group.

Insert rectangles and lines from the Shapes group.

Lines and shapes are in the Shapes group.

Insert text using the Type button in the Tools group.

Make drawings using pens in the Tools group.

OneNote Pages in the Notebook

Files syncing over the Internet

Microsoft OneDrive

Converting Handwriting to Text

When you use a pen tool to write on a notebook page, the text you enter is called **inked handwriting**. OneNote can convert inked handwriting to typed text when you use the **Ink to Text** button in the Convert group on the Draw tab, as shown in **Figure 4**. After OneNote converts the handwriting to text, you can use the Search box to find terms in the converted text or any other note in your notebooks.

Figure 4: Converting handwriting to text

On the Job Now

Use OneNote as a place to brainstorm ongoing work projects. If a notebook contains sensitive material, you can password-protect some or all of the notebook so that only certain people can open it.

Recording a Lecture

If your computer or mobile device has a microphone or camera, OneNote can record the audio or video from a lecture or business meeting as shown in **Figure 5**. When you record a lecture (with your instructor's permission), you can follow along, take regular notes at your own pace, and review the video recording later. You can control the start, pause, and stop motions of the recording when you play back the recording of your notes.

Figure 5: Video inserted in a notebook

Try This Now

Learn to use OneNote!
Links to companion **Sways**, featuring **videos** with hands-on instructions, are located on www.cengagebrain.com.

1: Taking Notes for a Week

As a student, you can get organized by using OneNote to take detailed notes in your classes. Perform the following tasks:

   a. Create a new OneNote notebook on your Microsoft OneDrive account (the default location for new notebooks). Name the notebook with your first name followed by "Notes," as in **Caleb Notes**.

   b. Create four section tabs, each with a different class name.

   c. Take detailed notes in those classes for one week. Be sure to include notes, drawings, and other types of content.

   d. Sync your notes with your OneDrive. Submit your assignment in the format specified by your instructor.

2: Using OneNote to Organize a Research Paper

You have a research paper due on the topic of three habits of successful students. Use OneNote to organize your research. Perform the following tasks:

   a. Create a new OneNote notebook on your Microsoft OneDrive account. Name the notebook **Success Research**.

   b. Create three section tabs with the following names:

- **Take Detailed Notes**
- **Be Respectful in Class**
- **Come to Class Prepared**

   c. On the web, research the topics and find three sources for each section. Copy a sentence from each source and paste the sentence into the appropriate section. When you paste the sentence, OneNote inserts it in a note with a link to the source.

   d. Sync your notes with your OneDrive. Submit your assignment in the format specified by your instructor.

3: Planning Your Career

Note: This activity requires a webcam or built-in video camera on any type of device.

Consider an occupation that interests you. Using OneNote, examine the responsibilities, education requirements, potential salary, and employment outlook of a specific career. Perform the following tasks:

   a. Create a new OneNote notebook on your Microsoft OneDrive account. Name the notebook with your first name followed by a career title, such as **Kara - App Developer**.

   b. Create four section tabs with the names **Responsibilities, Education Requirements, Median Salary**, and **Employment Outlook**.

   c. Research the responsibilities of your career path. Using OneNote, record a short video (approximately 30 seconds) of yourself explaining the responsibilities of your career path. Place the video in the Responsibilities section.

   d. On the web, research the educational requirements for your career path and find two appropriate sources. Copy a paragraph from each source and paste them into the appropriate section. When you paste a paragraph, OneNote inserts it in a note with a link to the source.

   e. Research the median salary for a single year for this career. Create a mathematical equation in the Median Salary section that multiplies the amount of the median salary times 20 years to calculate how much you will possibly earn.

   f. For the Employment Outlook section, research the outlook for your career path. Take at least four notes about what you find when researching the topic.

   g. Sync your notes with your OneDrive. Submit your assignment in the format specified by your instructor.

Introduction to Sway

Sway site | responsive design | Storyline | card | Creative Commons license | animation emphasis effects | Docs.com

Bottom Line
- Drag photos, videos, and files from your computer and content from Facebook and Twitter directly to your Sway presentation.
- Run Sway in a web browser or as an app on your smartphone, and save presentations as webpages.

Expressing your ideas in a presentation typically means creating PowerPoint slides or a Word document. Microsoft Sway gives you another way to engage an audience. Sway is a free Microsoft tool available at Sway.com or as an app in Office 365. Using Sway, you can combine text, images, videos, and social media in a website called a **Sway site** that you can share and display on any device. To get started, you create a digital story on a web-based canvas without borders, slides, cells, or page breaks. A Sway site organizes the text, images, and video into a **responsive design**, which means your content adapts perfectly to any screen size as shown in **Figure 6**. You store a Sway site in the cloud on OneDrive using a free Microsoft account.

Figure 6: Sway site with responsive design

You can display a Sway presentation in a web browser.

Sway uses responsive design to make sure pages fit perfectly on any device.

© iStock.com/marinello, © iStock.com/marekuliasz

Learn to use Sway!
Links to companion **Sways**, featuring **videos** with hands-on instructions, are located on www.cengagebrain.com.

Creating a Sway Presentation

You can use Sway to build a digital flyer, a club newsletter, a vacation blog, an informational site, a digital art portfolio, or a new product rollout. After you select your topic and sign into Sway with your Microsoft account, a **Storyline** opens, providing tools and a work area for composing your digital story. See **Figure 7**. Each story can include text, images, and videos. You create a Sway by adding text and media content into a Storyline section, or **card**. To add pictures, videos, or documents, select a card in the left pane and then select the Insert Content button. The first card in a Sway presentation contains a title and background image.

Figure 7: Creating a Sway site

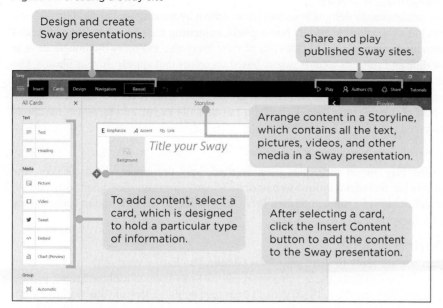

Design and create Sway presentations.

Share and play published Sway sites.

Arrange content in a Storyline, which contains all the text, pictures, videos, and other media in a Sway presentation.

To add content, select a card, which is designed to hold a particular type of information.

After selecting a card, click the Insert Content button to add the content to the Sway presentation.

Adding Content to Build a Story

As you work, Sway searches the Internet to help you find relevant images, videos, tweets, and other content from online sources such as Bing, YouTube, Twitter, and Facebook. You can drag content from the search results right into the Storyline. In addition, you can upload your own images and videos directly in the presentation. For example, if you are creating a Sway presentation about the market for commercial drones, Sway suggests content to incorporate into the presentation by displaying it in the left pane as search results. The search results include drone images tagged with **Creative Commons license** at online sources as shown in **Figure 8**. A Creative Commons license is a public copyright license that allows the free distribution of an otherwise copyrighted work. In addition, you can specify the source of the media. For example, you can add your own Facebook or OneNote pictures and videos in Sway without leaving the app.

On the Job Now

If you have a Microsoft Word document containing an outline of your business content, drag the outline into Sway to create a card for each topic.

Figure 8: Images in Sway search results

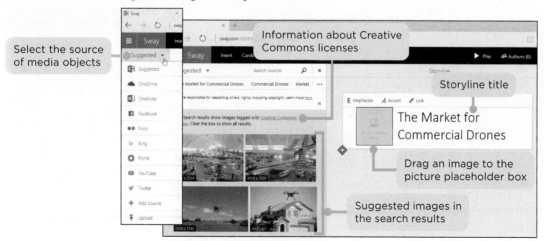

Select the source of media objects

Information about Creative Commons licenses

Storyline title

The Market for Commercial Drones

Drag an image to the picture placeholder box

Suggested images in the search results

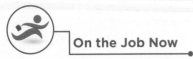

Designing a Sway

Sway professionally designs your Storyline content by resizing background images and fonts to fit your display, and by floating text, animating media, embedding video, and removing images as a page scrolls out of view. Sway also evaluates the images in your Storyline and suggests a color palette based on colors that appear in your photos. Use the Design button to display tools including color palettes, font choices, **animation emphasis effects**, and style templates to provide a personality for a Sway presentation. Instead of creating your own design, you can click the Remix button, which randomly selects unique designs for your Sway site.

Publishing a Sway

Use the Play button to display your finished Sway presentation as a website. The Address bar includes a unique web address where others can view your Sway site. As the author, you can edit a published Sway site by clicking the Edit button (pencil icon) on the Sway toolbar.

Sharing a Sway

When you are ready to share your Sway website, you have several options as shown in Figure 9. Use the Share slider button to share the Sway site publically or keep it private. If you add the Sway site to the Microsoft **Docs.com** public gallery, anyone worldwide can use Bing, Google, or other search engines to find, view, and share your Sway site. You can also share your Sway site using Facebook, Twitter, Google+, Yammer, and other social media sites. Link your presentation to any webpage or email the link to your audience. Sway can also generate a code for embedding the link within another webpage.

Figure 9: Sharing a Sway site

Try This Now

1: Creating a Sway Resume

Sway is a digital storytelling app. Create a Sway resume to share the skills, job experiences, and achievements you have that match the requirements of a future job interest. Perform the following tasks:

a. Create a new presentation in Sway to use as a digital resume. Title the Sway Storyline with your full name and then select a background image.
b. Create three separate sections titled **Academic Background, Work Experience**, and **Skills**, and insert text, a picture, and a paragraph or bulleted points in each section. Be sure to include your own picture.
c. Add a fourth section that includes a video about your school that you find online.
d. Customize the design of your presentation.
e. Submit your assignment link in the format specified by your instructor.

2: Creating an Online Sway Newsletter

Newsletters are designed to capture the attention of their target audience. Using Sway, create a newsletter for a club, organization, or your favorite music group. Perform the following tasks:

a. Create a new presentation in Sway to use as a digital newsletter for a club, organization, or your favorite music group. Provide a title for the Sway Storyline and select an appropriate background image.
b. Select three separate sections with appropriate titles, such as Upcoming Events. In each section, insert text, a picture, and a paragraph or bulleted points.
c. Add a fourth section that includes a video about your selected topic.
d. Customize the design of your presentation.
e. Submit your assignment link in the format specified by your instructor.

3: Creating and Sharing a Technology Presentation

To place a Sway presentation in the hands of your entire audience, you can share a link to the Sway presentation. Create a Sway presentation on a new technology and share it with your class. Perform the following tasks:

a. Create a new presentation in Sway about a cutting-edge technology topic. Provide a title for the Sway Storyline and select a background image.
b. Create four separate sections about your topic, and include text, a picture, and a paragraph in each section.
c. Add a fifth section that includes a video about your topic.
d. Customize the design of your presentation.
e. Share the link to your Sway with your classmates and submit your assignment link in the format specified by your instructor.

Introduction to Office Mix

add-in | clip | slide recording | Slide Notes | screen recording | free-response quiz

To enliven business meetings and lectures, Microsoft adds a new dimension to presentations with a powerful toolset called Office Mix, a free add-in for PowerPoint. (An **add-in** is software that works with an installed app to extend its features.) Using Office Mix, you can record yourself on video, capture still and moving images on your desktop, and insert interactive elements such as quizzes and live webpages directly into PowerPoint slides. When you post the finished presentation to OneDrive, Office Mix provides a link you can share with friends and colleagues. Anyone with an Internet connection and a web browser can watch a published Office Mix presentation, such as the one in **Figure 10**, on a computer or mobile device.

Figure 10: Office Mix presentation

Adding Office Mix to PowerPoint

To get started, you create an Office Mix account at the website mix.office.com using an email address or a Facebook or Google account. Next, you download and install the Office Mix add-in (see **Figure 11**). Office Mix appears as a new tab named Mix on the PowerPoint ribbon in versions of Office 2013 and Office 2016 running on personal computers (PCs).

Figure 11: Getting started with Office Mix

Capturing Video Clips

A **clip** is a short segment of audio, such as music, or video. After finishing the content on a PowerPoint slide, you can use Office Mix to add a video clip to animate or illustrate the content. Office Mix creates video clips in two ways: by recording live action on a webcam and by capturing screen images and movements. If your computer has a webcam, you can record yourself and annotate the slide to create a **slide recording** as shown in **Figure 12**.

Figure 12: Making a slide recording

Record your voice; also record video if your computer has a camera.

Use the Slide Notes button to display notes for your narration.

For best results, look directly at your webcam while recording video.

Use inking tools to write and draw on the slide as you record.

Choose a video and audio device to record images and sound.

When you are making a slide recording, you can record your spoken narration at the same time. The **Slide Notes** feature works like a teleprompter to help you focus on your presentation content instead of memorizing your narration. Use the Inking tools to make annotations or add highlighting using different pen types and colors. After finishing a recording, edit the video in PowerPoint to trim the length or set playback options.

The second way to create a video is to capture on-screen images and actions with or without a voiceover. This method is ideal if you want to show how to use your favorite website or demonstrate an app such as OneNote. To share your screen with an audience, select the part of the screen you want to show in the video. Office Mix captures everything that happens in that area to create a **screen recording**, as shown in **Figure 13**. Office Mix inserts the screen recording as a video in the slide.

Figure 13: Making a screen recording

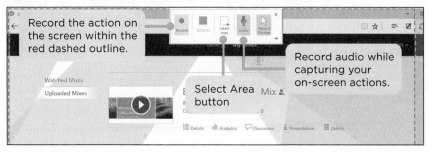

Record the action on the screen within the red dashed outline.

Record audio while capturing your on-screen actions.

Select Area button

Inserting Quizzes, Live Webpages, and Apps

To enhance and assess audience understanding, make your slides interactive by adding quizzes, live webpages, and apps. Quizzes give immediate feedback to the user as shown in **Figure 14**. Office Mix supports several quiz formats, including a **free-response quiz** similar to a short answer quiz, and true/false, multiple-choice, and multiple-response formats.

Figure 14: Creating an interactive quiz

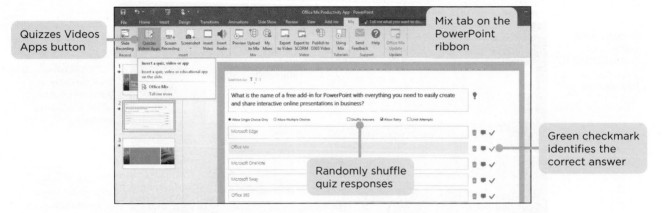

Sharing an Office Mix Presentation

When you complete your work with Office Mix, upload the presentation to your personal Office Mix dashboard as shown in **Figure 15**. Users of PCs, Macs, iOS devices, and Android devices can access and play Office Mix presentations. The Office Mix dashboard displays built-in analytics that include the quiz results and how much time viewers spent on each slide. You can play completed Office Mix presentations online or download them as movies.

Figure 15: Sharing an Office Mix presentation

Try This Now

Learn to use Office Mix!
Links to companion **Sways**, featuring **videos** with hands-on instructions, are located on www.cengagebrain.com.

1: Creating an Office Mix Tutorial for OneNote

Note: This activity requires a microphone on your computer.

Office Mix makes it easy to record screens and their contents. Create PowerPoint slides with an Office Mix screen recording to show OneNote 2016 features. Perform the following tasks:

   a. Create a PowerPoint presentation with the Ion Boardroom template. Create an opening slide with the title **My Favorite OneNote Features** and enter your name in the subtitle.
   b. Create three additional slides, each titled with a new feature of OneNote. Open OneNote and use the Mix tab in PowerPoint to capture three separate screen recordings that teach your favorite features.
   c. Add a fifth slide that quizzes the user with a multiple-choice question about OneNote and includes four responses. Be sure to insert a checkmark indicating the correct response.
   d. Upload the completed presentation to your Office Mix dashboard and share the link with your instructor.
   e. Submit your assignment link in the format specified by your instructor.

2: Teaching Augmented Reality with Office Mix

Note: This activity requires a webcam or built-in video camera on your computer.

A local elementary school has asked you to teach augmented reality to its students using Office Mix. Perform the following tasks:

   a. Research augmented reality using your favorite online search tools.
   b. Create a PowerPoint presentation with the Frame template. Create an opening slide with the title **Augmented Reality** and enter your name in the subtitle.
   c. Create a slide with four bullets summarizing your research of augmented reality. Create a 20-second slide recording of yourself providing a quick overview of augmented reality.
   d. Create another slide with a 30-second screen recording of a video about augmented reality from a site such as YouTube or another video-sharing site.
   e. Add a final slide that quizzes the user with a true/false question about augmented reality. Be sure to insert a checkmark indicating the correct response.
   f. Upload the completed presentation to your Office Mix dashboard and share the link with your instructor.
   g. Submit your assignment link in the format specified by your instructor.

3: Marketing a Travel Destination with Office Mix

Note: This activity requires a webcam or built-in video camera on your computer.

To convince your audience to travel to a particular city, create a slide presentation marketing any city in the world using a slide recording, screen recording, and a quiz. Perform the following tasks:

   a. Create a PowerPoint presentation with any template. Create an opening slide with the title of the city you are marketing as a travel destination and your name in the subtitle.
   b. Create a slide with four bullets about the featured city. Create a 30-second slide recording of yourself explaining why this city is the perfect vacation destination.
   c. Create another slide with a 20-second screen recording of a travel video about the city from a site such as YouTube or another video-sharing site.
   d. Add a final slide that quizzes the user with a multiple-choice question about the featured city with five responses. Be sure to include a checkmark indicating the correct response.
   e. Upload the completed presentation to your Office Mix dashboard and share your link with your instructor.
   f. Submit your assignment link in the format specified by your instructor.

Introduction to Microsoft Edge

Reading view | Hub | Cortana | Web Note | Inking | sandbox

Microsoft Edge is the default web browser developed for the Windows 10 operating system as a replacement for Internet Explorer. Unlike its predecessor, Edge lets you write on webpages, read webpages without advertisements and other distractions, and search for information using a virtual personal assistant. The Edge interface is clean and basic, as shown in **Figure 16**, meaning you can pay more attention to the webpage content.

Figure 16: Microsoft Edge tools

Forward button | New tab button | Web address in the Address bar | Add to favorites or reading list button

Back button | Reading view button | More button

Refresh (F5) button | Hub (Favorites, reading list, history, and downloads) button | Share Web Note button | Make a Web Note button

On the Job Now

Browsing the Web with Microsoft Edge

One of the fastest browsers available, Edge allows you to type search text directly in the Address bar. As you view the resulting webpage, you can switch to **Reading view**, which is available for most news and research sites, to eliminate distracting advertisements. For example, if you are catching up on technology news online, the webpage might be difficult to read due to a busy layout cluttered with ads. Switch to Reading view to refresh the page and remove the original page formatting, ads, and menu sidebars to read the article distraction-free.

Consider the **Hub** in Microsoft Edge as providing one-stop access to all the things you collect on the web, such as your favorite websites, reading list, surfing history, and downloaded files.

Locating Information with Cortana

Cortana, the Windows 10 virtual assistant, plays an important role in Microsoft Edge. After you turn on Cortana, it appears as an animated circle in the Address bar when you might need assistance, as shown in the restaurant website in **Figure 17**. When you click the Cortana icon, a pane slides in from the right of the browser window to display detailed information about the restaurant, including maps and reviews. Cortana can also assist you in defining words, finding the weather, suggesting coupons for shopping, updating stock market information, and calculating math.

Figure 17: Cortana providing restaurant information

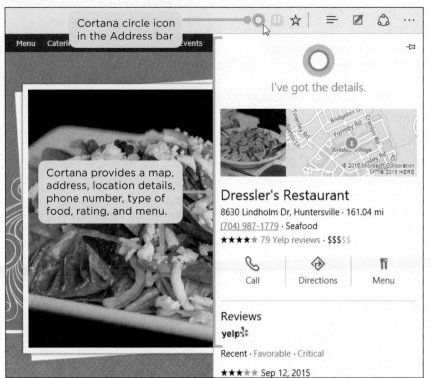

Cortana circle icon in the Address bar

Cortana provides a map, address, location details, phone number, type of food, rating, and menu.

I've got the details.

Dressler's Restaurant
8630 Lindholm Dr, Huntersville · 161.04 mi
(704) 987-1779 · Seafood
★★★★☆ 79 Yelp reviews · $$$$$

Call   Directions   Menu

Reviews
yelp⁙
Recent · Favorable · Critical
★★★☆☆ Sep 12, 2015

Annotating Webpages

One of the most impressive Microsoft Edge features are the **Web Note** tools, which you use to write on a webpage or to highlight text. When you click the Make a Web Note button, an **Inking** toolbar appears, as shown in **Figure 18**, that provides writing and drawing tools. These tools include an eraser, a pen, and a highlighter with different colors. You can also insert a typed note and copy a screen image (called a screen clipping). You can draw with a pointing device, fingertip, or stylus using different pen colors. Whether you add notes to a recipe, annotate sources for a research paper, or select a product while shopping online, the Web Note tools can enhance your productivity. After you complete your notes, click the Save button to save the annotations to OneNote, your Favorites list, or your Reading list. You can share the inked page with others using the Share Web Note button.

On the Job Now

To enhance security, Microsoft Edge runs in a partial sandbox, an arrangement that prevents attackers from gaining control of your computer. Browsing within the **sandbox** protects computer resources and information from hackers.

Figure 18: Web Note tools in Microsoft Edge

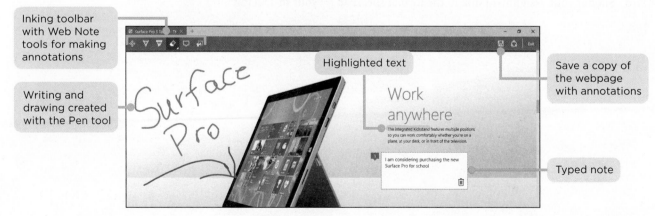

Inking toolbar with Web Note tools for making annotations

Writing and drawing created with the Pen tool

Highlighted text

Save a copy of the webpage with annotations

Typed note

Try This Now

Learn to use Edge!
Links to companion **Sways**, featuring **videos** with hands-on instructions, are located on www.cengagebrain.com.

1: Using Cortana in Microsoft Edge

Note: This activity requires using Microsoft Edge on a Windows 10 computer.

Cortana can assist you in finding information on a webpage in Microsoft Edge. Perform the following tasks:

a. Create a Word document using the Word Screen Clipping tool to capture the following screenshots.

- Screenshot A—Using Microsoft Edge, open a webpage with a technology news article. Right-click a term in the article and ask Cortana to define it.
- Screenshot B—Using Microsoft Edge, open the website of a fancy restaurant in a city near you. Make sure the Cortana circle icon is displayed in the Address bar. (If it's not displayed, find a different restaurant website.) Click the Cortana circle icon to display a pane with information about the restaurant.
- Screenshot C—Using Microsoft Edge, type **10 USD to Euros** in the Address bar without pressing the Enter key. Cortana converts the U.S. dollars to Euros.
- Screenshot D—Using Microsoft Edge, type **Apple stock** in the Address bar without pressing the Enter key. Cortana displays the current stock quote.

b. Submit your assignment in the format specified by your instructor.

2: Viewing Online News with Reading View

Note: This activity requires using Microsoft Edge on a Windows 10 computer.

Reading view in Microsoft Edge can make a webpage less cluttered with ads and other distractions. Perform the following tasks:

a. Create a Word document using the Word Screen Clipping tool to capture the following screenshots.

- Screenshot A—Using Microsoft Edge, open the website **mashable.com**. Open a technology article. Click the Reading view button to display an ad-free page that uses only basic text formatting.
- Screenshot B—Using Microsoft Edge, open the website **bbc.com**. Open any news article. Click the Reading view button to display an ad-free page that uses only basic text formatting.
- Screenshot C—Make three types of annotations (Pen, Highlighter, and Add a typed note) on the BBC article page displayed in Reading view.

b. Submit your assignment in the format specified by your instructor.

3: Inking with Microsoft Edge

Note: This activity requires using Microsoft Edge on a Windows 10 computer.

Microsoft Edge provides many annotation options to record your ideas. Perform the following tasks:

a. Open the website **wolframalpha.com** in the Microsoft Edge browser. Wolfram Alpha is a well-respected academic search engine. Type **US$100 1965 dollars in 2015** in the Wolfram Alpha search text box and press the Enter key.

b. Click the Make a Web Note button to display the Web Note tools. Using the Pen tool, draw a circle around the result on the webpage. Save the page to OneNote.

c. In the Wolfram Alpha search text box, type the name of the city closest to where you live and press the Enter key. Using the Highlighter tool, highlight at least three interesting results. Add a note and then type a sentence about what you learned about this city. Save the page to OneNote. Share your OneNote notebook with your instructor.

d. Submit your assignment link in the format specified by your instructor.

Office 2016 and Windows 10: Essential Concepts and Skills

Objectives

You will have mastered the material in this module when you can:

- Use a touch screen
- Perform basic mouse operations
- Start Windows and sign in to an account
- Identify the objects on the Windows 10 desktop
- Identify the apps in and versions of Microsoft Office 2016
- Run an app
- Identify the components of the Microsoft Office ribbon

- Create folders
- Save files
- Change screen resolution
- Perform basic tasks in Microsoft Office apps
- Manage files
- Use Microsoft Office Help and Windows Help

This introductory module covers features and functions common to Office 2016 apps, as well as the basics of Windows 10.

Roadmap

In this module, you will learn how to perform basic tasks in Windows and the Office apps. The following roadmap identifies general activities you will perform as you progress through this module:

1. SIGN IN to an account
2. USE WINDOWS
3. USE Office APPS
4. FILE and Folder MANAGEMENT
5. SWITCH between APPS

6. SAVE and Manage FILES
7. CHANGE SCREEN RESOLUTION
8. EXIT Office APPS
9. USE ADDITIONAL Office APPS
10. USE Office and Windows HELP

At the beginning of the step instructions throughout each module, you will see an abbreviated form of this roadmap. The abbreviated roadmap uses colors to indicate module progress: gray means the module is beyond that activity, blue means the task being shown is covered in that activity, and black means that activity is yet to be covered. For example, the following abbreviated roadmap indicates the module would be showing a task in the USE APPS activity.

1 SIGN IN | 2 USE WINDOWS | 3 USE APPS | 4 FILE MANAGEMENT | 5 SWITCH APPS | 6 SAVE FILES
7 CHANGE SCREEN RESOLUTION | 8 EXIT APPS | 9 USE ADDITIONAL APPS | 10 USE HELP

Use the abbreviated roadmap as a progress guide while you read or step through the instructions in this module.

Introduction to the Windows 10 Operating System

Windows 10 is the newest version of Microsoft Windows, which is a popular and widely used operating system (Figure 1). An **operating system (OS)** is a set of programs that coordinate all the activities among computer or mobile device hardware.

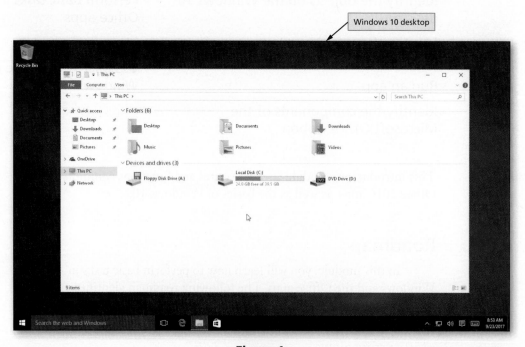

Windows 10 desktop

Figure 1

The Windows operating system simplifies the process of working with documents and apps by organizing the manner in which you interact with the computer. Windows is used to run apps. An application, or **app**, consists of programs designed to make users more productive and/or assist them with personal tasks, such as word processing or browsing the web.

Using a Touch Screen and a Mouse

Windows users who have computers or devices with touch screen capability can interact with the screen using gestures. A **gesture** is a motion you make on a touch screen with the tip of one or more fingers or your hand. Touch screens are convenient because they do not require a separate device for input. Table 1 presents common ways to interact with a touch screen.

Table 1 Touch Screen Gestures			
Motion	**Description**	**Common Uses**	**Equivalent Mouse Operation**
Tap	Quickly touch and release one finger one time.	Activate a link (built-in connection). Press a button. Run a program or an app.	Click
Double-tap	Quickly touch and release one finger two times.	Run a program or an app. Zoom in (show a smaller area on the screen, so that contents appear larger) at the location of the double-tap.	Double-click
Press and hold	Press and hold one finger to cause an action to occur, or until an action occurs.	Display a shortcut menu (immediate access to allowable actions). Activate a mode enabling you to move an item with one finger to a new location.	Right-click
Drag, or slide	Press and hold one finger on an object and then move the finger to the new location.	Move an item around the screen. Scroll.	Drag
Swipe	Press and hold one finger and then move the finger horizontally or vertically on the screen.	Select an object. Swipe from edge to display a bar such as the Action Center, Apps bar, and Navigation bar (all discussed later).	Drag
Stretch	Move two fingers apart.	Zoom in (show a smaller area on the screen, so that contents appear larger).	None
Pinch	Move two fingers together.	Zoom out (show a larger area on the screen, so that contents appear smaller).	None

Will your screen look different if you are using a touch screen?
The Windows and Microsoft Office interface varies slightly if you are using a touch screen. For this reason, you might notice that your screen looks slightly different from the screens in the module.

Windows users who do not have touch screen capabilities typically work with a mouse that has at least two buttons. For a right-handed user, the left button usually is

If you are using your finger on a touch screen and are having difficulty completing the steps in this module, consider using a stylus. Many people find it easier to be precise with a stylus than with a finger. In addition, with a stylus you see the pointer. If you still are having trouble completing the steps with a stylus, try using a mouse.

CONSIDER THIS

BTW
Pointer
If you are using a touch screen, the pointer may not appear on the screen as you perform touch gestures. The pointer will reappear when you begin using the mouse.

the primary mouse button, and the right mouse button is the secondary mouse button. Left-handed people, however, can reverse the function of these buttons.

Table 2 explains how to perform a variety of mouse operations. Some apps also use keys in combination with the mouse to perform certain actions. For example, when you hold down the CTRL key while rolling the mouse wheel, text on the screen may become larger or smaller based on the direction you roll the wheel. The function of the mouse buttons and the wheel varies depending on the app.

Table 2 Mouse Operations

Operation	Mouse Action	Example*	Equivalent Touch Gesture
Point	Move the mouse until the pointer on the desktop is positioned on the item of choice.	Position the pointer on the screen.	None
Click	Press and release the primary mouse button, which usually is the left mouse button.	Select or deselect items on the screen or run an app or app feature.	Tap
Right-click	Press and release the secondary mouse button, which usually is the right mouse button.	Display a shortcut menu.	Press and hold
Double-click	Quickly press and release the primary mouse button twice without moving the mouse.	Run an app or app feature.	Double-tap
Triple-click	Quickly press and release the primary mouse button three times without moving the mouse.	Select a paragraph.	Triple-tap
Drag	Point to an item, hold down the primary mouse button, move the item to the desired location on the screen, and then release the mouse button.	Move an object from one location to another or draw pictures.	Drag or slide
Right-drag	Point to an item, hold down the right mouse button, move the item to the desired location on the screen, and then release the right mouse button.	Display a shortcut menu after moving an object from one location to another.	Press and hold, then drag
Rotate wheel	Roll the wheel forward or backward.	Scroll vertically (up and down).	Swipe
Free-spin wheel	Whirl the wheel forward or backward so that it spins freely on its own.	Scroll through many pages in seconds.	Swipe
Press wheel	Press the wheel button while moving the mouse.	Scroll continuously.	None
Tilt wheel	Press the wheel toward the right or left.	Scroll horizontally (left and right).	None
Press thumb button	Press the button on the side of the mouse with your thumb.	Move forward or backward through webpages and/or control media, games, etc.	None

*Note: The examples presented in this column are discussed as they are demonstrated in this chapter.

© 2015 Cengage Learning

Figure 2

Scrolling

A **scroll bar** is a horizontal or vertical bar that appears when the contents of an area may not be visible completely on the screen (Figure 2). A scroll bar contains **scroll arrows** and a **scroll box** that enable you to view areas that currently cannot be seen on the screen. Clicking the up and down scroll arrows moves the screen content up or down one line. You also can click above or below the scroll box to move up or down a section, or drag the scroll box up or down to move to a specific location.

Keyboard Shortcuts

In many cases, you can use the keyboard instead of the mouse to accomplish a task. To perform tasks using the keyboard, you press one or more keyboard keys, sometimes identified as a **keyboard shortcut**. Some keyboard shortcuts consist of a single key, such as the F1 key. For example, to obtain help in many apps, you can press the F1 key. Other keyboard shortcuts consist of multiple keys, in which case a plus sign separates the key names, such as CTRL+ESC. This notation means to press and hold down the first key listed, press one or more additional keys, and then release all keys. For example, to display the Start menu, press CTRL+ESC, that is, hold down the CTRL key, press the ESC key, and then release both keys.

Starting Windows

It is not unusual for multiple people to use the same computer in a work, educational, recreational, or home setting. Windows enables each user to establish a **user account**, which identifies to Windows the resources, such as apps and storage locations, a user can access when working with the computer.

Each user account has a user name and may have a password and an icon, as well. A **user name** is a unique combination of letters or numbers that identifies a specific user to Windows. A **password** is a private combination of letters, numbers, and special characters associated with the user name that allows access to a user's account resources. An icon is a small image that represents an object; thus, a **user icon** is a picture associated with a user name.

When you turn on a computer, Windows starts and displays a **lock screen** consisting of the time and date (Figure 3). To unlock the screen, click the lock screen. Depending on your computer's settings, Windows may or may not display a sign-in screen that shows the user names and user icons for users who have accounts on the computer. This **sign-in screen** enables you to sign in to your user account and makes the computer available for use. Clicking the user icon begins the process of signing in, also called logging on, to your user account.

BTW

Minimize Wrist Injury
Computer users frequently switch between the keyboard and the mouse during a word processing session; such switching strains the wrist. To help prevent wrist injury, minimize switching. For instance, if your fingers already are on the keyboard, use keyboard keys to scroll. If your hand already is on the mouse, use the mouse to scroll. If your hand is on the touch screen, use touch gestures to scroll.

Figure 3

At the bottom of the sign-in screen is the 'Connect to Internet' button, 'Ease of access' button, and a Shut down button. Clicking the 'Connect to Internet' button displays a list of each network connection and its status. You also can connect to or disconnect from a network. Clicking the 'Ease of access' button displays the Ease of access menu, which provides tools to optimize a computer to accommodate the needs of the mobility, hearing, and vision impaired users. Clicking the Shut down button displays a menu containing commands related to putting the computer or mobile device in a low-power state, shutting it down, and restarting the computer or mobile device. The commands available on your computer or mobile device may differ.

- The Sleep command saves your work, turns off the computer fans and hard drive, and places the computer in a lower-power state. To wake the computer from sleep mode, press the power button or lift a laptop's cover, and sign in to your account.
- The Shut down command exits running apps, shuts down Windows, and then turns off the computer.
- The Restart command exits running apps, shuts down Windows, and then restarts Windows.

To Sign In to an Account

1 SIGN IN | 2 USE WINDOWS | 3 USE APPS | 4 FILE MANAGEMENT | 5 SWITCH APPS | 6 SAVE FILES
7 CHANGE SCREEN RESOLUTION | 8 EXIT APPS | 9 USE ADDITIONAL APPS | 10 USE HELP

The following steps, which use SCSeries as the user name, sign in to an account based on a typical Windows installation. *Why? After starting Windows, you might be required to sign in to an account to access the computer or mobile device's resources.* You may need to ask your instructor how to sign in to your account.

1

- Click the lock screen (shown in Figure 3) to display a sign-in screen.

- Click the user icon (for SCSeries, in this case) on the sign-in screen, which depending on settings, either will display a second sign-in screen that contains a Password text box (Figure 4) or will display the Windows desktop (Figure 5).

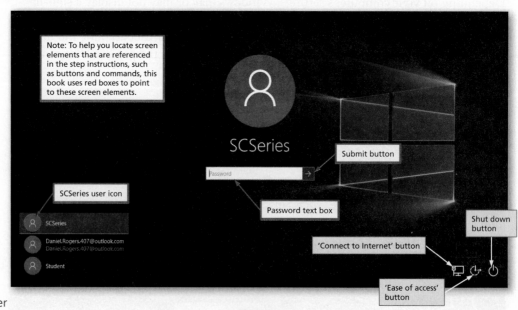

Note: To help you locate screen elements that are referenced in the step instructions, such as buttons and commands, this book uses red boxes to point to these screen elements.

SCSeries

SCSeries user icon

SCSeries

Daniel.Rogers.407@outlook.com
Daniel.Rogers.407@outlook.com

Student

Password text box

Submit button

Password

'Connect to Internet' button

Shut down button

'Ease of access' button

Figure 4

Q&A Why do I not see a user icon?
Your computer may require you to type a user name instead of clicking an icon.

What is a text box?
A text box is a rectangular box in which you type text.

Why does my screen not show a Password text box?
Your account does not require a password.

- If Windows displays a sign-in screen with a Password text box, type your password in the text box.

2
- Click the Submit button (shown in Figure 4) to sign in to your account and display the Windows desktop (Figure 5).

Q&A

Why does my desktop look different from the one in Figure 5?
The Windows desktop is customizable, and your school or employer may have modified the desktop to meet its needs. Also, your screen resolution, which affects the size of the elements on the screen, may differ from the screen resolution used in this book. Later in this module, you learn how to change screen resolution.

How do I type if my tablet has no keyboard?
You can use your fingers to press keys on a keyboard that appears on the screen, called an on-screen keyboard, or you can purchase a separate physical keyboard that attaches to or wirelessly communicates with the tablet.

Figure 5

The Windows Desktop

The Windows 10 desktop (Figure 5) and the objects on the desktop emulate a work area in an office. Think of the Windows desktop as an electronic version of the top of your desk. You can perform tasks such as placing objects on the desktop, moving the objects around the desktop, and removing items from the desktop.

When you run an app in Windows 10, it appears on the desktop. Some icons also may be displayed on the desktop. For instance, the icon for the **Recycle Bin**, the location of files that have been deleted, appears on the desktop by default. A **file** is a named unit of storage. Files can contain text, images, audio, and video. You can customize your desktop so that icons representing programs and files you use often appear on your desktop.

Introduction to Microsoft Office 2016

Microsoft Office 2016 is the newest version of Microsoft Office, offering features that provide users with better functionality and easier ways to work with the various files they create. This version of Office also is designed to work more optimally on mobile devices and online.

Microsoft Office 2016 Apps

Microsoft Office 2016 includes a wide variety of apps, such as Word, PowerPoint, Excel, Access, Outlook, Publisher, and OneNote:

- **Microsoft Word 2016**, or Word, is a full-featured word processing app that allows you to create professional-looking documents and revise them easily.

- **Microsoft PowerPoint 2016**, or PowerPoint, is a complete presentation app that enables you to produce professional-looking presentations and then deliver them to an audience.

- **Microsoft Excel 2016**, or Excel, is a powerful spreadsheet app that allows you to organize data, complete calculations, make decisions, graph data, develop professional-looking reports, publish organized data to the web, and access real-time data from websites.

- **Microsoft Access 2016**, or Access, is a database management system that enables you to create a database; add, change, and delete data in the database; ask questions concerning the data in the database; and create forms and reports using the data in the database.

- **Microsoft Outlook 2016**, or Outlook, is a communications and scheduling app that allows you to manage email accounts, calendars, contacts, and access to other Internet content.

- **Microsoft Publisher 2016**, or Publisher, is a desktop publishing app that helps you create professional-quality publications and marketing materials that can be shared easily.

- **Microsoft OneNote 2016**, or OneNote, is a note taking app that allows you to store and share information in notebooks with other people.

Microsoft Office 2016 Suites

A **suite** is a collection of individual apps available together as a unit. Microsoft offers a variety of Office suites, including a stand-alone desktop app, Microsoft Office 365, and Microsoft Office Online. **Microsoft Office 365**, or Office 365, provides plans that allow organizations to use Office in a mobile setting while also being able to communicate and share files, depending upon the type of plan selected by the organization. **Microsoft Office Online** includes apps that allow you to edit and share files on the web using the familiar Office interface.

During the Office 365 installation, you select a plan, and depending on your plan, you receive different apps and services. Office Online apps do not require a local installation and can be accessed through OneDrive and your browser. **OneDrive** is a cloud storage service that provides storage and other services, such as Office Online, to computer users.

 How do you sign up for a OneDrive account?

- Use your browser to navigate to onedrive.live.com.

- Create a Microsoft account by clicking the Sign up button and then entering your information to create the account.

- Sign in to OneDrive using your new account or use it in Office to save your files on OneDrive.

Apps in a suite, such as Microsoft Office, typically use a similar interface and share features. Once you are comfortable working with the elements and the interface and performing tasks in one app, the similarity can help you apply the knowledge and skills you have learned to another app(s) in the suite. For example, the process for saving a file in Word is the same in PowerPoint, Excel, and some of the other Office apps. While briefly showing how to use several Office apps, this module illustrates some of the common functions across the apps and identifies the characteristics unique to these apps.

Running and Using an App

To use an app, you must instruct the operating system to run the app. Windows provides many different ways to run an app, one of which is presented in this section (other ways to run an app are presented throughout this module). After an app is running, you can use it to perform a variety of tasks. The following pages use Word to discuss some elements of the Office interface and to perform tasks that are common to other Office apps.

Word

Word is a full-featured word processing app that allows you to create many types of personal and business documents, including flyers, letters, memos, resumes, reports, fax cover sheets, mailing labels, and newsletters. Word also provides tools that enable you to create webpages and save these webpages directly on a web server. Word has many features designed to simplify the production of documents and add visual appeal. Using Word, you easily can change the shape, size, and color of text. You also can include borders, shading, tables, images, pictures, charts, and web addresses in documents.

To Run an App Using the Start Menu and Create a Blank Document

1 SIGN IN | 2 USE WINDOWS | 3 USE APPS | 4 FILE MANAGEMENT | 5 SWITCH APPS | 6 SAVE FILES
7 CHANGE SCREEN RESOLUTION | 8 EXIT APPS | 9 USE ADDITIONAL APPS | 10 USE HELP

Across the bottom of the Windows 10 desktop is the taskbar. The taskbar contains the **Start button**, which you use to access apps, files, folders, and settings. A **folder** is a named location on a storage medium that usually contains related documents.

Clicking the Start button displays the Start menu. The **Start menu** allows you to access programs, folders, and files on the computer or mobile device and contains commands that allow you to start programs, store and search for documents, customize the computer or mobile device, and sign out of a user account or shut down the computer or mobile device. A **menu** is a list of related items, including folders, programs, and commands. Each **command** on a menu performs a specific action, such as saving a file or obtaining help. *Why? When you install an app, for example, the app's name will be added to the All apps list on the Start menu.*

The following steps, which assume Windows is running, use the Start menu to run an Office app and create a blank document based on a typical installation. You may need to ask your instructor how to run an Office app on your computer. Although the steps illustrate running the Word app, the steps to run any Office app are similar.

1
- Click the Start button on the Windows 10 taskbar to display the Start menu (Figure 6).

Figure 6

2

• Click All apps at the bottom of the left pane of the Start menu to display a list of apps installed on the computer or mobile device. If necessary, scroll to display the app you wish to run (Figure 7).

Figure 7

3

• If the app you wish to run is located in a folder, click or scroll to and then click the folder in the All apps list to display a list of the folder's contents.
• Click, or scroll to and then click, the program name (Microsoft Word 2016, in this case) in the list to run the selected program (Figure 8).

Figure 8

④

- Click the Blank document thumbnail on the Word start screen to create a blank Word document in the Word window (Figure 9).

Q&A

What happens when you run an app?

Some apps provide a means for you to create a blank document, as shown in Figure 8; others immediately display a blank document in an app window, such as the Word window shown in Figure 9. A **window** is a rectangular area that displays data and information. The top of a window has a **title bar**, which is a horizontal space that contains the window's name.

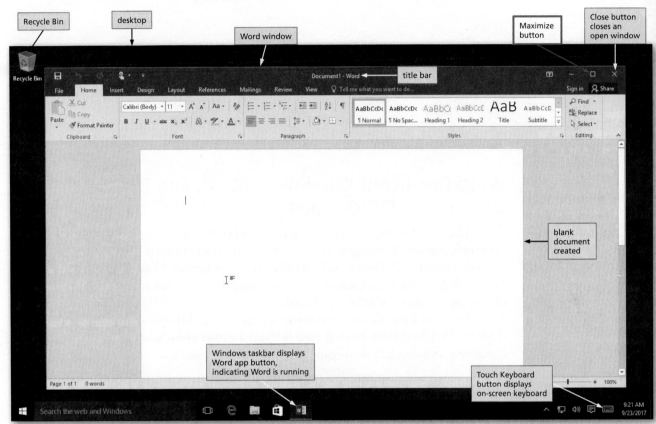

Figure 9

Other Ways

1. Type app name in search box, click app name in results list
2. Double-click file created in app you want to run

To Maximize a Window

Sometimes content is not visible completely in a window. One method of displaying the entire contents of a window is to **maximize** it, or enlarge the window so that it fills the entire screen. The following step maximizes the Word window; however, any Office app's window can be maximized using this step. *Why? A maximized window provides the most space available for using the app.*

Figure 10

• If the app window is not maximized already, click the Maximize button (shown in Figure 9) next to the Close button on the window's title bar (the Word window title bar, in this case) to maximize the window (Figure 10).

Q&A

What happened to the Maximize button?

It changed to a Restore Down button, which you can use to return a window to its size and location before you maximized it.

How do I know whether a window is maximized?

A window is maximized if it fills the entire display area and the Restore Down button is displayed on the title bar.

Other Ways

1. Double-click title bar

2. Drag title bar to top of screen

BTW
Touch Keyboard
To display the on-screen touch keyboard, click the Touch Keyboard button on the Windows taskbar. When finished using the touch keyboard, click the X button on the touch keyboard to close the keyboard.

Word Document Window, Ribbon, and Elements Common to Office Apps

The Word window consists of a variety of components to make your work more efficient and documents more professional. These include the document window, ribbon, Tell Me box, mini toolbar, shortcut menus, Quick Access Toolbar, and Microsoft Account area. Most of these components are common to other Microsoft Office apps; others are unique to Word.

You view a portion of a document on the screen through a **document window** (Figure 11). The default (preset) view is **Print Layout view**, which shows the document on a mock sheet of paper in the document window.

Scroll Bars　You use a scroll bar to display different portions of a document in the document window. At the right edge of the document window is a vertical scroll bar. If a document is too wide to fit in the document window, a horizontal scroll bar also appears at the bottom of the document window. On a scroll bar, the position of the scroll box reflects the location of the portion of the document that is displayed in the document window.

Status Bar　The **status bar**, located at the bottom of the document window above the Windows taskbar, presents information about the document, the progress of current tasks, and the status of certain commands and keys; it also provides controls for viewing the document. As you type text or perform certain tasks, various indicators and buttons may appear on the status bar.

The left side of the status bar in Figure 11 shows the current page followed by the total number of pages in the document, the number of words in the document, and an icon to check spelling and grammar. The right side of the status bar includes buttons and controls you can use to change the view of a document and adjust the size of the displayed document.

Ribbon　The ribbon, located near the top of the window below the title bar, is the control center in Word and other Office apps (Figure 12). The ribbon provides easy, central access to the tasks you perform while creating a document. The ribbon consists

Figure 11

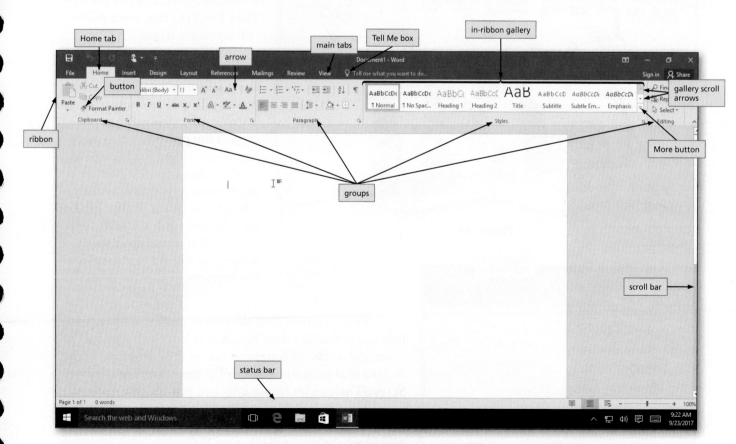

Figure 12

of tabs, groups, and commands. Each **tab** contains a collection of groups, and each **group** contains related commands. When you run an Office app, such as Word, it initially displays several main tabs, also called default or top-level tabs. All Office apps have a Home tab, which contains the more frequently used commands.

Figure 13

In addition to the main tabs, the Office apps display **tool tabs**, also called contextual tabs (Figure 13), when you perform certain tasks or work with objects such as pictures or tables. If you insert a picture in a Word document, for example, the Picture Tools tab and its related subordinate Format tab appear, collectively referred to as the Picture Tools Format tab. When you are finished working with the picture, the Picture Tools Format tab disappears from the ribbon. Word and other Office apps determine when tool tabs should appear and disappear based on tasks you perform. Some tool tabs, such as the Table Tools tab, have more than one related subordinate tab.

Figure 14

Items on the ribbon include buttons, boxes, and galleries (shown in Figure 12). A **gallery** is a set of choices, often graphical, arranged in a grid or in a list. You can scroll through choices in an in-ribbon gallery by clicking the gallery's scroll arrows. Or, you can click a gallery's More button to view more gallery options on the screen at a time.

Some buttons and boxes have arrows that, when clicked, also display a gallery; others always cause a gallery to be displayed when clicked. Most galleries support **live preview**, which is a feature that allows you to point to a gallery choice and see its effect in the document — without actually selecting the choice (Figure 14). Live preview works only if you are using a mouse; if you are using a touch screen, you will not be able to view live previews.

Some commands on the ribbon display an image to help you remember their function. When you point to a command on the ribbon, all or part of the command glows in a shade of gray, and a ScreenTip appears on the screen. A **ScreenTip** is an on-screen note that provides the name of the command, available keyboard shortcut(s), a description of the command, and sometimes instructions for how to obtain help about the command (Figure 15).

Figure 15

Some groups on the ribbon have a small arrow in the lower-right corner, called a **Dialog Box Launcher**, that when clicked, displays a dialog box or a task pane with additional options for the group (Figure 16). When presented with a dialog box, you make selections and must close the dialog box before returning to the document. A **task pane**, in contrast to a dialog box, is a window that can remain open and visible while you work in the document.

BTW
Touch Mode
The Office and Windows interfaces may vary if you are using touch mode. For this reason, you might notice that the function or appearance of your touch screen differs slightly from this module's presentation.

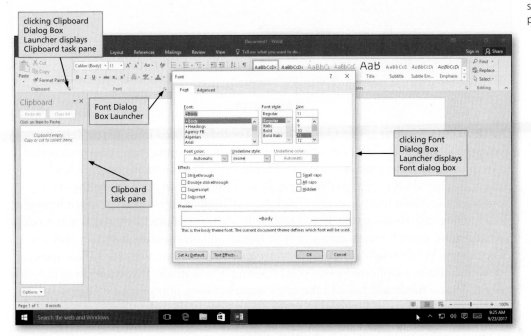

Figure 16

Tell Me Box   The **Tell Me box**, which appears to the right of the tabs on the ribbon, is a type of search box that helps you to perform specific tasks in an Office app (Figure 17). As you type in the Tell Me box, the word-wheeling feature displays search results that are refined as you type. For example, if you want to center text in a document, you can type "center" in the Tell Me box and then select the appropriate command. The Tell Me box also lists the last five commands accessed from the box.

Mini Toolbar   The **mini toolbar**, which appears automatically based on tasks you perform, contains commands related to changing the appearance of text in a document (Figure 18). If you do not use the mini toolbar, it disappears from the screen. The buttons, arrows, and boxes on the mini toolbar vary, depending on whether you are using Touch mode versus Mouse mode. If you right-click an item in the document window, Word displays both the mini toolbar and a shortcut menu, which is discussed in a later section in this module.

All commands on the mini toolbar also exist on the ribbon. The purpose of the mini toolbar is to minimize hand or mouse movement.

Figure 17

BTW
Turning Off the Mini Toolbar
If you do not want the mini toolbar to appear, click File on the ribbon to open the Backstage view, click the Options tab in the Backstage view, if necessary, click General (Options dialog box), remove the check mark from the 'Show Mini Toolbar on selection' check box, and then click the OK button.

Figure 18

Quick Access Toolbar   The **Quick Access Toolbar**, located initially (by default) above the ribbon at the left edge of the title bar, provides convenient, one-click access to frequently used commands (shown in Figure 15). The commands on the Quick Access Toolbar always are available, regardless of the task you are performing. The Touch/Mouse Mode button on the Quick Access Toolbar allows you to switch between Touch mode and Mouse mode. If you primarily are using touch gestures, Touch mode will add more space between commands in menus and on the ribbon so that they are easier to tap. While touch gestures are convenient ways to interact with Office apps, not all features are supported when you are using Touch mode. If you are using a mouse, Mouse mode will not add the extra space between buttons and commands. The Quick Access Toolbar is discussed in more depth later in the module.

KeyTips   If you prefer using the keyboard instead of the mouse, you can press the ALT key on the keyboard to display **KeyTips**, or keyboard code icons, for certain commands (Figure 19). To select a command using the keyboard, press the letter or number displayed in the KeyTip, which may cause additional KeyTips related to the selected command to appear. To remove KeyTips from the screen, press the ALT key or the ESC key until all KeyTips disappear, or click anywhere in the app window.

Microsoft Account Area   In this area, you can use the Sign in link to sign in to your Microsoft account. Once signed in, you will see your account information, as well as a picture if you have included one in your Microsoft account.

Figure 19

To Display a Different Tab on the Ribbon

1 SIGN IN | 2 USE WINDOWS | 3 USE APPS | 4 FILE MANAGEMENT | 5 SWITCH APPS | 6 SAVE FILES
7 CHANGE SCREEN RESOLUTION | 8 EXIT APPS | 9 USE ADDITIONAL APPS | 10 USE HELP

When you run Word, the ribbon displays nine main tabs: File, Home, Insert, Design, Layout, References, Mailings, Review, and View. The tab currently displayed is called the **active tab**.

The following step displays the Insert tab, that is, makes it the active tab. *Why? When working with an Office app, you may need to switch tabs to access other options for working with a document.*

1

- Click Insert on the ribbon to display the Insert tab (Figure 20).

Experiment

- Click the other tabs on the ribbon to view their contents. When you are finished, click Insert on the ribbon to redisplay the Insert tab.

Figure 20

Other Ways

1. Press ALT, press letter corresponding to tab to display
2. Press ALT, press LEFT ARROW or RIGHT ARROW until desired tab is displayed

To Collapse and Expand the Ribbon and Use Full Screen Mode

1 SIGN IN | 2 USE WINDOWS | 3 USE APPS | 4 FILE MANAGEMENT | 5 SWITCH APPS | 6 SAVE FILES
7 CHANGE SCREEN RESOLUTION | 8 EXIT APPS | 9 USE ADDITIONAL APPS | 10 USE HELP

To display more of a document or other item in the window of an Office app, some users prefer to collapse the ribbon, which hides the groups on the ribbon and displays only the main tabs, or to use **Full Screen mode**, which hides all the commands and just displays the document. Each time you run an Office app, the ribbon appears the same way it did the last time you used that Office app. The modules in this book, however, begin with the ribbon appearing as it did at the initial installation of the software.

The following steps collapse, expand, and restore the ribbon in an Office app and then switch to Full Screen mode. *Why? If you need more space on the screen to work with your document, you may consider collapsing the ribbon or switching to Full Screen mode to gain additional workspace.*

1

- Click the 'Collapse the Ribbon' button on the ribbon (shown in Figure 20) to collapse the ribbon (Figure 21).

Q&A What happened to the 'Collapse the Ribbon' button?
The 'Pin the ribbon' button replaces the 'Collapse the Ribbon' button when the ribbon is collapsed. You will see the 'Pin the ribbon' button only when you expand a ribbon by clicking a tab.

Figure 21

2

- Click Home on the ribbon to expand the Home tab (Figure 22).

Q&A | Why would I click the Home tab?
If you want to use a command on a collapsed ribbon, click the main tab to display the groups for that tab. After you select a command on the ribbon and resume working in the document, the groups will be collapsed once again. If you decide not to use a command on the ribbon, you can collapse the groups by clicking the same main tab or clicking in the app window.

Experiment

- Click Home on the ribbon to collapse the groups again. Click Home on the ribbon to expand the Home tab.

Figure 22

3

- Click the 'Pin the ribbon' button on the expanded Home tab to restore the ribbon.
- Click the 'Ribbon Display Options' button to display the Ribbon Display Options menu (Figure 23).

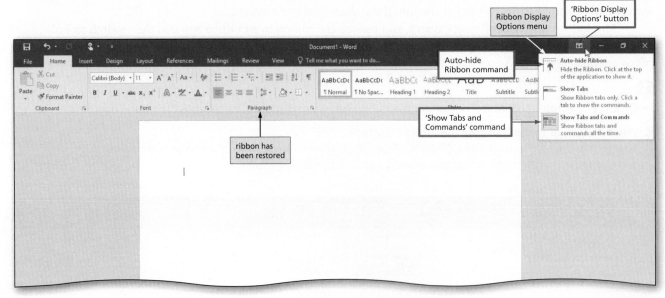

Figure 23

4

- Click Auto-hide Ribbon to hide all the commands from the screen (Figure 24).
- Click the ellipsis to temporarily display the ribbon.
- Click the 'Ribbon Display Options' button to display the Ribbon Display Options menu (shown in Figure 23).
- Click 'Show Tabs and Commands' to exit Full Screen mode.

Figure 24

Other Ways

1. Double-click a main tab on the ribbon
2. Press CTRL+F1

To Use a Shortcut Menu to Relocate the Quick Access Toolbar

1 SIGN IN | 2 USE WINDOWS | 3 USE APPS | 4 FILE MANAGEMENT | 5 SWITCH APPS | 6 SAVE FILES
7 CHANGE SCREEN RESOLUTION | 8 EXIT APPS | 9 USE ADDITIONAL APPS | 10 USE HELP

When you right-click certain areas of the Word and other Office app windows, a shortcut menu will appear. A **shortcut menu** is a list of frequently used commands that relate to an object. *Why? You can use shortcut menus to access common commands quickly.* When you right-click the status bar, for example, a shortcut menu appears with commands related to the status bar. When you right-click the Quick Access Toolbar, a shortcut menu appears with commands related to the Quick Access Toolbar. The following steps use a shortcut menu to move the Quick Access Toolbar, which by default is located on the title bar.

1

- Right-click the Quick Access Toolbar to display a shortcut menu that presents a list of commands related to the Quick Access Toolbar (Figure 25).

Figure 25

- Click 'Show Quick Access Toolbar Below the Ribbon' on the shortcut menu to display the Quick Access Toolbar below the ribbon (Figure 26).

Figure 26

- Right-click the Quick Access Toolbar to display a shortcut menu (Figure 27).

- Click 'Show Quick Access Toolbar Above the Ribbon' on the shortcut menu to return the Quick Access Toolbar to its original position (shown in Figure 25).

Figure 27

Other Ways

1. Click 'Customize Quick Access Toolbar' button on Quick Access Toolbar, click 'Show Below the Ribbon' or 'Show Above the Ribbon'

To Customize the Quick Access Toolbar

1 SIGN IN | 2 USE WINDOWS | 3 USE APPS | 4 FILE MANAGEMENT | 5 SWITCH APPS | 6 SAVE FILES
7 CHANGE SCREEN RESOLUTION | 8 EXIT APPS | 9 USE ADDITIONAL APPS | 10 USE HELP

The Quick Access Toolbar provides easy access to some of the more frequently used commands in the Office apps. By default, the Quick Access Toolbar contains buttons for the Save, Undo, and Redo commands. If your computer or mobile device has a touch screen, the Quick Access Toolbar also might display the Touch/Mouse Mode button. You can customize the Quick Access Toolbar by changing its location in the window, as shown in the previous steps, and by adding more buttons to reflect commands you would like to access easily. The following steps add the Quick Print button to the Quick Access Toolbar. *Why? Adding the Quick Print button to the Quick Access Toolbar speeds up the process of printing.*

- Click the 'Customize Quick Access Toolbar' button to display the Customize Quick Access Toolbar menu (Figure 28).

Q&A Which commands are listed on the Customize Quick Access Toolbar menu?
It lists commands that commonly are added to the Quick Access Toolbar.

Figure 28

2

- Click Quick Print on the Customize Quick Access Toolbar menu to add the Quick Print button to the Quick Access Toolbar (Figure 29).

Q&A How would I remove a button from the Quick Access Toolbar?
You would right-click the button you wish to remove and then click 'Remove from Quick Access Toolbar' on the shortcut menu or click the 'Customize Quick Access Toolbar' button on the Quick Access Toolbar and then click the button name in the Customize Quick Access Toolbar menu to remove the check mark.

Figure 29

To Enter Text in a Document

1 SIGN IN | 2 USE WINDOWS | 3 USE APPS | 4 FILE MANAGEMENT | 5 SWITCH APPS | 6 SAVE FILES
7 CHANGE SCREEN RESOLUTION | 8 EXIT APPS | 9 USE ADDITIONAL APPS | 10 USE HELP

The first step in creating a document is to enter its text by typing on the keyboard. By default, Word positions text at the left margin as you type. The following steps type this first line of a flyer. *Why? To begin creating a flyer, for example, you type the headline in the document window.*

1

- Type **VISIT NATIONAL MONUMENTS** as the text (Figure 30).

Q&A What is the blinking vertical bar to the right of the text?
The blinking bar is the insertion point, which indicates where text, graphics, and other items will be inserted in the document. As you type, the insertion point moves to the right, and when you reach the end of a line, it moves down to the beginning of the next line.

What if I make an error while typing?
You can press the BACKSPACE key until you have deleted the text in error and then retype the text correctly.

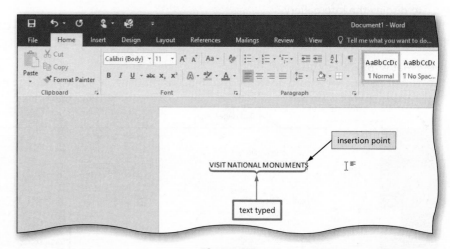

Figure 30

2

- Press the ENTER key to move the insertion point to the beginning of the next line (Figure 31).

Q&A Why did blank space appear between the entered text and the insertion point?
Each time you press the ENTER key, Word creates a new paragraph and inserts blank space between the two paragraphs. Depending on your settings, Office may or may not insert a blank space between the two paragraphs.

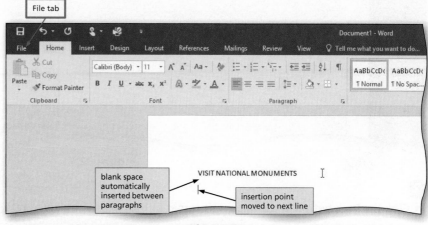

Figure 31

Document Properties

You can organize and identify your files by using **document properties**, which are the details about a file, such as the project author, title, and subject. For example, a class name or document topic can describe the file's purpose or content.

CONSIDER THIS

Why would you want to assign document properties to a document?

Document properties are valuable for a variety of reasons:

- Users can save time locating a particular file because they can view a file's document properties without opening the file.

- By creating consistent properties for files having similar content, users can better organize their files.

- Some organizations require users to add document properties so that other employees can view details about these files.

To Change Document Properties

1 SIGN IN | 2 USE WINDOWS | 3 USE APPS | 4 FILE MANAGEMENT | 5 SWITCH APPS | 6 SAVE FILES
7 CHANGE SCREEN RESOLUTION | 8 EXIT APPS | 9 USE ADDITIONAL APPS | 10 USE HELP

You can change the document properties while working with the file in an Office app. When you save the file, the Office app (Word, in this case) will save the document properties with the file. The following steps change document properties. **Why?** *Adding document properties will help you identify characteristics of the file without opening it.*

1

- Click File on the ribbon to open the Backstage view and then, if necessary, click the Info tab in the Backstage view to display the Info gallery.
- Click to the right of the Comments property in the Properties list, and type **CIS 101 Assignment** in the text box (Figure 32).

Q&A

What is the Backstage view?

The **Backstage view** contains a set of commands that enable you to manage documents and provides data about the documents.

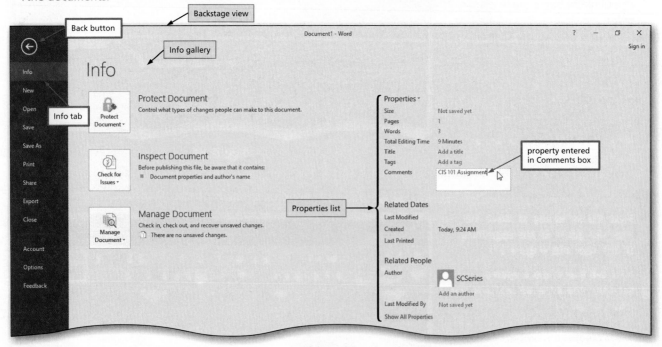

Figure 32

2

- Click the Back button in the upper-left corner of the Backstage view to return to the document window.

Printing, Saving, and Organizing Files

While you are creating a document, the computer or mobile device stores it in memory. When you save a document, the computer or mobile device places it on a storage medium, such as a hard disk, solid state drive (SSD), USB flash drive, or optical disc. The storage medium can be permanent in your computer, may be portable where you remove it from your computer, or may be on a web server you access through a network or the Internet.

A saved document is referred to as a file. A **file name** is the name assigned to a file when it is saved. When saving files, you should organize them so that you easily can find them later. Windows provides tools to help you organize files.

BTW
File Type
Depending on your Windows settings, the file type .docx may be displayed immediately to the right of the file name after you save the file. The file type .docx is a Word 2016 document.

Printing a Document

After creating a document, you may want to print it. Printing a document enables you to distribute it to others in a form that can be read or viewed but typically not edited.

What is the best method for distributing a document?

The traditional method of distributing a document uses a printer to produce a hard copy. A **hard copy** or **printout** is information that exists on a physical medium, such as paper. Hard copies can be useful for the following reasons:

- Some people prefer proofreading a hard copy of a document rather than viewing it on the screen to check for errors and readability.

- Hard copies can serve as a backup reference if your storage medium is lost or becomes corrupted and you need to recreate the document.

Instead of distributing a hard copy of a document, users can distribute the document as an electronic image that mirrors the original document's appearance. The electronic image of the document can be sent as an email attachment, posted on a website, or copied to a portable storage medium, such as a USB flash drive. Two popular electronic image formats, sometimes called fixed formats, are PDF by Adobe Systems and XPS by Microsoft. In Word, you can create electronic image files through the Save As dialog box and the Export, Share, and Print tabs in the Backstage view. Electronic images of documents, such as PDF and XPS, can be useful for the following reasons:

- Users can view electronic images of documents without the software that created the original document (e.g., Word). For example, to view a PDF file you use a program called Adobe Reader, which can be downloaded free from Adobe's website.

- Sending electronic documents saves paper and printer supplies. Society encourages users to contribute to **green computing**, which involves reducing the electricity consumed and environmental waste generated when using computers, mobile devices, and related technologies.

CONSIDER THIS

To Print a Document

1 SIGN IN | 2 USE WINDOWS | 3 USE APPS | 4 FILE MANAGEMENT | 5 SWITCH APPS | 6 SAVE FILES
7 CHANGE SCREEN RESOLUTION | 8 EXIT APPS | 9 USE ADDITIONAL APPS | 10 USE HELP

With the document opened, you may want to print it. *Why? Because you want to see how the text will appear on paper; you want to print a hard copy on a printer.* The following steps print a hard copy of the contents of the document.

- Click File on the ribbon to open the Backstage view.
- Click the Print tab in the Backstage view to display the Print gallery (Figure 33).

Q&A How can I print multiple copies of my document?
Increase the number in the Copies box in the Print gallery.

What if I decide not to print the document at this time?
Click the Back button in the upper-left corner of the Backstage view to return to the document window.

2

- Verify that the selected printer will print a hard copy of the document. If necessary, click the Printer Status button to display a list of available printer options and then click the desired printer to change the currently selected printer.

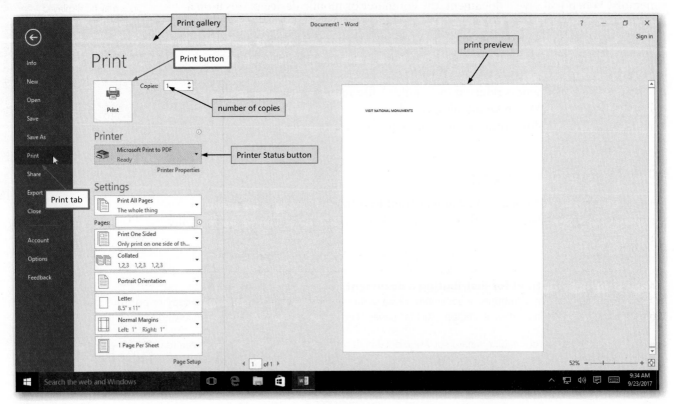

Figure 33

3

- Click the Print button in the Print gallery to print the document on the currently selected printer.
- When the printer stops, retrieve the hard copy (Figure 34).

Q&A   What if I want to print an electronic image of a document instead of a hard copy?

You would click the Printer Status button in the Print gallery and then select the desired electronic image option, such as Microsoft XPS Document Writer, which would create an XPS file.

VISIT NATIONAL MONUMENTS

Figure 34

Other Ways

1. Press CTRL+P

Organizing Files and Folders

A file contains data. This data can range from a research paper to an accounting spreadsheet to an electronic math quiz. You should organize and store files in folders to avoid misplacing a file and to help you find a file quickly.

If you are taking an introductory computer class (CIS 101, for example), you may want to design a series of folders for the different subjects covered in the class. To accomplish this, you can arrange the folders in a hierarchy for the class, as shown in Figure 35.

Figure 35

The hierarchy contains three levels. The first level contains the storage medium, such as a hard drive. The second level contains the class folder (CIS 101, in this case), and the third level contains seven folders, one each for a different Office app that will be covered in the class (Word, PowerPoint, Excel, Access, Outlook, Publisher, and OneNote).

When the hierarchy in Figure 35 is created, the storage medium is said to contain the CIS 101 folder, and the CIS 101 folder is said to contain the separate Office folders (i.e., Word, PowerPoint, Excel, etc.). In addition, this hierarchy easily can be expanded to include folders from other classes taken during additional semesters.

The vertical and horizontal lines in Figure 35 form a pathway that allows you to navigate to a drive or folder on a computer or network. A **path** consists of a drive letter (preceded by a drive name when necessary) and colon, to identify the storage device, and one or more folder names. A hard disk typically has a drive letter of C. Each drive or folder in the hierarchy has a corresponding path.

By default, Windows saves documents in the Documents folder, music in the Music folder, photos in the Pictures folder, videos in the Videos folder, and downloads in the Downloads folder.

The following pages illustrate the steps to organize the folders for this class and save a file in one of those folders:

1. Create the folder identifying your class.
2. Create the Word folder in the folder identifying your class.
3. Create the remaining folders in the folder identifying your class (one each for PowerPoint, Excel, Access, Outlook, Publisher, and OneNote).
4. Save a file in the Word folder.
5. Verify the location of the saved file.

To Create a Folder

When you create a folder, such as the CIS 101 folder shown in Figure 35, you must name the folder. A folder name should describe the folder and its contents. A folder name can contain spaces and any uppercase or lowercase characters, except a backslash (\), slash (/), colon (:), asterisk (*), question mark (?), quotation marks ("), less than symbol (<), greater than symbol (>), or vertical bar (|). Folder names cannot be CON, AUX, COM1, COM2, COM3, COM4, LPT1, LPT2, LPT3, PRN, or NUL. The same rules for naming folders also apply to naming files.

The following steps create a class folder (CIS 101, in this case) in the Documents folder. *Why? When storing files, you should organize the files so that it will be easier to find them later.*

1

- Click the File Explorer button on the taskbar to run the File Explorer.
- If necessary, double-click This PC in the navigation pane to expand the contents of your computer.
- Click the Documents folder in the navigation pane to display the contents of the Documents folder in the file list (Figure 36).

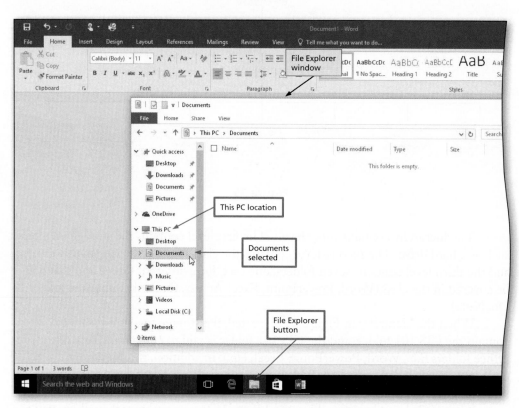

Figure 36

2

- Click the New folder button on the Quick Access Toolbar to create a new folder with the name, New folder, selected in a text box (Figure 37).

Q&A Why is the folder icon displayed differently on my computer or mobile device?
Windows might be configured to display contents differently on your computer or mobile device.

Figure 37

❸

- Type **CIS 101** (or your class code) in the text box as the new folder name.
- If requested by your instructor, add your last name to the end of the folder name.
- Press the ENTER key to change the folder name from New folder to a folder name identifying your class (Figure 38).

Q&A | What happens when I press the ENTER key?
The class folder (CIS 101, in this case) is displayed in the file list, which contains the folder name, date modified, type, and size.

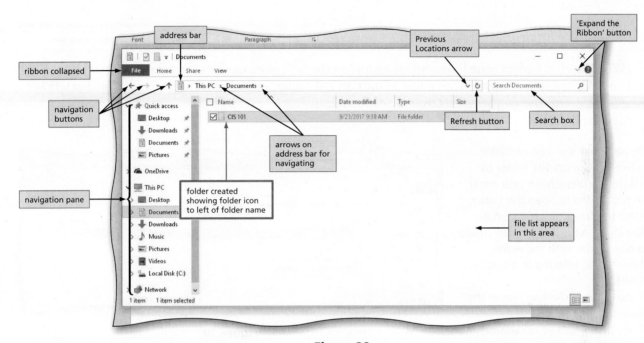

Figure 38

Other Ways

1. Press CTRL+SHIFT+N
2. Click the New folder button (Home tab | New group)

Folder Windows

The File Explorer window (shown in Figure 38) is called a folder window. Recall that a folder is a specific named location on a storage medium that contains related files. Most users rely on **folder windows** for finding, viewing, and managing information on their computers. Folder windows have common design elements, including the following (shown in Figure 38).

- The **address bar** provides quick navigation options. The arrows on the address bar allow you to visit different locations on the computer or mobile device.
- The buttons to the left of the address bar allow you to navigate the contents of the navigation pane and view recent pages.
- The **Previous Locations arrow** displays the locations you have visited.
- The **Refresh button** on the right side of the address bar refreshes the contents of the folder list.
- The **Search box** contains the dimmed words, Search Documents. You can type a term in the search box for a list of files, folders, shortcuts, and elements containing that term within the location you are searching.

- The **ribbon** contains four tabs used to accomplish various tasks on the computer related to organizing and managing the contents of the open window. This ribbon works similarly to the ribbon in the Office apps.
- The **navigation pane** on the left contains the Quick access area, the OneDrive area, the This PC area, and the Network area.
- The **Quick Access area** shows locations you access frequently. By default, this list contains links only to your Desktop, Downloads, Documents, and Pictures.

To Create a Folder within a Folder

1 SIGN IN | 2 USE WINDOWS | 3 USE APPS | 4 FILE MANAGEMENT | 5 SWITCH APPS | 6 SAVE FILES
7 CHANGE SCREEN RESOLUTION | 8 EXIT APPS | 9 USE ADDITIONAL APPS | 10 USE HELP

With the class folder created, you can create folders that will store the files you create using each Office app. The following step creates a Word folder in the CIS 101 folder (or the folder identifying your class). *Why? To be able to organize your files, you should create a folder structure.*

1

- Double-click the icon or folder name for the CIS 101 folder (or the folder identifying your class) in the file list to open the folder.
- Click the New folder button on the Quick Access Toolbar to create a new folder with the name, New folder, selected in a text box folder.
- Type **Word** in the text box as the new folder name.
- Press the ENTER key to rename the folder (Figure 39).

Figure 39

Other Ways
1. Press CTRL+SHIFT+N
2. Click the New folder button (Home tab | New group)

To Create the Remaining Folders

The following steps create the remaining folders in the folder identifying your class (in this case, CIS 101).

1 Click the New folder button on the Quick Access Toolbar to create a new folder with the name, New folder, selected in a text box.

2 Type **PowerPoint** in the text box as the new folder name.

3 Press the ENTER key to rename the folder.

4 Repeat Steps 1 through 3 to create each of the remaining folders, using Excel, Access, Outlook, Publisher, and OneNote as the folder names (Figure 40).

Figure 40

To Expand a Folder, Scroll through Folder Contents, and Collapse a Folder

Folder windows display the hierarchy of items and the contents of drives and folders in the file list. You might want to expand a folder in the navigation pane to view its contents, scroll through its contents, and collapse it when you are finished viewing its contents. *Why? When a folder is expanded, you can see all the folders it contains. By contrast, a collapsed folder hides the folders it contains.* The following steps expand, scroll through, and then collapse the folder identifying your class (CIS 101, in this case).

1

- Double-click the Documents folder in the This PC area of the navigation pane, which expands the folder to display its contents and displays a black arrow to the left of the Documents folder icon (Figure 41).

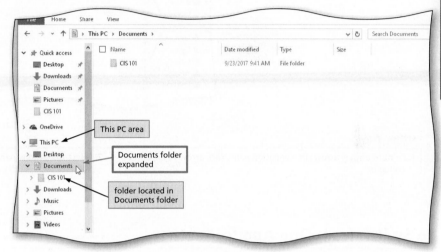

Figure 41

2

- Double-click the CIS 101 folder, which expands the folder to display its contents and displays a black arrow to the left of the folder icon (Figure 42).

Experiment

- Drag the scroll box down or click the down scroll arrow on the vertical scroll bar to display additional folders at the bottom of the navigation pane. Drag the scroll box up or click the scroll bar above the scroll box to move the scroll box to the top of the navigation pane. Drag the scroll box down the scroll bar until the scroll box is halfway down the scroll bar.

Figure 42

3

- Double-click the folder identifying your class (CIS 101, in this case) to collapse the folder (Figure 43).

Q&A Why are some folders indented below others?

A folder contains the indented folders below it.

Figure 43

Other Ways

1. Point to display arrows in navigation pane, click arrow to expand or collapse

2. Select folder to expand or collapse using arrow keys, press RIGHT ARROW to expand; press LEFT ARROW to collapse

To Switch from One App to Another

1 SIGN IN | 2 USE WINDOWS | 3 USE APPS | 4 FILE MANAGEMENT | 5 SWITCH APPS | 6 SAVE FILES
7 CHANGE SCREEN RESOLUTION | 8 EXIT APPS | 9 USE ADDITIONAL APPS | 10 USE HELP

The next step is to save the Word file containing the headline you typed earlier. Word, however, currently is not the active window. You can use the button on the taskbar and live preview to switch to Word and then save the document in the Word document window.

Why? *By clicking the appropriate app button on the taskbar, you can switch to the open app you want to use.* The steps below switch to the Word window; however, the steps are the same for any active Office app currently displayed as a button on the taskbar.

1

- Point to the Word app button on the taskbar to see a live preview of the open document(s) or the window title(s) of the open document(s), depending on your computer's configuration (Figure 44).

Q&A What if I am using a touch screen?

Live preview will not work if you are using a touch screen. If you are using a touch screen and do not have a mouse, proceed to Step 2.

Figure 44

2

- Click the button or the live preview to make the app associated with the app button the active window (Figure 45).

Q&A What if multiple documents are open in an app?
Click the desired live preview to switch to the window you want to use.

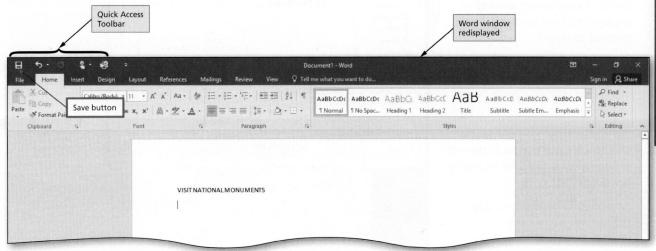

Figure 45

Other Ways
1. Press ALT+TAB until app you wish to display is selected

To Save a File in a Folder

1 SIGN IN | 2 USE WINDOWS | 3 USE APPS | 4 FILE MANAGEMENT | 5 SWITCH APPS | **6 SAVE FILES**
7 CHANGE SCREEN RESOLUTION | 8 EXIT APPS | 9 USE ADDITIONAL APPS | 10 USE HELP

With the folders for storing your files created, you can save the Word document. *Why? Without saving a file, you may lose all the work you have done and will be unable to reuse or share it with others later.* The following steps save a file in the Word folder contained in your class folder (CIS 101, in this case) using the file name, National Monuments.

1

- Click the Save button (shown in Figure 45) on the Quick Access Toolbar, which depending on settings, will display either the Save As gallery in the Backstage view (Figure 46) or the Save As dialog box (Figure 47).

Q&A What if the Save As gallery is not displayed in the Backstage view?
Click the Save As tab to display the Save As gallery.

How do I close the Backstage view?
Click the Back button in the upper-left corner of the Backstage view to return to the app window.

Figure 46

• If your screen displays the Backstage view, click This PC, if necessary, to display options in the right pane related to saving on your computer or mobile device; if your screen already displays the Save As dialog box, proceed to Step 3.

Q&A What if I wanted to save on OneDrive instead?
You would click OneDrive. Saving on OneDrive is discussed in a later section in this module.

• Click the Browse button in the left pane to display the Save As dialog box (Figure 47).

Q&A Why does a file name already appear in the File name box?
Word automatically suggests a file name the first time you save a document. The file name normally consists of the first few words contained in the document. Because the suggested file name is selected, you do not need to delete it; as soon as you begin typing, the new file name replaces the selected text.

Figure 47

❸

• Type **National Monuments** in the File name box (Save As dialog box) to change the file name. Do not press the ENTER key after typing the file name because you do not want to close the dialog box at this time (Figure 48).

Q&A What characters can I use in a file name?
The only invalid characters are the backslash (\), slash (/), colon (:), asterisk (*), question mark (?), quotation mark ("), less than symbol (<), greater than symbol (>), and vertical bar (|).

Figure 48

- Navigate to the desired save location (in this case, the Word folder in the CIS 101 folder [or your class folder] in the Documents folder) by performing the tasks in Steps 4a and 4b.

4a

- If the Documents folder is not displayed in the navigation pane, drag the scroll bar in the navigation pane until Documents appears.

- If the Documents folder is not expanded in the navigation pane, double-click Documents to display its folders in the navigation pane.

- If your class folder (CIS 101, in this case) is not expanded, double-click the CIS 101 folder to select the folder and display its contents in the navigation pane (Figure 49).

Figure 49

Q&A | What if I do not want to save in a folder?
Although storing files in folders is an effective technique for organizing files, some users prefer not to store files in folders. If you prefer not to save this file in a folder, select the storage device on which you wish to save the file and then proceed to Step 5.

4b

- Click the Word folder in the navigation pane to select it as the new save location and display its contents in the file list (Figure 50).

Figure 50

5

• Click the Save button (Save As dialog box) to save the document in the selected folder in the selected location with the entered file name (Figure 51).

Q&A How do I know that the file is saved?

While an Office app is saving a file, it briefly displays a message on the status bar indicating the amount of the file saved. In addition, the file name appears on the title bar.

Figure 51

Other Ways

1. Click File on ribbon, click Save As in Backstage view, click This PC, click Browse button, type file name (Save As dialog box), navigate to desired save location, click Save button
2. Press F12, type file name (Save As dialog box), navigate to desired save location, click Save button

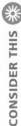

CONSIDER THIS

How often should you save a document?

It is important to save a document frequently for the following reasons:

• The document in memory might be lost if the computer is turned off or you lose electrical power while an app is running.

• If you run out of time before completing a project, you may finish it at a future time without starting over.

Navigating in Dialog Boxes

Navigating is the process of finding a location on a storage device. While saving the National Monuments file, for example, Steps 4a and 4b navigated to the Word folder located in the CIS 101 folder in the Documents folder. When performing certain functions in Windows apps, such as saving a file, opening a file, or inserting a picture in an existing document, you most likely will have to navigate to the location where you want to save the file or to the folder containing the file you want to open or insert. Most dialog boxes in Windows apps requiring navigation follow a similar procedure; that is, the way you navigate to a folder in one dialog box, such as the Save As dialog box, is similar to how you might navigate in another dialog box, such as the Open dialog box. If you chose to navigate to a specific location in a dialog box, you would follow the instructions in Steps 4a and 4b.

To Minimize and Restore a Window

1 SIGN IN | **2 USE WINDOWS** | 3 USE APPS | 4 FILE MANAGEMENT | 5 SWITCH APPS | 6 SAVE FILES
7 CHANGE SCREEN RESOLUTION | 8 EXIT APPS | 9 USE ADDITIONAL APPS | 10 USE HELP

Before continuing, you can verify that the Word file was saved properly. To do this, you will minimize the Word window and then open the CIS 101 window so that you can verify the file is stored in the CIS 101 folder on the hard drive. A **minimized window** is an open window that is hidden from view but can be displayed quickly by clicking the window's button on the taskbar.

In the following example, Word is used to illustrate minimizing and restoring windows; however, you would follow the same steps regardless of the Office app you are using. *Why? Before closing an app, you should make sure your file saved correctly so that you can find it later.*

The following steps minimize the Word window, verify that the file is saved, and then restore the minimized window.

- Click the Minimize button on the app's title bar (shown in Figure 51) to minimize the window (Figure 52).

Q&A Is the minimized window still available?
The minimized window, Word in this case, remains available but no longer is the active window. It is minimized as a button on the taskbar.

- If the File Explorer window is not open on the screen, click the File Explorer button on the taskbar to make the File Explorer window the active window.

Figure 52

- Double-click the Word folder in the file list to select the folder and display its contents (Figure 53).

Q&A Why does the File Explorer button on the taskbar change?
A selected app button indicates that the app is active on the screen. When the button is not selected, the app is running but not active.

- After viewing the contents of the selected folder, click the Word button on the taskbar to restore the minimized window (as shown in Figure 51).

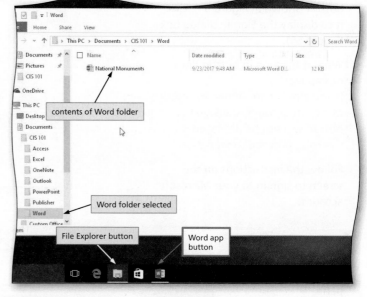

Figure 53

Other Ways

1. Right-click title bar, click Minimize on shortcut menu, click taskbar button in taskbar button area
2. Press WINDOWS+M, press WINDOWS+SHIFT+M
3. Click Word app button on taskbar to minimize window. Click Word app button again to restore window.

To Save a File on OneDrive

1 SIGN IN | 2 USE WINDOWS | 3 USE APPS | 4 FILE MANAGEMENT | 5 SWITCH APPS | **6 SAVE FILES**
7 CHANGE SCREEN RESOLUTION | 8 EXIT APPS | 9 USE ADDITIONAL APPS | 10 USE HELP

One of the features of Office is the capability to save files on OneDrive so that you can use the files on multiple computers or mobile devices without having to use an external storage device, such as a USB flash drive. Storing files on OneDrive also enables you to share files more efficiently with others, such as when using Office Online and Office 365.

In the following example, Word is used to save a file on OneDrive. *Why? Storing files on OneDrive provides more portability options than are available from storing files in the Documents folder.*

You can save files directly on OneDrive from within an Office app. The following steps save the current Word file on OneDrive. These steps require you have a Microsoft account and an Internet connection.

1

● Click File on the ribbon to open the Backstage view.

Q&A What is the purpose of the File tab?
The File tab opens the Backstage view for each Office app.

● Click the Save As tab in the Backstage view to display the Save As gallery.

● Click OneDrive to display OneDrive saving options or a Sign In button, if you are not signed in already to your Microsoft account (Figure 54).

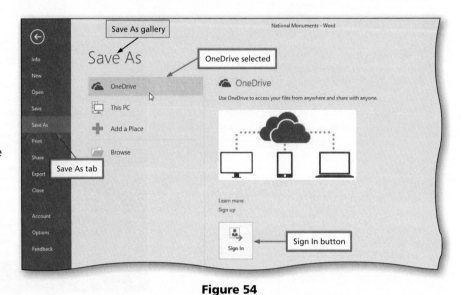

Figure 54

2

● If your screen displays a Sign In button (shown in Figure 54), click it to display the Sign in dialog box (Figure 55).

Q&A What if the Sign In button does not appear?
If you already are signed into your Microsoft account, the Sign In button will not be displayed. In this case, proceed to Step 3.

● Follow the instructions on the screen to sign in to your Microsoft account.

Figure 55

3

● If necessary, click OneDrive in the left pane.

● In the Backstage view, click the Documents folder in the right pane to display the Save As dialog box (Figure 56).

4

● Click the Save button (Save As dialog box) to save the file on OneDrive.

Figure 56

To Sign Out of a Microsoft Account

If you are using a public computer or otherwise wish to sign out of your Microsoft account, you should sign out of the account from the Accounts gallery in the Backstage view. Signing out of the account is the safest way to make sure that nobody else can access online files or settings stored in your Microsoft account. *Why? For security reasons, you should sign out of your Microsoft account when you are finished using a public or shared computer. Staying signed in to your Microsoft account might enable others to access your files.*

The following steps sign out of a Microsoft account from Word. You would use the same steps in any Office app. If you do not wish to sign out of your Microsoft account, read these steps without performing them.

1 Click File on the ribbon to open the Backstage view.

2 Click the Account tab to display the Account gallery (Figure 57).

3 Click the Sign out link, which displays the Remove Account dialog box. If a Can't remove Windows accounts dialog box appears instead of the Remove Account dialog box, click the OK button and skip the remaining steps.

Q&A Why does a Can't remove Windows accounts dialog box appear?
If you signed in to Windows using your Microsoft account, then you also must sign out from Windows, rather than signing out from within Word. When you are finished using Windows, be sure to sign out at that time.

4 Click the Yes button (Remove Account dialog box) to sign out of your Microsoft account on this computer.

Q&A Should I sign out of Windows after removing my Microsoft account?
When you are finished using the computer, you should sign out of Windows for maximum security.

5 Click the Back button in the upper-left corner of the Backstage view to return to the document.

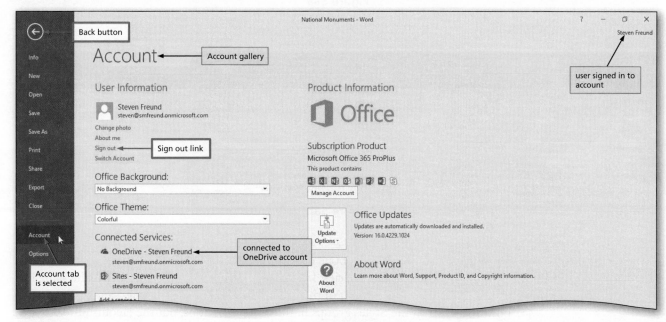

Figure 57

Screen Resolution

Screen resolution indicates the number of pixels (dots) that the computer uses to display the letters, numbers, graphics, and background you see on the screen. When you increase the screen resolution, Windows displays more information on the screen, but the information decreases in size. The reverse also is true: as you decrease the screen resolution, Windows displays less information on the screen, but the information increases in size.

Screen resolution usually is stated as the product of two numbers, such as 1366 × 768 (pronounced "thirteen sixty-six by seven sixty-eight"). A 1366 × 768 screen resolution results in a display of 1366 distinct pixels on each of 768 lines, or about 1,050,624 pixels. Changing the screen resolution affects how the ribbon appears in Office apps and some Windows dialog boxes. Figure 58 shows the Word ribbon at screen resolutions of 1366 × 768 and 1024 × 768. All of the same commands are available regardless of screen resolution. The app (Word, in this case), however, makes changes to the groups and the buttons within the groups to accommodate the various screen resolutions. The result is that certain commands may need to be accessed differently depending on the resolution chosen. A command that is visible on the ribbon and available by clicking a button at one resolution may not be visible and may need to be accessed using its Dialog Box Launcher at a different resolution.

Figure 58a

Figure 58b

Comparing the two ribbons in Figure 58, notice the changes in content and layout of the groups and galleries. In some cases, the content of a group is the same in each resolution, but the layout of the group differs. For example, the same gallery and buttons appear in the Styles groups in the two resolutions, but the layouts differ. In other cases, the content and layout are the same across the resolution, but the level of detail differs with the resolution.

To Change the Screen Resolution

If you are using a computer to step through the modules in this book and you want your screen to match the figures, you may need to change your screen's resolution. *Why? The figures in this book use a screen resolution of 1366 × 768.* The following steps change the screen resolution to 1366 × 768. Your computer already may be set to 1366 × 768. Keep in mind that many computer labs prevent users from changing the screen resolution; in that case, read the following steps for illustration purposes.

1

- Click the Show desktop button, which is located at the far-right edge of the taskbar, to display the Windows desktop.

- Right-click an empty area on the Windows desktop to display a shortcut menu that contains a list of commands related to the desktop (Figure 59).

Q&A Why does my shortcut menu display different commands?
Depending on your computer's hardware and configuration, different commands might appear on the shortcut menu.

Figure 59

2

- Click Display settings on the shortcut menu to open the Settings app window. If necessary, scroll to display the 'Advanced display settings' link (Figure 60).

Figure 60

- Click 'Advanced display settings' in the Settings window to display the advanced display settings.
- If necessary, scroll to display the Resolution box (Figure 61).

Figure 61

- Click the Resolution box to display a list of available screen resolutions (Figure 62).
- If necessary, scroll to and then click 1366 × 768 to select the screen resolution.

Q&A   What if my computer does not support the 1366 × 768 resolution? Some computers do not support the 1366 × 768 resolution. In this case, select a resolution that is close to the 1366 × 768 resolution.

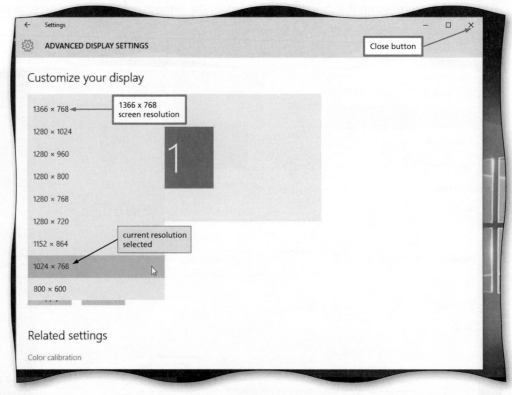

Figure 62

5

- Click the Apply button (Advanced Display Settings window) (shown in Figure 61) to change the screen resolution and display a confirmation message (Figure 63).
- Click the Keep changes button to accept the new screen resolution.
- Click the Close button (shown in Figure 62) to close the Settings app window.

Figure 63

Other Ways

1. Click Start button, click Settings, click System, click Display, click 'Advanced display settings,' select desired resolution in Resolution box, click Apply button, click Keep changes button

2. Type **screen resolution** in search box, click 'Change the screen resolution,' select desired resolution in Resolution box, click Apply, click Keep changes

---

To Exit an Office App with One Document Open

1 SIGN IN | 2 USE WINDOWS | 3 USE APPS | 4 FILE MANAGEMENT | 5 SWITCH APPS | 6 SAVE FILES
7 CHANGE SCREEN RESOLUTION | 8 EXIT APPS | 9 USE ADDITIONAL APPS | 10 USE HELP

When you exit an Office app, such as Word, if you have made changes to a file since the last time the file was saved, the Office app displays a dialog box asking if you want to save the changes you made to the file before it closes the app window. *Why? The dialog box contains three buttons with these resulting actions: the Save button saves the changes and then exits the Office app, the Don't Save button exits the Office app without saving changes, and the Cancel button closes the dialog box and redisplays the file without saving the changes.*

If no changes have been made to an open document since the last time the file was saved, the Office app will close the window without displaying a dialog box.

The following steps exit an Office app. In the following example, Word is used to illustrate exiting an Office app; however, you would follow the same steps regardless of the Office app you were using.

1

- If necessary, click the Word app button on the taskbar to display the Word window on the desktop (Figure 64).

Figure 64

• Click the Close button to close the document and exit Word. If a Microsoft Word dialog box appears, click the Save button to save any changes made to the document since the last save.

Q&A What if I have more than one document open in an Office app?

You could click the Close button for each open document. When you click the last open document's Close button, you also exit the Office app. As an alternative that is more efficient, you could right-click the app button on the taskbar and then click 'Close all windows' on the shortcut menu, or press ALT+F4 to close all open documents and exit the Office app.

Other Ways

1. Right-click the Office app button on Windows taskbar, click Close window on shortcut menu
2. Press ALT+F4

To Copy a Folder to OneDrive

1 SIGN IN | 2 USE WINDOWS | 3 USE APPS | **4 FILE MANAGEMENT** | 5 SWITCH APPS | 6 SAVE FILES
7 CHANGE SCREEN RESOLUTION | 8 EXIT APPS | **9 USE ADDITIONAL APPS** | **10 USE HELP**

To back up your files or easily make them available on another computer or mobile device, you can copy them to OneDrive. The following steps copy your CIS 101 folder to OneDrive. If you do not have access to a OneDrive account, read the following steps without performing them. *Why? It often is good practice to have a backup of your files so that they are available in case something happens to your original copies.*

1

• Click the File Explorer button on the taskbar to make the folder window the active window.

• Click Documents in the This PC area of the navigation pane to display the CIS 101 folder in the file list.

Q&A What if my CIS 101 folder is stored in a different location?

Use the navigation pane to navigate to the location of your CIS 101 folder. The CIS 101 folder should be displayed in the file list once you have located it.

• Click the CIS 101 folder in the file list to select it (Figure 65).

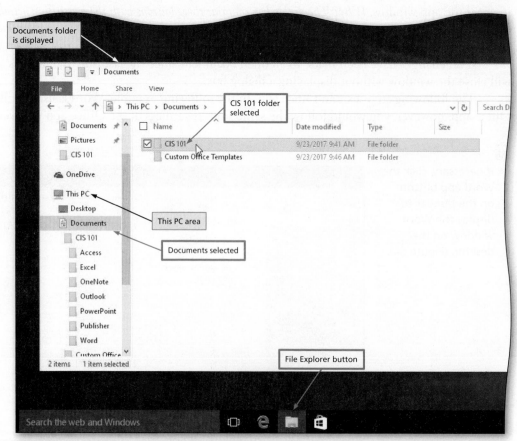

Figure 65

2

- Click Home on the ribbon to display the Home tab.
- Click the Copy to button (Home tab | Organize group) to display the Copy to menu (Figure 66).

Figure 66

3

- Click Choose location on the Copy to menu to display the Copy Items dialog box.
- Click OneDrive (Copy Items dialog box) to select it (Figure 67).

Figure 67

4

- Click the Copy button (Copy Items dialog box) to copy the selected folder to OneDrive.
- Click OneDrive in the navigation pane to verify the CIS 101 folder displays in the file list (Figure 68).

Q&A | Why does a Microsoft OneDrive dialog box display when I click OneDrive in the navigation pane?
If you are not currently signed in to Windows using a Microsoft account, you will manually need to sign in to a Microsoft account to save files to OneDrive. Follow the instructions on the screen to sign in to your Microsoft account.

Figure 68

Other Ways

1. In File Explorer, select folder to copy, click Copy button (Home tab | Clipboard group), display contents of OneDrive in file list, click Paste button (Home tab | Clipboard group)

2. In File Explorer, select folder to copy, press CTRL+C, display contents of OneDrive in file list, press CTRL+V

3. Drag folder to copy to OneDrive in navigation pane

To Unlink a OneDrive Account

If you are using a public computer and are not signed in to Windows with a Microsoft account, you should unlink your OneDrive account so that other users cannot access it. *Why? If you do not unlink your OneDrive account, other people using the same user account on the computer will be able to view, remove, and add to files stored in your OneDrive account.*

The following steps unlink your OneDrive account. If you do not wish to sign out of your Microsoft account, read these steps without performing them.

①

• Click the 'Show hidden icons' button on the Windows taskbar to show a menu of hidden icons (Figure 69).

Figure 69

②

• Right click the OneDrive icon (shown in Figure 69) to display a shortcut menu (Figure 70).

Figure 70

- Click Settings on the shortcut menu to display the Microsoft OneDrive dialog box (Figure 71).

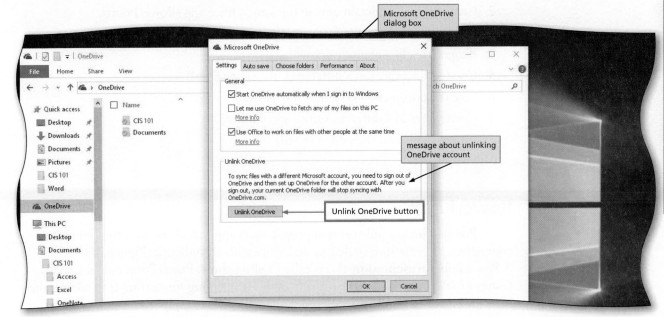

Figure 71

4

- If necessary, click the Settings tab.
- Click the Unlink OneDrive button (Microsoft OneDrive dialog box) to unlink the OneDrive account (Figure 72).
- When the Microsoft OneDrive dialog box appears with a Welcome to OneDrive message, click the Close button.
- Minimize the File Explorer window.

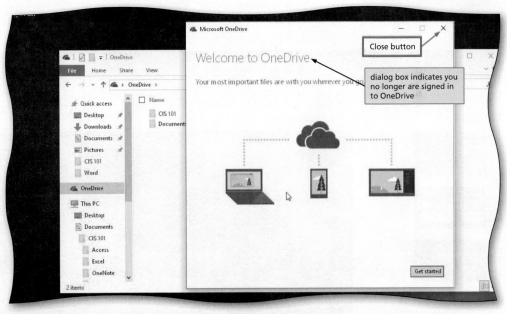

Figure 72

Break Point: If you wish to take a break, this is a good place to do so. To resume at a later time, continue to follow the steps from this location forward.

Additional Microsoft Office Apps

The previous section used Word to illustrate common features of Office and some basic elements unique to Word. The following sections present elements unique to PowerPoint, Excel, and Access, as well as illustrate additional common features of Office.

In the following pages, you will learn how to do the following:

1. Run an Office app (PowerPoint) using the search box.
2. Create two small documents in the same Office app (PowerPoint).
3. Close one of the documents.
4. Reopen the document just closed.
5. Create a document in a different Office app (Excel).
6. Save the document with a new file name.
7. Create a file in a different Office app (Access).
8. Close the file and then open the file.

PowerPoint

PowerPoint is a full-featured presentation app that allows you to produce compelling presentations to deliver and share with an audience (Figure 73). A PowerPoint **presentation** also is called a **slide show**. PowerPoint contains many features to design, develop, and organize slides, including formatting text, adding and editing video and audio clips, creating tables and charts, applying artistic effects to pictures, animating graphics, and collaborating with friends and colleagues. You then can turn your presentation into a video, broadcast your slide show on the web, or create a photo album.

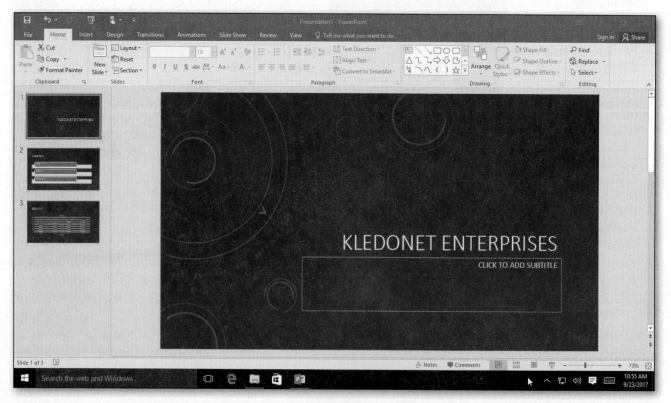

Figure 73

To Run an App Using the Search Box

The following steps, which assume Windows is running, use the search box to run the PowerPoint app based on a typical installation; however, you would follow similar steps to run any Office app. *Why? Some people prefer to use the search box to locate and run an app, as opposed to searching through a list of all apps on the Start menu.* You may need to ask your instructor how to run apps for your computer.

1

- Type **PowerPoint 2016** as the search text in the search box and watch the search results appear in the search results (Figure 74).

Q&A Do I need to type the complete app name or use correct capitalization?

No, you need to type just enough characters of the app name for it to appear in the search results. For example, you may be able to type PowerPoint or powerpoint, instead of PowerPoint 2016.

2

- Click the app name, PowerPoint 2016 in this case, in the search results to run PowerPoint (Figure 75).

Figure 74

Figure 75

- Click the Blank Presentation thumbnail to create a blank presentation and display it in the PowerPoint window.
- If the app window is not maximized, click the Maximize button on its title bar to maximize the window (Figure 76).

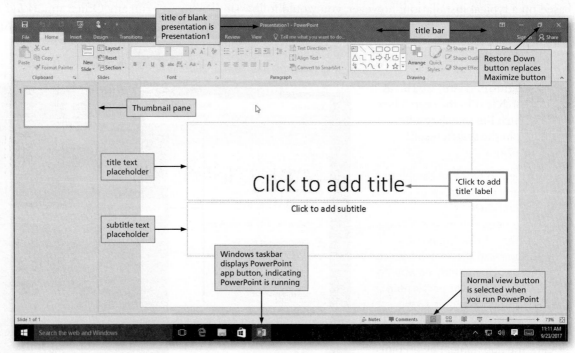

Figure 76

The PowerPoint Window and Ribbon

The PowerPoint window consists of a variety of components to make your work more efficient and documents more professional: the window, ribbon, mini toolbar, shortcut menus, Quick Access Toolbar, and Microsoft Account area. Many of these components are common to other Office apps and have been discussed earlier in this module. Other components, discussed in the following paragraphs and later in subsequent modules, are unique to PowerPoint.

The basic unit of a PowerPoint presentation is a **slide**. A slide may contain text and objects, such as graphics, tables, charts, and drawings. **Layouts** are used to position this content on the slide. When you create a new presentation, the default **Title Slide** layout appears (shown in Figure 76). The purpose of this layout is to introduce the presentation to the audience. PowerPoint includes several other built-in standard layouts.

The default slide layouts are set up in **landscape orientation**, where the slide width is greater than its height. In landscape orientation, the slide size is preset to 13.3 inches wide and 7.5 inches high when printed on a standard sheet of paper measuring 11 inches wide and 8.5 inches high.

Placeholders   **Placeholders** are boxes with dashed or solid borders that are displayed when you create a new slide. All layouts except the Blank slide layout contain placeholders. Depending on the particular slide layout selected, title and subtitle placeholders are displayed for the slide title and subtitle; a content placeholder is displayed for text or a table, chart, picture, graphic, or movie. The title slide in Figure 76 has two text placeholders for the main heading, or title, and the subtitle.

Ribbon   The ribbon in PowerPoint is similar to the one in Word and the other Microsoft Office apps. When you run PowerPoint, the ribbon displays nine main tabs: File, Home, Insert, Design, Transitions, Animations, Slide Show, Review, and View.

To Enter Content in a Title Slide

With the exception of a blank slide, PowerPoint assumes every new slide has a title. Many of PowerPoint's layouts have both a title text placeholder and at least one content placeholder. To make creating a presentation easier, any text you type after a new slide appears becomes title text in the title text placeholder. As you begin typing text in the title text placeholder, the title text also is displayed in the Slide 1 thumbnail in the Thumbnail pane. The title for this presentation is Mara's Marbles. The following step enters a presentation title on the title slide. **Why?** *In general, every presentation should have a title to describe what the presentation will be covering.*

1

- Click the 'Click to add title' label located inside the title text placeholder (shown in Figure 76) to select the placeholder.
- Type **Mara's Marbles** in the title text placeholder. Do not press the ENTER key because you do not want to create a new line of text (Figure 77).

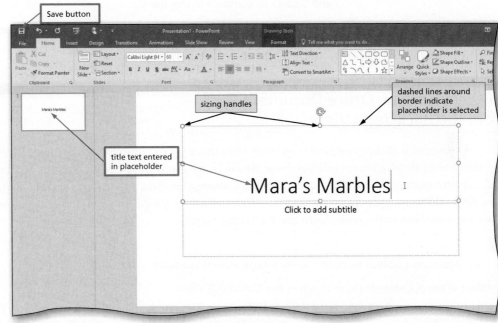

Figure 77

To Save a File in a Folder

The following steps save the presentation in the PowerPoint folder in the class folder (CIS 101, in this case) in the Documents folder using the file name, Mara's Marbles.

1 Click the Save button on the Quick Access Toolbar (shown in Figure 77), which depending on settings will display either the Save As gallery in the Backstage view or the Save As dialog box.

2 If your screen displays the Backstage view, click This PC, if necessary, to display options in the right pane related to saving on your computer; if your screen already displays the Save As dialog box, proceed to Step 4.

3 Click the Browse button in the left pane to display the Save As dialog box.

4 If necessary, type **Mara's Marbles** in the File name box (Save As dialog box) to change the file name. Do not press the ENTER key after typing the file name because you do not want to close the dialog box at this time.

5 Navigate to the desired save location (in this case, the PowerPoint folder in the CIS 101 folder [or your class folder] in the Documents folder). For specific instructions, perform the tasks in Steps 5a through 5e.

5a If the Documents folder is not displayed in the navigation pane, slide to scroll or drag the scroll bar in the navigation pane until Documents appears.

5b If the Documents folder is not expanded in the navigation pane, double-click Documents to display its folders in the navigation pane.

5c If the Documents folder is not expanded in the navigation pane, double-click Documents to display its folders in the navigation pane.

5d If your class folder (CIS 101, in this case) is not expanded, double-click the CIS 101 folder to select the folder and display its contents in the navigation pane.

5e Click the PowerPoint folder in the navigation pane to select it as the new save location and display its contents in the file list.

6 Click the Save button (Save As dialog box) to save the presentation in the selected folder in the selected location with the entered file name.

To Create a New Office Document from the Backstage View

1 SIGN IN | 2 USE WINDOWS | 3 USE APPS | 4 FILE MANAGEMENT | 5 SWITCH APPS | 6 SAVE FILES
7 CHANGE SCREEN RESOLUTION | 8 EXIT APPS | 9 USE ADDITIONAL APPS | 10 USE HELP

As discussed earlier, the Backstage view contains a set of commands that enable you to manage documents and data about the documents. *Why? From the Backstage view in PowerPoint, for example, you can create, open, print, and save presentations. You also can share documents, manage versions, set permissions, and modify document properties. In other Office 2016 apps, the Backstage view may contain features specific to those apps.* The following steps create a file, a blank presentation in this case, from the Backstage view.

1

● Click File on the ribbon to open the Backstage view (Figure 78).

Q&A | What is the purpose of the Info tab in the Backstage view?
The Info tab, which is selected by default when you click File on the ribbon, allows you to protect your document, inspect your document, and manage versions of your document as well as view all the file properties, such as when the file was created.

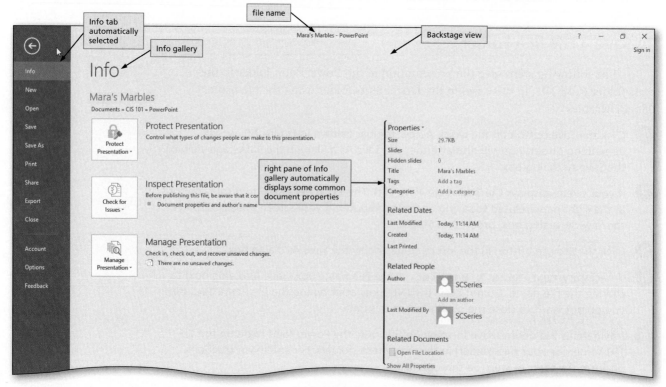

Figure 78

2

- Click the New tab in the Backstage view to display the New gallery (Figure 79).

Q&A Can I create documents through the Backstage view in other Office apps? Yes. If the Office app has a New tab in the Backstage view, the New gallery displays various options for creating a new file.

Figure 79

3

- Click the Blank Presentation thumbnail in the New gallery to create a new presentation.

Other Ways

1. Press CTRL + N

To Enter Content in a Title Slide of a Second PowerPoint Presentation

The presentation title for this presentation is Visiting National Monuments. The following steps enter a presentation title on the title slide.

1 Click the title text placeholder to select it.

2 Type **Visiting National Monuments** in the title text placeholder. Do not press the ENTER key.

To Save a File in a Folder

The following steps save the second presentation in the PowerPoint folder in the class folder (CIS 101, in this case) in the Documents folder using the file name, Visiting National Monuments.

1 Click the Save button on the Quick Access Toolbar, which depending on settings will display either the Save As gallery in the Backstage view or the Save As dialog box.

2 If your screen displays the Backstage view, click This PC, if necessary, to display options in the right pane related to saving on your computer; if your screen already displays the Save As dialog box, proceed to Step 4.

3 Click the Browse button in the left pane to display the Save As dialog box.

④ If necessary, type **Visiting National Monuments** in the File name box (Save As dialog box) to change the file name. Do not press the ENTER key after typing the file name because you do not want to close the dialog box at this time.

⑤ If necessary, navigate to the desired save location (in this case, the PowerPoint folder in the CIS 101 folder [or your class folder] in the Documents folder). For specific instructions, perform the tasks in Steps 5a through 5e in the previous section titled To Save a File in a Folder.

⑥ Click the Save button (Save As dialog box) to save the presentation in the selected folder on the selected drive with the entered file name.

To Close an Office File Using the Backstage View

1 SIGN IN | 2 USE WINDOWS | 3 USE APPS | 4 FILE MANAGEMENT | 5 SWITCH APPS | 6 SAVE FILES
7 CHANGE SCREEN RESOLUTION | 8 EXIT APPS | 9 USE ADDITIONAL APPS | 10 USE HELP

Sometimes, you may want to close an Office file, such as a PowerPoint presentation, entirely and start over with a new file. You also may want to close a file when you are done working with it. *Why? You should close a file when you are done working with it so that you do not make inadvertent changes to it.* The following steps close the current active Office file, that is, the Visiting National Monuments presentation, without exiting the active app (PowerPoint, in this case).

- Click File on the ribbon to open the Backstage view (Figure 80).

- Click Close in the Backstage view to close the open file (Visiting National Monuments, in this case) without exiting the active app.

Q&A

What if the Office app displays a dialog box about saving?
Click the Save button if you want to save the changes, click the Don't Save button if you want to ignore the changes since the last time you saved, and click the Cancel button if you do not want to close the document.

Can I use the Backstage view to close an open file in other Office apps, such as Word and Excel?
Yes.

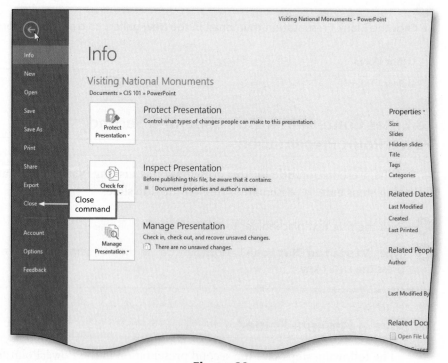

Figure 80

Other Ways

1. Press CTRL+F4

To Open a Recent Office File Using the Backstage View

1 SIGN IN | 2 USE WINDOWS | 3 USE APPS | 4 FILE MANAGEMENT | 5 SWITCH APPS | 6 SAVE FILES
7 CHANGE SCREEN RESOLUTION | 8 EXIT APPS | 9 USE ADDITIONAL APPS | 10 USE HELP

You sometimes need to open a file that you recently modified. *Why? You may have more changes to make, such as adding more content or correcting errors.* The Backstage view allows you to access recent files easily. The following steps reopen the Visiting National Monuments file just closed.

1

- Click File on the ribbon to open the Backstage view.
- Click the Open tab in the Backstage view to display the Open gallery (Figure 81).

2

- Click the desired file name in the Recent list, Visiting National Monuments in this case, to open the file.

Q&A Can I use the Backstage view to open a recent file in other Office apps, such as Word and Excel?
Yes, as long as the file name appears in the list of recent files.

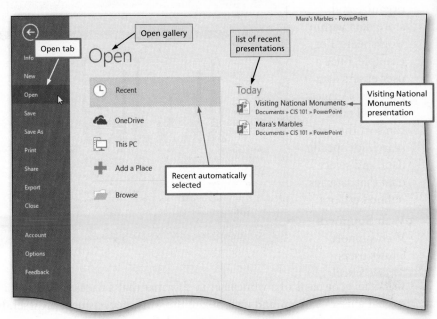

Figure 81

Other Ways

1. Click File on ribbon, click Open in Backstage view, click This PC, click Browse button, navigate to file (Open dialog box), click Open button

To Exit an Office App

You are finished using PowerPoint. Thus, you should exit this Office app. The following steps exit PowerPoint.

1 If you have one Office document open, click the Close button on the right side of the title bar to close the document and exit the Office app; or if you have multiple Office documents open, right-click the app button on the taskbar and then click 'Close all windows' on the shortcut menu, or press ALT+F4 to close all open documents and exit the Office app.

Q&A If I am using a touch screen, could I press and hold the Close button until all windows close and the app exits?
Yes.

2 If a dialog box appears, click the Save button to save any changes made to the document since the last save.

Excel

Excel is a powerful spreadsheet app that allows users to organize data, complete calculations, make decisions, graph data, develop professional-looking reports (Figure 82), publish organized data to the web, and access real-time data from websites. The four major parts of Excel are:

- **Workbooks and Worksheets:** A **workbook** is like a notebook. Inside the workbook are sheets, each of which is called a **worksheet**. Thus, a workbook is a collection of worksheets. Worksheets allow users to enter, calculate, manipulate, and analyze data, such as numbers and text. The terms worksheet and spreadsheet are interchangeable.
- **Charts:** Excel can draw a variety of charts, such as column charts and pie charts.

• **Tables:** Tables organize and store data within worksheets. For example, once a user enters data into a worksheet, an Excel table can sort the data, search for specific data, and select data that satisfies defined criteria.

Figure 82

• **Web Support:** Web support allows users to save Excel worksheets or parts of a worksheet in a format that a user can view in a browser, so that a user can view and manipulate the worksheet using a browser. Excel web support also provides access to real-time data, such as stock quotes, using web queries.

To Create a New Blank Office Document from File Explorer

1 SIGN IN | **2** USE WINDOWS | **3** USE APPS | **4** FILE MANAGEMENT | **5** SWITCH APPS | **6** SAVE FILES
7 CHANGE SCREEN RESOLUTION | **8** EXIT APPS | **9** USE ADDITIONAL APPS | **10** USE HELP

File Explorer provides a means to create a blank Office document without running an Office app. The following steps use File Explorer to create a blank Excel document. *Why? Sometimes you might need to create a blank document and then return to it later for editing.*

1

• If necessary, click the File Explorer button on the taskbar to make the folder window the active window.

• If necessary, double-click the Documents folder in the navigation pane to expand the Documents folder.

• If necessary, double-click your class folder (CIS 101, in this case) in the navigation pane to expand the folder.

• Click the Excel folder in the navigation pane to display its contents in the file list.

• With the Excel folder selected, right-click an open area in the file list to display a shortcut menu.

• Point to New on the shortcut menu to display the New submenu (Figure 83).

Figure 83

- Click 'Microsoft Excel Worksheet' on the New submenu to display an icon and text box for a new file in the current folder window with the file name, New Microsoft Excel Worksheet, selected (Figure 84).

Figure 84

- Type **Silver Sky Hardware** in the text box and then press the ENTER key to assign a new file name to the new file in the current folder (Figure 85).

Figure 85

To Run an App from File Explorer and Open a File

1 SIGN IN | 2 USE WINDOWS | 3 USE APPS | 4 FILE MANAGEMENT | 5 SWITCH APPS | 6 SAVE FILES
7 CHANGE SCREEN RESOLUTION | 8 EXIT APPS | 9 USE ADDITIONAL APPS | 10 USE HELP

Previously, you learned how to run an Office app using the Start menu and the search box. The following steps, which assume Windows is running, use File Explorer to run the Excel app based on a typical installation. *Why? Another way to run an Office app is to open an existing file from File Explorer, which causes the app in which the file was created to run and then open the selected file.* You may need to ask your instructor how to run Office apps for your computer.

- If necessary, display the file to open in the folder window in File Explorer (shown in Figure 85).
- Right-click the file icon or file name (Silver Sky Hardware, in this case) to display a shortcut menu (Figure 86).

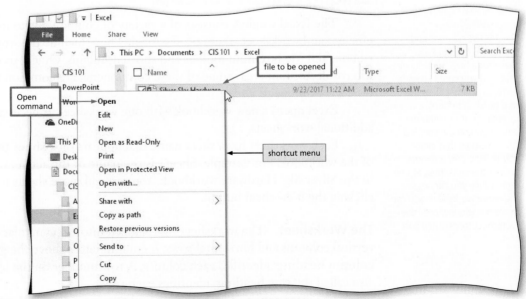

Figure 86

2

- Click Open on the shortcut menu to open the selected file in the app used to create the file, Excel in this case (Figure 87).
- If the window is not maximized, click the Maximize button on the title bar to maximize the window.

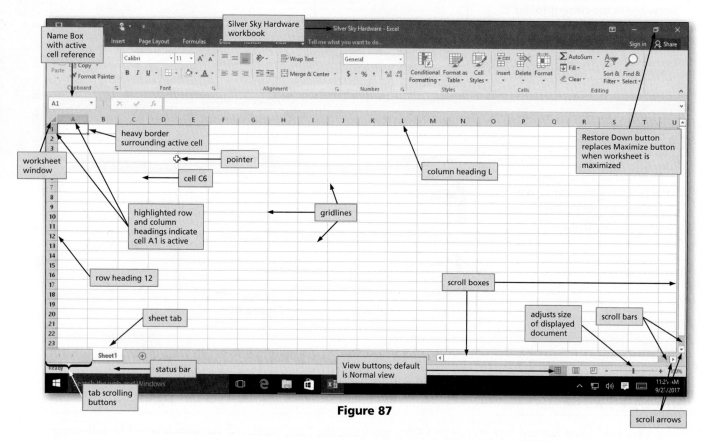

Figure 87

Q&A Instead of using File Explorer, can I run Excel using the same method shown previously for Word and PowerPoint?
Yes, you can use any method of running an Office app to run Excel.

Unique Features of Excel

The Excel window consists of a variety of components to make your work more efficient and worksheets more professional. These include the worksheet window, ribbon, Tell Me box, mini toolbar and shortcut menus, Quick Access Toolbar, and Microsoft Account area. Some of these components are common to other Office apps; others are unique to Excel.

Excel opens a new workbook with one worksheet. If necessary, you can add additional worksheets.

Each worksheet has a sheet name that appears on a **sheet tab** at the bottom of the workbook. For example, Sheet1 is the name of the active worksheet displayed in the Silver Sky Hardware workbook. You can add more sheets to the workbook by clicking the New sheet button.

The Worksheet The worksheet is organized into a rectangular grid containing vertical columns and horizontal rows. A column letter above the grid, also called the **column heading**, identifies each column. A row number on the left side of the grid, also called the **row heading**, identifies each row.

The intersection of each column and row is a cell. A **cell** is the basic unit of a worksheet into which you enter data. Each worksheet in a workbook has 16,384 columns and 1,048,576 rows for a total of 17,179,869,184 cells. Only a small fraction of the active worksheet appears on the screen at one time.

A cell is referred to by its unique address, or **cell reference**, which is the coordinates of the intersection of a column and a row. To identify a cell, specify the column letter first, followed by the row number. For example, cell reference C6 refers to the cell located at the intersection of column C and row 6 (Figure 87).

One cell on the worksheet, designated the **active cell**, is the one into which you can enter data. The active cell in Figure 87 is A1. The active cell is identified in three ways. First, a heavy border surrounds the cell; second, the active cell reference shows immediately above column A in the Name box; and third, the column heading A and row heading 1 are highlighted so that it is easy to see which cell is active (Figure 87).

The horizontal and vertical lines on the worksheet itself are called **gridlines**. Gridlines make it easier to see and identify each cell in the worksheet. If desired, you can turn the gridlines off so that they do not show on the worksheet. While learning Excel, gridlines help you to understand the structure of the worksheet.

The pointer in Figure 87 has the shape of a block plus sign. The pointer appears as a block plus sign whenever it is located in a cell on the worksheet. Another common shape of the pointer is the block arrow. The pointer turns into the block arrow when you move it outside the worksheet or when you drag cell contents between rows or columns.

Ribbon   When you run Excel, the ribbon displays eight main tabs: File, Home, Insert, Page Layout, Formulas, Data, Review, and View. The Formulas and Data tabs are specific to Excel. The Formulas tab allows you to work with Excel formulas, and the Data tab allows you to work with data processing features such as importing and sorting data.

Formula Bar   As you type, Excel displays the entry in the **formula bar**, which appears below the ribbon (Figure 88). You can make the formula bar larger by dragging the sizing handle at the bottom of the formula bar or clicking the expand button to the right of the formula bar. Excel also displays the active cell reference in the **Name box** on the left side of the formula bar.

BTW

Customizing the Ribbon
In addition to customizing the Quick Access Toolbar, you can add items to and remove items from the ribbon. To customize the ribbon, click File on the ribbon to open the Backstage view, click the Options tab in the Backstage view, and then click Customize Ribbon in the left pane of the Options dialog box. More information about customizing the ribbon is presented in a later module.

Figure 88

To Enter a Worksheet Title

1 SIGN IN | 2 USE WINDOWS | 3 USE APPS | 4 FILE MANAGEMENT | 5 SWITCH APPS | 6 SAVE FILES
7 CHANGE SCREEN RESOLUTION | 8 EXIT APPS | 9 USE ADDITIONAL APPS | 10 USE HELP

To enter data into a cell, you first must select it. The easiest way to select a cell (make it active) is to use the mouse to move the block plus sign pointer to the cell and then click. An alternative method is to use the arrow keys that are located just to the right of the typewriter keys on the keyboard. An arrow key selects the cell adjacent to the active cell in the direction of the arrow on the key.

In Excel, any set of characters containing a letter, hyphen (as in a telephone number), or space is considered text. **Text** is used to place titles, such as worksheet titles, column titles, and row titles, on the worksheet. The following steps enter the worksheet title in cell A1. *Why? A title informs others as to the contents of the worksheet, such as information regarding a company.*

1

- If it is not already the active cell, click cell A1 to make it the active cell.
- Type **Silver Sky Hardware** in cell A1 (Figure 89).

Figure 89

2

- Click the Enter button to complete the entry and enter the worksheet title in cell A1 (Figure 90).

Q&A | Why do some commands on the ribbon appear dimmed?
Excel dims the commands that are unavailable for use at the current time.

Figure 90

Other Ways

1. To complete entry, click any cell other than active cell

2. To complete entry, press ENTER, HOME, PAGE UP, PAGE DOWN, END, UP ARROW, DOWN ARROW, LEFT ARROW, or RIGHT ARROW

To Save an Existing Office File with the Same File Name

1 SIGN IN | 2 USE WINDOWS | 3 USE APPS | 4 FILE MANAGEMENT | 5 SWITCH APPS | 6 SAVE FILES
7 CHANGE SCREEN RESOLUTION | 8 EXIT APPS | 9 USE ADDITIONAL APPS | 10 USE HELP

Saving frequently cannot be overemphasized. *Why? You have made modifications to the file (spreadsheet) since you created it. Thus, you should save again. Similarly, you should continue saving files frequently so that you do not lose the changes you have made since the time you last saved the file.* You can use the same file name, such as Silver Sky Hardware, to save the changes made to the document. The following step saves a file again with the same file name.

1

- Click the Save button on the Quick Access Toolbar to overwrite the previously saved file (Silver Sky Hardware, in this case) in the Excel folder (Figure 91).

Figure 91

Other Ways

1. Press CTRL+S

2. Press SHIFT+F12

To Save a File with a New File Name

You might want to save a file with a different file name or to a different location. For example, you might start a homework assignment with a data file and then save it with a final file name for submission to your instructor, saving it to a location designated by your instructor. The following steps save a file with a different file name.

1 Click the File tab to open the Backstage view.

2 Click the Save As tab to display the Save As gallery.

3 If necessary, click This PC to display options in the right pane related to saving on your computer.

4 Click the Browse button in the left pane to display the Save As dialog box.

5 Type `Silver Sky Hardware Sales Summary` in the File name box (Save As dialog box) to change the file name. Do not press the ENTER key after typing the file name because you do not want to close the dialog box at this time.

6 If necessary, navigate to the desired save location (in this case, the Excel folder in the CIS 101 folder [or your class folder] in the Documents folder). For specific instructions, perform the tasks in Steps 5a through 5e in the previous section titled To Save a File in a Folder, replacing the PowerPoint folder with the Excel folder.

7 Click the Save button (Save As dialog box) to save the worksheet in the selected folder on the selected drive with the entered file name.

To Exit an Office App

You are finished using Excel. The following steps exit Excel.

1 If you have one Office document open, click the Close button on the right side of the title bar to close the document and exit the Office app; or if you have multiple Office documents open, right-click the app button on the taskbar and then click 'Close all windows' on the shortcut menu, or press ALT + F4 to close all open documents and exit the Office app.

2 If a dialog box appears, click the Save button to save any changes made to the file since the last save.

Access

The term **database** describes a collection of data organized in a manner that allows access, retrieval, and use of that data. **Access** is a database management system. A **database management system** is software that allows you to use a computer to create a database; add, change, and delete data in the database; create queries that allow you to ask questions concerning the data in the database; and create forms and reports using the data in the database.

To Run an App

The following steps, which assume Windows is running, run the Access app based on a typical installation. You may need to ask your instructor how to run apps for your computer.

1 Type **Access 2016** as the search text in the search box and watch the search results appear in the search results.

2 Click the app name, Access 2016 in this case, in the search results to run Access.

3 If the window is not maximized, click the Maximize button on its title bar to maximize the window (Figure 92).

Q&A Do I have to run Access using these steps?

No. You can use any previously discussed method of running an Office app to run Access.

Figure 92

Unique Elements in Access

You work on objects such as tables, forms, and reports in the **Access work area**. Figure 93 shows a work area with multiple objects open. **Object tabs** for the open objects appear at the top of the work area. You select an open object by clicking its tab. In the figure, the Customer List table is the selected object. To the left of the work area is the Navigation Pane, which contains a list of all the objects in the database. You use this pane to open an object. You also can customize the way objects are displayed in the Navigation Pane.

Because the Navigation Pane can take up space in the window, you may not have as much open space for working as you would with Word or Excel. You can use the 'Shutter Bar Open/Close Button' to minimize the Navigation Pane when you are not using it, which allows more space to work with tables, forms, reports, and other database elements.

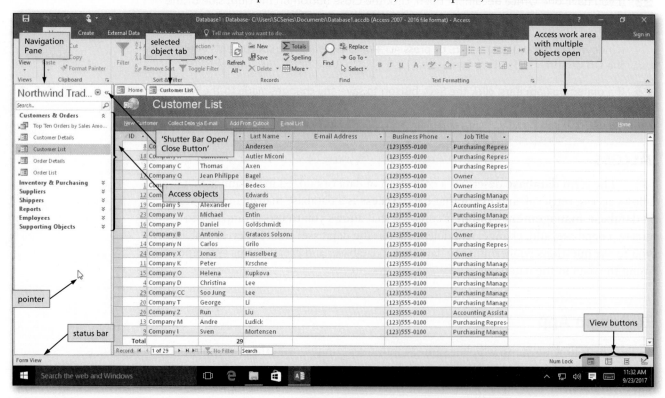

Figure 93

Ribbon   When you run Access, the ribbon displays five main tabs: File, Home, Create, External Data, and Database Tools. Access has unique groupings such as Sort & Filter and Records that are designed specifically for working with databases. Many of the formatting options are reserved for the tool tabs that appear when you are working with forms and reports.

To Create an Access Database

1 SIGN IN | 2 USE WINDOWS | 3 USE APPS | 4 FILE MANAGEMENT | 5 SWITCH APPS | 6 SAVE FILES
7 CHANGE SCREEN RESOLUTION | 8 EXIT APPS | 9 USE ADDITIONAL APPS | 10 USE HELP

Unlike the other Office apps, Access saves a database when you first create it. When working in Access, you will add data to an Access database. As you add data to a database, Access automatically saves your changes rather than waiting until you manually save the database or exit Access. Recall that in Word and Excel, you entered the data first and then saved it.

Because Access automatically saves the database as you add and change data, you do not always have to click the Save button on the Quick Access Toolbar. Instead, the Save button in Access is used for saving the objects (including tables, queries, forms, reports, and other database objects) a database contains. You can use either the 'Blank desktop database' option or a template to create a new database. If you already know the organization of your database, you would use the 'Blank desktop database' option. If not, you can use a template. Templates can guide you by suggesting some commonly used database organizations.

The following steps use the 'Blank desktop database' option to create a database named Rimitoein Electronics in the Access folder in the class folder (CIS 101, in this case) in the Documents folder. *Why? You have decided to use Microsoft Access to maintain large amounts of data.*

1

- Click the 'Blank desktop database' thumbnail (shown in Figure 92) to select the database type.
- Type **Rimitoein Electronics** in the File Name text box (Blank desktop database dialog box) to enter the new file name. Do not press the ENTER key after typing the file name because you do not want to create the database at this time (Figure 94).

Figure 94

2

- Click the 'Browse for a location to put your database' button to display the File New Database dialog box.
- Navigate to the location for the database, that is, the Documents folder, then to the folder identifying your class (CIS 101, in this case), and then to the Access folder (Figure 95). For specific instructions, perform the tasks in Steps 5a through 5e in the previous section titled To Save a File in a Folder, replacing the PowerPoint folder with the Access folder.

Q&A Why does the 'Save as type' box say Microsoft Access 2007-2016 Databases?
Microsoft Access database formats change with some new versions of Microsoft Access. The most recent format is the Microsoft Access 2007-2016 Databases format, which was released with Access 2007.

Figure 95

③

- Click the OK button (File New Database dialog box) to select the Access folder as the location for the database and close the dialog box (Figure 96).

④

- Click the Create button (Blank desktop database dialog box) to create the database on the selected drive in the selected folder with the file name, Rimitoein Electronics (Figure 97).

Q&A | How do I know that the Rimitoein Electronics database is created?
The file name of the database appears on the title bar.

Figure 96

Figure 97

To Close an Office File

Assume you need to close the Access database and return to it later. The following step closes an Office file.

① Click File on the ribbon to open the Backstage view and then click Close in the Backstage view to close the open file (Rimitoein Electronics, in this case) without exiting the active app.

Q&A | Why is Access still on the screen?
When you close a database, the app remains running.

To Open an Existing Office File

Assume you wish to continue working on an existing file, that is, a file you previously saved. Earlier in this module, you learned how to open a recently used file through the Backstage view. The following step opens a database, specifically the Rimitoein Electronics database, that recently was saved. *Why? Because the file has been created already, you just need to reopen it.*

1

- Click File on the ribbon to open the Backstage view and then click Open in the Backstage view to display the Open gallery in the Backstage view.
- Click This PC to display recent folders accessed on your computer.
- Click the Browse button to display the Open dialog box.
- If necessary, navigate to the location of the file to open.
- Click the file to open, Rimitoein Electronics in this case, to select the file (Figure 98).
- Click the Open button (Open dialog box) to open the file. If necessary, click the Enable Content button.

Q&A | Why did the Security Warning appear?
The Security Warning appears when you open an Office file that might contain harmful content. The files you create in this module are not harmful, but you should be cautious when opening files from other people.

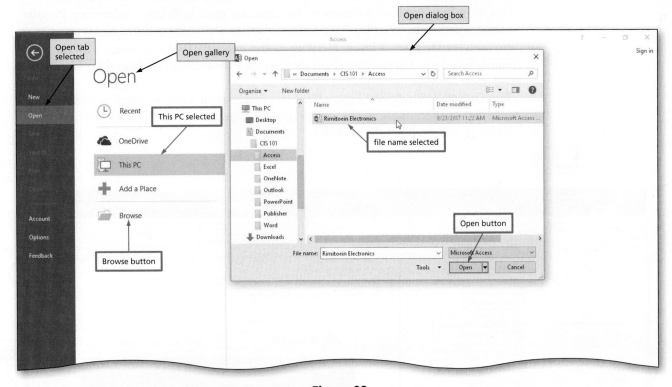

Figure 98

Other Ways

1. Press CTRL+O   2. Navigate to file in File Explorer window, double-click file name

To Exit an Office App

You are finished using Access. The following step exits Access.

1 Click the Close button on the right side of the title bar to close the file and exit the Office app.

Other Office Apps

In addition to the Office apps discussed thus far, three other apps are useful when collaborating and communicating with others: Outlook, Publisher, and OneNote.

Outlook

Outlook is a powerful communications and scheduling app that helps you communicate with others, keep track of contacts, and organize your calendar. Apps such as Outlook provide a way for individuals and workgroups to organize, find, view, and share information easily. Outlook allows you to send and receive email messages and provides a means to organize contacts. Users can track email messages, meetings, and notes related to a particular contact. Outlook's Calendar, People, Tasks, and Notes components aid in this organization. Contact information readily is available from the Outlook Calendar, Mail, People, and Task components by accessing the Search Contacts feature.

Email is the transmission of messages and files over a computer network. Email has become an important means of exchanging information and files between business associates, classmates and instructors, friends, and family. Businesses find that using email to send documents electronically saves both time and money. Parents with students away at college or relatives who live across the country find that communicating by email is an inexpensive and easy way to stay in touch with their family members. Exchanging email messages is a widely used service of the Internet.

The Outlook Window   Figure 99 shows an Outlook window, which is divided into three panes: the Navigation pane, the message pane to the left of center, and the Reading pane to the right of center.

Figure 99

When an email message is open in Outlook, it is displayed in a Message window (Figure 100). When you open a message, the Message tab on the ribbon appears, which contains the more frequently used commands.

Figure 100

Publisher

Publisher is a powerful desktop publishing (DTP) app that assists you in designing and producing professional-quality documents that combine text, graphics, illustrations, and photos. DTP software provides additional tools beyond those typically found in word processing apps, including design templates, graphic manipulation tools, color schemes or libraries, advanced layout and printing tools, and web components. For large jobs, businesses use DTP software to design publications that are camera ready, which means the files are suitable for outside commercial printing. In addition, DTP software can be used to create webpages and interactive web forms.

Publisher is used by people who regularly produce high-quality color publications, such as newsletters, brochures, flyers, logos, signs, catalogs, cards, and business forms. Publisher has many features designed to simplify production and make publications visually appealing. Using Publisher, you easily can change the shape, size, and color of text and graphics. You can include many kinds of graphical objects, including mastheads, borders, tables, images, pictures, charts, and web objects in publications, as well as integrate spreadsheets and databases.

The Publisher Window   Publisher initially displays a list of publication types. **Publication types** are typical publications used by desktop publishers. The more popular types are displayed in the center of the window.

Once you select a publication type, a dialog box is displayed to allow you to create the publication (Figure 101). Some templates are installed with Publisher, and others are available online. In Figure 101, the Business newsletter publication dialog box is displayed.

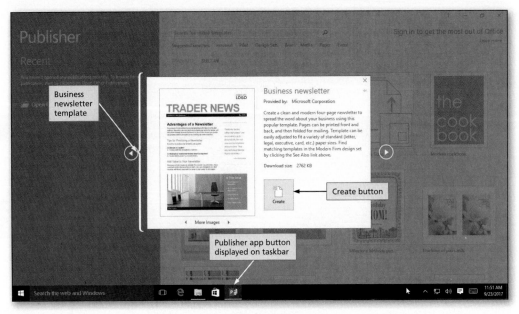

Figure 101

When you select the desired template, Publisher creates the publication and sets it up for you to edit. Figure 102 shows the Business newsletter publication that Publisher creates when default options are selected.

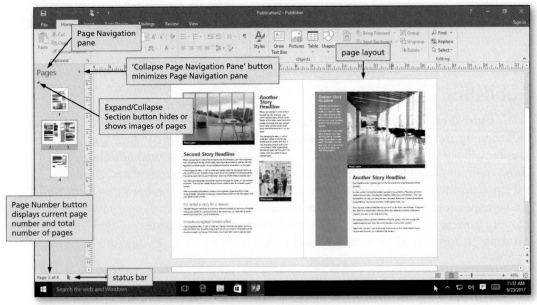

Figure 102

OneNote

OneNote is a note taking app that assists you in entering, saving, organizing, searching, and using notes. It enables you to create pages, which are organized in sections, just as in a physical notebook. In OneNote, you can type notes anywhere on a page and then easily move the notes around on the page. You can create lists and outlines, use handwriting to enter notes, and create drawings. If you use a tablet to add handwritten notes to a document, OneNote can convert the handwriting to text. It also can perform searches on the handwritten entries. Pictures and data from other apps easily are incorporated in your notes.

In addition to typing and handwriting, you can take audio notes. For example, you could record conversations during a meeting or lecture. As you record, you can take additional notes. When you play back the audio notes, you can synchronize the additional notes you took; that is, OneNote will show you during playback the exact points at which you added the notes. A variety of note flags, which are symbols that call your attention to notes on a page, enable you to flag notes as being important. You then can use the Note Flags summary to view the flagged notes, which can be sorted in a variety of ways.

OneNote includes tools to assist you with organizing a notebook and navigating its contents. It also includes a search feature, making it easy to find the specific notes in which you are interested. For short notes that you always want to have available readily, you can use Side Notes, which are used much like the sticky notes that you might use in a physical notebook.

OneNote Window   All activity in OneNote takes place in the **notebook** (Figure 103). Like a physical notebook, the OneNote notebook consists of notes that are placed on **pages**. The pages are grouped into **sections**, which can be further grouped into **folders**. (No folders are shown in the notebook in the figure.) You can use the Search box to search for specific text in your notes.

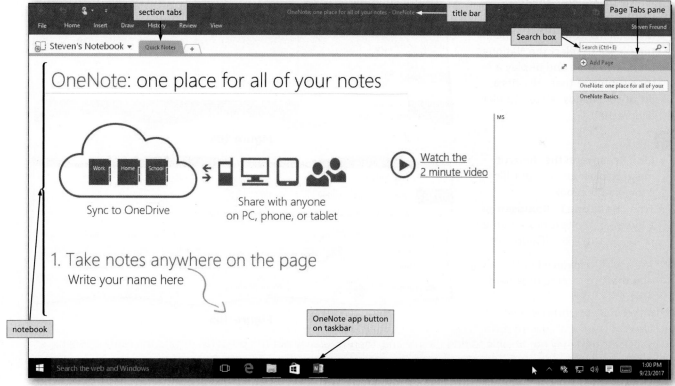

Figure 103

You can add pages to the notebook using the Add Page button in the Page Tabs pane. If page tabs are displayed, you can switch to a page by clicking its tab. Figure 103 shows the Quick Notes page being displayed for the notebook.

Break Point: If you wish to take a break, this is a good place to do so. To resume at a later time, continue to follow the steps from this location forward.

Renaming, Moving, and Deleting Files

Earlier in this module, you learned how to organize files in folders, which is part of a process known as **file management**. The following sections cover additional file management topics including renaming, moving, and deleting files.

To Rename a File

In some circumstances, you may want to change the name of, or rename, a file or a folder. *Why? You may want to distinguish a file in one folder or drive from a copy of a similar file, or you may decide to rename a file to better identify its contents.* The following steps change the name of the National Monuments file in the Word folder to National Monuments Flyer.

- If necessary, click the File Explorer button on the taskbar to make the folder window the active window.
- Navigate to the location of the file to be renamed (in this case, the Word folder in the CIS 101 [or your class folder] folder in the Documents folder) to display the file(s) it contains in the file list.
- Right-click the National Monuments icon or file name in the file list to select the National Monuments file and display a shortcut menu that presents a list of commands related to files (Figure 104).

Figure 104

- Click Rename on the shortcut menu to place the current file name in a text box.
- Type **National Monuments Flyer** in the text box and then press the ENTER key (Figure 105).

Q&A
Are any risks involved in renaming files that are located on a hard drive?
If you inadvertently rename a file that is associated with certain apps, the apps may not be able to find the file and, therefore, may not run properly. Always use caution when renaming files.

Can I rename a file when it is open?
No, a file must be closed to change the file name.

Figure 105

Other Ways

1. Select file, press F2, type new file name, press ENTER   2. Select file, click Rename (Home tab | Organize group), type new file name, press ENTER

To Move a File

Why? At some time, you may want to move a file from one folder, called the source folder, to another, called the destination folder. When you move a file, it no longer appears in the original folder. If the destination and the source folders are on the same media, you can move a file by dragging it. If the folders are on different media, then you will need to right-drag the file, and then click Move here on the shortcut menu. The following step moves the Silver Sky Hardware Sales Summary file from the Excel folder to the OneNote folder.

Office 2016 and Windows 10 Module

1

- In File Explorer, navigate to the location of the file to be moved (in this case, the Excel folder in the CIS 101 folder [or your class folder] in the Documents folder).
- Click the Excel folder in the navigation pane to display the files it contains in the right pane (Figure 106).
- Drag the Silver Sky Hardware Sales Summary file in the right pane to the OneNote folder in the navigation pane.

Figure 106

Other Ways

1. Right-click file to move, click Cut on shortcut menu, right-click destination folder, click Paste on shortcut menu

2. Select file to move, press CTRL+X, select destination folder, press CTRL+V

To Delete a File

1 SIGN IN | 2 USE WINDOWS | 3 USE APPS | **4 FILE MANAGEMENT** | 5 SWITCH APPS | 6 SAVE FILES
7 CHANGE SCREEN RESOLUTION | 8 EXIT APPS | 9 USE ADDITIONAL APPS | **10 USE HELP**

A final task you may want to perform is to delete a file. Exercise extreme caution when deleting a file or files. When you delete a file from a hard drive, the deleted file is stored in the Recycle Bin where you can recover it until you empty the Recycle Bin. If you delete a file from removable media, such as a USB flash drive, the file is deleted permanently. The next steps delete the Visiting National Monuments file from the PowerPoint folder. *Why? When a file no longer is needed, you can delete it to conserve space on your storage location.*

1

- In File Explorer, navigate to the location of the file to be deleted (in this case, the PowerPoint folder in the CIS 101 folder [or your class folder] in the Documents folder).
- Click the Visiting National Monuments icon or file name in the right pane to select the file.
- Right-click the selected file to display a shortcut menu (Figure 107).

2

- Click Delete on the shortcut menu to delete the file.
- If a dialog box appears, click the Yes button to delete the file.

Q&A Can I use this same technique to delete a folder?

Figure 107

Yes. Right-click the folder and then click Delete on the shortcut menu. When you delete a folder, all of the files and folders contained in the folder you are deleting, together with any files and folders on lower hierarchical levels, are deleted as well. For example, if you delete the CIS 101 folder, you will delete all folders and files inside the CIS 101 folder.

Other Ways

1. Select file, press DELETE

Microsoft Office and Windows Help

At any time while you are using one of the Office apps, you can use Office Help to display information about all topics associated with the app. To illustrate the use of Office Help, this section uses Word. Help in other Office apps operates in a similar fashion.

In Office, Help is presented in a window that has browser-style navigation buttons. Each Office app has its own Help home page, which is the starting Help page that is displayed in the Help window. If your computer is connected to the Internet, the contents of the Help page reflect both the local help files installed on the computer and material from Microsoft's website.

To Open the Help Window in an Office App

1 SIGN IN | 2 USE WINDOWS | 3 USE APPS | 4 FILE MANAGEMENT | 5 SWITCH APPS | 6 SAVE FILES
7 CHANGE SCREEN RESOLUTION | 8 EXIT APPS | 9 USE ADDITIONAL APPS | 10 USE HELP

The following step opens the Word Help window. *Why? You might not understand how certain commands or operations work in Word, so you can obtain the necessary information using help.*

1

- Run an Office app, in this case Word.
- Click the Blank document thumbnail to display a blank document.
- Press F1 to open the app's Help window (Figure 108).

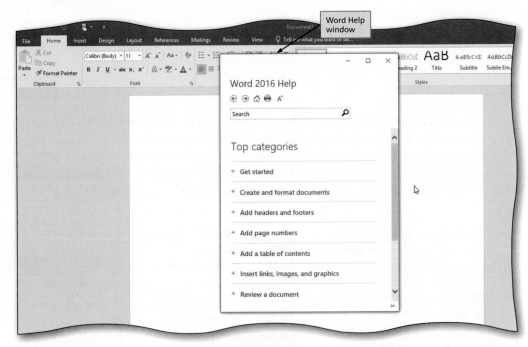

Figure 108

Moving and Resizing Windows

At times, it is useful, or even necessary, to have more than one window open and visible on the screen at the same time. You can resize and move these open windows so that you can view different areas of and elements in the window. In the case of the Help window, for example, it could be covering document text in the Word window that you need to see.

To Move a Window by Dragging

1 SIGN IN | 2 USE WINDOWS | 3 USE APPS | 4 FILE MANAGEMENT | 5 SWITCH APPS | 6 SAVE FILES
7 CHANGE SCREEN RESOLUTION | 8 EXIT APPS | 9 USE ADDITIONAL APPS | 10 USE HELP

You can move any open window that is not maximized to another location on the desktop by dragging the title bar of the window. *Why? You might want to have a better view of what is behind the window or just want to move the window so that you can see it better.* The following step drags the Word Help window to the upper-left corner of the desktop.

1

- Drag the window title bar (the Word Help window title bar, in this case) so that the window moves to the upper-left corner of the desktop, as shown in Figure 109.

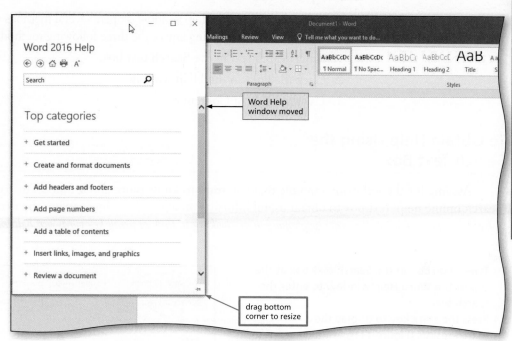

Figure 109

To Resize a Window by Dragging

1 SIGN IN | **2 USE WINDOWS** | 3 USE APPS | 4 FILE MANAGEMENT | 5 SWITCH APPS | 6 SAVE FILES
7 CHANGE SCREEN RESOLUTION | 8 EXIT APPS | 9 USE ADDITIONAL APPS | 10 USE HELP

A method used to change the size of the window is to drag the window borders. The following step changes the size of the Word Help window by dragging its borders. **Why?** *Sometimes, information is not visible completely in a window, and you want to increase the size of the window.*

1

- If you are using a mouse, point to the lower-right corner of the window (the Word Help window, in this case) until the pointer changes to a two-headed arrow.
- Drag the bottom border downward to display more of the active window (Figure 110).

Q&A Can I drag other borders on the window to enlarge or shrink the window?
Yes, you can drag the left, right, and top borders and any window corner to resize a window.

Q&A Will Windows remember the new size of the window after I close it?
Yes. When you reopen the window, Windows will display it at the same size it was when you closed it.

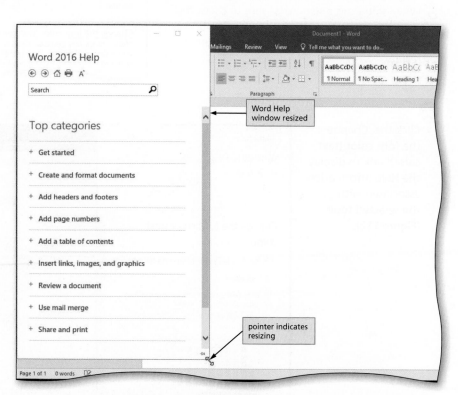

Figure 110

Using Office Help

Once an Office app's Help window is open, several methods exist for navigating Help. You can search for help by using any of the three following methods from the Help window:

1. Enter search text in the Search text box.

2. Click the links in the Help window.

3. Use the Table of Contents.

To Obtain Help Using the Search Text Box

Assume for the following example that you want to know more about fonts. The following steps use the 'Search online help' text box to obtain useful information about fonts by entering the word, fonts, as search text. *Why?* *You may not know the exact help topic you are looking to find, so using keywords can help narrow your search.*

- Type **fonts** in the Search text box at the top of the Word Help window to enter the search text.
- Press the ENTER key to display the search results (Figure 111).

Q&A Why do my search results differ?

If you do not have an Internet connection, your results will reflect only the content of the Help files on your computer. When searching for help online, results also can change as material is added, deleted, and updated on the online Help webpages maintained by Microsoft.

Q&A Why were my search results not very helpful?

When initiating a search, be sure to check the spelling of the search text; also, keep your search specific to return the most accurate results.

Figure 111

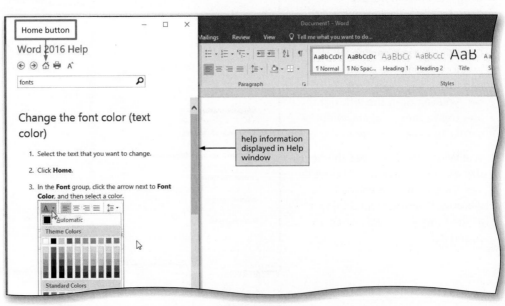

- Click the 'Change the font color (text color)' link to display the Help information associated with the selected topic (Figure 112).

Figure 112

3

- Click the Home button in the Help window to clear the search results and redisplay the Help home page (Figure 113).
- Click the Close button in the Word 2016 Help window to close the window.

Figure 113

Obtaining Help while Working in an Office App

Help in the Office apps provides you with the ability to obtain help directly, without opening the Help window and initiating a search. For example, you may be unsure about how a particular command works, or you may be presented with a dialog box that you are not sure how to use.

Figure 114 shows one option for obtaining help while working in an Office app. If you want to learn more about a command, point to its button and wait for the ScreenTip to appear. If the Help icon and 'Tell me more' link appear in the ScreenTip, click the 'Tell me more' link or press the F1 key while pointing to the button to open the Help window associated with that command.

Figure 115 shows a dialog box that contains a Help button. Clicking the Help button or pressing the F1 key while the dialog box is displayed opens a Help window. The Help window contains help about that dialog box, if available. If no help file is available for that particular dialog box, then the main Help window opens.

As mentioned previously, the Tell Me box is available in most Office apps and can perform a variety of functions. One of these functions is to provide easy access to commands by typing a description of the command.

Figure 114

Figure 115

To Obtain Help Using the Tell Me Box

1 SIGN IN | 2 USE WINDOWS | 3 USE APPS | 4 FILE MANAGEMENT | 5 SWITCH APPS | 6 SAVE FILES
7 CHANGE SCREEN RESOLUTION | 8 EXIT APPS | 9 USE ADDITIONAL APPS | 10 USE HELP

If you are having trouble finding a command in an Office app, you can use the Tell Me box to search for the function you are trying to perform. As you type, the Tell Me box will suggest commands that match the search text you are entering. *Why? You can use the Tell Me box to quickly access commands you otherwise may be unable to find on the ribbon.* The following step finds information about margins.

- Type **margins** in the Tell Me box and watch the search results appear.
- Point to Adjust Margins to display a submenu displaying the various margin settings (Figure 116).
- Click an empty area of the document window to close the search results.

- Exit Microsoft Word.

Figure 116

Using the Windows Search Box

One of the more powerful Windows features is the Windows search box. The search box is a central location from where you can type search text and quickly access related Windows commands or web search results. In addition, **Cortana** is a new search tool in Windows that you can access using the search box. It can act as a personal assistant by performing functions such as providing ideas; searching for apps, files, and folders; and setting reminders. In addition to typing search text in the search box, you also can use your computer or mobile device's microphone to give verbal commands.

To Use the Windows Search Box

1 SIGN IN | 2 USE WINDOWS | 3 USE APPS | 4 FILE MANAGEMENT | 5 SWITCH APPS | 6 SAVE FILES
7 CHANGE SCREEN RESOLUTION | 8 EXIT APPS | 9 USE ADDITIONAL APPS | 10 USE HELP

The following step uses the Windows search box to search for a Windows command. *Why? Using the search box to locate apps, settings, folders, and files can be faster than navigating windows and dialog boxes to search for the desired content.*

- Type **notification** in the search box to display the search results. The search results include related Windows settings, Windows Store apps, and web search results (Figure 117).
- Click an empty area of the desktop to close the search results.

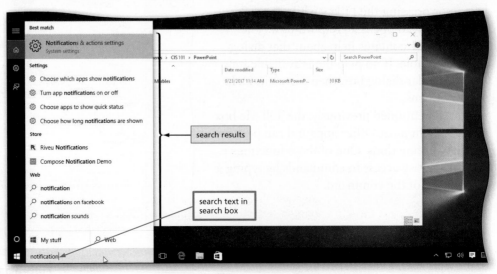

Figure 117

Office 2016 and Windows 10 Module

Summary

In this module, you learned how to use the Windows interface, several touch screen and mouse operations, file and folder management, some basic features of some Microsoft Office apps (including Word, PowerPoint, Excel, and Access), and discovered the common elements that exist among these different Office apps. You also were introduced to additional Office apps, including Outlook, Publisher, and OneNote. Topics covered included signing in, using Windows, using apps, file management, switching between apps, saving files, changing screen resolution, exiting apps, using additional apps, and using help.

CONSIDER THIS: PLAN AHEAD

What guidelines should you follow to plan your projects?

The process of communicating specific information is a learned, rational skill. Computers and software, especially Microsoft Office 2016, can help you develop ideas and present detailed information to a particular audience and minimize much of the laborious work of drafting and revising projects. No matter what method you use to plan a project, it is beneficial to follow some specific guidelines from the onset to arrive at a final product that is informative, relevant, and effective. Use some aspects of these guidelines every time you undertake a project, and others as needed in specific instances.

1. Determine the project's purpose.

   a) Clearly define why you are undertaking this assignment.

   b) Begin to draft ideas of how best to communicate information by handwriting ideas on paper; composing directly on a laptop, tablet, or mobile device; or developing a strategy that fits your particular thinking and writing style.

2. Analyze your audience.

   a) Learn about the people who will read, analyze, or view your work.

   b) Determine their interests and needs so that you can present the information they need to know and omit the information they already possess.

   c) Form a mental picture of these people or find photos of people who fit this profile so that you can develop a project with the audience in mind.

3. Gather possible content.

   a) Locate existing information that may reside in spreadsheets, databases, or other files.

   b) Conduct a web search to find relevant websites.

   c) Read pamphlets, magazine and newspaper articles, and books to gain insights of how others have approached your topic.

   d) Conduct personal interviews to obtain perspectives not available by any other means.

   e) Consider video and audio clips as potential sources for material that might complement or support the factual data you uncover.

4. Determine what content to present to your audience.

   a) Write three or four major ideas you want an audience member to remember after reading or viewing your project.

   b) Envision your project's endpoint, the key fact you wish to emphasize, so that all project elements lead to this final element.

   c) Determine relevant time factors, such as the length of time to develop the project, how long readers will spend reviewing your project, or the amount of time allocated for your speaking engagement.

   d) Decide whether a graph, photo, or artistic element can express or enhance a particular concept.

   e) Be mindful of the order in which you plan to present the content, and place the most important material at the top or bottom of the page, because readers and audience members generally remember the first and last pieces of information they see and hear.

CONSIDER THIS

How should you submit solutions to questions in the assignments identified with a symbol?

Every assignment in this book contains one or more questions with a symbol. These questions require you to think beyond the assigned file. Present your solutions to the question in the format required by your instructor. Possible formats may include one or more of these options: write the answer; create a document that contains the answer; present your answer to the class; discuss your answer in a group; record the answer as audio or video using a webcam, smartphone, or portable media player; or post answers on a blog, wiki, or website.

Apply Your Knowledge

Reinforce the skills and apply the concepts you learned in this module.

Creating a Folder and a Document

Instructions: You will create a PowerPoint Assignments folder and then create a PowerPoint presentation and save it in the folder.

Perform the following tasks:

1. Open the File Explorer window and then double-click to open the Documents folder.
2. Click the New folder button on the Quick Access Toolbar to display a new folder icon and text box for the folder name.
3. Type `PowerPoint Assignments` in the text box to name the folder. Press the ENTER key to create the folder in the Documents folder.
4. Run PowerPoint and create a new blank presentation.
5. Enter `Technology Update` in the title text placeholder (Figure 118).
6. Click the Save button on the Quick Access Toolbar. Navigate to the PowerPoint folder in the Documents folder and then save the document using the file name, Apply 1 Presentation.
7. If your Quick Access Toolbar does not show the Quick Print button, add the Quick Print button to the Quick Access Toolbar. Print the presentation using the Quick Print button on the Quick Access Toolbar. When you are finished printing, remove the Quick Print button from the Quick Access Toolbar.
8. Submit the printout to your instructor.
9. Exit PowerPoint.
10. ✺ What other commands might you find useful to include on the Quick Access Toolbar?

Figure 118

Extend Your Knowledge

Extend the skills you learned in this module and experiment with new skills. You will use Help to complete the assignment.

Using Help

Instructions: Use Office Help to perform the following tasks.

Perform the following tasks:
1. Run Word.
2. Click the Microsoft Word Help button to open the Word Help window (Figure 119).
3. Search Word Help to answer the following questions.
   a. What are the steps to create a hanging indent?
   b. What is mail merge?
4. With the Word app still running, run PowerPoint.
5. Click the Microsoft PowerPoint Help button on the title bar to open the PowerPoint Help window.
6. Search PowerPoint Help to answer the following questions.
   a. How can you create a Venn diagram?
   b. How do you add slide numbers to each slide?
7. Exit PowerPoint.
8. Run Excel.
9. Click the Microsoft Excel Help button to open the Excel Help window.
10. Search Excel Help to answer the following questions.
    a. What different types of charts are available in Excel?
    b. What is Flash Fill?
11. Exit Excel.
12. Run Access.
13. Click the Microsoft Access Help button to open the Access Help window.
14. Search Access Help to answer the following questions.
    a. What is a query?
    b. What are data types?
15. Exit Access.
16. Type the answers from your searches in a new blank Word document. Save the document with a new file name and then submit it in the format specified by your instructor.
17. Exit Word.
18. ✸ What search text did you use to perform the searches above? Did it take multiple attempts to search and locate the exact information for which you were searching?

Figure 119

Expand Your World
Creating Office Online Documents

Create a solution that uses cloud or web technologies by learning and investigating on your own from general guidance.

Instructions: Create the folders shown in Figure 120. Then, using the respective Office Online app, create a small file to save in each folder (i.e., create a Word document to save in the Word folder, a PowerPoint presentation to save in the PowerPoint folder, and so on).

Perform the following tasks:

1. Sign in to OneDrive in your browser.

2. Use the New button to create the folder structure shown in Figure 120.

3. In the Word folder, use the New button to create a Word document with the file name, Reminders, and containing the text, Lunch with Lucas on Tuesday.

4. Save the document and then exit the app.

5. Navigate to the PowerPoint folder.

Figure 120

6. Create a PowerPoint presentation called Widget Sales with one slide containing the title text, Online Presentation, and then exit the app.

7. Navigate to the Excel folder.

8. Create an Excel spreadsheet called Widget Sales Analysis containing the text, Sales Cost Analysis, in cell A1, and then exit the app.

9. Submit the assignment in the format specified by your instructor.

10. ✹ Based on your current knowledge of OneDrive, do you think you will use it? What about the Office Online apps?

In the Labs

Design, create, modify, and/or use files following the guidelines, concepts, and skills presented in this module. Labs 1 and 2, which increase in difficulty, require you to create solutions based on what you learned in the module; Lab 3 requires you to apply your creative thinking and problem-solving skills to design and implement a solution.

Lab 1: **Creating Folders for a Bookstore**

Problem: Your friend works for a local bookstore. He would like to organize his files in relation to the types of books available in the store. He has seven main categories: fiction, biography, children, humor, social science, nonfiction, and medical. You are to create a folder structure similar to Figure 121.

Perform the following tasks:

1. Click the File Explorer button on the taskbar and display the contents of the Documents folder.

2. In the Documents folder, create the main folder and name it Book Categories.

3. Navigate to the Book Categories folder.

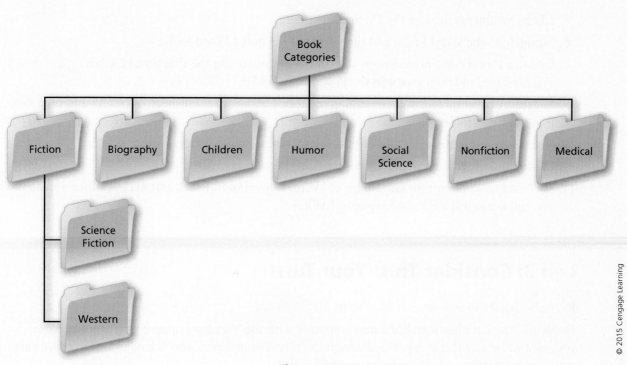

Figure 121

4. Within the Book Categories folder, create a folder for each of the following: Fiction, Biography, Children, Humor, Social Science, Nonfiction, and Medical.

5. Within the Fiction folder, create two additional folders, one for Science Fiction and the second for Western.

6. Submit the assignment in the format specified by your instructor.

7. ✹ Think about how you use your computer for various tasks (consider personal, professional, and academic reasons). What folders do you think will be required on your computer to store the files you save?

Lab 2: **Creating Office Documents and Saving Them in Appropriate Folders**

Problem: You are taking a class that requires you to create a Word, PowerPoint, Excel, and Access file. You will save these files to folders named for four different Office apps (Figure 122).

Perform the following tasks:

1. Create the folders shown in Figure 122.

2. Create a Word document containing the text, Week 1 Notes.

3. In the Backstage view, click Save As and then click This PC.

4. Click the Browse button to display the Save As dialog box.

Figure 122

5. Click Documents to open the Documents folder.

6. Navigate to the Word folder and then save the file in the Word folder.

7. Create a PowerPoint presentation with one slide containing the title text, In-Class Presentation, and then save it in the PowerPoint folder.

8. Create an Excel spreadsheet containing the text, Financial Spreadsheet, in cell A1 and then save it in the Excel folder.

9. Save an Access database named, My Movie Database, in the Access folder.

10. Submit the assignment in the format specified by your instructor.

11. ✸ Based on your current knowledge of Word, PowerPoint, Excel, and Access, which app do you think you will use most frequently? Why?

Lab 3: **Consider This: Your Turn**

Performing Research about Malware

Problem: You have just installed a new computer with the Windows operating system. Because you want to be sure that it is protected from the threat of malware, you decide to research malware, malware protection, and removing malware.

Part 1: Research the following three topics: malware, malware protection, and removing malware. Use the concepts and techniques presented in this module to use the search box to find information regarding these topics. Create a Word document that contains steps to properly safeguard a computer from malware, ways to prevent malware, as well as the different ways to remove malware or a virus should your computer become infected. Submit your assignment in the format specified by your instructor.

Part 2: You made several decisions while searching for this assignment. What decisions did you make? What was the rationale behind these decisions? How did you locate the required information about malware?

Figure 123

1 Creating, Formatting, and Editing a Word Document with a Picture

Objectives

You will have mastered the material in this module when you can:

- Enter text in a Word document
- Check spelling as you type
- Format paragraphs
- Format text
- Undo and redo commands or actions
- Change theme colors

- Insert digital pictures in a Word document
- Resize pictures
- Format pictures
- Add a page border
- Adjust spacing
- Correct errors and revise a document

Introduction

To advertise a sale, promote a business, publicize an event, or convey a message to the community, you may want to create a flyer and hand it out in person or post it in a public location. Libraries, schools, community organizations, grocery stores, coffee shops, and other places often provide bulletin boards or windows for flyers. You also see flyers posted on webpages, on social media, or in email messages.

Flyers announce personal items for sale or rent (car, boat, apartment); events, such as garage or block sales; services being offered (animal care, housecleaning, lessons, tours); membership, sponsorship, or donation requests (club, community organization, charity); and other messages, such as a lost or found pet.

Project — Flyer with a Picture

Individuals and businesses create flyers to gain public attention. Flyers, which usually are a single page in length, are an inexpensive means of reaching the community. Many flyers, however, go unnoticed because they are designed poorly.

The project in this module follows general guidelines and uses Word to create the flyer shown in Figure 1–1. This colorful, eye-catching flyer announces surfing lessons. The picture of the surfer riding a wave, taken with a digital camera, entices passersby or viewers to stop and look at the flyer. The headline on the flyer is large and colorful to draw attention into the text. The body copy below the picture briefly describes what is included in the lessons, along with a bulleted list that concisely highlights important information. The signature line of the flyer calls attention to the contact phone number. The word, expert, and the signature line are in a different color so that they stand apart from the rest of the text on the flyer. Finally, the graphical page border nicely frames and complements the contents of the flyer.

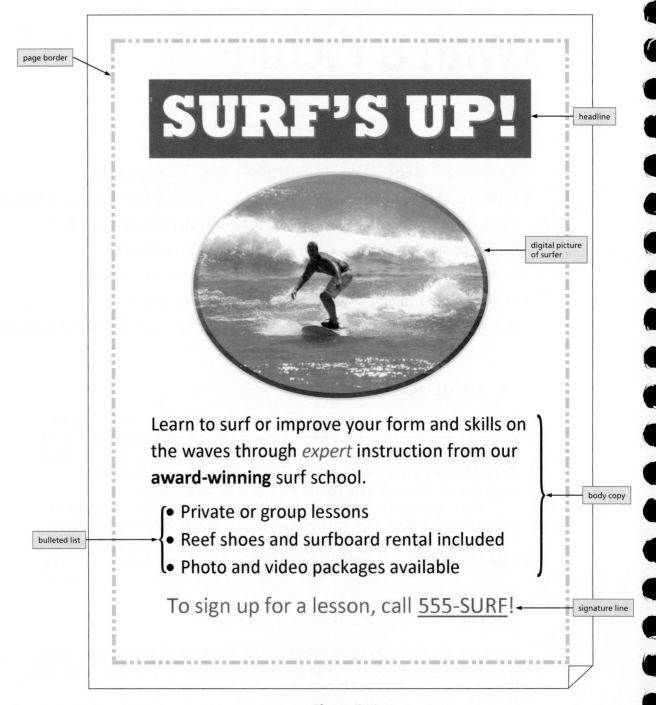

Figure 1–1

In this module, you will learn how to create the flyer shown in Figure 1–1. The following roadmap identifies general activities you will perform as you progress through this module:

1. ENTER TEXT in a new document.
2. FORMAT the TEXT in the flyer.
3. INSERT a PICTURE, called Surfer, in the flyer.
4. FORMAT the PICTURE in the flyer.
5. ENHANCE the PAGE with a border and spacing.
6. CORRECT errors AND REVISE text in the flyer.

To Run Word and Specify Settings

If you are using a computer to step through the project in this module and you want your screens to match the figures in this book, you should change your screen's resolution to 1366 × 768. For information about how to change a computer's resolution, refer to the Office and Windows module at the beginning of this book.

1 Run Word and create a blank document in the Word window.

2 If the Word window is not maximized, click the Maximize button on its title bar to maximize the window.

3 If the Print Layout button on the status bar is not selected (shown in Figure 1–2), click it so that your screen is in Print Layout view.

Q&A | What is Print Layout view?
The default (preset) view in Word is **Print Layout view**, which shows the document on a mock sheet of paper in the document window.

4 If Normal (Home tab | Styles group) is not selected in the Styles gallery (shown in Figure 1–2), click it so that your document uses the Normal style.

Q&A | What is the Normal style?
When you create a document, Word formats the text using a particular style. The default style in Word is called the **Normal style**, which is discussed later in this book.

What if rulers appear on my screen?
Click View on the ribbon to display the View tab and then remove the check mark from the View Ruler check box (View tab | Show group).

Entering Text

The first step in creating a document is to enter its text. With the projects in this book, you enter text by typing on the keyboard. By default, Word positions text you type at the left margin. In a later section of this module, you will learn how to format, or change the appearance of, the entered text.

For an introduction to Office and instructions about how to perform basic tasks in Office apps, read the Office and Windows module at the beginning of this book, where you can learn how to run an application, use the ribbon, save a file, open a file, print a file, exit an application, use Help, and much more.

For an introduction to Windows and instructions about how to perform basic Windows tasks, read the Office and Windows module at the beginning of this book, where you can learn how to resize windows, change screen resolution, create folders, move and rename files, use Windows Help, and much more.

BTW
The Word Window
The modules in this book begin with the Word window appearing as it did at the initial installation of the software. Your Word window may look different depending on your screen resolution and other Word settings.

To Type Text

To begin creating the flyer in this module, type the headline in the document window. *Why? The headline is the first line of text in the Surf Flyer.* The following steps type the first line of text in the document.

1

● Type **Surf's Up!** as the headline (Figure 1–2).

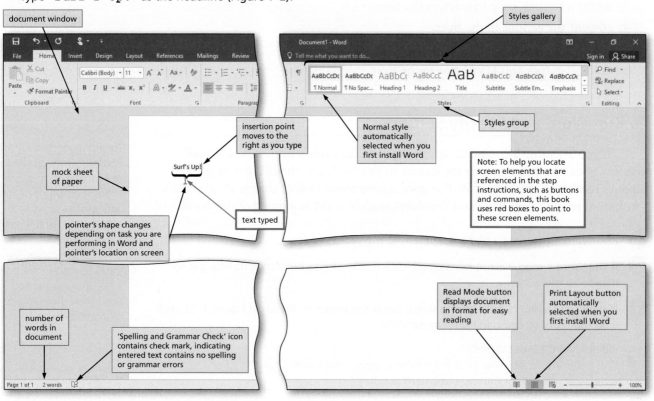

Figure 1–2

Q&A What if I make an error while typing?
You can press the BACKSPACE key until you have deleted the text in error and then retype the text correctly.

What is the purpose of the 'Spelling and Grammar Check' icon on the status bar?
The **'Spelling and Grammar Check' icon** displays either a check mark to indicate the entered text contains no spelling or grammar errors, or an X to indicate that it found potential errors. Word flags potential errors in the document with a red, green, or blue wavy underline. Later in this module, you will learn how to fix flagged errors.

2

● Press the ENTER key to move the insertion point to the beginning of the next line (Figure 1–3).

Q&A Why did blank space appear between the headline and the insertion point?
Each time you press the ENTER key, Word creates a new paragraph and inserts blank space between the two paragraphs. Later in this module, you will learn how to increase and decrease the spacing between paragraphs.

Figure 1–3

How do you use the touch keyboard with a touch screen?

To display the on-screen touch keyboard, tap the Touch Keyboard button on the Windows taskbar as shown in the Office and Windows module at the beginning of this book. When finished using the touch keyboard, tap the X button on the touch keyboard to close the keyboard.

To Display Formatting Marks

1 ENTER TEXT | **2 FORMAT TEXT** | **3 INSERT PICTURE**
4 FORMAT PICTURE | **5 ENHANCE PAGE** | **6 CORRECT & REVISE**

You may find it helpful to display formatting marks while working in a document. ***Why?*** *Formatting marks indicate where in a document you pressed the* ENTER *key,* SPACEBAR, *and other nonprinting characters.* A **formatting mark** is a character that Word displays on the screen but is not visible on a printed document. For example, the paragraph mark (¶) is a formatting mark that indicates where you pressed the ENTER key. A raised dot (·) shows where you pressed the SPACEBAR. Formatting marks are discussed as they appear on the screen.

Depending on settings made during previous Word sessions, your Word screen already may display formatting marks (Figure 1–4). The following step displays formatting marks, if they do not show already on the screen.

- If the Home tab is not the active tab, click Home on the ribbon to display the Home tab.
- If it is not selected already, click the 'Show/Hide ¶' button (Home tab | Paragraph group) to display formatting marks on the screen (Figure 1–4).

Q&A What if I do not want formatting marks to show on the screen?
You can hide them by clicking the 'Show/Hide ¶' button (Home tab | Paragraph group) again. It is recommended that you display formatting marks so that you visually can identify when you press the ENTER key, SPACEBAR, and other keys associated with nonprinting characters. Most of the document windows presented in this book, therefore, show formatting marks.

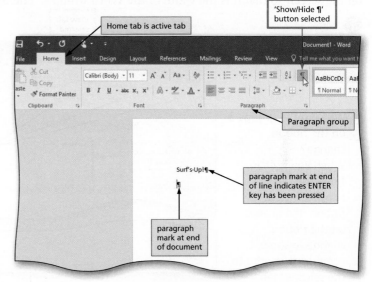

Home tab is active tab

'Show/Hide ¶' button selected

Paragraph group

paragraph mark at end of line indicates ENTER key has been pressed

paragraph mark at end of document

Surf's·Up!¶

Figure 1–4

Other Ways

1. Press CTRL+SHIFT+*

To Insert a Blank Line

1 ENTER TEXT | **2 FORMAT TEXT** | **3 INSERT PICTURE**
4 FORMAT PICTURE | **5 ENHANCE PAGE** | **6 CORRECT & REVISE**

In the flyer, the digital picture of the surfer appears between the headline and body copy. You will not insert this picture, however, until after you enter and format all text. ***Why?*** *Although you can format text and insert pictures in any order, for illustration purposes, this module formats all text first before inserting the picture. Thus, you leave a blank line in the document as a placeholder for the picture.*

To enter a blank line in a document, press the ENTER key without typing any text on the line. The following step inserts one blank line below the headline.

- Press the ENTER key to insert a blank line in the document (Figure 1–5).

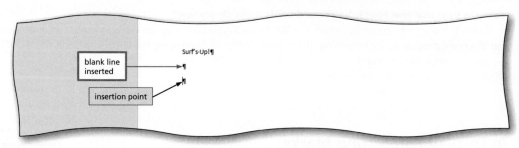

Figure 1–5

To Zoom Page Width

1 ENTER TEXT | 2 FORMAT TEXT | 3 INSERT PICTURE

4 FORMAT PICTURE | 5 ENHANCE PAGE | 6 CORRECT & REVISE

The next step in creating this flyer is to enlarge the contents that appear on the screen. *Why? You would like the text on the screen to be larger so that it is easier to read.* The document currently displays at 100% (shown in Figure 1–6). With Word, you can zoom page width, which zooms (enlarges or shrinks) the mock sheet of paper on the screen so that it is the width of the Word window. The following steps zoom page width.

- Click View on the ribbon to display the View tab (Figure 1–6).

Q&A Why did the groups on the ribbon change?
When you switch from one tab to another on the ribbon, the groups on the ribbon change to show commands related to the selected tab.

Figure 1–6

- Click the Page Width button (View tab | Zoom group) to display the page the same width as the document window (Figure 1–7).

Q&A If I change the zoom, will the document print differently?
Changing the zoom has no effect on the printed document.

Figure 1–7

Q&A What are the other predefined zoom options?

Through the View tab | Zoom group or the Zoom dialog box (Zoom button in Zoom group), you can zoom to one page (an entire single page appears in the document window), many pages (multiple pages appear at once in the document window), page width, text width, and a variety of set percentages. Whereas page width zoom places the edges of the page at the edges of the document window, text width zoom places the document contents at the edges of the document window.

Other Ways

1. Click Zoom button (View tab | Zoom group), click Page width (Zoom dialog box), click OK button

Wordwrap

Wordwrap allows you to type words in a paragraph continually without pressing the ENTER key at the end of each line. As you type, if a word extends beyond the right margin, Word also automatically positions that word on the next line along with the insertion point.

Word creates a new paragraph each time you press the ENTER key. Thus, as you type text in the document window, do not press the ENTER key when the insertion point reaches the right margin. Instead, press the ENTER key only in these circumstances:

1. To insert a blank line(s) in a document (as shown in previous steps)
2. To begin a new paragraph
3. To terminate a short line of text and advance to the next line
4. To respond to questions or prompts in Word dialog boxes, task panes, and other on-screen objects

BTW

Zooming
If text is too small for you to read on the screen, you can zoom the document by dragging the Zoom slider on the status bar or by clicking the Zoom Out or Zoom In buttons on the status bar. Changing the zoom has no effect on the printed document.

1 ENTER TEXT | 2 FORMAT TEXT | 3 INSERT PICTURE
4 FORMAT PICTURE | 5 ENHANCE PAGE | 6 CORRECT & REVISE

To Wordwrap Text as You Type

The next step in creating the flyer is to type the body copy. *Why? In many flyers, the body copy text appears below the headline.* The following steps illustrate how the body copy text wordwraps as you enter it in the document, which means you will not have to press the ENTER key at the end of the line.

1

- Type the first sentence of the body copy: `Learn to surf or improve your form and skills on the waves through expert instruction from our award-winning surf school.`

Q&A Why does my document wrap on different words?

The printer connected to a computer is one factor that can control where wordwrap occurs for each line in a document. Thus, it is possible that the same document could wordwrap differently if printed on different printers.

2

- Press the ENTER key to position the insertion point on the next line in the document (Figure 1–8).

Figure 1–8

Spelling and Grammar Check

As you type text in a document, Word checks your typing for possible spelling and grammar errors. If all of the words you have typed are in Word's dictionary and your grammar is correct, as mentioned earlier, the Spelling and Grammar Check icon on the status bar displays a check mark. Otherwise, the icon shows an X. In this case, Word flags the potential error(s) in the document window with a red, green, or blue wavy underline.

- A red wavy underline means the flagged text is not in Word's dictionary (because it is a proper name or misspelled).
- A green wavy underline indicates the text may be incorrect grammatically.
- A blue wavy underline indicates the text may contain a contextual spelling error, such as the misuse of homophones (words that are pronounced the same but that have different spellings or meanings, such as one and won).

Although you can check the entire document for spelling and grammar errors at once, you also can check flagged errors as they appear on the screen.

A flagged word is not necessarily misspelled. For example, many names, abbreviations, and specialized terms are not in Word's main dictionary. In these cases, you can instruct Word to ignore the flagged word. As you type, Word also detects duplicate words while checking for spelling errors. For example, if your document contains the phrase, to the the store, Word places a red wavy underline below the second occurrence of the word, the.

BTW

Automatic Spelling Correction

As you type, Word automatically corrects some misspelled words. For example, if you type recieve, Word automatically corrects the misspelling and displays the word, receive, when you press the SPACEBAR or type a punctuation mark. To see a complete list of automatically corrected words, click File on the ribbon to open the Backstage view, click the Options tab in the Backstage view, click Proofing in the left pane (Word Options dialog box), click the AutoCorrect Options button, and then scroll through the list near the bottom of the dialog box.

To Check Spelling and Grammar as You Type

1 ENTER TEXT | 2 FORMAT TEXT | 3 INSERT PICTURE
4 FORMAT PICTURE | 5 ENHANCE PAGE | 6 CORRECT & REVISE

In the following steps, the word, group, has been misspelled intentionally as goup. ***Why? These steps illustrate Word's check spelling as you type feature. If you are completing this project on a computer, your flyer may contain different or no misspelled words, depending on the accuracy of your typing.***

1

- Type **Private or goup** and then press the SPACEBAR, so that a red wavy line appears below the misspelled word (Figure 1–9).

Q&A What if Word does not flag my spelling and grammar errors with wavy underlines?

To verify that the check spelling and grammar as you type features are enabled, click File on the ribbon to open the Backstage view and then click the Options tab in the Backstage view. When the Word Options dialog box is displayed, click Proofing in the left pane and then ensure the 'Check spelling as you type' and 'Mark grammar errors as you type' check boxes contain check marks. Also ensure the 'Hide spelling errors in this document only' and 'Hide grammar errors in this document only' check boxes do not contain check marks. Click the OK button to close the Word Options dialog box.

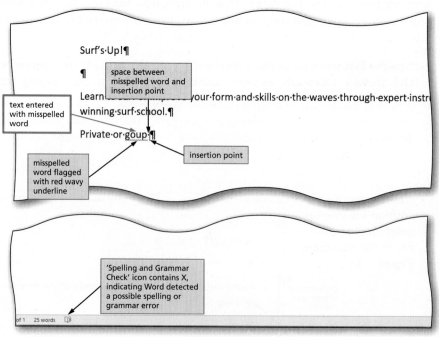

Figure 1–9

2

- Right-click the flagged word
  (goup, in this case) to display a
  shortcut menu that presents a list
  of suggested spelling corrections
  for the flagged word
  (Figure 1–10).

Q&A What if, when I right-click the
misspelled word, my desired
correction is not in the list on
the shortcut menu?
You can click outside the
shortcut menu to close the
shortcut menu and then retype
the correct word.

What if a flagged word actually is,
for example, a proper name and
spelled correctly?
Right-click it and then click Ignore All on the shortcut menu to instruct Word not to flag future occurrences
of the same word in this document.

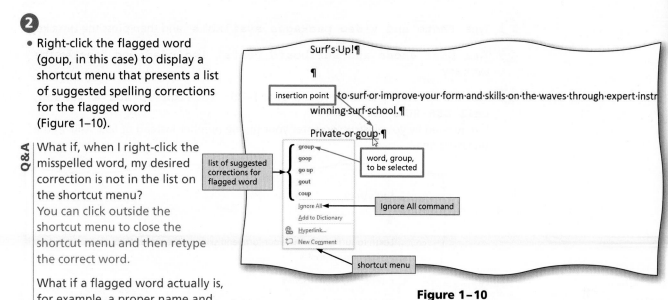

Figure 1–10

3

- Click group on
  the shortcut menu
  to replace the
  misspelled word in
  the document with
  a correctly spelled
  word (Figure 1–11).

Figure 1–11

Other Ways

1. Click 'Spelling and Grammar Check' icon on status bar, click desired word in Spelling pane, click Change button, click OK button

To Enter More Text

In the flyer, the text yet to be entered includes the remainder of the body copy,
which will be formatted as a bulleted list, and the signature line. The following steps
enter the remainder of text in the flyer.

1 Press the END key to move the insertion point to the end of the current line.

2 Type **lessons** and then press the ENTER key.

3 Type `Photo and video packages available` and then press the ENTER key.

4 Type `Reef shoes and surfboard rental included` and then press the ENTER key.

5 Type the signature line in the flyer (Figure 1–12): `To sign up for a lesson, call 555-SURF!`
If requested by your instructor, enter your phone number instead of 555-SURF in the signature line.

Surf's·Up!¶

¶

Learn·to·surf·or·improve·your·form·and·skills·on·the·waves·through·expert·instructi[
winning·surf·school.¶

three paragraphs of body copy that will be formatted as a bulleted list entered

Private·or·group·lessons¶

Photo·and·video·packages·available¶

Reef·shoes·and·surfboard·rental·included¶

signature line entered

To·sign·up·for·a·lesson,·call·555-SURF!¶

Figure 1–12

BTW
Organizing Files and Folders
You should organize and store files in folders so that you easily can find the files later. For example, if you are taking an introductory technology class called CIS 101, a good practice would be to save all Word files in a Word folder in a CIS 101 folder. For a discussion of folders and detailed examples of creating folders, refer to the Office and Windows module at the beginning of this book.

6 Save the flyer on your hard drive, OneDrive, or other storage location using Surf Flyer as the file name.

Q&A Why should I save the flyer at this time?
You have performed many tasks while creating this flyer and do not want to risk losing work completed thus far. For information about how to save, refer to the Office and Windows module at the beginning of this book.

CONSIDER THIS

How should you organize text in a flyer?
The text in a flyer typically is organized into three areas: headline, body copy, and signature line.

- The **headline** is the first line of text on the flyer. It conveys the product or service being offered (such as a car for sale, lessons, or sightseeing tours) or the benefit that will be gained (such as a convenience, better performance, greater security, higher earnings, or more comfort), or it can contain a message (such as a lost or found pet).

- The **body copy** consists of text between the headline and the signature line. This text highlights the key points of the message in as few words as possible. It should be easy to read and follow. While emphasizing the positive, the body copy must be realistic, truthful, and believable.

- The **signature line**, which is the last line of text on the flyer, contains contact information or identifies a call to action.

Navigating a Document

You view only a portion of a document on the screen through the document window. At some point when you type text or insert graphics, Word probably will **scroll** the top or bottom portion of the document off the screen. Although you cannot see the text and graphics once they scroll off the screen, they remain in the document.

You can use touch gestures, the keyboard, or a mouse to scroll to a different location in a document and/or move the insertion point around a document. If you are using a touch screen, simply use your finger to slide the document up or down to display a different location in the document and then tap to move the insertion point to a new location. When you use the keyboard, the insertion point automatically moves when you press the desired keys. For example, the previous steps used the END key to move the insertion point to the end of the current line. Table 1–1 outlines various techniques to navigate a document using the keyboard.

Table 1–1 Moving the Insertion Point with the Keyboard

Insertion Point Direction	Key(s) to Press	Insertion Point Direction	Key(s) to Press
Left one character	LEFT ARROW	Up one paragraph	CTRL+UP ARROW
Right one character	RIGHT ARROW	Down one paragraph	CTRL+DOWN ARROW
Left one word	CTRL+LEFT ARROW	Up one screen	PAGE UP
Right one word	CTRL+RIGHT ARROW	Down one screen	PAGE DOWN
Up one line	UP ARROW	To top of document window	ALT+CTRL+PAGE UP
Down one line	DOWN ARROW	To bottom of document window	ALT+CTRL+PAGE DOWN
To end of line	END	To beginning of document	CTRL+HOME
To beginning of line	HOME	To end of document	CTRL+END

© 2015 Cengage Learning

With the mouse, you can use the scroll arrows or the scroll box on the scroll bar to display a different portion of the document in the document window and then click the mouse to move the insertion point to that location. Table 1–2 explains various techniques for using the scroll bar to scroll vertically with the mouse.

Table 1–2 Using the Scroll Bar to Scroll Vertically with the Mouse

Scroll Direction	Mouse Action	Scroll Direction	Mouse Action
Up	Drag the scroll box upward.	Down one screen	Click anywhere below the scroll box on the vertical scroll bar.
Down	Drag the scroll box downward.	Up one line	Click the scroll arrow at the top of the vertical scroll bar.
Up one screen	Click anywhere above the scroll box on the vertical scroll bar.	Down one line	Click the scroll arrow at the bottom of the vertical scroll bar.

© 2015 Cengage Learning

Formatting Paragraphs and Characters

With the text for the flyer entered, the next step is to **format**, or change the appearance of, its text. A paragraph encompasses the text from the first character in the paragraph up to and including its paragraph mark (¶). **Paragraph formatting** is the process of changing the appearance of a paragraph. For example, you can center or add bullets to a paragraph. Characters include letters, numbers, punctuation marks, and symbols. **Character formatting** is the process of changing the way characters appear on the screen and in print. You use character formatting to emphasize certain words and improve readability of a document. For example, you can color, italicize, or underline characters. Often, you apply both paragraph and character formatting to the same text. For example, you may center a paragraph (paragraph formatting) and underline some of the characters in the same paragraph (character formatting).

Although you can format paragraphs and characters before you type, many Word users enter text first and then format the existing text. Figure 1–13a shows the flyer in this module before formatting its paragraphs and characters. Figure 1–13b shows the flyer after formatting. As you can see from the two figures, a document that is formatted is easier to read and looks more professional. The following sections discuss how to format the flyer so that it looks like Figure 1–13b.

BTW
Minimize Wrist Injury
Computer users frequently switch among the keyboard, the mouse, and touch gestures during a word processing session; such switching strains the wrist. To help prevent wrist injury, minimize switching. For instance, if your hand already is on the mouse, use the mouse to scroll. If your fingers already are on the keyboard, use keyboard keys to scroll. If your fingertips already are on the screen, use your finger to slide the document to a new location.

Figure 1–13a Unformatted Flyer

Figure 1–13b Formatted Flyer

Figure 1–13

BTW
Character Widths
Many word processing
documents use variable
character fonts, where some
characters are wider than
others; for example, the letter
w is wider than the letter i.

Font, Font Sizes, and Themes

Characters that appear on the screen are a specific shape and size. The **font**, or typeface, defines the appearance and shape of the letters, numbers, and special characters. In Word, the default font usually is Calibri (shown in Figure 1–14). You can leave characters in the default font or change them to a different font. **Font size** specifies the size of the characters and is determined by a measurement system called points. A single **point** is about 1/72 of one inch in height. The default font size in Word typically is 11 (Figure 1–14). Thus, a character with a font size of 11 is about 11/72 or a little less than 1/6 of one inch in height. You can increase or decrease the font size of characters in a document.

A document **theme** is a set of unified formats for fonts, colors, and graphics. Word includes a variety of document themes to assist you with coordinating these visual elements in a document. The default theme fonts are Calibri Light for headings and Calibri for body text. By changing the document theme, you quickly can give your document a new look. You also can define your own document themes.

CONSIDER THIS

How do I know which formats to use in a flyer?
In a flyer, consider the following formatting suggestions.

- **Increase the font size of characters.** Flyers usually are posted on a bulletin board or in a window. Thus, the font size should be as large as possible so that passersby easily can read the flyer. To give the headline more impact, its font size should be larger than the font size of the text in the body copy. If possible, make the font size of the signature line larger than the body copy but smaller than the headline.

- **Change the font of characters.** Use fonts that are easy to read. Try to use only two different fonts in a flyer; for example, use one for the headline and the other for all other text. Too many fonts can make the flyer visually confusing.

- **Change the paragraph alignment.** The default alignment for paragraphs in a document is **left-aligned**, that is, flush at the left margin of the document with uneven right edges. Consider changing the alignment of some of the paragraphs to add interest and variety to the flyer.

- **Highlight key paragraphs with bullets.** A bulleted paragraph is a paragraph that begins with a dot or other symbol. Use bulleted paragraphs to highlight important points in a flyer.

- **Emphasize important words.** To call attention to certain words or lines, you can underline them, italicize them, or bold them. Use these formats sparingly, however, because overuse will minimize their effect and make the flyer look too busy.

- **Use color.** Use colors that complement each other and convey the meaning of the flyer. Vary colors in terms of hue and brightness. Headline colors, for example, can be bold and bright. Signature lines should stand out more than body copy but less than headlines. Keep in mind that too many colors can detract from the flyer and make it difficult to read.

To Center a Paragraph

The headline in the flyer currently is left-aligned (shown in Figure 1–14). *Why? Word, by default, left-aligns text, unless you specifically change the alignment.* You want the headline to be **centered**, that is, positioned horizontally between the left and right margins on the page. Recall that Word considers a single short line of text, such as the one-word headline, a paragraph. Thus, you will center the paragraph containing the headline. The following steps center a paragraph.

1

- Click Home on the ribbon to display the Home tab.
- Click somewhere in the paragraph to be centered (in this case, the headline) to position the insertion point in the paragraph to be centered (Figure 1–14).

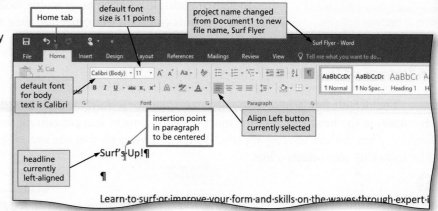

Figure 1–14

2

- Click the Center button (Home tab | Paragraph group) to center the paragraph containing the insertion point (Figure 1–15).

Q&A What if I want to return the paragraph to left-aligned?
You would click the Center button again or click the Align Left button (Home tab | Paragraph group).

Figure 1–15

Other Ways

1. Right-click paragraph (or if using touch, tap 'Show Context Menu' button on mini toolbar), click Paragraph on shortcut menu, click Indents and Spacing tab (Paragraph dialog box), click Alignment arrow, click Centered, click OK button

2. Click Paragraph Settings Dialog Box Launcher (Home tab or Layout tab | Paragraph group), click Indents and Spacing tab (Paragraph dialog box), click Alignment arrow, click Centered, click OK button

3. Press CTRL+E

To Center Another Paragraph

In the flyer, the signature line is to be centered to match the paragraph alignment of the headline. The following steps center the signature line.

1 Click somewhere in the paragraph to be centered (in this case, the signature line) to position the insertion point in the paragraph to be formatted.

2 Click the Center button (Home tab | Paragraph group) to center the paragraph containing the insertion point (shown in Figure 1–16).

BTW
File Type
Depending on your Windows settings, the file type .docx may be displayed on the title bar immediately to the right of the file name after you save the file. The file type .docx identifies a Word 2016 document.

BTW
The Ribbon and Screen Resolution
Word may change how the groups and buttons within the groups appear on the ribbon, depending on the computer or mobile device's screen resolution. Thus, your ribbon may look different from the ones in this book if you are using a screen resolution other than 1366 × 768.

Formatting Single versus Multiple Paragraphs and Characters

As shown in the previous sections, to format a single paragraph, simply position the insertion point in the paragraph to make it the current paragraph and then format the paragraph. Similarly, to format a single word, position the insertion point in the word to make it the current word, and then format the word.

To format multiple paragraphs or words, however, you first must select the paragraphs or words you want to format and then format the selection.

1 ENTER TEXT | 2 FORMAT TEXT | **3 INSERT PICTURE**
4 FORMAT PICTURE | 5 ENHANCE PAGE | 6 CORRECT & REVISE

To Select a Line

The default font size of 11 point is too small for a headline in a flyer. To increase the font size of the characters in the headline, you first must select the line of text containing the headline. *Why? If you increase the font size of text without selecting any text, Word will increase the font size only of the word containing the insertion point.* The following step selects a line.

- Move the pointer to the left of the line to be selected (in this case, the headline) until the pointer changes to a right-pointing block arrow (Figure 1–16).

Figure 1–16

2

- While the pointer is a right-pointing block arrow, click the mouse button to select the entire line to the right of the pointer (Figure 1–17).

Q&A

What if I am using a touch screen?
You would double-tap to the left of the line to be selected to select the line.

Why is the selected text shaded gray?
If your screen normally displays dark letters on a light background, which is the default setting in Word, then selected text is displayed with a light shading color, such as gray, on the dark letters. Note that the selection that appears on the text does not print.

Figure 1–17

Other Ways

1. Drag pointer through line   2. With insertion point at beginning of desired line, press CRTL+SHIFT+DOWN ARROW

To Change the Font Size of Selected Text

The next step is to increase the font size of the characters in the selected headline. **Why?** *You would like the headline to be as large as possible and still fit on a single line, which in this case is 72 point.* The following steps increase the font size of the headline from 11 to 72 point.

1

- With the text selected, click the Font Size arrow (Home tab | Font group) to display the Font Size gallery (Figure 1–18).

Q&A

What is the Font Size arrow?
The Font Size arrow is the arrow to the right of the Font Size box, which is the text box that displays the current font size.

Why are the font sizes in my Font Size gallery different from those in Figure 1–18?
Font sizes may vary depending on the current font and your printer driver.

What happened to the mini toolbar?
The mini toolbar disappears if you do not use it. These steps use the Font Size arrow on the Home tab instead of the Font Size arrow on the mini toolbar.

Figure 1–18

2

- Point to 72 in the Font Size gallery to display a live preview of the selected text at the selected point size (Figure 1–19).

Q&A

What is live preview?
Recall from the Office and Windows module at the beginning of this book that live preview is a feature that allows you to point to a gallery choice and see its effect in the document — without actually selecting the choice.

Can I use live preview on a touch screen?
Live preview is not available on a touch screen.

Surf's·Up!¶

Figure 1–19

Experiment

- Point to various font sizes in the Font Size gallery and watch the font size of the selected text change in the document window.

3

- Click 72 in the Font Size gallery to increase the font size of the selected text.

Other Ways

1. Click Font Size arrow on mini toolbar, click desired font size in Font Size gallery	2. Right-click selected text (or, if using touch, tap 'Show Context Menu' button on mini toolbar), click Font on shortcut menu, click Font tab (Font dialog box), select desired font size in Size list, click OK button	3. Click Font Dialog Box Launcher, (Home tab | Font group) click Font tab (Font dialog box), select desired font size in Size list, click OK button	4. Press CTRL+D, click Font tab (Font dialog box), select desired font size in Size list, click OK button

To Change the Font of Selected Text

The default theme font for headings is Calibri Light and for all other text, called body text in Word, is Calibri. Many other fonts are available, however, so that you can add variety to documents.

The following steps change the font of the headline from Calibri to Rockwell Extra Bold. *Why? To draw more attention to the headline, you change its font so that it differs from the font of other text in the flyer.*

❶

- With the text selected, click the Font arrow (Home tab | Font group) to display the Font gallery (Figure 1–20).

Q&A

Will the fonts in my Font gallery be the same as those in Figure 1–20?
Your list of available fonts may differ, depending on the type of printer you are using and other settings.

What if the text no longer is selected?
Follow the steps described earlier to select a line.

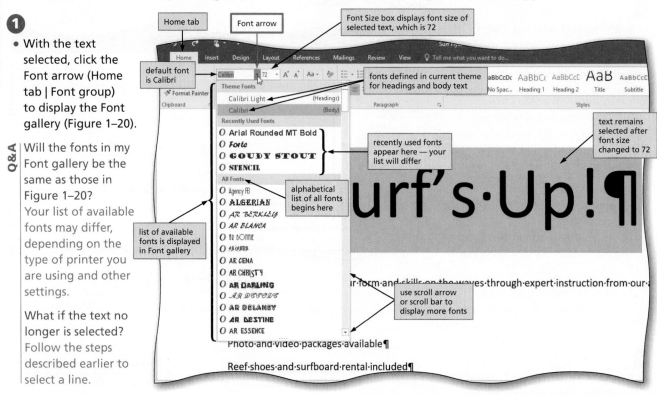

Figure 1–20

❷

- If necessary, scroll through the Font gallery to display Rockwell Extra Bold (or a similar font).
- Point to 'Rockwell Extra Bold' (or a similar font) to display a live preview of the selected text in the selected font (Figure 1–21).

Experiment

- Point to various fonts in the Font gallery and watch the font of the selected text change in the document window.

Figure 1–21

3

• Click 'Rockwell Extra Bold' (or a similar font) in the Font gallery to change the font of the selected text.

Q&A If the font I want to use appears in the Recently Used Fonts list in the Font gallery, could I click it there instead?
Yes.

Other Ways

1. Click Font arrow on mini toolbar, click desired font in Font gallery

2. Right-click selected text (or, if using touch, tap 'Show Context Menu' button on mini toolbar), click Font on shortcut menu, click Font tab (Font dialog box), select desired font in Font list, click OK button

3. Click Font Dialog Box Launcher (Home tab | Font group), click Font tab (Font dialog box), select desired font in Font list, click OK button

4. Press CTRL+D, click Font tab (Font dialog box), select desired font in Font list, click OK button

To Change the Case of Selected Text

1 ENTER TEXT | 2 FORMAT TEXT | 3 INSERT PICTURE
4 FORMAT PICTURE | 5 ENHANCE PAGE | 6 CORRECT & REVISE

The headline currently shows the first letter in each word capitalized, which sometimes is referred to as initial cap. The following steps change the headline to uppercase. *Why? To draw more attention to the headline, you would like the entire line of text to be capitalized, or in uppercase letters.*

1

• With the text selected, click the Change Case button (Home tab | Font group) to display the Change Case gallery (Figure 1–22).

Figure 1–22

2

• Click UPPERCASE in the Change Case gallery to change the case of the selected text (Figure 1–23).

Q&A What if a ruler appears on the screen or the pointer shape changes?
If you are using a mouse, depending on the position of your pointer and locations you click on the screen, a ruler may appear automatically or the pointer's shape may change. Simply move the mouse and the ruler should disappear and/or the pointer shape will change.

Figure 1–23

Other Ways

1. Right-click selected text (or, if using touch, tap 'Show Context Menu' button on mini toolbar), click Font on shortcut menu, click Font tab (Font dialog box), select All caps in Effects area, click OK button

2. Click Font Dialog Box Launcher (Home tab | Font group), click Font tab (Font dialog box), select All caps in Effects area, click OK button

3. Press SHIFT+F3 repeatedly until text is desired case

To Apply a Text Effect to Selected Text

Word provides many text effects to add interest and variety to text. The following steps apply a text effect to the headline. **Why?** *You would like the text in the headline to be even more noticeable.*

1

- With the text selected, click the 'Text Effects and Typography' button (Home tab | Font group) to display the Text Effects and Typography gallery (Figure 1–24).

Figure 1–24

2

- Point to 'Fill - White, Outline - Accent 2, Hard Shadow - Accent 2' (fourth text effect in third row) to display a live preview of the selected text with the selected text effect (Figure 1–25).

Figure 1–25

Experiment

- Point to various text effects in the Text Effects and Typography gallery and watch the text effects of the selected text change in the document window.

3

- Click 'Fill - White, Outline - Accent 2, Hard Shadow - Accent 2' to change the text effect of the selected text.

4

- Click anywhere in the document window to remove the selection from the selected text.

Other Ways

1. Right-click selected text (or, if using touch, tap 'Show Context Menu' button on mini toolbar), click Font on shortcut menu, click Font tab (Font dialog box), click Text Effects button, expand Text Fill or Text Outline section and then select the desired text effect(s) (Format Text Effects dialog box), click OK button, click OK button

2. Click Font Dialog Box Launcher (Home tab | Font group), click Font tab (Font dialog box), click Text Effects button, expand Text Fill or Text Outline section and then select desired text effect (Format Text Effects dialog box), click OK button, click OK button

To Shade a Paragraph

When you **shade** text, Word colors the rectangular area behind any text or graphics. If the text to shade is a paragraph, Word shades the area from the left margin to the right margin of the current paragraph. To shade a paragraph, place the insertion point in the paragraph. To shade any other text, you must first select the text to be shaded.

This flyer uses a shading color for the headline. *Why? To make the headline of the flyer more eye-catching, you shade it.* The following steps shade a paragraph.

1

- Click somewhere in the paragraph to be shaded (in this case, the headline) to position the insertion point in the paragraph to be formatted.

- Click the Shading arrow (Home tab | Paragraph group) to display the Shading gallery (Figure 1–26).

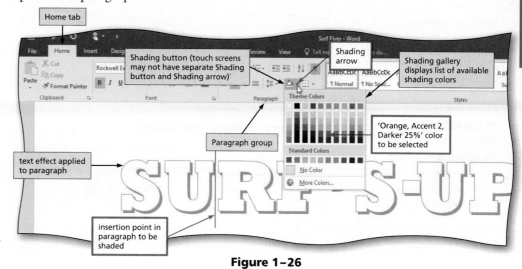

Figure 1–26

Q&A What if I click the Shading button by mistake?
Click the Shading arrow and proceed with Step 2. Note that if you are using a touch screen, you may not have a separate Shading button.

Why does my Shading gallery display different colors?
Your color scheme setting may display colors in a different order or may be different from Office, which is the default color scheme. To change the color scheme, click Design on the ribbon, click the Theme Colors button (Design tab | Document Formatting group), and then click Office in the Theme Colors gallery.

Experiment

- Point to various colors in the Shading gallery and watch the shading color of the current paragraph change.

2

- Click 'Orange, Accent 2, Darker 25%' (sixth color in fifth row) to shade the current paragraph (Figure 1–27).

Q&A What if I apply a dark shading color to dark text?
When the font color of text is Automatic, the color usually is black. If you select a dark shading color,

Figure 1–27

Word automatically may change the text color to white so that the shaded text is easier to read.

Other Ways

1. Click Borders arrow (Home tab | Paragraph group), click Borders and Shading, click Shading tab (Borders and Shading dialog box), click Fill arrow, select desired color, click OK button

To Select Multiple Lines

The next formatting step for the flyer is to increase the font size of the characters between the headline and the signature line. *Why? You want this text to be easier to read from a distance.*

To change the font size of the characters in multiple lines, you first must select all the lines to be formatted. The following steps select multiple lines.

1

- Scroll, if necessary, so that all text below the headline is displayed on the screen.

- Move the pointer to the left of the first paragraph to be selected until the pointer changes to a right-pointing block arrow (Figure 1–28).

Figure 1–28

Q&A What if I am using a touch screen?
You would tap to position the insertion point in the text to select.

2

- While the pointer is a right-pointing block arrow, drag downward to select all lines that will be formatted (Figure 1–29).

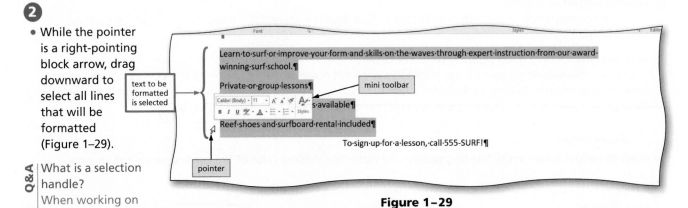

Figure 1–29

Q&A What is a selection handle?
When working on a touch screen, a **selection handle** (small circle) appears below the insertion point. Using a fingertip, you drag a selection handle to select text.

Other Ways

1. With insertion point at beginning of desired line, press SHIFT+DOWN ARROW repeatedly until all lines are selected

---

BTW
Formatting Marks
With some fonts, the formatting marks will not be displayed properly on the screen. For example, the raised dot that signifies a blank space between words may be displayed behind a character instead of in the blank space, causing the characters to look incorrect.

To Change the Font Size of Selected Text

The characters between the headline and the signature line in the flyer currently are 11 point. To make them easier to read from a distance, this flyer uses a 24-point font size for these characters. The following steps change the font size of the selected text.

1 With the text selected, click the Font Size arrow (Home tab | Font group) to display the Font Size gallery.

2 Click 24 in the Font Size gallery to increase the font size of the selected text.

3 Click anywhere in the document window to remove the selection from the text.

4 If necessary, scroll so that you can see all the resized text on the screen (Figure 1–30).

Figure 1–30

To Bullet a List of Paragraphs

1 ENTER TEXT | 2 FORMAT TEXT | **3 INSERT PICTURE**
4 FORMAT PICTURE | 5 ENHANCE PAGE | 6 CORRECT & REVISE

A **bulleted list** is a series of paragraphs, each beginning with a bullet character. The next step is to format the three paragraphs about the lessons that are above the signature line in the flyer as a bulleted list.

To format a list of paragraphs with bullets, you first must select all the lines in the paragraphs. *Why? If you do not select all paragraphs, Word will place a bullet only in the paragraph containing the insertion point.* The following steps bullet a list of paragraphs.

1

- Move the pointer to the left of the first paragraph to be selected until the pointer changes to a right-pointing block arrow.

- Drag downward until all paragraphs that will be formatted with a bullet character are selected (Figure 1–31).

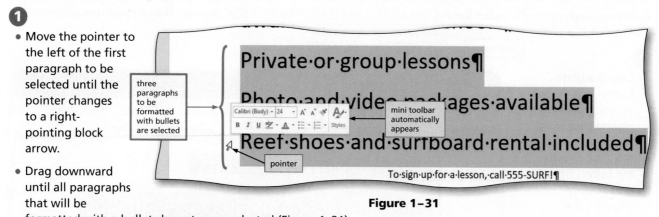

Figure 1–31

Q&A What if I am using a touch screen?

Tap to position the insertion point in the text to select and then drag the selection handle(s) as necessary to select the text that will be formatted.

2

- Click the Bullets button (Home tab | Paragraph group) to place a bullet character at the beginning of each selected paragraph (Figure 1–32).

Q&A Why does my screen display a Bullets gallery?
If you are using a touch screen, you may not have a separate Bullets button and Bullets arrow. In this case, select the desired bullet style in the Bullets gallery.

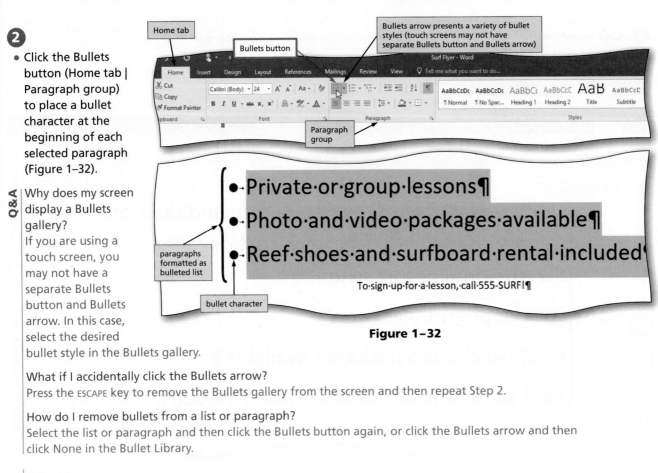

Figure 1–32

What if I accidentally click the Bullets arrow?
Press the ESCAPE key to remove the Bullets gallery from the screen and then repeat Step 2.

How do I remove bullets from a list or paragraph?
Select the list or paragraph and then click the Bullets button again, or click the Bullets arrow and then click None in the Bullet Library.

Other Ways

1. Right-click selected paragraphs, click Bullets button on mini toolbar

---

To Undo and Redo an Action

Word provides a means of canceling your recent command(s) or action(s). For example, if you format text incorrectly, you can undo the format and try it again. When you point to the Undo button, Word displays the action you can undo as part of a ScreenTip.

If, after you undo an action, you decide you did not want to perform the undo, you can redo the undone action. Word does not allow you to undo or redo some actions, such as saving or printing a document. The following steps undo the bullet format just applied and then redo the bullet format. *Why? These steps illustrate the undo and redo actions.*

1

- Click the Undo button on the Quick Access Toolbar to reverse your most recent action (in this case, remove the bullets from the paragraphs) (Figure 1–33).

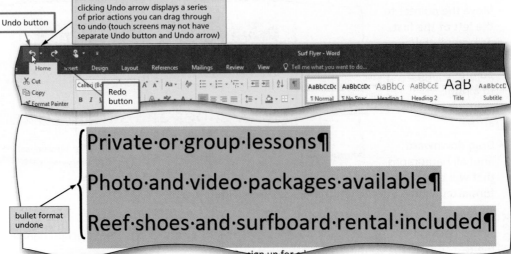

Figure 1–33

2

- Click the Redo button on the Quick Access Toolbar to reverse your most recent undo (in this case, place a bullet character on the paragraphs again) (shown in Figure 1–32).

Other Ways

1. Press CTRL+Z to undo; press CTRL+Y to redo

To Italicize Text

1 ENTER TEXT | 2 FORMAT TEXT | 3 INSERT PICTURE
4 FORMAT PICTURE | 5 ENHANCE PAGE | 6 CORRECT & REVISE

Italic text has a slanted appearance. The next step is to italicize the word, expert, in the flyer to further emphasize it. As with a single paragraph, if you want to format a single word, you do not need to select it. *Why?* *To format a single word, you simply position the insertion point somewhere in the word and apply the desired format.* The following step italicizes a word.

1

- Click somewhere in the word to be italicized (expert, in this case) to position the insertion point in the word to be formatted.

- Click the Italic button (Home tab | Font group) to italicize the word containing the insertion point (Figure 1–34).

Figure 1–34

Q&A How would I remove an italic format?
You would click the Italic button a second time, or you immediately could click the Undo button on the Quick Access Toolbar or press CTRL+Z.

How can I tell what formatting has been applied to text?
The selected buttons and boxes on the Home tab show formatting characteristics of the location of the insertion point. With the insertion point in the word, expert, the Home tab shows these formats: 24-point Calibri italic font.

Why did the appearance of the Redo button change?
It changed to a Repeat button. When it is a Repeat button, you can click it to repeat your last action. For example, you can select different text and then click the Repeat button to apply (repeat) the italic format to the selected text.

Other Ways

1. Click Italic button on mini toolbar	2. Right-click selected text (or, if using touch, tap 'Show Context Menu' button on mini toolbar), click Font on shortcut menu, click Font tab (Font dialog box), click Italic in Font style list, click OK button	3. Click Font Dialog Box Launcher (Home tab | Font group), click Font tab (Font dialog box), click Italic in Font style list, click OK button	4. Press CTRL+I

To Color Text

The following steps change the color of the word, expert. *Why? To emphasize the word even more, you change its color.*

1

- With the insertion point in the word to format, click the Font Color arrow (Home tab | Font group) to display the Font Color gallery (Figure 1–35).

Q&A What if I click the Font Color button by mistake?
Click the Font Color arrow and then proceed with Step 2. Note that you may not have a separate Font Color button if you are using a touch screen.

Figure 1–35

 Experiment

- If you are using a mouse, point to various colors in the Font Color gallery and watch the color of the current word change.

2

- Click 'Orange, Accent 2, Darker 25%' (sixth color in fifth row) to change the color of the text (Figure 1–36).

Q&A How would I change the text color back to black?
You would position the insertion point in the word or select the text, click the Font Color arrow (Home tab | Font group) again, and then click Automatic in the Font Color gallery.

Figure 1–36

Other Ways

1. Click Font Color arrow on mini toolbar, click desired color

2. Right-click selected text (or, if using touch, tap 'Show Context Menu' button on mini toolbar), click Font on shortcut menu, click Font tab (Font dialog box), click Font color arrow, click desired color, click OK button

3. Click Font Dialog Box Launcher (Home tab | Font group), click Font tab (Font dialog box), click Font color arrow, click desired color, click OK button

To Use the Mini Toolbar to Format Text

Recall from the Office and Windows module at the beginning of this book that the mini toolbar automatically appears based on certain tasks you perform. *Why? Word places commonly used buttons and boxes on the mini toolbar for your convenience. If you do not use the mini toolbar, it disappears from the screen.* All commands on the mini toolbar also exist on the ribbon.

The following steps use the mini toolbar to change the color and font size of text in the signature line of the flyer.

1

- Move the pointer to the left of the line to be selected until the pointer changes to a right-pointing block arrow and then click to select the line and display the mini toolbar (Figure 1–37).

Q&A What if I am using a touch screen? Double-tap to the left of the line to be selected to select the line and then tap the selection

Figure 1–37

to display the mini toolbar. If you are using a touch screen, the buttons and boxes on the mini toolbar differ. For example, it contains a 'Show Context Menu' button at the far-right edge, which you tap to display a shortcut menu.

2

- Click the Font Size arrow on the mini toolbar to display the Font Size gallery.
- Point to 28 in the Font Size gallery to display a live preview of the selected font size (Figure 1–38).

3

- Click 28 in the Font Size gallery to increase the font size of the selected text.

Figure 1–38

4

- With the text still selected and the mini toolbar still displayed, click the Font Color arrow on the mini toolbar to display the Font Color gallery.
- Point to 'Orange, Accent 2, Darker 25%' (sixth color in the fifth row) to display a live preview of the selected font color (Figure 1–39).

Figure 1–39

5

- Click 'Orange, Accent 2, Darker 25%' to change the color of the selected text.
- Click anywhere in the document window to remove the selection from the text.

To Select a Group of Words

1 ENTER TEXT | 2 FORMAT TEXT | **3 INSERT PICTURE**
4 FORMAT PICTURE | 5 ENHANCE PAGE | 6 CORRECT & REVISE

To emphasize the contact phone number (555-SURF), this text is underlined in the flyer. Because the phone number is separated with a hyphen, Word considers it a group of words. To format a group of words, you first must select them. ***Why?*** *If you underline text without selecting any text first, Word will underline only the word containing the insertion point.* The following steps select a group of words.

1

- Position the pointer immediately to the left of the first character of the text to be selected, in this case, the 5 in 555 (Figure 1–40).

Q&A Why did the shape of the pointer change?
The pointer's shape is an I-beam when positioned in unselected text in the document window.

Figure 1–40

2

- Drag the pointer through the last character of the text to be selected, in this case, the F in the phone number (Figure 1–41).

Q&A Why did the pointer shape change again?
When the pointer is positioned in selected text, its shape is a left-pointing block arrow.

Figure 1–41

Other Ways

1. With insertion point at beginning of first word in group, press CTRL+SHIFT+RIGHT ARROW repeatedly until all words are selected

To Underline Text

Underlined text prints with an underscore (_) below each character. In the flyer, the contact phone number, 555-SURF, in the signature line is underlined. *Why? Underlines are used to emphasize or draw attention to specific text.* The following step formats selected text with an underline.

1

- With the text selected, click the Underline button (Home tab | Font group) to underline the selected text (Figure 1–42).

Q&A What if my screen displays an Underline gallery?
If you are using a touch screen, you may not have a separate Underline button and Underline arrow. In this case, select the desired underline style in the Underline gallery.

If a button exists on the mini toolbar, can I click that instead of using the ribbon?
Yes.

How would I remove an underline?
You would click the Underline button a second time, or you immediately could click the Undo button on the Quick Access Toolbar.

Home tab

Underline arrow displays Underline gallery, which contains a variety of underline styles and colors (touch screens may not have separate Underline button and Underline arrow)

Underline button selected

Font group

Learn·to·surf·or·improve·your·form·and·skills·o

the·waves·through·*expert*·instruction·from·our·

award-winning·surf·school.¶

Private·············ns¶

·····and·video·pack······ailable¶

•·Reef·shoes·and·surfboard·rental·included¶

To·sign·up·for·a·lesson··call·555-SURF!

selected text underlined

Figure 1–42

Other Ways

1. Click Underline button on mini toolbar
2. Right-click text (or, if using touch, tap 'Show Context Menu' button on mini toolbar), click Font on shortcut menu, click Font tab (Font dialog box), click Underline style box arrow, click desired underline style, click OK button
3. Click Font Dialog Box Launcher (Home tab | Font group), click Font tab (Font dialog box), click Underline style arrow, click desired underline style, click OK button
4. Press CTRL+U

To Bold Text

Bold characters appear somewhat thicker and darker than those that are not bold. The following steps format the text, award-winning, in bold characters. *Why? To further emphasize this text, it is bold in the flyer.* Recall that if you want to format a single word, you simply position the insertion point in the word and then format the word. To format text that consists of more than one word, as you have learned previously, you select the text first.

1

- Select the text to be formatted (the text, award-winning, in this case); that is, position the pointer immediately to the left of the first character of the text to be selected and then drag the pointer through the last character of the text to be selected.

Q&A What if I am using a touch screen?
Tap to position the insertion point in the text you want to select and then drag the selection handle(s) to select the text to be formatted.

- With the text selected, click the Bold button (Home tab | Font group) to bold the selected text (Figure 1–43).

Q&A

How would I remove a bold format?

You would click the Bold button a second time, or you immediately could click the Undo button on the Quick Access Toolbar.

③

- Click anywhere in the document window to remove the selection from the screen.

Figure 1–43

Other Ways

1. Click Bold button on mini toolbar	2. Right-click selected text (or, if using touch, tap 'Show Context Menu' button on mini toolbar), click Font on shortcut menu, click Font tab (Font dialog box), click Bold in Font style list, click OK button	3. Click Font Dialog Box Launcher (Home tab | Font group), click Font tab (Font dialog box), click Bold in Font style list, click OK button	4. Press CTRL+B

1 ENTER TEXT | 2 FORMAT TEXT | **3 INSERT PICTURE**
4 FORMAT PICTURE | **5 ENHANCE PAGE** | **6 CORRECT & REVISE**

To Zoom One Page

Earlier in this module, you changed the zoom to page width so that the text on the screen was larger and easier to read. In the next set of steps, you want to see the entire page (as a mock sheet of paper) on the screen at once. *Why? You want be able to see the effect of adjusting colors in the document as a whole.* The next step displays a single page in its entirety in the document window as large as possible.

①

- Click View on the ribbon to display the View tab.
- Click the One Page button (View tab | Zoom group) to display the entire page in the document window as large as possible (Figure 1–44).

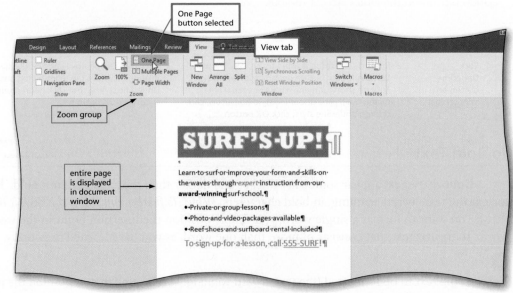

Figure 1–44

Other Ways

1. Click Zoom button (View tab | Zoom group), click Whole page (Zoom dialog box), click OK button

What colors should I choose when creating documents?

When choosing color, associate the meaning of the color with your message:

• Red expresses danger, power, or energy and often is associated with sports or physical exertion.

• Brown represents simplicity, honesty, and dependability.

• Orange denotes success, victory, creativity, and enthusiasm.

• Yellow suggests sunshine, happiness, hope, liveliness, and intelligence.

• Green symbolizes growth, healthiness, harmony, and healing and often is associated with safety or money.

• Blue indicates integrity, trust, importance, confidence, and stability.

• Purple represents wealth, power, comfort, extravagance, magic, mystery, and spirituality.

• White stands for purity, goodness, cleanliness, precision, and perfection.

• Black suggests authority, strength, elegance, power, and prestige.

• Gray conveys neutrality and, thus, often is found in backgrounds and other effects.

To Change Theme Colors

1 ENTER TEXT | 2 FORMAT TEXT | 3 INSERT PICTURE
4 FORMAT PICTURE | 5 ENHANCE PAGE | 6 CORRECT & REVISE

A **color scheme** in Word is a document theme that identifies complementary colors for text, background, accents, and links in a document. With more than 20 predefined color schemes, Word provides a simple way to coordinate colors in a document.

The default color scheme is called Office. In the flyer, you will change the color scheme. *Why? You want the colors in the flyer to represent integrity, trust, confidence, stability, healthiness, harmony, blooming, and safety, which are conveyed by shades of blues and greens. In Word, the Blue color scheme uses these colors.* The following steps change theme colors.

1

• Click Design on the ribbon to display the Design tab.

• Click the Theme Colors button (Design tab | Document Formatting group) to display the Theme Colors gallery.

• Point to Blue in the Theme Colors gallery to display a live preview of the selected theme color (Figure 1–45).

 Experiment

• Point to various color schemes in the Theme Colors gallery and watch the colors change in the document.

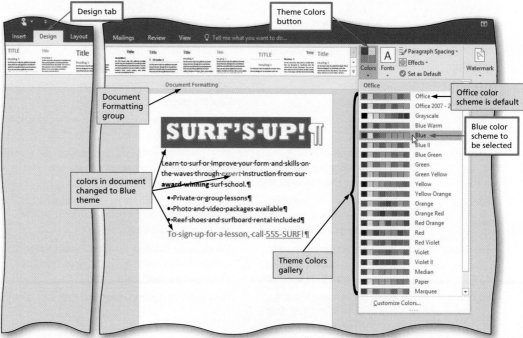

Figure 1–45

2

• Click Blue in the Theme Colors gallery to change the document theme colors.

◁ | What if I want to return to the original color scheme?
Q&A | You would click the Theme Colors button again and then click Office in the Theme Colors gallery.

To Zoom Page Width

Because the document contents are small when displayed on one page, the next steps zoom page width again.

BTW
**Selecting
Nonadjacent Items**
In Word, you can use keyboard keys to select nonadjacent items, that is, items not next to each other. This is helpful when you are applying the same formatting to multiple items. To select nonadjacent items (text or graphics), select the first item, such as a word or paragraph, as usual; then, press and hold down the CTRL key. While holding down the CTRL key, select additional items.

1 Click View on the ribbon to display the View tab.

2 Click the Page Width button (View tab | Zoom group) to display the page the same width as the document window (shown earlier in the module in Figure 1–7).

3 Save the flyer again on the same storage location with the same file name.

Q&A | Why should I save the flyer again?
You have made several modifications to the flyer since you last saved it; thus, you should save it again.

Selecting Text

In many of the previous steps, you have selected text. Table 1–3 summarizes the techniques used to select various items.

Table 1–3 Techniques for Selecting Text

Item to Select	Touch	Mouse	Keyboard (where applicable)
Block of text	Tap to position insertion point in text to select and then drag selection handle(s) to select text.	Click at beginning of selection, scroll to end of selection, position pointer at end of selection, hold down SHIFT key, and then click; or drag through the text.	
Character(s)	Tap to position insertion point in text to select and then drag selection handle(s) to select text.	Drag through character(s).	SHIFT+RIGHT ARROW or SHIFT+LEFT ARROW
Document		Move pointer to left of text until pointer changes to right-pointing block arrow and then triple-click.	CTRL+A
Graphic	Tap the graphic.	Click the graphic.	
Line	Double-tap to left of line to be selected.	Move pointer to left of line until pointer changes to right-pointing block arrow and then click.	HOME, then SHIFT+END or END, then SHIFT+HOME
Lines	Tap to position insertion point in text to select and then drag selection handle(s) to select text.	Move pointer to left of first line until pointer changes to right-pointing block arrow and then drag up or down.	HOME, then SHIFT+DOWN ARROW or END, then SHIFT+UP ARROW
Paragraph	Tap to position insertion point in text to select and then drag selection handle(s) to select text.	Triple-click paragraph; or move pointer to left of paragraph until pointer changes to right-pointing block arrow and then double-click.	CTRL+SHIFT+DOWN ARROW or CTRL+SHIFT+UP ARROW
Paragraphs	Tap to position insertion point in text to select and then drag selection handle(s) to select text.	Move pointer to left of paragraph until pointer changes to right-pointing block arrow, double-click, and then drag up or down.	CTRL+SHIFT+DOWN ARROW or CTRL+SHIFT+UP ARROW repeatedly
Sentence	Tap to position insertion point in text to select and then drag selection handle(s) to select text.	Press and hold down CTRL key and then click sentence.	
Word	Double-tap word.	Double-click word.	CTRL+SHIFT+RIGHT ARROW or CTRL+SHIFT+LEFT ARROW
Words	Tap to position insertion point in text to select and then drag selection handle(s) to select text.	Drag through words.	CTRL+SHIFT+RIGHT ARROW or CTRL+SHIFT+LEFT ARROW repeatedly

Inserting and Formatting a Picture in a Word Document

With the text formatted in the flyer, the next step is to insert a digital picture in the flyer and format the picture. Flyers usually contain a graphical image(s), such as a picture, to attract the attention of passersby. In the following sections, you will perform these tasks:

1. Insert a digital picture into the flyer.
2. Reduce the size of the picture.
3. Change the look of the picture.

CONSIDER THIS

How do I locate a graphic file to use in a document?

To use a graphic in a Word document, the image must be stored digitally in a file. Files containing graphics are available from a variety of sources:

• The web has images available, some of which are free, while others require a fee.

• You can take a picture with a digital camera or smartphone and **download** it, which is the process of copying the digital picture from the camera or phone to your computer.

• With a scanner, you can convert a printed picture, drawing, or diagram to a digital file.

If you receive a picture from a source other than yourself, do not use the file until you are certain it does not contain a virus. A **virus** is a computer program that can damage files and programs on your computer. Use an antivirus program to verify that any files you use are virus free.

To Center Another Paragraph

In the flyer, the digital picture of a surfer should be centered on the blank line below the headline. The blank paragraph below the headline currently is left-aligned. The following steps center this paragraph.

1 Click Home on the ribbon to display the Home tab.

2 Click somewhere in the paragraph to be centered (in this case, the blank line below the headline) to position the insertion point in the paragraph to be formatted.

3 Click the Center button (Home tab | Paragraph group) to center the paragraph containing the insertion point (shown in Figure 1–46).

To Insert a Picture

1 ENTER TEXT | 2 FORMAT TEXT | **3 INSERT PICTURE**
4 FORMAT PICTURE | 5 ENHANCE PAGE | 6 CORRECT & REVISE

The next step in creating the flyer is to insert a digital picture of a surfer in the flyer on the blank line below the headline. The picture, which was taken with a digital camera, is available on the Data Files. Please contact your instructor for information about accessing Data Files.

The following steps insert a picture, which, in this example, is located in the Module 01 folder in the Data Files folder. *Why? It is good practice to organize and store files in folders so that you easily can find the files at a later date.*

1

- If necessary, position the insertion point at the location where you want to insert the picture (in this case, on the centered blank paragraph below the headline).

- Click Insert on the ribbon to display the Insert tab (Figure 1–46).

Figure 1–46

2

- Click the From File button (Insert tab | Illustrations group) (shown in Figure 1–46) to display the Insert Picture dialog box (shown in Figure 1–47).

3

- Navigate to the desired picture location (in this case, the Module 01 folder in the Data Files folder). For a detailed example of this procedure, refer to Steps 4a and 4b in the To Save a File in a Folder section in the Office and Windows module at the beginning of this book.

Figure 1–47

- Click Surfing to select the file (Figure 1–47).

4

- Click the Insert button (Insert Picture dialog box) to insert the picture at the location of the insertion point in the document (Figure 1–48).

Q&A

What are the symbols around the picture?

A selected graphic appears surrounded by a **selection rectangle**, which has small squares and circles, called **sizing handles**, at each corner and middle location.

What is the purpose of the Layout Options button?

When you click the Layout Options button, Word provides options for changing how the graphic is positioned with text in the document.

Figure 1–48

How do you know where to position a graphic on a flyer?

The content, size, shape, position, and format of a graphic should capture the interest of passersby, enticing them to stop and read the flyer. Often, the graphic is the center of attention and visually the largest element on a flyer. If you use colors in the graphical image, be sure they are part of the document's color scheme.

---

1 ENTER TEXT | 2 FORMAT TEXT | 3 INSERT PICTURE
4 FORMAT PICTURE | 5 ENHANCE PAGE | 6 CORRECT & REVISE

To Zoom the Document

In the steps in the following sections, you will work with the picture just inserted. The next task is to adjust the zoom percentage. *Why? Currently, you can see only a small amount of text with the picture. Seeing more of the document at once helps you determine the appropriate size for the picture.* The following step zooms the document.

1

 Experiment

- Repeatedly click the Zoom Out and Zoom In buttons on the status bar and watch the size of the document change in the document window.

Q&A | What if I am using a touch screen?
Repeatedly pinch (move two fingers together on the screen) and stretch (move two fingers apart on the screen) and watch the size of the document change in the document window.

- Click the Zoom Out or Zoom In button as many times as necessary until the Zoom button on the status bar displays 40% on its face (Figure 1–49).

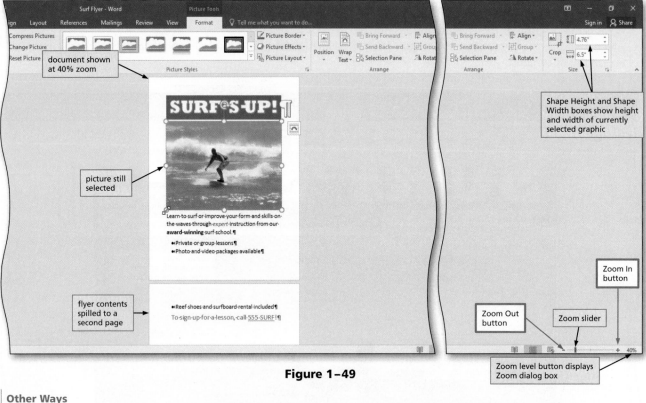

Figure 1–49

Other Ways

1. Drag Zoom slider on status bar
2. Click Zoom level button on status bar, select desired zoom percent or type (Zoom dialog box), click OK button
3. Click Zoom button (View tab | Zoom group), select desired zoom percent or type (Zoom dialog box), click OK button

To Resize a Graphic

1 ENTER TEXT | 2 FORMAT TEXT | 3 INSERT PICTURE
4 FORMAT PICTURE | 5 ENHANCE PAGE | 6 CORRECT & REVISE

Resizing includes both increasing and reducing the size of a graphic. The next step is to resize the picture so that it is smaller in the flyer. **Why?** *You want the graphic and all the text on the flyer to fit on a single sheet of paper.* The following steps resize a selected graphic.

1

- Be sure the graphic still is selected.

Q&A | What if my graphic (picture) is not selected?
To select a graphic, click it.

- Point to the lower-left corner sizing handle on the picture so that the pointer shape changes to a two-headed arrow (Figure 1–50).

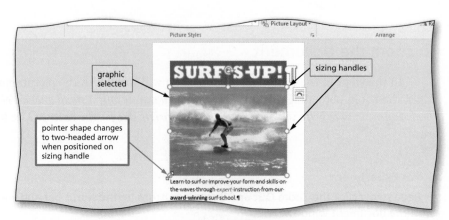

Figure 1–50

2

- Drag the sizing handle diagonally inward until the lower-left corner of the picture is positioned approximately as shown in Figure 1–51. Do not release the mouse button at this point.

Q&A What if I am using a touch screen?
Drag a corner of the graphic, without lifting your finger, until the graphic is the desired size.

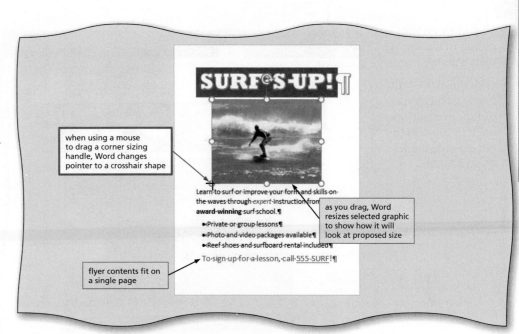

Figure 1–51

3

- Release the mouse button to resize the graphic, which, in this case, should have a height of about 3.7" and a width of about 5.06".

Q&A How can I see the height and width measurements?
Look in the Size group on the Picture Tools Format tab to see the height and width measurements of the currently selected graphic (shown in Figure 1–49).

What if the graphic is the wrong size?
Repeat Steps 1, 2, and 3, or enter the desired height and width values in the Shape Height and Shape Width boxes (Picture Tools Format tab | Size group).

What if I want to return a graphic to its original size and start again?
With the graphic selected, click the Size Dialog Box Launcher (Picture Tools Format tab | Size group), click the Size tab (Layout dialog box), click the Reset button, and then click the OK button.

Other Ways

1. Enter height and width of graphic in Shape Height and Shape Width boxes (Picture Tools Format tab | Size group)
2. Click Advanced Layout: Size Dialog Box Launcher (Picture Tools Format tab | Size group), click Size tab (Layout dialog box), enter desired height and width values in boxes, click OK button

1 ENTER TEXT | 2 FORMAT TEXT | 3 INSERT PICTURE
4 FORMAT PICTURE | **5 ENHANCE PAGE** | 6 CORRECT & REVISE

To Zoom 100%

In the next series of steps, you will format the picture. Earlier in this module, you changed the zoom to 40% so that you could see more of the page while resizing the graphic. The following step zooms the screen to 100%. **Why?** *You want the contents of the image to be enlarged a bit, while still seeing some of the text in the document.*

1

- Click View on the ribbon to display the View tab.

- Click the 100% button (View tab | Zoom group) to display the page at 100% in the document window (Figure 1–52).

Figure 1–52

Other Ways

1. Click Zoom button (View tab | Zoom group), click 100% (Zoom dialog box), click OK button

To Apply a Picture Style

A **style** is a named group of formatting characteristics. Word provides more than 25 picture styles. *Why? Picture styles enable you easily to change a picture's look to a more visually appealing style, including a variety of shapes, angles, borders, and reflections.* The flyer in this module uses a style that applies an oval shape to the picture. The following steps apply a picture style to a picture.

1

- Ensure the graphic still is selected and then click Picture Tools Format on the ribbon to display the Picture Tools Format tab (Figure 1–53).

Q&A
What if my graphic (picture) is not selected?
To select a graphic, click it.

What is the white circle attached to top of the selected graphic?
It is called a rotate handle. When you drag a graphic's **rotate handle,** the graphic moves in either a clockwise or counterclockwise direction.

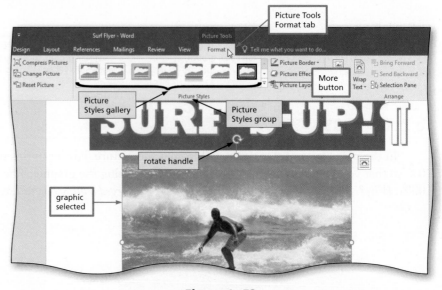

Figure 1–53

2

- Click the More button in the Picture Styles gallery (Picture Tools Format tab | Picture Styles group) (shown in Figure 1–53) to expand the gallery.

- Point to 'Soft Edge Oval' in the Picture Styles gallery to display a live preview of that style applied to the picture in the document (Figure 1–54).

Experiment

- Point to various picture styles in the Picture Styles gallery and watch the style of the picture change in the document window.

3

- Click 'Soft Edge Oval' in the Picture Styles gallery (sixth style in third row) to apply the style to the selected picture.

expanded gallery shows more options — your list may be arranged differently

pointer on 'Soft Edge Oval' picture style

picture format changes to Soft Edge Oval, showing live preview of style to which you are pointing in expanded gallery

Learn·to·surf·or·improve·your·form·and·skills·on·

Figure 1–54

Other Ways

1. Right-click picture, click 'Picture Styles' on mini toolbar, select desired style

To Apply Picture Effects

1 ENTER TEXT | 2 FORMAT TEXT | 3 INSERT PICTURE
4 FORMAT PICTURE | 5 ENHANCE PAGE | 6 CORRECT & REVISE

Word provides a variety of picture effects, such as shadows, reflections, glow, soft edges, bevel, and 3-D rotation. The difference between the effects and the styles is that each effect has several options, providing you with more control over the exact look of the image.

In this flyer, the picture has a slight lime green glow effect and beveled edges. The following steps apply picture effects to the selected picture. **Why?** *Picture effects enable you to further customize a picture.*

1

- With the picture still selected, click the Picture Effects button (Picture Tools Format tab | Picture Styles group) to display the Picture Effects menu.

- Point to Glow on the Picture Effects menu to display the Glow gallery.

- Point to 'Lime, 5 pt glow, Accent color 6' in the Glow Variations area (rightmost glow in first row) to display a live preview of the selected glow effect applied to the picture in the document window (Figure 1–55).

Experiment

- If you are using a mouse, point to various glow effects in the Glow gallery and watch the picture change in the document window.

Picture Tools Format tab

Picture Effects button

Picture Styles group

Picture Styles

selected picture shows live preview of glow effect to which you are pointing in gallery

Glow command

Picture Effects menu

Glow gallery

No Glow

Glow Variations area

Glow Variations

More Glow Colors

Glow Options...

pointer on 'Lime, 5 pt glow, Accent color 6'

Figure 1–55

②

• Click 'Lime, 5 pt glow, Accent color 6' in the Glow gallery to apply the selected picture effect.

Q&A
What if I wanted to discard formatting applied to a picture?

You would click the Reset Picture button (Picture Tools Format tab | Adjust group). To reset formatting and size, you would click the Reset Picture arrow (Picture Tools Format tab | Adjust group) and then click 'Reset Picture & Size' on the Reset Picture menu.

③

• Click the Picture Effects button (Picture Tools Format tab | Picture Styles group) to display the Picture Effects menu again.

• Point to Bevel on the Picture Effects menu to display the Bevel gallery.

• Point to Angle in the Bevel area (first effect in second row) to display a live preview of the selected bevel effect applied to the picture in the document window (Figure 1–56).

🔍 Experiment

• If you are using a mouse, point to various bevel effects in the Bevel gallery and watch the picture change in the document window.

Figure 1–56

④

• Click Angle in the Bevel gallery to apply the selected picture effect.

Other Ways

1. Right-click picture (or, if using touch, tap 'Show Context Menu' button on mini toolbar), click Format Object or Format Picture on shortcut menu, click Effects button (Format Picture task pane), select desired options, click Close button

2. Click Format Shape Dialog Box Launcher (Picture Tools Format tab | Picture Styles group), click Effects button (Format Picture task pane), select desired options, click Close button

---

BTW
Touch Screen Differences
The Office and Windows interfaces may vary if you are using a touch screen. For this reason, you might notice that the function or appearance of your touch screen differs slightly from this module's presentation.

Enhancing the Page

With the text and graphics entered and formatted, the next step is to look at the page as a whole and determine if it looks finished in its current state. As you review the page, answer these questions:

• Does it need a page border to frame its contents, or would a page border make it look too busy?

• Is the spacing between paragraphs and graphics on the page adequate? Do any sections of text or graphics look as if they are positioned too closely to the items above or below them?

• Does the flyer have too much space at the top or bottom? Should the contents be centered vertically?

You determine that a graphical, color-coordinated border would enhance the flyer. You also notice that the flyer would look better proportioned if it had a little more space above and below the picture. You also want to ensure that the contents are centered vertically. The following sections make these enhancements to the flyer.

To Add a Page Border

In Word, you can add a border around the perimeter of an entire page. The flyer in this module has a lime border. *Why? This border color complements the color of the flyer contents.* The following steps add a page border.

1
- Click Design on the ribbon to display the Design tab.
- Click the 'Borders and Shading' button (Design tab | Page Background group) to display the Borders and Shading dialog box (Figure 1–57).

Figure 1–57

2
- Scroll to, if necessary, and then click the sixth border style in the Style list (Borders and Shading dialog box) to select the style.
- Click the Color arrow to display a Color palette (Figure 1–58).

Figure 1–58

- Click 'Lime, Accent 6, Lighter 40%' (rightmost color in fourth row) in the Color palette to select the color for the page border.
- Click the Width arrow to display the Width list and then click 4 ½ pt to select the thickness of the page border (Figure 1–59).

4

- Click the OK button to add the border to the page (shown in Figure 1–60).

Q&A What if I wanted to remove the border?
You would click None in the Setting list in the Borders and Shading dialog box.

Figure 1–59

To Zoom One Page

The next steps zoom one page so that you can see the entire page on the screen at once.

1 Click View on the ribbon to display the View tab.

2 Click the One Page button (View tab | Zoom group) to display the entire page in the document window as large as possible.

To Change Spacing before and after Paragraphs

1 ENTER TEXT | 2 FORMAT TEXT | 3 INSERT PICTURE
4 FORMAT PICTURE | 5 ENHANCE PAGE | **6 CORRECT & REVISE**

The default spacing above (before) a paragraph in Word is 0 points and below (after) is 8 points. In the flyer, you want to increase the spacing below the paragraph containing the headline and above the signature line. **Why?** *The flyer spacing will look more balanced with spacing increased above and below these paragraphs.* The following steps change the spacing above and below a paragraph.

1

- Position the insertion point in the paragraph to be adjusted, in this case, the paragraph containing the headline.

Q&A What happened to the Picture Tools Format tab?
When you click outside of a graphic or press a key to scroll through a document, Word deselects the graphic and removes the Picture Tools Format tab from the screen. That is, this tab appears only when a graphic is selected.

- Click Layout on the ribbon to display the Layout tab.
- Click the Spacing After up arrow (Layout tab | Paragraph group) so that 12 pt is displayed in the Spacing After box to increase the space below the current paragraph (Figure 1–60).

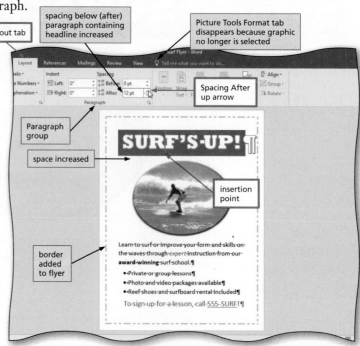

Figure 1–60

2

- Position the insertion point in the paragraph to be adjusted, in this case, the paragraph containing the signature line.

- Click the Spacing Before up arrow (Layout tab | Paragraph group) as many times as necessary so that 12 pt is displayed in the Spacing Before box to increase the space above the current paragraph (Figure 1–61).

- If the text flows to two pages, reduce the spacing above and below paragraphs as necessary.

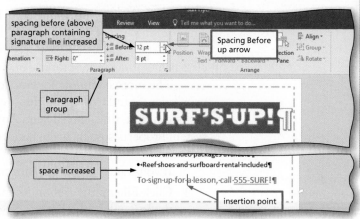

Figure 1–61

Other Ways

1. Right-click paragraph (or, if using touch, tap 'Show Context Menu' button on mini toolbar), click Paragraph on shortcut menu, click Indents and Spacing tab (Paragraph dialog box), enter spacing before and after values, click OK button

2. Click Paragraph Settings Dialog Box Launcher (Home tab or Layout tab | Paragraph group), click Indents and Spacing tab (Paragraph dialog box), enter spacing before and after values, click OK button

To Center Page Contents Vertically

1 ENTER TEXT | 2 FORMAT TEXT | 3 INSERT PICTURE
4 FORMAT PICTURE | 5 ENHANCE PAGE | **6 CORRECT & REVISE**

In Word, you can center the page contents vertically. *Why? This places the same amount of space at the top and bottom of the page.* The following steps center page contents vertically.

1

- If necessary, click Layout on the ribbon to display the Layout tab.

- Click the Page Setup Dialog Box Launcher (Layout tab | Page Setup group) to display the Page Setup dialog box.

- Click the Layout tab (Page Setup dialog box) to display the Layout sheet (Figure 1–62).

Figure 1–62

2

- Click the Vertical alignment arrow (Page Setup dialog box) to display the list of alignment options and then click Center in the list (Figure 1–63).

3

- Click the OK button to center the page contents vertically on the screen (shown in Figure 1–1 at the beginning of this module).

Q&A What if I wanted to change the alignment back?
You would select the Top vertical alignment from the Vertical alignment list in the Layout sheet (Page Setup dialog box).

Figure 1–63

TO CHANGE DOCUMENT PROPERTIES

Word helps you organize and identify your files by using **document properties**, which, as discussed in the Office and Windows module at the beginning of this book, are the details about a file, such as the project author, title, and subject. For example, a class name or document topic can describe the file's purpose or content.

The more common document properties are standard and automatically updated properties. **Standard properties** are associated with all Microsoft Office files and include author, title, and subject. **Automatically updated properties** include file system properties, such as the date you create or change a file, and statistics, such as the file size.

If you wanted to change document properties, you would follow these steps.

1. Click File on the ribbon to open the Backstage view and then, if necessary, click the Info tab in the Backstage view to display the Info gallery.

2. If the property you wish to change is displayed in the Properties list in the right pane of the Info gallery, try to click to the right of the property. If a text box appears to the right of the property, type the text for the property in the text box and then click the Back button in the upper-left corner of the Backstage view to return to the Word window. Skip the remaining steps.

3. If the property you wish to change is not displayed in the Properties list in the right pane of the Info gallery or you cannot change it in the Info gallery, click the Properties button in the right pane to display the Properties menu and then click Advanced Properties on the Properties menu to display the Properties dialog box. If necessary, click the Summary tab (Properties dialog box) to display the Summary sheet, fill in the appropriate text boxes, and then click the OK button.

Q&A Why are some of the document properties in the dialog box already filled in?
The person who installed Office 2016 on your computer or network may have set or customized the properties.

BTW
Printing Document Properties
To print document properties, click File on the ribbon to open the Backstage view, click the Print tab in the Backstage view to display the Print gallery, click the first button in the Settings area to display a list of options specifying what you can print, click Document Info in the list to specify you want to print the document properties instead of the actual document, and then click the Print button in the Print gallery to print the document properties on the currently selected printer.

To Save the Document and Exit Word

Although you still need to make some edits to this document, you want to exit Word and resume working on the project at a later time. Thus, the following steps save the document and exit Word. For a detailed example of the procedure summarized below, refer to the Office and Windows module at the beginning of this book.

1 Save the flyer again on the same storage location with the same file name.

2 Close the open document and exit Word.

Break Point: If you wish to take a break, this is a good place to do so. To resume at a later time, continue following the steps from this location forward.

Correcting Errors and Revising a Document

After creating a document, you may need to change it. For example, the document may contain an error, or new circumstances may require you to add text to the document.

Types of Changes Made to Documents

The types of changes made to documents normally fall into one of the three following categories: additions, deletions, or modifications.

Additions Additional words, sentences, or paragraphs may be required in a document. Additions occur when you omit text from a document and want to insert it later. For example, you may want to add your email address to the flyer.

Deletions Sometimes, text in a document is incorrect or no longer is needed. For example, you may discover that the lessons no longer include reef shoes. In this case, you would delete the words, reef shoes, from the flyer.

Modifications If an error is made in a document or changes take place that affect the document, you might have to revise a word(s) in the text. For example, the phone number may change.

To Run Word, Open a Document, and Specify Settings

Once you have created and saved a document, you may need to retrieve it from storage. For example, you might want to revise the document or distribute it. Earlier in this module you saved the flyer using the file name, Surf Flyer. The following steps run Word, open this document, and specify settings. For a detailed example of the procedures summarized below for running Word or opening a document, refer to the Office and Windows module.

1 Run Word.

2 Open the document named Surf Flyer from the Recent list or use the Open dialog box to navigate to the location of the file and then open it in the Word window.

3 If the Word window is not maximized, click the Maximize button on its title bar to maximize the window.

4 Click View on the ribbon to display the View tab and then click the 100% button (View tab | Zoom group) to display the page at 100% in the document window.

> **BTW**
> **Word Help**
> At any time while using Word, you can find answers to questions and display information about various topics through Word Help. Used properly, this form of assistance can increase your productivity and reduce your frustrations by minimizing the time you spend learning how to use Word. For instructions about Word Help and exercises that will help you gain confidence in using it, read the Office and Windows module at the beginning of this book.

To Insert Text in an Existing Document

1 ENTER TEXT | 2 FORMAT TEXT | 3 INSERT PICTURE
4 FORMAT PICTURE | 5 ENHANCE PAGE | **6 CORRECT & REVISE**

Word inserts text to the left of the insertion point. The text to the right of the insertion point moves to the right and downward to fit the new text. The following steps insert the word, today, to the left of the word, or, in the flyer. **Why?** *These steps illustrate the process of inserting text.*

1

- Scroll through the document and then click to the left of the location of text to be inserted (in this case, the o in or) to position the insertion point where text should be inserted (Figure 1–64).

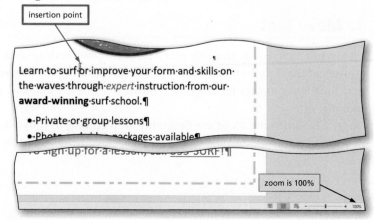

Figure 1–64

2

- Type **today** and then press the SPACEBAR to insert the word to the left of the insertion point (Figure 1–65).

Q&A | Why did the text move to the right as I typed?
In Word, the default typing mode is **insert mode**, which means as you type a character, Word moves all the characters to the right of the typed character one position to the right.

Learn·to·surf·today·or·improve·your·form·and· skills·on·the·waves·through·*expert*·instruction· from·our·**award-winning**·surf·school.¶

Figure 1–65

To Delete Text

1 ENTER TEXT | 2 FORMAT TEXT | 3 INSERT PICTURE
4 FORMAT PICTURE | 5 ENHANCE PAGE | **6 CORRECT & REVISE**

It is not unusual to type incorrect characters or words in a document. As discussed earlier in this module, you can click the Undo button on the Quick Access Toolbar to undo a command or action immediately — this includes typing. Word also provides other methods of correcting typing errors.

To delete an incorrect character in a document, simply click next to the incorrect character and then press the BACKSPACE key to erase to the left of the insertion point, or press the DELETE key to erase to the right of the insertion point.

To delete a word or phrase, you first must select the word or phrase. The following steps select the word, today, which was just added in the previous steps, and then delete the selection. **Why?** *These steps illustrate the process of selecting a word and then deleting selected text.*

1

- Double-click the word to be selected (in this case, today) to select the word (Figure 1–66).

2

- Press the DELETE key to delete the selected text.

Q&A | What if I am using a touch screen?
Tap the selected text to display the mini toolbar and then tap the Cut button on the mini toolbar to delete the selected text.

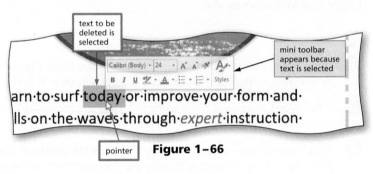

Figure 1–66

Other Ways

1. Right-click selected item, click Cut on shortcut menu
2. Select item, press BACKSPACE to delete to left of insertion point or press DELETE to delete to right of insertion point
3. Select item, press CTRL+X

To Move Text

1 ENTER TEXT | 2 FORMAT TEXT | 3 INSERT PICTURE
4 FORMAT PICTURE | 5 ENHANCE PAGE | **6 CORRECT & REVISE**

An efficient way to move text a short distance is drag-and-drop editing. With **drag-and-drop editing**, you select the item to be moved, drag the selected item to the new location, and then drop, or insert, it in the new location. Another technique for moving text is the cut-and-paste technique, which is discussed in the next module.

The following steps use drag-and-drop editing to move text. **Why?** *While proofreading the flyer, you realize that the body copy would read better if the last two bulleted paragraphs were reversed.*

1

- Position the pointer in the paragraph to be moved (in this case, the last bulleted item) and then triple-click to select the paragraph.

- With the pointer in the selected text, press and hold down the mouse button, which displays a small dotted box with the pointer (Figure 1–67).

Figure 1–67

2

- Drag the insertion point to the location where the selected text is to be moved, as shown in Figure 1–68.

Figure 1–68

3

- Release the mouse button to move the selected text to the location of the dotted insertion point (Figure 1–69).

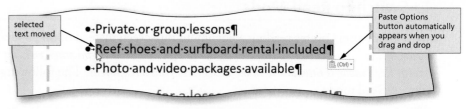

Figure 1–69

Q&A What if I accidentally drag text to the wrong location?

Click the Undo button on the Quick Access Toolbar and try again.

Can I use drag-and-drop editing to move any selected item?

Yes, you can select words, sentences, phrases, and graphics and then use drag-and-drop editing to move them.

What is the purpose of the Paste Options button?

If you click the Paste Options button, a menu appears that allows you to change the format of the item that was moved. The next module discusses the Paste Options menu.

- Click anywhere in the document window to remove the selection from the bulleted item.

Q&A What if I am using a touch screen?

If you have a stylus, you can follow Steps 1 through 3 using the stylus. If you are using your finger, you will need to use the cut-and-paste technique: tap to position the insertion point in the text to be moved and then drag the selection handles as necessary to select the text that you want to move; tap the selection to display the mini toolbar and then tap the Cut button on the mini toolbar to remove the text; tap to position the insertion point at the location where you want to move the text; display the Home tab and then tap the Paste button on the Home tab to place the text at the location of the insertion point. The next module discusses this procedure in more depth.

Other Ways

1. Click Cut button (Home tab | Clipboard group), click where text or object is to be pasted, click Paste button (Home tab | Clipboard group)

2. Right-click selected text, click Cut on mini toolbar or shortcut menu, right-click where text or object is to be pasted, click Paste on mini toolbar or 'Keep Source Formatting' on shortcut menu

3. Press CTRL+X, position insertion point where text or object is to be pasted, press CTRL+V

To Save and Print the Document

It is a good practice to save a document before printing it, in the event you experience difficulties printing. The following steps save and print the document. For a detailed example of the procedure summarized next for saving and printing a document, refer to the Office and Windows module at the beginning of this book.

BTW
Conserving Ink and Toner
If you want to conserve ink or toner, you can instruct Word to print draft quality documents by clicking File on the ribbon to open the Backstage view, clicking the Options tab in the Backstage view to display the Word Options dialog box, clicking Advanced in the left pane (Word Options dialog box), scrolling to the Print area in the right pane, placing a check mark in the 'Use draft quality' check box, and then clicking the OK button. Then, use the Backstage view to print the document as usual.

1 Save the flyer again on the same storage location with the same file name.

2 If requested by your instructor, print the flyer.

Q&A What if one or more of my borders do not print?

Click the Page Borders button (Design tab | Page Background group), click the Options button (Borders and Shading dialog box), click the Measure from arrow and click Text, change the four text boxes to 15 pt, and then click the OK button in each dialog box. Try printing the document again. If the borders still do not print, adjust the boxes in the dialog box to a number smaller than 15 point.

1 ENTER TEXT | 2 FORMAT TEXT | 3 INSERT PICTURE
4 FORMAT PICTURE | 5 ENHANCE PAGE | **6 CORRECT & REVISE**

To Switch to Read Mode

Some users prefer reading a document on-screen instead of on paper. *Why? If you are not composing a document, you can switch to* **Read mode**, *which hides the ribbon and other writing tools so that more content fits on the screen. Read mode is intended to make it easier to read a document.* The following step switches from Print Layout view to Read mode.

- Click the Read Mode button on the status bar to switch to Read mode (Figure 1–70).

Experiment

- Click the arrows to advance forward and then move backward through the document.

Q&A Besides reading, what can I do in Read mode?

You can zoom, copy text, highlight text, search, add comments, and more.

Figure 1–70

BTW
Distributing a Document
Instead of printing and distributing a hard copy of a document, you can distribute the document electronically. Options include sending the document via email; posting it on cloud storage (such as OneDrive) and sharing the file with others; posting it on social media, a blog, or other website; and sharing a link associated with an online location of the document. You also can create and share a PDF or XPS image of the document, so that users can view the file in Acrobat Reader or XPS Viewer instead of in Word.

1 ENTER TEXT | 2 FORMAT TEXT | 3 INSERT PICTURE
4 FORMAT PICTURE | 5 ENHANCE PAGE | **6 CORRECT & REVISE**

To Switch to Print Layout View

The next steps switch back to Print Layout view. *Why? If you want to show the document on a mock sheet of paper in the document window, along with the ribbon and other writing tools, you should switch to Print Layout view.* The following step switches to Print Layout view.

1

- Click the Print Layout button on the status bar to switch to Print Layout view (Figure 1–71).

- Because the project now is complete, you can exit Word.

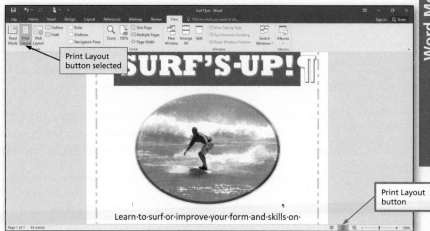

Figure 1–71

Other Ways

1. Click Print Layout button (View tab | Views group)   2. Click View on the ribbon, click Edit Document

Summary

In this module, you have learned how to enter text in a document, correct spelling errors as you type, format paragraphs and characters, insert and format a picture, add a page border, adjust paragraph and page spacing, and correct errors and revise a document.

What decisions will you need to make when creating your next flyer?

Use these guidelines as you complete the assignments in this module and create your own flyers outside of this class.

1. Choose the text for the headline, body copy, and signature line — using as few words as possible to make a point.

2. Format various elements of the text.

    a) Select appropriate font sizes for text in the headline, body copy, and signature line.

    b) Select appropriate fonts for text in the headline, body copy, and signature line.

    c) Adjust paragraph alignment, as appropriate.

    d) Highlight key paragraphs with bullets.

    e) Emphasize important words.

    f) Use color to convey meaning and add appeal.

3. Find an eye-catching graphic(s) that conveys the overall message and meaning of the flyer.

4. Establish where to position and how to format the graphical image(s) so that the image grabs the attention of passersby and draws them into reading the flyer.

5. Determine whether the flyer needs enhancements, such as a graphical, color-coordinated border, or spacing adjustments to improve readability or overall appearance.

6. Correct errors and revise the document as necessary.

    a) Post the flyer on a wall and make sure all text and images are legible from a distance.

    b) Ask someone else to read the flyer and give you suggestions for improvements.

7. Determine the best method for distributing the document, such as printing, sending via email, or posting on the web or social media.

CONSIDER THIS: PLAN AHEAD

STUDENT ASSIGNMENTS

Apply Your Knowledge

Reinforce the skills and apply the concepts you learned in this module.

Modifying Text and Formatting a Document

Note: To complete this assignment, you will be required to use the Data Files. Please contact your instructor for information about accessing the Data Files.

Instructions: Run Word. Open the document, Apply 1–1 Graduation Flyer Unformatted, which is located in the Data Files. The flyer you open contains an unformatted flyer. You are to modify text, format paragraphs and characters, and insert a picture in the flyer to create the flyer shown in Figure 1–72.

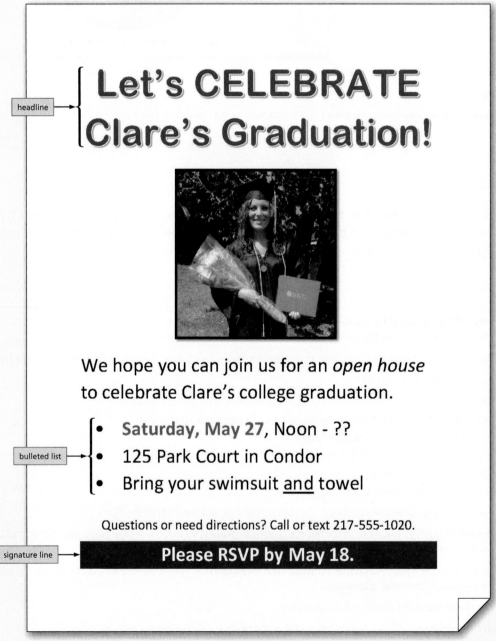

Figure 1–72

Perform the following tasks:

1. Correct each spelling (red wavy underline) and grammar (green and blue wavy underlines) error by right-clicking the flagged text and then clicking the appropriate correction on the shortcut menu.

2. Delete the word, degree, in the sentence below the headline.

3. Insert the word, need, between the words, or directions (so that it reads: Questions or need directions?), in the second to last line of the flyer.

4. Change the word, on, to the word, by, in the last line so that the text reads: Please RSVP by May 18.

5. If requested by your instructor, change the phone number in the flyer to your phone number.

6. Center the headline and the last two paragraphs of the flyer.

7. Select the third, fourth, and fifth paragraphs of text in the flyer and add bullets to the selected paragraphs.

8. Change the theme colors to the Blue II color scheme.

9. Change the font and font size of the headline to 48-point Arial Rounded MT Bold, or a similar font. Change the case of the word, Celebrate, in the headline to uppercase letters. Apply the text effect called Fill - Dark Green, Accent 1, Outline - Background 1, Hard Shadow - Accent 1 to the entire headline. Change the font color of the headline text to Dark Green, Accent 5, Darker 25%.

10. Change the font size of the sentence below the headline, the bulleted list, and the last line of flyer to 26 point.

11. Use the mini toolbar to change the font size of the sentence below the bulleted list to 18 point.

12. Switch the last two bulleted paragraphs. That is, select the '125 Park Court in Condor' bullet and move it so that it is the second bulleted paragraph.

13. Select the words, open house, in the paragraph below the headline and italicize these words. Undo this change and then redo the change.

14. Select the text, Saturday, May 27, in the first bulleted paragraph and bold this text. Change the font color of this same text to Dark Red.

15. Underline the word, and, in the third bulleted paragraph.

16. Bold the text, Please RSVP by May 18., in the last line of the flyer. Shade this same text Dark Green, Accent 5, Darker 50%. If the font color does not automatically change to a lighter color, change its color to White, Background 1.

17. Change the zoom so that the entire page is visible in the document window.

18. Insert the picture of the graduate centered on the blank line below the headline. The picture is called Graduation and is available on the Data Files. Resize the picture so that it is approximately 2.9" × 2.89". Apply the Simple Frame, Black picture style to the inserted picture.

19. Change the spacing before the first bulleted paragraph to 12 points and the spacing after the last bulleted paragraph to 24 points.

20. The entire flyer should fit on a single page. If it flows to two pages, resize the picture or decrease spacing before and after paragraphs until the entire flyer text fits on a single page.

21. Change the zoom to text width, then page width, then 100% and notice the differences.

22. If requested by your instructor, enter the text, Graduation Open House, as the keywords in the document properties. Change the other document properties, as specified by your instructor.

23. Click File on the ribbon and then click Save As. Save the document using the file name, Apply 1–1 Graduation Flyer Formatted.

24. Print the document. Switch to Read Mode and browse pages through the document. Switch to Print Layout view.

25. Submit the revised document, shown in Figure 1–72, in the format specified by your instructor.

26. Exit Word.

27. ✹ If this flyer were announcing a victory parade instead of a graduation, which color scheme would you apply and why?

STUDENT ASSIGNMENTS

Extend Your Knowledge

Extend the skills you learned in this module and experiment with new skills. You may need to use Help to complete the assignment.

Modifying Text and Picture Formats and Adding Page Borders

Note: To complete this assignment, you will be required to use the Data Files. Please contact your instructor for information about accessing the Data Files.

add art page border

change border color and add shadow effect; change color saturation and color tone

use 'Increase Font Size' button to increase font size

change to picture bullets

change underline style and color

remove bullet

Figure 1–73

Instructions: Run Word. Open the document, Extend 1–1 Painting Lessons Flyer Draft, from the Data Files. You will enhance the look of the flyer shown in Figure 1–73. *Hint:* Remember, if you make a mistake while formatting the picture, you can reset it by using the Reset Picture button or Reset Picture arrow (Picture Tools Format tab | Adjust group).

Perform the following tasks:

1. Use Help to learn about the following: remove bullets, grow font, shrink font, art page borders, decorative underline(s), picture bullets, picture border shading, picture border color, shadow picture effects, and color saturation and tone.

2. Remove the bullet from the last paragraph of the flyer.

3. Select the text, Painting Lessons, and use the 'Increase Font Size' button (Home tab | Font group) to increase its font size.

4. Add an art page border to the flyer. If the border is not in color, add color to it if the border supports color.

5. Change the solid underline below the word, all, to a decorative underline. Change the color of the underline.

6. Change the style of the bullets to picture bullet(s). Adjust the hanging indent, if necessary, to align the text in the bulleted list.

7. Change the color of the picture border. Add a shadow picture effect to the picture.

8. Change the color saturation and color tone of the picture.

9. If requested by your instructor, change the name of the art studio (Bakersfield) to your last name.

10. Save the revised document with the file name, Extend 1–1 Painting Lessons Flyer Final, and then submit it in the format specified by your instructor.

11. ✴ In this assignment, you changed the bullets to picture bullets. Which bullet character did you select and why?

Expand Your World

Create a solution that uses cloud or web technologies by learning and investigating on your own from general guidance.

Using Word Online to Create a Flyer with a Picture

Note: To complete this assignment, you will be required to use the Data Files. Please contact your instructor for information about accessing the Data Files.

Instructions: You will use Word Online to prepare a flyer. The text for the unformatted flyer is shown in Figure 1–74. You will enter the text in Word Online and then use its tools to enhance the look of the flyer.

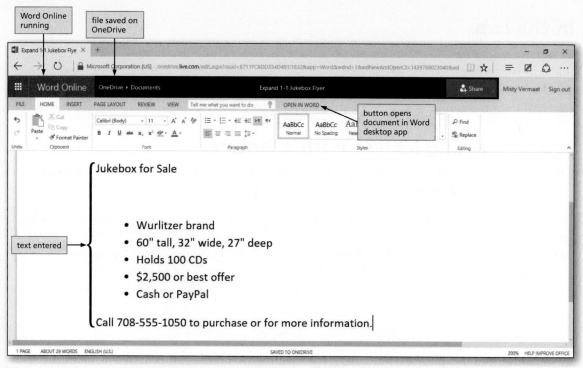

Figure 1–74

Perform the following tasks:

1. Run a browser. Search for the text, Word Online, using a search engine. Visit several websites to learn about Word Online. Navigate to the Office Online website. You will need to sign in to your OneDrive account.

2. Create a new blank Word document using Word Online. Name the document Expand 1–1 Jukebox Flyer.

3. Notice the differences between Word Online and the Word desktop app you used to create the project in this module.

4. Enter the text in the flyer, shown in Figure 1–74, checking spelling as you type.

5. Insert the picture called Jukebox, which is located in the Data Files.

Continued >

Expand Your World *continued*

6. Use the features available in Word Online, along with the concepts and techniques presented in this module, to format this flyer. Be sure to change the font and font size of text, center a paragraph(s), italicize text, color text, underline text, and apply a picture style. Resize the picture. Adjust spacing above and below paragraphs as necessary. The flyer should fit on a single page.

7. If requested by your instructor, replace the phone number in the flyer with your phone number.

8. Save the document again. Click the button to open the document in the Word desktop app. If necessary, sign in to your Microsoft account when prompted. Notice how the document appears in the Word desktop app.

9. Using either Word Online or the Word desktop app, submit the document in the format requested by your instructor. Exit Word Online. If necessary, sign out of your OneDrive account and your Microsoft account in Word.

10. ✹ What is Word Online? Which features that are covered in this module are not available in Word Online? Do you prefer using Word Online or the Word desktop app? Why?

In the Labs

Design, create, modify, and/or use a document following the guidelines, concepts, and skills presented in this module. Labs 1 and 2, which increase in difficulty, require you to create solutions based on what you learned in the module; Lab 3 requires you to apply your creative thinking and problem-solving skills to design and implement a solution.

Lab 1: **Creating a Flyer with a Picture**

Note: To complete this assignment, you will be required to use the Data Files. Please contact your instructor for information about accessing the Data Files.

Problem: Your boss asked you to prepare a flyer that advertises the company's commodity trading seminars. First, you prepare the unformatted flyer shown in Figure 1–75a, and then you format it so that it looks like Figure 1–75b. *Hint:* Remember, if you make a mistake while formatting the flyer, you can use the Undo button on the Quick Access Toolbar to undo your last action.

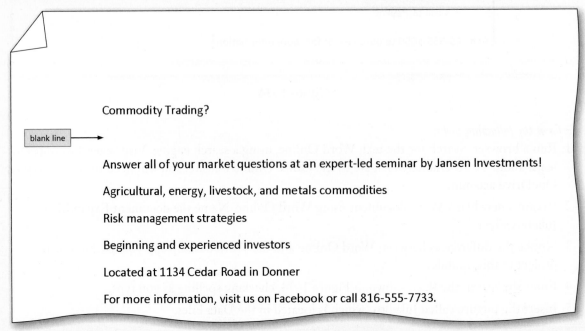

Commodity Trading?

blank line →

Answer all of your market questions at an expert-led seminar by Jansen Investments!

Agricultural, energy, livestock, and metals commodities

Risk management strategies

Beginning and experienced investors

Located at 1134 Cedar Road in Donner

For more information, visit us on Facebook or call 816-555-7733.

Figure 1–75a Unformatted Text

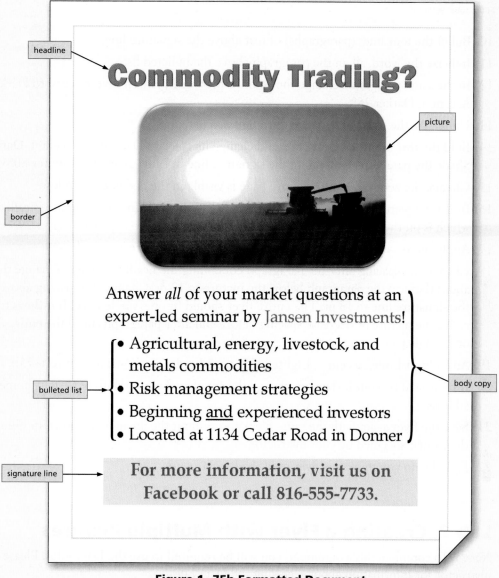

Figure 1–75b Formatted Document

Perform the following tasks:

1. Run Word. Display formatting marks on the screen.

2. Type the flyer text, unformatted, as shown in Figure 1–75a, inserting a blank line between the headline and the body copy. If Word flags any misspelled words as you type, check their spelling and correct them.

3. Save the document using the file name, Lab 1–1 Commodity Trading Flyer.

4. Center the headline and the signature line.

5. Change the theme colors to Green.

6. Change the font size of the headline to 48 point and the font to Franklin Gothic Heavy or a similar font. Apply the text effect called Fill - Dark Teal, Accent 4, Soft Bevel.

7. Change the font size of body copy between the headline and the signature line to 24 point.

8. Change the font size of the signature line to 26 point.

9. Change the font of the body copy and signature line to Book Antiqua.

Continued >

In the Labs *continued*

10. Bullet the four lines (paragraphs) of text above the signature line.

11. Italicize the word, all, in the paragraph above the bulleted list.

12. In the same paragraph, change the color of the words, Jansen Investments, to Dark Teal, Accent 4, Darker 25%.

13. Underline the word, and, in the third bulleted paragraph.

14. Bold the text in the signature line and change its color to Dark Teal, Accent 4, Darker 25%. Shade the paragraph containing the signature line in Lime, Accent 2, Lighter 80%.

15. Change the zoom so that the entire page is visible in the document window.

16. Insert the picture centered on a blank line below the headline. The picture is called Harvest, which is on the Data Files. Reduce the size of the picture to approximately 3.29" × 5.11".

17. Apply the Bevel Rectangle picture style to the inserted picture.

18. Change the spacing after the paragraph containing the headline to 0 pt. Change the spacing above (before) the paragraph below the picture to 12 pt. Change the spacing above (before) the signature line to 18 pt. The entire flyer should fit on a single page. If it flows to two pages, resize the picture or decrease spacing before and after paragraphs until the entire flyer text fits on a single page.

19. Add a ½-pt Lime, Accent 3, Lighter 40% page border, as shown in Figure 1–75b.

20. If requested by your instructor, change the street address in the flyer to your home street address.

21. Save the flyer again with the same file name. Submit the document, shown in Figure 1–75b, in the format specified by your instructor.

22. ❀ Why do you think this flyer used shades of green?

Lab 2: **Creating a Flyer with Multiple Pictures**

Note: To complete this assignment, you will be required to use the Data Files. Please contact your instructor for information about accessing the Data Files.

Problem: Your boss at Gingham Travel has asked you to prepare a flyer that promotes its business. You prepare the flyer shown in Figure 1–76. *Hint*: Remember, if you make a mistake while formatting the flyer, you can use the Undo button on the Quick Access Toolbar to undo your last action.

Perform the following tasks:

1. Run Word. Type the flyer text, unformatted. If Word flags any misspelled words as you type, check their spelling and correct them.

2. Save the document using the file name, Lab 1–2 Spring Break Flyer.

3. Change the theme colors to the Aspect color scheme.

4. Add bullets to the four paragraphs shown in the figure. Center all paragraphs, except the paragraphs containing the bulleted list.

5. Change the font size of both lines in the headline to 48 point. Change the font of the first line in the headline to Ravie, or a similar font, and the second line in the headline to Arial Rounded MT Bold, or a similar font. Apply this text effect to the first line in the headline: Fill - Dark Purple, Accent 1, Outline - Background 1, Hard Shadow - Accent 1. Shade the second line of the headline to the Dark Green, Accent 4 color, and change the font color to White, Background 1.

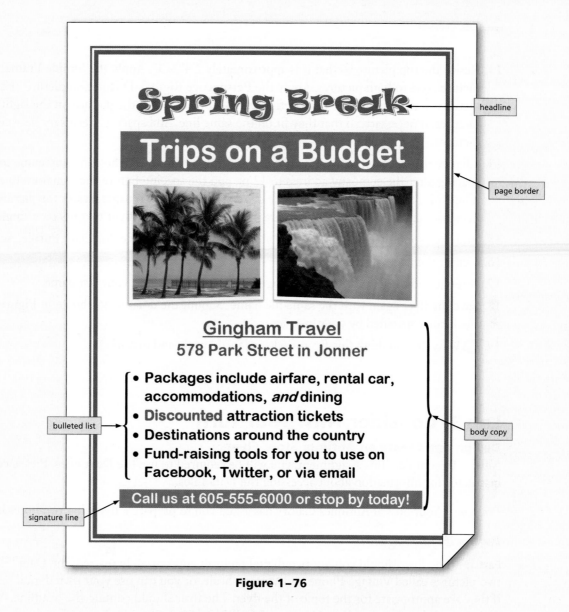

Figure 1–76

6. Change the font of all text below the headline to Arial Rounded MT Bold. Change the font size of the company name to 28 point, the company address to 24 point, and the bulleted list and signature line to 22 point.

7. Change the color of the company name and address to Dark Green, Accent 4, Darker 25%. Underline the company name.

8. Italicize the word, and, in the first bulleted paragraph.

9. Bold the word, Discounted, in the second bulleted paragraph. Change the color of this same word to Dark Purple, Accent 5.

10. Shade the signature line to the Dark Green, Accent 4 color, and change the font color to White, Background 1.

11. Change the zoom so that the entire page is visible in the document window.

12. Insert two pictures on the same blank line below the headline. The pictures are called Spring Break - Florida and Spring Break - New York, which are both in the Data Files.

Continued >

In the Labs *continued*

13. Resize the top picture so that it is approximately 2.4" × 3". Apply the Simple Frame, White picture style to both pictures. Apply the Perspective Right 3-D Rotation picture effect to the picture on the left and the Perspective Left 3-D Rotation to the picture on the right. Resize the pictures, if necessary, so that they fit on the same line. Add space as necessary between the two pictures.

14. Change the spacing before and after the paragraph containing the company name to 0 pt, the spacing after the company address to 12 pt, and the spacing before the signature line to 12 pt. The entire flyer should fit on a single page. If it flows to two pages, resize the pictures or decrease spacing before and after paragraphs until the entire flyer text fits on a single page.

15. Add the 6-point page border shown in Figure 1–76, using the color Dark Purple, Accent 5.

16. Center the page contents vertically.

17. If requested by your instructor, change the company name to your last name.

18. Save the flyer again with the same file name. Submit the document, shown in Figure 1–76, in the format specified by your instructor.

19. ✸ Why do you think this flyer used shades of purple and green?

Lab 3: **Consider This: Your Turn**

Design and Create an Antique Store Flyer

Note: To complete this assignment, you will be required to use the Data Files. Please contact your instructor for information about accessing the Data Files.

Problem: Your boss at Antiques Galore has asked you to prepare a flyer that promotes its business.

Perform the following tasks:

Part 1: The flyer should contain two digital pictures appropriately resized; the Data Files contains two pictures called Vintage Phone and Vintage Scale, or you can use your own digital pictures if they are appropriate for the topic of the flyer. The flyer should contain the headline, Antiques Galore, and this signature line: Questions? Call 312-555-2000 or find us on Facebook. The body copy consists of the following text, in any order: We sell all types of vintage items and also buy items individually or as an entire estate. Bring your items in for a free appraisal!; 1,200 square foot shop; Collectibles, costume jewelry, furniture, paintings, pottery, toys, and more!; Affordable items with new inventory daily; Located at 229 Center Street in Snow Hill; Open from 9:00 a.m. to 8:00 p.m. daily.

Use the concepts and techniques presented in this module to create and format this flyer. Be sure to check spelling and grammar. Submit your assignment and answers to the Part 2 critical thinking questions in the format specified by your instructor.

Part 2: ✸ You made several decisions while creating the flyer in this assignment: where to place text, how to format the text (i.e., font, font size, paragraph alignment, bulleted paragraphs, underlines, italics, bold, color, etc.), which graphics to use, where to position the graphics, how to format the graphics, and which page enhancements to add (i.e., borders and spacing). What was the rationale behind each of these decisions? When you proofread the document, what further revisions did you make and why? How would you recommend distributing this flyer?

2 Creating a Research Paper with References and Sources

Objectives

You will have mastered the material in this module when you can:

- Describe the MLA documentation style for research papers
- Modify a style
- Change line and paragraph spacing in a document
- Use a header to number pages of a document
- Apply formatting using keyboard shortcuts
- Modify paragraph indentation

- Insert and edit citations and their sources
- Add a footnote to a document
- Insert a manual page break
- Create a bibliographical list of sources
- Cut, copy, and paste text
- Find text and replace text
- Find a synonym
- Check spelling and grammar at once
- Look up information

Introduction

In both academic and business environments, you will be asked to write reports. Business reports range from proposals to cost justifications to five-year plans to research findings. Academic reports focus mostly on research findings.

A **research paper** is a document you can use to communicate the results of research findings. To write a research paper, you learn about a particular topic from a variety of sources (research), organize your ideas from the research results, and then present relevant facts and/or opinions that support the topic. Your final research paper combines properly credited outside information along with personal insights. Thus, no two research papers — even if they are about the same topic — will or should be the same.

Project — Research Paper

When preparing a research paper, you should follow a standard documentation style that defines the rules for creating the paper and crediting sources. A variety of documentation styles exists, depending on the nature of the research paper. Each style requires the same basic information; the differences in styles relate to requirements for presenting the information. For example, one documentation style uses the term, bibliography, for the list of sources, whereas another uses the term, references, and yet a third prefers the term, works cited. Two popular documentation styles for research papers are the **Modern Language Association of America** (**MLA**) and **American Psychological Association** (**APA**) styles. This module uses the MLA documentation style because it is used in a wide range of disciplines.

The project in this module follows research paper guidelines and uses Word to create the short research paper shown in Figure 2–1. This paper, which discusses using headphones and earbuds safely, follows the MLA documentation style. Each page contains a page number. The first two pages present the name and course information (student name, instructor name, course name, and paper due date), paper title, an introduction with a thesis statement, details that support the thesis, and a conclusion. This section of the paper also includes references to research sources and a footnote. The third page contains a detailed, alphabetical list of the sources referenced in the research paper. All pages include a header at the upper-right edge of the page.

In this module, you will learn how to create the research paper shown in Figure 2–1. The following roadmap identifies general activities you will perform as you progress through this module:

1. CHANGE the DOCUMENT SETTINGS.
2. CREATE the HEADER for each page of the research paper.
3. TYPE the RESEARCH PAPER text WITH CITATIONS.
4. CREATE an ALPHABETICAL WORKS CITED page.
5. PROOFREAD AND REVISE the RESEARCH PAPER.

MLA Documentation Style

The research paper in this project follows the guidelines presented by the MLA. To follow the MLA documentation style, use a 12-point Times New Roman or similar font. Double-space text on all pages of the paper using one-inch top, bottom, left, and right margins. Indent the first word of each paragraph one-half inch from the left margin. At the right margin of each page, place a page number one-half inch from the top margin. On each page, precede the page number with your last name.

The MLA documentation style does not require a title page. Instead, place your name and course information in a block at the left margin beginning one inch from the top of the page. Center the title one double-spaced line below your name and course information.

In the text of the paper, place author references in parentheses with the page number(s) of the referenced information. The MLA documentation style uses in-text **parenthetical references** instead of noting each source at the bottom of the page or at the end of the paper. In the MLA documentation style, notes are used only for optional content or bibliographic notes.

If used, content notes elaborate on points discussed in the paper, and bibliographic notes direct the reader to evaluations of statements in a source or provide a means for identifying multiple sources. Use a superscript (raised number) both to signal that a note exists and to sequence the notes (shown in Figure 2–1). Position notes at the bottom of the page as footnotes or at the end of the paper as endnotes. Indent the first line of each note one-half inch from the left margin. Place one space following the superscripted number before beginning the note text. Double-space the note text (shown in Figure 2–1).

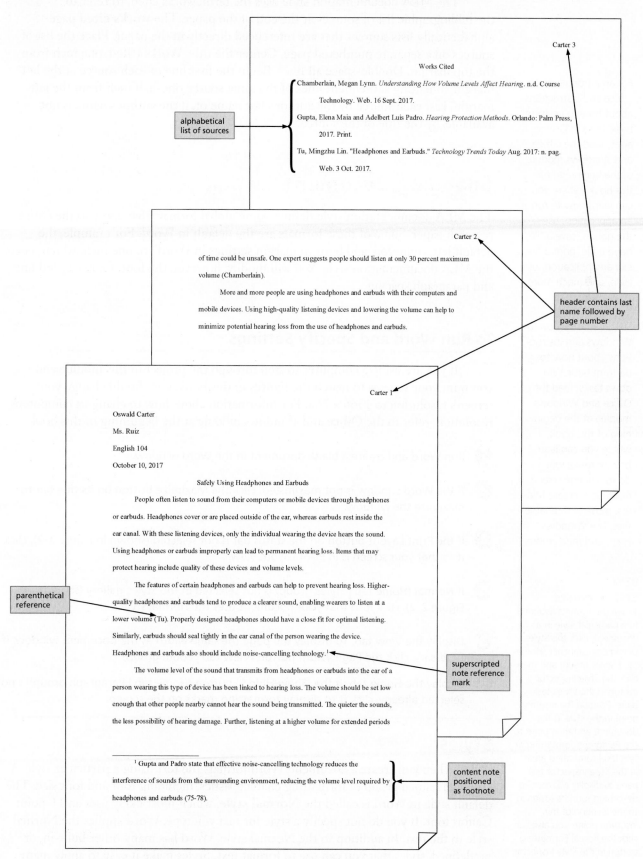

Figure 2–1

The MLA documentation style uses the term, works cited, to refer to the bibliographic list of sources at the end of the paper. The **works cited** page alphabetically lists sources that are referenced directly in the paper. Place the list of sources on a separate numbered page. Center the title, Works Cited, one inch from the top margin. Double-space all lines. Begin the first line of each source at the left margin, indenting subsequent lines of the same source one-half inch from the left margin. List each source by the author's last name or, if the author's name is not available, by the title of the source.

Changing Document Settings

The MLA documentation style defines some global formats that apply to the entire research paper. Some of these formats are the default in Word. For example, the default left, right, top, and bottom margin settings in Word are one inch, which meets the MLA documentation style. You will modify, however, the font, font size, and line and paragraph spacing.

To Run Word and Specify Settings

If you are using a computer to step through the project in this module and you want your screens to match the figures in this book, you should change your screen's resolution to 1366 × 768. For information about how to change a computer's resolution, refer to the Office and Windows module at the beginning of this book.

1. Run Word and create a blank document in the Word window.

2. If the Word window is not maximized, click the Maximize button on its title bar to maximize the window.

3. If the Print Layout button on the status bar is not selected (shown in Figure 2–2), click it so that your screen is in Print Layout view.

4. If Normal (Home tab | Styles group) is not selected in the Styles gallery (shown in Figure 2–2), click it so that your document uses the Normal style.

5. Display the View tab. To display the page the same width as the document window, if necessary, click the Page Width button (View tab | Zoom group).

6. Display the Home tab. If the 'Show/Hide ¶' button (Home tab | Paragraph group) is not selected already, click it to display formatting marks on the screen.

Styles

When you create a document, Word formats the text using a particular style. A **style** is a named group of formatting characteristics, including font and font size. The default style in Word is called the **Normal style**, which most likely uses an 11-point Calibri font. If you do not specify a style for text you type, Word applies the Normal style to the text. In addition to the Normal style, Word has many other built-in, or predefined, styles that you can use to format text. Styles make it easy to apply many formats at once to text. You can modify existing styles and create your own styles. Styles are discussed as they are used in this book.

For an introduction to Office and instructions about how to perform basic tasks in Office apps, read the Office and Windows module at the beginning of this book, where you can learn how to run an application, use the ribbon, save a file, open a file, print a file, exit an application, use Help, and much more.

For an introduction to Windows and instructions about how to perform basic Windows tasks, read the Office and Windows module at the beginning of this book, where you can learn how to resize windows, change screen resolution, create folders, move and rename files, use Windows Help, and much more.

BTW
Style Formats
To see the formats assigned to a particular style in a document, click the Styles Dialog Box Launcher (Home tab | Styles group) and then click the Style Inspector button in the Styles task pane. Position the insertion point in the style in the document and then point to the Paragraph formatting or Text level formatting areas in the Style Inspector task pane to display a ScreenTip describing formats assigned to the location of the insertion point. You also can click the Reveal Formatting button in the Style Inspector task pane or press SHIFT+F1 to display the Reveal Formatting task pane.

To Modify a Style

The MLA documentation style requires that all text in the research paper use a 12-point Times New Roman or similar font. If you change the font and font size using buttons on the ribbon, you will need to make the change many times during the course of creating the paper. *Why? Word formats various areas of a document based on the Normal style, which uses an 11-point Calibri font. For example, body text, headers, and bibliographies all display text based on the Normal style.*

Thus, instead of changing the font and font size for various document elements, a more efficient technique is to change the Normal style for this document to use a 12-point Times New Roman font. *Why? By changing the Normal style, you ensure that all text in the document will use the format required by the MLA.* The following steps change the Normal style.

1

- Right-click Normal in the Styles gallery (Home tab | Styles group) to display a shortcut menu related to styles (Figure 2–2).

Figure 2–2

2

- Click Modify on the shortcut menu to display the Modify Style dialog box (Figure 2–3).

Figure 2–3

3

- Click the Font arrow (Modify Style dialog box) to display the Font list. Scroll to and then click Times New Roman in the list to change the font for the style being modified.
- Click the Font Size arrow (Modify Style dialog box) and then click 12 in the Font Size list to change the font size for the style being modified.
- Ensure that the 'Only in this document' option button is selected (Figure 2–4).

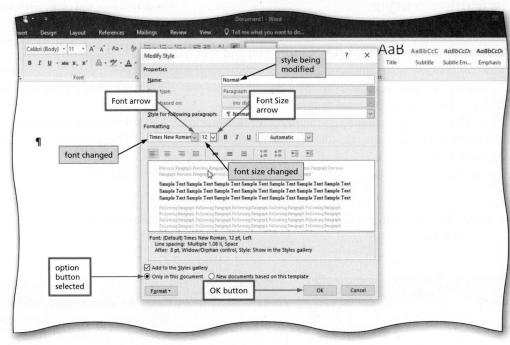

Figure 2–4

Q&A Will all future documents use the new font and font size?

No, because the 'Only in this document' option button is selected. If you wanted all future documents to use a new setting, you would select the 'New documents based on this template' option button.

4

- Click the OK button (Modify Style dialog box) to update the Normal style to the specified settings.

Other Ways

1. Click Styles Dialog Box Launcher, click arrow next to style name, click Modify on menu, change settings (Modify Style dialog box), click OK button

2. Press ALT+CTRL+SHIFT+S, click arrow next to style name, click Modify on menu, change settings (Modify Style dialog box), click OK button

---

BTW
Line Spacing
If the top of a set of characters or a graphical image is chopped off, then line spacing may be set to Exactly. To remedy the problem, change line spacing to 1.0, 1.15, 1.5, 2.0, 2.5, 3.0, or At least (in the Paragraph dialog box), all of which accommodate the largest font or image.

Adjusting Line and Paragraph Spacing

Line spacing is the amount of vertical space between lines of text in a paragraph. **Paragraph spacing** is the amount of space above and below a paragraph. By default, the Normal style places 8 points of blank space after each paragraph and inserts a vertical space equal to 1.08 lines between each line of text. It also automatically adjusts line height to accommodate various font sizes and graphics.

The MLA documentation style requires that you double-space the entire research paper. That is, specifying a document use **double-space** means that the amount of vertical space between each line of text and above and below paragraphs should be equal to one blank line. The next sets of steps adjust line spacing and paragraph spacing according to the MLA documentation style.

1 CHANGE DOCUMENT SETTINGS | 2 CREATE HEADER | 3 TYPE RESEARCH PAPER WITH CITATIONS

To Change Line Spacing

4 CREATE ALPHABETICAL WORKS CITED | 5 PROOFREAD & REVISE RESEARCH PAPER

The following steps change the line spacing to 2.0 to double-space lines in a paragraph. **Why?** *The lines of the research paper should be double-spaced, according to the MLA documentation style.*

1

- Click the 'Line and Paragraph Spacing' button (Home tab | Paragraph group) to display the Line and Paragraph Spacing gallery (Figure 2–5).

Q&A What do the numbers in the Line and Paragraph Spacing gallery represent?

The options 1.0, 2.0, and 3.0 set line spacing to single, double, and triple, respectively. Similarly, the 1.15, 1.5, and 2.5 options set line spacing to 1.15, 1.5, and 2.5 lines. All of these options adjust line spacing automatically to accommodate the largest font or graphic on a line.

Figure 2–5

2

- Click 2.0 in the Line and Paragraph Spacing gallery to change the line spacing at the location of the insertion point.

Q&A Can I change the line spacing of existing text?

Yes. Select the text first and then change the line spacing as described in these steps.

Other Ways

1. Right-click paragraph (or, if using touch, tap 'Show Context Menu' on mini toolbar), click Paragraph on shortcut menu, or click Indents and Spacing tab (Paragraph dialog box), click Line spacing arrow, select desired spacing, click OK button

2. Click Paragraph Settings Dialog Box Launcher (Home tab or Layout tab | Paragraph group), click Indents and Spacing tab (Paragraph dialog box), click Line spacing arrow, select desired spacing, click OK button

3. Press CTRL+2 for double-spacing

To Remove Space after a Paragraph

1 CHANGE DOCUMENT SETTINGS | 2 CREATE HEADER | 3 TYPE RESEARCH PAPER WITH CITATIONS
4 CREATE ALPHABETICAL WORKS CITED | 5 PROOFREAD & REVISE RESEARCH PAPER

The following steps remove space after a paragraph. **Why?** *The research paper should not have additional blank space after each paragraph, according to the MLA documentation style.*

1

- Click the 'Line and Paragraph Spacing' button (Home tab | Paragraph group) to display the Line and Paragraph Spacing gallery (Figure 2–6).

Q&A Why does a check mark appear to the left of 2.0 in the gallery?

The check mark indicates the currently selected line spacing.

Figure 2–6

- Click 'Remove Space After Paragraph' in the Line and Paragraph Spacing gallery so that no blank space appears after paragraphs.

Q&A Can I remove space after existing paragraphs?
Yes. Select the paragraphs first and then remove the space as described in these steps.

Other Ways

1. Adjust Spacing After arrows (Layout tab | Paragraph group) until 0 pt is displayed

2. Right-click paragraph (or, if using touch, tap 'Show Context Menu' on mini toolbar), click Paragraph on shortcut menu, click Indents and Spacing tab (Paragraph dialog box), adjust After arrows until 0 pt is displayed, click OK button

3. Click Paragraph Settings Dialog Box Launcher (Home tab or Layout tab | Paragraph group), click Indents and Spacing tab (Paragraph dialog box), adjust After arrows until 0 pt is displayed, click OK button

---

To Update a Style to Match a Selection

1 CHANGE DOCUMENT SETTINGS | **2 CREATE HEADER** | 3 TYPE RESEARCH PAPER WITH CITATIONS
4 CREATE ALPHABETICAL WORKS CITED | 5 PROOFREAD & REVISE RESEARCH PAPER

To ensure that all paragraphs in the paper will be double-spaced and do not have space after the paragraphs, you want the Normal style to include the line and paragraph spacing changes made in the previous two sets of steps. The following steps update the Normal style. *Why? You can update a style to reflect the settings of the location of the insertion point or selected text. Because no text has been typed in the research paper yet, you do not need to select text prior to updating the Normal style.*

- Right-click Normal in the Styles gallery (Home tab | Styles group) to display a shortcut menu (Figure 2–7).

- Click 'Update Normal to Match Selection' on the shortcut menu to update the selected (or current) style to reflect the settings at the location of the insertion point.

Figure 2–7

Other Ways

1. Click Styles Dialog Box Launcher, click arrow next to style name, click 'Update Normal to Match Selection'

2. Press ALT+CTRL+SHIFT+S, click arrow next to style name in Styles pane, click 'Update Normal to Match Selection'

Creating a Header

BTW
The Ribbon and Screen Resolution
Word may change how the groups and buttons within the groups appear on the ribbon, depending on the computer or mobile device's screen resolution. Thus, your ribbon may look different from the ones in this book if you are using a screen resolution other than 1366 x 768.

A **header** is text and/or graphics that print at the top of each page in a document. Similarly, a **footer** is text and/or graphics that print at the bottom of every page. In Word, headers print in the top margin one-half inch from the top of every page, and footers print in the bottom margin one-half inch from the bottom of each page, which meets the MLA documentation style. In addition to text and graphics, headers and footers can include document information, such as the page number, current date, current time, and author's name.

In this research paper, you are to precede the page number with your last name placed one-half inch from the upper-right edge of each page. The procedures in the following sections enter your name and the page number in the header, as specified by the MLA documentation style.

To Switch to the Header

The following steps switch from editing the document text to editing the header. *Why? To enter text in the header, you instruct Word to edit the header.*

1

- Click Insert on the ribbon to display the Insert tab.
- Click the 'Add a Header' button (Insert tab | Header & Footer group) to display the Add a Header gallery (Figure 2–8)

🔍 **Experiment**

- Click the down scroll arrow in the Add a Header gallery to see the available built-in headers.

Q&A Can I use a built-in header for this research paper?

None of the built-in headers adheres to the MLA documentation style; thus, you should enter your own header content instead of using a built-in header for this research paper.

How would I remove a header from a document?
You would click Remove Header in the Add a Header gallery. Similarly, to remove a footer, you would click Remove Footer in the Add a Footer gallery.

Figure 2–8

2

- Click Edit Header in the Add a Header gallery to switch from the document text to the header, which allows you to edit the contents of the header (Figure 2–9).

Q&A How do I remove the Header & Footer Tools Design tab from the ribbon?

When you are finished editing the header, you will close it, which removes the Header & Footer Tools Design tab.

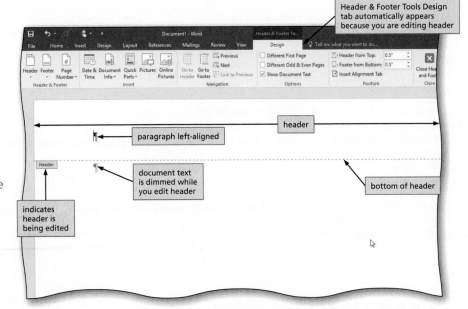

Figure 2–9

Other Ways

1. Double-click dimmed header

2. Right-click header in document, click Edit Header button that appears

To Right-Align a Paragraph

1 CHANGE DOCUMENT SETTINGS | 2 CREATE HEADER | 3 TYPE RESEARCH PAPER WITH CITATIONS
4 CREATE ALPHABETICAL WORKS CITED | 5 PROOFREAD & REVISE RESEARCH PAPER

The paragraph in the header currently is left-aligned (shown in Figure 2–9). The following steps right-align this paragraph. ***Why?*** *Your last name and the page number should print **right-aligned**; that is, they should print at the right margin, according to the MLA documentation style.*

1

- Click Home on the ribbon to display the Home tab.

2

- Click the Align Right button (Home tab | Paragraph group) to right-align the current paragraph (Figure 2–10).

Q&A What if I wanted to return the paragraph to left-aligned?
You would click the Align Right button again, or click the Align Left button (Home tab | Paragraph group).

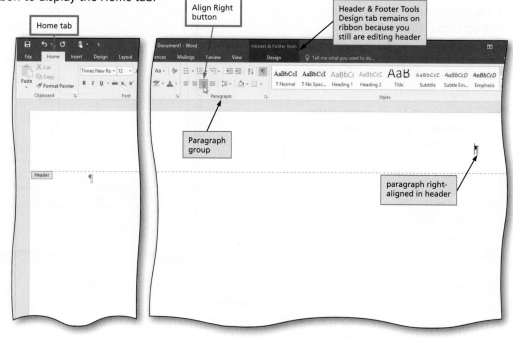

Figure 2–10

Other Ways

1. Right-click paragraph (or, if using touch, tap 'Show Context Menu' button on mini toolbar), click Paragraph on shortcut menu, click Indents and Spacing tab (Paragraph dialog box), click Alignment arrow, click Right, click OK button

2. Click Paragraph Settings Dialog Box Launcher (Home tab or Layout tab | Paragraph group), click Indents and Spacing tab (Paragraph dialog box), click Alignment arrow, click Right, click OK button

3. Press CTRL+R

BTW
Footers
If you wanted to create a footer, you would click the 'Add a Footer' button (Insert tab | Header & Footer group) and then select the desired built-in footer or click Edit Footer in the Add a Footer gallery to create a customized footer; or, you could double-click the dimmed footer.

To Enter Text

The following step enters the last name right-aligned in the header area.

1 Type **Carter** and then press the SPACEBAR to enter the last name in the header.

If requested by your instructor, enter your last name instead of Carter in the header.

To Insert a Page Number

1 CHANGE DOCUMENT SETTINGS | 2 CREATE HEADER | 3 TYPE RESEARCH PAPER WITH CITATIONS
4 CREATE ALPHABETICAL WORKS CITED | 5 PROOFREAD & REVISE RESEARCH PAPER

The following steps insert a page number at the location of the insertion point. ***Why?*** *The MLA documentation style requires a page number following the last name in the header.*

1

- Click Header & Footer Tools Design on the ribbon to display the Header & Footer Tools Design tab.
- Click the 'Add Page Numbers' button (Header & Footer Tools Design tab | Header & Footer group) to display the Add Page Numbers menu.

Q&A Why does the button name in the step differ from the name on the face of the button in the figure?
The text that appears on the face of the button may vary, depending on screen resolution. The name that appears in the ScreenTip (when you point to the button), however, never changes. For this reason, this book uses the name that appears in the ScreenTip to identify buttons, boxes, and other on-screen elements.

- Point to Current Position on the Add Page Numbers menu to display the Current Position gallery (Figure 2–11).

🔍 **Experiment**

- Click the down scroll arrow in the Current Position gallery to see the available page number formats.

Figure 2–11

2

- If necessary, scroll to the top of the Current Position gallery.
- Click Plain Number in the Current Position gallery to insert an unformatted page number at the location of the insertion point (Figure 2–12).

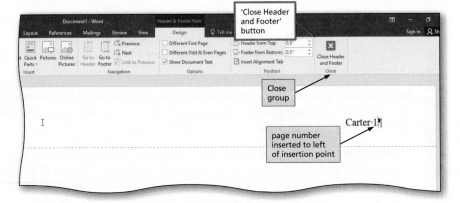

Figure 2–12

Other Ways

1. Click 'Add Page Numbers' button (Insert tab | Header & Footer group)

2. Click 'Explore Quick Parts' button (Insert tab | Text group or Header & Footer Tools Design tab | Insert group), click Field on Explore Quick Parts menu, select Page in Field names list (Field dialog box), select desired format in Format list, click OK button

To Close the Header

The next task is to switch back to the document text. *Why? You are finished entering text in the header.* The following step closes the header.

1

- Click the 'Close Header and Footer' button (Header & Footer Tools Design tab | Close group) (shown in Figure 2–12) to close the header and switch back to the document text (Figure 2–13).

Q&A
How do I make changes to existing header text? Switch to the header using the steps described previously in the section titled To Switch to the Header, edit the header as you would edit text in the document window, and then switch back to the document text.

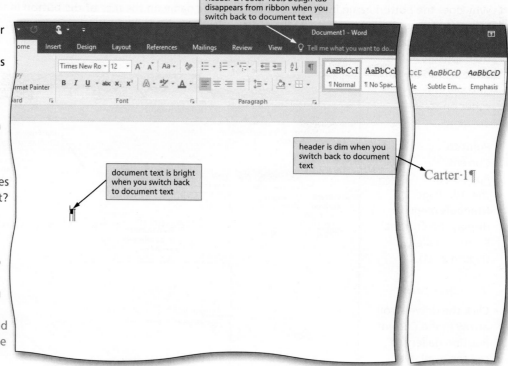

Figure 2–13

Other Ways

1. Double-click dimmed document text

Typing the Research Paper Text

The text of the research paper in this module encompasses the first two pages of the paper. You will type the text of the research paper and then modify it later in the module, so that it matches Figure 2–1 shown at the beginning of this module.

CONSIDER THIS

What should you consider when writing the first draft of a research paper?
As you write the first draft of a research paper, be sure it includes the proper components, uses credible sources, and does not contain any plagiarized material.

- **Include an introduction, body, and conclusion.** The first paragraph of the paper introduces the topic and captures the reader's attention. The body, which follows the introduction, consists of several paragraphs that support the topic. The conclusion summarizes the main points in the body and restates the topic.

- **Evaluate sources for authority, currency, and accuracy.** Be especially wary of information obtained on the web. Any person, company, or organization can publish a webpage on the Internet. When considering the source, consider the following:

  - Authority: Does a reputable institution or group support the source? Is the information presented without bias? Are the author's credentials listed and verifiable?

  - Currency: Is the information up to date? Are dates of sources listed? What is the last date revised or updated?

  - Accuracy: Is the information free of errors? Is it verifiable? Are the sources clearly identified?

- **Acknowledge all sources of information; do not plagiarize.** Sources of research include books, magazines, newspapers, and the Internet. As you record facts and ideas, list details about the source: title, author, place of publication, publisher, date of publication, etc. When taking notes, be careful not to **plagiarize**. That is, do not use someone else's work and claim it to be your own. If you copy information directly, place it in quotation marks and identify its source. Not only is plagiarism unethical, but it is considered an academic crime that can have severe punishments, such as failing a course or being expelled from school.

When you summarize, paraphrase (rewrite information in your own words), present facts, give statistics, quote exact words, or show a map, chart, or other graphic, you must acknowledge the source. Information that commonly is known or accessible to the audience constitutes common knowledge and does not need to be acknowledged. If, however, you question whether certain information is common knowledge, you should document it — just to be safe.

To Enter Name and Course Information

As discussed earlier in this module, the MLA documentation style does not require a separate title page for research papers. Instead, place your name and course information in a block at the top of the page, below the header, at the left margin. The following steps enter the name and course information in the research paper.

1 Type **Oswald Carter** as the student name and then press the ENTER key.

2 Type **Ms. Ruiz** as the instructor name and then press the ENTER key.

3 Type **English 104** as the course name and then press the ENTER key.

4 Type **October 10, 2017** as the paper's due date and then press the ENTER key (Figure 2–14).

If requested by your instructor, enter your name and course information instead of the information shown above.

Q&A Why did the word, October, appear on the screen as I began typing the month name?
Word has an AutoComplete feature, where it predicts some words or phrases as you are typing and displays its prediction in a ScreenTip. If the AutoComplete prediction is correct, you can press the ENTER key (or, if using touch, tap the ScreenTip) to instruct Word to finish your typing with the word or phrase that appears in the ScreenTip.

BTW

Date Formats
The MLA style prefers the day-month-year (10 October 2017) or month-day-year (October 10, 2017) format.

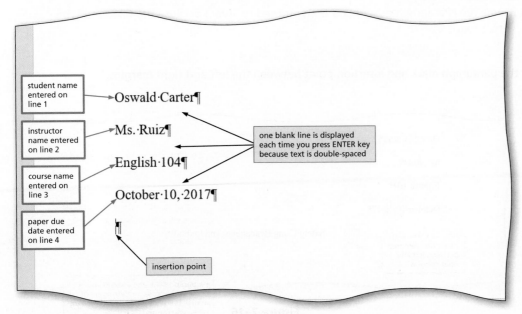

student name entered on line 1 → Oswald·Carter¶

instructor name entered on line 2 → Ms.·Ruiz¶

one blank line is displayed each time you press ENTER key because text is double-spaced

course name entered on line 3 → English·104¶

paper due date entered on line 4 → October·10,·2017¶

¶

insertion point

Figure 2–14

To Click and Type

The next task is to enter the title of the research paper centered between the page margins. In Module 1, you used the Center button (Home tab | Paragraph group) to center text and graphics. As an alternative, if you are using a mouse, you can use Word's Click and Type feature to format and enter text, graphics, and other items. *Why? With **Click and Type**, you can double-click a blank area of the document window and Word automatically formats the item you type or insert according to the location where you double-clicked.* The following steps use Click and Type to center and then type the title of the research paper.

1

🔎 **Experiment**

- Move the pointer around the document below the entered name and course information and observe the various icons that appear with the I-beam.

- Position the pointer in the center of the document at the approximate location for the research paper title until a center icon appears below the I-beam (Figure 2–15).

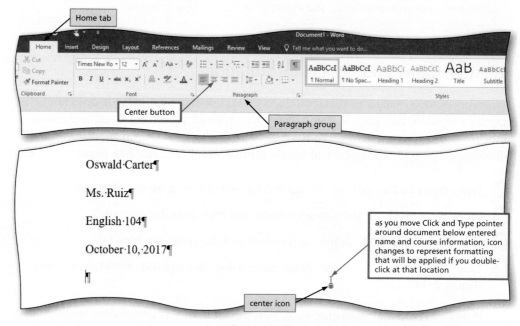

Figure 2–15

What are the other icons that appear in the Click and Type pointer?
A left-align icon appears to the right of the I-beam when the Click and Type pointer is in certain locations on the left side of the document window. A right-align icon appears to the left of the I-beam when the Click and Type pointer is in certain locations on the right side of the document window.

What if I am using a touch screen?
Tap the Center button (Home tab | Paragraph group) and then proceed to Step 3 because the Click and Type feature does not work with a touch screen.

2

- Double-click to center the paragraph mark and insertion point between the left and right margins.

3

- Type **Safely Using Headphones and Earbuds** as the paper title and then press the ENTER key to position the insertion point on the next line (Figure 2–16).

Figure 2–16

Keyboard Shortcuts

Word has many **keyboard shortcuts**, sometimes called shortcut keys or keyboard key combinations, for your convenience while typing. Table 2–1 lists the common keyboard shortcuts for formatting characters. Table 2–2 lists common keyboard shortcuts for formatting paragraphs.

Table 2–1 Keyboard Shortcuts for Formatting Characters

Character Formatting Task	Keyboard Shortcut	Character Formatting Task	Keyboard Shortcut
All capital letters	CTRL+SHIFT+A	Italic	CTRL+I
Bold	CTRL+B	Remove character formatting (plain text)	CTRL+SPACEBAR
Case of letters	SHIFT+F3	Small uppercase letters	CTRL+SHIFT+K
Decrease font size	CTRL+SHIFT+<	Subscript	CTRL+EQUAL SIGN
Decrease font size 1 point	CTRL+[	Superscript	CTRL+SHIFT+PLUS SIGN
Double-underline	CTRL+SHIFT+D	Underline	CTRL+U
Increase font size	CTRL+SHIFT+>	Underline words, not spaces	CTRL+SHIFT+W
Increase font size 1 point	CTRL+]		

© 2015 Cengage Learning

Table 2–2 Keyboard Shortcuts for Formatting Paragraphs

Paragraph Formatting	Keyboard Shortcut	Paragraph Formatting	Keyboard Shortcut
1.5 line spacing	CTRL+5	Justify paragraph	CTRL+J
Add/remove one line above paragraph	CTRL+0 (ZERO)	Left-align paragraph	CTRL+L
Center paragraph	CTRL+E	Remove hanging indent	CTRL+SHIFT+T
Decrease paragraph indent	CTRL+SHIFT+M	Remove paragraph formatting	CTRL+Q
Double-space lines	CTRL+2	Right-align paragraph	CTRL+R
Hanging indent	CTRL+T	Single-space lines	CTRL+1
Increase paragraph indent	CTRL+M		

© 2015 Cengage Learning

To Format Text Using a Keyboard Shortcut

The paragraphs below the paper title should be left-aligned, instead of centered. Thus, the next step is to left-align the paragraph below the paper title. When your fingers already are on the keyboard, you may prefer using keyboard shortcuts to format text as you type it.

The following step left-aligns a paragraph using the keyboard shortcut CTRL+L. (Recall from Module 1 that a notation such as CTRL+L means to press the letter L on the keyboard while holding down the CTRL key.)

1 Press CTRL+L to left-align the current paragraph, that is, the paragraph containing the insertion point (shown in Figure 2–17).

Q&A Why would I use a keyboard shortcut instead of the ribbon to format text?
Switching between the mouse and the keyboard takes time. If your hands are already on the keyboard, use a keyboard shortcut. If your hand is on the mouse, use the ribbon.

2 Save the research paper on your hard drive, OneDrive, or other storage location using the file name, Headphones and Earbuds Paper.

Q&A Why should I save the research paper at this time?
You have performed many tasks while creating this flyer and do not want to risk losing work completed thus far.

BTW
Keyboard Shortcuts
To print a complete list of keyboard shortcuts in Word, press F1 to display the Word Help window, type **keyboard shortcuts** in the Search box in the Word Help window, press the ENTER key, click the Keyboard shortcuts for Microsoft Word link, click the Print button in the Help window, and then click the Print button in the Print dialog box.

To Display the Rulers

1 CHANGE DOCUMENT SETTINGS | 2 CREATE HEADER | 3 TYPE RESEARCH PAPER WITH CITATIONS
4 CREATE ALPHABETICAL WORKS CITED | 5 PROOFREAD & REVISE RESEARCH PAPER

According to the MLA documentation style, the first line of each paragraph in the research paper is to be indented one-half inch from the left margin. Although you can use a dialog box to indent paragraphs, Word provides a quicker way through the **horizontal ruler**. This ruler is displayed at the top edge of the document window just below the ribbon. Word also provides a **vertical ruler** that is displayed along the left edge of the Word window. The following step displays the rulers. **Why?** *You want to use the horizontal ruler to indent paragraphs.*

- If necessary, scroll the document so that the research paper title is at the top of the document window.
- Click View on the ribbon to display the View tab.
- If the rulers are not displayed, click the View Ruler check box (View tab | Show group) to place a check mark in the check box and display the horizontal and vertical rulers on the screen (Figure 2–17).

Q&A What tasks can I accomplish using the rulers?
You can use the rulers to indent paragraphs, set tab stops, change page margins, and adjust column widths.

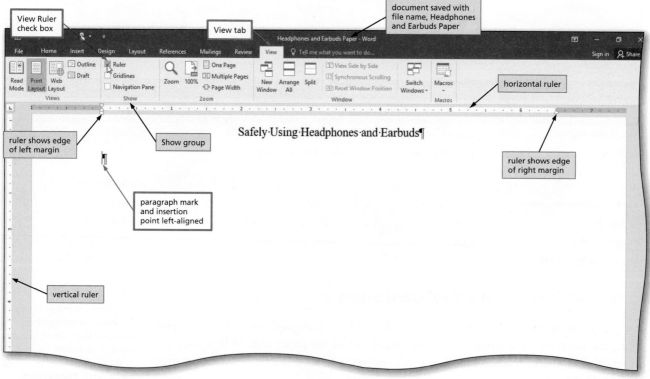

Figure 2–17

To First-Line Indent Paragraphs

1 CHANGE DOCUMENT SETTINGS | 2 CREATE HEADER | 3 TYPE RESEARCH PAPER WITH CITATIONS
4 CREATE ALPHABETICAL WORKS CITED | 5 PROOFREAD & REVISE RESEARCH PAPER

If you are using a mouse, you can use the horizontal ruler, usually simply called the **ruler**, to indent just the first line of a paragraph, which is called a **first-line indent**. The left margin on the ruler contains two triangles above a square. The **'First Line Indent' marker** is the top triangle at the 0" mark on the ruler (shown in Figure 2–18). The bottom triangle is discussed later in this module. The small square at the 0" mark is the Left Indent marker. The **Left Indent marker** allows you to change the entire left margin, whereas the 'First Line Indent' marker indents only the first line of the paragraph.

The following steps first-line indent paragraphs in the research paper. **Why?** *The first line of each paragraph in the research paper is to be indented one-half inch from the left margin, according to the MLA documentation style.*

1

- With the insertion point on the paragraph mark below the research paper title, point to the 'First Line Indent' marker on the ruler (Figure 2–18).

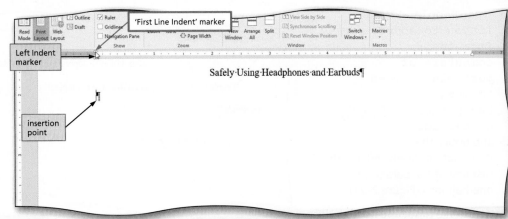

Figure 2–18

2

- Drag the 'First Line Indent' marker to the .5" mark on the ruler to display a vertical dotted line in the document window, which indicates the proposed indent location of the first line of the paragraph (Figure 2–19).

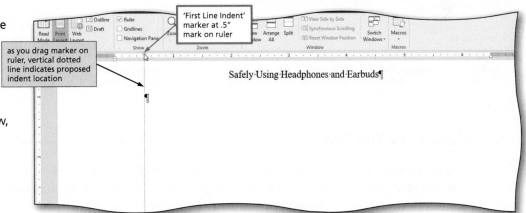

Figure 2–19

3

- Release the mouse button to place the 'First Line Indent' marker at the .5" mark on the ruler, or one-half inch from the left margin (Figure 2–20).

Q&A What if I am using a touch screen?

If you are using a touch screen, you cannot drag the 'First Line Indent' marker and must follow these steps instead: tap the Paragraph Settings Dialog Box Launcher (Home tab or Layout tab | Paragraph group) to display the Paragraph dialog box, tap the Indents and Spacing tab (Paragraph dialog box), tap the Special arrow, tap First line, and then tap the OK button.

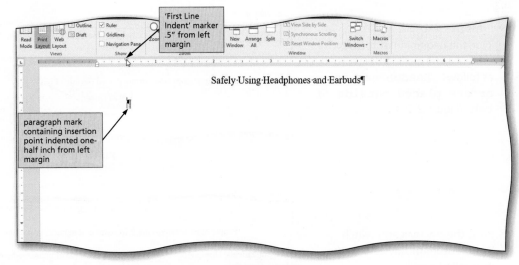

Figure 2–20

4

- Type `People often listen to sound from their computers or portable devices through headphones or earbuds.` and notice that Word automatically indents the first line of the paragraph by one-half inch (Figure 2–21).

Figure 2–21

Q&A

Will I have to set a first-line indent for each paragraph in the paper?

No. Each time you press the ENTER key, paragraph formatting in the previous paragraph carries forward to the next paragraph. Thus, once you set the first-line indent, its format carries forward automatically to each subsequent paragraph you type.

Other Ways

1. Right-click paragraph (or, if using touch, tap 'Show Context Menu' button on mini toolbar), click Paragraph on shortcut menu, click Indents and Spacing tab (Paragraph dialog box), click Special arrow, click First line, click OK button

2. Click Paragraph Settings Dialog Box Launcher (Home tab or Layout tab | Paragraph group), click Indents and Spacing tab (Paragraph dialog box), click Special arrow, click First line, click OK button

---

To AutoCorrect as You Type

1 CHANGE DOCUMENT SETTINGS | 2 CREATE HEADER | 3 TYPE RESEARCH PAPER WITH CITATIONS
4 CREATE ALPHABETICAL WORKS CITED | 5 PROOFREAD & REVISE RESEARCH PAPER

Word has predefined many commonly misspelled words, which it automatically corrects for you. ***Why?*** *As you type, you may make typing, spelling, capitalization, or grammar errors. Word's **AutoCorrect** feature automatically corrects these kinds of errors as you type them in the document. For example, if you type the characters, ahve, Word automatically changes it to the correct spelling, have, when you press the SPACEBAR or a punctuation mark key, such as a period or comma.*

The following steps intentionally misspell the word, the, as teh to illustrate the AutoCorrect feature.

1

- Press the SPACEBAR.
- Type the beginning of the next sentence, misspelling the word, the, as follows: `Headphones cover or are placed outside of teh` (Figure 2–22).

Figure 2–22

2

- Press the SPACEBAR and watch Word automatically correct the misspelled word.
- Type the rest of the sentence (Figure 2–23): `ear, whereas earbuds rest inside the ear canal.`

Figure 2–23

To Use the AutoCorrect Options Button

1 CHANGE DOCUMENT SETTINGS | 2 CREATE HEADER | 3 TYPE RESEARCH PAPER WITH CITATIONS
4 CREATE ALPHABETICAL WORKS CITED | 5 PROOFREAD & REVISE RESEARCH PAPER

The following steps illustrate the AutoCorrect Options button and menu. ***Why?*** *If you are using a mouse, when you position the pointer on text that Word automatically corrected, a small blue box appears below the text. If you point to the small blue box, Word displays the AutoCorrect Options button. When you click the **AutoCorrect Options button***, *Word displays a menu that allows you to undo a correction or change how Word handles future automatic corrections of this type.*

1

- Position the pointer in the text automatically corrected by Word (the word, the, in this case) to display a small blue box below the automatically corrected word (Figure 2–24).

Figure 2–24

2

- Point to the small blue box to display the AutoCorrect Options button.
- Click the AutoCorrect Options button to display the AutoCorrect Options menu (Figure 2–25).
- Press the ESC key to remove the AutoCorrect Options menu from the screen.

Q&A Do I need to remove the AutoCorrect Options button from the screen?
No. When you move the pointer, the AutoCorrect Options button will disappear from the screen. If, for some reason, you wanted to remove the AutoCorrect Options button from the screen, you could press the ESC key a second time.

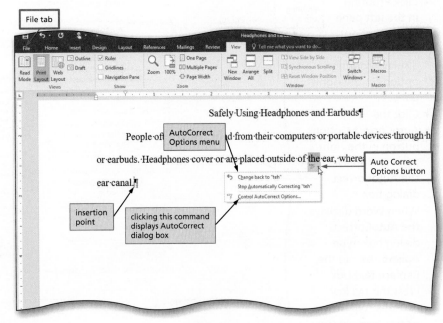

Figure 2–25

To Create an AutoCorrect Entry

1 CHANGE DOCUMENT SETTINGS | 2 CREATE HEADER | 3 TYPE RESEARCH PAPER WITH CITATIONS
4 CREATE ALPHABETICAL WORKS CITED | 5 PROOFREAD & REVISE RESEARCH PAPER

The next steps create an AutoCorrect entry. ***Why?*** *In addition to the predefined list of AutoCorrect spelling, capitalization, and grammar errors, you can create your own AutoCorrect entries to add to the list. For example, if you tend to mistype the word computer as comptuer, you should create an AutoCorrect entry for it.*

1

- Click File on the ribbon (shown in Figure 2–25) to open the Backstage view (Figure 2–26).

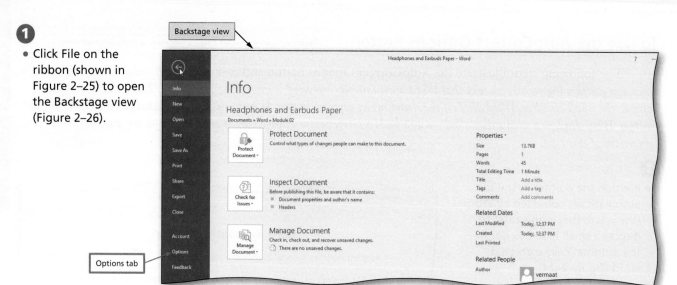

Figure 2–26

2

- Click the Options tab in the Backstage view to display the Word Options dialog box.
- Click Proofing in the left pane (Word Options dialog box) to display proofing options in the right pane.
- Click the AutoCorrect Options button in the right pane to display the AutoCorrect dialog box.
- When Word displays the AutoCorrect dialog box, type **comptuer** in the Replace text box.
- Press the TAB key and then type **computer** in the With text box (Figure 2–27).

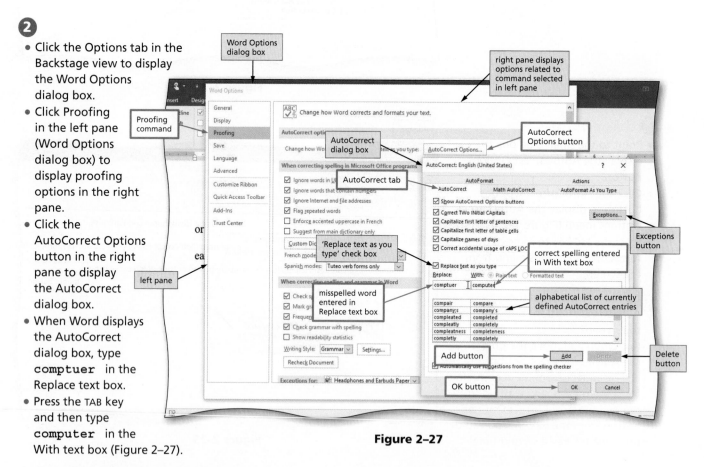

Figure 2–27

Q&A How would I delete an existing AutoCorrect entry?
You would select the entry to be deleted in the list of defined entries in the AutoCorrect dialog box and then click the Delete button (AutoCorrect dialog box).

3

- Click the Add button (AutoCorrect dialog box) to add the entry alphabetically to the list of words to correct automatically as you type. (If your dialog box displays a Replace button instead, click it and then click the Yes button in the Microsoft Word dialog box to replace the previously defined entry.)
- Click the OK button (AutoCorrect dialog box) to close the dialog box.
- Click the OK button (Word Options dialog box) to close the dialog box.

The AutoCorrect Dialog Box

In addition to creating AutoCorrect entries for words you commonly misspell or mistype, you can create entries for abbreviations, codes, and so on. For example, you could create an AutoCorrect entry for asap, indicating that Word should replace this text with the phrase, as soon as possible.

If, for some reason, you do not want Word to correct automatically as you type, you can turn off the Replace text as you type feature by clicking the Options tab in the Backstage view, clicking Proofing in the left pane (Word Options dialog box), clicking the AutoCorrect Options button in the right pane (shown in Figure 2–27), removing the check mark from the 'Replace text as you type' check box, and then clicking the OK button in each open dialog box.

The AutoCorrect sheet in the AutoCorrect dialog box (Figure 2–27) contains other check boxes that correct capitalization errors if the check boxes are selected:

- If you type two capital letters in a row, such as TH, Word makes the second letter lowercase, Th.
- If you begin a sentence with a lowercase letter, Word capitalizes the first letter of the sentence.
- If you type the name of a day in lowercase letters, such as tuesday, Word capitalizes the first letter in the name of the day, Tuesday.
- If you leave the CAPS LOCK key on and begin a new sentence, such as after, Word corrects the typing, After, and turns off the CAPS LOCK key.

If you do not want Word to perform any of these corrections automatically, simply remove the check mark from the appropriate check box in the AutoCorrect dialog box.

Sometimes, you do not want Word to AutoCorrect a particular word or phrase. For example, you may use the code, WD., in your documents. Because Word automatically capitalizes the first letter of a sentence, the character you enter following the period will be capitalized (in the previous sentence, it would capitalize the letter i in the word, in). To allow the code, WD., to be entered into a document and still leave the AutoCorrect feature turned on, you would set an exception. To set an exception to an AutoCorrect rule, click the Options tab in the Backstage view, click Proofing in the left pane (Word Options dialog box), click the AutoCorrect Options button in the right pane, click the Exceptions button (Figure 2–27), click the appropriate tab in the AutoCorrect Exceptions dialog box, type the exception entry in the text box, click the Add button, click the Close button (AutoCorrect Exceptions dialog box), and then click the OK button in each of the remaining dialog boxes.

To Enter More Text

The next task is to continue typing text in the research paper up to the location of the in-text parenthetical reference. The following steps enter this text.

1 With the insertion point positioned at the end of the first paragraph in the paper, as shown in Figure 2–25, press the SPACEBAR and then type these three sentences, intentionally misspelling the word sound as sould: `With these listening devices, only the individual wearing the device hears the sould. Using headphones or earbuds improperly can lead to permanent hearing loss. Items that may protect hearing include quality of these devices and volume levels.`

Q&A Why is the word, sound, misspelled?
Later in this module, you will use Word's check spelling and grammar at once feature to check the entire document for errors.

BTW
Automatic Corrections
If you do not want to keep a change made automatically by Word and you immediately notice the automatic correction, you can undo the change by clicking the Undo button on the Quick Access Toolbar or pressing CTRL+Z. You also can undo a correction through the AutoCorrect Options button (Word Options dialog box) (shown in Figure 2–27).

BTW
Spacing after Punctuation
Because word processing documents use variable character fonts, it often is difficult to determine in a printed document how many times someone has pressed the SPACEBAR between sentences. Thus, the rule is to press the SPACEBAR only once after periods, colons, and other punctuation marks.

2 Press the ENTER key to start a new paragraph.

3 Type **The features of certain headphones and earbuds can help to prevent hearing loss. Higher-quality headphones and earbuds tend to produce a clearer sound, enabling wearers to listen at a lower volume** and then press the SPACEBAR (Figure 2–28).

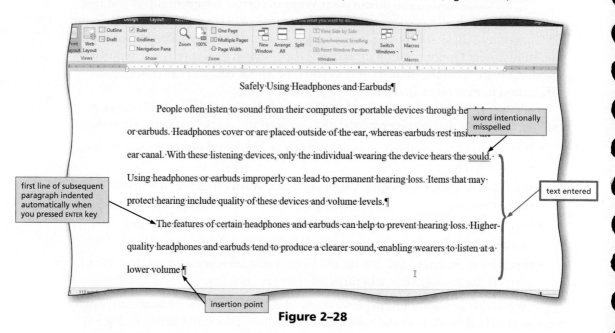

Figure 2–28

BTW
Word Help
At any time while using Word, you can find answers to questions and display information about various topics through Word Help. Used properly, this form of assistance can increase your productivity and reduce your frustrations by minimizing the time you spend learning how to use Word. For instructions about Word Help and exercises that will help you gain confidence in using it, read the Office and Windows module at the beginning of this book.

Citations

Both the MLA and APA guidelines suggest the use of in-text parenthetical references (placed at the end of a sentence), instead of footnoting each source of material in a paper. These parenthetical references, called citations in Word, guide the reader to the end of the paper for complete information about the source.

Word provides tools to assist you with inserting citations in a paper and later generating a list of sources from the citations. With a documentation style selected, Word automatically formats the citations and list of sources according to that style. The process for adding citations in Word is as follows:

1. Modify the documentation style, if necessary.
2. Insert a citation placeholder.
3. Enter the source information for the citation.

You can combine Steps 2 and 3, where you insert the citation placeholder and enter the source information at once. Or, you can insert the citation placeholder as you write and then enter the source information for the citation at a later time. While creating the research paper in this module, you will use both methods.

To Change the Bibliography Style

1 CHANGE DOCUMENT SETTINGS | 2 CREATE HEADER | 3 TYPE RESEARCH PAPER WITH CITATIONS
4 CREATE ALPHABETICAL WORKS CITED | 5 PROOFREAD & REVISE RESEARCH PAPER

The first step in inserting a citation is to be sure the citations and sources will be formatted using the correct documentation style, called the bibliography style in Word. *Why? You want to ensure that Word is using the MLA documentation style for this paper.* The following steps change the specified documentation style.

1

- Click References on the ribbon to display the References tab.
- Click the Bibliography Style arrow (References tab | Citations & Bibliography group) to display the Bibliography Style gallery, which lists predefined documentation styles (Figure 2–29).

2

- Click 'MLA Seventh Edition' in the Bibliography Style gallery to change the documentation style to MLA.

Q&A

What if I am using a different edition of a documentation style shown in the Bibliography Style gallery?
Select the closest one and then, if necessary, perform necessary edits before submitting the paper.

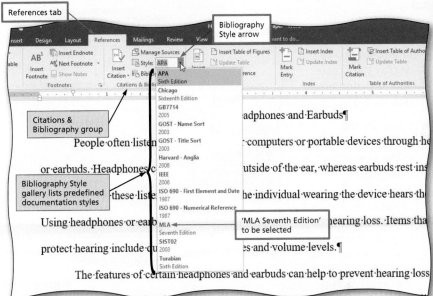

Figure 2–29

What details are required for sources?
During your research, be sure to record essential publication information about each of your sources. Following is a sample list of types of required information for the MLA documentation style.

- Book: full name of author(s), complete title of book, edition (if available), volume (if available), publication city, publisher name, publication year, and publication medium

- Magazine: full name of author(s), complete title of article, magazine title, issue number (if available), date of magazine, page numbers of article, publication medium, and date viewed (if medium is a website)

- Website: full name of author(s), title of website, website publisher or sponsor (if none, write N.p.), publication date (if none, write n.d.), publication medium, and date viewed

CONSIDER THIS

To Insert a Citation and Create Its Source

1 CHANGE DOCUMENT SETTINGS | 2 CREATE HEADER | **3 TYPE RESEARCH PAPER WITH CITATIONS**
4 CREATE ALPHABETICAL WORKS CITED | 5 PROOFREAD & REVISE RESEARCH PAPER

With the documentation style selected, the next task is to insert a citation at the location of the insertion point and enter the source information for the citation. You can accomplish these steps at once by instructing Word to add a new source. The following steps add a new source for a magazine (periodical) article on the web. *Why? The material preceding the insertion point was summarized from an online magazine article.*

1

- With the insertion point at the location for the citation (as shown in Figure 2–28), click the Insert Citation button (References tab | Citations & Bibliography group) to display the Insert Citation menu (Figure 2–30).

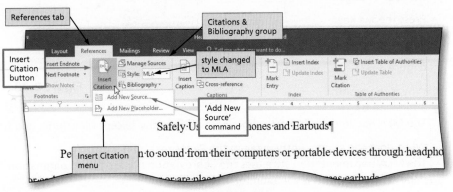

Figure 2–30

2

- Click 'Add New Source' on the Insert Citation menu to display the Create Source dialog box (Figure 2–31).

Q&A What are the Bibliography Fields in the Create Source dialog box?
A **field** is a placeholder for data whose contents can change. You enter data in some fields; Word supplies data for others. In this case, you enter the contents of the fields for a particular source, for example, the author name in the Author field.

Figure 2–31

 Experiment

- Click the 'Type of Source' arrow and then click one of the source types in the list, so that you can see how the list of fields changes to reflect the type of source you selected.

3

- If necessary, click the 'Type of Source' arrow (Create Source dialog box) and then click 'Article in a Periodical', so that the list shows fields required for a magazine (periodical).

- Click the Author text box. Type **Tu, Mingzhu Lin** as the author.

- Click the Title text box. Type **Headphones and Earbuds** as the article title.

- Press the TAB key and then type **Technology and Trends Today** as the periodical title.

- Press the TAB key and then type **2017** as the year.

- Press the TAB key and then type **Aug.** as the month.

- Press the TAB key twice and then type **n. pag.** as the number of pages.

- Press the TAB key and then type **Web** as the medium (Figure 2–32).

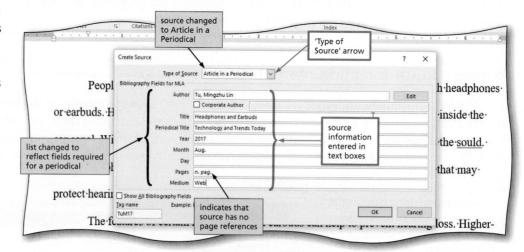

Figure 2–32

Q&A Why is the month abbreviated?
The MLA documentation style abbreviates all months, except May, June, and July, when they appear in a source.

What does the n. pag. entry mean in the Pages text box?
The MLA documentation style uses the abbreviation n. pag. for no pagination, which indicates the source has no page references. This is common for web sources.

4

- Place a check mark in the 'Show All Bibliography Fields' check box so that Word displays all fields available for the selected source, including the date viewed (accessed) fields.

- If necessary, scroll to the bottom of the Bibliography Fields list to display the date viewed (accessed) fields.

- Click the Year Accessed text box. Type **2017** as the year.

- Press the TAB key and then type **Oct.** as the month accessed.

- Press the TAB key and then type **3** as the day accessed (Figure 2–33).

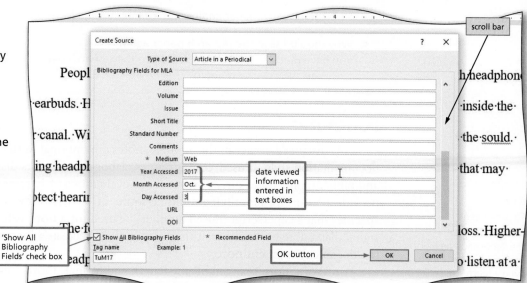

Figure 2–33

Q&A What if some of the text boxes disappear as I enter the fields?
With the 'Show All Bibliography Fields' check box selected, the dialog box may not be able to display all fields at the same time. In this case, some may scroll up off the screen.

5

- Click the OK button to close the dialog box, create the source, and insert the citation in the document at the location of the insertion point.
- Press the END key to move the insertion point to the end of the line, if necessary, which also deselects the citation.
- Press the PERIOD key to end the sentence (Figure 2–34).

Figure 2–34

To Enter More Text

The next task is to continue typing text in the research paper up to the location of the footnote. The following steps enter this text.

1 Press the SPACEBAR.

2 Type the next sentences (Figure 2–35): **Properly designed headphones**

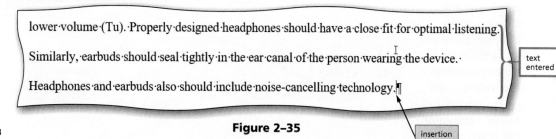

Figure 2–35

should have a close fit for optimal listening. Similarly, earbuds should seal tightly in the ear canal of the person wearing the device. Headphones and earbuds also should include noise-cancelling technology.

3 Save the research paper again on the same storage location with the same file name.

Q&A | Why should I save the research paper again?
You have made several modifications to the research paper since you last saved it; thus, you should save it again.

Footnotes

As discussed earlier in this module, notes are optional in the MLA documentation style. If used, content notes elaborate on points discussed in the paper, and bibliographic notes direct the reader to evaluations of statements in a source or provide a means for identifying multiple sources. The MLA documentation style specifies that a superscript (raised number) be used for a **note reference mark** to signal that a note exists either at the bottom of the page as a **footnote** or at the end of the document as an **endnote**.

In Word, **note text** can be any length and format. Word automatically numbers notes sequentially by placing a note reference mark both in the body of the document and to the left of the note text. If you insert, rearrange, or remove notes, Word renumbers any subsequent note reference marks according to their new sequence in the document.

BTW
Touch Screen Differences
The Office and Windows interfaces may vary if you are using a touch screen. For this reason, you might notice that the function or appearance of your touch screen differs slightly from this module's presentation.

To Insert a Footnote Reference Mark

1 CHANGE DOCUMENT SETTINGS | 2 CREATE HEADER | 3 TYPE RESEARCH PAPER WITH CITATIONS
4 CREATE ALPHABETICAL WORKS CITED | 5 PROOFREAD & REVISE RESEARCH PAPER

The following step inserts a footnote reference mark in the document at the location of the insertion point and at the location where the footnote text will be typed. *Why? You will insert a content note elaborating on noise-cancelling technology, which you want to position as a footnote.*

1
• With the insertion point positioned as shown in Figure 2–35, click the Insert Footnote button (References tab | Footnotes group) to display a note reference mark (a superscripted 1) in two places: (1) in the document window at the location of the insertion point and (2) at the bottom of the page where the footnote will be positioned, just below a separator line (Figure 2–36).

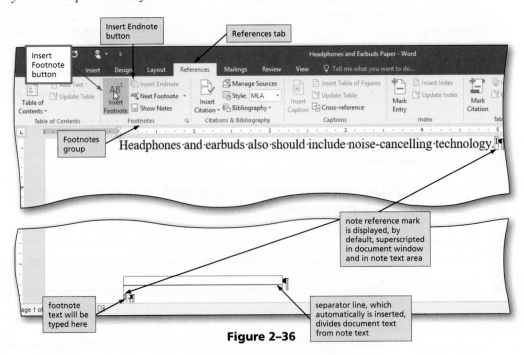

Figure 2–36

Q&A What if I wanted notes to be positioned as endnotes instead of as footnotes?

You would click the Insert Endnote button (References tab | Footnotes group), which places the separator line and the endnote text at the end of the document, instead of the bottom of the page containing the reference.

Other Ways

1. Press ALT+CTRL+F

To Enter Footnote Text

The following step types the footnote text to the right of the note reference mark below the separator line.

1 Type the footnote text up to the citation (shown in Figure 2–37): `Gupta and Padro state that effective noise-cancelling technology reduces the interference of sounds from the surrounding environment, reducing the volume level required by headphones and earbuds` and then press the SPACEBAR.

To Insert a Citation Placeholder

1 CHANGE DOCUMENT SETTINGS | 2 CREATE HEADER | 3 TYPE RESEARCH PAPER WITH CITATIONS
4 CREATE ALPHABETICAL WORKS CITED | 5 PROOFREAD & REVISE RESEARCH PAPER

Earlier in this module, you inserted a citation and its source at once. In Word, you also can insert a citation without entering the source information. *Why? Sometimes, you may not have the source information readily available and would prefer to enter it at a later time.*

The following steps insert a citation placeholder in the footnote, so that you can enter the source information later.

1

- With the insertion point positioned as shown in Figure 2–37, click the Insert Citation button (References tab | Citations & Bibliography group) to display the Insert Citation menu (Figure 2–37).

Figure 2–37

2

Figure 2–38

- Click 'Add New Placeholder' on the Insert Citation menu to display the Placeholder Name dialog box.
- Type **Gupta** as the tag name for the source (Figure 2–38).

Q&A | What is a tag name?

A tag name is an identifier that links a citation to a source. Word automatically creates a tag name when you enter a source. When you create a citation placeholder, enter a meaningful tag name, which will appear in the citation placeholder until you edit the source.

3

- Click the OK button (Placeholder Name dialog box) to close the dialog box and insert the entered tag name in the citation placeholder in the document (shown in Figure 2–39).
- Press the PERIOD key to end the sentence.

Q&A | What if the citation is in the wrong location?

Click the citation to select it and then drag the citation tab (on the upper-left corner of the selected citation) to any location in the document.

Footnote Text Style

When you insert a footnote, Word formats it using the Footnote Text style, which does not adhere to the MLA documentation style. For example, notice in Figure 2–37 that the footnote text is single-spaced, left-aligned, and a smaller font size than the text in the research paper. According to the MLA documentation style, notes should be formatted like all other paragraphs in the paper.

You could change the paragraph formatting of the footnote text to first-line indent and double-spacing and then change the font size from 10 to 12 point. If you use this technique, however, you will need to change the format of the footnote text for each footnote you enter into the document.

A more efficient technique is to modify the format of the Footnote Text style so that every footnote you enter in the document will use the formats defined in this style.

To Modify a Style Using a Shortcut Menu

1 CHANGE DOCUMENT SETTINGS | 2 CREATE HEADER | 3 TYPE RESEARCH PAPER WITH CITATIONS
4 CREATE ALPHABETICAL WORKS CITED | 5 PROOFREAD & REVISE RESEARCH PAPER

The Footnote Text style specifies left-aligned single-spaced paragraphs with a 10-point font size for text. The following steps modify the Footnote Text style. *Why? To meet MLA documentation style, the footnotes should be double-spaced with a first-line indent and a 12-point font size for text.*

1

- Right-click the note text in the footnote to display a shortcut menu related to footnotes (Figure 2–39).

Gupta and Padro state that effective noise-cancelling technology reduces the interference of sounds from the surrounding environment, reducing the volume level required by headphones and earbuds (Gupta).

Figure 2–39

2

- Click Style on the shortcut menu to display the Style dialog box. If necessary, click the Category arrow, click All styles in the Category list, and then click Footnote Text in the Styles list to select the style to modify.

- Click the Modify button (Style dialog box) to display the Modify Style dialog box.

- Click the Font Size arrow (Modify Style dialog box) to display the Font Size list and then click 12 in the Font Size list to change the font size.

- Click the Double Space button to change the line spacing.

- Click the Format button to display the Format menu (Figure 2–40).

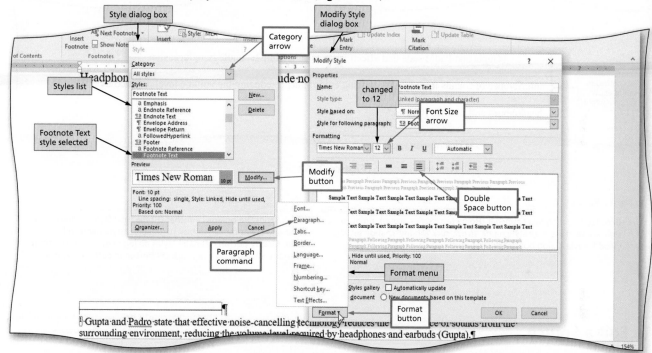

Figure 2–40

3

- Click Paragraph on the Format menu (Modify Style dialog box) to display the Paragraph dialog box.

- Click the Special arrow in the Indentation area (Paragraph dialog box) and then click First line (Figure 2–41).

Figure 2–41

4

- Click the OK button (Paragraph dialog box) to close the dialog box.
- Click the OK button (Modify Style dialog box) to close the dialog box.
- Click the Apply button (Style dialog box) to apply the style changes to the footnote text (Figure 2–42).

Q&A Will all footnotes use this modified style?
Yes. Any future footnotes entered in the document will use a 12-point font with the paragraphs first-line indented and double-spaced.

Footnote Text style modified to match research paper paragraphs

¶ Gupta and Padro state that effective noise-cancelling technology reduces the interference of sounds from the surrounding environment, reducing the volume level required by headphones and earbuds (Gupta).¶

Page 1 of 1   175 words

Figure 2–42

Other Ways

1. Click Styles Dialog Box Launcher (Home tab | Styles group), point to style name in list, click style name arrow, click Modify, change settings (Modify Style dialog box), click OK button

2. Click Styles Dialog Box Launcher (Home tab | Styles group), click Manage Styles button in task pane, select style name in list, click Modify button (Manage Styles dialog box), change settings (Modify Style dialog box), click OK button in each dialog box

---

1 CHANGE DOCUMENT SETTINGS | 2 CREATE HEADER | 3 TYPE RESEARCH PAPER WITH CITATIONS
4 CREATE ALPHABETICAL WORKS CITED | 5 PROOFREAD & REVISE RESEARCH PAPER

To Edit a Source

When you typed the footnote text for this research paper, you inserted a citation placeholder for the source. The following steps edit a source. *Why? Assume you now have the source information and are ready to enter it.*

1

- Click somewhere in the citation placeholder to be edited, in this case (Gupta), to select the citation placeholder.

- Click the Citation Options arrow to display the Citation Options menu (Figure 2–43).

Q&A What is the purpose of the tab to the left of the selected citation?
If, for some reason, you wanted to move a citation to a different location in the document, you would select the citation and then drag the citation tab to the desired location.

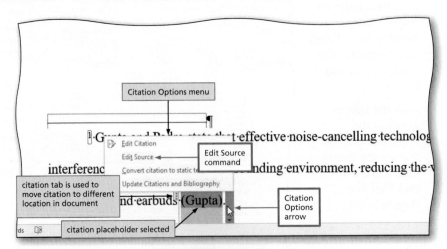

Citation Options menu

Edit Citation
Edit Source — Edit Source command
Convert citation to static te...
Update Citations and Bibliography

citation tab is used to move citation to different location in document

...effective noise-cancelling technolog...
...nding environment, reducing the...

nd earbuds (Gupta).

Citation Options arrow

citation placeholder selected

Figure 2–43

2

- Click Edit Source on the Citation Options menu to display the Edit Source dialog box.

- If necessary, click the 'Type of Source' arrow (Edit Source dialog box) and then click Book, so that the list shows fields required for a book.

- Because this source has two authors, click the Edit button to display the Edit Name dialog box, which assists you with entering multiple author names.

- Type `Gupta` as the first author's last name; press the TAB key and then type `Elena` as the first name; press the TAB key and then type `Maia` as the middle name (Figure 2–44).

Q&A What if I already know how to punctuate the author entry properly?
You can enter the name directly in the Author box.

Figure 2–44

3

- Click the Add button (Edit Name dialog box) to add the first author name to the Names list.

- Type `Padro` as the second author's last name; press the TAB key and then type `Adelbert` as the first name; press the TAB key and then type `Luis` as the middle name.

- Click the Add button (Edit Name dialog box) to add the second author name to the Names list (Figure 2–45).

Figure 2–45

4

- Click the OK button (Edit Name dialog box) to add the author names that appear in the Names list to the Author box in the Edit Source dialog box.

- Click the Title text box (Edit Source dialog box). Type **Hearing Protection Methods** as the book title.

- Press the TAB key and then type **2017** as the year.

- Press the TAB key and then type **Orlando** as the city.

- Press the TAB key and then type **Palm Press** as the publisher.

- Press the TAB key and then type **Print** as the medium (Figure 2–46).

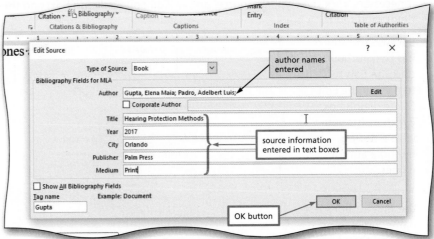

Figure 2–46

5

- Click the OK button to close the dialog box, create the source, and update the citation to display both author last names (shown in Figure 2–47).

Other Ways

1. Click Manage Sources button (References tab | Citations & Bibliography group), click placeholder source in Current List, click Edit button (Source Manager dialog box)

To Edit a Citation

1 CHANGE DOCUMENT SETTINGS | 2 CREATE HEADER | 3 TYPE RESEARCH PAPER WITH CITATIONS
4 CREATE ALPHABETICAL WORKS CITED | 5 PROOFREAD & REVISE RESEARCH PAPER

In the MLA documentation style, if a source has page numbers, you should include them in the citation. Thus, Word provides a means to enter the page numbers to be displayed in the citation. Also, if you reference the author's name in the text, you should not list it again in the parenthetical citation. Instead, just list the page number(s) in the citation. To do this, you instruct Word to suppress author and title. *Why? If you suppress the author, Word automatically displays the title, so you need to suppress both the author and title if you want just the page number(s) to be displayed.* The following steps edit the citation, suppressing the author and title but displaying the page numbers.

1

- If necessary, click somewhere in the citation to be edited, in this case somewhere in (Gupta and Padro), which selects the citation and displays the Citation Options arrow.

- Click the Citation Options arrow to display the Citation Options menu (Figure 2–47).

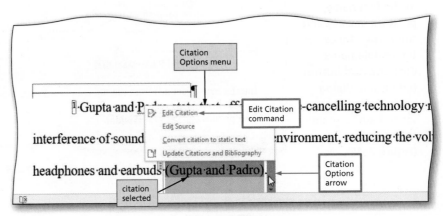

Figure 2–47

2

- Click Edit Citation on the Citation Options menu to display the Edit Citation dialog box.

- Type **75-78** in the Pages text box (Edit Citation dialog box).

- Click the Author check box to place a check mark in it.

- Click the Title check box to place a check mark in it (Figure 2–48).

Figure 2–48

3

- Click the OK button to close the dialog box, remove the author names from the citation in the footnote, suppress the title from showing, and add page numbers to the citation.

- Press the END key to move the insertion point to the end of the line, which also deselects the citation (Figure 2–49).

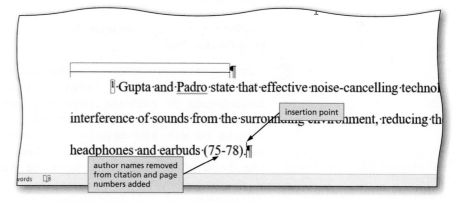

Figure 2–49

Working with Footnotes and Endnotes

You edit footnote text just as you edit any other text in the document. To delete or move a note reference mark, however, the insertion point must be in the document text (not in the footnote text).

To delete a note, select the note reference mark in the document text (not in the footnote text) by dragging through the note reference mark and then click the Cut button (Home tab | Clipboard group). Or, click immediately to the right of the note reference mark in the document text and then press the BACKSPACE key twice, or click immediately to the left of the note reference mark in the document text and then press the DELETE key twice.

To move a note to a different location in a document, select the note reference mark in the document text (not in the footnote text), click the Cut button (Home tab | Clipboard group), click the location where you want to move the note, and then click the Paste button (Home tab | Clipboard group). When you move or delete notes, Word automatically renumbers any remaining notes in the correct sequence.

If you are using a mouse and position the pointer on the note reference mark in the document text, the note text is displayed above the note reference mark as a ScreenTip. To remove the ScreenTip, move the pointer.

If, for some reason, you wanted to change the format of note reference marks in footnotes or endnotes (i.e., from 1, 2, 3 to A, B, C), you would click the Footnote & Endnote Dialog Box Launcher (References tab | Footnotes group) to display the Footnote and Endnote dialog box, click the Number format arrow (Footnote and Endnote dialog box), click the desired number format in the list, and then click the Apply button.

BTW

Footnote and Endnote Location
You can change the location of footnotes from the bottom of the page to the end of the text by clicking the Footnote & Endnote Dialog Box Launcher (References tab | Footnotes group), clicking the Footnotes arrow (Footnote and Endnote dialog box), and then clicking Below text. Similarly, clicking the Endnotes arrow (Footnote and Endnote dialog box) enables you to change the location of endnotes from the end of the document to the end of a section.

If, for some reason, you wanted to change a footnote number, you would click the Footnote & Endnote Dialog Box Launcher (References tab | Footnotes group) to display the Footnote and Endnote dialog box, enter the desired number in the Start at box, and then click the Apply button (Footnote and Endnote dialog box).

If, for some reason, you wanted to convert footnotes to endnotes, you would click the Footnote & Endnote Dialog Box Launcher (References tab | Footnotes group) to display the Footnote and Endnote dialog box, click the Convert button (Footnote and Endnote dialog box), select the 'Convert all footnotes to endnotes' option button (Convert Notes dialog box), click the OK button (Convert Notes dialog box), and then click the Close button (Footnote and Endnote dialog box).

To Enter More Text

The next task is to continue typing text in the body of the research paper. The following steps enter this text.

1 Position the insertion point after the note reference mark in the document and then press the ENTER key.

2 Type the first three sentences in the third paragraph of the research paper (shown in Figure 2–50): **The volume level of the sound that transmits from headphones or earbuds into the ear of a person wearing this type of device has been linked to hearing loss. The volume should be set low enough that other people nearby cannot hear the sound being transmitted. The quieter the sounds, the less possibility of hearing damage.**

To Count Words

1 CHANGE DOCUMENT SETTINGS | 2 CREATE HEADER | 3 TYPE RESEARCH PAPER WITH CITATIONS
4 CREATE ALPHABETICAL WORKS CITED | 5 PROOFREAD & REVISE RESEARCH PAPER

Often when you write papers, you are required to compose the papers with a minimum number of words. The minimum requirement for the research paper in this module is 275 words. You can look on the status bar and see the total number of words thus far in a document. For example, Figure 2–50 shows the research paper has 231 words, but you are not sure if that count includes the words in your footnote. The following steps display the Word Count dialog box. **Why?** *You want to verify that the footnote text is included in the count.*

1
• Click the Word Count indicator on the status bar to display the Word Count dialog box.

• If necessary, place a check mark in the 'Include textboxes, footnotes and endnotes' check box (Word Count dialog box) (Figure 2–50).

Why do the statistics in my Word Count dialog box differ from those in Figure 2–50?
Depending on the accuracy of your typing, your statistics may differ.

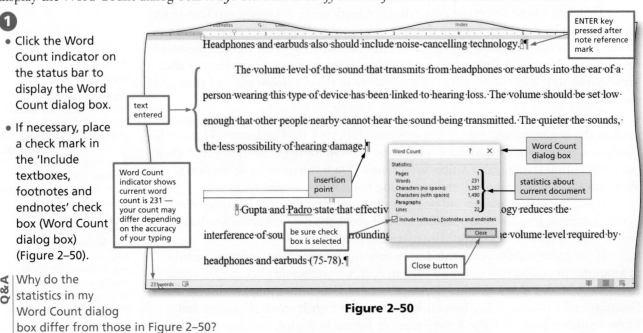

Figure 2–50

2

- Click the Close button (Word Count dialog box) to close the dialog box.

Q&A Can I display statistics for just a section of the document?
Yes. Select the section and then click the Word Count indicator on the status bar to display statistics about the selected text.

Other Ways

1. Click Word Count button (Review tab | Proofing group)   2. Press CTRL+SHIFT+G

Automatic Page Breaks

As you type documents that exceed one page, Word automatically inserts page breaks, called **automatic page breaks** or **soft page breaks**, when it determines the text has filled one page according to paper size, margin settings, line spacing, and other settings. If you add text, delete text, or modify text on a page, Word recalculates the location of automatic page breaks and adjusts them accordingly.

Word performs page recalculation between the keystrokes, that is, in between the pauses in your typing. Thus, Word refers to the automatic page break task as **background repagination**. An automatic page break will occur in the next set of steps.

To Enter More Text and Insert a Citation Placeholder

The next task is to type the remainder of the third paragraph in the body of the research paper. The following steps enter this text and a citation placeholder at the end of the paragraph.

1 With the insertion point positioned at the end of the third sentence in the third paragraph, as shown in Figure 2–50, press the SPACEBAR.

2 Type the rest of the third paragraph: **Further, listening at a higher volume for extended periods of time could be unsafe. One expert suggests people should listen at only 30 percent maximum** and then press the SPACEBAR.

Q&A Why does the text move from the second page to the first page as I am typing?
Word, by default, will not allow the first line of a paragraph to be by itself at the bottom of a page (an **orphan**) or the last line of a paragraph to be by itself at the top of a page (a **widow**). As you type, Word adjusts the placement of the paragraph to avoid orphans and widows.

3 Click the Insert Citation button (References tab | Citations & Bibliography group) to display the Insert Citation menu. Click 'Add New Placeholder' on the Insert Citation menu to display the Placeholder Name dialog box.

4 Type **Chamberlain** as the tag name for the source.

5 Click the OK button (Placeholder Name dialog box) to close the dialog box and insert the tag name in the citation placeholder (shown in Figure 2–51).

6 Press the PERIOD key to end the sentence.

BTW
Page Break Locations
As you type, your page break may occur at different locations depending on Word settings and the type of printer connected to the computer.

To Hide and Show White Space

With the page break and header, it is difficult to see the entire third paragraph at once on the screen. With the screen in Print Layout view, you can hide white space, which is the space that is displayed at the top and bottom of pages (including headers and footers) and also the space between pages. The following steps hide white space, if your screen displays it, and then shows white space. *Why? You want to see as much of the third paragraph as possible at once, which spans the bottom of the first page and the top of the second page.*

1

- Position the pointer in the document window in the space between pages so that the pointer changes to a 'Hide White Space' button (Figure 2–51).

Q&A What if I am using a touch screen?
Proceed to step 2.

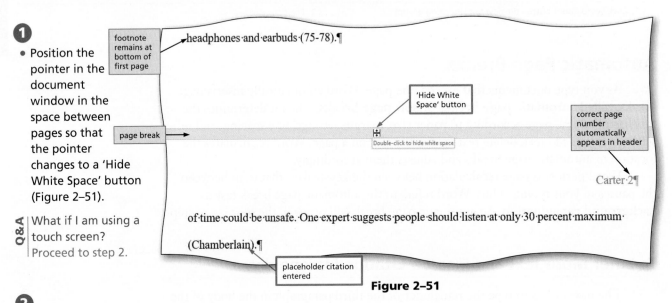

Figure 2–51

2

- Double-click while the pointer is a 'Hide White Space' button to hide white space.

Q&A What if I am using a touch screen?
Double-tap in the space between pages.

Does hiding white space have any effect on the printed document?
No.

3

- Position the pointer in the document window on the page break between pages so that the pointer changes to a 'Show White Space' button (Figure 2–52).

Figure 2–52

4

- Double-click while the pointer is a 'Show White Space' button to show white space.

Q&A | What if I am using a touch screen?
Double-tap the page break.

Other Ways

1. Click File on ribbon, click Options tab in Backstage view, click Display in left pane (Word Options dialog box), remove or select check mark from 'Show white space between pages in Print Layout view' check box, click OK button

---

To Edit a Source

When you typed the third paragraph of the research paper, you inserted a citation placeholder, Chamberlain, for the source. You now have the source information, which is for a website, and are ready to enter it. The following steps edit the source for the Chamberlain citation placeholder.

1 Click somewhere in the citation placeholder to be edited, in this case (Chamberlain), to select the citation placeholder.

2 Click the Citation Options arrow to display the Citation Options menu.

3 Click Edit Source on the Citation Options menu to display the Edit Source dialog box.

4 If necessary, click the 'Type of Source' arrow (Edit Source dialog box); scroll to and then click Web site, so that the list shows fields required for a Web site.

5 Place a check mark in the 'Show All Bibliography Fields' check box to display more fields related to Web sites.

6 Click the Author text box. Type **Chamberlain, Megan Lynn** as the author.

7 Click the 'Name of Web Page' text box. Type **Understanding How Volume Levels Affect Hearing** as the webpage name.

8 Click the Production Company text box. Type **Course Technology** as the production company.

9 Click the Year Accessed text box. Type **2017** as the year accessed (Figure 2–53).

Figure 2–53

10 Press the TAB key and then type `Sept.` as the month accessed.

11 Press the TAB key and then type `16` as the day accessed.

12 Press the TAB key as many times as necessary to move the insertion point to the Medium text box and then type `Web` as the Medium.

Q&A Do I need to enter a web address (URL)?
The latest MLA documentation style update does not require the web address in the source.

13 Click the OK button to close the dialog box and create the source.

BTW
Organizing Files and Folders
You should organize and store files in folders so that you easily can find the files later. For example, if you are taking an introductory technology class called CIS 101, a good practice would be to save all Word files in a Word folder in a CIS 101 folder. For a discussion of folders and detailed examples of creating folders, refer to the Office and Windows module at the beginning of this book.

To Enter More Text

The next task is to type the last paragraph of text in the research paper. The following steps enter this text.

1 Press the END key to position the insertion point at the end of the third paragraph and then press the ENTER key.

2 Type the last paragraph of the research paper (Figure 2–54): `More and more people are using headphones and earbuds with their computers and portable devices. Using high-quality listening devices and lowering the volume can help to lessen potential hearing loss from the use of headphones and earbuds.`

3 Save the research paper again on the same storage location with the same file name.

Figure 2–54

Break Point: If you wish to take a break, this is a good place to do so. You can exit Word now. To resume at a later time, run Word, open the file called Headphones and Earbuds Paper, and continue following the steps from this location forward. For a detailed example of exiting Word, running Word, and opening a file, refer to the Office and Windows module at the beginning of the book.

Creating an Alphabetical Works Cited Page

According to the MLA documentation style, the **works cited page** is a list of sources that are referenced directly in a research paper. You place the list on a separate numbered page with the title, Works Cited, centered one inch from the top margin. The works are to be alphabetized by the author's last name or, if the work has no author, by the work's title. The first line of each entry begins at the left margin. Indent subsequent lines of the same entry one-half inch from the left margin.

What is a bibliography?

A **bibliography** is an alphabetical list of sources referenced in a paper. Whereas the text of the research paper contains brief references to the source (the citations), the bibliography lists all publication information about the source. Documentation styles differ significantly in their guidelines for preparing a bibliography. Each style identifies formats for various sources, including books, magazines, pamphlets, newspapers, websites, television programs, paintings, maps, advertisements, letters, memos, and much more. You can find information about various styles and their guidelines in printed style guides and on the web.

To Page Break Manually

1 CHANGE DOCUMENT SETTINGS | 2 CREATE HEADER | 3 TYPE RESEARCH PAPER WITH CITATIONS
4 CREATE ALPHABETICAL WORKS CITED | **5 PROOFREAD & REVISE RESEARCH PAPER**

The next step is to insert a manual page break following the body of the research paper. *Why? According to the MLA documentation style, the works cited are to be displayed on a separate numbered page.*

A **manual page break**, or **hard page break**, is one that you force into the document at a specific location. Word never moves or adjusts manual page breaks. Word, however, does adjust any automatic page breaks that follow a manual page break. Word inserts manual page breaks immediately above or to the left of the location of the insertion point. The following step inserts a manual page break after the text of the research paper.

1

- Verify that the insertion point is positioned at the end of the text of the research paper, as shown in Figure 2–54.

- Click Insert on the ribbon to display the Insert tab.

- Click the 'Insert a Page Break' button (Insert tab | Pages group) to insert a manual page break immediately to the left of the insertion point and position the insertion point immediately below the manual page break (Figure 2–55).

Figure 2–55

Other Ways

1. Press CTRL+ENTER

To Apply a Style

The works cited title is to be centered between the margins of the paper. If you simply issue the Center command, the title will not be centered properly. *Why? It will be to the right of the center point because earlier you set the first-line indent for paragraphs to one-half inch.*

To properly center the title of the works cited page, you could drag the 'First Line Indent' marker back to the left margin before centering the paragraph, or you could apply the Normal style to the location of the insertion point. Recall that you modified the Normal style for this document to 12-point Times New Roman with double-spaced, left-aligned paragraphs that have no space after the paragraphs.

To apply a style to a paragraph, first position the insertion point in the paragraph and then apply the style. The following step applies the modified Normal style to the location of the insertion point.

1

- Click Home on the ribbon to display the Home tab.

- With the insertion point on the paragraph mark at the top of page 3 (as shown in Figure 2–55) even if Normal is selected, click Normal in the Styles gallery (Home tab | Styles group) to apply the Normal style to the paragraph containing the insertion point (Figure 2–56).

Figure 2–56

Other Ways

1. Click Styles Dialog Box Launcher (Home tab | Styles group), select desired style in Styles task pane

2. Press CTRL+SHIFT+S, click Style Name arrow in Apply Styles task pane, select desired style in list

To Center Text

The next task is to enter the title, Works Cited, centered between the margins of the paper. The following steps use a keyboard shortcut to format the title.

1 Press CTRL+E to center the paragraph mark.

2 Type **Works Cited** as the title.

3 Press the ENTER key.

4 Press CTRL+L to left-align the paragraph mark (shown in Figure 2–57).

To Create a Bibliographical List

While typing the research paper, you created several citations and their sources. The next task is to use Word to format the list of sources and alphabetize them in a **bibliographical list**. *Why? Word can create a bibliographical list with each element of the source placed in its correct position with proper punctuation, according to the specified style, saving you time looking up style guidelines. For example, in this research paper, the book source will list, in* *this order; the author name(s), book title, publisher city, publishing company name, and publication year with the correct punctuation between each element according to the MLA documentation style.* The following steps create an MLA-styled bibliographical list from the sources previously entered.

1

- Click References on the ribbon to display the References tab.

- With the insertion point positioned as shown in Figure 2–57, click the Bibliography button (References tab | Citations & Bibliography group) to display the Bibliography gallery (Figure 2–57).

Q&A Will I select the Works Cited option from the Bibliography gallery? No. The title it inserts is not formatted according to the MLA documentation style. Thus, you will use the Insert Bibliography command instead.

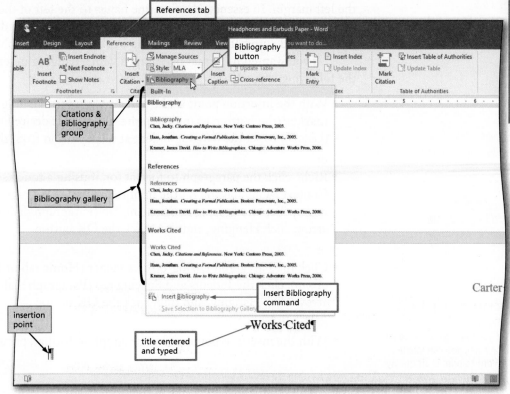

Figure 2–57

2

- Click Insert Bibliography in the Bibliography gallery to insert a list of sources at the location of the insertion point.

- If necessary, scroll to display the entire list of sources in the document window (Figure 2–58).

Q&A What is the n.d. in the first work? The MLA documentation style uses the abbreviation n.d. for no date (for example, no date appears on the webpage).

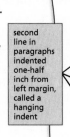

Figure 2–58

- Save the research paper again on the same storage location with the same file name.

To Format Paragraphs with a Hanging Indent

Notice in Figure 2–58 that the first line of each source entry begins at the left margin, and subsequent lines in the same paragraph are indented one-half inch from the left margin. In essence, the first line hangs to the left of the rest of the paragraph; thus, this type of paragraph formatting is called a **hanging indent**. The Bibliography style in Word automatically formats the works cited paragraphs with a hanging indent.

If you wanted to format paragraphs with a hanging indent, you would use one of the following techniques.

- With the insertion point in the paragraph to format, drag the **Hanging Indent marker** (the bottom triangle) on the ruler to the desired mark on the ruler (i.e., .5") to set the hanging indent at that location from the left margin.

or

- Right-click the paragraph to format (or, if using a touch screen, tap the 'Show Context Menu' button on the mini toolbar), click Paragraph on the shortcut menu, click the Indents and Spacing tab (Paragraph dialog box), click the Special arrow, click Hanging, and then click the OK button.

or

- Click the Paragraph Dialog Box Launcher (Home tab or Layout tab | Paragraph group), click the Indents and Spacing tab (Paragraph dialog box), click the Special arrow, click Hanging, and then click the OK button.

or

- With the insertion point in the paragraph to format, press CTRL+T.

BTW
Conserving Ink and Toner
If you want to conserve ink or toner, you can instruct Word to print draft quality documents by clicking File on the ribbon to open the Backstage view, clicking the Options tab in the Backstage view to display the Word Options dialog box, clicking Advanced in the left pane (Word Options dialog box), scrolling to the Print area in the right pane, placing a check mark in the 'Use draft quality' check box, and then clicking the OK button. Then, use the Backstage view to print the document as usual.

Proofreading and Revising the Research Paper

As discussed in Module 1, once you complete a document, you might find it necessary to make changes to it. Before submitting a paper to be graded, you should proofread it. While **proofreading**, ensure all the source information is correct and look for grammatical, typographical, and spelling errors. Also ensure that transitions between sentences flow smoothly and the sentences themselves make sense.

To assist you with the proofreading effort, Word provides several tools. You can go to a page, copy text, find text, replace text, insert a synonym, check spelling and grammar, and look up information. The following pages discuss these tools.

CONSIDER THIS

What should you consider when proofreading and revising a paper?
As you proofread the paper, look for ways to improve it. Check all grammar, spelling, and punctuation. Be sure the text is logical and transitions are smooth. Where necessary, add text, delete text, reword text, and move text to different locations. Ask yourself these questions:

- Does the title suggest the topic?
- Is the thesis clear?
- Is the purpose of the paper clear?
- Does the paper have an introduction, body, and conclusion?
- Does each paragraph in the body relate to the thesis?
- Is the conclusion effective?
- Are sources acknowledged correctly?

To Modify a Source

While proofreading the paper, you notice an error in the magazine title; specifically, the word, and, should be removed. If you modify the contents of any source, the list of sources automatically updates. ***Why?*** *Word automatically updates the contents of fields, and the bibliography is a field.* The following steps delete a word from the title of the magazine article.

①
- Click the Manage Sources button (References tab | Citations & Bibliography group) to display the Source Manager dialog box.
- Click the source you wish to edit in the Current List, in this case the article by Tu, to select the source.
- Click the Edit button (Source Manager dialog box) to display the Edit Source dialog box.
- In the Periodical Title text box, delete the word, and, from the title (Figure 2–59).

Figure 2–59

②
- Click the OK button (Edit Source dialog box) to close the dialog box.
- If a Microsoft Word dialog box appears, click its Yes button to update all occurrences of the source.
- Click the Close button (Source Manager dialog box) to update the list of sources and close the dialog box.

To Update a Field

Depending on settings, the bibliography field may not automatically reflect the edited magazine title. Thus, the following steps update the bibliography field. ***Why?*** *Because the bibliography is a field, you may need to instruct Word to update its contents.*

1

• Right-click anywhere in the bibliography text to display a shortcut menu related to fields (Figure 2–60).

Q&A What if I am using a touch screen?
Press and hold anywhere in the bibliography text and then tap the 'Show Context Menu' button on the mini toolbar.

Figure 2–60

Why are all the words in the bibliography shaded gray?
By default, Word shades selected fields gray.

What if the bibliography field is not shaded gray?
Click File on the ribbon to open the Backstage view, click the Options tab in the Backstage view, click Advanced in the left pane (Word Options dialog box), scroll to the 'Show document content' area, click the Field shading arrow, click When selected, and then click the OK button.

2

• Click Update Field on the shortcut menu to update the selected field (Figure 2–61).

Q&A Can I update all fields in a document at once?
Yes. Select the entire document and then follow these steps.

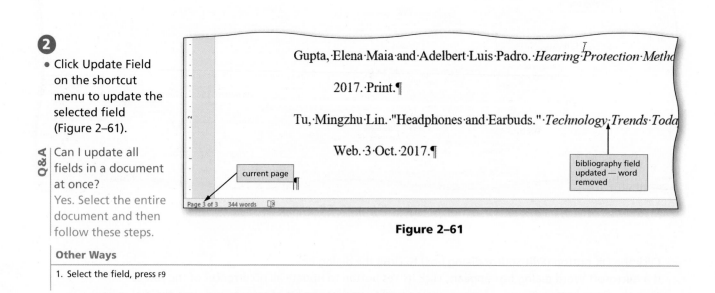

Figure 2–61

Other Ways

1. Select the field, press F9

TO CONVERT A FIELD TO REGULAR TEXT

If, for some reason, you wanted to convert a field, such as the bibliography field, to regular text, you would perform the following steps. Keep in mind, though, once you convert the field to regular text, it no longer is a field that can be updated.

1. Click somewhere in the field to select it, in this case, somewhere in the bibliography.

2. Press CTRL+SHIFT+F9 to convert the selected field to regular text.

To Go to a Page

The next task in revising the paper is to modify text on the second page of the document. *Why? You want to copy text from one location to another on the second page.* You could scroll to the desired location in the document, or you can use the Navigation Pane to browse through pages in a document. The following steps display the top of the second page in the document window and position the insertion point at the beginning of that page.

1

- Click View on the ribbon to display the View tab.

- Place a check mark in the 'Open the Navigation Pane' check box (View tab | Show group) to open the Navigation Pane on the left side of the Word window.

- If necessary, click the Pages tab in the Navigation Pane to display thumbnails of the pages in the document.

- Scroll to, if necessary, and then click the thumbnail of the second page to display the top of the selected page in the top of the document window (Figure 2–62).

Q&A What is the Navigation Pane?
The Navigation Pane is a window that enables you to browse through headings in a document, browse through pages in a document, or search for text in a document.

Figure 2–62

2

- Click the Close button in the Navigation Pane to close the pane.

Other Ways

1. Click Find arrow (Home tab | Editing group), click Go To on Find menu, click Go To tab (Find and Replace dialog box), enter page number, click Go To button

2. Click Page Number indicator on status bar, click Pages tab in Navigation Pane, click thumbnail of desired page (Navigation Pane)

3. Press CTRL+G, enter page number (Find and Replace dialog box), click Go To button

Copying, Cutting, and Pasting

While proofreading the research paper, you decide it would read better if the word, volume, in the second sentence of the last paragraph also appeared after the word, maximum, in the last sentence of the previous paragraph. You could type the word at the desired location, but you decide to use the Office Clipboard. The **Office Clipboard** is a temporary storage area that holds up to 24 items (text or graphics) copied from any Office program. The Office Clipboard works with the copy, cut, and paste commands:

- **Copying** is the process of placing items on the Office Clipboard, leaving the item in the document.

- **Cutting** removes the item from the document before placing it on the Office Clipboard.

- **Pasting** is the process of copying an item from the Office Clipboard into the document at the location of the insertion point.

To Copy and Paste

In the research paper, you copy a word from one location to another. *Why? The sentence reads better with the word, volume, inserted after the word, maximum.* The following steps copy and paste a word.

1

- Select the item to be copied (the word, volume, in this case).

- Click Home on the ribbon to display the Home tab.

- Click the Copy button (Home tab | Clipboard group) to copy the selected item in the document to the Office Clipboard (Figure 2–63).

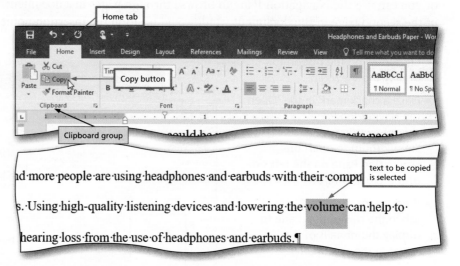

Figure 2–63

2

- Position the insertion point at the location where the item should be pasted (immediately following the space to the right of the word, maximum, in this case) (Figure 2–64).

Figure 2–64

3

- Click the Paste button (Home tab | Clipboard group) to paste the copied item in the document at the location of the insertion point (Figure 2–65).

Q&A

What if I click the Paste arrow by mistake?
Click the Paste arrow again to remove the Paste menu and repeat Step 3.

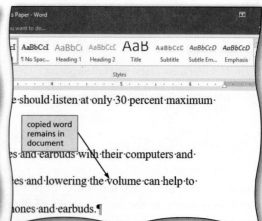

Figure 2–65

Other Ways

1. Click Copy on shortcut menu (or, if using touch, tap Copy on mini toolbar), right-click where item is to be pasted, click 'Keep Source Formatting' in Paste Options area on shortcut menu (or, if using touch, tap Paste on mini toolbar)

2. Select item, press CTRL+C, position insertion point at paste location, press CTRL+V

To Display the Paste Options Menu

When you paste an item or move an item using drag-and-drop editing, which was discussed in the previous module, Word automatically displays a Paste Options button near the pasted or moved text (shown in Figure 2–65). *Why? The Paste Options button allows you to change the format of a pasted item. For example, you can instruct Word to format the pasted item the same way as where it was copied (the source) or format it the same way as where it is being pasted (the destination).* The following steps display the Paste Options menu.

1

• Click the Paste Options button to display the Paste Options menu (Figure 2–66).

Q&A What are the functions of the buttons on the Paste Options menu?

In general, the left button indicates the pasted item should look the same as it did in its original location (the source). The second button formats the pasted text to match the rest of the item where it was pasted (the destination). The third button removes all formatting from the pasted item. The 'Set Default Paste' command displays the Word Options dialog box. Keep in mind that the buttons shown on a Paste Options menu will vary, depending on the item being pasted.

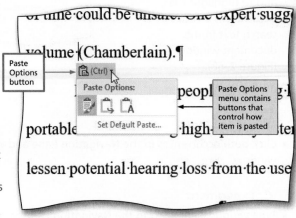

Figure 2–66

2

• Click anywhere to remove the Paste Options menu from the window.

Other Ways

1. CTRL or ESC (to remove the Paste Options menu)

To Find Text

While proofreading the paper, you would like to locate all occurrences of the word, portable. *Why? You are contemplating changing occurrences of this word to the word, mobile.* The following steps find all occurrences of specific text in a document.

1

• Click the Find button (Home tab | Editing group) to display the Navigation Pane.

Q&A What if I am using a touch screen?

Tap the Find button (Home tab | Editing group) and then tap Find on the menu.

• If necessary, click the Results tab in the Navigation Pane, which displays a Search box where you can type text for which you want to search (Figure 2–67).

Figure 2–67

- Type **portable** in the Navigation Pane Search box to display all occurrences of the typed text, called the search text, in the Navigation Pane and to highlight the occurrences of the search text in the document window (Figure 2–68).

Figure 2–68

🔍 **Experiment**

- Click both occurrences in the Navigation Pane and watch Word display the associated text in the document window.

🔍 **Experiment**

- Type various search text in the Navigation Pane Search box, and watch Word both list matches in the Navigation Pane and highlight matches in the document window.
- Click the Close button in the Navigation Pane to close the pane.

Other Ways
1. Click Find arrow (Home tab | Editing group), click Find on Find menu, enter search text in Navigation Pane	2. Click Page Number indicator on status bar, enter search text in Navigation Pane	3. Press CTRL+F, enter search text in Navigation Pane

1 CHANGE DOCUMENT SETTINGS | 2 CREATE HEADER | 3 TYPE RESEARCH PAPER WITH CITATIONS
4 CREATE ALPHABETICAL WORKS CITED | 5 PROOFREAD & REVISE RESEARCH PAPER

To Replace Text

You decide to change all occurrences of the word, portable, to the word, mobile. *Why? The term, mobile devices, is more commonly used than portable devices.* Word's find and replace feature locates each occurrence of a word or phrase and then replaces it with text you specify. The following steps find and replace text.

- Click the Replace button (Home tab \| Editing group) to display the Replace sheet in the Find and Replace dialog box.
- If necessary, type **portable** in the Find what box (Find and Replace dialog box).
- Type **mobile** in the Replace with box (Figure 2–69).

Figure 2–69

2

- Click the Replace All button to instruct Word to replace all occurrences of the Find what text with the Replace with text (Figure 2–70). If Word displays a dialog box asking if you want to continue searching from the beginning of the document, click the Yes button.

Figure 2–70

Q&A Does Word search the entire document?
If the insertion point is at the beginning of the document, Word searches the entire document; otherwise, Word may search from the location of the insertion point to the end of the document and then display a dialog box asking if you want to continue searching from the beginning. You also can search a section of text by selecting the text before clicking the Replace or Replace All button.

3

- Click the OK button (Microsoft Word dialog box) to close the dialog box.
- Click the Close button (Find and Replace dialog box) to close the dialog box.

Other Ways

1. Press CTRL+H

Find and Replace Dialog Box

The Replace All button (Find and Replace dialog box) replaces all occurrences of the Find what text with the Replace with text. In some cases, you may want to replace only certain occurrences of a word or phrase, not all of them. To instruct Word to confirm each change, click the Find Next button (Find and Replace dialog box) (shown in Figure 2–70), instead of the Replace All button. When Word locates an occurrence of the text, it pauses and waits for you to click either the Replace button or the Find Next button. Clicking the Replace button changes the text; clicking the Find Next button instructs Word to disregard the replacement and look for the next occurrence of the Find what text.

If you accidentally replace the wrong text, you can undo a replacement by clicking the Undo button on the Quick Access Toolbar. If you used the Replace All button, Word undoes all replacements. If you used the Replace button, Word undoes only the most recent replacement.

BTW
Finding Formatting
To search for formatting or a special character, click the More button in the Find and Replace dialog box (shown in Figure 2–69). To find formatting, use the Format button in the Find dialog box. To find a special character, use the Special button.

To Find and Insert a Synonym

1 CHANGE DOCUMENT SETTINGS | 2 CREATE HEADER | 3 TYPE RESEARCH PAPER WITH CITATIONS
4 CREATE ALPHABETICAL WORKS CITED | 5 PROOFREAD & REVISE RESEARCH PAPER

In this project, you would like a synonym for the word, lessen, in the last paragraph of the research paper. *Why? When writing, you may discover that you used the same word in multiple locations or that a word you used was not quite appropriate, which is the case here.* In these instances, you will want to look up a **synonym**, or a word similar in meaning, to the duplicate or inappropriate word. A **thesaurus** is a book of synonyms. Word provides synonyms and a thesaurus for your convenience. The following steps find a suitable synonym.

- Right-click the word for which you want to find a synonym (in this case, lessen) to display a shortcut menu.
- Point to Synonyms on the shortcut menu to display a list of synonyms for the word you right-clicked (Figure 2–71).

Q&A What if I am using a touch screen?
Press and hold the word for which you want a synonym, tap the 'Show Context Menu' button on the mini toolbar, and then tap Synonyms on the shortcut menu.

Figure 2–71

- Click the synonym you want (in this case, minimize) on the Synonyms submenu to replace the selected word in the document with the selected synonym (Figure 2–72).

Q&A What if the synonyms list on the shortcut menu does not display a suitable word?
You can display the thesaurus in the Thesaurus task pane by clicking Thesaurus on the Synonyms submenu. The Thesaurus task pane displays a complete thesaurus, in which you can look up synonyms for various meanings of a word. You also can look up an antonym, or word with an opposite meaning.

More and more people are using headphones and earbuds with the mobile devices. Using high-quality listening devices and lowering the vol minimize potential hearing loss from the use of headphones and earbuds.¶

word, lessen, changed to minimize

Figure 2–72

Other Ways

1. Click Thesaurus button (Review tab | Proofing group)
2. Press SHIFT+F7

To Check Spelling and Grammar at Once

1 CHANGE DOCUMENT SETTINGS | 2 CREATE HEADER | 3 TYPE RESEARCH PAPER WITH CITATIONS
4 CREATE ALPHABETICAL WORKS CITED | 5 PROOFREAD & REVISE RESEARCH PAPER

As discussed in Module 1, Word checks spelling and grammar as you type and places a wavy underline below possible spelling or grammar errors. Module 1 illustrated how to check these flagged words immediately. The next steps check spelling and grammar at once. *Why? Some users prefer to wait and check their entire document for spelling and grammar errors at once.*

Note: In the following steps, the word, sound, has been misspelled intentionally as sould to illustrate the use of Word's check spelling and grammar at once feature. If you are completing this project on a computer or mobile device, your research paper may contain different misspelled words, depending on the accuracy of your typing.

1

- Press CTRL+HOME because you want the spelling and grammar check to begin from the top of the document.
- Click Review on the ribbon to display the Review tab.

- Click the 'Spelling & Grammar' button (Review tab | Proofing group) to begin the spelling and grammar check at the location of the insertion point, which, in this case, is at the beginning of the document.

- Click the desired word in the list of suggestions in the Spelling task pane (sound, in this case) (Figure 2–73).

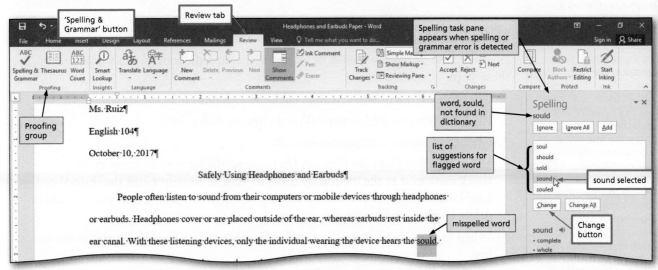

Figure 2–73

2

- With the word, sound, selected in the list of suggestions, click the Change button (Spelling task pane) to change the flagged word to the selected suggestion and then continue the spelling and grammar check until the next error is identified or the end of the document is reached (Figure 2–74).

3

- Because the flagged word is a proper noun and spelled correctly, click the Ignore All button (Spelling task pane) to ignore this and future occurrences of the flagged proper noun and then continue the spelling and grammar check until the next error is identified or the end of the document is reached.

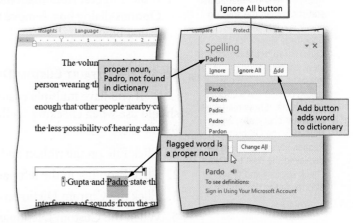

Figure 2–74

4

- When the spelling and grammar check is finished and Word displays a dialog box, click its OK button.

Q&A Can I check spelling of just a section of a document?

Yes, select the text before starting the spelling and grammar check.

Other Ways
1. Click 'Spelling and Grammar Check' icon on status bar   2. Press F7

The Main and Custom Dictionaries

As shown in the previous steps, Word may flag a proper noun as an error because the proper noun is not in its main dictionary. You may want to add some proper nouns that you use repeatedly, such as a company name or employee names, to Word's dictionary. To prevent Word from flagging proper nouns as errors, you can add the proper nouns to the custom dictionary. To add a correctly spelled word to the custom dictionary, click the Add button (Spelling task pane) or right-click the flagged word

BTW
Readability Statistics
You can instruct Word to display readability statistics when it has finished a spelling and grammar check on a document. Three readability statistics presented are the percent of passive sentences, the Flesch Reading Ease score, and the Flesch-Kincaid Grade Level score. The Flesch Reading Ease score uses a 100-point scale to rate the ease with which a reader can understand the text in a document. A higher score means the document is easier to understand. The Flesch-Kincaid Grade Level score rates the text in a document on a U.S. school grade level. For example, a score of 10.0 indicates a student in the tenth grade can understand the material. To show readability statistics when the spelling check is complete, open the Backstage view, click the Options tab in the Backstage view, click Proofing in the left pane (Word Options dialog box), place a check mark in the 'Show readability statistics' check box, and then click the OK button. Readability statistics will be displayed the next time you check spelling and grammar at once in the document.

(or, if using touch, press and hold and then tap 'Show Context Menu' button on the mini toolbar) and then click 'Add to Dictionary' on the shortcut menu. Once you have added a word to the custom dictionary, Word no longer will flag it as an error.

To View or Modify Entries in a Custom Dictionary

To view or modify the list of words in a custom dictionary, you would follow these steps.

1. Click File on the ribbon and then click the Options tab in the Backstage view.
2. Click Proofing in the left pane (Word Options dialog box).
3. Click the Custom Dictionaries button.
4. When Word displays the Custom Dictionaries dialog box, if necessary, place a check mark next to the dictionary name to view or modify. Click the 'Edit Word List' button (Custom Dictionaries dialog box). (In this dialog box, you can add or delete entries to and from the selected custom dictionary.)
5. When finished viewing and/or modifying the list, click the OK button in the dialog box.
6. Click the OK button (Custom Dictionaries dialog box).
7. If the 'Suggest from main dictionary only' check box is selected in the Word Options dialog box, remove the check mark. Click the OK button (Word Options dialog box).

To Set the Default Custom Dictionary

If you have multiple custom dictionaries, you can specify which one Word should use when checking spelling. To set the default custom dictionary, you would follow these steps.

1. Click File on the ribbon and then click the Options tab in the Backstage view.
2. Click Proofing in the left pane (Word Options dialog box).
3. Click the Custom Dictionaries button.
4. When the Custom Dictionaries dialog box is displayed, place a check mark next to the desired dictionary name. Click the Change Default button (Custom Dictionaries dialog box).
5. Click the OK button (Custom Dictionaries dialog box).
6. If the 'Suggest from main dictionary only' check box is selected in the Word Options dialog box, remove the check mark. Click the OK button (Word Options dialog box).

To Look Up Information

1 CHANGE DOCUMENT SETTINGS | 2 CREATE HEADER | 3 TYPE RESEARCH PAPER WITH CITATIONS
4 CREATE ALPHABETICAL WORKS CITED | 5 PROOFREAD & REVISE RESEARCH PAPER

If you are connected to the Internet, you can use the Insights task pane to search through various forms of reference information, including images, on the web and/or look up a definition of a word. The following steps use the Insights task pane to look up a definition of a word. *Why? Assume you want to see some images and know more about the word, headphones.*

1

- Position the insertion point in the word you want to look up (in this case, headphones).
- Click the Smart Lookup button (Review tab | Insights group) to open the Insights task pane (Figure 2–75).

Q&A Why does my Insights task pane look different? Depending on your settings, your Insights task pane may appear different from the figure shown here.

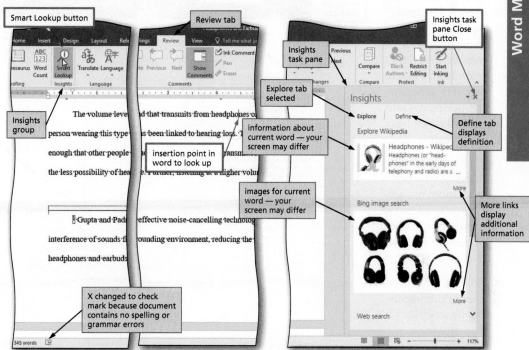

Figure 2–75

Experiment

- With the Explore tab selected in the Insights task pane, scroll through the information and images that appear in the Insights task pane. Click the Define tab in the Insights task pane to see a definition of the current word. Click the Explore tab to redisplay information from the web and images of the current word. Click one of the More links in the Insights task pane to view additional information. Click the Back button at the top of the Insights task pane to return to the previous display.

Q&A Can I copy information from the Insights task pane into my document?
Yes, you can use the Copy and Paste commands. When using Word to insert material from the Insights task pane or any other online reference, however, be careful not to plagiarize.

2

- Click the Close button in the Insights task pane.

Q&A Is the Research task pane from previous Word editions still available?
Yes. While holding down the ALT key, you can click the word you want to look up (such as headphones) to open the Research task pane and display a dictionary entry for the ALT+clicked word.

To Zoom Multiple Pages

1 CHANGE DOCUMENT SETTINGS | 2 CREATE HEADER | 3 TYPE RESEARCH PAPER WITH CITATIONS
4 CREATE ALPHABETICAL WORKS CITED | 5 PROOFREAD & REVISE RESEARCH PAPER

The next steps display multiple pages in the document window at once. *Why? You want to be able to see all pages in the research paper on the screen at the same time. You also hide formatting marks and the rulers so that the display is easier to view.*

1

- Click Home on the ribbon to display the Home tab.
- If the 'Show/Hide ¶' button (Home tab | Paragraph group) is selected, click it to hide formatting marks.
- Click View on the ribbon to display the View tab.

- If the rulers are displayed, click the View Ruler check box (View tab | Show group) to remove the check mark from the check box and remove the horizontal and vertical rulers from the screen.

- Click the Multiple Pages button (View tab | Zoom group) to display all three pages at once in the document window (Figure 2–76).

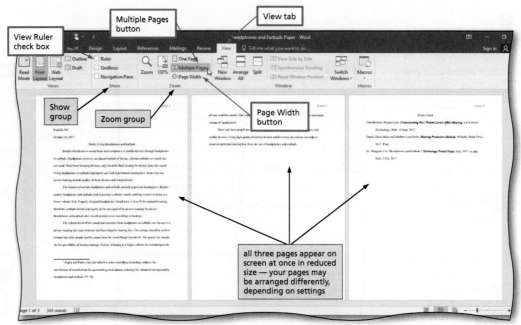

Figure 2–76

Why do the pages appear differently on my screen? Depending on settings, Word may display all the pages as shown in Figure 2–76 or may show the pages differently.

- When finished, click the Page Width button (View tab | Zoom group) to return to the page width zoom.

To Change Read Mode Color

1 CHANGE DOCUMENT SETTINGS | 2 CREATE HEADER | 3 TYPE RESEARCH PAPER WITH CITATIONS
4 CREATE ALPHABETICAL WORKS CITED | 5 PROOFREAD & REVISE RESEARCH PAPER

You would like to read the entire research paper using Read mode but would like to change the background color of the Read mode screen. *Why? You prefer a different background color for reading on the screen.* The following steps change the color of the screen in Read mode.

- Click the Read Mode button on the status bar to switch to Read mode.
- Click the View tab to display the View menu.
- Point to Page Color on the View menu to display the Page Color submenu (Figure 2–77).

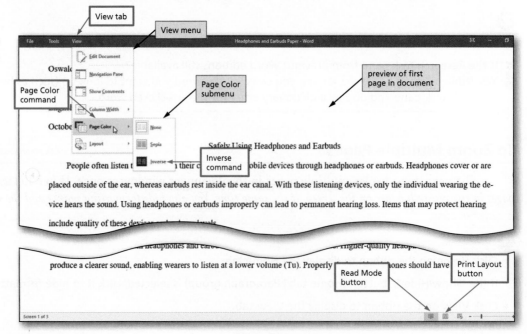

Figure 2–77

2

- Click Inverse on the Page Color submenu to change the color of the Read mode screen to inverse (Figure 2–78).

3

- When finished, click the Print Layout button (shown in Figure 2–77) on the status bar to return to Print Layout view.

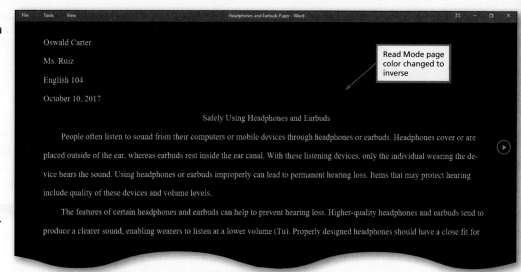

Figure 2–78

To Save and Print the Document and Exit Word

The following steps save and print the document and then exit Word. For a detailed example of the procedure summarized below, refer to the Office and Windows module at the beginning of this book.

1 Save the research paper again on the same storage location with the same file name.

2 If requested by your instructor, print the research paper.

3 Exit Word.

Summary

In this module, you have learned how to modify styles, adjust line and paragraph spacing, use headers to number pages, insert and edit citations and their sources, add footnotes, create a bibliographical list of sources, update a field, go to a page, copy and paste text, find and replace text, check spelling and grammar, and look up information.

What decisions will you need to make when creating your next research paper?
Use these guidelines as you complete the assignments in this module and create your own research papers outside of this class.

1. Select a topic.

 a) Spend time brainstorming ideas for a topic.

 b) Choose a topic you find interesting.

 c) For shorter papers, narrow the scope of the topic; for longer papers, broaden the scope.

 d) Identify a tentative thesis statement, which is a sentence describing the paper's subject matter.

2. Research the topic and take notes, being careful not to plagiarize.

3. Organize your notes into related concepts, identifying all main ideas and supporting details in an outline.

4. Write the first draft from the outline, referencing all sources of information and following the guidelines identified in the required documentation style.

5. Create the list of sources, using the formats specified in the required documentation style.

6. Proofread and revise the paper.

CONSIDER THIS: PLAN AHEAD

Apply Your Knowledge

Reinforce the skills and apply the concepts you learned in this module.

Revising Text and Paragraphs in a Document

Note: To complete this assignment, you will be required to use the Data Files. Please contact your instructor for information about accessing the Data Files.

Instructions: Run Word. Open the document, Apply 2-1 3-D Printers Paragraph Draft, which is located in the Data Files. The document you open contains a paragraph of text. You are to revise the document as follows: move a word, move another word and change the format of the moved word, change paragraph indentation, change line spacing, find all occurrences of a word, replace all occurrences of a word with another word, locate a synonym, and edit the header. The modified paragraph is shown in Figure 2–79.

Figure 2–79

Perform the following tasks:

1. Copy the text, printers, from the second sentence and paste it in the third sentence after the underlined word, liquid.

2. Select the underlined word, liquid, in the third sentence. Use drag-and-drop editing to move the selected word, liquid, so that it is before the word, polymer, in the last sentence. (If you are using a touch screen, use the cut and paste commands to move the word.) Click the Paste Options button that displays to the right of the moved word, liquid. Remove the underline format from the moved word by clicking 'Keep Text Only' on the Paste Options menu.

3. Display the ruler, if necessary. Use the ruler to indent the first line of the paragraph one-half inch. (If you are using a touch screen, use the Paragraph dialog box.)

4. Change the line spacing of the paragraph to double.

5. Use the Navigation Pane to find all occurrences of the word, printer. How many are there?

6. Use the Find and Replace dialog box to replace all occurrences of the word, 3D, with the word, 3-D. How many replacements were made?

7. Use the Navigation Pane to find the word, finished. Use Word's thesaurus to change the word, finished, to the word, complete. What other words are in the list of synonyms?

8. Switch to the header so that you can edit it. In the first line of the header, change the word, Draft, to the word, Modified, so that it reads: 3-D Printers Paragraph Modified.

9. In the second line of the header, insert a page number (a plain number with no formatting) one space after the word, Page.

10. Change the alignment of both lines of text in the header from left-aligned to right-aligned. Switch back to the document text.

11. If requested by your instructor, enter your first and last name on a separate line below the page number in the header.

12. Click File on the ribbon and then click Save As. Save the document using the file name, Apply 2-1 3-D Printers Paragraph Modified.

13. Submit the modified document, shown in Figure 2–79, in the format specified by your instructor.

14. Use the Insights task pane to look up the word prosthetics. Click the Explore tab in the Insights task pane. Which web articles appeared? What images appeared? Click the Define tab in the Insights task pane. Which dictionary was used?

15. ✳ Answer the questions posed in #5, #6, #7, and #14. How would you find and replace a special character, such as a paragraph mark?

Extend Your Knowledge

Extend the skills you learned in this module and experiment with new skills. You may need to use Help to complete the assignment.

Working with References and Proofing Tools
Note: To complete this assignment, you will be required to use the Data Files. Please contact your instructor for information about accessing the Data Files.

Instructions: Run Word. Open the document, Extend 2-1 Databases Paper Draft, from the Data Files. You will add another footnote to the paper, convert the footnotes to endnotes, modify the Endnote Text style, change the format of the note reference marks, use Word's readability statistics, translate the document to another language (Figure 2–80), and convert the document from MLA to APA documentation style.

Perform the following tasks:
1. Use Help to learn more about footers, footnotes and endnotes, readability statistics, bibliography styles, AutoCorrect, and Word's translation features.

2. Delete the footer from the document.

3. Insert a second footnote at an appropriate place in the research paper. Use the following footnote text: A data warehouse is a huge database that stores and manages the data required to analyze past and current transactions.

4. Change the location of the footnotes from bottom of page to below text. How did the placement of the footnotes change?

5. Convert the footnotes to endnotes. Where are the endnotes positioned?

6. Modify the Endnote Text style to 12-point Times New Roman font, double-spaced text with a hanging-line indent.

7. Change the format of the note reference marks to capital letters (A, B, etc.).

Continued >

Extend Your Knowledge continued

8. Add an AutoCorrect entry that replaces the word, buziness, with the word, business. Type the following sentence as the first sentence in the last paragraph of the paper, misspelling the word, business, as buziness to test the AutoCorrect entry: `Organizations often use a database to manage buziness or other functions.` Delete the AutoCorrect entry that replaces buziness with the word, business.

9. Display the Word Count dialog box. How many words, characters without spaces, characters with spaces, paragraphs, and lines are in the document? Be sure to include footnote and endnote text in the statistics.

10. Check spelling of the document, displaying readability statistics. What are the Flesch-Kincaid Grade Level and the Flesch Reading Ease score? Modify the paper to increase the reading ease score. How did you modify the paper? What are the new statistics?

11. If requested by your instructor, change the student name at the top of the paper to your name, including the last name in the header.

12. Save the revised document with the file name, Extend 2-1 Databases Paper Modified, and then submit it in the format specified by your instructor.

13. If you have an Internet connection, translate the research paper into a language of your choice using the Translate button (Review tab | Language group), as shown in Figure 2–80. Submit the translated document in the format specified by your instructor. Use the Mini Translator to hear how to pronounce three words in your paper.

14. Select the entire document and then change the documentation style from MLA to APA. Save the APA version of the document with a new file name. Compare the APA version to the MLA version. If you have a hard copy of each and your instructor requests it, circle the differences between the two documents.

15. ✳ Answer the questions posed in #4, #5, #9, and #10. Where did you insert the second footnote and why?

Figure 2–80

Expand Your World

Create a solution that uses cloud or web technologies by learning and investigating on your own from general guidance.

Using an Online Bibliography Tool to Create a List of Sources

Instructions: Assume you are using a computer or mobile device that does not have Word but has Internet access. To make use of time between classes, you use an online bibliography tool to create a list of sources that you can copy and paste into the Works Cited pages of a research paper that is due tomorrow.

Perform the following tasks:

1. Run a browser. Search for the text, online bibliography tool, using a search engine. Visit several of the online bibliography tools and determine which you would like to use to create a list of sources. Navigate to the desired online bibliography tool.

2. Use the online bibliography tool to enter list of sources shown below (Figure 2–81):

   Alverez, Juan and Tracy Marie Wilson. *Radon in the Home*. Chicago: Martin Publishing, 2017. Print.

   Buchalski, Leonard Adam. *Radon and Your Health*. Los Angeles: Coastal Works, 2017. Print.

   Johnson, Shantair Jada. "Radon Facts." *Environment Danger* Aug. 2017. Web. 31 Aug. 2017.

   Slobovnik, Vincent Alexander. *The Radon Guide*. Aug. 2017. Course Technology. Web. 18 Sept. 2017.

   Wakefield, Ginger Lynn and Bethany Olivia Ames. "Radon Removal Systems." *Living Well Today* Aug. 2017. Web. 3 Oct. 2017.

   Zhao, Shen Li. *Radon Testing Procedures*. Sept. 2017. Course Technology. Web. 8 Sept. 2017.

3. If requested by your instructor, replace the name in one of the sources above with your name.

4. Search for another source that discusses radon issues in the home. Add that source.

5. Copy and paste the list of sources into a Word document.

6. Save the document with the file name, Expand 2-1 Radon Issues Sources. Submit the document in the format specified by your instructor.

7. ☀ Which online bibliography tools did you evaluate? Which one did you select to use and why? Do you prefer using the online bibliography tool or Word to create sources? Why? What differences, if any, did you notice between the list of sources created with the online bibliography tool and the lists created when you use Word?

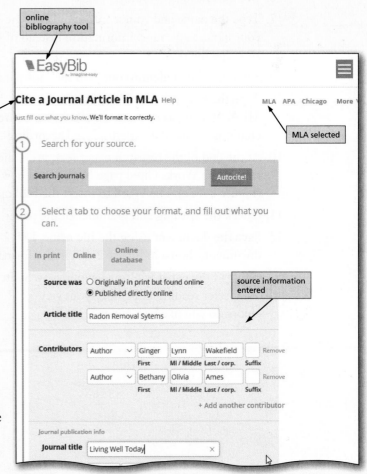

Figure 2–81

In the Labs

Design, create, modify, and/or use a document following the guidelines, concepts, and skills presented in this module. Labs 1 and 2, which increase in difficulty, require you to create solutions based on what you learned in the module; Lab 3 requires you to apply your creative thinking and problem-solving skills to design and implement a solution.

Lab 1: **Preparing a Short Research Paper**

Problem: You are a college student currently enrolled in an introductory English class. Your assignment is to prepare a short research paper (300–350 words) in any area of interest to you. The requirements are that the paper be presented according to the MLA documentation style and have three references. At least one of the three references must be from the web. You prepare the paper shown in Figure 2–82, which discusses wearable devices.

Perform the following tasks:

1. Run Word. If necessary, display formatting marks on the screen.

2. Modify the Normal style to the 12-point Times New Roman font.

3. Adjust line spacing to double.

4. Remove space below (after) paragraphs.

5. Update the Normal style to reflect the adjusted line and paragraph spacing.

6. Create a header to number pages.

7. Type the name and course information at the left margin. If requested by your instructor, use your name and course information instead of the information shown in Figure 2–82a. Center and type the title.

8. Set a first-line indent to one-half inch for paragraphs in the body of the research paper.

9. Type the research paper as shown in Figures 2–82a and 2–82b. Change the bibliography style to MLA. As you insert citations, enter their source information (shown in Figure 2–82c). Edit the citations so that they are displayed according to Figures 2–82a and 2–82b.

10. At the end of the research paper text, press the ENTER key and then insert a manual page break so that the Works Cited page begins on a new page. Enter and format the works cited title (Figure 2–82c). Use Word to insert the bibliographical list (bibliography).

11. Check the spelling and grammar of the paper at once.

12. Save the document using the file name, Lab 2–1 Wearable Devices Paper. Submit the document, shown in Figure 2–82, in the format specified by your instructor.

13. ⊛ Read the paper in Print Layout view. Switch to Read mode and scroll through the pages. Do you prefer reading in Print Layout view or Read mode? Why? In Read mode, which of the page colors do you like best and why?

Hakimi 1

Farrah Iman Hakimi

Mr. Danshov

English 103

November 15, 2017

Wearable Devices

A wearable device or wearable is a small, mobile computing device designed to be worn by a consumer. These devices often communicate with a mobile device or computer using Bluetooth. Three popular types of wearable devices are activity trackers, smartwatches, and smart glasses.

An activity tracker is a wearable device that monitors fitness-related activities such as distance walked, heart rate, pulse, calories consumed, and sleep patterns. These devices typically sync, usually wirelessly, with a web or mobile app on your computer or mobile device to extend the capability of the wearable device (Pappas 32-41).

A smartwatch is a wearable device that, in addition to keeping time, can communicate wirelessly with a smartphone to make and answer phone calls, read and send messages, access the web, play music, work with apps such as fitness trackers and GPS, and more. Most include a touch screen (Carter and Schmidt).

Smart glasses, also called smart eyewear, are wearable head-mounted eyeglass-type devices that enable the user to view information or take photos and videos that are projected to a miniature screen in the user's field of vision. For example, the device wearer could run an app while wearing smart glasses that display flight status information when he or she walks into an airport. Users control the device through voice commands or by touching controls on its frame. Some smart glasses also include mobile apps, such as fitness trackers and GPS (Yazzie).

Figure 2–82a

Continued >

In the Labs *continued*

Hakimi 2

Activity trackers, smartwatches, and smart eyewear are available from a variety of

manufacturers. Before making a purchase, consumers should research costs and features of all

options to determine the device that best suits their requirements.

Figure 2–82b

Hakimi 3

Works Cited

Carter, Calvin J. and Karl Hans Schmidt. "Smartwatch Review." *Technology Trends* Aug. 2017:

n. pag. Web. 12 October 2017.

Pappas, Anastasia Maria. *Activity Trackers and Other Wearable Devices*. Dallas: Western Star

Publishing, 2017. Print.

Yazzie, Nina Tamaya. *Evaluating Today's Smart Glasses*. 25 Aug. 2017. Course Technology.

Web. 25 Sept. 2017.

Figure 2–82c

Lab 2: **Preparing a Research Report with a Footnote**

Problem: You are a college student enrolled in an introductory technology class. Your assignment is to prepare a short research paper (350–400 words) in any area of interest to you. The requirements are that the paper be presented according to the MLA documentation style, contain at least one note positioned as a footnote, and have three references. At least one of the three references must be from the web. You prepare a paper about two-step verification (Figure 2–83).

Perform the following tasks:
1. Run Word. Modify the Normal style to the 12-point Times New Roman font. Adjust line spacing to double and remove space below (after) paragraphs. Update the Normal style to include the adjusted line and paragraph spacing. Create a header to number pages. Type the name and course information at the left margin. If requested by your instructor, use your name and course information instead of the information shown in Figure 2–83a. Center and type the title. Set a first-line indent for paragraphs in the body of the research paper.

2. Type the research paper as shown in Figures 2–83a and 2–83b. Insert the footnote as shown in Figure 2–83a. Change the Footnote Text style to the format specified in the MLA documentation

Wagner 1

Bryan Wagner

Dr. Rosenberg

Technology 104

October 27, 2017

Two-Step Verification

In an attempt to protect personal data and information from online thieves, many

organizations, such as financial institutions or universities, that store sensitive or confidential

items use a two-step verification process. With two-step verification, a computer or mobile

device uses two separate methods, one after the next, to verify the identity of a user.

ATMs (automated teller machines) usually require a two-step verification. Users first

insert their ATM card into the ATM (Step 1) and then enter a PIN, or personal identification

number, (Step 2) to access their bank account. If someone steals these cards, the thief must enter

the user's PIN to access the account (Tanaka).

Another use of two-step verification requires a mobile phone and a computer or mobile

device.[1] When users sign in to an account on a computer or mobile device, they enter a user

name and password (Step 1). Next, they are prompted to enter another authentication code (Step

2), which is sent as a text or voice message or via an app on a smartphone. This second code

generally is valid for a set time, sometimes only for a few minutes or hours. If users do not sign

in during this time limit, they must repeat the process and request another verification code

---

[1] According to Moore and O'Sullivan, users should register an alternate mobile phone

number, landline phone number, email address, or other form of contact beyond a mobile phone

number so that they still can access their accounts even if they lose their mobile phone (54).

Figure 2–83a

Wagner 2

(Marcy). Microsoft and Google commonly use two-step verification when users sign in to these

websites (Moore and O'Sullivan).

Some organizations use two separate methods to verify the identity of users. These two-

step verification procedures are designed to protect users' sensitive and confidential items from

online thieves.

Figure 2–83b

Continued >

In the Labs *continued*

style. Change the bibliography style to MLA. As you insert citations, use the following source information, entering it according to the MLA style:

a. Type of Source: Article
    in a Periodical
    Author: Hana Kei
    Tanaka
    Article Title: Safeguards
    against Unauthorized
    Access and Use
    Periodical Title:
    Technology Today
    Year: 2017
    Month: Sept.
    Pages: no pages used
    Medium: Web
    Year Accessed: 2017
    Month Accessed: Oct.
    Day Accessed: 3

b. Type of Source: Web site
    Author: Fredrick Lee
    Marcy
    Name of webpage:
    Two-Step Verification
    Year/Month/Date: none
    given
    Production Company:
    Course Technology
    Medium: Web
    Year Accessed: 2017
    Month Accessed: Sept.
    Day Accessed: 18

c. Type of Source: Book
    Author: Aaron Bradley
    Moore and Brianna
    Clare O'Sullivan
    Title: Authentication
    Techniques
    Year: 2017
    City: Detroit
    Publisher: Great Lakes
    Press
    Medium: Print

3. At the end of the research paper text, press the ENTER key once and insert a manual page break so that the Works Cited page begins on a new page. Enter and format the works cited title. Use Word to insert the bibliographical list.

4. Check the spelling and grammar of the paper.

5. Save the document using the file name, Lab 2–2 Two-Step Verification Paper. Submit the document, shown in Figure 2–83, in the format specified by your instructor.

6. ✹ This paper uses web sources. What factors should you consider when selecting web sources?

Lab 3: Consider This: Your Turn

Create a Research Paper about Wireless Communications

Note: To complete this assignment, you will be required to use the Data Files. Please contact your instructor for information about accessing the Data Files.

Problem: As a student in an introductory computer class, your instructor has assigned a brief research paper that discusses wireless communications.

Perform the following tasks:
Part 1: The source for the text in your research paper is in a file called Lab 2–3 Consider This Your Turn Wireless Communications Notes, which is located in the Data Files. If your instructor requests, use the Insights task pane to obtain information from another source and include that information as a note positioned as a footnote in the paper, along with entering its corresponding source information as appropriate. Add an AutoCorrect entry to correct a word you commonly mistype. If necessary, set the default dictionary. Add one of the source last names to the dictionary.

Using the concepts and techniques presented in this module, organize the notes in the text in the file on the Data Files, rewording as necessary, and then create and format this research paper according to the MLA documentation style. Be sure to check spelling and grammar of the finished paper. Submit your assignment and answers to the critical thinking questions in the format specified by your instructor.

Part 2: ✹ You made several decisions while creating the research paper in this assignment: how to organize the notes, where to place citations, how to format sources, and which source on the web to use for the footnote text (if requested by your instructor). What was the rationale behind each of these decisions? When you proofread the document, what further revisions did you make and why?

1 Creating and Editing a Presentation with Pictures

Objectives

You will have mastered the material in this module when you can:

- Select and change a document theme and variant
- Create a title slide and a text slide with a multilevel bulleted list
- Add new slides and change slide layouts
- Insert pictures into slides with and without content placeholders
- Move and resize pictures

- Change font size and color
- Bold and italicize text
- Duplicate a slide
- Arrange slides
- Select slide transitions
- View a presentation in Slide Show view

Introduction

A PowerPoint **presentation**, also called a **slide show**, can help you deliver a dynamic, professional-looking message to an audience. PowerPoint allows you to produce slides to use in an academic, business, or other environment. The collection of slides in a presentation is called a **deck**, resembling a deck of cards that are stacked on top of each other. A common use of slide decks is to enhance an oral presentation. A speaker might desire to convey information, such as urging students to volunteer at a fund-raising event, explaining changes in employee compensation packages, or describing a new laboratory procedure. The PowerPoint slides should reinforce the speaker's message and help the audience retain the information presented. Custom slides can fit your specific needs and contain diagrams, charts, tables, pictures, shapes, video, sound, and animation effects to make your presentation more effective. An accompanying handout gives audience members reference notes and review material for your presentation.

Project — Presentation with a Bulleted List and Pictures

In this module's project, you will follow proper design guidelines and learn to use PowerPoint to create, save, and view the slides shown in Figures 1–1a through 1–1e. The objective is to produce a presentation, titled Tall Oaks, to promote three programs at the nature center. This slide show has a variety of pictures and visual elements to add interest and give facts about the events. Some of the text has formatting and color enhancements. Transitions help one slide flow gracefully into the next during a slide show.

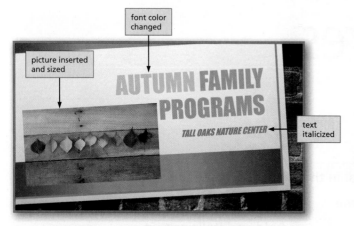

(a) Slide 1 (Title Slide with Picture)

(b) Slide 2 (Multilevel Bulleted List with Picture)

(c) Slide 3 (Comparison Layout and Pictures)

(d) Slide 4 (Title and Illustration)

(e) Slide 5 (Closing Slide)

Figure 1–1

In this module, you will learn how to perform basic tasks using PowerPoint. The following roadmap identifies general activities you will perform as you progress through this module:

1. INSERT the four PRESENTATION SLIDES, using various layouts.
2. ENTER the TEXT for the slides.
3. FORMAT the TEXT on each slide.
4. INSERT GRAPHICAL ELEMENTS, including pictures.
5. SIZE AND POSITION the graphical elements.
6. ENHANCE the SLIDE SHOW by adding a closing slide and transition.
7. DISPLAY the SLIDES.

> For an introduction to Office and instructions about how to perform basic tasks in Office apps, read the Office and Windows module at the beginning of this book, where you can learn how to run an application, use the ribbon, save a file, open a file, print a file, exit an application, use Help, and much more.

Choosing a Document Theme and Variant

You easily can give the slides in a presentation a professional and integrated appearance by using a theme. A document **theme** is a specific design with coordinating colors, fonts, and special effects such as shadows and reflections. Several themes are available when you run PowerPoint, each with a specific name. Using one of the formatted themes makes creating a professional-looking presentation easier and quicker than using the Blank Presentation template, where you would need to make all design decisions.

Each theme has a set of four alternate designs, called **variants**. Each variant has the same overall composition, but the colors, fonts, and design elements differ. Once you select a theme, you then can select a variation that best fits your overall design needs. If you later decide that another theme or variant would better fit the presentation's general theme, you can change these elements while you are developing slides.

> For an introduction to Windows and instructions about how to perform basic Windows tasks, read the Office and Windows module at the beginning of this book, where you can learn how to resize windows, change screen resolution, create folders, move and rename files, use Windows Help, and much more.

To Choose a Document Theme and Variant

1 INSERT PRESENTATION SLIDES | 2 ENTER TEXT | 3 FORMAT TEXT | 4 INSERT GRAPHICAL ELEMENTS
5 SIZE & POSITION | 6 ENHANCE SLIDE SHOW | 7 DISPLAY SLIDES

When you begin creating a new PowerPoint presentation, you need to select a theme. You either can start with no design elements by using the Blank Presentation, or you can select one of the available professionally designed themes. The following steps apply the Berlin theme and then change the variant. *Why? The title slide will have text and a picture, so you want to select a theme, like Berlin, with an uncluttered background. The presentation discusses three events occurring at the nature center, and green is the color commonly associated with nature's forests and grasslands. The default Berlin theme is predominantly orange and black, but one of its variants is green and is an appropriate choice to relate to the nature concept.*

> BTW
> **The PowerPoint Window**
> The modules in this book begin with the PowerPoint window appearing as it did at the initial installation of the software. Your PowerPoint window may look different depending on your screen resolution and other PowerPoint settings.

1

- Run PowerPoint and point to the Berlin theme on the Recent screen (Figure 1–2).

◄ | I do not see the Berlin theme. What should I do?
Q&A | Your list of available templates may differ from those shown in the figure. You may need to scroll down to locate
| the Berlin theme or enter "Berlin" in the Search box.

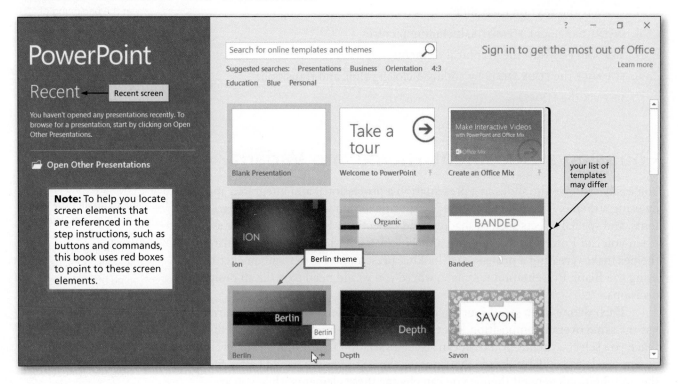

Figure 1–2

2

- Click the Berlin theme to display a theme preview dialog box with a thumbnail view of the theme and its variants
(Figure 1–3).

◄ | Can I see previews of other themes?
Q&A | Yes. Click the right or left arrows on the sides of the theme preview dialog box.

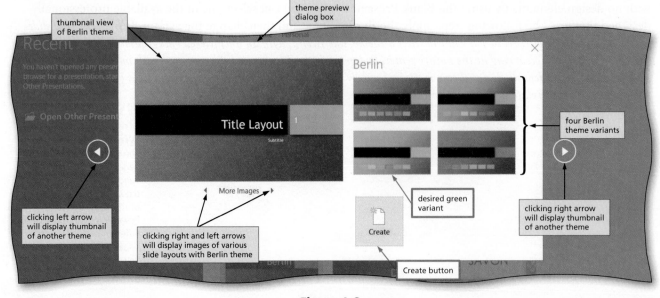

Figure 1–3

3

- Click the lower-left (green) variant to view a preview of that style applied to the thumbnail.

Q&A Can I see previews of the Berlin theme and green variant applied to layouts other than the title slide?
Yes. Click the right or left arrows beside the words, More Images, below the thumbnail. Three other layouts will be displayed: Title and Content, Two Content, and Photo.

- Click the Create button to apply the Berlin theme and green variant to the presentation and to display Slide 1 (Figure 1–4).

Figure 1–4

Creating a Title Slide

When you open a new presentation, the default **Title Slide** layout appears. The purpose of this layout is to introduce the presentation to the audience. PowerPoint includes other standard layouts for each of the themes. The slide layouts are set up in **landscape orientation**, where the slide width is greater than its height. In landscape orientation, the slide size is preset to 10 inches wide and 7.5 inches high when printed on a standard sheet of paper measuring 11 inches wide and 8.5 inches high.

    Placeholders are boxes with dotted or hatch-marked borders that are displayed when you create a new slide. Most layouts have both a title text placeholder and at least one content placeholder. Depending on the particular slide layout selected, title and subtitle placeholders are displayed for the slide title and subtitle; a content text placeholder is displayed for text, art, or a table, chart, picture, graphic, or movie. The title slide has two text placeholders where you can type the main heading, or title, of a new slide and the subtitle.

    With the exception of the Blank slide layout, PowerPoint assumes every new slide has a title. To make creating a presentation easier, any text you type after a new slide appears becomes title text in the title text placeholder. The following steps create the title slide for this presentation.

BTW
PowerPoint Screen Resolution
If you are using a computer or mobile device to step through the project in this module and you want your screens to match the figures in this book, you should change your screen's resolution to 1366 x 768. For information about how to change a computer's resolution, refer to the Office and Windows module at the beginning of this book.

How do I choose the words for the slide?

All presentations should follow the 7 × 7 rule, which states that each slide should have a maximum of seven lines, and each line should have a maximum of seven words. PowerPoint designers must choose their words carefully and, in turn, help viewers read the slides easily.

Avoid line wraps. Your audience's eyes want to stop at the end of a line. Thus, you must plan your words carefully or adjust the font size so that each point displays on only one line.

To Enter the Presentation Title

1 INSERT PRESENTATION SLIDES | 2 ENTER TEXT | 3 FORMAT TEXT | 4 INSERT GRAPHICAL ELEMENTS
5 SIZE & POSITION | 6 ENHANCE SLIDE SHOW | 7 DISPLAY SLIDES

The presentation title for Project 1 is Autumn Family Programs. *Why? The presentation discusses three programs that will be held during the fall months.* The following steps create the slide show's title.

- Click the label, 'Click to add title', located inside the title text placeholder to select the placeholder (Figure 1–5).

Figure 1–5

- Type **Autumn Family Programs** in the title text placeholder. Do not press the ENTER key (Figure 1–6).

Figure 1–6

Correcting a Mistake When Typing

If you type the wrong letter, press the BACKSPACE key to erase all the characters back to and including the one that is incorrect. If you mistakenly press the ENTER key after typing the title and the insertion point is on the new line, simply press the BACKSPACE key to return the insertion point to the right of the last letter in the word, Programs.

By default, PowerPoint allows you to reverse up to the last 20 changes by clicking the Undo button on the Quick Access Toolbar. The ScreenTip that appears when you point to the Undo button changes to indicate the type of change just made. For example, if you type text in the title text placeholder and then point to the Undo button, the ScreenTip that appears is Undo Typing. For clarity, when referencing the Undo button in this project, the name displaying in the ScreenTip is used. You can reapply a change that you reversed with the Undo button by clicking the Redo button on the Quick Access Toolbar. Clicking the Redo button reverses the last undo action. The ScreenTip name reflects the type of reversal last performed.

BTW
Touch Screen Differences
The Office and Windows interfaces may vary if you are using a touch screen. For this reason, you might notice that the function or appearance of your touch screen differs slightly from this module's presentation.

Paragraphs

Text in the subtitle text placeholder supports the title text. It can appear on one or more lines in the placeholder. To create more than one subtitle line, you press the ENTER key after typing some words. PowerPoint creates a new line, which is the second paragraph in the placeholder. A **paragraph** is a segment of text with the same format that begins when you press the ENTER key and ends when you press the ENTER key again. This new paragraph is the same level as the previous paragraph. A **level** is a position within a structure, such as an outline, that indicates the magnitude of importance. PowerPoint allows for five paragraph levels.

How do you use the touch keyboard with a touch screen?
To display the on-screen keyboard, tap the Touch Keyboard button on the Windows taskbar. When finished using the touch keyboard, tap the X button on the touch keyboard to close the keyboard.

CONSIDER THIS

To Enter the Presentation Subtitle Paragraph

1 INSERT PRESENTATION SLIDES | 2 ENTER TEXT | 3 FORMAT TEXT | 4 INSERT GRAPHICAL ELEMENTS
5 SIZE & POSITION | 6 ENHANCE SLIDE SHOW | 7 DISPLAY SLIDES

The first subtitle paragraph is related to the title. *Why? The subtitle gives an additional detail, the nature center's name.* The following steps enter the presentation subtitle.

1

- Click the label, 'Click to add subtitle', located inside the subtitle text placeholder to select the placeholder (Figure 1–7).

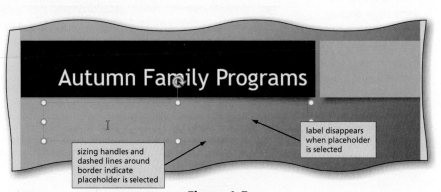

sizing handles and dashed lines around border indicate placeholder is selected

label disappears when placeholder is selected

Figure 1–7

• Type **Tall Oaks Nature Center** but do not press the ENTER key (Figure 1–8).

Autumn Family Programs

Tall Oaks Nature Center

> subtitle text entered in placeholder

Figure 1–8

To Zoom a Slide

1 INSERT PRESENTATION SLIDES | 2 ENTER TEXT | 3 FORMAT TEXT | 4 INSERT GRAPHICAL ELEMENTS
5 SIZE & POSITION | 6 ENHANCE SLIDE SHOW | 7 DISPLAY SLIDES

You can **zoom** the view of the slide on the screen so that the text or other content is enlarged or shrunk. When you zoom in, you get a close-up view of your slide; when you zoom out, you see more of the slide at a reduced size. You will be modifying the text and other slide components as you create the presentation, so you can enlarge the slide on the screen. *Why? Zooming the slide can help you see slide elements more clearly so that you can position them precisely where desired.* The following step changes the zoom to 70 percent.

Experiment

• Repeatedly click the Zoom In and Zoom Out buttons on the status bar and watch the size of the slide change in the Slide pane.

• Click the Zoom In or Zoom Out button as many times as necessary until the Zoom button on the status bar displays 70% on its face (Figure 1–9).

Q&A If I change the zoom percentage, will the slide display differently when I run the presentation?
No. Changing the zoom helps you develop the slide content and does not affect the slide show.

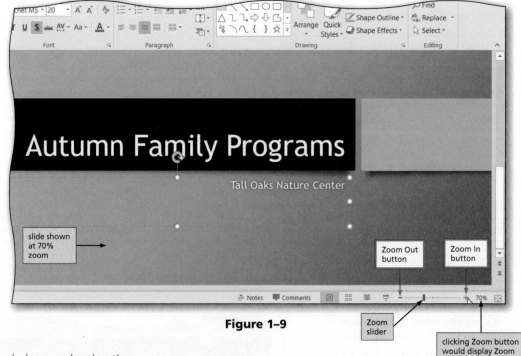

Autumn Family Programs

Tall Oaks Nature Center

> slide shown at 70% zoom

> Zoom Out button

> Zoom In button

> Zoom slider

> clicking Zoom button would display Zoom dialog box

Figure 1–9

Other Ways			
1. Drag Zoom slider on status bar	2. Click Zoom level button on status bar, select desired zoom percent or type (Zoom dialog box), click OK button	3. Click Zoom button (View tab | Zoom group), select desired zoom percent or type (Zoom dialog box), click OK button	4. For touch screens: Pinch two fingers together in Slide pane (zoom out) or stretch two fingers apart (zoom in)

Formatting Characters in a Presentation

Recall that each document theme determines the color scheme, font set, and layout of a presentation. You can use a specific document theme and then change the characters' formats any time before, during, or after you type the text.

Fonts and Font Styles

Characters that appear on the screen are a specific shape and size. Examples of how you can modify the appearance, or **format**, of these typed characters on the screen and in print include changing the font, style, size, and color. The **font**, or typeface, defines the appearance and shape of the letters, numbers, punctuation marks, and symbols. **Style** indicates how the characters are formatted. PowerPoint's text font styles include regular, italic, bold, and bold italic. **Size** specifies the height of the characters and is gauged by a measurement system that uses points. A **point** is 1/72 of an inch in height. Thus, a character with a font size of 36 is 36/72 (or 1/2) of an inch in height. **Color** defines the hue of the characters.

This presentation uses the Berlin document theme, which has particular font styles and font sizes. The Berlin document theme default title text font is named Trebuchet MS. It has no special effects, and its size is 54 point. The Berlin default subtitle text font also is Trebuchet MS with a font size of 20 point.

To Select a Paragraph

1 INSERT PRESENTATION SLIDES | 2 ENTER TEXT | 3 FORMAT TEXT | 4 INSERT GRAPHICAL ELEMENTS
5 SIZE & POSITION | 6 ENHANCE SLIDE SHOW | 7 DISPLAY SLIDES

You can use many techniques to format characters. When you want to apply the same formats to multiple words or paragraphs, it is helpful to select these words. ***Why?*** *It is efficient to select the desired text and then make the desired changes to all the characters simultaneously.* The first formatting change you will make will apply to the title slide subtitle. The following step selects this paragraph.

- Triple-click the paragraph, Tall Oaks Nature Center, in the subtitle text placeholder to select the paragraph (Figure 1–10).

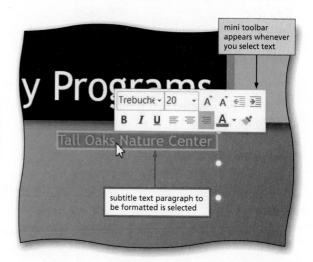

Figure 1–10

Other Ways
1. Position pointer to left of first paragraph and drag to end of line

To Italicize Text

Different font styles often are used on slides. *Why? These style changes make the words more appealing to the reader and emphasize particular text.* **Italic** text has a slanted appearance. Used sparingly, it draws the readers' eyes to these characters. The following step adds emphasis to the line of the subtitle text by changing regular text to italic text.

- With the subtitle text still selected, click the Italic button on the mini toolbar to italicize that text on the slide (Figure 1–11).

Q&A If I change my mind and decide not to italicize the text, how can I remove this style?
Immediately click the Undo button on the Quick Access Toolbar, click the Italic button a second time, or press CTRL+Z.

Figure 1–11

Other Ways

1. Right-click selected text, click Italic button in mini toolbar near shortcut menu	2. Select text, click Italic button (Home tab | Font group)	3. Click Font dialog box launcher (Home tab | Font group), click Font tab (Font dialog box), click Italic in Font style list, click OK button	4. Select text, press CTRL+I

To Increase Font Size

Why? To add emphasis, you increase the font size for the subtitle text. The 'Increase Font Size' button on the mini toolbar increases the font size in preset increments. The following step uses this button to increase the font size.

- With the text, Tall Oaks Nature Center, selected, click the 'Increase Font Size' button on the mini toolbar four times to increase the font size of the selected text from 20 to 36 point (Figure 1–12).

Figure 1–12

Other Ways

1. Click Font Size arrow on mini toolbar, click desired font size in Font Size gallery	2. Click 'Increase Font Size' button (Home tab | Font group)	3. Click Font Size arrow (Home tab | Font group), click desired font size in Font size gallery	4. Press CTRL+SHIFT+>

To Select a Word

PowerPoint designers use many techniques to emphasize words and characters on a slide. To accentuate the word, Autumn, on your slide, you want to increase the font size and change the font color to orange for this word in the title text. To make these changes, you should begin by selecting the word, Autumn. *Why? You could perform these actions separately, but it is more efficient to select the word and then change the font attributes.* The following step selects a word.

1

- Position the pointer somewhere in the word to be selected (in this case, in the word, Autumn).

- Double-click the word to select it (Figure 1–13).

Figure 1–13

Other Ways

1. Position pointer before first character, press CTRL+SHIFT+RIGHT ARROW   2. Position pointer before first character, drag right to select word

---

To Change the Text Color

PowerPoint allows you to use one or more text colors in a presentation. You decide to change the color of the word you selected, Autumn. *Why? The color, orange, is associated with that season, and you want to add more emphasis, subtly, to this word in your title slide text.* The following steps add emphasis to this word by changing the font color from white to orange.

1

- With the word, Autumn, selected, click the Font Color arrow on the mini toolbar to display the Font Color gallery, which includes Theme Colors and Standard Colors (Figure 1–14).

Q&A If the mini toolbar disappears from the screen, how can I display it once again?
Right-click the text, and the mini toolbar should appear.

🔎 **Experiment**

- Point to various colors in the gallery and watch the word's font color change.

Figure 1–14

- Click Orange in the Standard Colors row on the mini toolbar (third color from left) to change the font color to Orange (Figure 1–15).

Figure 1–15

Q&A

Why did I select the color Orange?
Orange is one of the 10 standard colors associated with every document theme, and it is a universal color representing the fall colors. The new color will emphasize the fact that the presentation focuses on programs suited for this time of year.

What is the difference between the colors shown in the Theme Colors area and the Standard Colors?
The 10 colors in the top row of the Theme Colors area are two text, two background, and six accent colors in the Berlin theme; the five colors in each column under the top row display different transparencies. The Standard Colors are available in every document theme.

3

- Click outside the selected area to deselect the word.

4

- Save the presentation on your hard disk, OneDrive, or other storage location using Tall Oaks as the file name.

Q&A

Why should I save the presentation at this time?
You have performed many tasks while creating this presentation and do not want to risk losing work completed thus far.

Other Ways

1. Right-click selected text, click Font on shortcut menu, click Font Color button, click desired color

2. Click Font Color arrow (Home tab | Font group), click desired color

BTW

Organizing Files and Folders
You should organize and store files in folders so that you easily can find the files later. For example, if you are taking an introductory technology class called CIS 101, a good practice would be to save all PowerPoint files in a PowerPoint folder in a CIS 101 folder. For a discussion of folders and detailed examples of creating folders, refer to the Office and Windows module at the beginning of this book.

Adding a New Slide to a Presentation

With the text for the title slide for the presentation created, the next step is to add the first text slide immediately after the title slide. Usually, when you create a presentation, you add slides with text, pictures, graphics, or charts. Some placeholders allow you to double-click the placeholder and then access other objects, such as videos, charts, diagrams, and organization charts. You can change the layout for a slide at any time during the creation of a presentation.

To Add a New Text Slide with a Bulleted List

1 INSERT PRESENTATION SLIDES | 2 ENTER TEXT | 3 FORMAT TEXT | **4 INSERT GRAPHICAL ELEMENTS**
5 SIZE & POSITION | 6 ENHANCE SLIDE SHOW | 7 DISPLAY SLIDES

When you add a new slide, PowerPoint uses the Title and Content slide layout. This layout provides a title placeholder and a content area for text, art, charts, and other graphics. A vertical scroll bar appears in the Slide pane when you add the second slide. *Why? The scroll bar allows you to move from slide to slide easily.* A small image of this slide also appears in the Slides tab. The following step adds a new slide with the Title and Content slide layout.

1

- Click the New Slide button (Home tab | Slides group) to insert a new slide with the Title and Content layout (Figure 1–16).

Q&A Why does the bullet character display a white dot?
The Berlin document theme determines the bullet characters. Each paragraph level has an associated bullet character.

I clicked the New Slide arrow instead of the New Slide button. What should I do?
Click the Title and Content slide thumbnail in the Berlin layout gallery.

How do I know which slide number I am viewing?
The left edge of the status bar shows the current slide number followed by the total number of slides in the document. In addition, the slide number is displayed to the left of the slide thumbnail.

What are those six icons grouped in the middle of the Slide pane?
You can click one of the icons to insert a specific type of content: table, chart, SmartArt graphic, pictures, online pictures, or video.

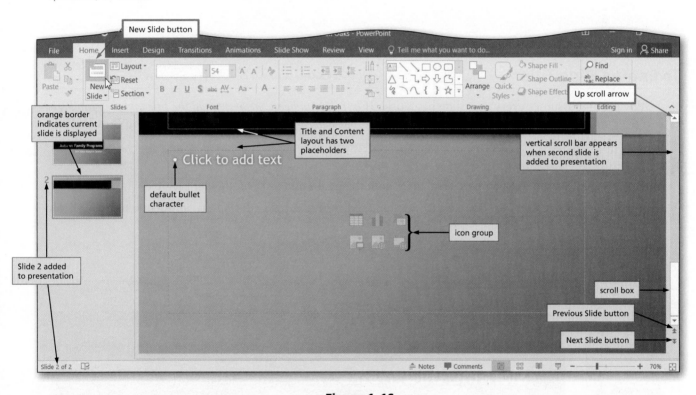

Figure 1–16

Other Ways

1. Click New Slide button (Insert tab | Slides group)   2. Press CTRL+M

Creating a Text Slide with a Multilevel Bulleted List

The information in the Slide 2 text placeholder is presented in a bulleted list with three levels. A **bulleted list** is a list of paragraphs, each of which may be preceded by a bullet character, such as a dot, arrow, or checkmark. Most themes display a bullet character at the start of a paragraph by default. A slide that consists of more than one

BTW
The Ribbon and Screen Resolution
PowerPoint may change how the groups and buttons within the groups appear on the ribbon, depending on the computer or mobile device's screen resolution. Thus, your ribbon may look different from the ones in this book if you are using a screen resolution other than 1366 x 768.

BTW
File Type
Depending on your Windows settings, the file type .pptx may be displayed on the title bar immediately to the right of the file name after you save the file. The file type .pptx identifies a PowerPoint document.

level of bulleted text is called a **multilevel bulleted list slide**. In a multilevel bulleted list, a lower-level paragraph is a subset of a higher-level paragraph. It usually contains information that supports the topic in the paragraph immediately above it.

As you can see in Figure 1–1b, two of the Slide 2 paragraphs appear at the same level, called the first level: Enjoy a hike on natural surface trails, and 9 a.m. every Saturday. Beginning with the second level, each paragraph indents to the right of the preceding level and is pushed down to a lower level. For example, if you increase the indent of a first-level paragraph, it becomes a second-level paragraph. The second and fourth paragraphs on Slide 2 are second-level paragraphs. The last paragraph, Extra supplies will be available, is a third-level paragraph.

Creating a text slide with a multilevel bulleted list requires several steps. Initially, you enter a slide title in the title text placeholder. Next, you select the content text placeholder. Then, you type the text for the multilevel bulleted list, increasing and decreasing the indents as needed. The next several sections add a slide with a multilevel bulleted list.

To Enter a Slide Title

1 INSERT PRESENTATION SLIDES | **2 ENTER TEXT** | 3 FORMAT TEXT | **4 INSERT GRAPHICAL ELEMENTS**
5 SIZE & POSITION | **6 ENHANCE SLIDE SHOW** | **7 DISPLAY SLIDES**

PowerPoint assumes every new slide has a title. *Why? The audience members read the title and then can begin to focus their attention on the information being presented on that slide.* The title for Slide 2 is Morning Bird Walks. The following step enters this title.

- If necessary, click the Up scroll arrow several times until the entire title text placeholder is visible.

- Click the label 'Click to add title', to select it and then type **Morning Bird Walks** in the title text placeholder. Do not press the ENTER key (Figure 1–17).

Figure 1–17

To Select a Text Placeholder

1 INSERT PRESENTATION SLIDES | 2 ENTER TEXT | 3 FORMAT TEXT | 4 INSERT GRAPHICAL ELEMENTS
5 SIZE & POSITION | 6 ENHANCE SLIDE SHOW | 7 DISPLAY SLIDES

Why? Before you can type text into a content placeholder, you first must select it. The following step selects the text placeholder on Slide 2.

1

- Click the label, 'Click to add text', to select the content placeholder (Figure 1–18).

Q&A Why does my pointer have a different shape?
If you move the pointer away from the bullet, it will change shape.

Figure 1–18

Other Ways

1. Press CTRL+ENTER

To Type a Multilevel Bulleted List

1 INSERT PRESENTATION SLIDES | 2 ENTER TEXT | 3 FORMAT TEXT | 4 INSERT GRAPHICAL ELEMENTS
5 SIZE & POSITION | 6 ENHANCE SLIDE SHOW | 7 DISPLAY SLIDES

The content placeholder provides an area for the text characters. When you click inside a placeholder, you then can type or paste text. As discussed previously, a bulleted list is a list of paragraphs, each of which is preceded by a bullet. A paragraph is a segment of text ended by pressing the ENTER key. The theme determines the bullets for each level. *Why? The bullet variations are determined by the specific paragraph levels, and they generally vary in size, shape, and color.*

The content text placeholder is selected, so the next step is to type the multilevel bulleted list that consists of six paragraphs, as shown in Figure 1–1b. Creating a lower-level paragraph is called **demoting** text; creating a higher-level paragraph is called **promoting** text. The following steps create a multilevel bulleted list consisting of three levels.

1

- Type **Enjoy a hike on natural surface trails** and then press the ENTER key (Figure 1–19).

Figure 1–19

• Click the 'Increase
List Level' button
(Home tab |
Paragraph group)
to indent the
second paragraph
below the first and
create a second-
level paragraph
(Figure 1–20).

Q&A

Why does the bullet
for this paragraph
have a different
size?
A different bullet
is assigned to each
paragraph level.

Figure 1–20

❸

• Type
**Approximately
1.5 miles** and
then press the ENTER
key (Figure 1–21).

Figure 1–21

❹

• Click the 'Decrease
List Level' button
(Home tab |
Paragraph group)
so that the second-
level paragraph
becomes a first-
level paragraph
(Figure 1–22).

Q&A

Can I delete bullets
on a slide?
Yes. If you do
not want bullets
to display in
a particular
paragraph, click the
Bullets button (Home
tab | Paragraph group) or right-click the paragraph
and then click the Bullets button on the shortcut menu.

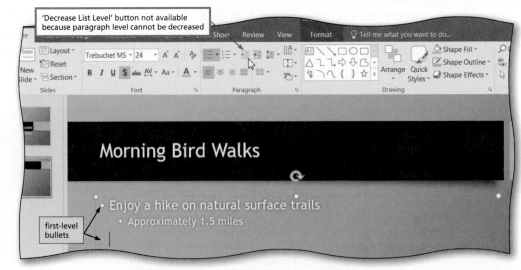

Figure 1–22

Other Ways

1. Press TAB to promote paragraph; press SHIFT+TAB to demote paragraph

To Type the Remaining Text for Slide 2

The following steps complete the text for Slide 2.

1 Type `9 a.m. every Saturday` and then press the ENTER key.

2 Click the 'Increase List Level' button (Home tab | Paragraph group) to demote the paragraph to the second level.

3 Type `Bring binoculars and a field guide` and then press the ENTER key to add a new paragraph at the same level as the previous paragraph.

4 Click the 'Increase List Level' button (Home tab | Paragraph group) to demote the paragraph to the third level.

5 Type `Extra supplies will be available` but do not press the ENTER key (Figure 1–23).

Q&A I pressed the ENTER key in error, and now a new bullet appears after the last entry on this slide. How can I remove this extra bullet?
Press the BACKSPACE key twice.

Figure 1–23

BTW
Automatic Spelling Correction
As you type, PowerPoint automatically corrects some misspelled words. For example, if you type availalbe, PowerPoint automatically corrects the misspelling and displays the word, available, when you press the SPACEBAR or type a punctuation mark. To see a complete list of automatically corrected words, click File on the ribbon to open the Backstage view, click the Options tab in the Backstage view, click Proofing in the left pane (PowerPoint Options dialog box), click the AutoCorrect Options button, and then scroll through the list near the bottom of the dialog box.

To Select a Group of Words

1 INSERT PRESENTATION SLIDES | 2 ENTER TEXT | 3 FORMAT TEXT | 4 INSERT GRAPHICAL ELEMENTS
5 SIZE & POSITION | 6 ENHANCE SLIDE SHOW | 7 DISPLAY SLIDES

PowerPoint designers use many techniques to emphasize words and characters on a slide. To highlight the day of the week when the walks are held, you want to bold and increase the font size of the words, every Saturday, in the body text. The following steps select two words. *Why? You could perform these actions separately, but it is more efficient to select the words and then change the font attributes.*

1

• Position the pointer immediately to the left of the first character of the text to be selected (in this case, the e in the word, every) (Figure 1–24).

Figure 1–24

• Drag the pointer through the last character of the text to be selected (in this case, the y in the word, Saturday) (Figure 1–25).

text to be formatted is selected

Figure 1–25

Other Ways

1. Press CTRL+SHIFT+RIGHT ARROW repeatedly until desired words are selected

---

1 INSERT PRESENTATION SLIDES | 2 ENTER TEXT | 3 FORMAT TEXT | 4 INSERT GRAPHICAL ELEMENTS
5 SIZE & POSITION | 6 ENHANCE SLIDE SHOW | 7 DISPLAY SLIDES

To Bold Text

Why? *Bold characters display somewhat thicker and darker than those that display in a regular font style.* Clicking the Bold button on the mini toolbar is an efficient method of bolding text. To add more emphasis to the fact that the body needs nature for cooling purposes, you want to bold the words, every Saturday. The following step bolds this text.

• With the words, every Saturday, selected, click the Bold button on the mini toolbar to bold the two words (Figure 1–26).

default font size is 24 point

Bold button selected

selected words are bolded

Figure 1–26

Other Ways

1. Right-click selected text, click Font on shortcut menu, click Font tab (Font dialog box), click Bold in Font style list, click OK button

2. Select text, click Bold button (Home tab | Font group)

3. Click Font dialog box launcher (Home tab | Font group), click Font tab (Font dialog box), click Bold in Font style list, click OK button

4. Select text, press CTRL+B

To Increase Font Size

The following steps increase the font size from 24 to 28 point. ***Why?*** *To add emphasis, you increase the font size for the words, every Saturday.*

1 With the words, every Saturday, still selected, click the 'Increase Font Size' button on the mini toolbar once (Figure 1–27).

2 Click outside the selected area to deselect the two words.

Figure 1–27

Adding New Slides, Changing Slide Layouts, and Changing the Theme

Slide 3 in Figure 1–1c contains two pictures: a grasshopper and a dragonfly. Slide 4 in Figure 1–1d contains an illustration of a firefly and does not contain a bulleted list. When you add a new slide, PowerPoint applies the Title and Content layout. This layout and the Title Slide layout for Slide 1 are the default styles. A **layout** specifies the arrangement of placeholders on a slide. These placeholders are arranged in various configurations and can contain text, such as the slide title or a bulleted list, or they can contain content, such as SmartArt graphics, pictures, charts, tables, and shapes. The placement of the text, in relationship to content, depends on the slide layout. You can specify a particular slide layout when you add a new slide to a presentation or after you have created the slide.

Using the **layout gallery**, you can choose a slide layout. The nine layouts in this gallery have a variety of placeholders to define text and content positioning and formatting. Three layouts are for text: Title Slide, Section Header, and Title Only. Five are for text and content: Title and Content, Two Content, Comparison, Content with Caption, and Picture with Caption. The Blank layout has no placeholders. If none of these standard layouts meets your design needs, you can create a **custom layout**. A custom layout specifies the number, size, and location of placeholders, background content, and optional slide and placeholder-level properties.

When you change the layout of a slide, PowerPoint retains the text and objects and repositions them into the appropriate placeholders. Using slide layouts eliminates the need to resize objects and the font size because PowerPoint automatically sizes the objects and text to fit the placeholders. At any time when creating the slide content, you can change the theme and variant to give the presentation a different look and feel.

To Add a New Slide and Enter a Slide Title and Headings

1 INSERT PRESENTATION SLIDES | 2 ENTER TEXT | 3 FORMAT TEXT | **4 INSERT GRAPHICAL ELEMENTS**
5 SIZE & POSITION | 6 ENHANCE SLIDE SHOW | 7 DISPLAY SLIDES

The text on Slide 3 in Figure 1–1c consists of a title and two headings. The appropriate layout for this slide is named Comparison. *Why? The Comparison layout has two headings and two text placeholders adjacent to each other, so an audience member easily can compare and contrast the items shown side by side.* The following steps add Slide 3 to the presentation with the Comparison layout and then enter the title and heading text for this slide.

BTW

Customizing a Slide Layout

PowerPoint provides a wide variety of slide layouts for each theme, but you can customize the layouts to make your deck unique. Display the View tab, click Slide Master (View tab | Master Views group), select the thumbnail below the slide master in the left pane that you would like to customize, and then make the desired modifications.

1

- Click the New Slide arrow in the Slides group to display the Berlin layout gallery (Figure 1–28).

Figure 1–28

2

- Click Comparison to add Slide 3 and apply that layout (Figure 1–29).

Figure 1–29

❸
- Type **Afternoon Insect Identification** in the title text placeholder.
- Click the left heading placeholder with the label, 'Click to add text', to select this placeholder (Figure 1–30).

Figure 1–30

❹
- Type **Grasshoppers** and then press the ENTER key.
- Type **(also known as locusts)** but do not press the ENTER key.
- Select the right heading placeholder and then type **Dragonflies** and press the ENTER key.

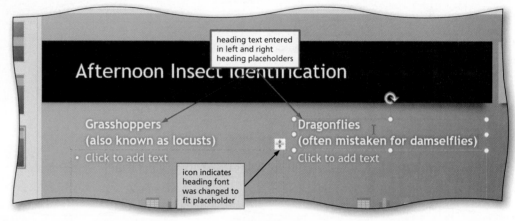

Figure 1–31

- Type **(often mistaken for damselflies)** but do not press the ENTER key (Figure 1–31).

Q&A | What is the white box with the arrow between the placeholders?
The text is too large to fit in the placeholder using the default font and paragraph attributes, so PowerPoint adjusts the text so it displays properly. That icon informs you that the font was altered.

To Add a Slide with the Title Only Layout

1 INSERT PRESENTATION SLIDES | 2 ENTER TEXT | 3 FORMAT TEXT | **4 INSERT GRAPHICAL ELEMENTS**
5 SIZE & POSITION | 6 ENHANCE SLIDE SHOW | 7 DISPLAY SLIDES

The following steps add Slide 4 to the presentation with the Title Only slide layout style. *Why? The only text on the slide is the title, and the majority of the slide content is the illustration.*

1

- If necessary, click Home on the ribbon to display the Home tab.
- Click the New Slide arrow (Home tab | Slides group) to display the Berlin layout gallery (Figure 1–32).

Figure 1–32

2

- Click Title Only to add a new slide and apply that layout to Slide 4 (Figure 1–33).

Figure 1–33

To Enter a Slide Title

The only text on Slide 4 is the title. The following step enters the title text for this slide.

1 Type **Twilight Firefly Hikes** as the title text but do not press the ENTER key (Figure 1–34).

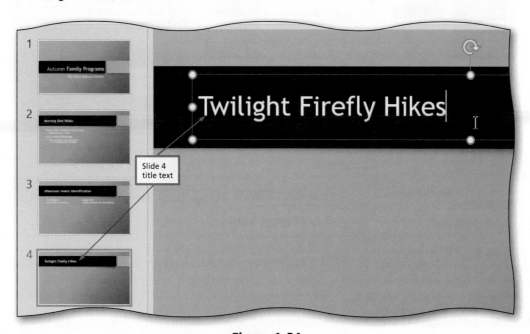

Figure 1–34

1 INSERT PRESENTATION SLIDES | 2 ENTER TEXT | 3 FORMAT TEXT | 4 INSERT GRAPHICAL ELEMENTS
5 SIZE & POSITION | 6 ENHANCE SLIDE SHOW | 7 DISPLAY SLIDES

To Change the Theme

A theme provides consistency in design and color throughout the entire presentation by setting the color scheme, font set, and layout of a presentation. This collection of formatting choices includes a set of colors (the Theme Colors group), a set of heading and content text fonts (the Theme Fonts group), and a set of lines and fill effects (the Theme Effects group). These groups allow you to choose and change the appearance of all the slides or individual slides in your presentation. *Why? At any time while creating the slide deck, you may decide to switch the theme so that the slides have a totally different appearance.* The following steps change the theme for this presentation from Berlin to Main Event.

1

• Click Design on the ribbon to display the Design tab (Figure 1–35).

Figure 1–35

2

• Click the More button (Design tab | Themes group) to expand the gallery, which shows more theme gallery options. If necessary, scroll down to the bottom of the gallery to view the Main Event thumbnail (Figure 1–36).

Experiment

• Point to various document themes in the Themes gallery and watch the colors and fonts change on the title slide.

Figure 1–36

Q&A | Are the themes displayed in a specific order?
No. Your themes might be in a different order than shown here.

How can I determine the theme names?
If you point to a theme, a ScreenTip with the theme's name appears on the screen.

3

• Click the Main Event theme to apply this theme to all four slides (Figure 1–37).

Q&A | If I decide at some future time that this design does not fit the theme of my presentation, can I apply a different design?
Yes. You can repeat these steps at any time while creating your presentation.

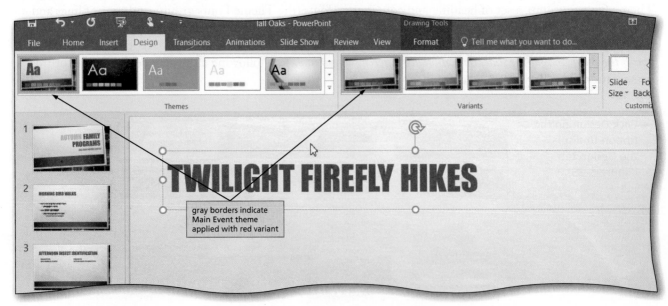

Figure 1–37

To Change the Variant

When you began creating this presentation, you selected the Berlin theme and then chose a green variant. You can change the color variation at any time for any theme. *Why? The new Main Event theme has a default red color, but you want to emphasize the green color associated with nature, just like you initially did when you chose the green variant for the Berlin theme.* The following steps change the variant from red to green.

1

- Point to the green variant (Design tab | Variants group) to see a preview of the green variant on Slide 4 (Figure 1–38).

 Experiment

- Point to the orange, green, and blue variants and watch the colors change on the slide.

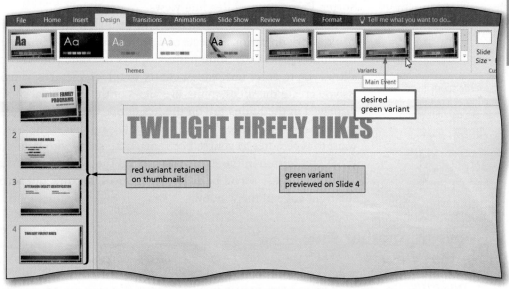

Figure 1–38

2

- Click the green variant to apply this color to all four slides (Figure 1–39).

Q&A If I decide at some future time that this color variation does not fit the theme of my presentation, can I apply a different variant?
Yes. You can repeat these steps at any time.

Figure 1–39

3

- Save the presentation again on the same storage location with the same file name.

Q&A Why should I save the presentation again?
You have made several modifications to the presentation since you last saved it. Thus, you should save it again.

Break Point: If you wish to take a break, this is a good place to do so. You can exit PowerPoint now. To resume at a later time, run PowerPoint, open the file called Tall Oaks, and continue following the steps from this location forward. For a detailed example of exiting PowerPoint, running PowerPoint, and opening a file, refer to the Office and Windows module at the beginning of the book.

PowerPoint Views

The PowerPoint window display varies depending on the view. A **view** is the mode in which the presentation appears on the screen. You will use some views when you are developing slides and others when you are delivering your presentation. When creating a presentation, you most likely will use Normal, Slide Sorter, Notes Pane, and Outline views. When presenting your slides to an audience, you most likely will use Slide Sorter, Presenter, and Reading views.

The default view is **Normal view**, which is composed of three areas that allow you to work on various aspects of a presentation simultaneously. The large area in the middle, called the **Slide pane**, displays the slide you currently are developing and allows you to enter text, tables, charts, graphics, pictures, video, and other elements. As you create the slides, miniature views of the individual slides, called thumbnails, are displayed in the **Slides tab** on the left of the screen. You can rearrange the thumbnails in this pane. The **Notes pane**, by default, is hidden at the bottom of the window. If you want to type notes to yourself or remarks to share with your audience, you can click the Notes button in the status bar to open the Notes pane. After you have created at least two slides, a **scroll bar** containing **scroll arrows** and **scroll boxes** will appear on the right edge of the window.

To Move to Another Slide in Normal View

1 INSERT PRESENTATION SLIDES | 2 ENTER TEXT | 3 FORMAT TEXT | 4 INSERT GRAPHICAL ELEMENTS
5 SIZE & POSITION | 6 ENHANCE SLIDE SHOW | 7 DISPLAY SLIDES

Why? *When creating or editing a presentation in Normal view (the view you are currently using), you often want to display a slide other than the current one.* Before continuing with developing this project, you want to display the title slide. You can click the desired slide in the Slides tab or drag the scroll box on the vertical scroll bar; if you are using a touch screen, you can tap the desired slide in the Slides tab. When you drag the scroll box, the **slide indicator** shows the number and title of the slide you are about to display. Releasing shows the slide. The following steps move from Slide 4 to Slide 1 using the scroll box in the Slide pane.

1

- Position the pointer on the scroll box.

- Press and hold down the mouse button so that Slide: 4 of 4 Twilight Firefly Hikes appears in the slide indicator (Figure 1–40).

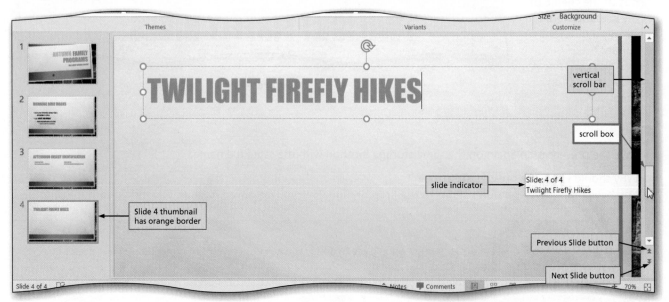

Figure 1–40

2

- Drag the scroll box up the vertical scroll bar until Slide: 1 of 4 Autumn Family Programs appears in the slide indicator (Figure 1–41).

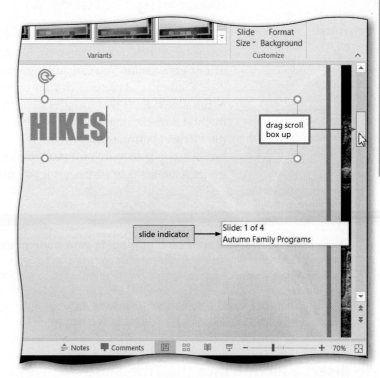

Figure 1–41

3

- Release so that Slide 1 appears in the Slide pane and the Slide 1 thumbnail has an orange border in the Slides tab (Figure 1–42).

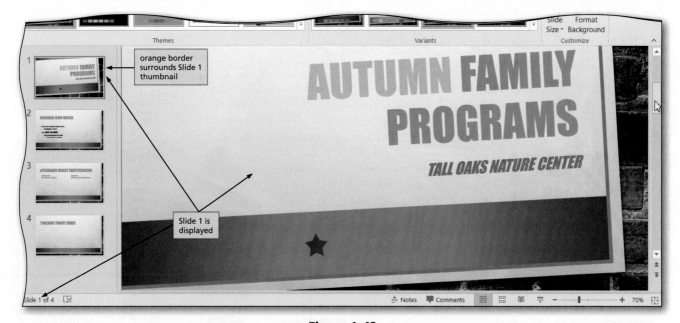

Figure 1–42

Other Ways

1. Click Next Slide button or Previous Slide button to move forward or back one slide

2. Click slide in Slides tab

3. Press PAGE DOWN or PAGE UP to move forward or back one slide

BTW
Microsoft Clip Organizer
Previous versions of Microsoft Office stored photos, illustrations, animations, videos, and other media in the Clip Organizer. Office 2016 has replaced this feature with the Insert Pictures dialog box, which is displayed when you click the Online Pictures button (Insert tab | Images group). You then can search for and insert files using Bing Image Search.

Inserting Pictures into Slides

Adding pictures can help increase the visual and audio appeal of many slides. These images may include photographs, illustrations, and other artwork. If you have a Microsoft account, you can add pictures from websites, including Flickr and OneDrive.

You can add pictures to your presentation in two ways. One way is by selecting one of the slide layouts that includes a content placeholder with a Pictures button. A second method is by clicking the Pictures button in the Images area on the Insert tab. Clicking the Pictures button opens the Insert Picture dialog box. The **Insert Picture dialog box** allows you to search for picture files that are stored on your computer or a storage device. Contact your instructor if you need the pictures used in the following steps.

CONSIDER THIS

How can you design a title slide that holds your audience's attention?

Develop a slide that reflects the content of your presentation but does so in a thought-provoking way. A title, at the very least, should prepare your audience for the material they are about to see and hear. Look for ways to focus attention on your theme and the method in which you plan to present this theme. A unique photograph or graphic can help generate interest. You may decide to introduce your topic with a startling fact, a rhetorical question, or a quotation. The device you choose depends upon your audience, the occasion, and the presentation's purpose.

To Insert a Picture into the Title Slide

1 INSERT PRESENTATION SLIDES | 2 ENTER TEXT | 3 FORMAT TEXT | 4 INSERT GRAPHICAL ELEMENTS
5 SIZE & POSITION | 6 ENHANCE SLIDE SHOW | 7 DISPLAY SLIDES

Slide 1 uses the Title Slide layout, which has two placeholders for text but none for graphical content. You desire to place a graphic on Slide 1. *Why? It is likely that your viewers will see an image on this slide before they read any text, so you want to include a picture to create interest in the presentation and introduce your audience to the topic.* For this presentation, you will insert a photograph of several leaves that have changed colors. Later in this module, you will resize and position the picture in an appropriate location. The following steps add a picture to Slide 1.

- Click Insert on the ribbon to display the Insert tab.
- Click the Pictures button (Insert tab | Images group) to display the Insert Picture dialog box.

Q&A | What should I do if no pictures are displayed when I click the Pictures button?
You may need to click the Online Pictures button instead of the Pictures button.

- Navigate to the Data Files and the Module 01 folder. Click the Autumn Leaves picture to select that file (Figure 1–43).

Q&A | Why do I see only a list of file names and not thumbnails of the pictures in my folder?
Your view is different from the view shown in Figure 1–43.

Figure 1–43

3

- Click the Insert button (Insert Picture dialog box) to insert the picture into Slide 1 (Figure 1–44).

Q&A Can I double-click the picture or file name instead of selecting it and clicking the Insert button?
Yes. Either method inserts the picture.

Why is this picture displayed in this location on the slide?
The slide layout does not have a content placeholder, so PowerPoint inserts the file in an area of the slide. You will move and resize the picture later in this module.

Figure 1–44

To Insert a Picture into a Slide without a Content Placeholder

The next step is to add an owl picture to Slide 2. This slide has a bulleted list in the text placeholder, so the icon group does not display in the center of the placeholder. Later in this module, you will resize the inserted picture. The following steps add one picture to Slide 2.

1 Click the Slide 2 thumbnail in the Slides tab to display Slide 2.

2 Click Insert on the ribbon to display the Insert tab and then click the Pictures button (Insert tab | Images group) to display the Insert Picture dialog box.

3 If necessary, scroll down the list of files, click Owl to select the file, and then click the Insert button to insert the picture into Slide 2 (Figure 1–45).

Q&A Why is my picture a different size from the one shown in Figure1-1b?
The clip was inserted into the slide and not into a content placeholder. You will resize the picture later in this module.

BTW

Wrapping Text around a Photo
PowerPoint does not allow you to wrap text around a picture or other graphics, such as tables, shapes, and charts. This feature, however, is available in Word.

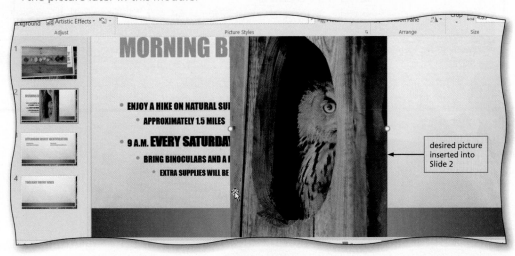

Figure 1–45

To Insert a Picture
into a Content Placeholder

Slide 3 uses the Comparison layout, which has a content placeholder below each of the two headings. You desire to insert pictures into both content placeholders. *Why? You want to display two insects that participants likely will identify during the program at the nature center.* The following steps insert a picture of a grasshopper into the left content placeholder and a dragonfly into the right content placeholder on Slide 3.

1

- Click the Slide 3 thumbnail in the Slides tab to display Slide 3 (Figure 1–46).

Figure 1–46

2

- Click the Pictures icon in the left content placeholder to select that placeholder and to open the Insert Picture dialog box.

- If necessary, scroll down the list of files, click Grasshopper to select the file, and then double-click to insert the picture into the left content placeholder (Figure 1–47).

Q&A Do I need to select the file name before double-clicking to insert the picture?
No. You just can double-click the file name.

Skitter Photo/StockSnap.io

Figure 1–47

3
- Click the Pictures icon in the right content placeholder to select that placeholder and to open the Insert Picture dialog box.

- If necessary, scroll down the list to display the Dragonfly file name and then insert this picture into the right content placeholder (Figure 1–48).

Figure 1–48

To Insert a Picture into a Slide without a Content Placeholder

Next, you will add a picture to Slide 4. This picture is an illustration, not an actual photograph, of a firefly. You will not insert this file into a content placeholder, so it will display in the center of the slide. Later in this module, you will resize this picture. You locate and insert illustrations in the same manner you used to insert photos. The following steps add an illustration picture to Slide 4.

1 Click the Slide 4 thumbnail in the Slides tab.

2 Display the Insert tab, click the Pictures button, and then insert the Firefly file into Slide 4 (Figure 1–49).

Figure 1–49

> **Break Point:** If you wish to take a break, this is a good place to do so. You can save your presentation and then exit PowerPoint now. To resume at a later time, run PowerPoint, open the file called Tall Oaks, and continue following the steps from this location forward.

Resizing Photos and Illustrations

Sometimes it is necessary to change the size of pictures and illustrations. **Resizing** includes enlarging or reducing the size of a graphic. You can resize these images using a variety of techniques. One method involves changing the size of a picture by specifying exact dimensions in a dialog box. Another method involves sliding or dragging one of the graphic's sizing handles to the desired location. A selected graphic appears surrounded by a **selection rectangle**, which has small circles, called **sizing handles** or move handles, at each corner and middle location.

To Proportionally Resize Pictures

1 INSERT PRESENTATION SLIDES | 2 ENTER TEXT | 3 FORMAT TEXT | 4 INSERT GRAPHICAL ELEMENTS
5 SIZE & POSITION | 6 ENHANCE SLIDE SHOW | 7 DISPLAY SLIDES

Why? *On Slides 1, 2, and 4, the picture and illustration sizes are too large to display aesthetically on the slides.* At times it is important to maintain the proportions of a picture, such as when a person is featured prominently. To change the size of a picture and keep the width and height in proportion to each other, drag the corner sizing handles to view how the image will look on the slide. Using these corner handles maintains the graphic's original proportions. If, however, the proportions do not need to be maintained precisely, as with the owl picture on Slide 2, drag the side sizing handles to alter the proportions so that the graphic's height and width become larger or smaller. The following steps proportionally decrease the size of the Slide 1 picture using a corner sizing handle.

- Click the Slide 1 thumbnail in the Slides tab to display Slide 1.
- Click the leaves picture to select it and display the selection rectangle.
- Point to the lower-right corner sizing handle on the picture so that the pointer changes to a two-headed arrow (Figure 1–50).

Q&A I am using a touch screen and do not see a two-headed arrow when I press and hold the lower-right sizing handle. Why?
Touch screens may not display pointers; you can just press and slide sizing handles to resize.

Figure 1–50

2

- Drag the sizing handle diagonally toward the upper-left corner of the slide until the lower-right sizing handle or the crosshair is positioned approximately as shown in Figure 1–51.

 Q&A What if the picture is not the same size as the one shown in Figure 1–51?
Repeat Steps 1 and 2.

Can I drag any corner sizing handle diagonally inward toward the opposite corner to resize the picture?
Yes.

3

- Release to resize the picture.

Figure 1–51

To Nonproportionally Resize the Photograph on Slide 2

1 INSERT PRESENTATION SLIDES | 2 ENTER TEXT | 3 FORMAT TEXT | 4 INSERT GRAPHICAL ELEMENTS
5 SIZE & POSITION | **6 ENHANCE SLIDE SHOW** | 7 DISPLAY SLIDES

Why? *The height of the owl picture in Slide 2 extends from the top to the bottom of the slide. The width, however, will cover some of the text when the picture is positioned on the right side of the slide.* The width of this picture can be decreased slightly without negatively distorting the original image. You can decrease the width of a picture by sliding or dragging one of the sizing handles on the sides of the image. The following steps resize the width of the nature bottle picture using a sizing handle along the side of the image.

1

- Display Slide 2 and then click the owl picture to select it and display the selection rectangle.

- Click the Zoom Out button as many times as necessary until the Zoom level is 50%.

- Point to the middle sizing handle on the bottom edge of the picture so that the pointer changes to a two-headed arrow (Figure 1–52).

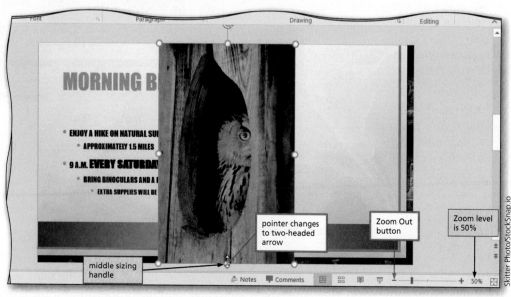

Figure 1–52

2

• Drag the sizing handle upward until the sizing handle or crosshair is positioned on the top of the green bar, as shown in Figure 1–53.

Q&A What if the picture is not the same size as the one shown in Figure 1–53? Repeat Steps 1 and 2.

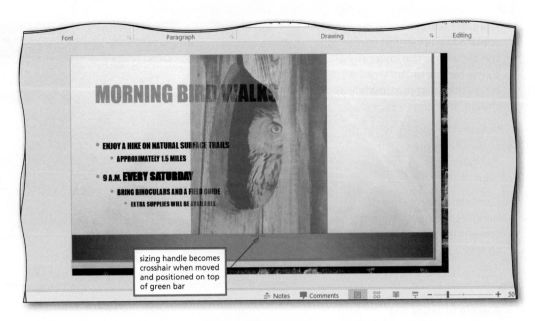

Figure 1–53

3

• Release to resize the picture.

• Click outside the picture to deselect it (Figure 1–54).

Q&A What if I want to return the picture to its original size and start again? With the picture selected, click the Reset Picture arrow (Picture Tools Format tab | Adjust group) and then click Reset Picture & Size in the Reset Picture gallery.

What happened to the Picture Tools Format tab? When you click outside the picture, PowerPoint deselects the object and removes the Picture Tools Format tab from the screen.

Figure 1–54

To Resize the Illustration on Slide 4

The firefly picture illustration on Slide 4 can be reduced slightly to fit entirely on the slide. You resize an illustration in the same manner that you resize a photograph. You want to maintain the proportions of the character and nature in this illustration, so you will drag one of the corner sizing handles. The following steps resize this illustration using a corner sizing handle.

1 Display Slide 4 and then click the firefly illustration to select it.

2 Drag any corner sizing handle on the illustration diagonally inward until the illustration is positioned and resized approximately as shown in Figure 1–55.

Figure 1–55

To Move Pictures

1 INSERT PRESENTATION SLIDES | 2 ENTER TEXT | 3 FORMAT TEXT | 4 INSERT GRAPHICAL ELEMENTS
5 SIZE & POSITION | **6 ENHANCE SLIDE SHOW** | **7 DISPLAY SLIDES**

Why? *After you insert a photo or an illustration on a slide, you might want to reposition it. The leaves picture on Slide 1 could be moved to the lower-left side of the slide, the owl on Slide 2 could be moved to the right side of the slide, and the illustration on Slide 4 could be positioned in the center of the slide.* PowerPoint displays **Smart Guides** automatically when a picture, shape, or other object is moved and is close to lining up with another slide element. These layout guides, which display as dashed lines, help you align slide elements vertically and horizontally. They display when aligning to the left, right, top, bottom, and middle of placeholders and other objects on a slide. For example, a Smart Guide will display to help you align the right or left edge of a picture in relation to a text placeholder or to another picture. The following steps center the illustration on Slide 4 and move the pictures on Slides 2 and 1.

1

- If necessary, click the firefly illustration on Slide 4 to select it.

- With the four-headed arrow displaying, drag the illustration downward and toward the left until the horizontal Smart Guide is displayed under the title text placeholder and the vertical Smart Guide is displayed through the center of the slide, as shown in Figure 1–56, and then release.

- If necessary, select the illustration and then use the ARROW keys to position it precisely as shown in Figure 1–56.

Q&A The firefly still is not located exactly where I want it to display. What can I do to align the image?
Press the CTRL key while you press the ARROW keys. This key combination moves the illustration in smaller increments than when you press only an ARROW key.

Figure 1–56

2

- Display Slide 2 and then click the owl picture to select it.

- Drag the picture downward and to the right until the horizontal Smart Guide is displayed above the title text placeholder and the right edge is aligned with the vertical gray bar on the right side of the slide (Figure 1–57).

Figure 1–57

3

- Display Slide 1 and then click the leaves picture to select it.

- Drag the picture downward until the horizontal Smart Guide is displayed under the title text placeholder and the vertical Smart Guide is displayed near the left side of the slide, as shown in Figure 1–58, and then release.

Figure 1–58

 Q&A Can I move the picture in small increments?

Yes. To move or nudge the picture in very small increments, hold down the CTRL key with the picture selected while pressing the ARROW keys. You cannot perform this action using a touch screen.

To Rotate a Picture

1 INSERT PRESENTATION SLIDES | 2 ENTER TEXT | 3 FORMAT TEXT | 4 INSERT GRAPHICAL ELEMENTS
5 SIZE & POSITION | 6 ENHANCE SLIDE SHOW | 7 DISPLAY SLIDES

Why? *The Main Event Title Slide layout is angled, so the picture would complement the design by being angled, too.* Dragging the **rotation handle** above a selected object allows you to rotate an object in any direction. The following steps rotate the leaves picture.

1

- With the leaves picture selected, position the mouse pointer over the rotation handle so that it changes to a Free Rotate pointer (Figure 1–59).

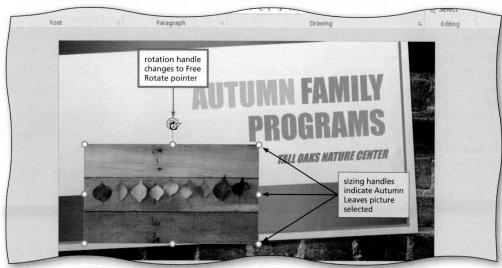

Figure 1–59

2

- Drag the rotation handle counterclockwise and then move the picture so that it is displayed as shown in Figure 1–60.

Figure 1–60

Ending a Slide Show with a Closing Slide

All the text for the slides in the Tall Oaks slide show has been entered. This presentation thus far consists of a title slide, one text slide with a multilevel bulleted list, a third slide with a Comparison layout, and a fourth slide for an illustration. A closing slide that resembles the title slide is the final slide to create.

What factors should you consider when developing a closing slide for the presentation?

After the last slide appears during a slide show, the default PowerPoint setting is to end the presentation with a **black slide**. This black slide appears only when the slide show is running and concludes the slide show, so your audience never sees the PowerPoint window. It is a good idea, however, to end your presentation with a final closing slide to display at the end of the presentation. This slide ends the presentation gracefully and should be an exact copy, or a very similar copy, of your title slide. The audience will recognize that the presentation is drawing to a close when this slide appears. It can remain on the screen when the audience asks questions, approaches the speaker for further information, or exits the room.

CONSIDER THIS

To Duplicate a Slide

Why? *When two slides contain similar information and have the same format, duplicating one slide and then making minor modifications to the new slide saves time and increases consistency.* Slide 5 will have the same layout and design as Slide 1. The most expedient method of creating this slide is to copy Slide 1 and then make minor modifications to the new slide. The following steps duplicate the title slide.

1

• With Slide 1 selected, click the New Slide arrow (Home tab | Slides group) to display the Main Event layout gallery (Figure 1–61).

Figure 1–61

2

• Click 'Duplicate Selected Slides' in the Main Event layout gallery to create a new Slide 2, which is a duplicate of Slide 1 (Figure 1–62).

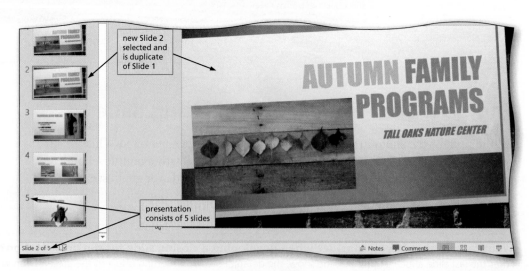

Figure 1–62

To Arrange a Slide

The new Slide 2 was inserted directly below Slide 1 because Slide 1 was the selected slide. This duplicate slide needs to display at the end of the presentation directly after the final title and content slide. *Why?* *It is a closing slide that reinforces the concept presented in Slide 1 and indicates to your audiences that your presentation is ending.*

Changing slide order is an easy process and is best performed in the Slides tab. When you click the thumbnail and begin to drag it to a new location, the remaining thumbnails realign to show the new sequence. When you release, the slide drops into the desired location. Hence, this process of sliding or dragging and then dropping the thumbnail in a new location is called **drag and drop**. You can use the drag-and-drop method to move any selected item, including text and graphics. The following step moves the new Slide 2 to the end of the presentation so that it becomes a closing slide.

1

- With Slide 2 selected, drag the Slide 2 slide thumbnail below the last slide in the Slides tab so that it becomes the new Slide 5 (Figure 1–63).

cursor shape indicates drag-and-drop method

Figure 1–63

Other Ways

1. Click Slide Sorter button on status bar, drag thumbnail to new location

2. Click Slide Sorter button (View tab | Presentation Views group), click slide thumbnail, drag thumbnail to new location

Break Point: If you wish to take a break, this is a good place to do so. Be sure to save the Tall Oaks file again and then you can exit PowerPoint. To resume at a later time, run PowerPoint, open the file called Tall Oaks, and continue following the steps from this location forward.

Making Changes to Slide Text Content

After creating slides in a presentation, you may find that you want to make changes to the text. Changes may be required because a slide contains an error, the scope of the presentation shifts, or the style is inconsistent. This section explains the types of changes that commonly occur when creating a presentation.

You generally make three types of changes to text in a presentation: additions, replacements, and deletions.

- Additions are necessary when you omit text from a slide and need to add it later. You may need to insert text in the form of a sentence, word, or single character. For example, you may want to add the presenter's middle name on the title slide.

- Replacements are needed when you want to revise the text in a presentation. For example, you may want to substitute the word, *their*, for the word, *there*.

• Deletions are required when text on a slide is incorrect or no longer is relevant to the presentation. For example, a slide may look cluttered. Therefore, you may want to remove one of the bulleted paragraphs to add more space.

Editing text in PowerPoint basically is the same as editing text in a word processing program. The following sections illustrate the most common changes made to text in a presentation.

BTW
Selecting
Nonadjacent Text
In PowerPoint, you can use keyboard keys to select letters, numbers, or special characters not next to each other. This is especially helpful when you are applying the same formatting to multiple words. To select nonadjacent text, select the first item, such as a word or paragraph, as usual; then, press and hold down the CTRL key. While holding down the CTRL key, select additional items.

Replacing Text in an Existing Slide

When you need to correct a word or phrase, you can replace the text by selecting the text to be replaced and then typing the new text. As soon as you press any key on the keyboard, the selected text is deleted and the new text is displayed.

PowerPoint inserts text to the left of the insertion point. The text to the right of the insertion point moves to the right (and shifts downward if necessary) to accommodate the added text.

Deleting Text

You can delete text using one of many methods. One is to use the BACKSPACE key to remove text just typed. The second is to position the insertion point to the left of the text you want to delete and then press the DELETE key. The third method is to drag through the text you want to delete and then click the Cut button on the mini toolbar, press DELETE or BACKSPACE key, or press CTRL+X. Use the third method when deleting large sections of text.

To Delete Text in a Placeholder

1 INSERT PRESENTATION SLIDES | 2 ENTER TEXT | **3 FORMAT TEXT** | 4 INSERT GRAPHICAL ELEMENTS
5 SIZE & POSITION | 6 ENHANCE SLIDE SHOW | **7 DISPLAY SLIDES**

Why? *To keep the ending slide clean and simple, you want to edit a few words in the slide title and subtitle text.* The following steps change Autumn to Register For and then change Tall Oaks Nature Center to Call 555-8928 today! in the placeholders.

• With Slide 5 selected, position the pointer immediately to the left of the first character of the text to be selected in the title text placeholder (in this case, the A in the word, Autumn).

• Drag the pointer through the last character of the text to be selected (in this case, the n in the word, Autumn) (Figure 1–64).

Q&A
Can I drag from left to right or right to left?
Yes. Either direction will select the letters.

Could I also have selected the word, Autumn, by double-clicking it?
Yes. Either method works to select a word.

Figure 1–64

2

- Press the DELETE key to delete the selected text.

- Type **Register for** as the first words in the title text placeholder (Figure 1–65).

Q&A Could I have typed these words while the word, Autumn, was selected without cutting the text first?

Yes. Either method works to replace words. You will use this alternate method in the next step.

Why does the text display with all capital letters despite the fact that I am typing uppercase and lowercase letters?

The Main Event theme uses the All Caps effect for the title and subtitle text. This effect converts lowercase letters to uppercase letters.

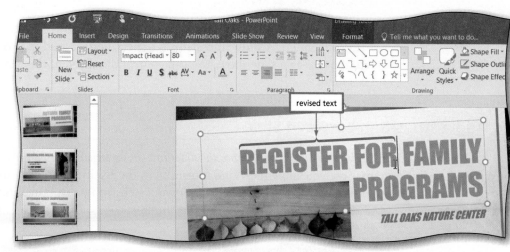

Figure 1–65

3

- Position the pointer anywhere in the subtitle text placeholder other than on the picture and then triple-click to select all the text, Tall Oaks Nature Center (Figure 1–66).

Figure 1–66

4

- Type **Call 816-555-8928 today!** as the new subtitle text (Figure 1-67).

- If requested by your instructor, change the last four digits of the phone number in the subtitle text placeholder, 8928, to the last four digits of your phone number.

Figure 1–67

Other Ways

1. Right-click selected text, click Cut on shortcut menu   2. Select text, press DELETE or BACKSPACE key   3. Select text, press CTRL+X

Adding a Transition

PowerPoint includes a wide variety of visual and sound effects that can be applied to text or content. A **slide transition** is a special effect used to progress from one slide to the next in a slide show. You can control the speed of the transition effect and add a sound.

To Add a Transition between Slides

Why? Transitions add interest when you advance the slides in a presentation and make a slide show presentation look professional. In this presentation, you apply the Wind transition in the Exciting category to all slides and change the transition speed from 2 seconds to 3 seconds. The following steps apply this transition to the presentation.

- Click the Transitions tab on the ribbon and then point to the More button (Transitions tab | Transition to This Slide group) in the Transition to This Slide gallery (Figure 1–68).

Q&A
Is a transition applied now?
No. None, the first slide icon in the Transition to This Slide group, is selected, which indicates no transition has been applied.

Figure 1–68

2

- Click the More button to expand the Transitions gallery.

- Point to the Wind transition in the Exciting category in the Transitions gallery (Figure 1–69).

Figure 1–69

3

- Click Wind in the Exciting category in the Transitions gallery to view a preview of this transition and to apply this transition to the closing slide.

Q&A Why does a star appear next to Slide 5 in the Slides tab? The star indicates that a transition animation effect is applied to that slide.

- Click the Duration up arrow (Transitions tab | Timing group) four times to change the transition speed from 02.00 seconds to 03.00 seconds (Figure 1–70).

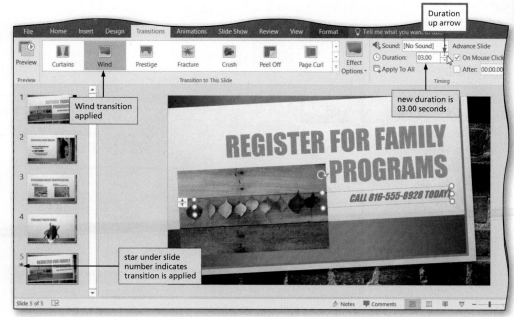

Figure 1–70

Q&A Why did the time change from the default 02.00 to 03.00?
Each transition has a default duration time. The default Wind transition time is 02.00 seconds.

4

- Click the Preview Transitions button (Transitions tab | Preview area) to view the transition and the new transition time (Figure 1–71).

Q&A Can I adjust the duration time I just set?
Yes. Click the Duration up or down arrows or type a speed in the Duration box and preview the transition until you find the time that best fits your presentation.

Figure 1–71

5

- Click the 'Apply To All' button (Transitions tab | Timing group) to apply the Wind transition and the increased transition time to Slides 1 through 4 in the presentation (Figure 1–72).

Q&A What if I want to apply a different transition and duration to each slide in the presentation? Repeat Steps 2 and 3 for each slide individually.

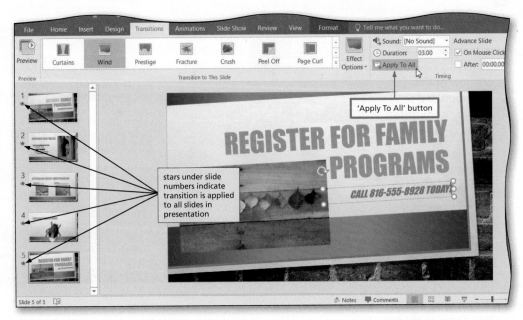

Figure 1–72

Document Properties

PowerPoint helps you organize and identify your files by using **document properties**, which are the details about a file such as the project author, title, and subject. For example, a class name or presentation topic can describe the file's purpose or content.

Why would you want to assign document properties to a presentation?

Document properties are valuable for a variety of reasons:

- Users can save time locating a particular file because they can view a file's document properties without opening the presentation.

- By creating consistent properties for files having similar content, users can better organize their presentations.

- Some organizations require PowerPoint users to add document properties so that other employees can view details about these files.

The more common document properties are standard and automatically updated properties. **Standard properties** are associated with all Microsoft Office files and include author, title, and subject. **Automatically updated properties** include file system properties, such as the date you create or change a file, and statistics, such as the file size.

BTW

Printing Document Properties

PowerPoint 2016 does not allow you to print document properties. This feature, however, is available in other Office 2016 apps, including Word and Excel.

To Change Document Properties

To change document properties, you would follow these steps.

1. Click File on the ribbon to open the Backstage view and then, if necessary, click the Info tab in the Backstage view to display the Info gallery.

2. If the property you wish to change is displayed in the Properties list in the right pane of the Info gallery, try to click that property. If a text box with that property is displayed, type the text for the property in the box, and then click the Back button in the upper-left corner of the Backstage view to return to the PowerPoint window. Skip the remaining steps.

3. If the property you wish to change is not displayed in the Properties list in the right pane of the Info gallery or you cannot change it in the Info gallery, click the Properties button in the right pane to display the Properties menu, and then click Advanced Properties on the Properties menu to display the Summary tab in the Properties dialog box.

Q&A Why are some of the document properties in my Document Information Panel already filled in?
The person who installed Office 2016 on your computer or network may have set or customized the properties.

4. Type the desired text in the appropriate property boxes.

5. Click the OK button (Properties dialog box) to close the dialog box

6. Click the Back button in the upper-left corner of the Backstage view to return to the PowerPoint presentation window.

Viewing the Presentation in Slide Show View

The 'Start From Beginning' button, located in the Quick Access Toolbar, allows you to show a presentation using a computer. As the name implies, the first slide to be displayed always will be Slide 1. You also can run a presentation starting with the slide currently displaying when you click the Slide Show button on the status bar. In either case, PowerPoint displays the slides on the full screen without any of the PowerPoint window objects, such as the ribbon. The full-screen slide hides the toolbars, menus, and other PowerPoint window elements.

> **BTW**
> **PowerPoint Help**
> At any time while using PowerPoint, you can find answers to questions and display information about various topics through PowerPoint Help. Used properly, this form of assistance can increase your productivity and reduce your frustrations by minimizing the time you spend learning how to use PowerPoint. For instructions about PowerPoint Help and exercises that will help you gain confidence in using it, read the Office and Windows module at the beginning of this book.

To Start Slide Show View

| 1 INSERT PRESENTATION SLIDES | 2 ENTER TEXT | 3 FORMAT TEXT | 4 INSERT GRAPHICAL ELEMENTS |
| 5 SIZE & POSITION | 6 ENHANCE SLIDE SHOW | 7 DISPLAY SLIDES |

Why? You run a presentation for your audience so they can see the slides in their entirety and view any transitions or other effects added to the slides. When making a presentation, you use **Slide Show view**. You can start Slide Show view from Normal view or Slide Sorter view. Slide Show view begins when you click the 'Start From Beginning' button or the Slide Show button. The following steps start Slide Show view starting with Slide 1.

1

• Point to the 'Start From Beginning' button (Figure 1–73).

Q&A What would have displayed if I had clicked the Slide Show button instead of the 'Start From Beginning' button?
When you click the Slide Show button to start the presentation, PowerPoint begins the show with the currently displayed slide, which in this case is Slide 5. Only Slide 5 would display during the slide show.

Figure 1–73

● Click the 'Start From Beginning'
button to display the transition
and the title slide (Figure 1–74).

Q&A Where is the PowerPoint window?
When you run a slide show, the
PowerPoint window is hidden. It
will reappear once you end your
slide show.

transition
displayed as title
slide appears in
Slide Show view

Figure 1–74

Other Ways

1. Display Slide 1, click Slide Show button on status bar
2. Click 'Start From Beginning' button (Slide Show tab | Start Slide Show group)
3. Press F5

To Move Manually through Slides in a Slide Show

1 INSERT PRESENTATION SLIDES | 2 ENTER TEXT | 3 FORMAT TEXT | 4 INSERT GRAPHICAL ELEMENTS

5 SIZE & POSITION | 6 ENHANCE SLIDE SHOW | **7 DISPLAY SLIDES**

After you begin Slide Show view, you can move forward or backward through the slides. PowerPoint allows you to advance through the slides manually or automatically. During a slide show, each slide in the presentation shows on the screen, one slide at a time. Each time you click, the next slide appears. The following steps move manually through the slides. *Why? You can control the length of time each slide is displayed and change the preset order if you need to review a slide already shown or jump ahead to another slide designed to display later in the presentation.*

● Click each slide until Slide 5
(Register for Family Programs) is
displayed (Figure 1–75).

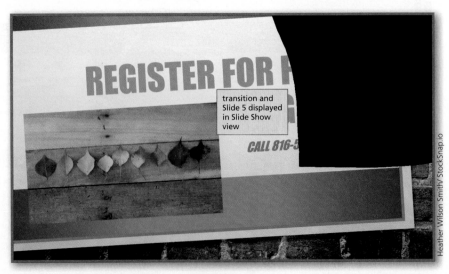

REGISTER FOR F

transition and
Slide 5 displayed
in Slide Show
view

CALL 816-5

Heather Wilson Smith/ StockSnap.io

Figure 1–75

2

- Click Slide 5 so that the black slide appears with a message announcing the end of the slide show (Figure 1–76).

Q&A I see a small toolbar in the lower-left corner of my slide. What is this toolbar?

You may see the Slide Show toolbar when you begin running a slide show and then click a slide or move the pointer. The buttons on this toolbar allow you to navigate to the next slide or the previous slide, to mark up the current slide, or to change the current display. If you do not see the toolbar, hover the mouse near the lower-left corner of the screen.

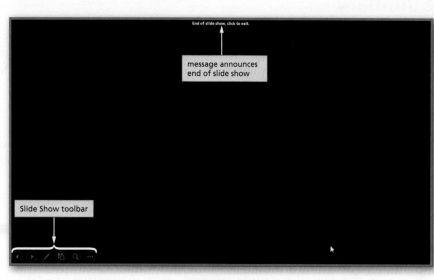

Figure 1–76

3

- Click the black slide to return to Normal view in the PowerPoint window.

Other Ways
1. Press PAGE DOWN to advance one slide at a time, or press PAGE UP to go back one slide at a time	2. Press RIGHT ARROW or DOWN ARROW to advance one slide at a time, or press LEFT ARROW or UP ARROW to go back one slide at a time	3. If Slide Show toolbar is displayed, click Next Slide or Previous Slide button on toolbar

To Save and Print the Presentation

It is a good practice to save a presentation before printing it, in the event you experience difficulties printing. For a detailed example of the procedure summarized below for saving and printing a presentation, refer to the Office and Windows module at the beginning of this book.

1 Save the presentation again on the same storage location with the same file name.

2 Print the presentation.

Q&A Do I have to wait until my presentation is complete to print it?

No, you can print a presentation at any time while you are creating it.

3 Because the project now is complete, you can exit PowerPoint.

BTW

Conserving Ink and Toner

If you want to conserve ink or toner, you can instruct PowerPoint to print draft quality documents by clicking File on the ribbon to open the Backstage view, clicking the Options tab in the Backstage view to display the PowerPoint Options dialog box, clicking Advanced in the left pane (PowerPoint Options dialog box), scrolling to the Print area in the right pane, not placing a check mark in the High quality check box, and then clicking the OK button. Then, use the Backstage view to print the document as usual.

BTW

Distributing a Document

Instead of printing and distributing a hard copy of a document, you can distribute the document electronically. Options include sending the document via email; posting it on cloud storage (such as OneDrive) and sharing the file with others; posting it on social media, a blog, or other website; and sharing a link associated with an online location of the document. You also can create and share a PDF or XPS image of the document, so that users can view the file in Acrobat Reader or XPS Viewer instead of in PowerPoint.

Summary

In this module, you learned how to use PowerPoint to create and enhance a presentation. Topics covered included applying and changing a document theme and variant, creating a title slide and text slides with a bulleted list, inserting pictures and then resizing and moving them on a slide, formatting and editing text, adding a slide transition, and viewing the presentation in Slide Show view.

CONSIDER THIS: PLAN AHEAD

What decisions will you need to make when creating your next presentation?
Use these guidelines as you complete the assignments in this module and create your own slide show decks outside of this class.

1. Determine the content you want to include on your slides.

2. Determine which theme and variant are appropriate.

3. Identify the slide layouts that best communicate your message.

4. Format various text elements to emphasize important points.

    a) Select appropriate font sizes.

    b) Emphasize important words with bold or italic type and color.

5. Locate graphical elements, such as pictures, that reinforce your message.

    a) Size and position them aesthetically on slides.

6. Determine a storage location for the presentation.

7. Determine the best method for distributing the presentation.

Apply Your Knowledge

Reinforce the skills and apply the concepts you learned in this module.

Modifying Character Formats and Paragraph Levels and Moving an Illustration

Note: To complete this assignment, you will be required to use the Data Files. Please contact your instructor for information about accessing the Data Files.

Instructions: Run PowerPoint. Open the presentation called Apply 1-1 Email Fraud, which is located in the Data Files.

The two slides in the presentation discuss phishing, which is a scam in which a perpetrator attempts to obtain an individual's personal and/or financial information. The document you open is an unformatted presentation. You are to modify the document theme, indent the paragraphs, resize and move the image, and format the text so the slides look like Figure 1–77.

Perform the following tasks:

1. Change the document theme to Droplet. Select the blue (third) variant.
2. On the title slide, use your name in place of Student Name and bold and italicize your name.
3. If requested by your instructor, change your first name to your grandmother's first name on the title slide.
4. Increase the title text font size to 60 point and then bold this text. Resize and position the illustration using the Smart Guides to align the image with the bottom of the subtitle placeholder and the right edge of the placeholders, as shown in Figure 1–77a.
5. On Slide 2, increase the indent of the second, third, and fourth paragraphs to second-level paragraphs. Then combine paragraphs six and seven (Work related and Personal) to read, **Work and personal messages can contain threats**, as shown in Figure 1–77b. Increase the indent of this paragraph to second level.

(a) Slide 1 (Title Slide with a Picture)

(b) Slide 2 (Multilevel Bulleted List)

Figure 1–77

6. Apply the Ripple transition in the Exciting category to both slides. Change the duration to 3.00 seconds. Click the 'Start From Beginning' button to start the show from the first slide. Then click to display each slide and again to end the presentation.

Continued >

Apply Your Knowledge *continued*

7. Save the presentation using the file name, Apply 1-1 Phishing.

8. Submit the revised document in the format specified by your instructor.

9. ✹ In Step 5 you combined two paragraphs and added text. How did this action improve the slide content?

Extend Your Knowledge

Extend the skills you learned in this module and experiment with new skills. You may need to use Help to complete the assignment.

Changing Slide Theme, Layout, and Text

Note: To complete this assignment, you will be required to use the Data Files. Please contact your instructor for information about accessing the Data Files.

Instructions: Run PowerPoint. Open the presentation called Extend 1-1 Waterfalls, which is located in the Data Files. Slide 1 is shown in Figure 1-78. You are aware that geologists have classified many types of waterfalls, including cascade and cataract, and the three slides in this file are part of a presentation you are developing for your geology class on this topic. Choose a theme, format the slides, and create a closing slide.

Perform the following tasks:

1. Change the document theme to Slice and the variant to green.

2. On Slide 1, format the text using techniques you learned in this module, such as changing the font size and color and bolding and italicizing words.

3. Replace the text, Student Name, with your name. In addition, delete the bullet preceding your name because, in most cases, a bullet is displayed as the first character in a list consisting of several paragraphs, not just one line of text. To delete the bullet, position the insertion point in the paragraph and then click the Bullets button (Home tab | Paragraph group).

4. Resize the picture and move it to an appropriate area on the slide.

5. On Slide 2, add bullets to the three paragraphs. To add bullets, select the paragraphs and then click the Bullets button (Home tab | Paragraph group). Insert the picture called Cascade, which is located in the Data Files, resize it, and then move it to an appropriate area on the slide.

6. On Slide 3, add bullets to the two paragraphs. Insert the picture called Cataract, which is located in the Data Files, resize it, and then move it to an appropriate area on the slide.

7. Create a closing slide using the title slide as a guide. Change the subtitle text to Natural Wonders and then underline this text. Insert the two waterfall pictures, Cascade and Cataract, and then size and move all three pictures to appropriate places on the slide.

Figure 1–78

8. Apply the Drape transition in the Exciting category to all slides and then change the duration for Slide 1 to 3.50 seconds. Click the 'Start From Beginning' button to start the show from the first slide. Then click to display each slide and again to end the presentation.

9. Save the presentation using the file name, Extend 1-1 Natural Wonders.

10. Submit the revised document in the format specified by your instructor.

11. If requested by your instructor, replace your last name on Slide 1 with the name of your hometown.

12. ✸ How did you determine the appropriate size and location of the three pictures on the closing slide?

Expand Your World

Create a solution that uses cloud and web technologies by learning and investigating on your own from general guidance.

Modifying and Exporting a Presentation

Note: To complete this assignment, you will be required to use the Data Files. Please contact your instructor for information about accessing the Data Files.

Instructions: Run PowerPoint. Open the presentation called Expand 1-1 Youth Group, which is located in the Data Files. The local youth group in your community is sponsoring a talent show, and you are part of a committee to publicize the event. You want to share the one slide you developed with some of the participants, so you have decided to store the file on OneDrive. You are going to modify the slide you have created, shown in Figure 1–79, and save it to OneDrive.

Perform the following tasks:

1. Insert the pictures called Musician and Singers, which are located in the Data Files. Size and then move them to the areas indicated in Figure 1–79. Use the guides to help you position the pictures.

2. If requested to do so by your instructor, change the words, Phoenix, AZ, to the town and state where you were born.

3. Save the presentation using the file name, Expand 1-1 Talent Show.

4. Export the file to your OneDrive account.

5. Submit the assignment in the format specified by your instructor.

6. ✸ When would you save one of your files for school or your job to OneDrive? Do you think using OneDrive enhances collaboration efforts? Why?

Figure 1–79

In the Labs

Design, create, modify, and/or use a presentation following the guidelines, concepts, and skills presented in this module. Labs 1 and 2, which increase in difficulty, require you to create solutions based on what you learned in the module; Lab 3 requires you to apply your creative thinking and problem-solving skills to design and implement a solution.

Lab 1: **Creating a Presentation with Pictures**

Note: To complete this assignment, you will be required to use the Data Files. Please contact your instructor for information about accessing the Data Files.

Problem: Your friend, Bobby, has expanded her Bake Shoppe and wants to publicize new offerings. She has asked you to help her create a presentation that showcases pastries and breads. You prepare the PowerPoint presentation shown in Figure 1–80.

Perform the following tasks:

1. Run PowerPoint. Create a new presentation using the Retrospect document theme. Do not change the variant.
2. Using Figure 1–80a, create the title slide. Type the title text and subtitle text shown in the figure. Decrease the font size of the title text to 60 point and bold this text. Change the font color to Orange, Accent 1 (in Theme Colors row).

(a) Slide 1 (Title Slide)

(b) Slide 2

(c) Slide 3

(d) Slide 4 (Closing Slide)

Figure 1–80

3. On Slide 1, insert the illustration called Bakery, which is located in the Data Files. Move the illustration up to the top of the slide and then use the Smart Guides to align its left and right edges with the sides of the text placeholders. Use the lower-center sizing handle to resize this illustration so that it fits above the title text.

4. Replace the words, Anytown, USA, with your hometown city and state.

5. Create Slide 2 using the Title Only layout. Type the title text, Fresh Daily, bold this text, and then change the font color to Orange, Accent 1 (in Theme Colors row). Insert the picture called Doughnut, which is located in the Data Files, resize it as shown in Figure 1–80b, and then move it to the left side of the slide. Insert the picture called Muffin, which is located in the Data Files, and then resize and move it to the right side of the slide, as shown in the figure.

6. Using Figure 1–80c as a guide, create Slide 3 using the Picture with Caption layout. Insert the picture called Bread, which is located in the Data Files. Type the title text, Artisan Breads, increase the font size to 48 point, and then bold this text. Type `All natural ingredients` as the subtitle text, press the Tab key four times, and then type `No preservatives` in the placeholder. Increase this subtitle text size to 28 point.

7. Create a closing slide by duplicating Slide 1. Change the subtitle text using Figure 1–80d as a guide.

8. Apply the Clock transition in the Exciting category to all slides. Change the duration to 2.00 seconds.

9. Click the 'Start From Beginning' button to start the show from the first slide. Then click to display each slide and again to end the presentation.

10. Save the presentation using the file name, Lab 1-1 Bake. Submit the document in the format specified by your instructor.

11. ✸ What is the significance of changing the font color on Slides 1 and 2 but not Slide 3?

Lab 2: Creating a Presentation with Bulleted Lists and Pictures

Note: To complete this assignment, you will be required to use the Data Files. Please contact your instructor for information about accessing the Data Files.

Problem: The history museum in your town is a popular destination for residents, tourists, and researchers. Among the more popular exhibits are the dinosaurs, mummies, and antiques. You want to highlight these three attractions, so you create the presentation shown in Figure 1–81.

Perform the following tasks:

1. Run PowerPoint. Create a new presentation using the Quotable document theme.

2. Using Figure 1–81, create the title slide. Use your name in place of Student Name.

3. If requested by your instructor, substitute the name of your hometown in place of your last name.

4. On Slide 1 (Figure 1–81a), italicize the text, History Museum. Increase the font size of the subtitle text, Popular Exhibits, to 32 point and the font size of your name to 24 point. Change the font color of the title text to Dark Blue (in Standard Colors row).

5. Create the three slides shown in Figures 1-81b, 1-81c, and 1-81d. Use the Comparison layout for Slide 2, the Section Header layout for Slide 3, and the Two Content layout for Slide 4. Change the color of the title text on these three text slides to Dark Blue. Increase the font size of the subtitle text on Slides 2 and 3 to 24 point.

Continued >

In the Labs *continued*

(a) Slide 1 (Title Slide)

(b) Slide 2

(c) Slide 3

(d) Slide 4

Sergey Zolkin/Unsplash.com, Gabe Rodriguez/Unsplash.com

Figure 1–81

6. Add the pictures shown in Figures 1-81a through 1-81d using the guides on Slides 1 and 3 to help align them. The pictures to be inserted are called Museum Icon, Girls in Museum, T-rex Skeleton, T-rex 3D, Pharaoh, Car, and Typewriter, and they are located in the Data Files. Zoom the slides and then resize the pictures when necessary.

7. Apply the Gallery transition in the Exciting category to all slides. Change the duration to 2.25 seconds.

8. Click the 'Start From Beginning' button to start the show from the first slide. Then click to display each slide and again to end the presentation.

9. Save the presentation using the file name, Lab 1-2 History Museum.

10. Submit the revised document in the format specified by your instructor.

11. ❁ How does changing the title text font color to Dark Blue complement the theme color?

Lab 3: **Consider This: Your Turn**

Design and Create a Presentation about the Building Construction Technology Program

Note: To complete this assignment, you will be required to use the Data Files. Please contact your instructor for information about accessing the Data Files.

Part 1: Your school is expanding the courses offered in the Building Construction Technology Program, and the department chair has asked you to help promote the program. He informs you that students obtain hands-on experience using the latest methods of construction, and they receive instruction in the classroom and in the lab. The capstone courses are held in the field, where students build an actual energy-efficient home from the ground up. The skills learned and experience gained prepare students for careers in carpentry, masonry, plumbing, electrical, project supervision, cost estimating, and drafting. Use the concepts and techniques presented in this module to prepare a presentation with a minimum of four slides that showcase the Building Construction Technology program. Select a suitable theme, and include a title slide, bulleted list, closing slide, and transition. The presentation should contain pictures and illustrations resized appropriately. Several pictures are available in the Data Files: Backhoe, Concrete, Hammer, Hard Hat, Measuring Tape, Nail, and Tool Belt. Review and revise your presentation as needed. Submit your assignment in the format specified by your instructor.

Part 2: 🌼 You made several decisions while creating the presentation in this assignment: what theme to use, where to place text, how to format the text (font, font size, paragraph alignment, bulleted paragraphs, italics, bold, color). You decided which images to use and where to position them. You also chose a transition. What was the rationale behind each of these decisions? When you reviewed the slides, what further revisions did you make and why? Where would you recommend showing this slide show?

2 Enhancing a Presentation with Pictures, Shapes, and WordArt

Objectives

You will have mastered the material in this module when you can:

- Search for and download an online theme
- Insert and format pictures
- Insert and size a shape
- Apply effects to a shape
- Add text to a shape

- Change the text font
- Insert a picture to create a background
- Insert and format WordArt
- Format slide backgrounds
- Find and replace text and check spelling
- Add and print speaker notes

Introduction

In our visually oriented culture, audience members enjoy viewing effective graphics. Whether reading a document or viewing a PowerPoint presentation, people increasingly want to see photographs, artwork, graphics, and a variety of typefaces. Researchers have known for decades that documents with visual elements are more effective than those that consist of only text because the illustrations motivate audiences to study the material. People remember at least one-third more information when the document they are seeing or reading contains visual elements. These graphics help clarify and emphasize details, so they appeal to audience members with differing backgrounds, reading levels, attention spans, and motivations.

Project — Presentation with Pictures, Shapes, and WordArt

The project in this module focuses on publicizing a basketball camp held each summer for children living in the park district. Professionals teach boys and girls a variety of offensive and defensive skills during this fun and educational event. The presentation shown in Figure 2–1 follows graphical guidelines and has a variety of illustrations and visual elements that are colorful and appealing to child athletes and their parents. For example, the pictures have particular shapes and effects. The enhanced type has a style that blends well with the formatted background and illustrations. Pictures and type are formatted using picture styles and WordArt, which give the presentation a professional look. You plan to present the material during winter and spring sports tournaments, so you want to add notes explaining concepts you will be discussing during these events.

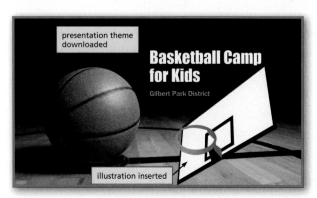

(a) Slide 1 (Title Slide)

(b) Slide 2 (Formatted Picture)

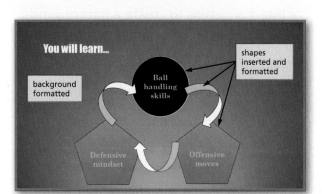

(c) Slide 3 (Shapes Inserted and Formatted)

(d) Slide 4 (Picture Background)

Figure 2–1

For an introduction to Windows and instructions about how to perform basic Windows tasks, read the Office and Windows module at the beginning of this book, where you can learn how to resize windows, change screen resolution, create folders, move and rename files, use Windows Help, and much more.

In this module, you will learn how to create the slides shown in Figure 2–1. The following roadmap identifies general activities you will perform as you progress through this module:

1. DOWNLOAD a theme and SELECT SLIDES for the presentation.

2. INSERT and FORMAT PICTURES for the slides.

3. INSERT and FORMAT SHAPES on one slide.

4. FORMAT SLIDE BACKGROUNDS with a gradient, texture, and picture fill.

5. INSERT and FORMAT WORDART by changing the shape, fill, and outline.

6. REVIEW, REVISE, and PRINT SLIDES by finding a synonym, checking spelling, and adding speaker notes.

Downloading a Theme and Editing Slides

In Module 1, you selected a theme and then typed the content for the title and text slides. In this module, you will type the slide content for the title and text slides, select a background, insert and format pictures and shapes, and then insert and format WordArt. To begin creating the four slides in this presentation, you will download a theme, delete unneeded slides in this downloaded presentation, and then enter text in three of the four slides.

To Search for and Download an Online Theme

1 DOWNLOAD & SELECT SLIDES | 2 INSERT & FORMAT PICTURES | 3 INSERT & FORMAT SHAPES

4 FORMAT SLIDE BACKGROUNDS | 5 INSERT & FORMAT WORDART | 6 REVIEW, REVISE, & PRINT SLIDES

PowerPoint displays many themes that are varied and appealing and give you an excellent start at designing a presentation. At times, however, you may have a specific topic and design concept and could use some assistance in starting to develop the presentation. Microsoft offers hundreds of predesigned themes and templates that could provide you with an excellent starting point. *Why? You can search for one of these ready-made presentations, or you can browse one of the predefined categories, such as business and education. The themes and templates can save you time and help you develop content.* The following steps search for a theme with a basketball concept.

1

- Run PowerPoint and then type **basketball** in the 'Search for online templates and themes' box (Figure 2–2).

Q&A Why are my theme thumbnails displaying in a different order?
The order changes as you choose themes for presentations. In addition, Microsoft occasionally adds and modifies the themes, so the order may change.

Can I choose one of the keywords listed below the 'Search for online templates and themes' box?
Yes. Click one of the terms in the Suggested searches list to display a variety of templates and themes relating to those topics.

Figure 2–2

- Click the Start searching button (the magnifying glass) or press the ENTER key to search for and display all themes with the keyword, basketball.

- Click the 'Basketball presentation (widescreen)' theme to display a theme preview dialog box with a thumbnail view of the theme (Figure 2–3).

Figure 2–3

Q&A Can I see previews of the slides in this theme?
Yes. Click the right or left arrows beside the words, More Images, below the thumbnail. On some devices, a preview of all slides starts automatically after you tap the theme.

- Click the Create button to download the theme and open a presentation with that theme in PowerPoint.

To Delete a Slide

1 DOWNLOAD & SELECT SLIDES | 2 INSERT & FORMAT PICTURES | 3 INSERT & FORMAT SHAPES
4 FORMAT SLIDE BACKGROUNDS | 5 INSERT & FORMAT WORDART | 6 REVIEW, REVISE, & PRINT SLIDES

The downloaded theme has nine slides with a variety of layouts. You will use four different layouts in your Basketball Camp presentation, so you can delete the slides you downloaded that you will not need. *Why? Deleting the extra slides now helps reduce clutter and helps you focus on the layouts you will use.* The following steps delete the extra slides.

- Click the Slide 3 thumbnail in the Slides tab to select this slide.

- Press and hold the SHIFT key, scroll down, and then click the thumbnail for Slide 7 to select slides 3 through 7 (Figure 2–4).

Q&A Do I need to select consecutive slides?
No. You can select an individual slide to delete. You also can select nonconsecutive slides by pressing and holding the CTRL key down and then clicking the thumbnails of the slides you want to delete.

Why did I press and hold down the SHIFT key instead of the CTRL key?
Holding down the SHIFT key selects consecutive slides between the first and last selected slides, whereas holding the CTRL key selects only the slides you click.

Figure 2–4

2

- Right-click any selected slide to display the shortcut menu (Figure 2–5).

Figure 2–5

3

- Click Delete Slide to delete the selected slides from the presentation (Figure 2–6).

Figure 2–6

Other Ways	
1. Select slide(s), press DELETE	2. Select slide(s), press BACKSPACE

To Create a Title Slide

Recall from Module 1 that the title slide introduces the presentation to the audience. In addition to introducing the presentation, this project uses the title slide to capture the audience's attention by using title text and an illustration. *Why? The presentation focuses on basketball, so the picture of a ball and court on the title slide can be supplemented with a backboard illustration that you will insert later on this slide.* The following steps create the slide show's title slide.

1 Display Slide 1, select the text in the title text placeholder, and then type **Basketball Camp for Kids** as the title text.

◄ | Why do I have to select the text in the placeholder before typing?
Q&A | This downloaded template includes text in some of the placeholders that must be replaced with your own text.

For an introduction to Office and instructions about how to perform basic tasks in Office apps, read the Office and Windows module at the beginning of this book, where you can learn how to run an application, use the ribbon, save a file, open a file, print a file, exit an application, use Help, and much more.

BTW
PowerPoint Screen Resolution
If you are using a computer or mobile device to step through the project in this module and you want your screens to match the figures in this book, you should change your screen's resolution to 1366 x 768. For information about how to change a computer's resolution, refer to the Office and Windows module at the beginning of this book.

② Click the subtitle text placeholder, select the text in that placeholder, and then type **Gilbert Park District** as the subtitle text (Figure 2–7).

- If requested by your instructor, type the name of the city or county in which you were born instead of the word, Gilbert.

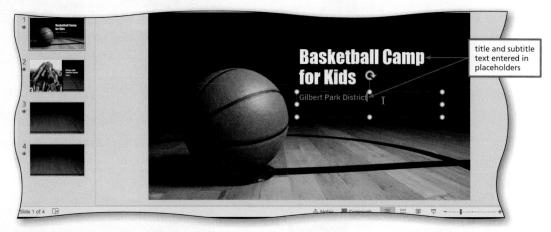

Figure 2–7

To Create the First Text Slide

The first text slide you create in Module 2 emphasizes two benefits of attending the weekly camp: receiving professional instruction and developing friendships. The following steps create the Slide 2 text slide using the Picture with Caption layout.

① Display Slide 2, select the text in the title text placeholder, and then type **Learn from pros and make acquaintances** in the placeholder.

② Select the text in the caption placeholder and then type **Classes meet weekday mornings throughout the summer** in this placeholder (Figure 2–8).

Figure 2–8

To Create the Second Text Slide

The second text slide you create shows three skills that will be taught: ball handling, offensive moves, and defensive strategies. The following steps add a title to Slide 3, which uses the Title Only layout, and save the presentation.

1 Display Slide 3 and then type **You will lern…** in the title text placeholder. The word, lern, is misspelled intentionally; the red wavy line indicates the misspelling (Figure 2-9).

2 Save the presentation using **Basketball Camp** as the file name.

Figure 2-9

Inserting and Formatting Pictures in a Presentation

With the text entered in three of the four slides, the next step is to insert pictures into Slides 1 and 2 and then format the pictures. These graphical images draw the viewers' eyes to the slides and help them retain the information presented.

In the following pages, you will perform these tasks:

1. Insert an illustration into Slide 1.
2. Resize the illustration.
3. Change the Slide 2 photo.
4. Change the photo's brightness and contrast.
5. Change the photo's style and effect.
6. Add and modify the photo's border.

BTW
Organizing Files and Folders
You should organize and store files in folders so that you easily can find the files later. For example, if you are taking an introductory technology class called CIS 101, a good practice would be to save all PowerPoint files in a PowerPoint folder in a CIS 101 folder. For a discussion of folders and detailed examples of creating folders, refer to the Office and Windows module at the beginning of this book.

To Insert a Picture into a Slide without a Content Placeholder

1 DOWNLOAD & SELECT SLIDES | 2 INSERT & FORMAT PICTURES | **3 INSERT & FORMAT SHAPES**
4 FORMAT SLIDE BACKGROUNDS | 5 INSERT & FORMAT WORDART | 6 REVIEW, REVISE, & PRINT SLIDES

In Module 1, you inserted photos and an illustration into slides without a content placeholder. *Why? Some slide layouts do not have a content placeholder, so you must insert and move the pictures to appropriate locations on the slide.* The illustration for Slide 1 is available in the Data Files. Contact your instructor if you need the pictures used in the following steps. The instructions in this module show the required files in the Module 02 folder in the Data Files folder. The following steps insert an illustration into the title slide.

- Display Slide 1 and then click Insert on the ribbon to display the Insert tab.
- Click the Pictures button (Insert tab | Images group) to display the Insert Picture dialog box.

2

- If necessary, navigate to the PowerPoint Module 02 folder and then click Backboard to select the file name (Figure 2–10).

Q&A

What if Backboard is not displayed in the navigation pane?
Drag the navigation pane scroll bar (Insert Picture dialog box) until Backboard appears. If this file is not in the list, see your instructor.

Why do I see just file names and not thumbnails of the pictures in my folder?
Your view is different from the view shown in Figure 2–10.

Figure 2–10

3

- Click the Insert button (Insert Picture dialog box) to insert the illustration into Slide 1.
- Drag the upper-left sizing handle diagonally toward the lower-right corner of the slide until the crosshair is positioned approximately as shown in Figure 2–11.

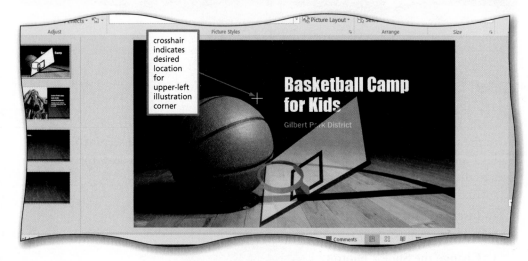

Figure 2–11

4

- Release to resize the illustration.
- Drag the illustration to the right until the vertical Smart Guide is displayed near the right side of the slide, as shown in Figure 2–12, and then release.

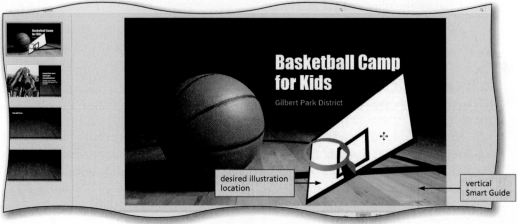

Figure 2–12

To Change a Picture

Why? *The downloaded theme included the photo of several team members on Slide 2. You need to change the photo because those players are wearing green uniforms, which are not the clothes your camp participants will wear.* The next task in the presentation is to change the default picture on Slide 2 to one of the pictures in the Data Files. The following steps change the Slide 2 photo to the Teamwork photo, which, in this example, is located in the Module 02 folder in the Data Files folder.

1

- Display Slide 2 and then right-click the picture to display the shortcut menu (Figure 2–13).

Q&A

Why are the Style and Crop buttons displayed near the shortcut menu on my screen?
These two buttons display either above or below the shortcut menu depending upon where you right-click on the screen.

Figure 2–13

2

- Click Change Picture to display the Insert Pictures dialog box (Figure 2–14).

Figure 2–14

3

- Click the Browse button in the 'From a file' area to display the Insert Picture dialog box.
- If necessary, navigate to the PowerPoint Module 02 folder, scroll down, and then click Teamwork to select the file (Figure 2–15).

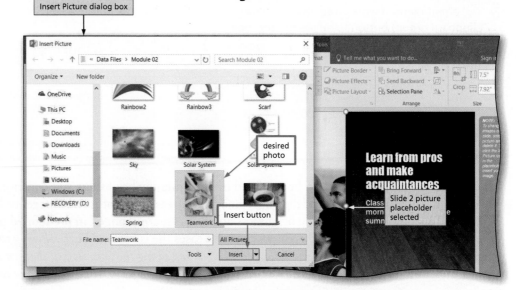

Figure 2–15

4

- Click the Insert button (Insert Picture dialog box) to insert the photo into the Slide 2 picture placeholder.
- Click the gray text box on the right side of the slide to select this object (Figure 2–16).

Q&A | Why should I select and then delete this gray text box?
When you delete the box, the slide will expand to the right to fill that space and you will be able to view a larger slide image.

Figure 2–16

5

- Press the DELETE key to delete this text box.

Q&A | Could I have followed the directions in the gray box on the right to change the image?
Yes, either method works. You also could have selected the gray box and then clicked the Cut button (Home tab | Clipboard group) button to delete the text box.

Other Ways

1. Click Change Picture button (Picture Tools Format tab | Adjust group)

To Correct a Picture

1 DOWNLOAD & SELECT SLIDES | 2 INSERT & FORMAT PICTURES | 3 INSERT & FORMAT SHAPES
4 FORMAT SLIDE BACKGROUNDS | 5 INSERT & FORMAT WORDART | 6 REVIEW, REVISE, & PRINT SLIDES

A photo's color intensity can be modified by changing the brightness and contrast. **Brightness** determines the overall lightness or darkness of the entire image, whereas **contrast** is the difference between the darkest and lightest areas of the image. The brightness and contrast are changed in predefined percentage increments. The following step decreases the brightness and increases the contrast. *Why?* *Altering the photo's brightness will coordinate with the dark colors on the basketball court while increasing the contrast will sharpen the image. It is important for the audience to recognize the basketball and the players' overlapping hands but not focus on each aspect of this photo.*

1

- Select the Teamwork photo on Slide 2 and then click Format on the ribbon to display the Picture Tools Format tab.

- Click the Corrections button (Picture Tools Format tab | Adjust group) to display the Corrections gallery.

- Scroll down to display the last row of images in the Corrections gallery and then

Figure 2–17

point to Brightness: −20% Contrast: +40% (second picture in last Brightness/Contrast row) to display a live preview of these corrections on the picture (Figure 2–17).

Q&A Can I use live preview on a touch screen?
Live preview is not available on a touch screen.

Why is a gray border surrounding the pictures in the center of the Sharpen/Soften and Brightness/Contrast areas of the gallery?
The image on Slide 2 currently has normal sharpness, brightness, and contrast (0%), which is represented by these center images in the gallery.

Experiment

- Point to various pictures in the Brightness/Contrast area and watch the brightness and contrast change on the picture in Slide 2.

- Click Brightness: −20% Contrast: +40% to apply this correction to the Teamwork photo.

Q&A How can I remove all effects from the picture?
Click the Reset Picture button (Picture Tools Format tab | Adjust group).

Other Ways

1. Click Picture Corrections Options (Corrections gallery), move Brightness or Contrast sliders or enter number in box next to slider (Format Picture pane)

To Apply a Picture Style

1 DOWNLOAD & SELECT SLIDES | 2 INSERT & FORMAT PICTURES | 3 INSERT & FORMAT SHAPES
4 FORMAT SLIDE BACKGROUNDS | 5 INSERT & FORMAT WORDART | 6 REVIEW, REVISE, & PRINT SLIDES

A **style** is a named group of formatting characteristics. The picture on Slide 2 emphasizes the concept of teamwork in this sport, and you can increase its visual appeal by applying a style. *Why? PowerPoint provides more than 25 picture styles that enable you easily to change a picture's look to a more visually appealing style, including a variety of shapes, angles, borders, and reflections.* You want to use a style that applies a shadow to the Teamwork photo. The following steps apply a picture style to the Slide 2 photo.

- With the Slide 2 picture selected and the Picture Tools Format tab displaying, click the More button in the Picture Styles gallery (Picture Tools Format tab | Picture Styles group) (shown in Figure 2–17) to expand the gallery.
- Point to Bevel Rectangle in the Picture Styles gallery (last style in third row) to display a live preview of that style applied to the picture in the document (Figure 2–18).

Figure 2–18

Experiment

- Point to various picture styles in the Picture Styles gallery and watch the style of the picture change in the document window.

- Click Bevel Rectangle in the Picture Styles gallery to apply the style to the selected picture.

To Add a Picture Border

1 DOWNLOAD & SELECT SLIDES | 2 INSERT & FORMAT PICTURES | 3 INSERT & FORMAT SHAPES
4 FORMAT SLIDE BACKGROUNDS | 5 INSERT & FORMAT WORDART | 6 REVIEW, REVISE, & PRINT SLIDES

The next step is to add a border to the Slide 2 picture. *Why? Some picture styles do not have a border; others, such as the Bevel Rectangle style you applied to this picture, do have this edging. This border is small, and you want a larger edge around the photo to draw attention to the graphic.* The following steps add a border to the Teamwork picture.

- With the Slide 2 picture still selected, click the Picture Border arrow (Picture Tools Format tab | Picture Styles group) to display the Picture Border gallery.

◁ | What if the Picture Tools Format tab no longer is displayed on my ribbon?
Q&A | Click the picture to display the Picture Tools Format tab.

2

- Point to Weight on the Picture Border gallery to display the Weight gallery.

- Point to 6 pt to display a live preview of this line weight on the picture (Figure 2–19).

Q&A Can I make the line width more than 6 pt?
Yes. Click More Lines, Click Solid line in the Line section of the Format Picture pane, and then increase the amount in the Width box.

Figure 2–19

Experiment

- Point to various line weights in the Weight gallery and watch the line thickness change.

3

- Click 6 pt to add this line weight to the picture.

To Change a Picture Border Color

1 DOWNLOAD & SELECT SLIDES | 2 INSERT & FORMAT PICTURES | 3 INSERT & FORMAT SHAPES
4 FORMAT SLIDE BACKGROUNDS | 5 INSERT & FORMAT WORDART | 6 REVIEW, REVISE, & PRINT SLIDES

The default color for the border you added to the Slide 2 picture is white, but you will change the border color to black. *Why? The black color coordinates with other elements on the slide, especially the lines on the basketball and the court.* The following steps change the Slide 2 picture border color.

1

- With the Slide 2 photo still selected, click the Picture Border arrow (Picture Tools Format tab | Picture Styles group) to display the Picture Border gallery again.

2

- Point to Black, Background 1 (first color in first row) in the Picture Border gallery to display a live preview of that border color on the picture (Figure 2–20).

Figure 2–20

Experiment

- Point to various colors in the Picture Border gallery and watch the border on the picture change in the slide.

3

- Click Black, Background 1 in the Picture Border gallery to change the picture border color.

To Apply Picture Effects

1 DOWNLOAD & SELECT SLIDES | 2 INSERT & FORMAT PICTURES | 3 INSERT & FORMAT SHAPES
4 FORMAT SLIDE BACKGROUNDS | 5 INSERT & FORMAT WORDART | 6 REVIEW, REVISE, & PRINT SLIDES

Why? *Picture effects allow you to further customize a picture.* PowerPoint provides a variety of picture effects, including shadows, reflections, glow, soft edges, bevel, and 3-D rotation. The difference between the effects and the styles is that each effect has several options, providing you with more control over the exact look of the image.

In this presentation, the photo on Slide 2 has a brown glow effect and a bevel applied to its edges. The following steps apply picture effects to the selected picture.

1

- With the Slide 2 picture still selected, click the Picture Effects button (Picture Tools Format tab | Picture Styles group) to display the Picture Effects menu.

Q&A What if the Picture Tools Format tab no longer is displayed on my ribbon?
Click the picture to display the Picture Tools Format tab.

- Point to Glow on the Picture Effects menu to display the Glow gallery.

- Point to Brown, 18 pt glow, Accent color 3 in the Glow Variations area (third glow in last row) to display a live preview of the selected glow effect applied to the picture in the document window (Figure 2–21).

Figure 2–21

Experiment

- Point to various glow effects in the Glow gallery and watch the picture change in the document window.

2

• Click Brown, 18 pt glow, Accent color 3 in the Glow gallery to apply the selected picture effect.

3

• Click the Picture Effects button (Picture Tools Format tab | Picture Styles group) to display the Picture Effects menu again.

• Point to Bevel on the Picture Effects menu to display the Bevel gallery.

• Point to Angle (first bevel in second Bevel row) to display a live preview of the selected bevel effect applied to the Slide 2 picture (Figure 2–22).

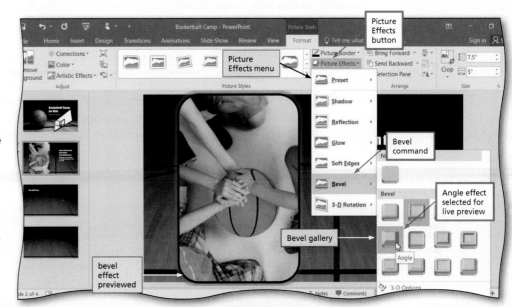

Figure 2–22

Experiment

• Point to various bevel effects in the Bevel gallery and watch the picture change in the slide.

4

• Click Angle in the Bevel gallery to apply the selected picture effect.

Other Ways
1. Right-click picture, click Format Picture on shortcut menu, select desired options (Format Picture pane), click Close button	2. Click Format Shape pane launcher (Picture Tools Format tab | Picture Styles group), select desired options (Format Picture pane), click Close button

Break Point: If you wish to take a break, this is a good place to do so. Be sure to save the Basketball Camp file again and then you can exit PowerPoint. To resume at a later time, run PowerPoint, open the file called Basketball Camp, and continue following the steps from this location forward.

Inserting and Formatting a Shape

One method of getting the audience's attention and reinforcing the major concepts being presented is to have graphical elements on the slide. PowerPoint provides a wide variety of predefined shapes that can add visual interest to a slide. Shape elements include lines, basic geometrical shapes, arrows, equation shapes, flowchart symbols, stars, banners, and callouts. After adding a shape to a slide, you can change its default characteristics by adding text, bullets, numbers, and styles. You also can combine multiple shapes to create a more complex graphic.

The predefined shapes are found in the Shapes gallery. This collection is found on the Home tab | Drawing group and the Insert tab | Illustrations group. Once you have inserted and selected a shape, the Drawing Tools Format tab is displayed, and the Shapes gallery also is displayed in the Insert Shapes group.

BTW

Inserting Special Characters
Along with adding shapes to a slide, you can insert characters not found on your keyboard, such as the section sign (§), the copyright sign (©), and Greek capital letters (e.g., Δ, Ω, and ß). To insert these characters, click the Insert tab and then click the Symbol button (Insert tab | Symbols group). When the Symbol dialog box is displayed, you can use the same font you currently are using in your presentation, or you can select another font. The Webdings, Wingdings, Wingdings 2, and Wingdings 3 fonts have a variety of symbols.

Slide 3 in this presentation is enhanced in a variety of ways. First, an oval, an arrow, and a pentagon shape are inserted on the slide and formatted. Then, text is added to the oval and pentagon and formatted. The pentagon is copied, and the text is modified in this new shape. Finally, the arrow shape is duplicated twice and moved into position.

To Add a Shape

1 DOWNLOAD & SELECT SLIDES | 2 INSERT & FORMAT PICTURES | 3 INSERT & FORMAT SHAPES
4 FORMAT SLIDE BACKGROUNDS | 5 INSERT & FORMAT WORDART | 6 REVIEW, REVISE, & PRINT SLIDES

Many of the shapes included in the Shapes gallery can direct the viewer to important aspects of the presentation. The following steps add an oval shape, which displays as a circle, to Slide 3. *Why? A circle shape complements the basketball photo on Slide 1 and helps reinforce the presentation's basketball theme.*

1

• Display Slide 3 and then, if necessary, click the Home tab (Figure 2–23).

Figure 2–23

2

• Click the Shapes More button (Home tab | Drawing group) shown in Figure 2–23 to display the Shapes gallery (Figure 2–24).

Q&A
I do not see a Shapes More button and the three rows of the shapes shown in Figure 2–24. Instead, I have a Shapes button. Why?
Monitor dimensions and resolution affect how buttons display on the ribbon. Click the Shapes button to display the entire Shapes gallery.

Figure 2–24

- Click the Oval shape in the Basic Shapes area of the Shapes gallery.

Q&A Why did my pointer change shape?
The pointer changed to a plus shape to indicate the Oval shape has been added to the Clipboard.

- Position the pointer (a crosshair) near the center of the slide, as shown in Figure 2–25.

Figure 2–25

- Click Slide 3 to insert the Oval shape.

Other Ways

1. Click Shapes button (Insert tab | Illustrations group)

To Resize a Shape

1 DOWNLOAD & SELECT SLIDES | 2 INSERT & FORMAT PICTURES | 3 INSERT & FORMAT SHAPES
4 FORMAT SLIDE BACKGROUNDS | 5 INSERT & FORMAT WORDART | 6 REVIEW, REVISE, & PRINT SLIDES

The next step is to resize the Oval shape. **Why?** *The oval should be enlarged so that it is a focal point in the middle area of the slide.* The following steps resize the selected shape.

1

- Press and hold down the SHIFT key and then drag the upper-left corner sizing handle until the shape is resized approximately as shown in Figure 2–26 and the top is aligned with a horizontal Smart Guide.

Q&A Why did I need to press the SHIFT key while enlarging the shape?
Holding down the SHIFT key while dragging keeps the proportions of the original shape.

What if my shape is not selected?
To select a shape, click it.

If I am using a touch screen, how can I maintain the shape's original proportion?
If you drag one of the corner sizing handles, the object should stay in proportion.

Figure 2–26

2

- Release to resize the shape.
- Drag the shape until the vertical Smart Guide is displayed in the middle of the oval and the horizontal Smart Guide is displayed at the top of the oval, as shown in Figure 2–27, and then release.

Q&A What if I want to move the shape to a precise location on the slide?
With the shape selected, press the ARROW keys or the CTRL+ARROW keys to move the shape to the desired location.

Figure 2–27

Other Ways

1. Enter shape height and width in Height and Width boxes (Drawing Tools Format tab | Size group)
2. Click Size and Position pane launcher (Drawing Tools Format tab | Size group), click Size tab, enter desired height and width values in boxes, click Close button

To Add Other Shapes

1 DOWNLOAD & SELECT SLIDES | 2 INSERT & FORMAT PICTURES | 3 INSERT & FORMAT SHAPES
4 FORMAT SLIDE BACKGROUNDS | 5 INSERT & FORMAT WORDART | 6 REVIEW, REVISE, & PRINT SLIDES

Ovals, squares, arrows, stars, and equation shapes are among the items included in the Shapes gallery. These shapes can be combined to show relationships among the elements, and they can help illustrate the basic concepts presented in your slide show. *Why?* *Arrows are especially useful in showing the relationship among slide elements and guiding the viewer's eyes to move from one shape to the next.* More than two dozen arrow shapes are displayed in the Block Arrows section of the Shapes gallery. The following steps add one of these arrows and the pentagon shapes to Slide 3.

1

- Click the Shapes More button (Drawing Tools Format tab | Insert Shapes group) shown in Figure 2–27 to display the Shapes gallery (Figure 2–28).

Q&A When I inserted the Oval shape, I selected it on the Home tab. Is the same Shapes gallery also displayed on the Drawing Tools Format tab?
Yes. The Shapes gallery is displayed on this tab once an object is inserted and selected on the slide.

Figure 2–28

2

- Click the Curved Left Arrow shape in the Block Arrows area of the Shapes gallery.
- Position the pointer to the right of the oval shape in Slide 3 and then click to insert the Curved Left Arrow shape.

3

- Press and hold down the SHIFT key and then drag a corner sizing handle until the arrow shape is approximately the size shown in Figure 2–29.

Q&A If I am using a touch screen, how can I maintain the Oval shape's original proportion?
The object should stay in proportion when you drag one of the corner sizing handles.

- If necessary, drag the Curved Left Arrow shape to the right side of the oval, as shown in Figure 2–29, and then release.

Figure 2–29

4

- Display the Shapes gallery and then click the Regular Pentagon shape in the Basic Shapes area of the gallery (shown in Figure 2–28).
- Position the pointer toward the lower-left side of the Curved Left Arrow shape and then click to insert the Regular Pentagon shape.

5

- Press and hold down the SHIFT key and then drag a corner sizing handle to resize the pentagon shape so that it is the size shown in Figure 2–30.
- Drag the pentagon shape so that its tip is placed at the intersection of the horizontal Smart Guide above the pentagon and the vertical Smart Guide in the middle of the shape, as shown in Figure 2–30, and then release.

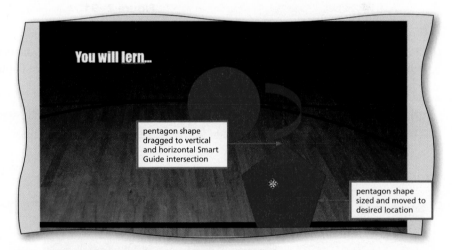

Figure 2–30

To Apply a Shape Style

1 DOWNLOAD & SELECT SLIDES | 2 INSERT & FORMAT PICTURES | 3 INSERT & FORMAT SHAPES
4 FORMAT SLIDE BACKGROUNDS | 5 INSERT & FORMAT WORDART | 6 REVIEW, REVISE, & PRINT SLIDES

Formatting text in a shape follows the same techniques as formatting text in a placeholder. You can change font, font color and size, and alignment. You later will add information about a skill to the Oval shape, but first you want to apply a shape style. **Why?** *The style will give depth and dimension to the object.* The Quick Styles gallery has a variety of styles that change depending upon the theme applied to the presentation. The following steps apply a style to the oval.

1

- Display the Home tab, click the oval to select it, and then click the Quick Styles button (Home tab | Drawing group) (Figure 2–31).

Figure 2–31

2

- Point to Light 1 Outline, Colored Fill – Black, Dark 1 in the Quick Styles gallery (first shape in third Theme Styles row) to display a live preview of that style applied to the oval in the slide (Figure 2–32).

Figure 2–32

Experiment

• Point to various styles in the Quick Styles gallery and watch the style of the shape change.

3

• Click Light 1 Outline, Colored Fill – Black, Dark 1 in the Quick Styles gallery to apply the selected style to the oval.

Other Ways

1. Click Shape Styles More button (Drawing Tools Format tab | Shape Styles group), select style
2. Right-click shape, click Style button on mini toolbar, select desired style

---

To Apply Another Style

You later will add text to the oval and pentagon about particular skills taught at the camp, but now you want to format the arrow and pentagon shapes. *Why? You can apply shape styles to the arrow and pentagon that will coordinate with the oval's style. A light style color in the arrow shape will help join darker style colors of the oval and rectangle. This formatting will add interest and emphasize the relationship between basketball playing skills.* The following steps apply styles to the arrow and pentagon shapes.

1 Click the arrow shape to select it.

2 Click the Quick Styles button (Home tab | Drawing group) to display the Quick Styles gallery and then apply the Colored Outline – Black, Dark 1 style (first style in first Theme Styles row) to the arrow shape.

3 Click the pentagon shape to select it and then click the Quick Styles button.

4 Click Subtle Effect – Black, Dark 1 (first style in fourth Theme Styles row) to apply that style to the pentagon shape (Figure 2–33).

BTW

Deleting a Shape
If you want to delete a shape you have added to a slide, click that shape to select it and then press the delete key. If you want to DELETE multiple shapes, press the CTRL key while clicking the undesired shapes and then press the DELETE key.

Figure 2–33

To Add Text to a Shape

The three shapes on Slide 3 help call attention to the key aspects of your presentation. *Why? Your goal is to emphasize key skills the campers will learn.* The next step is to add this information to Slide 3. The following steps add text to the oval and pentagon shapes.

1

- With the pentagon selected, type **Offensive moves** to add the text in the shape.

2

- Click the oval to select it and then type **Ball handling skills** to add the text in the shape (Figure 2–34).

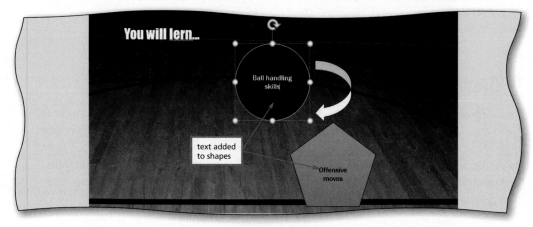

Figure 2–34

To Change the Font

The default theme font is Franklin Gothic Medium. To draw more attention to text in the shapes and to help differentiate these slide elements from the title text, you want to change the font to Century Schoolbook. *Why? Century Schoolbook is a serif typeface, meaning the ends of some of the letter are adorned with small decorations, called serifs. These adornments slow down the viewer's reading speed, which might help them retain the information they saw.* To change the font, you must select the letters you want to format. In Module 1, you selected a paragraph and then formatted the characters, and you follow the same procedure to change the font. The following steps change the text font in the shape.

1

- With the oval selected, triple-click the text to select all the characters and display the mini toolbar (Figure 2–35).

Figure 2–35

2

- Click the Font arrow to display the Font gallery (Figure 2–36).

Q&A Will the fonts in my Font gallery be the same as those shown in Figure 2–36?
Your list of available fonts may differ, depending on what fonts you have installed and the type of printer you are using.

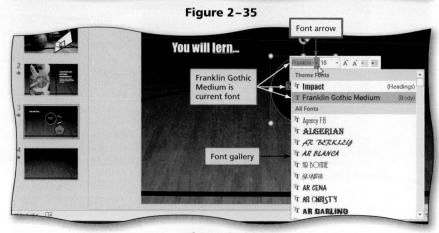

Figure 2–36

3

- Drag or scroll through the Font gallery and then point to Century Schoolbook (or a similar font) to display a live preview of the title text in the Century Schoolbook font (Figure 2–37).

🔎 **Experiment**

- Point to various fonts in the Font gallery and watch the subtitle text font change in the slide.

- Click Century Schoolbook (or a similar font) to change the font of the selected text to Century Schoolbook.

Figure 2–37

Other Ways

1. Click Font arrow (Home tab | Font group), click desired font in Font gallery
2. Right-click selected text, click Font on shortcut menu (Font dialog box), click Font tab, select desired font in Font list, click OK button
3. Click Font dialog box launcher (Home tab | Font group), click Font tab (Font dialog box), select desired font in Font list, click OK button
4. Press CTRL+SHIFT+F, click Font tab (Font dialog box), select desired font in the Font list, click OK button
5. Right-click selected text, click Font arrow on mini toolbar, select desired font

To Format the Text

To increase readability, you can format the oval text by increasing the font size, bolding the characters, and changing the font color to orange. The following steps format the oval text.

1 With the oval text selected, click the Increase Font Size button (Home tab | Font group) two times to increase the font size to 24 pt.

2 Click the Bold button (Home tab | Font group) to bold the text.

3 Click the Font Color arrow and change the color to Orange (third color in Standard Colors row) (Figure 2–38).

Q&A What should I do if one or more letters of the word, handling, wrap to the third line in the shape?
Press and hold down the SHIFT key and then drag a corner sizing handle outward slightly to resize the oval shape.

Could I also add a shadow behind the text to add depth and help the letters display prominently?
Yes. Select the text and then click the Text Shadow button (Home tab | Font group).

BTW
Text in a Shape
When you add text to a shape, it becomes part of the shape. If you rotate or flip the shape, the text also rotates or flips.

Figure 2–38

Other Ways

1. Right-click selected text, click desired text format button on mini toolbar

Format Painter

To save time and avoid formatting errors, you can use the Format Painter to apply custom formatting to other places in your presentation quickly and easily. You can use this feature in three ways:

- To copy only character attributes, such as font and font effects, select text that has these qualities.
- To copy both character attributes and paragraph attributes, such as alignment and indentation, select the entire paragraph.
- To apply the same formatting to multiple words, phrases, or paragraphs, double-click the Format Painter button and then select each item you want to format. You then can press the ESC key or click the Format Painter button to turn off this feature.

To Format Text Using the Format Painter

1 DOWNLOAD & SELECT SLIDES | 2 INSERT & FORMAT PICTURES | 3 INSERT & FORMAT SHAPES
4 FORMAT SLIDE BACKGROUNDS | 5 INSERT & FORMAT WORDART | 6 REVIEW, REVISE, & PRINT SLIDES

Why? *To save time and duplicated effort, you quickly can use the Format Painter to copy formatting attributes from the oval shape text and apply them to pentagon shape text.* The following steps use the Format Painter to copy formatting features.

- With the oval text still selected, double-click the Format Painter button (Home tab | Clipboard group).
- Move the pointer off the ribbon (Figure 2–39).

Q&A Why does the Format Painter button on my screen display only a paint brush and not the words, Format Painter?
Monitor dimensions and resolution affect how buttons display on the ribbon.

Why did my pointer change shape?
The pointer changed shape by adding a paintbrush to indicate that the Format Painter function is active.

Figure 2–39

2

- Triple-click the pentagon text to apply the format to all characters (Figure 2–40).
- Click the Format Painter button or press the ESC key to turn off the Format Painter feature.

Q&A | What should I do if one or more letters of the word, Offensive, wrap to a second line in the shape?
Press and hold down the SHIFT key and then drag a corner sizing handle outward slightly to resize the pentagon shape.

Figure 2–40

Other Ways

1. Select text, double-click Format Painter button on mini toolbar

To Copy and Paste a Shape

1 DOWNLOAD & SELECT SLIDES | 2 INSERT & FORMAT PICTURES | 3 INSERT & FORMAT SHAPES
4 FORMAT SLIDE BACKGROUNDS | 5 INSERT & FORMAT WORDART | 6 REVIEW, REVISE, & PRINT SLIDES

Good basketball players have both offensive and defensive skills. You already have created the shape stating the campers will work on refining their offensive talents. You now need to create a second shape with information about defensive instruction that will be provided at the camp. The following steps copy the pentagon shape and then change the text. *Why? You could repeat all the steps you performed to create the first pentagon, but it is much more efficient to duplicate the shape and then edit the text.*

1

- With the pentagon shape selected, click the Copy button (Home tab | Clipboard group) (Figure 2–41).

Figure 2–41

2

- Click the Paste button (Home tab | Clipboard group) to insert a duplicate Regular Pentagon shape on Slide 3.
- Drag the new pentagon shape to the left of the original pentagon shape, as shown in Figure 2–42.
- In the left pentagon shape, select the text, Offensive moves, and then type `Defensive mindset` as the replacement text (Figure 2–42).

Q&A | What should I do if one or more letters of the word, Defensive, wrap to a second line in the shape?
Press and hold down the SHIFT key and then drag a corner sizing handle outward slightly to resize the pentagon shape.

Figure 2–42

3

- Select the arrow shape and then click the Copy button (Home tab | Clipboard group) (Figure 2–43).

Figure 2–43

4

- Click the Paste button (Home tab | Clipboard group) two times to insert two duplicate arrow shapes on Slide 3.
- Drag one of the duplicate arrow shapes between the two pentagon shapes and then drag the other duplicate arrow shape between the left pentagon shape and the oval shape (Figure 2–44).

Figure 2–44

5

- With the left arrow selected, drag its rotation handle clockwise or counterclockwise so that it is displayed as shown in Figure 2–45. Repeat this procedure for the other two arrows, and then adjust the shapes' locations on Slide 3 so that the arrows touch their adjacent shapes (Figure 2–45).

Figure 2–45

- If the end of an arrow is underneath an oval or a pentagon shape, select the arrow, click the Drawing Tools Format tab, and then click the Bring Forward button (Drawing Tools Format tab | Arrange group) to bring the arrow on top of the shape.

Other Ways

1. Right-click selected shape, click Copy on shortcut menu, right-click blank area, click Paste on shortcut menu
2. Select shape, press CTRL+C, press CTRL+V

Break Point: If you wish to take a break, this is a good place to do so. Be sure to save the Basketball Camp file again and then you can exit PowerPoint. To resume at a later time, run PowerPoint, open the file called Basketball Camp, and continue following the steps from this location forward.

Formatting Slide Backgrounds

A slide's background is an integral part of a presentation because it can generate audience interest. Every slide can have the same background, or different backgrounds can be used in a presentation. This background is considered **fill**, which is the content that makes up the interior of a shape, line, or character. Four fills are available: solid, gradient, picture or texture, and pattern. **Solid fill** is one color used throughout the entire slide. **Gradient fill** is one color shade gradually progressing to another shade of the same color or one color progressing to another color. **Picture or texture fill** uses a specific file or an image that simulates a material, such as cork, granite, marble, or canvas. **Pattern fill** adds designs, such as dots or dashes, which repeat in rows across the slide.

Once you add a fill, you can adjust its appearance. For example, you can adjust its **transparency**, which allows you to see through the background, so that any text on the slide is visible. You also can select a color that is part of the theme or a custom color. You can use an **offset**, another background feature, to move the background away from the slide borders in varying distances by percentage. A **tiling option** repeats the background image many times vertically and horizontally on the slide; the smaller the tiling percentage, the greater the number of times the image is repeated.

To Insert a Texture Fill

1 DOWNLOAD & SELECT SLIDES | 2 INSERT & FORMAT PICTURES | 3 INSERT & FORMAT SHAPES
4 FORMAT SLIDE BACKGROUNDS | **5 INSERT & FORMAT WORDART** | 6 REVIEW, REVISE, & PRINT SLIDES

Why? *Various texture fills are available to give your background a unique look.* The 24 pictures in the Texture gallery give the appearance of a physical object, such as water drops, sand, tissue paper, and a paper bag. You also can use your own texture pictures for custom backgrounds. The following steps insert the Brown marble texture fill on Slide 2 in the presentation.

1

• Display Slide 2. Click the Design tab and then click the Format Background button (Design tab | Customize group) to display the Format Background pane (Figure 2–46).

Figure 2–46

2

- With the Fill section displaying (Format Background pane), if necessary, click 'Picture or texture fill' and then click the Texture button to display the Texture gallery (Figure 2–47).

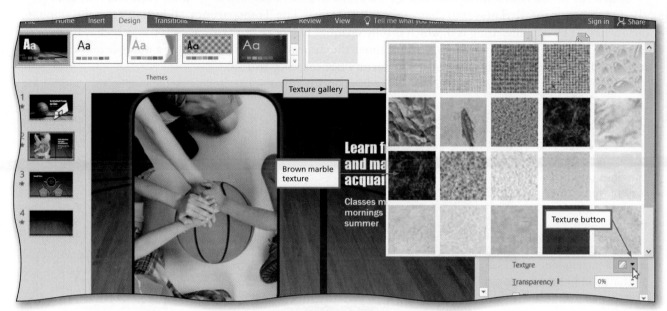

Figure 2–47

3

- Click the Brown marble texture (first texture in third row) to insert this texture fill as the background on Slide 2 (Figure 2–48).

Q&A Is a live preview available to see the various textures on this slide?
No. Live preview is not an option with the background textures and fills.

Could I insert this background on all four slides simultaneously?
Yes. You would click the 'Apply to All' button to insert the Brown marble background on all slides.

Figure 2–48

Other Ways

1. Right-click background, click Format Background on shortcut menu, select desired options (Format Background pane)

To Format the Background Texture Fill Transparency

Why? *The Brown marble texture on Slide 2 is dark, and its pattern may detract from the photo and text.* One method of reducing this darkness is to change the transparency. The **Transparency slider** indicates the amount of opaqueness. The default setting is 0, which is fully opaque. The opposite extreme is 100%, which is fully transparent. To change the transparency, you can move the Transparency slider or enter a number in the box next to the slider. The following step adjusts the texture transparency to 15%.

1

- Click the Transparency slider (Format Background pane) and drag it to the right until 15% is displayed in the Transparency box (Figure 2–49).

Q&A Can I move the slider in small increments so that I can get a precise percentage easily?
Yes. Click the up or down arrows in the Transparency box to move the slider in 1% increments.

Figure 2–49

To Insert a Gradient Fill

Although you selected Brown marble texture fill on Slide 2 and changed the transparency, you decide that another type of background may be more suitable for Slide 3. **Why?** *The Brown marble texture does not offer sufficient contrast with the oval symbol and may detract from the messages presented in the three symbols.* For each theme, PowerPoint provides 30 preset **gradient fills** with five designs for each of the six major theme colors. Each fill has one dark color shade that gradually lightens to either another shade of the same color or another color. The following steps replace the background on Slide 3 to a preset gradient fill.

1

- Display Slide 3. With the Fill section displaying (Format Background pane), click Gradient fill in the Format Background pane (shown in Figure 2–49) and then click the Preset gradients button to display the Preset gradients gallery (Figure 2–50).

Q&A Are the backgrounds displayed in a specific order?
Yes. The first row has light colors at the top of the background; the middle rows have darker fills at the bottom; the bottom row has overall dark fills on all edges.

Is a live preview available to see the various gradients on this slide?
No. Live preview is not an option with the background textures and fills.

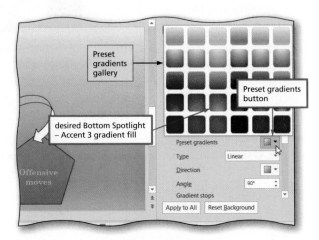

Figure 2–50

2

- Click Bottom Spotlight – Accent 3 (third fill in fourth row) to apply that style to Slide 3 (Figure 2–51).

Q&A If I decide later that this background gradient does not fit the theme of my presentation, can I apply a different background?
Yes. You can repeat these steps at any time while creating your presentation.

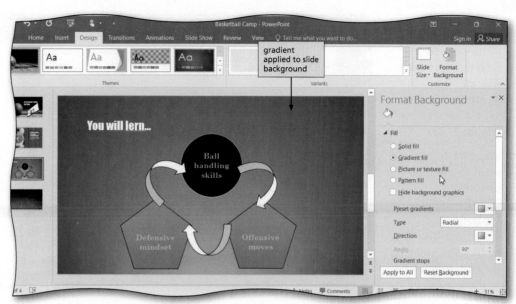

Figure 2–51

Other Ways

1. Click Design tab on ribbon, click Format Background button (Customize group), select desired options (Format Background pane)
2. Right-click background, click Format Background on shortcut menu, select desired options (Format Background pane)

To Insert a Picture to Create a Background

Why? *For variety and interest, you want to use an illustration as the Slide 4 background.* This picture is stored in the Data Files folder. PowerPoint will stretch the height and width of this picture to fill the slide area. The following steps insert the illustration, Basketball Boy, on Slide 4 only.

1

- Display Slide 4. With the Fill section displaying (Format Background pane), if necessary, click 'Picture or texture fill' and then click the File button (Format Background pane) to display the Insert Picture dialog box. If necessary, navigate to the Module 02 folder in the Data Files folder or the location where your data files are located.

Figure 2–52

- Click Basketball Boy to select the file name (Figure 2–52).

2

- Click the Insert button (Insert Picture dialog box) to insert the Basketball Boy illustration as the Slide 4 background (Figure 2–53).

Q&A What if I do not want to use this picture?
Click the Undo button on the Quick Access Toolbar or click the Reset Background button at the bottom of the Format Background pane.

Figure 2–53

To Format the Background Picture Fill Transparency

1 DOWNLOAD & SELECT SLIDES | 2 INSERT & FORMAT PICTURES | 3 INSERT & FORMAT SHAPES
4 FORMAT SLIDE BACKGROUNDS | **5 INSERT & FORMAT WORDART** | 6 REVIEW, REVISE, & PRINT SLIDES

Why? *The Basketball Boy illustration on Slide 4 has vibrant colors that will conflict with the WordArt you will add later in this project.* You can adjust the transparency of picture in the same manner that you change the transparency of a slide texture. The following steps adjust the transparency of the background picture to 30% and then close the Format Background pane.

1

- Click the Transparency slider and drag it to the right until 30% is displayed in the Transparency box (Figure 2–54).

2

- Click the Close button (Format Background pane) to close the pane and return to Slide 4.

Figure 2–54

Inserting and Formatting WordArt

One method of adding appealing visual elements to a presentation is by using **WordArt** styles. This feature is found in other Microsoft Office applications, including Word and Excel. This gallery of decorative effects allows you to type new text or convert existing text to WordArt. You then can add elements such as fills, outlines, and effects.

WordArt **fill** in the interior of a letter can consist of a solid color, texture, picture, or gradient. The WordArt **outline** is the exterior border surrounding each letter or symbol. PowerPoint allows you to change the outline color, weight, and style. You also can add an **effect**, which helps add emphasis or depth to the characters. Some effects are shadows, reflections, glows, bevels, and 3-D rotations.

To Insert WordArt

1 DOWNLOAD & SELECT SLIDES | 2 INSERT & FORMAT PICTURES | 3 INSERT & FORMAT SHAPES
4 FORMAT SLIDE BACKGROUNDS | 5 INSERT & FORMAT WORDART | 6 REVIEW, REVISE, & PRINT SLIDES

The basketball camp is a very popular event among boys and girls in the community, and the sessions fill every year. Parents need to register their student early to reserve a place. You want to emphasize this concept, and the last slide in the presentation is an excellent location to urge your audience to take action. *Why? Audience members remember the first and last things they see and hear.* You quickly can add a visual element to the slide by selecting a WordArt style from the WordArt Styles gallery and then applying it to some text. The following steps insert WordArt.

1
- Display the Insert tab and then click the WordArt button (Insert tab | Text group) to display the WordArt gallery (Figure 2–55).

Figure 2–55

2
- Click 'Fill – Red, Accent 2, Outline – Accent 2' (third style in first row) to insert the WordArt object (Figure 2–56).

Figure 2–56

3
- Type **Register today!** in the object as the WordArt text (Figure 2–57).

Q&A Why did the Drawing Tools Format tab appear automatically in the ribbon?
It appears when you select text to which you could add a WordArt style or other effect.

Figure 2–57

To Change the WordArt Shape

Why? *The WordArt text is useful to emphasize the need to register children early for camp. You further can emphasize this text by changing its shape.* PowerPoint provides a variety of graphical shapes that add interest to WordArt text. The following steps change the WordArt shape to Chevron Up.

1

- With the WordArt object still selected, click the Text Effects button (Drawing Tools Format tab | WordArt Styles group) to display the Text Effects menu (Figure 2–58).

Figure 2–58

2

- Point to Transform in the Text Effects menu to display the WordArt Transform gallery (Figure 2–59).

Figure 2–59

3

- Point to the Chevron Up effect in the Warp area (first effect in second row in Warp area) to display a live preview of that text effect applied to the WordArt object (Figure 2–60).

Figure 2–60

🔍 Experiment

- Point to various effects in the Transform gallery and watch the format of the text and borders change.

Q&A | How can I see the preview of a Transform effect if the gallery overlays the WordArt letters?
Move the WordArt box to the left or right side of the slide and then repeat Steps 1 and 2.

4

- Click the Chevron Up shape to apply this text effect to the WordArt object.

Q&A | Can I change the shape I applied to the WordArt?
Yes. Position the insertion point in the box and then repeat Steps 1 and 2.

5

- Drag the lower-right sizing handle diagonally toward the lower-right corner of the slide until the crosshair is positioned approximately as shown in Figure 2–61.

crosshair indicates lower-right WordArt location

Figure 2–61

6

- Release to resize the WordArt object.
- Drag the WordArt object toward the right side of the slide until it is positioned approximately as shown in Figure 2–62.

WordArt object moved to desired location

Figure 2–62

To Apply a WordArt Text Fill

1 DOWNLOAD & SELECT SLIDES | 2 INSERT & FORMAT PICTURES | 3 INSERT & FORMAT SHAPES
4 FORMAT SLIDE BACKGROUNDS | 5 INSERT & FORMAT WORDART | 6 REVIEW, REVISE, & PRINT SLIDES

Various texture fills are available to give your WordArt characters a unique look. You used a texture fill to add interest to the Slide 3 background. The following steps add the Medium wood texture as a fill for the WordArt characters. *Why? The brown fill coordinates well with the red WordArt outline and is similar to the color of the basketball court in the Slide 1 and Slide 2 backgrounds.*

①

- With the WordArt object selected, click the Text Fill arrow (Drawing Tools Format tab | WordArt Styles group) to display the Text Fill gallery.
- Point to Texture in the Text Fill gallery to display the Texture gallery.

②

- If necessary, scroll down and then point to the Medium wood texture (last texture in last row) to display a live preview of that texture applied to the WordArt object (Figure 2–63).

Figure 2–63

🔎 Experiment

- Point to various styles in the Texture gallery and watch the fill change.

③

- Click the Medium wood texture to apply this texture as the fill for the WordArt object.

Q&A Can I apply this texture simultaneously to text that appears in more than one place on my slide?
Yes. You can select one area of text, press and then hold the CTRL key while you select the other text, and then apply the texture.

To Change the Weight of the WordArt Outline

1 DOWNLOAD & SELECT SLIDES | 2 INSERT & FORMAT PICTURES | 3 INSERT & FORMAT SHAPES
4 FORMAT SLIDE BACKGROUNDS | 5 INSERT & FORMAT WORDART | **6 REVIEW, REVISE, & PRINT SLIDES**

The letters in the WordArt style applied have an outline around the edges. You can increase the width of the outlines. *Why? The thicker line will emphasize this characteristic and add another visual element.* As with fonts, lines also are measured in points, and PowerPoint gives you the option to change the line **weight**, or thickness, starting with ¼ point (pt) and increasing in ¼-point increments. Other outline options include modifying the color and the line style, such as changing to dots or dashes or a combination of dots and dashes. The following steps change the WordArt outline weight to 6 pt.

1

- With the WordArt object still selected, click the Text Outline arrow (Drawing Tools Format tab | WordArt Styles group) to display the Text Outline gallery.
- Point to Weight in the gallery to display the Weight list.
- Point to 6 pt to display a live preview of this line weight on the WordArt text outline (Figure 2–64).

Figure 2–64

Q&A Can I make the line width more than 6 pt?
Yes. Click More Lines and increase the amount in the Width box.

Experiment

- Point to various line weights in the Weight list and watch the line thickness change.

2

- Click 6 pt to apply this line weight to the WordArt text outline.

Q&A Must my text have an outline?
No. To delete the outline, click No Outline in the Text Outline gallery.

To Change the Color of the WordArt Outline

1 DOWNLOAD & SELECT SLIDES | 2 INSERT & FORMAT PICTURES | 3 INSERT & FORMAT SHAPES
4 FORMAT SLIDE BACKGROUNDS | 5 INSERT & FORMAT WORDART | 6 REVIEW, REVISE, & PRINT SLIDES

Why? *The WordArt outline color and the boy's shorts are similar, so you can add contrast by changing one of these slide elements.* The following steps change the WordArt outline color.

1

- With the WordArt object still selected, display the Text Outline gallery.
- Point to Black, Background 1 (first color in Theme Colors row) to display a live preview of this outline color (Figure 2–65).

Figure 2–65

Figure 2–66

- Point to various colors in the gallery and watch the outline colors change.

2

- Click Black, Background 1 to apply this color to the WordArt outline.
- Click outside of the WordArt box to deselect this slide element (Figure 2–66).

Reviewing and Revising Individual Slides

The text, pictures, and shapes for all slides in the Basketball Camp presentation have been entered. Once you complete a slide show, you might decide to change elements. PowerPoint provides several tools to assist you with making changes. They include finding and replacing text, inserting a synonym, checking spelling, and printing speaker notes. The following pages discuss these tools.

Replace Dialog Box

BTW
Finding and Replacing Text
When finding and replacing text, you do not need to display the slide that contains the word for which you are searching. You can perform this action when any slide is displayed. To see the results of the search and replace action, however, you need to display the slide where the change occurred.

At times, you might want to change all occurrences of a word or phrase to another word or phrase. For example, an instructor may have one slide show to accompany a lecture for several introductory classes, and he wants to update slides with the particular class name and section that appear on several slides. He manually could change the characters, but PowerPoint includes an efficient method of replacing one word with another. The Find and Replace feature automatically locates specific text and then replaces it with desired text.

In some cases, you may want to replace only certain occurrences of a word or phrase, not all of them. To instruct PowerPoint to confirm each change, click the Find Next button in the Replace dialog box instead of the Replace All button. When PowerPoint locates an occurrence of the text, it pauses and waits for you to click either the Replace button or the Find Next button. Clicking the Replace button changes the text; clicking the Find Next button instructs PowerPoint to disregard that particular instance and look for the next occurrence of the Find what text.

To Find and Insert a Synonym

1 DOWNLOAD & SELECT SLIDES | 2 INSERT & FORMAT PICTURES | 3 INSERT & FORMAT SHAPES
4 FORMAT SLIDE BACKGROUNDS | 5 INSERT & FORMAT WORDART | **6 REVIEW, REVISE, & PRINT SLIDES**

Why? *When reviewing your slide show, you may decide that a particular word does not express the exact usage you intended or that you used the same word on multiple slides.* In these cases, you could find a **synonym**, or word similar in meaning, to replace the inappropriate or duplicate word. PowerPoint provides a **thesaurus**, which is a list of synonyms and antonyms, to help you find a replacement word.

In this project, you want to find a synonym to replace the word, acquaintances, on Slide 2. The following steps locate an appropriate synonym and replace the word.

1

- Display Slide 2 and then place the insertion point in the word, acquaintances.
- Right-click to display a shortcut menu related to the word, acquaintances. Then, point to Synonyms on the shortcut menu to display a list of synonyms for this word (Figure 2–67).

Q&A How do I locate a synonym for multiple words?
You need to select all the words and then right-click to display the shortcut menu.

If I am using a touch screen, how do I find a synonym?
Tap the Thesaurus button (Review tab | Proofing group) to display the Thesaurus pane for the selected word. Then, in the pane, tap the arrow next to the word to display a shortcut menu.

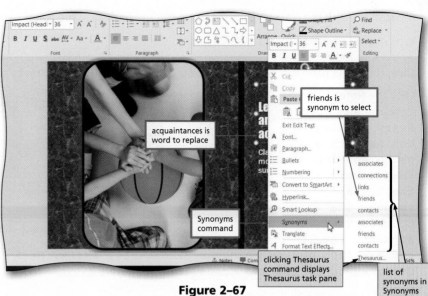

Figure 2–67

2

- Click the synonym you want (friends) on the Synonyms submenu to replace the word, acquaintances, in the presentation with the word, friends (Figure 2–68).

Q&A What if a suitable word does not display in the Synonyms submenu?
You can display the Thesaurus pane by clicking Thesaurus on the Synonyms submenu. A complete thesaurus with synonyms displays in the pane along with an antonym, which is a word with an opposite meaning.

Learn from pros and make friends

Classes meet weekday mornings throughout the summer

Figure 2–68

Other Ways

1. Click Thesaurus (Review tab | Proofing group)   2. Press SHIFT+F7

To Add Notes

1 DOWNLOAD & SELECT SLIDES | 2 INSERT & FORMAT PICTURES | 3 INSERT & FORMAT SHAPES
4 FORMAT SLIDE BACKGROUNDS | 5 INSERT & FORMAT WORDART | 6 REVIEW, REVISE, & PRINT SLIDES

Why? As you create slides, you may find material you want to state verbally and do not want to include on the slide. After adding these comments, you can print a set of speaker notes that will print below a small image of the slide. You can type and format comments in the **Notes pane** as you work in Normal view and then print this information as **notes pages**. The Notes pane is hidden until you click the Notes button on the status bar to open the pane. If you want to close the Notes pane, click the Notes button again. Charts, tables, and pictures added to the Notes pane also print on these pages. The following steps add text to the Notes pane on Slides 2, 3, and 4.

Note: In the following step, the word, skills, has been misspelled intentionally as skils to illustrate the use of PowerPoint's spell check feature. Your slides may contain different misspelled words, depending upon the accuracy of your typing.

1

- If necessary, click the Notes button on the status bar to display the Notes pane for Slide 2.

Q&A Why might I need to click the Notes button?
By default, the Notes pane is closed when you begin a new presentation. Once you display the Notes pane for any slide, the Notes pane will remain open unless you click the Notes button to close it.

- Click the Notes pane and then type `Every morning begins with a group session that covers the day's agenda. The coaches then separate the campers into groups to cover fundamental skils. Each morning ends with a contest designed to be fun and competitive.` (Figure 2–69).

Figure 2–69

Q&A What if I cannot see all the lines I typed?
You can drag the splitter bar up to enlarge the Notes pane. Clicking the Notes pane scroll arrows or swiping up or down on the Notes pane allows you to view the entire text.

2

- Display Slide 3, click the Notes pane, and then type `Campers will gain confidence while learning sportsmanship and strategies.` (Figure 2–70).

Figure 2–70

3

- Display Slide 4 and then type `Space is limited. Every camper will receive a t-shirt, snacks, and water. Parents are encouraged to attend the awards ceremony at the end of the camp session.` in the Notes pane (Figure 2–71).

Figure 2–71

To Find and Replace Text

1 DOWNLOAD & SELECT SLIDES | 2 INSERT & FORMAT PICTURES | 3 INSERT & FORMAT SHAPES
4 FORMAT SLIDE BACKGROUNDS | 5 INSERT & FORMAT WORDART | 6 REVIEW, REVISE, & PRINT SLIDES

While reviewing your slides, you realize that the camp will be held in the afternoon, not in the morning. To change this word throughout a presentation, you could view each slide, look for the word, morning, delete the word, and then type the replacement word, afternoon. A more efficient and effective method of performing this action is to use PowerPoint's Find and Replace feature. *Why?* *This method locates each occurrence of a word or phrase automatically and then replaces it with specified text.* The word, morning, displays three times in the slides and notes. The following steps use Find and Replace to replace all occurrences of the word, morning, with the word, afternoon.

1

- If necessary, display the Home tab and then click the Replace button (Home tab | Editing group) to display the Replace dialog box.

- Type **morning** in the Find what box (Replace dialog box).

- Click the Replace with box and then type **afternoon** in the box (Figure 2–72).

Figure 2–72

2

- Click the Replace All button (Replace dialog box) to instruct PowerPoint to replace all occurrences of the Find what word, morning, with the Replace with word, afternoon (Figure 2–73).

Q&A If I accidentally replaced the wrong text, can I undo this replacement?
Yes. Press CTRL+Z or click the Undo button on the Quick Access Toolbar to undo all replacements. If you had clicked the Replace button instead of the Replace All button, PowerPoint would undo only the most recent replacement.

Figure 2–73

3

- Click the OK button (Microsoft PowerPoint dialog box).

- Click the Close button (Replace dialog box).

Other Ways

1. Press CTRL+H

Checking Spelling

After you create a presentation, you should check it visually for spelling errors and style consistency. In addition, you can use PowerPoint's Spelling tool to identify possible misspellings on the slides and in the notes. You should proofread your presentation carefully by pointing to each word and saying it aloud as you point to it. Be mindful of commonly misused words such as its and it's, through and though, and to and too.

PowerPoint checks the entire presentation for spelling mistakes using a standard dictionary contained in the Microsoft Office group. This dictionary is shared with the other Microsoft Office applications such as Word and Excel. A custom dictionary is available if you want to add special words such as proper names, cities, and acronyms.

BTW
Formatting Notes Pane Text
You can format text in the Notes pane in the same manner you format text on a slide. To add emphasis, for example, you can italicize key words or change the font color and size.

When checking a presentation for spelling errors, PowerPoint opens the standard dictionary and the custom dictionary file, if one exists. When a word appears in the Spelling pane, you can perform one of several actions, as described in Table 2–1.

The standard dictionary contains commonly used English words. It does not, however, contain many proper names, abbreviations, technical terms, poetic contractions, or antiquated terms. PowerPoint treats words not found in the dictionaries as misspellings.

Table 2–1   Spelling Pane Buttons and Actions

Button Name/Action	When to Use	Action
Ignore	Word is spelled correctly but not found in dictionaries	PowerPoint continues checking rest of the presentation but will flag that word again if it appears later in document.
Ignore All	Word is spelled correctly but not found in dictionaries	PowerPoint ignores all occurrences of the word and continues checking rest of presentation.
Add	Add word to custom dictionary	PowerPoint opens custom dictionary, adds word, and continues checking rest of presentation.
Change	Word is misspelled	Click proper spelling of the word in Suggestions list. PowerPoint corrects word, continues checking rest of presentation, but will flag that word again if it appears later in document.
Change All	Word is misspelled	Click proper spelling of word in Suggestions list. PowerPoint changes all occurrences of misspelled word and continues checking rest of presentation.
Listen to the pronunciation	To hear the pronunciation of a word	Click the audio speaker icon next to the properly spelled word near the bottom of the Spelling pane.
View synonyms	See some synonyms for the correctly spelled word	View the bullet list of synonyms below the correctly spelled word near the bottom of the Spelling pane.
Close	Stop spelling checker	PowerPoint closes spelling checker and returns to PowerPoint window.

To Check Spelling

1 DOWNLOAD & SELECT SLIDES | 2 INSERT & FORMAT PICTURES | 3 INSERT & FORMAT SHAPES
4 FORMAT SLIDE BACKGROUNDS | 5 INSERT & FORMAT WORDART | **6 REVIEW, REVISE, & PRINT SLIDES**

Why? Although PowerPoint's spelling checker is a valuable tool, it is not infallible. You should not rely on the spelling checker to catch all your mistakes. The following steps check the spelling on all slides in the Basketball Camp presentation.

1
• Click Review on the ribbon to display the Review tab.

• Click the Spelling button (Review Tab | Proofing group) to start the spelling checker and display the Spelling pane (Figure 2–74).

Figure 2–74

2

• With the word, skils, selected in the list and in the Notes pane, click the Change button (Spelling pane) to replace the misspelled flagged word, skils, with the selected correctly spelled word, skills, and then continue the spelling check (Figure 2–75).

Figure 2–75

Q&A | Could I have clicked the Change All button instead of the Change button?

Yes. When you click the Change All button, you change the current and future occurrences of the misspelled word. The misspelled word, skils, appears only once in the presentation, so clicking the Change or the Change All button in this instance produces identical results.

Occasionally a correctly spelled word is flagged as a possible misspelled word. Why?

Your custom dictionary does not contain the word, so it is seen as spelled incorrectly. You can add this word to a custom dictionary to prevent the spelling checker from flagging it as a mistake.

3

• Replace the misspelled word, lern, with the word, learn.
• Continue checking all flagged words in the presentation. When the Microsoft PowerPoint dialog box appears, click the OK button (Microsoft PowerPoint dialog box) to close the spelling checker and return to the slide where a possible misspelled word appeared.

Other Ways

1. Click Spell Check icon on status bar	2. Right-click flagged word, click correct word	3. Press F7

To Insert a Slide Number

PowerPoint can insert the slide number on your slides automatically to indicate where the slide is positioned within the presentation. The number location on the slide is determined by the presentation theme. You have the option to not display this slide number on the title slide. To insert a slide number on all slides except the title slide, you would follow these steps.

1. Display the Insert tab and then click the Slide Number button (Insert tab | Text group) to display the Header and Footer dialog box.

2. Click the Slide number check box (Header and Footer dialog box) to place a check mark in it.

Q&A | Can I prevent the slide number from being displayed on the title slide?

Yes. Click the 'Don't show on title slide' check box (Header and Footer dialog box) to place a check mark in it.

3. Click the 'Apply to All' button (Header and Footer dialog box) to close the dialog box and insert the slide number.

Q&A | How does clicking the 'Apply to All' button differ from clicking the Apply button?

The Apply button inserts the slide number only on the currently displayed slide, whereas the 'Apply to All' button inserts the slide number on every slide.

BTW

PowerPoint Help
At any time while using PowerPoint, you can find answers to questions and display information about various topics through PowerPoint Help. Used properly, this form of assistance can increase your productivity and reduce your frustrations by minimizing the time you spend learning how to use PowerPoint. For instructions about PowerPoint Help and exercises that will help you gain confidence in using it, read the Office and Windows module at the beginning of this book.

Other Ways

1. Click 'Header & Footer' button (Insert tab | Text group), click Slide tab, if necessary (Header and Footer dialog box), click Slide number and 'Don't show on title slide' check boxes, click 'Apply to All' button

To Add a Transition between Slides

A final enhancement you will make in this presentation is to change the transition from Fade to Wipe for all slides and increase the transition duration. The following steps apply this transition to the presentation.

1 Click Transitions on the ribbon and then click the Wipe transition (Transitions tab | Transition to This Slide group) to apply this transition.

2 Click the Duration up arrow in the Timing group four times to change the transition speed from 01.00 to 02.00.

3 Click the Preview Transitions button (Transitions tab | Preview area) to view the new transition and time.

4 Click the 'Apply To All' button (Transitions tab | Timing group) to apply this transition and speed to all four slides in the presentation (Figure 2–76).

Q&A Can I apply a particular transition or duration to one slide and then change the transition or timing for a different slide in the presentation?
Yes. Select a slide and then select a transition and duration. Do not click the 'Apply To All' button. Repeat this process to apply the transition and duration to individual slides.

Figure 2–76

How can I use handouts to organize my speech?
As you develop a lengthy presentation with many visuals, handouts can help you organize your material. Print handouts with the maximum number of slides per page. Use scissors to cut each thumbnail and then place these miniature slide images adjacent to each other on a flat surface. Any type on the thumbnails will be too small to read, so the images will need to work with only the support of the verbal message you provide. You can rearrange these thumbnails as you organize your speech. When you return to your computer, you can rearrange the slides on your screen to match the order of your thumbnail printouts. Begin speaking the actual words you want to incorporate in the body of the talk. This process of glancing at the thumbnails and hearing yourself say the key ideas of the speech is one of the best methods of organizing and preparing for the actual presentation. Ultimately, when you deliver your speech in front of an audience, the images on the slides or on your note cards should be sufficient to remind you of the accompanying verbal message.

To Print Speaker Notes

Why? *Comments added to slides in the Notes pane give the speaker information that supplements the text on the slide.* They will print with a small image of the slide at the top and the comments below the slide. The following steps print the speaker notes.

1

- Display Slide 1, click File on the ribbon to open the Backstage view, and then click the Print tab in the Backstage view to display Slide 1 in the Print gallery.

- Click 'Full Page Slides' in the Settings area to display the Print gallery (Figure 2–77).

Q&A Why does the preview of my slide appear in black and white?

Your printer determines how the preview appears. If your printer is not capable of printing color images, the preview will not appear in color.

Figure 2–77

2

- Click Notes Pages in the Print Layout area to select this option and then click the Next Page button three times to display a preview of Slide 4 (Figure 2–78).

Q&A Can I preview Slides 1, 2, or 3 now?

Yes. Click the Previous Page button to preview the other slides.

Figure 2–78

- Verify that the printer listed on the Printer Status button will print a hard copy of the presentation. If necessary, click the Printer Status button to display a list of available printer options and then click the desired printer to change the currently selected printer.
- Click the Print button in the Print gallery to print the notes pages on the currently selected printer.
- When the printer stops, retrieve the hard copy.

Q&A   I am not using a color printer, so why do the background images display in the figures but not in my printout?
Graphics are displayed depending upon the settings in the Print gallery. For example, the background will print if Color is specified whereas it will not with a Grayscale or Pure Black and White setting.

Other Ways

1. Press CTRL+P, select desired options

To Save and Print the Presentation

It is a good practice to save a presentation before printing it, in the event you experience difficulties printing. For a detailed example of the procedure summarized below for saving and printing a presentation, refer to the Office and Windows module at the beginning of this book.

1 Save the presentation again on the same storage location with the same file name.

2 Print the presentation.

Q&A   Do I have to wait until my presentation is complete to print it?
No, you can follow these steps to print a presentation at any time while you are creating it.

3 Because the project now is complete, you can exit PowerPoint.

BTW
Conserving Ink and Toner
If you want to conserve ink or toner, you can instruct PowerPoint to print draft quality documents by clicking File on the ribbon to open the Backstage view, clicking the Options tab in the Backstage view to display the PowerPoint Options dialog box, clicking Advanced in the left pane (PowerPoint Options dialog box), scrolling to the Print area in the right pane, not placing a check mark in the High quality check box, and then clicking the OK button. Then, use the Backstage view to print the document as usual.

BTW
Distributing a Document
Instead of printing and distributing a hard copy of a document, you can distribute the document electronically. Options include sending the document via email; posting it on cloud storage (such as OneDrive) and sharing the file with others; posting it on social media, a blog, or other website; and sharing a link associated with an online location of the document. You also can create and share a PDF or XPS image of the document, so that users can view the file in Acrobat Reader or XPS Viewer instead of in PowerPoint.

BTW
Printing Document Properties
PowerPoint 2016 does not allow you to print document properties. This feature, however, is available in other Office 2016 apps, including Word and Excel.

Summary

In this module, you have learned how to insert and format pictures, add and format shapes, insert and format WordArt, add and format slide backgrounds, find and replace text, check spelling, add notes, and print speaker notes.

What decisions will you need to make when creating your next presentation?

Use these guidelines as you complete the assignments in this module and create your own slide show decks outside of this class.

1. Determine if an online theme can help you design and develop the presentation efficiently and effectively.

2. Identify personal pictures that would create interest and promote the message being presented.

3. Consider modifying pictures.

    a) Add corrections.

    b) Add styles.

    c) Add effects.

    d) Add and format borders.

4. Locate shapes that supplement the verbal and written message.

    a) Size and position them aesthetically on slides.

    b) Add styles.

5. Develop WordArt that emphasizes major presentation messages.

    a) Modify the shape.

    b) Change the weight and color to coordinate with slide elements.

6. Format individual slide backgrounds.

    a) Add and modify fills.

    b) Insert a picture background.

7. Change fonts to emphasize particular slide components.

8. Search for synonyms that help express your thoughts.

9. Create speaker notes.

10. Check spelling.

Apply Your Knowledge

Reinforce the skills and apply the concepts you learned in this module.

Changing the Background and Adding Photos and WordArt

Note: To complete this assignment, you will be required to use the Data Files. Please contact your instructor for information about accessing the Data Files.

Instructions: Run PowerPoint. Open the presentation called Apply 2–1 Bees, which is located in the Data Files. The four slides in the presentation discuss bee stings. The document you open is an unformatted presentation. You are to add pictures, apply picture styles, add WordArt, change slide layouts, and apply a transition so the slides look like Figure 2–79.

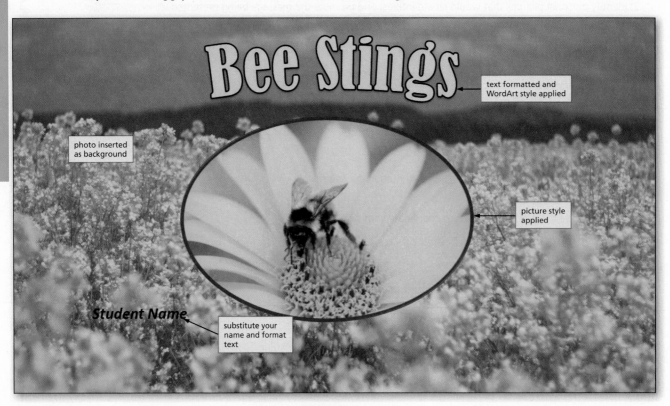

(a) Slide 1

Figure 2–79

Perform the following tasks:

1. On the title slide, use your name in place of Student Name and then bold and italicize this text (Figure 2–79a).

2. If requested to do so by your instructor, change your first name to your mother's first name on the title slide.

3. Increase the title text font size to 96 point and change the font to Bernard MT Condensed. Apply the WordArt style, Fill – White, Outline – Accent 1, Shadow (in first row). Change text fill color to Yellow (in Standard Colors row). Change text outline to Black, Text 1 (in first Theme Colors row) and then change the outline weight to 2¼ pt. Apply the Transform text effect, Arch Up (in Follow Path row) to this text.

4. Apply the Beveled Oval, Black picture style to the picture on Slide 1 and then move the picture to the center of the slide as shown in Figure 2–79a. Use the vertical Smart Guide to align the picture in this location.

5. Create a background on Slide 1 by inserting the photo, Spring, which is located in the Data Files.

6. On Slide 2, change the layout to Title and Content. Increase the title text font to 54 point, change the font color to Green (in Standard Colors row), and then bold this text. Increase the list font size to 32 point, as shown in Figure 2–79b.

7. Create a background on Slides 2 and 3 by inserting the Light Gradient – Accent 4 gradient fill (in first Preset gradients row).

8. On Slide 2, insert the picture, Bee2, move it to the right side of the slide, and then apply the Soft Edge Rectangle picture style to the picture.

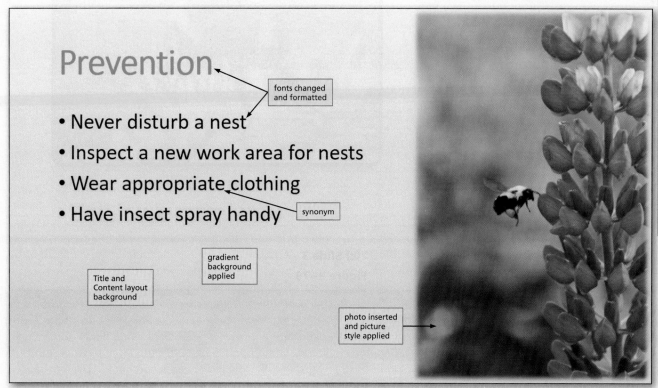

(b) Slide 2

Figure 2–79

9. On Slide 2, type **Wear long pants and a long-sleeved shirt when hiking or working outside.** in the Notes pane.

10. Replace the word, proper, with the synonym, appropriate.

11. On Slide 3 (Figure 2–79c), increase the title text font to 54 point, change the font color to Green (in Standard Colors row), and then bold this text. Increase the list font size to 24 point. Insert the photo, Bee3, and then apply the Reflected Bevel, Black picture style and change the picture brightness to Brightness: +20% Contrast: 0% (Normal) (in Brightness/Contrast area).

12. Type **Apply ice to control swelling.** in the Notes pane.

13. Create a new Slide 4 with the blank layout. Create a background on Slide 4 by inserting the photo, Hiking. Insert the illustration, Bee4. Resize this illustration and move it to the woman's right arm, as shown in Figure 2–79d.

14. On Slide 4, insert the Oval Callout shape (in first row in Callouts area) and then move it to the right side of the woman's head. Apply the Subtle Effect – Gold, Accent 4 (in fourth row) shape style to the callout. Size the shape as shown in the figure. Type **I am glad I have insect repellent in my backpack** in the shape. Bold and italicize this text and then change the font size to 20 point, as shown in Figure 2–79d.

15. Apply the Wind transition in the Exciting category to all slides. Change the duration to 2.50 seconds.

Continued >

Apply Your Knowledge *continued*

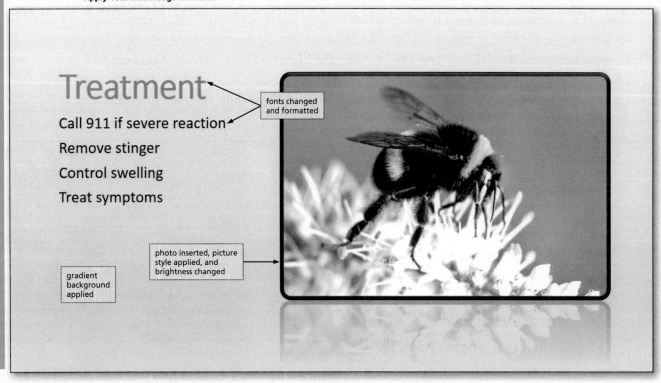

(c) Slide 3

Figure 2–79

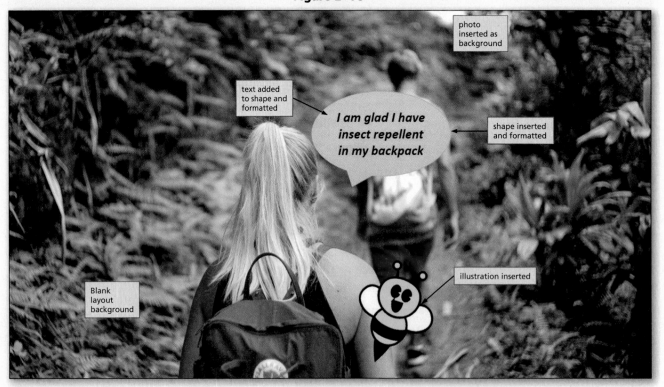

(d) Slide 4

Figure 2–79

16. Save the presentation using the file name, Apply 2–1 Bee Stings.

17. Submit the revised document in the format specified by your instructor.

18. ✦ In Step 4 you applied the Beveled Oval, Black picture style to the photo on Slide 1. How did this style enhance the photo and the slide?

Extend Your Knowledge

Extend the skills you learned in this module and experiment with new skills. You may need to use Help to complete the assignment.

Changing Slide Backgrounds, Inserting Shapes and WordArt, and Finding and Replacing Text

Note: To complete this assignment, you will be required to use the Data Files. Please contact your instructor for information about accessing the Data Files.

Instructions: Run PowerPoint. Open the presentation, Extend 2–1 Monarch, which is located in the Data Files. You will create backgrounds including inserting a photo to create a background, apply a WordArt Style and effect, add shapes, and find and replace text to create the presentation.

Perform the following tasks:

1. Change the document theme to Basis and choose the orange variant (third variant).

2. Find and replace the words, stay alive, with the word, survive, on all slides.

3. On all slides, create a background by inserting the photo, Sky. Change the transparency to 25%.

4. On the title slide (Figure 2–80a), apply the WordArt style, Fill - Black, Text 1, Outline – Background 1, Hard Shadow – Accent 1 (second style in third row), to the title text, and then increase the font size to 72 point. Apply the WordArt Glow text effect, Red, 18 pt glow, Accent color 3 (in Glow Variations area), and then italicize this text. Also, align the text in the middle of the text box by clicking the Align Text button (Home tab | Paragraph group) and then selecting Middle in the Align Text gallery. You may need to use Help for assistance in aligning this text.

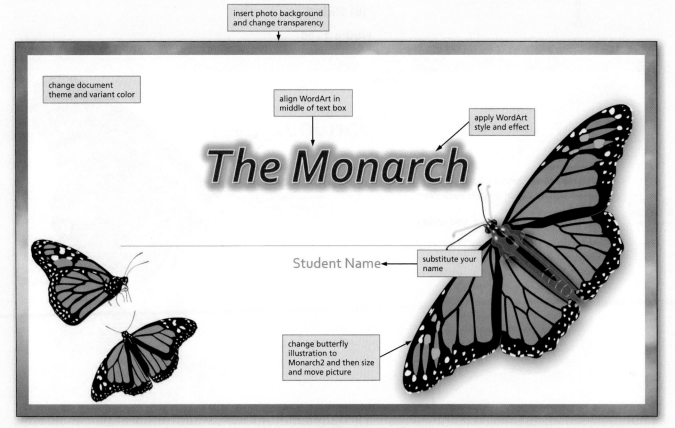

(a) Slide 1

Figure 2–80

Continued >

Extend Your Knowledge *continued*

5. If requested to do so by your instructor, add your current or previous pet's name as the Slide 1 subtitle text in place of Student Name.

(b) Slide 2

Figure 2–80

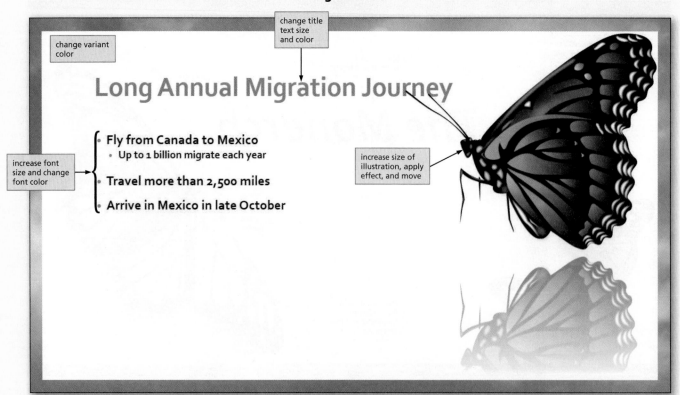

(c) Slide 3

Figure 2–80

(d) Slide 4

Figure 2–80

6. On Slide 1, move the butterfly illustration in the upper-left corner to the lower-left corner of the slide. Change the butterfly illustration in the upper-right corner of the slide to the illustration, Monarch2. Increase the size of this illustration to approximately 6.26" × 5.44" and move it to the lower-right side of the slide as shown in Figure 2–80a. *Hint*: Use the Size group on the Picture Tools Format tab to enter these measurements for the illustration.

7. On Slides 2 and 3, increase the font size of the first-level paragraphs to 20 point and the one second-level paragraph on Slide 3 to 16 point. Also, change the color of this text to Black, Text 1 (in first Theme Colors row) and then bold this text.

8. On Slide 2 (Figure 2–80b), increase the size of the illustration to approximately 4.14" × 5.53", apply the Reflected Bevel, Black picture style, and then move it under the title text.

9. On Slide 3 (Figure 2–80c), increase the size of the illustration to approximately 4.35" × 5.2", apply the Half Reflection, 8 pt offset reflection picture effect (Reflection Variations area), and then move this illustration to the upper-right corner of the slide.

10. On Slides 2, 3, and 4, decrease the size of the title text to 40 point and then bold this text.

11. On Slide 4 (Figure 2–80d), insert the Right Arrow shape (in Block Arrows area) and position it on the globe illustration near the Canada–United States border. Size the shape as shown in the figure. Type **Canada to Mexico** in the shape. Bold this text and then change the font size to 24 point. Apply the Light 1 Outline, Colored Fill – Orange, Accent 4 shape style (in third Theme Styles row) to the shape.

12. On Slide 4, insert a Curved Arrow Connector shape by displaying the Shapes gallery, clicking this shape (in Lines area), and then positioning the pointer over central Canada in the globe illustration. Then, click and drag the pointer to central Mexico. Size this arrow so it is approximately 0.84" × 1.91". Hint: You can size a shape in the same manner as you size a picture or illustration.

Continued >

Extend Your Knowledge *continued*

13. With the Curved Arrow Connector selected, click the Shape Outline button (Drawing Tools Format tab | Shape Styles group) to display the Shape Outline gallery and then click the Red, Accent 1 style (in first Theme Styles row) to apply this style to this arrow shape. Change the shape outline weight to 6 pt.

14. Apply an appropriate transition to all slides.

15. Save the presentation using the file name, Extend 2–1 Monarch Migration.

16. Submit the revised document in the format specified by your instructor.

17. ✳ In this assignment, you changed the transparency of the inserted background picture on all the slides to 25%. How did this transparency change enhance your slides?

Expand Your World

Create a solution that uses cloud and web technologies by learning and investigating on your own from general guidance.

Modifying a Presentation Using PowerPoint Online

Note: To complete this assignment, you will be required to use the Data Files. Please contact your instructor for information about accessing the Data Files.

Instructions: The park district director in your community is planning a basketball camp for next summer. He has asked you to help him promote this event, and he wants to focus on the skills boys and girls will learn and develop. You inform him that you have created a Basketball Camp presentation for your computer class, and he would like you to customize the content of these slides slightly to promote the summer camp.

Perform the following tasks:

1. Run a browser. Search for the text, PowerPoint Online, using a search engine. Visit several websites to learn about PowerPoint Online. Navigate to the Office Online website. You will need to sign in to your Microsoft account. Run PowerPoint Online.

2. Locate the Basketball Camp presentation in the Recent list and then click the file name to open the file. Click the Edit Presentation button and then click 'Edit in PowerPoint Online' and display the ribbon. Modify the presentation you created for the Basketball Camp presentation by adding the name and address of the nearest park district headquarters on the title slide. In addition, add the date that is the first Saturday in June next year and a starting time of 1 p.m.

3. If requested by your instructor, add the name of one of your high school teachers as the park district director's name on the title slide.

4. Save the presentation using the file name, Expand 2–1 Basketball Camp.

5. Submit the assignment in the format specified by your instructor.

6. ✳ Other than the content the director asked you to include on the title slide, how does the presentation you created using PowerPoint Online differ from the presentation you created in the Module 2 project? Which tabs are not available in PowerPoint Online? View the Home, Design, and Transitions tabs. Do you think the formatting functions, themes, and transitions are adequate to develop effective presentations? Why or why not?

In the Labs

Design, create, modify, and/or use a presentation following the guidelines, concepts, and skills presented in this module. Labs 1 and 2, which increase in difficulty, require you to create solutions based on what you learned in the module; Lab 3 requires you to apply your creative thinking and problem-solving skills to design and implement a solution.

Lab 1: Creating a Presentation, Inserting Photos, Applying Picture Styles, and Inserting Shapes

Note: To complete this assignment, you will be required to use the Data Files. Please contact your instructor for information about accessing the Data Files.

Problem: Your astronomy class is studying the dwarf planet, Pluto, and the New Horizon probe that has been taking photographs of this planet. Prepare the PowerPoint presentation shown in Figure 2–81.

Perform the following tasks:

1. Run PowerPoint. Create a new presentation using the Celestial theme.

2. On Slide 1, insert the photo, Pluto1, as shown in Figure 2–81a. Apply the Metal Oval picture style to the picture, decrease the size of the picture slightly, and then move it to the left side of the slide as shown in the figure.

3. Type **Pluto Up Close** as the Slide 1 title text. Press the ENTER key after the words, PLUTO and UP, so the text is displayed on three lines. Change the font to Britannic Bold and increase the font size to 88 point. Apply the WordArt style Gradient Fill – Gray (first style in

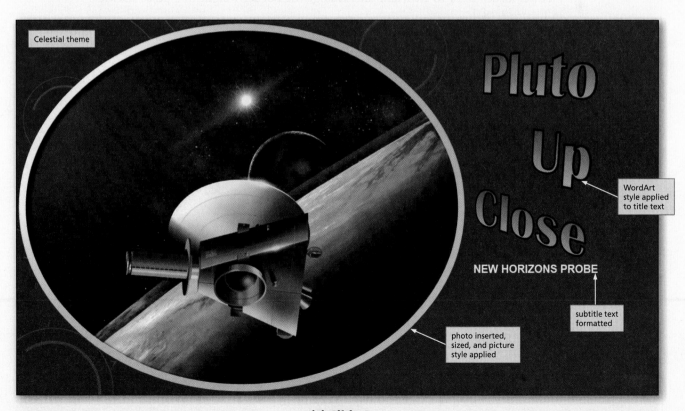

(a) Slide 1

Figure 2–81

Continued >

In the Labs *continued*

second row). Change the text outline color to Black, Background 1 (in Theme Colors row) and the text outline weight to 3 pt. Also, apply the Perspective Heroic Extreme Left 3-D Rotation (in Perspective area) to this text. Type **New Horizons Probe** as the subtitle text. Change the font to Arial, decrease the font size to 16 point, and then bold this text.

4. Insert four new slides. Create Slides 2 and 5 with the Two Content layout, Slide 3 with the Panoramic Picture with Caption layout, and Slide 4 with the Title Only layout.

5. Using Figures 2–81b through 2–81e as a guide, type the title and content text. On Slide 2, change the title font to Arial, increase the font size to 44 point, and then change the font color to Red (in Standard Colors row). Use the Format Painter to apply these formatting changes to the title text on Slides 4 and 5.

6. On Slide 3, change the font size of the two paragraphs to 24 point and then bold this text.

7. On Slide 5, change the bulleted list font size to 28 point and then bold this text.

8. Using Figures 2–81b through 2–81e as a guide, insert all illustrations on Slides 2 through 5. The pictures and illustration to be inserted, which are available in the Data Files, are called Pluto2 (for Slide 2), Solar System (for Slide 3), Pluto3 (for Slide 4), and Solar System2 (for Slide 5).

9. Size the pictures and then use the Smart Guides to position these images. You may want to zoom the slides to help you align these graphic elements.

10. On Slide 2, apply the Bevel Perspective picture style to the picture, change the picture border color to Red, and then change the border weight to 3 pt, as shown in Figure 2–81b.

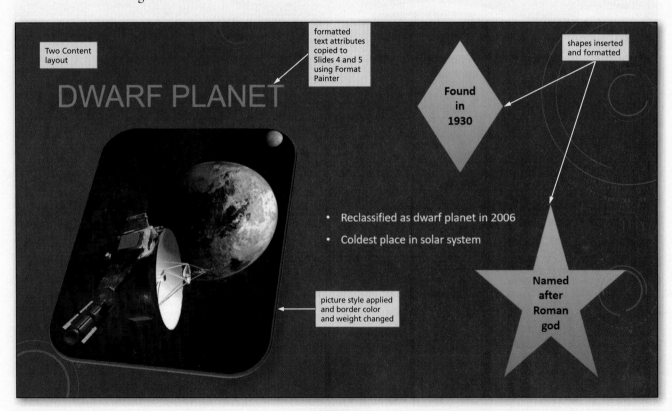

(b) Slide 2

Figure 2–81

11. On Slide 2, insert the Diamond shape located in the Basic Shapes area to the right of the title text. Apply the Subtle Effect – Olive Green, Accent 4 shape style (in Theme Styles area) to the shape, type **`Found in 1930`** in the shape, and then bold this text. Insert the 5-Point Star shape located in the Stars and Banners area in the lower-right corner of the slide. Apply the Subtle Effect – Blue, Accent 2 shape style (in Theme Styles area) to the shape, type **`Named after Roman god`** in the shape, and then bold this text. Adjust the size and position of these two shapes, as shown in the figure.

12. On Slide 3, insert the Sun shape located in the Basic Shapes area on the lower-right corner of the slide. Apply the Intense Effect – Gold, Accent 5 shape style (in Theme Styles area) to the shape. Size the shape as shown in the figure. Type the text, **`Pluto takes 248 earth years to orbit the sun`** in the shape and then bold this text, as shown in Figure 2–81c.

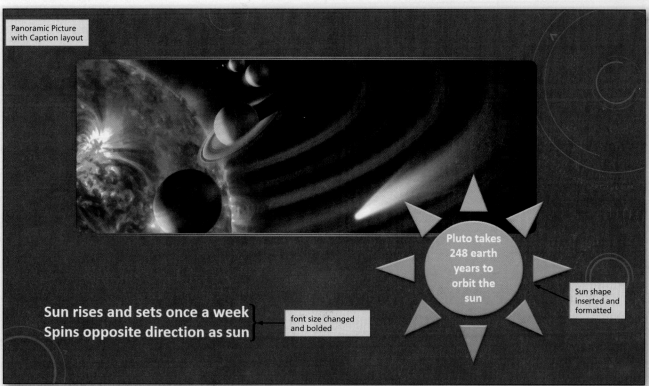

(c) Slide 3

Figure 2–81

13. On Slide 4, insert the Oval shape. Select this shape, hold down the SHIFT key, and then draw a circle .75" × .75", as shown in Figure 2–81d. *Hint*: Use the Size group in the Drawing Tools Format tab to enter the exact measurement of the shape. Change the shape fill gradient to Linear Down (in first Light Variations area). Then copy and paste this shape four times. Move the five shapes around the Pluto illustration, as shown in the figure.

14. On Slide 5, apply the Simple Frame, White picture style to the illustration. Insert the Left Arrow shape located in the Block Arrows area to the right of the illustration. Change the shape fill to Red. Size the shape as shown in the figure. Type **`Pluto`** in the shape and then bold this text, as shown in Figure 2–81e.

15. On Slide 2, type **`Pluto was discovered on February 18, 1930, by Clyde Tombaugh of the Lowell Observatory.`** in the Notes pane.

16. On Slide 3, type **`It takes five hours for the sun's rays to reach Pluto. It takes only eight minutes for the sun's rays to reach Earth.`** in the Notes pane.

Continued >

In the Labs *continued*

(d) Slide 4

Figure 2–81

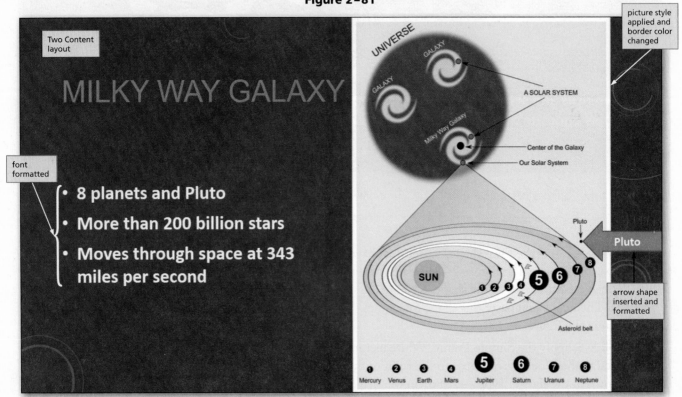

(e) Slide 5

Figure 2–81

17. If requested by your instructor, type the name of the city or county in which you were born into the title placeholder on Slide 3.

18. Apply the Vortex transition in the Exciting category to all slides. Change the duration to 3.0 seconds.

19. Check the spelling and correct any errors. Save the presentation using the file name, Lab 2–1 Pluto Up Close.

20. Print the notes pages.

21. Submit the document in the format specified by your instructor.

22. ✸ In Step 2, you applied the Metal Oval picture style to the picture. How did this improve the design of the slide? Why did you put a 3 pt red border on the picture on Slide 2?

Lab 2: Creating a Presentation Using an Online Theme Template, Shapes, and WordArt

Note: To complete this assignment, you will be required to use the Data Files. Please contact your instructor for information about accessing the Data Files.

Problem: Your local library has hired a singer for the summer reading program. Her weekly show is centered around music and art, and one of her songs is about the colors of the rainbow. In addition to her backdrop of rainbow colors, you decide to develop a presentation to teach the children more about rainbows. You create the presentation shown in Figure 2–82.

Perform the following tasks:

1. Run PowerPoint and then search for an online template by typing **nature** in the 'Search for online templates and themes' box. Choose the template called Nature presentation, illustrated landscape design (widescreen).

2. Delete Slides 12 and 13, delete Slides 6 through 10, and then delete Slides 3 and 4. Duplicate Slide 2 and then move Slide 4 to the end of the presentation.

3. Type the title and text content for all slides, as shown in Figures 2–82a through 2–82e.

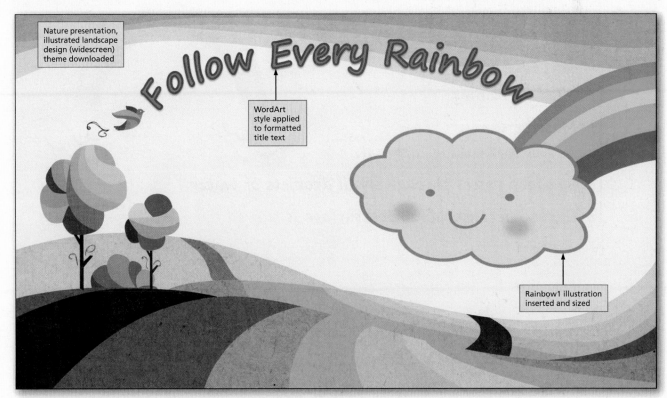

(a) Slide 1

Figure 2–82

Continued >

In the Labs *continued*

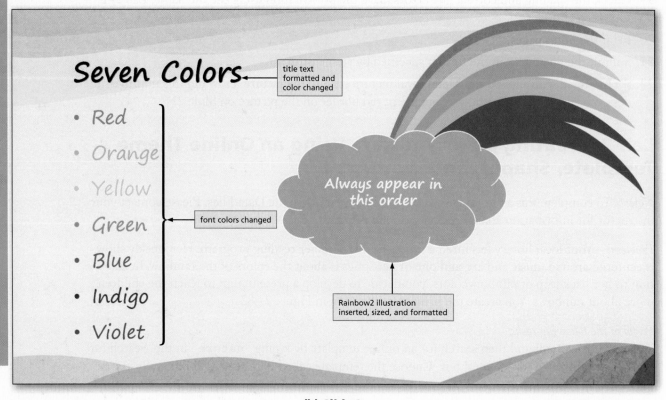

(b) Slide 2

Figure 2–82

(c) Slide 3

Figure 2–82

4. Insert the illustrations shown in Figures 2–82b through 2–82d from the Data Files. The illustrations are called Rainbow1 (for Slide 1), Rainbow2 (for Slide 2), Rainbow3 (for Slide 3), and People (for Slide 4). Size the illustrations using Figure 2–82 as a guide.

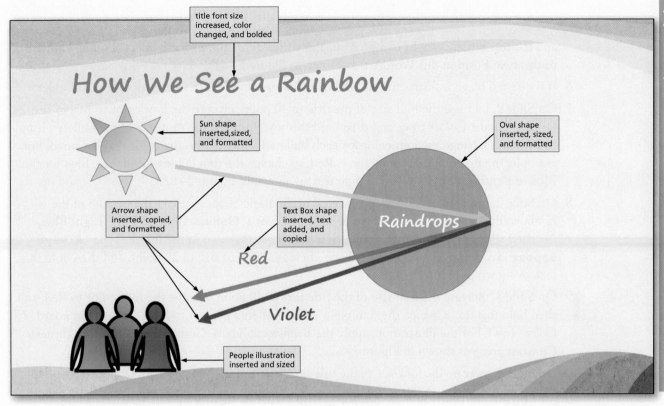

(d) Slide 4

Figure 2–82

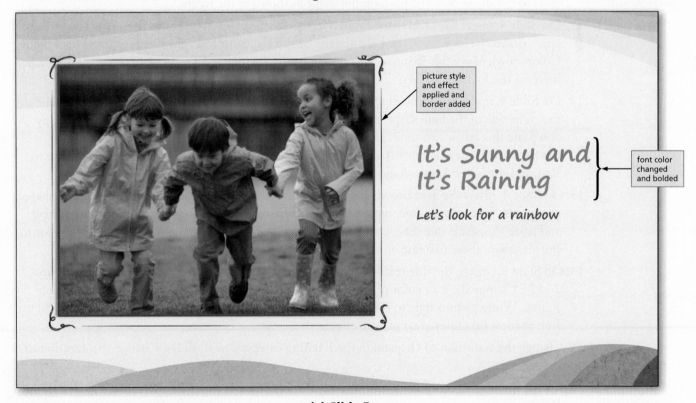

(e) Slide 5

Figure 2–82

5. On the title slide, select the title text and then apply the WordArt style Fill – White, Outline – Accent 1, Shadow (fourth style in first row). Increase the font size to 72 point. Change the text fill to Red (in Standard Colors row), the text outline color to Purple (in Standard Colors row),

Continued >

In the Labs *continued*

and the text outline weight to 3 pt. Also, apply the Arch Up transform effect (Follow Path area), to this text. Position this WordArt, as shown in Figure 2–82a.

6. If requested by your instructor, add the name of your hometown in the subtitle placeholder.

7. On Slide 2, increase the font size of the title to 40 point, change the font color to Black, Text 2 (in first Theme Colors row), and then bold this text. Increase the font size of the bulleted list to 28 point. Change the font color for each bulleted paragraph to the color that is named. For example, the first bulleted paragraph is Red, so change the font color to Red. Use Blue for the Blue text and Dark Blue for the Indigo text, as shown in Figure 2–82b.

8. On Slide 2, insert the Cloud shape, located in the Basic Shapes area, at the bottom of the rainbow illustration. Change the shape style to Light 1, Outline, Colored Fill – Light Blue, Accent 2 (in third Theme Styles row). Size the shape as shown in the figure. Type **Always appear in this order** in the shape, increase the font size to 20 point, and then bold this text, as shown in Figure 2–82b.

9. On Slide 3, increase the font size of the title text to 40 point, change the font color to Red, and then bold this text. Change the font color of the bulleted list text to Dark Blue (in Standard Colors row). For the illustration, apply the Brightness: +20% Contrast: +40% (in Brightness/ Contrast area), as shown in Figure 2–82c.

10. On Slide 4, increase the font size of the title text to 40 point, change the font color to Red, and then bold this text, as shown in Figure 2–82d. Insert the Sun shape, located in the Basic Shapes area, in the upper left area of the slide below the title text. Change the shape fill color to Yellow (in Standard Colors row) and then apply the From Top Left Corner gradient (in Dark Variations area) to the shape. Size and position the shape as shown in the figure.

11. On Slide 4, insert the Oval shape located in the Basic Shapes area, resize the shape so that it is approximately 3" × 3", and then change the Shape Fill color to Light Blue, Accent 2 (in Theme Colors row). Move this shape to the area shown in the figure. Type **Raindrops** in the shape, increase the font size to 24 point, and then bold this text.

12. On Slide 4, insert the Arrow shape, located in the Lines area, from the edge of the sun shape to the right side of the blue shape, as shown in Figure 2–82d. Change the weight to 6 pt. Copy and paste this arrow two times and use the sizing handles to position the arrows, as shown in the figure. Change the upper Arrow shape outline color to Yellow, the middle Arrow shape to Red, and the lower Arrow shape to Purple.

13. On Slide 4, insert the Text Box shape, located in the Basic Shapes area, type **Red** in the shape, change the font color to Red, increase the font size to 24 point, and then bold this text. Copy and paste this shape one time, change the text to **Violet,** and then change the font color to Purple. Move these two text box shapes to the areas shown in the figure.

14. On Slide 5, change the title text font color to Red and then bold this text, as shown in Figure 2–82e. Change the font color of the text to Purple and then bold this text. Apply the Simple Frame, White picture style to the picture. Add a 3 pt Purple border and then apply the Offset Left shadow (in Outer area) picture effect.

15. Change the transition to Origami in the Exciting category to all slides. Change the duration to 2.5 seconds.

16. Check spelling and correct all errors. Save the presentation using the file name, Lab 2–2 About Rainbows.

17. Submit the revised document in the format specified by your instructor.

18. ✳ You searched for an online rainbow theme. Do you think any of the other themes would have worked well for your presentation? Does choosing specific slide layouts while beginning the exercise help save time creating the presentation?

Lab 3: **Consider This: Your Turn**

Design and Create a Presentation about Learning to Knit and Crochet

Note: To complete this assignment, you will be required to use the Data Files. Please contact your instructor for information about accessing the Data Files.

Part 1: More than 50 million people knit or crochet to create fun and useful items, to relax, or to exchange ideas with fellow hobbyists at a regional guild or group. The local craft store in your community is offering a series of classes on knitting and crocheting techniques, and the manager has asked you to help promote the event. The introductory course includes instruction on selecting yarn, hooks, and needles; reading patterns; and making basic stitches. The intermediate and advanced courses include knitting in the round; making sleeves, button holes, and cables; and bead and filet crocheting. Classes are scheduled for four weeks on consecutive Saturdays beginning the first week of every month. All students will learn new skills and complete a fashionable project, which could include creating afghans, hats, and scarves for community residents in need. Use the concepts and techniques presented in this module to prepare a presentation to promote the classes. Select a suitable theme, and include a title slide, bulleted lists, shapes, and WordArt. The presentation should contain photos and illustrations appropriately resized. Six photos and illustrations are available in the Data Files: Green Yarn, Mitten, Two Mittens, Penguin, Quilt, and Scarf. Apply picture styles and effects. Add a title slide and closing slide to complete your presentation. Format the title slide with a shape. Format the background with at least one picture and apply a background texture to at least one slide. Review and revise your presentation as needed. Submit your assignment in the format specified by your instructor.

Part 2: ✳ You made several decisions while creating the presentation in this assignment: where to place text, how to format the text (such as font, font size, and where to use WordArt), which graphical image(s) to use, what styles and effects to apply, where to position the graphical images, how to format the graphical images, and which shapes to use to add interest to the presentation. What was the rationale behind each of these decisions? When you reviewed the document, what further revisions did you make and why? Where would you recommend showing this slide show?

1 Creating a Worksheet and a Chart

Objectives

You will have mastered the material in this module when you can:

- Describe the Excel worksheet
- Enter text and numbers
- Use the Sum button to sum a range of cells
- Enter a simple function
- Copy the contents of a cell to a range of cells using the fill handle
- Apply cell styles
- Format cells in a worksheet

- Create a 3-D pie chart
- Change a worksheet name and sheet tab color
- Change document properties
- Preview and print a worksheet
- Use the AutoCalculate area to display statistics
- Correct errors on a worksheet

Introduction

Almost every organization collects vast amounts of data. Often, data is consolidated into a summary so that people in the organization better understand the meaning of the data. An Excel worksheet allows data to be summarized and charted easily. A **chart** conveys a visual representation of data. In this module, you will create a worksheet that includes a chart. The data in the worksheet and chart comprise a personal budget that contains monthly estimates for each income and expense category.

Project — Personal Budget Worksheet and Chart

The project in this module follows proper design guidelines and uses Excel to create the worksheet and chart shown in Figure 1–1a and Figure 1–1b. The worksheet contains budget data for Linda Fox. She has compiled a list of her expenses and sources of income and wants to use this information to create an easy-to-read worksheet to see how much she will be ahead or behind each month. In addition, she would like a 3-D pie chart to show her estimated expenses by category for each of the 12 months.

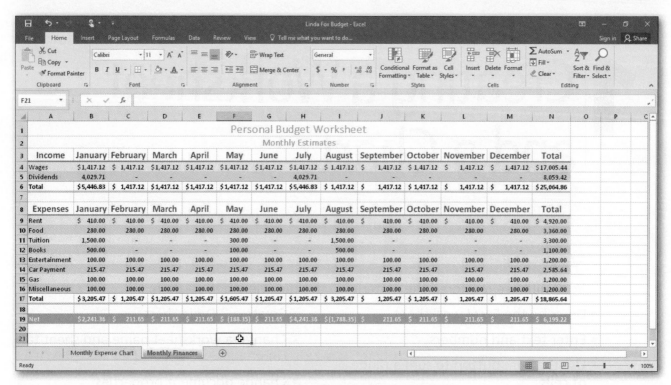

Figure 1–1(a) Personal Budget Worksheet

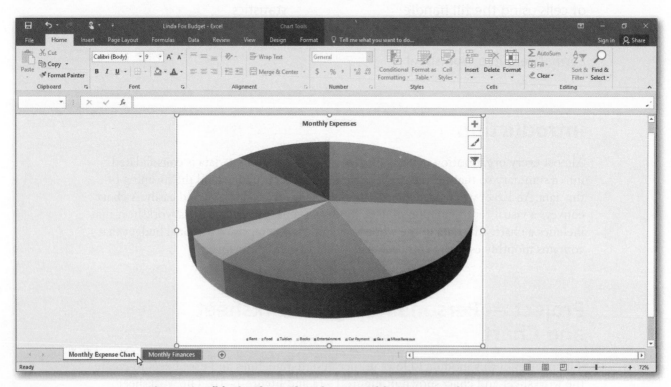

Figure 1–1(b) Pie Chart Showing Monthly Expenses by Category

The first step in creating an effective worksheet is to make sure you understand what is required. The person or persons requesting the worksheet may supply their requirements in a requirements document, or you can create one. A requirements document includes a needs statement, a source of data, a summary of calculations, and any other special requirements for the worksheet, such as charting and web support. Figure 1–2 shows the requirements document for the new workbook to be created in this module.

Worksheet Title	Personal Budget Worksheet
Word	A yearly projection of Linda Fox's personal budget
Source of data	Data supplied by Linda Fox includes monthly estimates for income and expenses
Calculations	The following calculations must be made: 1. For each month, a total for income and expenses 2. For each budget item, a total for the item 3. For the year, total all income and expenses 4. Net = income − expenses

Figure 1–2

In this module, you will learn how to perform basic workbook tasks using Excel. The following roadmap identifies general activities you will perform as you progress through this module:

1. ENTER TEXT in a blank worksheet.

2. CALCULATE SUMS AND USE FORMULAS in the worksheet.

3. FORMAT TEXT in the worksheet.

4. INSERT a pie CHART into the worksheet.

5. Assign a NAME to the sheet TAB.

6. PREVIEW AND PRINT the WORKSHEET.

For an introduction to Windows and instructions about how to perform basic Windows tasks, read the Office and Windows module at the beginning of this book, where you can learn how to resize windows, change screen resolution, create folders, move and rename files, use Windows Help, and much more.

Why is it important to plan a worksheet?
The key to developing a useful worksheet is careful planning. Careful planning can reduce your effort significantly and result in a worksheet that is accurate, easy to read, flexible, and useful. When analyzing a problem and designing a worksheet solution, what steps should you follow?

• Define the problem, including need, source of data, calculations, charting, and web or special requirements.

• Design the worksheet.

• Enter the data and formulas.

• Test the worksheet.

CONSIDER THIS

After carefully reviewing the requirements document (Figure 1–2) and making the necessary decisions, the next step is to design a solution or draw a sketch of the worksheet based on the requirements, including titles, column and row headings, the location of data values, and the 3-D pie chart, as shown in Figure 1–3. The dollar signs and commas that you see in the sketch of the worksheet indicate formatted numeric values.

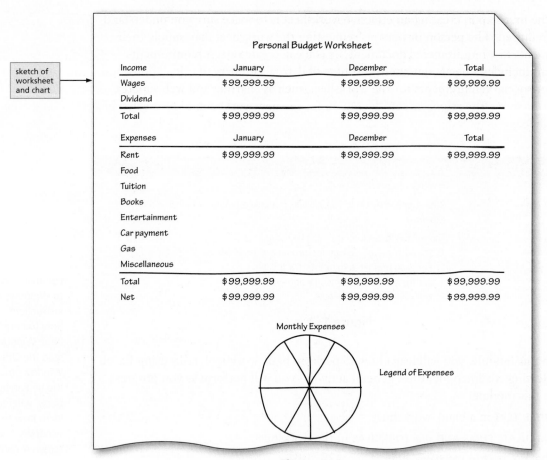

sketch of worksheet and chart

Personal Budget Worksheet

Income	January	December	Total
Wages	$99,999.99	$99,999.99	$99,999.99
Dividend			
Total	$99,999.99	$99,999.99	$99,999.99
Expenses	January	December	Total
Rent	$99,999.99	$99,999.99	$99,999.99
Food			
Tuition			
Books			
Entertainment			
Car payment			
Gas			
Miscellaneous			
Total	$99,999.99	$99,999.99	$99,999.99
Net	$99,999.99	$99,999.99	$99,999.99

Monthly Expenses

Legend of Expenses

Figure 1–3

For an introduction to Office and instructions about how to perform basic tasks in Office apps, read the Office and Windows module at the beginning of this book, where you can learn how to run an application, use the ribbon, save a file, open a file, print a file, exit an application, use Help, and much more.

BTW
Touch Screen Differences
The Office and Windows interfaces may vary if you are using a touch screen. For this reason, you might notice that the function or appearance of your touch screen differs slightly from this module's presentation.

With a good understanding of the requirements document, an understanding of the necessary decisions, and a sketch of the worksheet, the next step is to use Excel to create the worksheet and chart.

Selecting a Cell

To enter data into a cell, you first must select it. The easiest way to **select** a cell (make it active) is to use the mouse to move the block plus sign pointer to the cell and then click.

An alternative method is to use the arrow keys that are located just to the right of the alphanumeric keys on a standard keyboard. An arrow key selects the cell adjacent to the active cell in the direction of the arrow on the key.

You know a cell is selected, or active, when a heavy border surrounds the cell and the active cell reference appears in the Name box on the left side of the formula bar. Excel also changes the color of the active cell's column and row headings to a darker shade.

Entering Text

In Excel, any set of characters containing a letter, hyphen (as in a telephone number), or space is considered **text**. Text is used for titles, such as column and row titles, on the worksheet.

Worksheet titles and subtitles should be as brief and meaningful as possible. A worksheet title could include the name of the organization, department, or a description of the content of the worksheet. A worksheet subtitle, if included, could include a more detailed description of the content of the worksheet. Examples of worksheet titles are January 2018 Payroll and Year 2018 Projected Budget, and examples of subtitles are Finance Department and Monthly Projections, respectively.

As shown in Figure 1–4, data in a worksheet is identified by row and column titles so that the meaning of each entry is clear. Rows typically contain information such as categories of data. Columns typically describe how data is grouped in the worksheet, such as by month or by department.

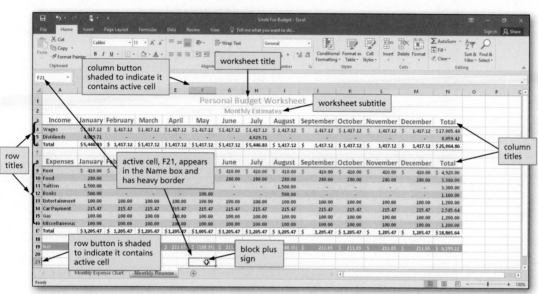

Figure 1–4

BTW

Excel Screen Resolution

If you are using a computer to step through the project in this module and you want your screens to match the figures in this book, you should change your screen's resolution to 1366 x 768. For information about how to change a computer's resolution, refer to the Office and Windows module at the beginning of this book.

To Enter the Worksheet Titles

1 ENTER TEXT | 2 CALCULATE SUMS & USE FORMULAS | 3 FORMAT TEXT
4 INSERT CHART | 5 NAME TAB | 6 PREVIEW & PRINT WORKSHEET

As shown in Figure 1–4, the worksheet title, Personal Budget Worksheet, identifies the purpose of the worksheet. The worksheet subtitle, Monthly Estimates, identifies the type of data contained in the worksheet. *Why? A title and subtitle help the reader to understand clearly what the worksheet contains.* The following steps enter the worksheet titles in cells A1 and A2. Later in this module, the worksheet titles will be formatted so that they appear as shown in Figure 1–4.

1

- Run Excel and create a blank workbook in the Excel window.

- If necessary, click cell A1 to make cell A1 the active cell (Figure 1–5).

Figure 1–5

- Type **Personal Budget Worksheet** in cell A1 (Figure 1–6).

Q&A

Why did the appearance of the formula bar change?

Excel displays the title in the formula bar and in cell A1. When you begin typing a cell entry, Excel enables two additional boxes in the formula bar: the Cancel button and the Enter button. Clicking the Enter button completes an entry. Clicking the Cancel button cancels an entry.

Figure 1–6

- Click the Enter button to complete the entry and enter the worksheet title (Figure 1–7).

Q&A

Why does the entered text appear in three cells?

When the text is longer than the width of a cell, Excel displays the overflow characters in adjacent cells to the right as long as those adjacent cells contain no data. If the adjacent cells contain data, Excel hides the overflow characters. The overflow characters are visible in the formula bar whenever that cell is active.

Figure 1–7

- Click cell A2 to select it.

- Type **Monthly Estimates** as the cell entry.

- Click the Enter button to complete the entry and enter the worksheet subtitle (Figure 1–8).

Q&A

What happens when I click the Enter button?

When you complete an entry by clicking the Enter button, the insertion point disappears and the cell in which the text is entered remains the active cell.

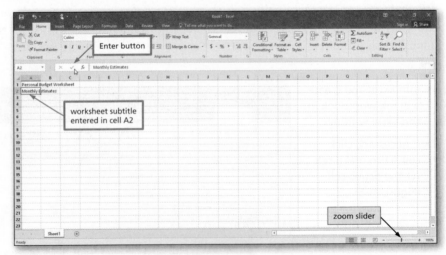

Figure 1–8

Other Ways

1. To complete entry, click any cell other than active cell

2. To complete entry, press ENTER

3. To complete entry, press HOME, PAGE UP, PAGE DOWN, END, UP ARROW, DOWN ARROW, LEFT ARROW, or RIGHT ARROW

Why is it difficult to read the text on my screen?

If you are having trouble reading the cell values in your spreadsheet, you can zoom in to make the cells larger. When you zoom in, fewer columns and rows display on your screen, and you might have to scroll more often. To zoom in, drag the zoom slider on the right of the status bar, or click the plus button on the zoom slider, until you reach your desired zoom level. In addition to the zoom slider, you also can zoom by clicking the Zoom button (View tab | Zoom group), selecting a desired zoom percentage (Zoom dialog box), and then clicking the OK button (Zoom dialog box).

AutoCorrect

The **AutoCorrect** feature of Excel works behind the scenes, correcting common mistakes when you complete a text entry in a cell. AutoCorrect makes three types of corrections for you:

1. Corrects two initial uppercase letters by changing the second letter to lowercase.

2. Capitalizes the first letter in the names of days.

3. Replaces commonly misspelled words with their correct spelling. For example, it will change the misspelled word *recieve* to *receive* when you complete the entry. AutoCorrect will correct the spelling of hundreds of commonly misspelled words automatically.

BTW

The Ribbon and Screen Resolution
Excel may change how the groups and buttons within the groups appear on the ribbon, depending on the computer's screen resolution. Thus, your ribbon may look different from the ones in this book if you are using a screen resolution other than 1366 x 768.

To Enter Column Titles

1 ENTER TEXT | 2 CALCULATE SUMS & USE FORMULAS | 3 FORMAT TEXT
4 INSERT CHART | 5 NAME TAB | 6 PREVIEW & PRINT WORKSHEET

The worksheet is divided into two parts, income and expense, as shown in Figure 1–4. Grouping income and expense data by month is a common method for organizing budget data. The column titles shown in row 3 identify the income section of the worksheet and indicate that the income values will be grouped by month. Likewise, row 8 is clearly identified as the expense section and similarly indicates that the expense values will be estimated on a per month basis. The following steps enter the column titles in row 3. **Why?** *Data entered in columns should be identified using column titles to identify what the column contains.*

1

- Click cell A3 to make it the active cell.

- Type **Income** to begin entry of a column title in the active cell (Figure 1–9).

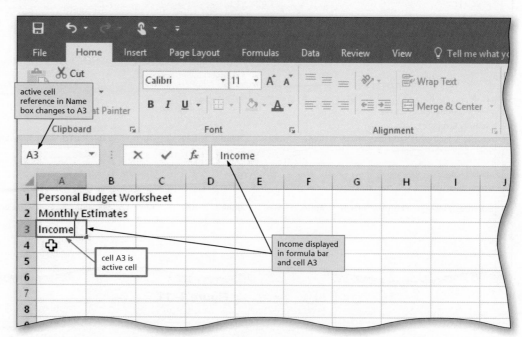

Figure 1–9

2

- Press the RIGHT ARROW key to enter the column title and make the cell to the right the active cell (Figure 1–10).

Why is the RIGHT ARROW key used to complete the entry in the cell?

Pressing an arrow key to complete an entry makes the adjacent cell in the direction of the arrow (up, down, left, or right) the next active cell. However, if your next entry is in a nonadjacent cell, you can complete your current entry by clicking the next cell in which you plan to enter data. You also can press the ENTER key and then click the appropriate cell for the next entry.

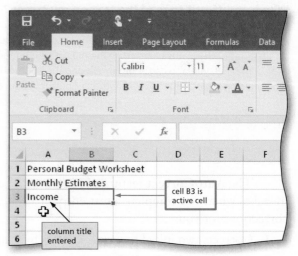

Figure 1–10

3

- Repeat Steps 1 and 2 to enter the remaining column titles; that is, enter **January** in cell B3, **February** in cell C3, **March** in cell D3, **April** in cell E3, **May** in cell F3, **June** in cell G3, **July** in cell H3, **August** in cell I3, **September** in cell J3, **October** in cell K3, **November** in cell L3, **December** in cell M3, and **Total** in cell N3 (complete the last entry in cell N3 by clicking the Enter button in the formula bar).

- Click cell A8 to select it.

- Repeat Steps 1 and 2 to enter the remaining column titles; that is, enter **Expenses** in cell A8, **January** in cell B8, **February** in cell C8, **March** in cell D8, **April** in cell E8, **May** in cell F8, **June** in cell G8, **July** in cell H8, **August** in cell I8, **September** in cell J8, **October** in cell K8, **November** in cell L8, **December** in cell M8, and **Total** in cell N8 (complete the last entry in cell N8 by clicking the Enter button in the formula bar) (Figure 1–11).

Figure 1–11

To Enter Row Titles

The next step in developing the worksheet for this project is to enter the row titles in column A. For the Personal Budget Worksheet data, the row titles contain a list of income types and expense types. Each income or expense item should be placed in its own row. ***Why?*** *Entering one item per row allows for maximum flexibility, in case more income or expense items are added in the future.* The following steps enter the row titles in the worksheet.

1

- Click cell A4 to select it.

- Type **Wages** and then click cell A5 or press the DOWN ARROW key to enter a row title (Figure 1–12).

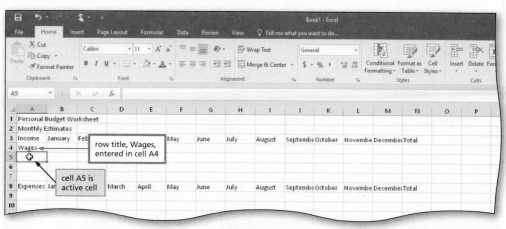

Figure 1–12

2

- Repeat Step 1 to enter the remaining row titles in column A; that is, enter **Dividends** in cell A5, **Total** in cell A6, **Rent** in cell A9, **Food** in cell A10, **Tuition** in cell A11, **Books** in cell A12, **Entertainment** in cell A13, **Car Payment** in cell A14, **Gas** in cell A15, **Miscellaneous** in cell A16, **Total** in cell A17, and **Net** in cell A19 (Figure 1–13).

Q&A
Why is the text left-aligned in the cells?
Excel automatically left-aligns the text in the cell. Excel treats any combination of numbers, spaces, and nonnumeric characters as text. For example, Excel would recognize the following entries as text: 401AX21, 921–231, 619 321, 883XTY. How to change the text alignment in a cell is discussed later in this module.

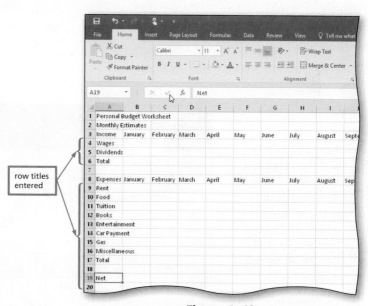

Figure 1–13

Entering Numbers

In Excel, you enter a **number** into a cell to represent an amount or value. A number can contain only the following characters:

    0 1 2 3 4 5 6 7 8 9 + – ( ) , / . $ % E e

If a cell entry contains any other keyboard character (including spaces), Excel interprets the entry as text and treats it accordingly. The use of special characters is explained when they are used in this book.

To Enter Numbers

The Personal Budget Worksheet numbers used in Module 1 are summarized in Table 1–1. These numbers, which represent yearly income and expense amounts, are entered in rows 4–5 and 9–16. *Why?* *One of the most powerful features of Excel is the ability to perform calculations on numeric data. Before you can perform calculations, you first must enter the data.* The following steps enter the numbers in Table 1–1 one row at a time.

Table 1–1 Personal Budget Worksheet

Income	January	February	March	April	May	June	July	August	September	October	November	December
Wages	1417.12	1417.12	1417.12	1417.12	1417.12	1417.12	1417.12	1417.12	1417.12	1417.12	1417.12	1417.12
Dividends	4029.71	0	0	0	0	0	4029.71	0	0	0	0	0

Expenses	January	February	March	April	May	June	July	August	September	October	November	December
Rent	410	410	410	410	410	410	410	410	410	410	410	410
Food	280	280	280	280	280	280	280	280	280	280	280	280
Tuition	1500	0	0	0	300	0	0	1500	0	0	0	0
Books	500	0	0	0	100	0	0	500	0	0	0	0
Entertainment	100	100	100	100	100	100	100	100	100	100	100	100
Car Payment	215.47	215.47	215.47	215.47	215.47	215.47	215.47	215.47	215.47	215.47	215.47	215.47
Gas	100	100	100	100	100	100	100	100	100	100	100	100
Miscellaneous	100	100	100	100	100	100	100	100	100	100	100	100

1

- Click cell B4 to select it.

- Type **1417.12** and then press the RIGHT ARROW key to enter the data in the selected cell and make the cell to the right (cell C4) the active cell (Figure 1–14).

Q&A Do I need to enter dollar signs, commas, or trailing zeros for the amounts?
You are not required to type dollar signs, commas, or trailing zeros. When you enter a dollar value that has cents, however, you must add the decimal point and the numbers representing the cents. Later in this module, you will learn how to format numbers with dollar signs, commas, and trailing zeros to improve their appearance and readability.

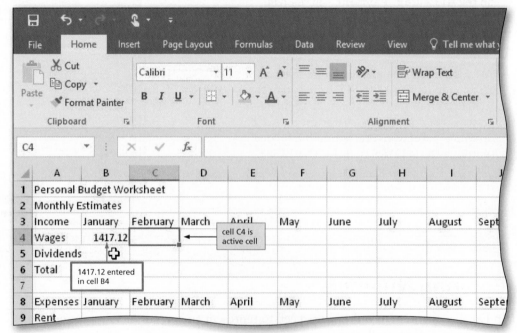

Figure 1–14

2

- Enter   `1417.12`   in cells C4, D4, E4, F4, G4, H4, I4, J4, K4, L4, and M4 to complete the first row of numbers in the worksheet (Figure 1–15).

Q&A

Why are the numbers right-aligned?

When you enter numeric data in a cell, Excel recognizes the values as numbers and automatically right-aligns the values in order to vertically align decimal and integer values.

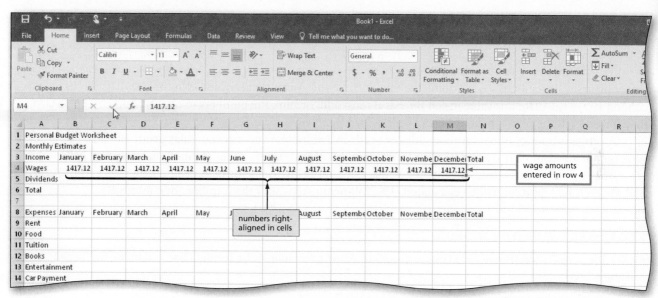

Figure 1–15

3

- Click cell B5 to select it and complete the entry in the previously selected cell.

- Enter the remaining numbers provided in Table 1–1 for each of the nine remaining budget items in row 5 and rows 9–16 (Figure 1–16).

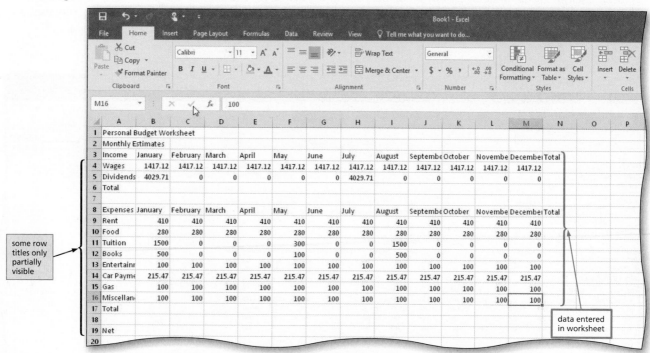

Figure 1–16

Calculating a Sum

The next step in creating the worksheet is to perform any necessary calculations, such as calculating the column and row totals. In Excel, you easily can perform calculations using a **function**, or a predefined formula. When you use functions, Excel performs the calculations for you, which helps to prevent errors and allows you to work more efficiently.

To Sum a Column of Numbers

1 ENTER TEXT | 2 CALCULATE SUMS & USE FORMULAS | 3 FORMAT TEXT
4 INSERT CHART | 5 NAME TAB | 6 PREVIEW & PRINT WORKSHEET

As stated in the requirements document in Figure 1–2, totals are required for each month and each budget item. The first calculation is to determine the total income for Wages and Dividends in the month of January (column B). To calculate this value in cell B6, Excel must add, or sum, the numbers in cells B4 and B5. The **SUM function** adds all the numbers in a range of cells. **Why?** *Excel's SUM function is an efficient means to accomplish this task.*

A **range** is a series of two or more adjacent cells in a column, row or rectangular group of cells. For example, the group of adjacent cells B4 and B5 is a range. Many Excel operations are performed on a range of cells.

After calculating the total income for January, the monthly totals for income and expenses and the yearly total for each budget item will be calculated. The following steps sum the numbers in column B.

1

- Click cell B6 to make it the active cell.

- Click the Sum button (Home tab | Editing group) to enter a formula in the formula bar and in the active cell (Figure 1–17).

Q&A

What if my screen displays the Sum menu?

If you are using a touch screen, you may not have a separate Sum button and Sum arrow. In this case, select the desired option (Sum) on the Sum menu.

How does Excel know which cells to sum?

Excel automatically selects what it considers to be your choice of the range to sum. When proposing the range, Excel first looks for a range of cells with numbers above the active cell and then to the left. If Excel proposes the wrong range, you can correct it by dragging through the correct range before pressing the ENTER key. You also can enter the correct range by typing the beginning cell reference, a colon (:), and the ending cell reference.

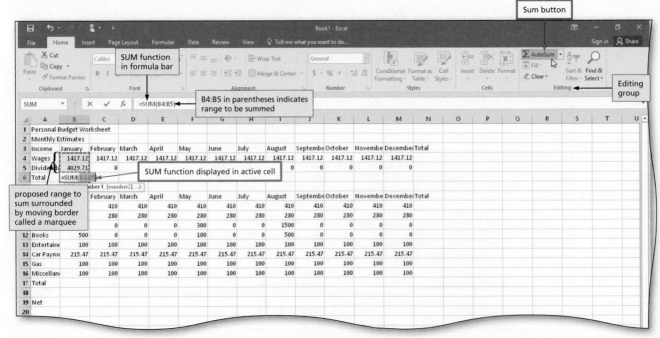

Figure 1–17

2

- Click the Enter button in the formula bar to enter the sum in the active cell.

Q&A What is the purpose of the arrow next to the Sum button on the ribbon?

The Sum arrow (shown in Figure 1–17) displays a list of functions that allow you to easily determine the average of a range of numbers, the number of items in a selected range, or the maximum or minimum value of a range.

3

- Repeat Steps 1 and 2 to enter the SUM function in cell B17 (Figure 1–18).

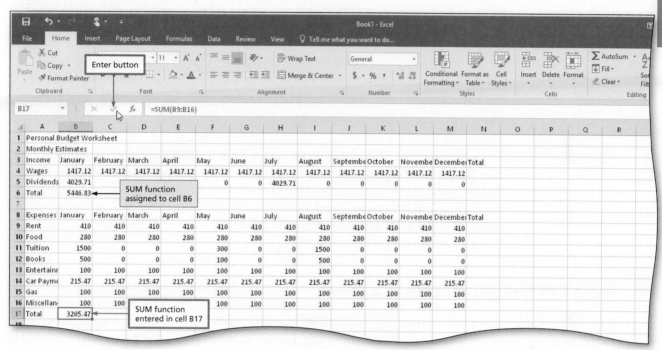

Figure 1–18

Other Ways

1. Click Insert Function button in formula bar, select SUM in Select a function list, click OK button (Insert Function dialog box), click OK button

2. Click Sum arrow (Home tab | Editing group), click More Functions in list, scroll to and (Function Arguments dialog box)

then click SUM (Insert Function dialog box), click OK button, select range (Function Arguments dialog box), click OK button

3. Type **=S** in cell, select SUM in list, select range, click Enter button

4. Press ALT+EQUAL SIGN (=) twice

Using the Fill Handle to Copy a Cell to Adjacent Cells

You want to calculate the totals for income during each month in cells C6:M6. Table 1–2 illustrates the similarities between the function and range used in cell B6 and the function and ranges required to sum the totals in cells C6, D6, E6, F6, G6, H6, I6, J6, K6, L6, and M6.

To calculate each total for each range across the worksheet, you could follow the same steps shown previously in Figure 1–17 and Figure 1–18. A more efficient method, however, would be to copy the SUM function from cell B6 to the range C6:M6. The cell being copied is called the **source area** or **copy area**. The range of cells receiving the copy is called the **destination area** or **paste area**.

Table 1–2 Sum Function Entries in Row 6		
Cell	**SUM Function Entries**	**Result**
B6	=SUM(B4:B5)	Sums cells B4 and B5
C6	=SUM(C4:C5)	Sums cells C4 and C5
D6	=SUM(D4:D5)	Sums cells D4 and D5
E6	=SUM(E4:E5)	Sums cells E4 and E5
F6	=SUM(F4:F5)	Sums cells F4 and F5
G6	=SUM(G4:G5)	Sums cells G4 and G5
H6	=SUM(H4:H5)	Sums cells H4 and H5
I6	=SUM(I4:I5)	Sums cells I4 and I5
J6	=SUM(J4:J5)	Sums cells J4 and J5
K6	=SUM(K4:K5)	Sums cells K4 and K5
L6	=SUM(L4:L5)	Sums cells L4 and L5
M6	=SUM(M4:M5)	Sums cells M4 and M5

Although the SUM function entries in Table 1–2 are similar to each other, they are not exact copies. The range in each SUM function entry uses cell references that are one column to the right of the previous column. When you copy formulas that include cell references, Excel automatically adjusts them for each new position, resulting in the SUM function entries illustrated in Table 1–2. Each adjusted cell reference is called a **relative reference**.

1 ENTER TEXT | 2 CALCULATE SUMS & USE FORMULAS | 3 FORMAT TEXT
4 INSERT CHART | 5 NAME TAB | 6 PREVIEW & PRINT WORKSHEET

To Copy a Cell to Adjacent Cells in a Row

The easiest way to copy the SUM formula from cell B6 to cells C6:M6 is to use the fill handle. *Why?* *Using the fill handle copies content to adjacent cells more efficiently.* The **fill handle** is the small green square located in the lower-right corner of the heavy border around the active cell. The following steps use the fill handle to copy cell B6 to the adjacent cells C6:M6.

1

• With cell B6 active, point to the fill handle to activate it. Your pointer changes to a crosshair (Figure 1–19).

Q&A Why is my fill handle not a green square?
If you are using a touch screen, the fill handle appears as a black and white rectangle with a blue down arrow in it.

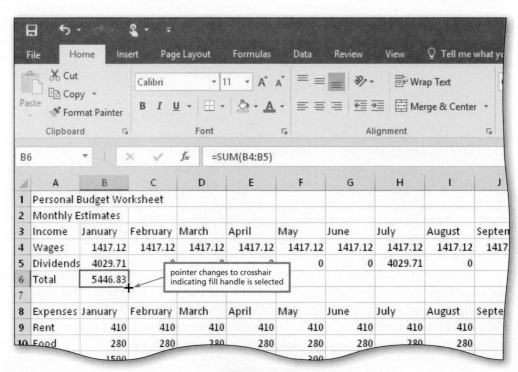

Figure 1–19

2

- Drag the fill handle to select the destination area, range C6:M6, which will draw a heavy green border around the source area and the destination area (Figure 1–20). Do not release the mouse button.

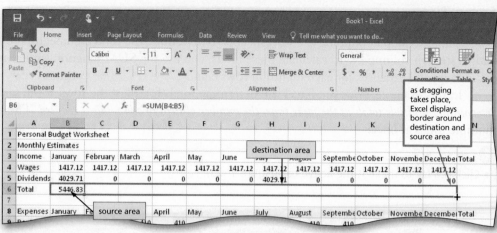

Figure 1–20

3

- Release the mouse button to copy the SUM function from the active cell to the destination area and calculate the sums (Figure 1–21).

Q&A

What is the purpose of the 'Auto Fill Options' button? The 'Auto Fill Options' button allows you to choose whether you want to copy the values from the source area to the destination area with the existing formatting, without the formatting, or with the formatting but without the functions.

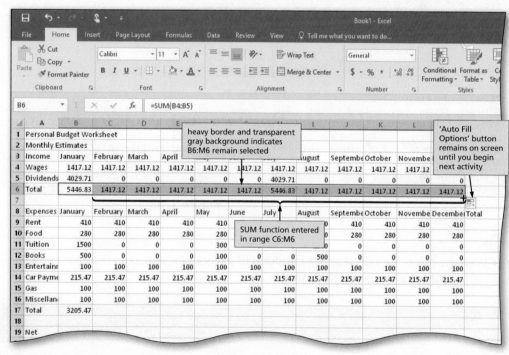

Figure 1–21

4

- Repeat Steps 1–3 to copy the SUM function from cell B17 to the range C17:M17 (Figure 1–22).

Figure 1–22

Other Ways

1. Select source area, click Copy button (Home tab | Clipboard group), select destination area, click Paste button (Home tab | Clipboard group)

2. Right-click source area, click Copy on shortcut menu, select and right-click destination area, click Paste on shortcut menu

To Calculate Multiple Totals at the Same Time

The next step in building the worksheet is to determine the total income, total expenses, and total for each budget item in column N. To calculate these totals, you use the SUM function similar to how you used it to total the income and expenses for each month in rows 6 and 17.

In this example, however, Excel will determine totals for all of the rows at the same time. *Why? By determining multiple totals at the same time, the number of steps to add totals is reduced.* The following steps sum multiple totals at once.

1

• Click cell N4 to make it the active cell (Figure 1–23).

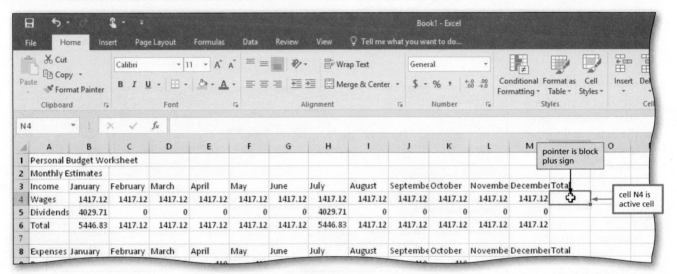

Figure 1–23

2

• With the pointer in cell N4 and in the shape of a block plus sign, drag the pointer down to cell N6 to highlight the range with a transparent view (Figure 1–24).

Figure 1–24

3

• Click the Sum button (Home tab | Editing group) to calculate the sums of the corresponding rows (Figure 1–25).

Q&A

How does Excel create unique totals for each row?

If each cell in a selected range is adjacent to a row of numbers, Excel assigns the SUM function to each cell when you click the Sum button.

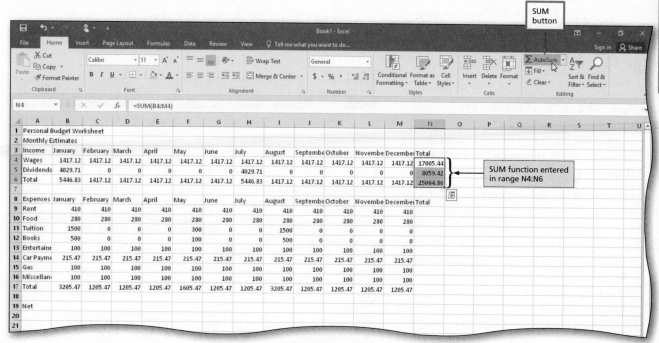

Figure 1–25

4

• Repeat Steps 1–3 to select cells N9 to N17 and calculate the sums of the corresponding rows (Figure 1–26).

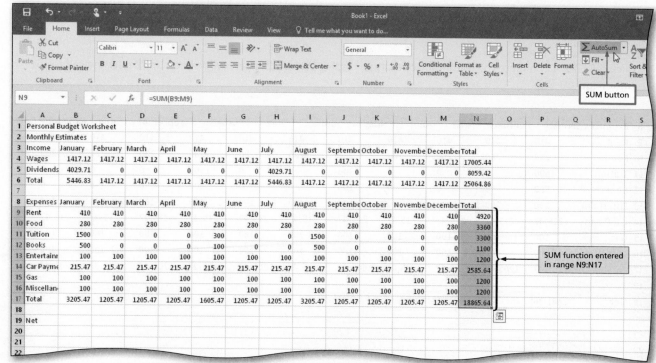

Figure 1–26

To Enter a Formula Using the Keyboard

The net for each month, which will appear in row 19, is equal to the income total in row 6 minus the expense total in row 17. The formula needed in the worksheet is noted in the requirements document as follows:

Net (row 19) = Income (row 6) – Expenses (row 17)

The following steps enter the net formula in cell B19 using the keyboard. *Why? Sometimes a predefined function does not fit your needs; therefore, you enter a formula of your own.*

1

- Select cell B19 to deselect the selected range.

- Type `=b6-b17` in the cell. The formula is displayed in the formula bar and the current cell, and colored borders are drawn around the cells referenced in the formula (Figure 1–27).

Q&A

What occurs on the worksheet as I enter the formula?

The equal sign (=) preceding b6–b17 in the formula alerts Excel that you are entering a formula or function and not text. Because the most common error when entering a formula is to reference the wrong cell, Excel highlights the cell references in the formula in color, and uses same colors to highlight the borders of the cells to help you ensure that your cell references are correct. The minus sign (–) following b6 in the formula is the arithmetic operator that directs Excel to perform the subtraction operation.

Figure 1–27

2

- Click cell C19 to complete the arithmetic operation, display the result in the worksheet, and select the cell to the right (Figure 1–28).

8	Expenses	January	February	March	April	May	June	July	August	Septembe	October	Novembe	Dec
9	Rent	410	410	410	410	410	410	410	410	410	410	410	
10	Food	280	280	280	280	280	280	280	280	280	280	280	
11	Tuition	1500	0	0	0	300	0	0	1500	0	0	0	
12	Books	500	0	0	0	100	0	0	500	0	0	0	
13	Entertainr	100	100	100	100	100	100	100	100	100	100	100	
14	Car Payme	215.47	215.47	215.47	215.47	215.47	215.47	215.47	215.47	215.47	215.47	215.47	
15	Gas	100	100	100	100	100	100	100	100	100	100	100	
16	Miscellan	100	100	100	100	100	100	100	100	100	100	100	
17	Total	3205.47	1205.47	1205.47	1205.47	1605.47	1205.47	1205.47	3205.47	1205.47	1205.47	1205.47	12
18													
19	Net	2241.36											
20													
21													
22													
23													

Figure 1–28

To Copy a Cell to Adjacent Cells in a Row

The easiest way to copy the SUM formula from cell B19 to cells C19, D19, E19, F19, G19, H19, I19, J19, K19, L19, M19, and N19 is to use the fill handle. The following steps use the fill handle to copy the formula in cell B19 to the adjacent cells C19:N19.

1 Select cell B19.

2 Drag the fill handle to select the destination area, range C19:N19, which draws a shaded border around the source area and the destination area. Release the mouse button to copy the simple formula function from the active cell to the destination area and calculate the results.

3 Save the worksheet on your hard drive, OneDrive, or other storage location using Linda Fox Budget as the file name.

Q&A | Why should I save the workbook at this time?
You have performed many tasks while creating this workbook and do not want to risk losing work completed thus far.

Break Point: If you wish to take a break, this is a good place to do so. You can exit Excel. To resume at a later time, run Excel, open the file called Linda Fox Budget, and continue following the steps from this location forward.

Formatting the Worksheet

The text, numeric entries, and functions for the worksheet now are complete. The next step is to format the worksheet. You **format** a worksheet to emphasize certain entries and make the worksheet easier to read and understand.

Figure 1–29a shows the worksheet before formatting. Figure 1–29b shows the worksheet after formatting. As you can see from the two figures, a worksheet that is formatted not only is easier to read but also looks more professional.

To change the unformatted worksheet in Figure 1–29a so that it looks like the formatted worksheet in Figure 1–29b, the following tasks must be completed:

What steps should I consider when formatting a worksheet?
The key to formatting a worksheet is to consider the ways you can enhance the worksheet so that it appears professional. When formatting a worksheet, consider the following steps:

• Identify in what ways you want to emphasize various elements of the worksheet.

• Increase the font size of cells.

• Change the font color of cells.

• Center the worksheet titles, subtitles, and column headings.

• Modify column widths to best fit text in cells.

• Change the font style of cells.

CONSIDER THIS

(a) Unformatted Worksheet

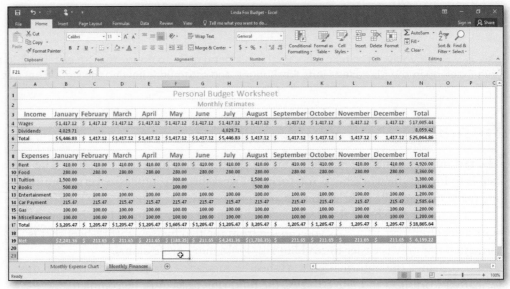

(b) Formatted Worksheet

Figure 1–29

1. Change the font, change the font style, increase the font size, and change the font color of the worksheet titles in cells A1 and A2.

2. Center the worksheet titles in cells A1 and A2 across columns A through N.

3. Format the body of the worksheet. The body of the worksheet, range A3:N19, includes the column titles, row titles, and numbers. Formatting the body of the worksheet changes the numbers to use a dollars-and-cents format, with dollar signs in rows 4 and 9 and in the total rows (row 6 and 17); changes the styles of some rows; adds underlining that emphasizes portions of the worksheet; and modifies the column widths to fit the text in the columns and make the text and numbers readable.

Although the formatting procedures are explained in the order described above, you could make these format changes in any order. Modifying the column widths, however, usually is done last because other formatting changes may affect the size of data in the cells in the column.

Font Style, Size, and Color

The characters that Excel displays on the screen are a specific font, style, size, and color. The **font**, or font face, defines the appearance and shape of the letters, numbers, and special characters. Examples of fonts include Calibri, Cambria, Times New Roman, Arial, and Courier. **Font style** indicates how the characters are emphasized. Common font styles include regular, bold, underline, and italic. The **font size** specifies the size of the characters. Font size is gauged by a measurement system called points. A single point is 1/72 of one inch in height. Thus, a character with a **point size** of 10 is 10/72 of one inch in height. Finally, Excel has a wide variety of **font colors** from which to choose to define the color of the characters.

When Excel first runs, the default font for the entire workbook is Calibri, with a font size, font style, and font color of 11-point regular black. You can change the font characteristics in a single cell, a range of cells, the entire worksheet, or the entire workbook.

To Change a Cell Style

1 ENTER TEXT | 2 CALCULATE SUMS & USE FORMULAS | 3 FORMAT TEXT
4 INSERT CHART | 5 NAME TAB | 6 PREVIEW & PRINT WORKSHEET

You can change several characteristics of a cell, such as the font, font size, and font color, all at once by assigning a predefined cell style to a cell. A **cell style** is a predefined font, font size, and font color that you can apply to a cell. *Why? Using the predefined styles provides a consistent appearance to common portions of your worksheets, such as worksheet titles, worksheet subtitles, column headings, and total rows.* The following steps assign the Title cell style to the worksheet title in cell A1.

1

- Click cell A1 to make cell A1 the active cell.
- Click the Cell Styles button (Home tab | Styles group) to display the Cell Styles gallery (Figure 1–30).

Figure 1–30

2

- Point to the Title cell style in the Titles and Headings area of the Cell Styles gallery to see a live preview of the cell style in the active cell (Figure 1–31).

Q&A Can I use live preview on a touch screen?
Live preview is not available on a touch screen.

Experiment

- Point to other cell styles in the Cell Styles gallery to see a live preview of those cell styles in cell A1.

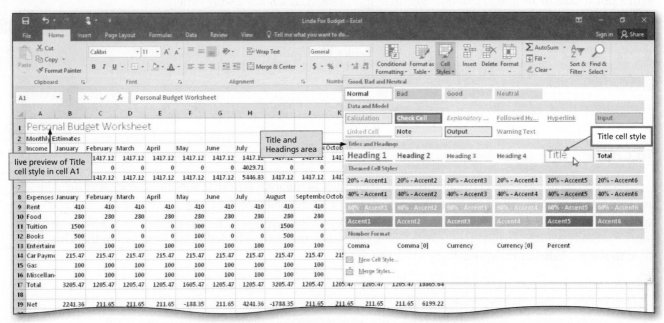

Figure 1–31

3

- Click the Title cell style to apply the cell style to the active cell (Figure 1–32).

Q&A Why do settings in the Font group on the ribbon change?
The font and font size change to reflect the font changes applied to the active cell, cell A1, as a result of applying the Title cell style.

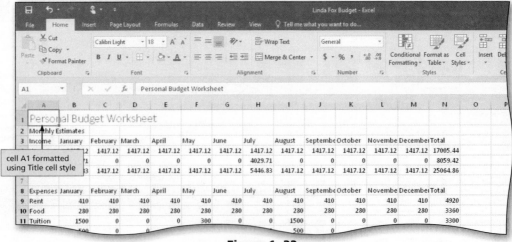

Figure 1–32

1 ENTER TEXT | 2 CALCULATE SUMS & USE FORMULAS | 3 FORMAT TEXT
4 INSERT CHART | 5 NAME TAB | 6 PREVIEW & PRINT WORKSHEET

To Change the Font

Why? *Different fonts often are used in a worksheet to make it more appealing to the reader and to relate or distinguish data in the worksheet.* The following steps change the worksheet subtitle's font to Calibri Light.

1

- Click cell A2 to make it the active cell.

- Click the Font arrow (Home tab | Font group) to display the Font gallery. If necessary, scroll to Calibri Light.

- Point to Calibri Light in the Font gallery to see a live preview of the selected font in the active cell (Figure 1–33).

🔎 **Experiment**

- Point to several other fonts in the Font gallery to see a live preview of the other fonts in the selected cell.

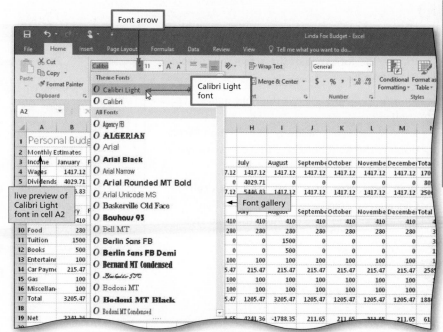

Figure 1–33

2

- Click Calibri Light in the Font gallery to change the font of the worksheet subtitle to Calibri Light (Figure 1–34).

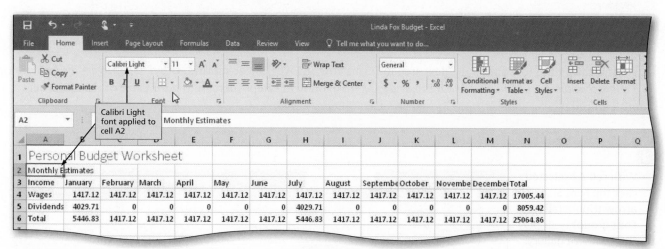

Figure 1–34

Other Ways

1. Click Font Settings Dialog Box Launcher, click Font tab (Format Cells dialog box), click desired font in Font list, click OK button

2. Right-click cell to display mini toolbar, click Font box arrow on mini toolbar, click desired font in Font gallery

3. Right-click selected cell, click Format Cells on shortcut menu, click Font tab (Format Cells dialog box), click desired font, click OK button

1 ENTER TEXT | **2** CALCULATE SUMS & USE FORMULAS | **3** FORMAT TEXT
4 INSERT CHART | **5** NAME TAB | **6** PREVIEW & PRINT WORKSHEET

To Apply Bold Style to a Cell

Bold, or boldface, text has a darker appearance than normal text. ***Why?*** *You apply bold style to a cell to emphasize it or make it stand out from the rest of the worksheet.* The following steps apply bold style to the worksheet title and subtitle.

1

- Click cell A1 to make it active and then click the Bold button (Home tab | Font group) to change the font style of the active cell to bold (Figure 1–35).

Q&A What if a cell already has the bold style applied?
If the active cell contains bold text, then Excel displays the Bold button with a darker gray background.

How do I remove the bold style from a cell?
Clicking the Bold button (Home tab | Font group) a second time removes the bold style.

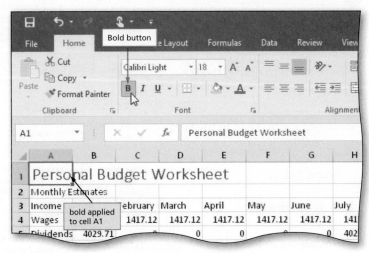

Figure 1–35

2

- Repeat Step 1 to bold cell A2.

Other Ways

1. Click Font Settings Dialog Box Launcher, click Font tab (Format Cells dialog box), click Bold in Font style list, click OK button
2. Right-click selected cell, click Bold button on mini toolbar
3. Right-click selected cell, click Format Cells on shortcut menu, click Font tab (Format Cells dialog box), click Bold, click OK button
4. Press CTRL+B

To Increase the Font Size of a Cell Entry

1 ENTER TEXT | **2** CALCULATE SUMS & USE FORMULAS | **3** FORMAT TEXT
4 INSERT CHART | **5** NAME TAB | **6** PREVIEW & PRINT WORKSHEET

Increasing the font size is the next step in formatting the worksheet subtitle. **Why?** *You increase the font size of a cell so that the entry stands out and is easier to read.* The following steps increase the font size of the worksheet subtitle in cell A2.

1

- With cell A2 selected, click the Font Size arrow (Home tab | Font group) to display the Font Size gallery.

- Point to 14 in the Font Size gallery to see a live preview of the active cell with the selected font size (Figure 1–36).

Experiment

- If you are using a mouse, point to several other font sizes in the Font Size list to see a live preview of those font sizes in the selected cell.

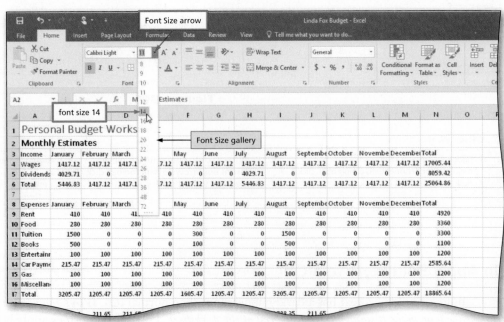

Figure 1–36

1

- Click 14 in the Font Size gallery to change the font size in the active cell (Figure 1–37).

Q&A Can I choose a font size that is not in the Font Size gallery? Yes. An alternative to selecting a font size in the Font Size gallery is to click the Font Size box (Home tab | Font group), type the font size you want, and then press the ENTER key.

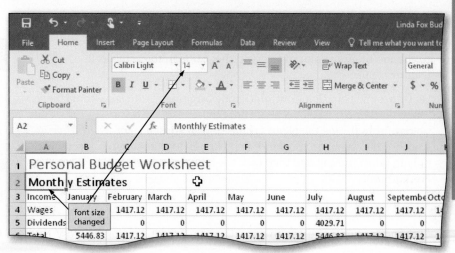

Figure 1–37

Other Ways

1. Click 'Increase Font Size' button (Home tab | Font group) or 'Decrease Font Size' button (Home tab | Font group)	2. Click Font Settings Dialog box Launcher, click Font tab (Format Cells dialog box), click desired size in Size list, click OK button	3. Right-click cell to display mini toolbar, click Font Size arrow on mini toolbar, click desired font size in Font Size gallery	4. Right-click selected cell, click Format Cells on shortcut menu, click Font tab (Format Cells dialog box), select font size in Size box, click OK button

1 ENTER TEXT | **2** CALCULATE SUMS & USE FORMULAS | **3** FORMAT TEXT
4 INSERT CHART | **5** NAME TAB | **6** PREVIEW & PRINT WORKSHEET

To Change the Font Color of a Cell Entry

The next step is to change the color of the font in cells A1 and A2 to orange. *Why? Changing the font color of cell entries can help the text stand out more. You also can change the font colors to match the company or product's brand colors.* The following steps change the font color of a cell entry.

1

- Click cell A1 and then click the Font Color arrow (Home tab | Font group) to display the Font Color gallery.

- Point to 'Orange, Accent 2' (column 6, row 1) in the Theme Colors area of the Font Color gallery to see a live preview of the font color in the active cell (Figure 1–38).

Experiment

- Point to several other colors in the Font Color gallery to see a live preview of other font colors in the active cell.

Q&A How many colors are in the Font Color gallery? You can choose from approximately 70 different font colors in the Font Color gallery. Your Font Color gallery may have more or fewer colors, depending on the color settings of your operating system. The Theme Colors area contains colors that are included in the current workbook's theme.

Figure 1–38

2

- Click 'Orange, Accent 2' (column 6, row 1) in the Font Color gallery to change the font color of the worksheet title in the active cell (Figure 1–39).

Q&A Why does the Font Color button change after I select the new font color?
When you choose a color on the Font Color gallery, Excel changes the Font Color button (Home tab | Font group) to your chosen color. Then when you want to change the font color of another cell to the same color, you need only to select the cell and then click the Font Color button (Home tab | Font group).

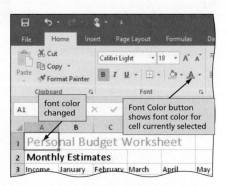

Figure 1–39

3

- Click the Font Color button to apply Orange, Accent 2 (column 6, row 1) to cell A2.

Other Ways

1. Click Font Settings Dialog Box Launcher, click Font tab (Format Cells dialog box), click desired color in Color list, click OK button

2. Right-click the cell to display mini toolbar, click Font Color arrow on mini toolbar, click desired font color in Font Color gallery

3. Right-click selected cell, click Format Cells on shortcut menu, click Font tab (Format Cells dialog box), select color in Font Color gallery, click OK button

To Center Cell Entries across Columns by Merging Cells

1 ENTER TEXT | 2 CALCULATE SUMS & USE FORMULAS | 3 FORMAT TEXT
4 INSERT CHART | 5 NAME TAB | 6 PREVIEW & PRINT WORKSHEET

The final step in formatting the worksheet title and subtitle is to center them across columns A through N. **Why?** *Centering a title across the columns used in the body of the worksheet improves the worksheet's appearance.* To do this, the 14 cells in the range A1:N1 are combined, or merged, into a single cell that is the width of the columns in the body of the worksheet. The 14 cells in the range A2:N2 are merged in a similar manner. **Merging cell**s involves creating a single cell by combining two or more selected cells. The following steps center the worksheet title and subtitle across columns by merging cells.

1

- Select cell A1 and then drag to cell N1 to highlight the range to be merged and centered (Figure 1–40).

Q&A What if a cell in the range B1:N1 contains data?
For the 'Merge & Center' button (Home tab | Alignment group) to work properly, all the cells except the leftmost cell in the selected range must be empty.

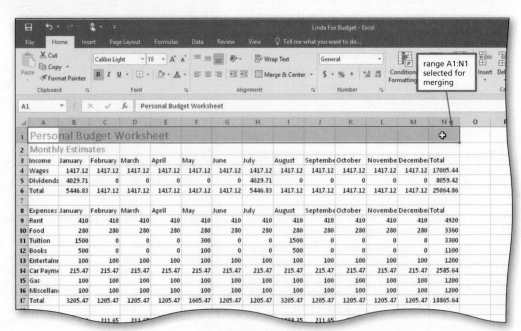

Figure 1–40

2

- Click the 'Merge & Center' button (Home tab | Alignment group) to merge cells A1 through N1 and center the contents of the leftmost cell across the selected columns (Figure 1–41).

Q&A What if my screen displays a Merge & Center menu?

Select the desired option on the Merge & Center menu if you do not have a separate 'Merge & Center' button and 'Merge & Center' arrow.

What happened to cells B1 through N1?

After the merge, cells B1 through N1 no longer exist. The new cell A1 now extends across columns A through N.

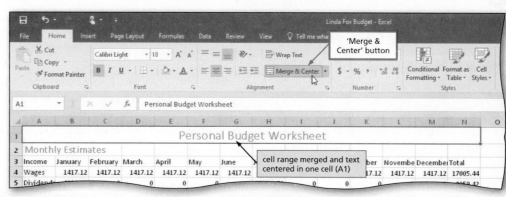

Figure 1–41

3

- Repeat Steps 1 and 2 to merge and center the worksheet subtitle across cells A2 through N2 (Figure 1–42).

Q&A Are cells B1 through N1 and B2 through N2 lost forever?

No. The opposite of merging cells is **splitting** a merged cell. After you have merged multiple cells into one cell, you can unmerge, or split, the cell to display the original range of cells. You

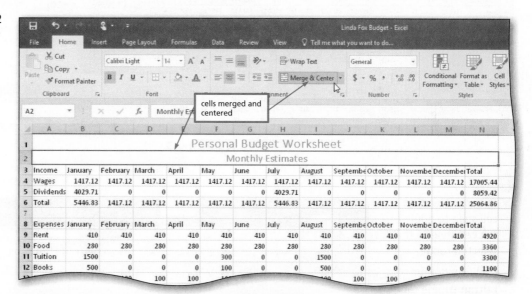

Figure 1–42

split a merged cell by selecting it and clicking the 'Merge & Center' button. For example, if you click the 'Merge & Center' button a second time in Step 2, it will split the merged cell A1 into cells A1, B1, C1, D1, E1, F1, G1, H1, I1, J1, K1, L1, M1, and N1, and move the title to it's original location in cell A1.

Other Ways

1. Right-click selection, click 'Merge & Center' button on mini toolbar

2. Right-click selected cell, click Format Cells on shortcut menu, click Alignment tab (Format Cells dialog box), select 'Center Across Selection' in Horizontal list, click OK button

1 ENTER TEXT | 2 CALCULATE SUMS & USE FORMULAS | 3 FORMAT TEXT
4 INSERT CHART | 5 NAME TAB | 6 PREVIEW & PRINT WORKSHEET

To Format Rows Using Cell Styles

The next step to format the worksheet is to format the rows. **Why?** *Row titles and the total row should be formatted so that the column titles and total row can be distinguished from the data in the body of the worksheet. Data rows can be formatted to make them easier to read as well.* The following steps format the column titles and total row using cell styles in the default worksheet theme.

1

- Click cell A3 and then drag to cell N3 to select the range.
- Click the Cell Styles button (Home tab | Styles group) to display the Cell Styles gallery.
- Point to the Heading 1 cell style in the Titles and Headings area of the Cell Styles gallery to see a live preview of the cell style in the selected range (Figure 1–43).

Experiment

- Point to other cell styles in the Titles and Headings area of the Cell Styles gallery to see a live preview of other styles.

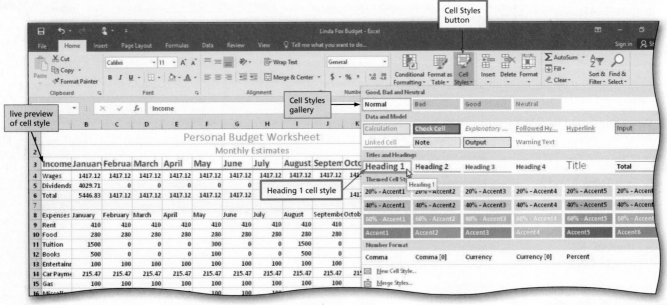

Figure 1–43

2

- Click the Heading 1 cell style to apply the cell style to the selected range.
- Click the Center button (Home tab | Alignment group) to center the column headings in the selected range.
- Select the range A8 to N8 (Figure 1–44).

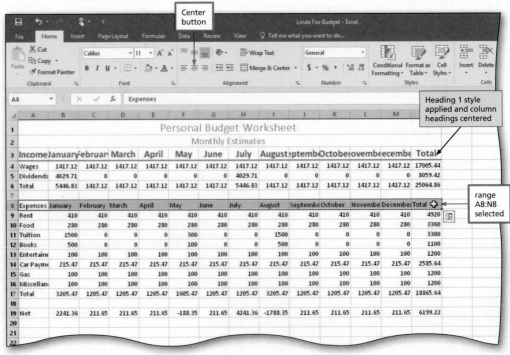

Figure 1–44

3

- Apply the Heading 1 cell style format and then center the headings (Figure 1–45).

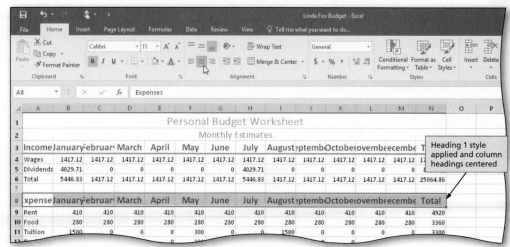

Figure 1–45

4

- Format the range A6:N6 and A17:N17 with the Total cell style format.

- Format the range A19:N19 with the Accent2 cell style format.

- Format the range A4:N4, A9:N9, A11:N11, A13:N13, A15:N15 with the 20% - Accent2 cell style format.

- Format the range A5:N5, A10:N10, A12:N12, A14:N14, A16:N16 with the 40% - Accent2 cell style format. Deselect the selected ranges

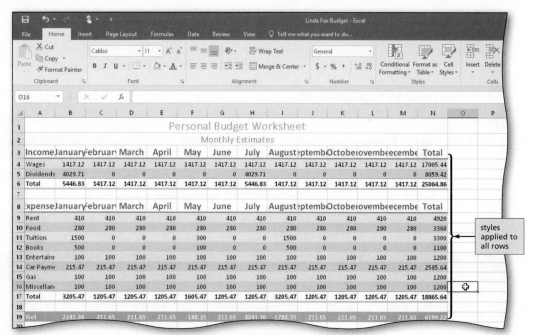

Figure 1–46

To Format Numbers in the Worksheet

1 ENTER TEXT | 2 CALCULATE SUMS & USE FORMULAS | 3 FORMAT TEXT
4 INSERT CHART | 5 NAME TAB | 6 PREVIEW & PRINT WORKSHEET

The requirements document requested that numbers in the first row and last row of each section should be formatted to use a dollar-and-cents format, while other numbers receive a comma format. *Why? Using a dollar-and-cents format for selected cells makes it clear to users of the worksheet that the numbers represent dollar values without cluttering the entire worksheet with dollar signs, and applying the comma format makes larger numbers easier to read.* Excel allows you to apply various number formats, many of which are discussed in later modules. The following steps use buttons on the ribbon to format the numbers in the worksheet.

1

- Select the range B4:N4.

- Click the 'Accounting Number Format' button (Home tab | Number group) to apply the accounting number format to the cells in the selected range.

Q&A What if my screen displays an Accounting Number Format menu?

If you are using a touch screen, you may not have a separate 'Accounting Number Format' button and 'Accounting Number Format' arrow. In this case, select the desired option on the Accounting Number Format menu.

What effect does the accounting number format have on the selected cells?
The accounting number format causes numbers to be displayed with two decimal places and to align vertically. Cell widths are adjusted automatically to accommodate the new formatting.

- Select the range B5:N5 (Figure 1–47).

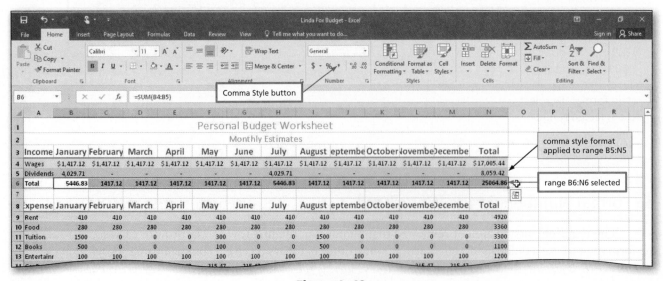

Figure 1–47

2

- Click the Comma Style button (Home tab | Number group) to apply the comma style format to the selected range.

Q&A What effect does the comma style format have on the selected cells?
The comma style format formats numbers to have two decimal places and commas as thousands separators.

- Select the range B6:N6 to make it the active range (Figure 1–48).

Figure 1–48

3

- Click the 'Accounting Number Format' button (Home tab | Number group) to apply the accounting number format to the cells in the selected range.

4

- Format the ranges B9:N9, B17:N17, and B19:N19 with the accounting number format.

- Format the range B10:N16 with the comma style format. Click cell A1 to deselect the selected ranges (Figure 1–49).

Q&A How do I select the range B10:N16?

Select this range the same way as you select a range of cells in a column or row; that is, click the first cell in the range (B10, in this case) and drag to the last cell in the range (N16, in this case).

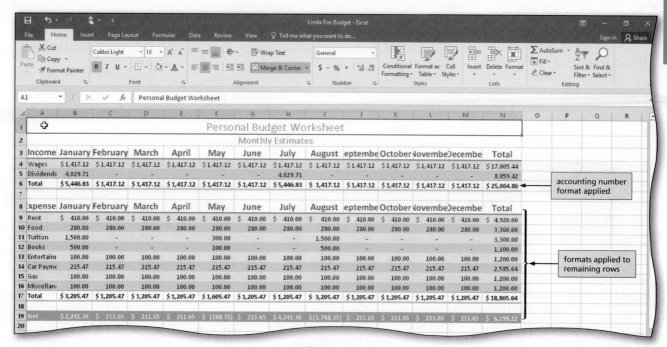

Figure 1–49

Other Ways

1. Click 'Accounting Number Format' or Comma Style button on mini toolbar

2. Right-click selected cell, click Format Cells on shortcut menu, click Number tab (Format Cells dialog box), select Accounting in Category list or select Number and click 'Use 1000 Separator', click OK button

1 ENTER TEXT | 2 CALCULATE SUMS & USE FORMULAS | 3 FORMAT TEXT
4 INSERT CHART | 5 NAME TAB | 6 PREVIEW & PRINT WORKSHEET

To Adjust the Column Width

The last step in formatting the worksheet is to adjust the width of the columns so that each title is visible. *Why? To make a worksheet easy to read, the column widths should be adjusted appropriately.* Excel offers other methods for adjusting cell widths and row heights, which are discussed later in this book. The following steps adjust the width of columns A through N so that the contents of the columns are visible.

1

- Point to the boundary on the right side of the column A heading above row 1 to change the pointer to a split double arrow (Figure 1–50).

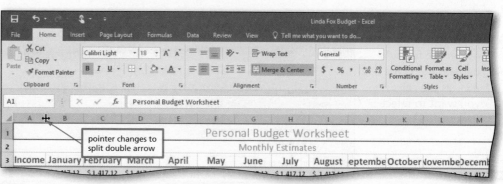

Figure 1–50

2

- Double-click the boundary to adjust the width of the column to accommodate the width of the longest item in the column (Figure 1–51).

Q&A

What if all of the items in the column are already visible?
If all of the items are shorter in length than the width of the column and you double-click the column boundary, Excel will reduce the width of the column.

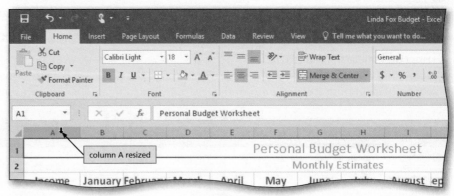

Figure 1–51

3

- Repeat Steps 1 and 2 to adjust the column width of columns B through N (Figure 1–52).

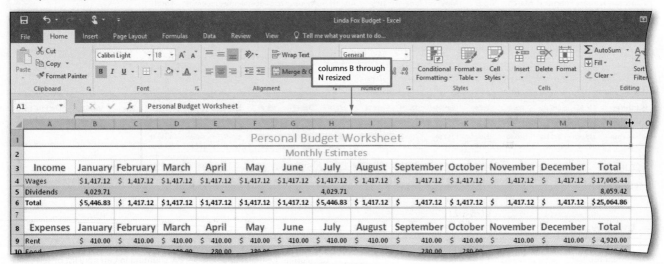

Figure 1–52

To Use the Name Box to Select a Cell

1 ENTER TEXT | 2 CALCULATE SUMS & USE FORMULAS | 3 FORMAT TEXT
4 INSERT CHART | 5 NAME TAB | 6 PREVIEW & PRINT WORKSHEET

The next step is to chart the monthly expenses. To create the chart, you need to identify the range of the data you want to feature on the chart and then select it. In this case you want to start with cell A3. Rather than clicking cell A3 to select it, you will select the cell by using the Name box, which is located to the left of the formula bar. **Why?** *You might want to use the Name box to select a cell if you are working with a large worksheet and it is faster to type the cell name rather than scrolling to and clicking it.* The following steps select cell A3 using the Name box.

1

- Click the Name box in the formula bar and then type **a3** as the cell you want to select (Figure 1–53).

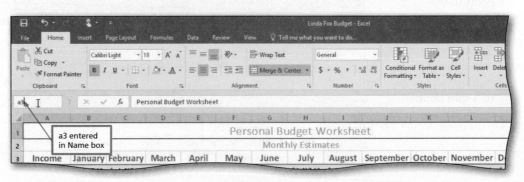

Figure 1–53

2

- Press the ENTER key to change the active cell in the Name box and make cell A3 the active cell (Figure 1–54).

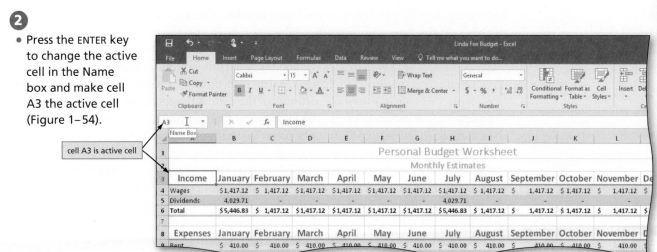

Figure 1–54

Other Ways to Select Cells

As you will see in later modules, in addition to using the Name box to select any cell in a worksheet, you also can use it to assign names to a cell or range of cells. Excel supports several additional ways to select a cell, as summarized in Table 1–3.

Table 1–3 Selecting Cells in Excel

Key, Box, or Command	Function
ALT+PAGE DOWN	Selects the cell one worksheet window to the right and moves the worksheet window accordingly.
ALT+PAGE UP	Selects the cell one worksheet window to the left and moves the worksheet window accordingly.
ARROW	Selects the adjacent cell in the direction of the arrow on the key.
CTRL+ARROW	Selects the border cell of the worksheet in combination with the arrow keys and moves the worksheet window accordingly. For example, to select the rightmost cell in the row that contains the active cell, press CTRL+RIGHT ARROW. You also can press the END key, release it, and then press the appropriate arrow key to accomplish the same task.
CTRL+HOME	Selects cell A1 or the cell one column and one row below and to the right of frozen titles and moves the worksheet window accordingly.
Find command on Find & Select menu (Home tab | Editing group) or SHIFT+F5	Finds and selects a cell that contains specific contents that you enter in the Find and Replace dialog box. If necessary, Excel moves the worksheet window to display the cell. You also can press CTRL+F to display the Find and Replace dialog box.
Go To command on Find & Select menu (Home tab | Editing group) or F5	Selects the cell that corresponds to the cell reference you enter in the Go To dialog box and moves the worksheet window accordingly. You also can press CTRL+G to display the Go To dialog box.
HOME	Selects the cell at the beginning of the row that contains the active cell and moves the worksheet window accordingly.
Name box	Selects the cell in the workbook that corresponds to the cell reference you enter in the Name box.
PAGE DOWN	Selects the cell down one worksheet window from the active cell and moves the worksheet window accordingly.
PAGE UP	Selects the cell up one worksheet window from the active cell and moves the worksheet window accordingly.

© 2014 Cengage Learning

Break Point: If you wish to take a break, this is a good place to do so. Be sure to save the Linda Fox Budget file again and then you can exit Excel. To resume at a later time, run Excel, open the file called Linda Fox Budget, and continue following the steps from this location forward.

Adding a Pie Chart to the Worksheet

Excel includes 15 chart types from which you can choose, including column, line, pie, bar, area, X Y (scatter), stock, surface, radar, treemap, sunburst,

BTW

Excel Help
At any time while using
Excel, you can find answers
to questions and display
information about various
topics through Excel Help.
Used properly, this form of
assistance can increase your
productivity and reduce your
frustrations by minimizing the
time you spend learning how
to use Excel. For instructions
about Excel Help and
exercises that will help you
gain confidence in using it,
read the Office and Windows
module at the beginning of
this book.

histogram, box & whisker, waterfall, and combo. The type of chart you choose
depends on the type and quantity of data you have and the message or analysis you
want to convey.

A column or cylinder chart is a good way to compare values side by side. A line
chart often is used to illustrate changes in data over time. Pie charts show the contribution
of each piece of data to the whole, or total, of the data. A pie chart can go even further
in comparing values across categories by showing each pie piece in comparison with
the others. Area charts, like line charts, illustrate changes over time, but often are used
to compare more than one set of data, and the area below the lines is filled in with a
different color for each set of data. An X Y (scatter) chart is used much like a line chart,
but each piece of data is represented by a dot and is not connected with a line. Scatter
charts are typically used for viewing scientific, statistical, and engineering data. A stock
chart provides a number of methods commonly used in the financial industry to show
fluctuations in stock market data. A surface chart compares data from three columns
and/or rows in a 3-D manner. A radar chart can compare aggregate values of several sets
of data in a manner that resembles a radar screen, with each set of data represented by a
different color. A combo chart allows you to combine multiple types of charts.

Excel 2016 includes five new charts. Treemap and sunburst charts are hierarchy
charts, used to compare parts to a whole. A treemap chart uses nested rectangles to
show data in a hierarchy. A sunburst chart stacks multiple pie charts on one another
to illustrate related data. New statistical charts include histogram and box & whisker
charts. A histogram chart shows the distribution of data. A box & whisker chart, or box
plot, is used to display variation within a set of data. The new waterfall chart is used to
visualize increases and decreases within a set of data and is grouped with stock charts.

As outlined in the requirements document in Figure 1–2, the budget worksheet
should include a pie chart to graphically represent the yearly expense totals for each
item in Linda Fox's budget. The pie chart shown in Figure 1–55 is on its own sheet
in the workbook. The pie chart resides on a separate sheet, called a **chart sheet**, which
contains only the chart.

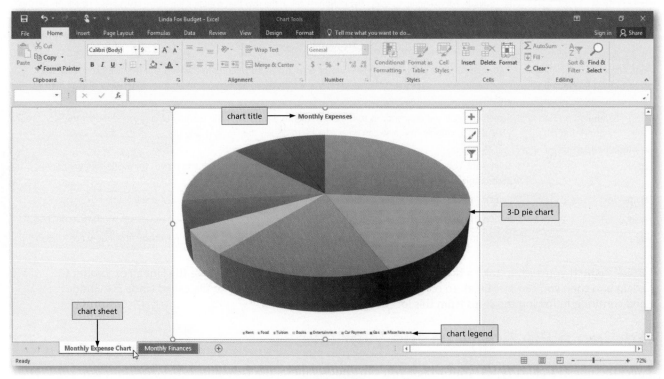

Figure 1–55

In this worksheet, the ranges you want to chart are the nonadjacent ranges A9:A16 (expense titles) and N9:N16 (yearly expense totals). The expense titles in the range A9:A16 will identify the slices of the pie chart; these entries are called category names. The range N9:N16 contains the data that determines the size of the slices in the pie; these entries are called the **data series**. Because eight budget items are being charted, the 3-D pie chart contains eight slices.

To Add a 3-D Pie Chart

1 ENTER TEXT | 2 CALCULATE SUMS & USE FORMULAS | 3 FORMAT TEXT
4 INSERT CHART | 5 NAME TAB | 6 PREVIEW & PRINT WORKSHEET

Why? *When you want to see how each part relates to the whole, you use a pie chart.* The following steps draw the 3-D pie chart.

1

- Select the range A9:A16 to identify the range of the category names for the 3-D pie chart.

- While holding down the CTRL key, select the nonadjacent range N9:N16.

- Click Insert on the ribbon to display the Insert tab.

- Click the 'Insert Pie or Doughnut Chart' button (Insert tab | Charts group) to display the Insert Pie or Doughnut Chart gallery (Figure 1–56).

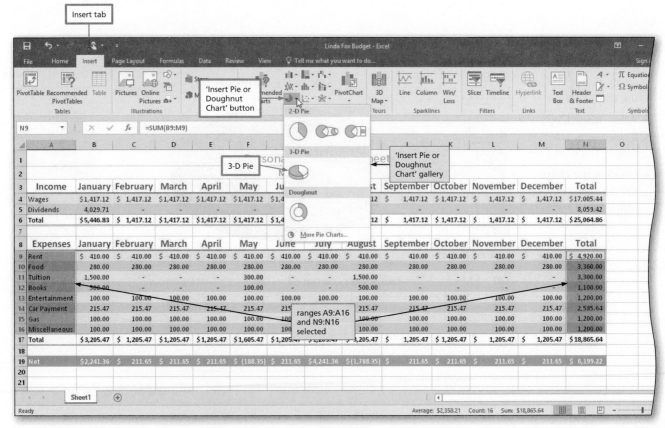

Figure 1–56

2

- Click 3-D Pie in the Insert Pie or Doughnut Chart gallery to insert the chart in the worksheet (Figure 1–57).

Q&A

Why have new tabs appeared on the ribbon?
The new tabs provide additional options and functionality when you are working with certain objects, such as charts, and only display when you are working with those objects.

Figure 1–57

3

- Click and drag to select all the text in the chart title.

- Type **Monthly Expenses** to specify the title.

- Deselect the chart title to view the new title (Figure 1–58).

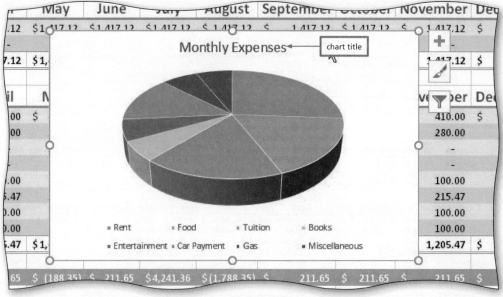

Figure 1–58

1 ENTER TEXT | 2 CALCULATE SUMS & USE FORMULAS | 3 FORMAT TEXT
4 INSERT CHART | 5 NAME TAB | 6 PREVIEW & PRINT WORKSHEET

To Apply a Style to a Chart

Why? *If you want to enhance the appearance of a chart, you can apply a chart style.* The following steps apply Style 5 to the 3-D pie chart.

1

- Click the Chart Styles button to display the Chart Styles gallery.
- Scroll in the Chart Style gallery to display the Style 5 chart style (Figure 1–59).

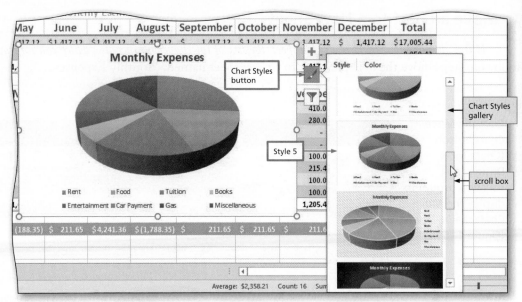

Figure 1–59

2

- Click Style 5 in the Chart Styles gallery to change the chart style to Style 5 (Figure 1–60).

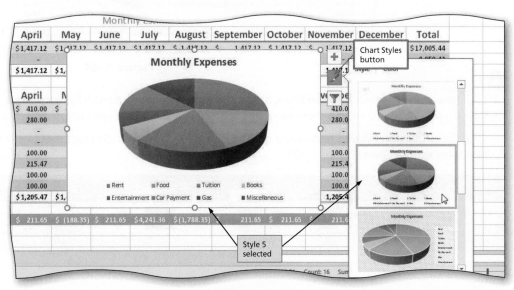

Figure 1–60

3

- Click the Chart Styles button to close the Chart Styles gallery.

Changing the Sheet Tab Names

The sheet tabs at the bottom of the window allow you to navigate between any worksheet in the workbook. You click the sheet tab of the worksheet you want to view in the Excel window. By default, the worksheets are named Sheet1, Sheet2, and so on. The worksheet names become increasingly important as you move toward more sophisticated workbooks, especially workbooks in which you reference cells between worksheets.

BTW

Exploding a Pie Chart

If you want to draw attention to a particular slice in a pie chart, you can offset the slice so that it stands out from the rest. A pie chart with one or more slices offset is referred to as an exploded pie chart. To offset a slice, click the slice two times to select it (do not double-click) and then drag the slice outward.

To Move a Chart to a New Sheet

Why? *By moving a chart to its own sheet, the size of the chart will increase, which can improve readability.* The following steps move the 3-D pie chart to a chart sheet named, Monthly Expenses.

1

- Click the Move Chart button (Chart Tools Design tab | Location group) to display the Move Chart dialog box (Figure 1–61).

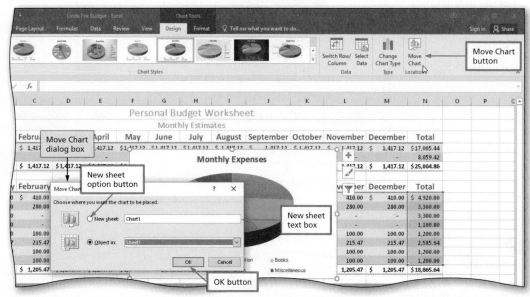

Figure 1–61

2

- Click New sheet to select it (Move Chart dialog box) and then type **Monthly Expense Chart** in the New sheet text box to enter a sheet tab name for the worksheet that will contain the chart.

- Click the OK button (Move Chart dialog box) to move the chart to a new chart sheet with the sheet tab name, Monthly Expense Chart (Figure 1–62).

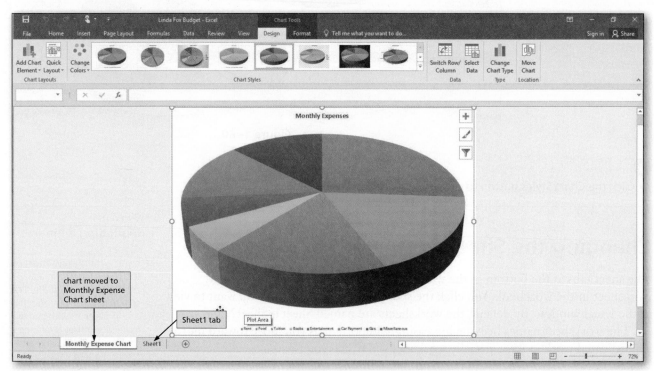

Figure 1–62

To Change the Sheet Tab Name

You decide to change the name of the Sheet1 tab to Monthly Finances. ***Why?*** *Use simple, meaningful names for each sheet tab. Sheet tab names often match the worksheet title. If a worksheet includes multiple titles in multiple sections of the worksheet, use a sheet tab name that encompasses the meaning of all of the sections.* The following steps rename the sheet tab.

1

- Double-click the sheet tab labeled Sheet1 in the lower-left corner of the window.

- Type **Monthly Finances** as the sheet tab name and then press the ENTER key to assign the new name to the sheet tab (Figure 1–63).

Q&A What is the maximum length for a sheet tab name?
Sheet tab names can be up to 31 characters (including spaces) in length. Longer worksheet names, however, mean that fewer sheet tabs will display on your screen. If you have multiple worksheets with long sheet tab names, you may have to scroll through sheet tabs.

Figure 1–63

2

- Right-click the sheet tab labeled, Monthly Finances, in the lower-left corner of the window to display a shortcut menu.

- Point to Tab Color on the shortcut menu to display the Tab Color gallery (Figure 1–64).

Figure 1–64

3

- Click a color that matches your shirt in the Theme Colors area to change the color of the tab (Figure 1–65).

- If necessary, click Home on the ribbon to display the Home tab.

- Save the workbook again on the same storage location with the same file name.

Q&A Why should I save the workbook again?
You have made several modifications to the workbook since you last saved it. Thus, you should save it again.

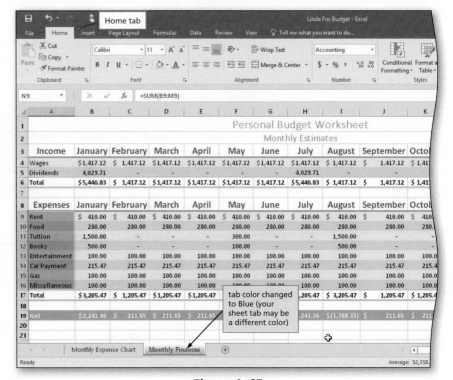

Figure 1–65

Document Properties

Excel helps you organize and identify your files by using **document properties**, which are the details about a file such as the project author, title, and subject. For example, you could use the class name or topic to describe the workbook's purpose or content in the document properties.

CONSIDER THIS

Why would you want to assign document properties to a workbook?

Document properties are valuable for a variety of reasons:

- Users can save time locating a particular file because they can view a file's document properties without opening the workbook.

- By creating consistent properties for files having similar content, users can better organize their workbooks.

- Some organizations require Excel users to add document properties so that other employees can view details about these files.

Common document properties include standard properties and those that are automatically updated. **Standard properties** are associated with all Microsoft Office files and include author, title, and subject. **Automatically updated properties** include file system properties, such as the date you create or change a file, and statistics, such as the file size.

TO CHANGE DOCUMENT PROPERTIES

To change document properties, you would follow these steps.

1. Click File on the ribbon to open the Backstage view and then, if necessary, click the Info tab in the Backstage view to display the Info gallery. The Properties list is found in the right pane of the Info gallery.

2. If the property you wish to change is in the Properties list, click to the right of the property category to display a text box. (Note that not all properties are editable.) Type the desired text for the property and then click anywhere in the Info gallery to enter the data, or press TAB to navigate to the next property. Click the Back button in the upper-left corner of the Backstage view to return to the Excel window.

3. If the property you wish to change is not in the Properties list or you cannot edit it, click the Properties button to display the Properties menu, and then click Advanced Properties to display the Summary tab in the Properties dialog box. Type your desired text in the appropriate property text boxes. Click the OK button (Properties dialog box) to close the dialog box and then click the Back button in the upper-left corner of the Backstage view to return to the workbook.

Q&A | Why do some of the document properties in my Properties dialog box contain data? Depending on where you are using Office 2016, your school, university, or place of employment may have customized the properties.

Printing a Worksheet

After creating a worksheet, you may want to print it. Printing a worksheet enables you to distribute the worksheet to others in a form that can be read or viewed but not edited. It is a good practice to save a workbook before printing a worksheet, in the event you experience difficulties printing.

What is the best method for distributing a workbook?

The traditional method of distributing a workbook uses a printer to produce a hard copy. A **hard copy** or **printout** is information that exists on paper. Hard copies can be useful for the following reasons:

• Some people prefer proofreading a hard copy of a workbook rather than viewing it on the screen to check for errors and readability.

• Hard copies can serve as a backup reference if your storage medium is lost or becomes corrupted and you need to recreate the workbook.

Instead of distributing a hard copy of a workbook, users can distribute the workbook as an electronic image that mirrors the original workbook's appearance. An electronic image of a workbook is not an editable file; it simply displays a picture of the workbook. The electronic image of the workbook can be sent as an email attachment, posted on a website, or copied to a portable storage medium such as a USB flash drive. Two popular electronic image formats, sometimes called fixed formats, are PDF by Adobe Systems and XPS by Microsoft. In Excel, you can create electronic image files through the Save As dialog box and the Export, Share, and Print tabs in the Backstage view. Electronic images of workbooks, such as PDF and XPS, can be useful for the following reasons:

• Users can view electronic images of workbooks without the software that created the original workbook (e.g., Excel). Specifically, to view a PDF file, you use a program called Adobe Reader, which can be downloaded free from Adobe's website. Similarly, to view an XPS file, you use a program called XPS Viewer, which is included in the latest version of Windows.

• Sending electronic workbooks saves paper and printer supplies. Society encourages users to contribute to **green computing**, which involves reducing the electricity consumed and environmental waste generated when using computers, mobile devices, and related technologies.

To Preview and Print a Worksheet in Landscape Orientation

1 ENTER TEXT | 2 CALCULATE SUMS & USE FORMULAS | 3 FORMAT TEXT
4 INSERT CHART | 5 NAME TAB | 6 PREVIEW & PRINT WORKSHEET

Pages printed in **portrait orientation** have the short (8½") edge at the top of the printout; the printed page is taller than it is wide. **Landscape orientation** prints the long (11") edge at the top of the paper; the printed page is wider than it is tall. With the completed workbook saved, you may want to print it. *Why? Because the worksheet is included in a report delivered in person, you will print a hard copy on a printer.* The following steps print a hard copy of the contents of the worksheet.

1

• Click File on the ribbon to open the Backstage view.

• Click the Print tab in the Backstage view to display the Print gallery (Figure 1–66).

Q&A How can I print multiple copies of my worksheet?
Increase the number in the Copies box in the Print gallery.

What if I decide not to print the worksheet at this time?
Click the Back button in the upper-left corner of the Backstage view to return to the workbook window.

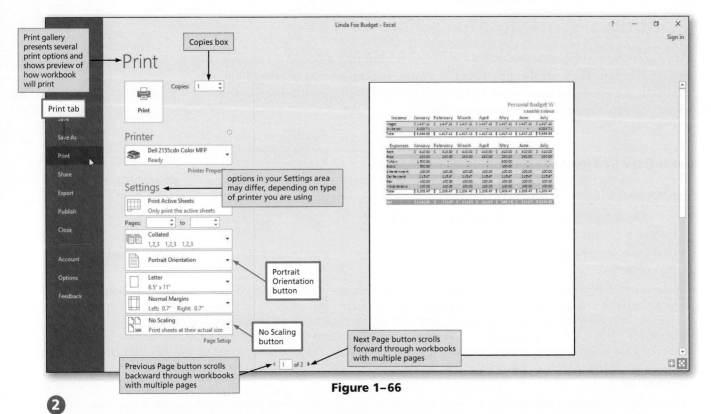

Figure 1–66

2

- Verify that the printer listed on the Printer Status button will print a hard copy of the workbook. If necessary, click the Printer Status button to display a list of available printer options and then click the desired printer to change the currently selected printer.

3

- Click the Portrait Orientation button in the Settings area and then select Landscape Orientation to change the orientation of the page to landscape.

- Click the No Scaling button and then select 'Fit Sheet on One Page' to print the entire worksheet on one page (Figure 1–67).

Figure 1–67

4

- Click the Print button in the Print gallery to print the worksheet in landscape orientation on the currently selected printer.

- When the printer stops, retrieve the hard copy (Figure 1–68).

Q&A Do I have to wait until my worksheet is complete to print it?
No, you can print a document at any time while you are creating it.

Personal Budget Worksheet
Monthly Estimates

Income	January	February	March	April	May	June	July	August	September	October	November	December	Total
Wages	$ 1,417.12	$ 1,417.12	$ 1,417.12	$ 1,417.12	$ 1,417.12	$ 1,417.12	$ 1,417.12	$ 1,417.12	1,417.12	$ 1,417.12	1,417.12	$ 1,417.12	$ 17,005.44
Dividends	4,029.71	-	-	-	-	-	4,029.71	-	-	-	-	-	8,059.42
Total	**$ 5,446.83**	**$ 1,417.12**	**$ 1,417.12**	**$ 1,417.12**	**$ 1,417.12**	**$ 1,417.12**	**$ 5,446.83**	**$ 1,417.12**	**1,417.12**	**$ 1,417.12**	**1,417.12**	**$ 1,417.12**	**$ 25,064.86**

Expenses	January	February	March	April	May	June	July	August	September	October	November	December	Total
Rent	$ 410.00	$ 410.00	$ 410.00	$ 410.00	$ 410.00	$ 410.00	$ 410.00	$ 410.00	$ 410.00	$ 410.00	$ 410.00	$ 410.00	$ 4,920.00
Food	280.00	280.00	280.00	280.00	280.00	280.00	280.00	280.00	280.00	280.00	280.00	280.00	3,360.00
Tuition	1,500.00	-	-	-	300.00	-	-	1,500.00	-	-	-	-	3,300.00
Books	500.00	-	-	-	100.00	-	-	500.00	-	-	-	-	1,100.00
Entertainment	100.00	100.00	100.00	100.00	100.00	100.00	100.00	100.00	100.00	100.00	100.00	100.00	1,200.00
Car Payment	215.47	215.47	215.47	215.47	215.47	215.47	215.47	215.47	215.47	215.47	215.47	215.47	2,585.64
Gas	100.00	100.00	100.00	100.00	100.00	100.00	100.00	100.00	100.00	100.00	100.00	100.00	1,200.00
Miscellaneous	100.00	100.00	100.00	100.00	100.00	100.00	100.00	100.00	100.00	100.00	100.00	100.00	1,200.00
Total	**$ 3,205.47**	**$ 1,205.47**	**$ 1,205.47**	**$ 1,205.47**	**$ 1,605.47**	**$ 1,205.47**	**$ 1,205.47**	**$ 3,205.47**	**1,205.47**	**$ 1,205.47**	**1,205.47**	**$ 1,205.47**	**$ 18,865.64**

| Net | $ 2,241.36 | $ 211.65 | $ 211.65 | $ 211.65 | $ (188.35) | $ 211.65 | $ 4,241.36 | $ (1,788.35) | $ 211.65 | $ 211.65 | $ 211.65 | $ 211.65 | $ 6,199.22 |

Figure 1–68

Other Ways

1. Press CTRL+P to open Print Gallery, press ENTER

Autocalculate

You easily can obtain a total, an average, or other information about the numbers in a range by using the **AutoCalculate area** on the status bar. First, select the range of cells containing the numbers you want to check. Next, right-click the AutoCalculate area to display the Customize Status Bar shortcut menu (Figure 1–69). The check marks indicate that the calculations are displayed in the status bar; more than one may be selected. The functions of the AutoCalculate commands on the Customize Status Bar shortcut menu are described in Table 1–4.

Table 1–4 Commonly Used Status Bar Commands

Command	Function
Average	AutoCalculate area displays the average of the numbers in the selected range
Count	AutoCalculate area displays the number of non-empty cells in the selected range
Numerical Count	AutoCalculate area displays the number of cells containing numbers in the selected range
Minimum	AutoCalculate area displays the lowest value in the selected range
Maximum	AutoCalculate area displays the highest value in the selected range
Sum	AutoCalculate area displays the sum of the numbers in the selected range

BTW
Distributing a Workbook
Instead of printing and distributing a hard copy of a workbook, you can distribute the workbook electronically. Options include sending the workbook via email; posting it on cloud storage (such as OneDrive) and sharing the file with others; posting it on social media, a blog, or other website; and sharing a link associated with an online location of the workbook. You also can create and share a PDF or XPS image of the workbook, so that users can view the file in Acrobat Reader or XPS Viewer instead of in Excel.

To Use the AutoCalculate Area to Determine a Maximum

The following steps determine the largest monthly total in the budget. *Why? Sometimes, you want a quick analysis, which can be especially helpful when your worksheet contains a lot of data.*

1

- Select the range B19:M19. Right-click the status bar to display the Customize Status Bar shortcut menu (Figure 1–69).

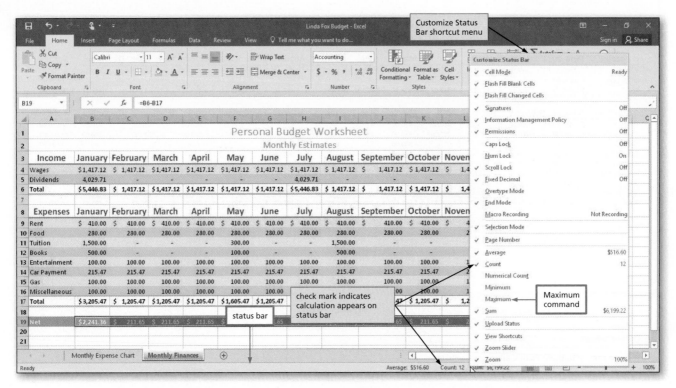

Figure 1–69

2

- Click Maximum on the shortcut menu to display the Maximum value in the range B19:M19 in the AutoCalculate area of the status bar.

- Click anywhere on the worksheet to close the shortcut menu (Figure 1–70).

	280.00	280.00	280.00	280.00	280.00	280.00	280.00	280.00	3,500.00
-	300.00	-	-	1,500.00	-	-	-	-	3,300.00
-	100.00	-	-	500.00	-	-	-	-	1,100.00
100.00	100.00	100.00	100.00	100.00	100.00	100.00	100.00	100.00	1,200.00
215.47	215.47	215.47	215.47	215.47	215.47	215.47	215.47	215.47	2,585.64
100.00	100.00	100.00	100.00	100.00	100.00	100.00	100.00	100.00	1,200.00
100.00	100.00	100.00	100.00	100.00	100.00	100.00	100.00	100.00	1,200.00
$1,205.47	$1,605.47	$1,205.47	$1,205.47	$ 3,205.47	$ 1,205.47	$1,205.47	$ 1,205.47	$ 1,205.47	$18,865.64
$ 211.65	$ (188.35)	$ 211.65	$4,241.36	$(1,78...		$ 211.65	$ 211.65	211.65	$ 6,199.22

maximum value displayed in AutoCalculate area

nances   (+)   ◀

Average: $516.60   Count: 12   Max: $4,241.36   Sum: $6,199.22

Figure 1–70

3

- Right-click the AutoCalculate area and then click Maximum on the shortcut menu to deselect it. The Maximum value will no longer appear on the status bar.

- Close the shortcut menu.

4

- Save the workbook using the same file name in the same storage location.

- If desired, sign out of your Microsoft account.

- Exit Excel.

Correcting Errors

You can correct data entry errors on a worksheet using one of several methods. The method you choose will depend on the extent of the error and whether you notice it while entering the data or after you have entered the incorrect data into the cell.

Correcting Errors while Entering Data into a Cell

If you notice an error while you are entering data into a cell, press the BACKSPACE key to erase the incorrect character(s) and then enter the correct character(s). If the error is a major one, click the Cancel box in the formula bar or press the ESC key to erase the entire entry and then reenter the data.

Correcting Errors after Entering Data into a Cell

If you find an error in the worksheet after entering the data, you can correct the error in one of two ways:

1. If the entry is short, select the cell, retype the entry correctly, and then click the Enter button or press the ENTER key. The new entry will replace the old entry.

2. If the entry in the cell is long and the errors are minor, using Edit mode may be a better choice than retyping the cell entry. In **Edit mode**, Excel displays the active cell entry in the formula bar and a flashing insertion point in the active cell, and you can edit the contents directly in the cell — a procedure called **in-cell editing.**

   a. Double-click the cell containing the error to switch Excel to Edit mode (Figure 1–71).

   b. Make corrections using the following in-cell editing methods.

      (1) To insert new characters between two characters, place the insertion point between the two characters and begin typing. Excel inserts the new characters to the left of the insertion point.

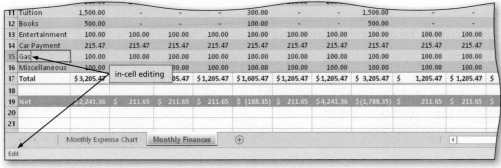

Figure 1–71

(2) To delete a character in the cell, move the insertion point to the left of the character you want to delete and then press the DELETE key, or place the insertion point to the right of the character you want to delete and then press the BACKSPACE key. You also can drag to select the character or adjacent characters you want to delete and then press the DELETE key or CTRL+X, or click the Cut button (Home tab | Clipboard group).

(3) When you are finished editing an entry, click the Enter button or press the ENTER key.

There are two ways for entering data in Edit mode: Insert mode and Overtype mode. In the default **Insert mode**, as you type a character, Excel inserts the character and moves all characters to the right of the typed character one position to the right. You can change to Overtype mode by pressing the INSERT key. In **Overtype mode**, Excel replaces, or overtypes, the character to the right of the insertion point. The INSERT key toggles the keyboard between Insert mode and Overtype mode.

While in Edit mode, you may have reason to move the insertion point to various points in the cell, select portions of the data in the cell, or switch from inserting characters to overtyping characters. Table 1–5 summarizes the more common tasks performed during in-cell editing.

Table 1–5 Summary of In-Cell Editing Tasks

	Task	Mouse Operation	Keyboard
1.	Move the insertion point to the beginning of data in a cell.	Point to the left of the first character and click.	Press HOME
2.	Move the insertion point to the end of data in a cell.	Point to the right of the last character and click.	Press END
3.	Move the insertion point anywhere in a cell.	Point to the appropriate position and click the character.	Press RIGHT ARROW or LEFT ARROW
4.	Highlight one or more adjacent characters.	Drag through adjacent characters.	Press SHIFT+RIGHT ARROW or SHIFT+LEFT ARROW
5.	Select all data in a cell.	Double-click the cell with the insertion point in the cell if the data in the cell contains no spaces.	
6.	Delete selected characters.	Click the Cut button (Home tab | Clipboard group).	Press DELETE
7.	Delete characters to the left of the insertion point.		Press BACKSPACE
8.	Delete characters to the right of the insertion point.		Press DELETE
9.	Toggle between Insert and Overtype modes.		Press INSERT

Undoing the Last Cell Entry

The Undo button on the Quick Access Toolbar (Figure 1–72) allows you to erase recent cell entries. Thus, if you enter incorrect data in a cell and notice it immediately, click the Undo button and Excel changes the cell entry to what it was prior to the incorrect data entry.

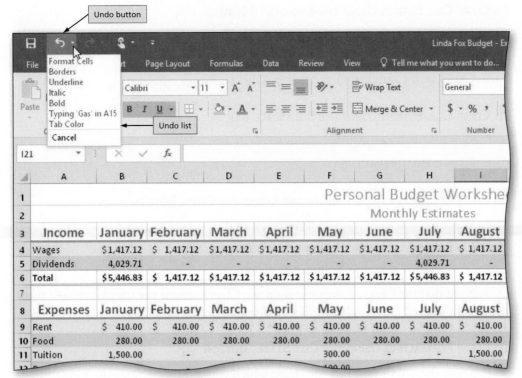

Figure 1–72

Excel remembers the last 100 actions you have completed. Thus, you can undo up to 100 previous actions by clicking the Undo arrow to display the Undo list and then clicking the action to be undone (Figure 1–72). You can drag through several actions in the Undo list to undo all of them at once. If no actions are available for Excel to undo, then the dimmed appearance of the Undo button indicates that it is unavailable.

The Redo button, next to the Undo button on the Quick Access Toolbar, allows you to repeat previous actions; that is, if you accidentally undo an action, you can use the Redo button to perform the action again.

Clearing a Cell or Range of Cells

If you enter data into the wrong cell or range of cells, you can erase, or clear, the data using one of the first four methods listed below. The fifth method clears the formatting from the selected cells. To clear a cell or range of cells, you would perform the following steps:

To CLEAR CELL ENTRIES USING THE FILL HANDLE

1. Select the cell or range of cells and then point to the fill handle so that the pointer changes to a crosshair.
2. Drag the fill handle back into the selected cell or range until a shadow covers the cell or cells you want to erase.

TO CLEAR CELL ENTRIES USING THE SHORTCUT MENU

1. Select the cell or range of cells to be cleared.
2. Right-click the selection.
3. Click Clear Contents on the shortcut menu.

TO CLEAR CELL ENTRIES USING THE BACKSPACE KEY

1. Select the cell or range of cells to be cleared.
2. Press the BACKSPACE key.

TO CLEAR CELL ENTRIES AND FORMATTING USING THE CLEAR BUTTON

1. Select the cell or range of cells to be cleared.
2. Click the Clear button (Home tab | Editing group).
3. Click Clear Contents on the Clear menu.

Note that the Clear All command on the Clear menu is the only command that clears both the cell entry and the cell formatting.

TO CLEAR FORMATTING USING THE CELL STYLES BUTTON

1. Select the cell or range of cells from which you want to remove the formatting.
2. Click the Cell Styles button (Home tab | Styles group) and then click Normal in the Cell Styles gallery.

As you are clearing cell entries, always remember that you should *never press the SPACEBAR to clear a cell*. Pressing the SPACEBAR enters a blank character. A blank character is interpreted by Excel as text and is different from an empty cell, even though the cell may appear empty.

Clearing the Entire Worksheet

If the required worksheet edits are extremely extensive or if the requirements drastically change, you may want to clear the entire worksheet and start over. To clear the worksheet or delete an embedded chart, you would use the following steps.

TO CLEAR THE ENTIRE WORKSHEET

1. Click the Select All button on the worksheet. The Select All button is located above the row 1 identifier and to the left of the column A heading.
2. Click the Clear button (Home tab | Editing group) and then click Clear All on the menu to delete both the entries and formats.

The Select All button selects the entire worksheet. Instead of clicking the Select All button, you can press CTRL+A. To clear an unsaved workbook, click the Close Window button on the workbook's title bar or click the Close button in the Backstage view. Click the No button if the Microsoft Excel dialog box asks if you want to save changes. To start a new, blank workbook, click the New button in the Backstage view.

Summary

In this module you have learned how to create a personal budget worksheet and chart. Topics covered included selecting a cell, entering text, entering numbers, calculating a sum, using the fill handle, formatting a worksheet, adding a pie chart, changing sheet tab names, printing a worksheet, AutoCalculate, and correcting errors.

CONSIDER THIS: PLAN AHEAD

What decisions will you need to make when creating workbooks and charts in the future?

1. Determine the workbook structure.

   a) Determine the data you will need for your workbook.

   b) Sketch a layout of your data and your chart.

2. Create the worksheet.

   a) Enter titles, subtitles, and headings.

   b) Enter data, functions, and formulas.

3. Format the worksheet.

   a) Format the titles, subtitles, and headings using styles.

   b) Format the totals.

   c) Format the numbers.

   d) Format the text.

   e) Adjust column widths.

4. Create the chart.

   a) Determine the type of chart to use.

   b) Determine the chart title and data.

   c) Format the chart.

Apply Your Knowledge

Reinforce the skills and apply the concepts you learned in this module.

Changing the Values in a Worksheet

Note: To complete this assignment, you will be required to use the Data Files. Please contact your instructor for information about accessing the required files.

Instructions: Run Excel. Open the workbook Apply 1–1 Lima Wholesale (Figure 1–73a). The workbook you open contains sales data for Lima Wholesale. You are to apply formatting to the worksheet and move the chart to a new sheet tab.

Table 1–6 New Worksheet Data	
Cell	**Change Cell Contents To**
A2	Monthly Departmental Sales
B5	15242.36
C7	114538.23
D5	25747.85
E6	39851.44
F7	29663.77
G6	19885.41

Perform the following tasks:

1. Make the changes to the worksheet described in Table 1–6 so that the worksheet appears as shown in Figure 1–73b. As you edit the values in the cells containing numeric data, watch the totals in row 8, the totals in column H, and the chart change.

2. Change the worksheet title in cell A1 to the Title cell style and then merge and center it across columns A through H.

3. Use buttons in the Font group on the Home tab on the ribbon to change the worksheet subtitle in cell A2 to 16-point font and then center it across columns A through H. Change the font color of cell A2 to Dark Blue, Text 2, Darker 25%.

4. Apply the worksheet name, Monthly Sales, and the Dark Blue, Text 2, Darker 25% color to the sheet tab.

5. Move the chart to a new sheet called Sales Analysis Chart (Figure 1–73c). Change the chart title to SALES TOTALS.

6. If requested by your instructor, replace Lima in cell A1 with your last name.

7. Save the workbook using the file name, Apply 1–1 Lima Wholesale Sales Analysis.

8. Submit the revised workbook as specified by your instructor and exit Excel.

9. ✳ Besides the styles used in the worksheet, what other changes could you make to enhance the worksheet?

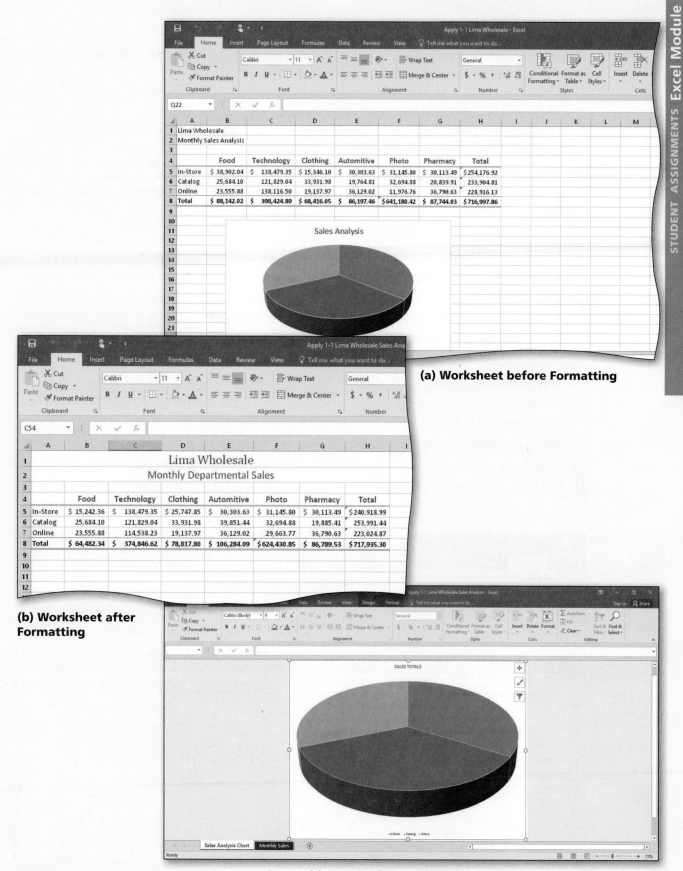

(a) **Worksheet before Formatting**

(b) **Worksheet after Formatting**

(c) **3-D Pie Chart on Separate Sheet**

Figure 1–73

Extend Your Knowledge

Extend the skills you learned in this module and experiment with new skills. You may
need to use Help to complete the assignment.

Creating Styles and Formatting a Worksheet

Note: To complete this assignment, you will be required to use the Data Files. Please contact your
instructor for information about accessing the required files.

Instructions: Run Excel. Open the workbook Extend 1–1 Dasminne Grocery (Figure 1–74). The
workbook you open contains sales data for Dasminne Grocery. You are to create styles and format a
worksheet using them.

Perform the following tasks:

1. Select cell A4. Use the New Cell Style command in the Cell Styles gallery to create a style that
   uses the Blue, Accent 1, Darker 50% font color (row 6, column 5). Name the style, MyHeadings.

2. Select cell A5. Use the New Cell style dialog box to create a style that uses the Blue, Accent 1,
   Darker 25% (row 5, column 5) font color. Name the style, MyRows.

3. Select cell ranges B4:G4 and A5:A8. Apply the MyHeadings style to the cell ranges.

4. Select the cell range B5:G7. Apply the MyRows style to the cell range.

5. Apply a worksheet name to the sheet tab and apply a color of your choice to the sheet tab.

6. If requested by your instructor, change the font color for the text in cells A1 and A2 to the color
   of your eyes, if available.

7. Save the workbook using the file name, Extend 1–1 Dasminne Grocery Third Quarter.

8. Submit the revised workbook as specified by your instructor and exit Excel.

9. ✸ What other styles would you create to improve the worksheet's appearance?

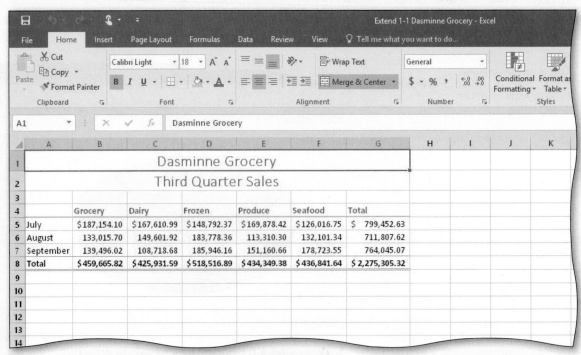

Figure 1–74

Expand Your World

Create a solution that uses cloud or web technologies by learning and investigating on your own from general guidance.

College Loan Calculator

Instructions: You are tasked with determining how long it will take you to pay back your college loans. You decide to download and use one of Excel's templates to create your worksheet.

Perform the following tasks:

1. Click the New tab in the Backstage view and then search for and click the College loan calculator template to download it.

2. Enter data for your estimated salary after graduation, the date you will begin paying back loans, as well as fictitious (but realistic) information for four loans, including loan number, lender, loan amount, annual interest rate, beginning date, and length (in years).

3. Save the file as Expand 1-1: College Loans. Print the worksheet.

4. Submit the assignment as specified by your instructor.

5. ✳ Which template would you use if you wanted to plan and keep track of a budget for a wedding?

In the Labs

Design, create, modify, and/or use a workbook following the guidelines, concepts, and skills presented in this module. Labs 1 and 2, which increase in difficulty, require you to create solutions based on what you learned in the module; Lab 3 requires you to apply your creative thinking and problem-solving skills to design and implement a solution.

Lab 1: First Quarter Revenue Analysis Worksheet

Problem: You work as a spreadsheet specialist for Katie's Kicks, which has four regional shops in the state of Florida. Your manager has asked you to develop a first quarter revenue analysis similar to the one shown in Figure 1–75.

Perform the following tasks:

1. Run Excel and create a new blank workbook. Enter the worksheet title, Katie's Kicks, in cell A1 and the worksheet subtitle, First Quarter Revenue Analysis, in cell A2. Beginning in row 4, enter the region data shown in Table 1–7.

Table 1–7 Katie's Kicks				
	North	**South**	**East**	**West**
Sneakers	72714.58	77627.29	76607.31	49008.32
Shoes	45052.23	69165.66	76243.41	84844.01
Sandals	77630.94	78684.24	56601.25	72716.68
Accessories	65423.73	77690.69	58383.67	54433.07
Miscellaneous	55666.92	78618.97	47317.09	68594.40

2. Create totals for each region, product, and company grand total.

3. Format the worksheet title with the Title cell style. Center the title across columns A through F.

Continued >

In the Labs *continued*

4. Format the worksheet subtitle to 16-point Calibri Light, and change the font color to Blue-Gray, Text 2. Center the subtitle across columns A through F.

5. Use Cell Styles to format the range A4:F4 with the Heading 3 cell style, the range B4:F4 with the Accent1 cell style, and the range A10:F10 with the Total cell style.

6. Center the column titles in row 4. Apply the accounting number format to the ranges B5:F5 and B10:F10. Apply the comma style format to the range B6:F9. Adjust any column widths to the widest text entry in each column.

7. Select the ranges B4:E4 and B10:E10 and then insert a 3-D pie chart. Apply the Style 3 chart style to the chart. Move the chart to a new worksheet named Revenue Analysis Chart. Change the chart title to First Quarter Revenue Analysis.

8. Rename the Sheet1 tab, First Quarter, and apply the Green color to the sheet tab.

9. If requested by your instructor, change the font color of the text in cells A1 and A2 to the color of the shirt you currently are wearing.

10. Save the workbook using the file name, Lab 1-1 Katie's Kicks.

11. Preview and print the worksheet in landscape orientation.

12. ✹ If you wanted to chart the item totals instead of the regions, which ranges would you use to create the chart?

13. Submit the assignment as specified by your instructor.

(a) Worksheet

(b) Pie Chart

Figure 1–75

Lab 2: **Sales Analysis Worksheet**

Problem: As the chief accountant for Davis Mobile Concepts, a leading car audio dealer serving four states, you have been asked by the vice president to create a worksheet to analyze the yearly sales for each state (Figure 1–76). The packages and corresponding sales by state for the year are shown in Table 1–8.

(a) Worksheet

(b) Pie Chart

Figure 1–76

Perform the following tasks:

1. Create the worksheet shown in Figure 1–76a using the data in Table 1–8.

Table 1–8 Davis Mobile Concepts				
	Alarm	**Audio**	**Light**	**Ultimate**
California	860358.71	431758.35	375708.22	247826.28
Nevada	345024.13	863814.87	786253.39	511277.11
Oregon	396157.67	326159.07	500255.40	383514.73
Washington	395428.36	804908.29	279091.37	342965.38

Continued >

2. Use the SUM function to determine total revenue for each of the four packages, the totals for each state, and the company total. Add column and row headings for the totals row and totals column, as appropriate.

3. Format the worksheet title and subtitle with the Title cell style and center them across columns A through F. Use the Font group on the ribbon to format the worksheet title and subtitle as 18-point Arial Black. Format the title and subtitle with Green, Accent 6 font color. Center the titles across columns A through F.

4. Format the range B4:F4 with the Heading 2 cell style and center the text in the cells. Format the range A5:F8 with the 20% - Accent6 cell style and the range A9:F9 with the Total cell style. Format cells B5:F5 and B9:F9 with the accounting number format and cells B6:F8 with the comma style format. If necessary, resize all columns to fit the data.

5. Create a 3-D pie chart on its own sheet that shows the total sales contributions of each state. Chart the state names (A5:A8) and corresponding totals (F5:F8). Use the sheet tab name, Yearly Sales Chart. Apply a chart style of your choosing. Change the chart title to Yearly Sales by State.

6. Change the Sheet1 tab name to Yearly Sales and apply the Orange color to the sheet tab.

7. If requested by your instructor, change the state in cell A8 to the state in which you were born. If your state already is listed in the spreadsheet, choose a different state.

8. Save the workbook using the file name, Lab 1-2 Davis Mobile Concepts. Print the worksheet in landscape orientation.

9. ✳ If you wanted to make a distinction between the rows in the table, what could you do?

10. Submit the assignment as specified by your instructor.

Lab 3: **Consider This: Your Turn**

Apply your creative thinking and problem-solving skills to design and implement a solution.

✳ **Comparing Televisions**

Part 1: You are shopping for a new television and want to compare the prices of three televisions. Research new televisions. Create a worksheet that compares the type, size, and the price for each television, as well as the costs to add an extended warranty. Use the concepts and techniques presented in this module to calculate the average price of a television and average cost of an extended warranty and to format the worksheet. Submit your assignment in the format specified by your instructor.

Part 2: Based upon the data you found, how could you chart the information to show the comparisons? Which chart would be the best to use? Include a chart to compare the different television costs.

2 | Formulas, Functions, and Formatting

Objectives

You will have mastered the material in this module when you can:

- Use Flash Fill
- Enter formulas using the keyboard
- Enter formulas using Point mode
- Apply the MAX, MIN, and AVERAGE functions
- Verify a formula using Range Finder
- Apply a theme to a workbook
- Apply a date format to a cell or range

- Add conditional formatting to cells
- Change column width and row height
- Check the spelling on a worksheet
- Change margins and headers in Page Layout view
- Preview and print versions and sections of a worksheet

Introduction

In Module 1, you learned how to enter data, sum values, format a worksheet to make it easier to read, and draw a chart. This module continues to illustrate these topics and presents some new ones.

The new topics covered in this module include using formulas and functions to create a worksheet. Recall from Module 1 that a function is a prewritten formula that is built into Excel. Other new topics include using option buttons, verifying formulas, applying a theme to a worksheet, adding borders, formatting numbers and text, using conditional formatting, changing the widths of columns and heights of rows, checking spelling, generating alternative worksheet displays and printouts, and adding page headers and footers to a worksheet. One alternative worksheet display and printout shows the formulas in the worksheet instead of the values. When you display the formulas in the worksheet, you see exactly what text, data, formulas, and functions you have entered into it.

Project — Worksheet with Formulas and Functions

The project in this module follows proper design guidelines and uses Excel to create the worksheet shown in Figure 2–1. Every two weeks, the owners of Olivia's Art Supply create a salary report by hand, where they keep track of employee payroll data. Before paying employees, the owners must summarize the hours worked, pay rate, and tax information for each employee to ensure that the business properly compensates its employees. This report also includes the following information for each employee: name, email address, number of dependents, hours worked, hourly pay rate, tax information, net pay, and hire date. As the complexity of creating the salary report increases, the owners want to use Excel to make the process easier.

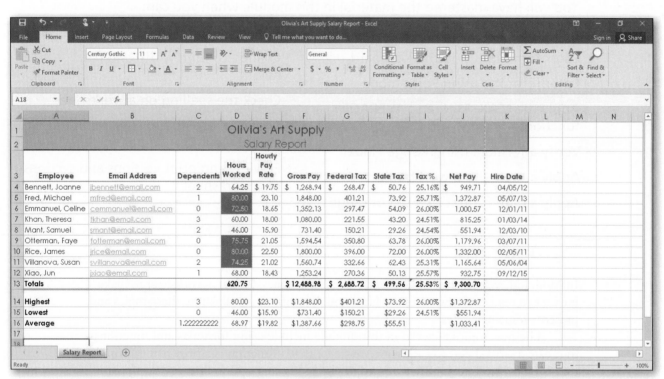

Figure 2–1

Recall that the first step in creating an effective worksheet is to make sure you understand what is required. The people who request the worksheet usually provide the requirements. The requirements document for the Olivia's Art Supply Salary Report worksheet includes the following needs: source of data, summary of calculations, and other facts about its development (Figure 2–2).

Worksheet Title	Olivia's Art Supply Salary Report
Needs	An easy-to-read worksheet that summarizes the company's salary report (Figure 2–3). For each employee, the worksheet is to include the employee's name, email address, number of dependents, hours worked, hourly pay rate, gross pay, federal tax, state tax, total tax percent, net pay, and hire date. The worksheet also should include the total pay for all employees, as well as the highest value, lowest value, and average for each category of data.
Source of Data	Supplied data includes employee names, number of dependents, hours worked, hourly pay rate, and hire dates.
Calculations	The following calculations must be made for each of the employees: 1. Gross Pay = Hours Worked * Hourly Pay Rate 2. Federal Tax = 0.22 * (Gross Pay * Number of Dependents * 24.32) 3. State Tax = 0.04 * Gross Pay 4. Tax % = (Federal Tax + State Tax) / Gross Pay 5. Net Pay = Gross Pay * (Federal Tax + State Tax) 6. Compute the totals for hours worked, gross pay, federal tax, state tax, and net pay 7. Compute the total tax percent 8. Use the MAX and MIN functions to determine the highest and lowest values for number of dependents, hours worked, hourly pay rate, gross pay, federal tax, state tax, total tax percent, and net pay 9. Use the AVERAGE function to determine the average for hours worked, number of dependents, hourly pay rate, gross pay, federal tax, state tax, and net pay

Figure 2–2

In addition, using a sketch of the worksheet can help you visualize its design. The sketch for the Olivia's Art Supply Salary Report worksheet includes a title, a subtitle, column and row headings, and the location of data values (Figure 2–3). It also uses specific characters to define the desired formatting for the worksheet, as follows:

1. The row of Xs below the leftmost column heading defines the cell entries as text, such as employee names.

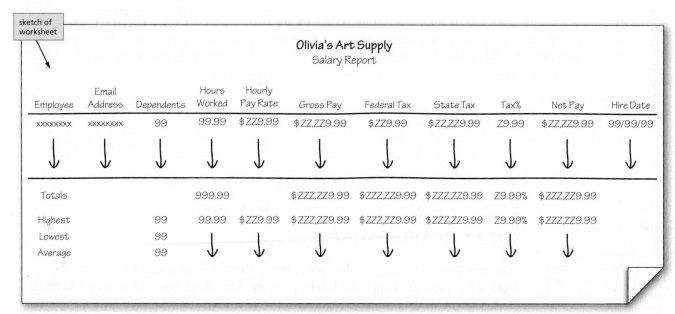

Figure 2–3

For an introduction to Windows and instructions about how to perform basic Windows tasks, read the Office and Windows module at the beginning of this book, where you can learn how to resize windows, change screen resolution, create folders, move and rename files, use Windows Help, and much more.

2. The rows of Zs and 9s with slashes, dollar signs, decimal points, commas, and percent signs in the remaining columns define the cell entries as numbers. The Zs indicate that the selected format should instruct Excel to suppress leading 0s. The 9s indicate that the selected format should instruct Excel to display any digits, including 0s.

3. The decimal point means that a decimal point should appear in the cell entry and indicates the number of decimal places to use.

4. The slashes in the last column identify the cell entry as a date.

5. The dollar signs that are adjacent to the Zs below the totals row signify a floating dollar sign, or one that appears next to the first significant digit.

6. The commas indicate that the selected format should instruct Excel to display a comma separator only if the number has sufficient digits (values in the thousandths) to the left of the decimal point.

7. The percent sign (%) in the Tax % column indicates a percent sign should appear after the number.

For an introduction to Office and instructions about how to perform basic tasks in Office apps, read the Office and Windows module at the beginning of this book, where you can learn how to run an application, use the ribbon, save a file, open a file, print a file, exit an application, use Help, and much more.

In this module, you will learn how to use functions and create formulas. The following roadmap identifies general activities you will perform as you progress through this module:

1. ENTER FORMULAS in the worksheet.

2. ENTER FUNCTIONS in the worksheet.

3. VERIFY FORMULAS in the worksheet.

4. FORMAT the WORKSHEET.

5. CHECK SPELLING.

6. PRINT the WORKSHEET.

CONSIDER THIS

What is the function of an Excel worksheet?

The function, or purpose, of a worksheet is to provide a user with direct ways to accomplish tasks. In designing a worksheet, functional considerations should supersede visual aesthetics. Consider the following when designing your worksheet:

• Avoid the temptation to use flashy or confusing visual elements within the worksheet.

• Understand the requirements document.

• Choose the proper functions and formulas.

• Build the worksheet.

BTW
Touch Screen Differences
The Office and Windows interfaces may vary if you are using a touch screen. For this reason, you might notice that the function or appearance of your touch screen differs slightly from this module's presentation.

Entering the Titles and Numbers into the Worksheet

The first step in creating the worksheet is to enter the titles and numbers into the worksheet. The following sets of steps enter the worksheet title and subtitle and then the salary report data shown in Table 2–1.

To Enter the Worksheet Title and Subtitle

With a good comprehension of the requirements document, an understanding of the necessary decisions, and a sketch of the worksheet, the next step is to use Excel to create the worksheet. The following steps enter the worksheet title and subtitle into cells A1 and A2.

1 Run Excel and create a blank workbook in the Excel window.

2 If necessary, select cell A1. Type **Olivia's Art Supply** in the selected cell and then press the DOWN ARROW key to enter the worksheet title.

3 Type **Salary Report** in cell A2 and then press the DOWN ARROW key to enter the worksheet subtitle.

To Enter the Column Titles

The column titles in row 3 begin in cell A3 and extend through cell K3. The employee names and the row titles begin in cell A4 and continue down to cell A16. The employee data is entered into rows 4 through 12 of the worksheet. The remainder of this section explains the steps required to enter the column titles, payroll data, and row titles, as shown in Figure 2–4, and then to save the workbook. The following steps enter the column titles.

1 With cell A3 selected, type **Employee** and then press the RIGHT ARROW key to enter the column heading.

2 Type **Email Address** in cell B3 and then press the RIGHT ARROW key.

3 In cell C3, type **Dependents** and then press the RIGHT ARROW key.

4 In cell D3, type **Hours** and then press the ALT+ENTER keys to enter the first line of the column heading. Type **Worked** and then press the RIGHT ARROW key to enter the column heading.

Q&A Why do I use the ALT+ENTER keys?
You press ALT+ENTER in order to start a new line in a cell. The final line can be completed by clicking the Enter button, pressing the ENTER key, or pressing one of the arrow keys. When you see ALT+ENTER in a step, press the ENTER key while holding down the ALT key and then release both keys.

5 Type **Hourly** in cell E3, press the ALT+ENTER keys, type **Pay Rate,** and then press the RIGHT ARROW key.

6 Type **Gross Pay** in cell F3 and then press the RIGHT ARROW key.

7 Type **Federal Tax** in cell G3 and then press the RIGHT ARROW key.

8 Type **State Tax** in cell H3 and then press the RIGHT ARROW key.

9 Type **Tax %** in cell I3 and then press the RIGHT ARROW key.

10 Type **Net Pay** in cell J3 and then press the RIGHT ARROW key.

11 Type **Hire Date** in cell K3 and then press the RIGHT ARROW key.

BTW
Screen Resolution
If you are using a computer or mobile device to step through the project in this module and you want your screens to match the figures in this book, you should change your screen's resolution to 1366 x 768. For information about how to change a computer's resolution, refer to the Office and Windows module at the beginning of this book.

BTW
Wrapping Text
If you have a long text entry, such as a paragraph, you can instruct Excel to wrap the text in a cell. This method is easier than your pressing ALT+ENTER to end each line of text within the paragraph. To wrap text, right-click in the cell, click Format Cells on a shortcut menu, click the Alignment tab, and then click Wrap text. Excel will increase the height of the cell automatically so that the additional lines will fit. If you want to control where each line ends in the cell, rather than letting Excel wrap the text based on the cell width, you must end each line with ALT+ENTER.

To Enter the Salary Data

The salary data in Table 2-1 includes a hire date for each employee. Excel considers a date to be a number and, therefore, it displays the date right-aligned in the cell. The following steps enter the data for each employee, except their email addresses, which will be entered later in this module.

① Select cell A4. Type **Bennett, Joanne** and then press the RIGHT ARROW key two times to enter the employee name and make cell C4 the active cell.

② Type **2** in cell C4 and then press the RIGHT ARROW key.

③ Type **64.25** in cell D4 and then press the RIGHT ARROW key.

④ Type **19.75** in cell E4.

⑤ Click cell K4 and then type **4/5/12**.

⑥ Enter the payroll data in Table 2–1 for the eight remaining employees in rows 5 through 12.

Q&A In Step 5, why did the date change from 4/5/12 to 4/5/2012?
When Excel recognizes a date in mm/dd/yy format, it formats the date as mm/dd/yyyy. Most professionals prefer to view dates in mm/dd/yyyy format as opposed to mm/dd/yy format to avoid confusion regarding the intended year. For example, a date displayed as 3/3/50 could imply a date of 3/3/1950 or 3/3/2050.

Table 2–1 Olivia's Art Supply Salary Report Data

Employee	Email Address	Dependents	Hours Worked	Hourly Pay Rate	Hire Date
Bennett, Joanne		2	64.25	19.75	4/5/12
Fred, Michael		1	80.00	23.10	5/7/13
Emmanuel, Celine		0	72.50	18.65	12/1/11
Khan, Theresa		3	60.00	18.00	1/3/14
Mant, Samuel		2	46.00	15.90	12/3/10
Otterman, Faye		0	75.75	21.05	3/7/11
Rice, James		0	80.00	22.50	2/5/11
Villanova, Susan		2	74.25	21.02	5/6/04
Xiao, Jun		1	68.00	18.43	9/12/15

Flash Fill

When you are entering data in a spreadsheet, occasionally Excel will recognize a pattern in the data you are entering. **Flash Fill** is an Excel feature that looks for patterns in the data and automatically fills or formats data in remaining cells. For example if column A contains a list of 10 phone numbers without parentheses around the area code or dashes after the prefix, Flash Fill can help create formatted phone numbers with relative ease. To use Flash Fill, simply start entering formatted phone numbers in cells next to the unformatted numbers. After entering a few formatted phone numbers, Flash Fill will suggest similarly formatted phone numbers for the remaining cells in the column. If you do not want to wait for Excel to offer suggestions, type one or two examples and then click the Flash Fill button (Data tab | Data Tools group). Flash fill will autocomplete the remaining cells. If Flash Fill makes a mistake, simply click the Undo button, enter a few more examples, and try again. In addition to formatting data, Flash Fill can perform tasks such as concatenating data from multiple cells and separating data from one cell into multiple cells.

To Use Flash Fill

In the Olivia's Art Supply Salary Report worksheet, you can use Flash Fill to generate email addresses using first and last names from another column in the worksheet. *Why? The Flash Fill feature is a convenient way to avoid entering a lot of data manually.* The following steps use Flash Fill to generate employee email addresses using the names entered in column A.

1
- Click cell B4 to select it.
- Type **jbennett@ email.com** and then press the DOWN ARROW key to select cell B5.
- Type **mfred@ email.com** and then click the Enter button to enter Michael Fred's email address in cell B5 (Figure 2–4).

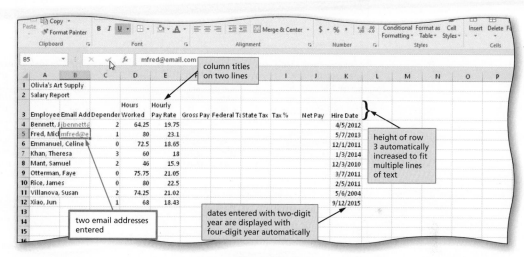

Figure 2–4

2
- Click Data on the ribbon to select the Data tab.
- Click Flash Fill (Data tab | Data Tools group) to enter similarly formatted email addresses in the range B6:B12.
- Remove the entries from cells B1 and B2 (Figure 2–5).

Q&A | Why was I unable to click the Flash Fill button after entering the first email address?

Figure 2–5

One entry might not have been enough for Excel to recognize a pattern. For instance, Flash Fill might have used the letter *j* before each last name in the email address, instead of using the first initial and last name.

What would have happened if I kept typing examples without clicking the Flash Fill button?
As soon as Excel recognized a pattern, it would have displayed suggestions for the remaining cells. Pressing the ENTER key when the suggestions appear will populate the remaining cells.

To Enter the Row Titles

The following steps add row titles for the rows that will contain the totals, highest, lowest, and average amounts.

1 Select cell A13. Type `Totals` and then press the DOWN ARROW key to enter a row header.

2 Type `Highest` in cell A14 and then press the DOWN ARROW key.

3 Type `Lowest` in cell A15 and then press the DOWN ARROW key.

4 Type `Average` in cell A16 and then press the DOWN ARROW key (Figure 2–6).

Figure 2–6

To Change the Sheet Tab Name and Color

The following steps change the sheet tab name, change the tab color, and save the workbook in the Excel folder (for your assignments).

1 Double-click the Sheet1 tab and then enter `Salary Report` as the sheet tab name and then press the ENTER key.

2 Right-click the sheet tab to display the shortcut menu.

3 Point to Tab Color on the shortcut menu to display the Tab Color gallery. Click Green (column 6, row 7) in the Standard Colors area to apply the color to the sheet tab.

4 Save the workbook in your hard drive, OneDrive, or other storage location using Olivia's Art Supply Salary Report as the file name.

Q&A Why should I save the workbook at this time?
You have performed many tasks while creating this workbook and do not want to risk losing work completed thus far.

Entering Formulas

One of the reasons Excel is such a valuable tool is that you can assign a formula to a cell, and Excel will calculate the result. A **formula** consists of cell references, numbers, and arithmetic operators that instruct Excel to perform a calculation. Consider, for example, what would happen if you had to multiply 64.25 by 19.75 and then manually enter the product for Gross Pay, 1,268.94, in cell F4. Every time the values in cells D4 or E4 changed, you would have to recalculate the product and enter the new value in cell F4. By contrast, if you enter a formula in cell F4 to multiply the values in cells D4 and E4, Excel recalculates the product whenever new values are entered into those cells and displays the result in cell F4.

A formula in a cell that contains a reference back to itself is called a **circular reference**. Excel warns you when you create circular references. In almost all cases, circular references are the result of an incorrect formula. A circular reference can be direct or indirect. For example, placing the formula =A1 in cell A1 results in a direct circular reference. A **direct circular reference** occurs when a formula refers to the same cell in which it is entered. An **indirect circular reference** occurs when a formula in a cell refers to another cell or cells that include a formula that refers back to the original cell.

BTW
Entering Numbers in a Range
An efficient way to enter data into a range of cells is to select a range and then enter the first number in the upper-left cell of the range. Excel responds by accepting the value and moving the active cell selection down one cell. When you enter the last value in the first column, Excel moves the active cell selection to the top of the next column.

To Enter a Formula Using the Keyboard

1 ENTER FORMULAS | 2 ENTER FUNCTIONS | 3 VERIFY FORMULAS
4 FORMAT WORKSHEET | 5 CHECK SPELLING | 6 PRINT WORKSHEET

The formulas needed in the worksheet are noted in the requirements document as follows:

1. Gross Pay (column F) = Hours Worked × Hourly Pay Rate
2. Federal Tax (column G) = 0.22 × (Gross Pay − Dependents × 24.32)
3. State Tax (column H) = 0.04 × Gross Pay
4. Tax % (column I) = (Federal Tax + State Tax) / Gross Pay
5. Net Pay (column J) = Gross Pay − (Federal Tax + State Tax)

The gross pay for each employee, which appears in column F, is equal to hours worked in column D times hourly pay rate in column E. Thus, the gross pay for Joanne Bennett in cell F4 is obtained by multiplying 64.25 (cell D4) by 19.75 (cell E4) or = C4 × D4. The following steps enter the initial gross pay formula in cell F4 using the keyboard. **Why?** *In order for Excel to perform the calculations, you must first enter the formulas.*

1

- With cell F4 selected, type **=d4*e4** in the cell to display the formula in the formula bar and the current cell and to display colored borders around the cells referenced in the formula (Figure 2–7).

Q&A What happens when I enter the formula?
The **equal sign** (=) preceding d4*e4 alerts Excel that you are entering a formula or function — not text. Because the most common error when entering a formula is to reference the wrong cell, Excel colors the cells referenced in the formula. The colored cells help you determine whether the cell references are correct. The asterisk (*) following d4 is the arithmetic operator for multiplication.

Is there a function, similar to the SUM function, that calculates the product of two or more numbers?
Yes. The **PRODUCT function** calculates the product of two or more numbers. For example, the function, =PRODUCT(D4,E4) will calculate the product of cells D4 and E4.

Figure 2–7

2

- Press the RIGHT ARROW key to complete the arithmetic operation indicated by the formula, display the result in the worksheet, and select the cell to the right (Figure 2–8). The number of decimal places on your screen may be different than shown in Figure 2–8, but these values will be adjusted later in this module.

Figure 2–8

BTW
Automatic Recalculation
Every time you enter a value into a cell in the worksheet, Excel automatically recalculates all formulas. You can change to manual recalculation by clicking the Calculation Options button (Formulas tab | Calculation group) and then clicking Manual. In manual calculation mode, pressing the F9 key instructs Excel to recalculate all formulas.

Arithmetic Operations

Excel provides powerful functions and capabilities that allow you to perform arithmetic operations easily and efficiently. Table 2–2 describes multiplication and other valid Excel arithmetic operators.

Table 2–2 Arithmetic Operations Listed in Order of Operations			
Arithmetic Operator	**Meaning**	**Example of Usage**	**Result**
–	Negation	–78	Negative 78
%	Percentage	=23%	Multiplies 23 by 0.01
^	Exponentiation	=3 ^ 4	Raises 3 to the fourth power
*	Multiplication	=61.5 * C5	Multiplies the contents of cell C5 by 61.5
/	Division	=H3 / H11	Divides the contents of cell H3 by the contents of cell H11
+	Addition	=11 + 9	Adds 11 and 9
–	Subtraction	=22 – F15	Subtracts the contents of cell F15 from 22

BTW
Troubling Formulas
If Excel does not accept a formula, remove the equal sign from the left side and complete the entry as text. Later, after you have entered additional data in the cells reliant on the formula or determined the error, reinsert the equal sign to change the text back to a formula and edit the formula as needed.

Order of Operations

When more than one arithmetic operator is involved in a formula, Excel follows the same basic order of operations that you use in algebra. The **order of operations** is the collection of rules that define which mathematical operations take precedence over the others in expressions with multiple operations. Moving from left to right in a formula, the order of operations is as follows: first negation (–), then all percentages (%), then all exponentiations (^), then all multiplications (*) and divisions (/), and, finally, all additions (+) and subtractions (–).

As in algebra, you can use parentheses to override the order of operations. For example, if Excel follows the order of operations, 8 * 3 + 2 equals 26. If you use parentheses, however, to change the formula to 8 * (3 + 2), the result is 40, because the parentheses instruct Excel to add 3 and 2 before multiplying by 8. Table 2–3 illustrates several examples of valid Excel formulas and explains the order of operations.

Table 2–3 Examples of Excel Formulas

Formula	Result
=G15	Assigns the value in cell G15 to the active cell.
=2^4 + 7	Assigns the sum of 16 + 7 (or 23) to the active cell.
=100 + D2 or =D2 +100 or =(100 + D2)	Assigns 100 plus the contents of cell D2 to the active cell.
=25% * 40	Assigns the product of 0.25 times 40 (or 10) to the active cell.
– (K15 * X45)	Assigns the negative value of the product of the values contained in cells K15 and X45 to the active cell. *Tip:* You do not need to type an equal sign before an expression that begins with a minus sign, which indicates a negation.
=(U8 – B8) * 6	Assigns the difference between the values contained in cells U8 and B8 times 6 to the active cell.
=J7 / A5 + G9 * M6 – Z2 ^ L7	Completes the following operations, from left to right: exponentiation (Z2 ^ L7), then division (J7 / A5), then multiplication (G9 * M6), then addition (J7 / A5) + (G9 * M6), and finally subtraction (J7 / A5 + G9 * M6) – (Z2 ^ L7). If cells A5 = 6, G9 = 2, J7 = 6, L7 = 4, M6 = 5, and Z2 = 2, then Excel assigns the active cell the value –5; that is, 6 / 6 + 2 * 5 – 2 ^ 4 = –5.

BTW
Parentheses
Remember that you can use parentheses to override the order of operations. You cannot use brackets or braces in place of parentheses in arithmetic operations.

To Enter Formulas Using Point Mode

1 ENTER FORMULAS | 2 ENTER FUNCTIONS | 3 VERIFY FORMULAS
4 FORMAT WORKSHEET | 5 CHECK SPELLING | 6 PRINT WORKSHEET

The sketch of the worksheet in Figure 2–3 calls for the federal tax, state tax, tax percentage, and net pay for each employee to appear in columns G, H, I, and J, respectively. All four of these values are calculated using formulas in row 4:

Federal Tax (cell G4) = 0.22 × (Gross Pay − Dependents × 24.32) or = 0.22 * (F4 − C4 * 24.32)
State Tax (cell H4) = 0.04 × Gross Pay or = 0.04 * F4
Tax % (cell I4) = (Federal Tax + State Tax) / Gross Pay or = (G4 + H4) / F4
Net Pay (cell J4) = Gross Pay − (Federal Tax + State Tax) or = F4 − (G4 + H4)

An alternative to entering the formulas in cells G4, H4, I4, and J4 using the keyboard is to enter the formulas using the pointer and Point mode. **Point mode** allows you to select cells for use in a formula by using the pointer. The following steps enter formulas using Point mode. *Why? Using Point mode makes it easier to create formulas without worrying about typographical errors when entering cell references.*

1

- With cell G4 selected, type =0.22*(to begin the formula and then click cell F4 to add a cell reference in the formula (Figure 2–9).

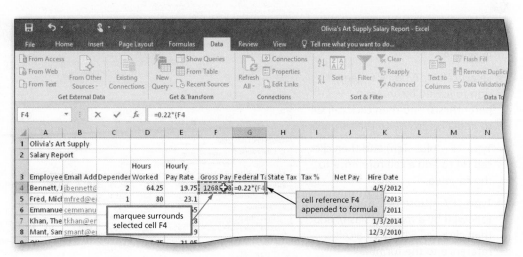

Figure 2–9

2

- Type **–** (minus sign) and then click cell C4 to add a subtraction operator and a reference to another cell to the formula.

- Type ***24.32)** to complete the formula (Figure 2–10).

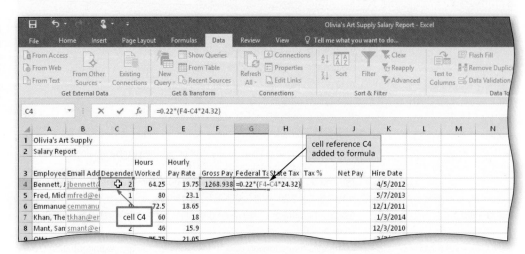

Figure 2–10

3

- Click the Enter button in the formula bar and then select cell H4 to prepare to enter the next formula.

- Type **=0.04*** and then click cell F4 to add a cell reference to the formula (Figure 2–11).

 Q&A

Why should I use Point mode to enter formulas?

Using Point mode to enter formulas often is faster and more accurate than using the keyboard, but only when the cell you want to select does not require you to scroll. In many instances, as in these steps, you may want to use

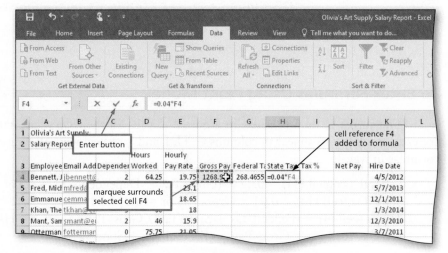

Figure 2–11

both the keyboard and pointer when entering a formula in a cell. You can use the keyboard to begin the formula, for example, and then use the pointer to select a range of cells.

4

- Click the Enter button in the formula bar to enter the formula in cell H4.

- Select cell I4. Type **= (** (equal sign followed by an open parenthesis) and then click cell G4 to add a reference to the formula.

- Type **+** (plus sign) and then click cell H4 to add a cell reference to the formula.

- Type **) /** (close parenthesis followed by a forward slash), and then click cell F4 to add a cell reference to the formula.

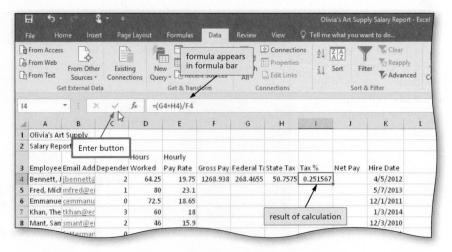

Figure 2–12

- Click the Enter button in the formula bar to enter the formula in cell I4 (Figure 2–12).

5

- Click cell J4, type = (equal sign) and then click cell F4.

- Type – ((minus sign followed by an open parenthesis) and then click cell G4.

- Type + (plus sign), click cell H4, and then type) (close parenthesis) to complete the formula (Figure 2–13).

- Click the Enter button.

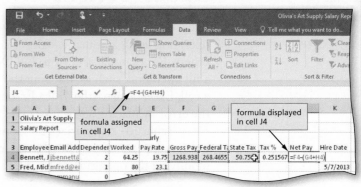

Figure 2–13

To Copy Formulas Using the Fill Handle

The five formulas for Joanne Bennett in cells F4, G4, H4, I4, and J4 now are complete. The next step is to copy them to the range F5:J12. When copying formulas in Excel, the source area is the cell, or range, from which data or formulas are being copied. When a range is used as a source, it sometimes is called the **source range**. The destination area is the cell, or range, to which data or formulas are being copied. When a range is used as a destination, it sometimes is called the **destination range**. Recall from Module 1 that the fill handle is a small square in the lower-right corner of the active cell or active range. The following steps copy the formulas using the fill handle.

1 Select the source range, F4:J4 in this case, activate the fill handle, drag the fill handle down through cell J12, and then continue to hold the mouse button to select the destination range.

2 Release the mouse button to copy the formulas to the destination range (Figure 2–14).

Q&A How does Excel adjust the cell references in the formulas in the destination area?
Recall that when you copy a formula, Excel adjusts the cell references so that the new formulas contain new cell references corresponding to the new locations and perform calculations using the appropriate values. Thus, if you copy downward, Excel adjusts the row portion of cell references relative to the source cell. If you copy across, then Excel adjusts the column portion of cell references relative to the source cell. Cell references that adjust relative to the location of the source cell are called **relative cell references**.

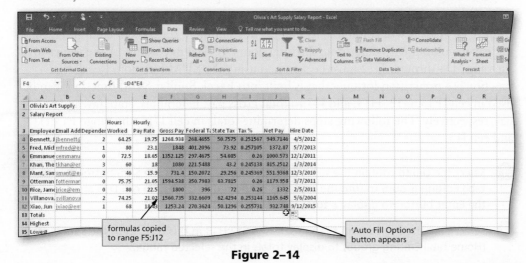

Figure 2–14

Option Buttons

Excel displays option buttons in a worksheet to indicate that you can complete an operation using automatic features such as AutoCorrect, Auto Fill, error checking, and others. For example, the 'Auto Fill Options' button shown in Figure 2–14 appears after a fill operation, such as dragging the fill handle. When an error occurs in a formula in a cell, Excel displays the Trace Error button next to the cell and identifies the cell with the error by placing a green triangle in the upper left of the cell.

Table 2–4 summarizes the option buttons available in Excel. When one of these buttons appears on your worksheet, click its arrow to produce the list of options for modifying the operation or to obtain additional information.

Table 2–4 Option Buttons in Excel

Name	Menu Function
Auto Fill Options	Provides options for how to fill cells following a fill operation, such as dragging the fill handle
AutoCorrect Options	Undoes an automatic correction, stops future automatic corrections of this type, or causes Excel to display the AutoCorrect Options dialog box
Insert Options	Lists formatting options following an insertion of cells, rows, or columns
Paste Options	Specifies how moved or pasted items should appear (for example, with original formatting, without formatting, or with different formatting)
Trace Error	Lists error-checking options following the assignment of an invalid formula to a cell

CONSIDER THIS

Why is the Paste Options button important?

The Paste Options button provides powerful functionality. When performing copy and paste operations, the button allows you great freedom in specifying what it is you want to paste. You can choose from the following options:

- Paste an exact copy of what you copied, including the cell contents and formatting.

- Copy only formulas.

- Copy only formatting.

- Copy only values.

- Copy a combination of these options.

- Copy a picture of what you copied.

BTW

Selecting a Range
You can select a range using the keyboard. Press the F8 key and then use the arrow keys to select the desired range. After you are finished, make sure to press the F8 key to turn off the selection process or you will continue to select ranges.

To Determine Totals Using the Sum Button

The next step is to determine the totals in row 13 for the hours worked in column D, gross pay in column F, federal tax in column G, state tax in column H, and net pay in column J. To determine the total hours worked in column D, the values in the range D4 through D12 must be summed using the SUM function. Recall that a function is a prewritten formula that is built into Excel. Similar SUM functions can be used in cells F13, G13, H13, and J13 to total gross pay, federal tax, state tax, and net pay, respectively. The following steps determine totals in cell D13, the range F13:H13, and cell J13.

1 Select the cell to contain the sum, cell D13 in this case. Click the Sum button (Home tab | Editing group) to sum the contents of the range D4:D12 in cell D13 and then click the Enter button to display a total in the selected cell.

2 Select the range to contain the sums, range F13:H13 in this case. Click the Sum button (Home tab | Editing group) to display totals in the selected range.

3 Select the cell to contain the sum, cell J13 in this case. Click the Sum button (Home tab | Editing group) to sum the contents of the range J4:J12 in cell J13 and then click the Enter button to display a total in the selected cell (Figure 2–15).

Q&A Why did I have to click the Enter button?
When calculating a sum for a single column, you click the Enter button. If you are calculating the sum for multiple ranges, you click the Sum button.

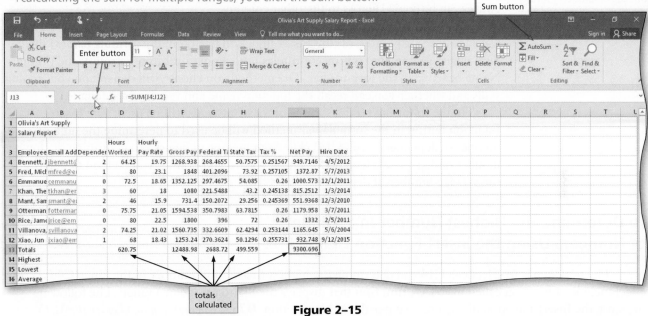

Figure 2–15

To Determine the Total Tax Percentage

With the totals in row 13 determined, the next step is to copy the tax percentage formula in cell I12 to cell I13. The following step copies the tax percentage formula.

1 Select the cell to be copied, I12 in this case, and then drag the fill handle down through cell I13 to copy the formula (Figure 2–16).

Q&A Why was the SUM function not used for tax percentage in I13?
The total tax percentage is calculated using the totals of the Gross Pay, Federal Tax and State Tax columns, not by summing the tax percentage column.

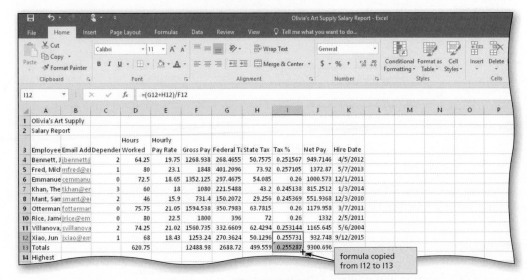

Figure 2–16

BTW
Statistical Functions
Excel usually considers a
blank cell to be equal to
0. The statistical functions,
however, ignore blank cells.
Excel thus calculates the
average of three cells with
values of 10, blank, and 8 to
be 9 [(10 + 8) / 2] and not 6
[(10 + 0 + 8) / 3].

Using the AVERAGE, MAX, and MIN Functions

The next step in creating the Olivia's Art Supply Salary Report worksheet is to compute the highest value, lowest value, and average value for the number of dependents listed in the range C4:C12 using the MAX, MIN, and AVERAGE functions in the range C14:C16. Once the values are determined for column C, the entries can be copied across to the other columns.

With Excel, you can enter functions using one of five methods: (1) keyboard, touch gesture, or pointer; (2) the Insert Function button in the formula bar; (3) the Sum menu; (4) the Sum button (Formulas tab | Function Library group); and (5) the Name box area in the formula bar. The method you choose will depend on your typing skills and whether you can recall the function name and required arguments.

In the following sections, three of these methods will be used. The Insert Function button in the formula bar method will be used to determine the highest number of dependents (cell C14). The Sum menu will be used to determine the lowest number of dependents (cell C15). The keyboard and pointer will be used to determine the average number of dependents (cell C16).

To Determine the Highest Number in a Range of Numbers Using the Insert Function Dialog Box

1 ENTER FORMULAS | 2 ENTER FUNCTIONS | 3 **VERIFY FORMULAS**
4 FORMAT WORKSHEET | 5 CHECK SPELLING | 6 PRINT WORKSHEET

The next step is to select cell C14 and determine the highest (maximum) number in the range C4:C12. Excel includes a function called the **MAX function** that displays the highest value in a range. The following steps use the Insert Function dialog box to enter the MAX function. *Why? Although you could enter the MAX function using the keyboard and Point mode as described previously, an alternative method to entering the function is to use the Insert Function button in the formula bar to open the Insert Function dialog box. The Insert Function dialog box is helpful if you do not remember the name of a function or need to search for a particular function by what it does.*

- Select the cell to contain the maximum number, cell C14 in this case.

- Click the Insert Function button in the formula bar to display the Insert Function dialog box.

- Click MAX in the Select a function list (Insert Function dialog box; Figure 2–17). You may need to scroll.

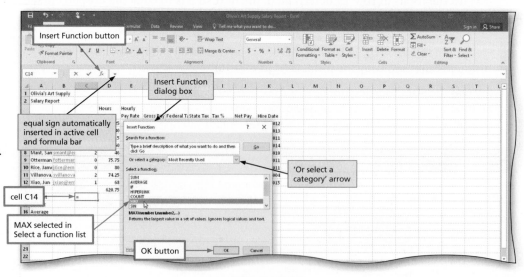

Figure 2–17

Q&A

What if the MAX function is not in the Select a function list?

Click the 'Or select a category' arrow to display the list of function categories, select All, and then scroll down and select the MAX function in the Select a function list.

How can I learn about other functions?

Excel has more than 400 functions that perform nearly every type of calculation you can imagine. These functions are categorized in the Insert Function dialog box shown in Figure 2–17. To view the categories, click the 'Or select a category' arrow. Click the name of a function in the Select a function list to display a description of the function.

2

- Click the OK button (Insert Function dialog box) to display the Function Arguments dialog box.

- Replace the text in the Number1 box with the text, **c4:c12** (Function Arguments dialog box) to enter the first argument of the function (Figure 2–18).

Q&A What are the numbers that appear to the right of the Number1 box in the Function Arguments dialog box?
The numbers shown to the right of the Number1 box are the values in the selected range (or if the range is large, the first few numbers only). Excel also displays the value the MAX function will return to cell C14 in the Function Arguments dialog box, shown in Figure 2–18.

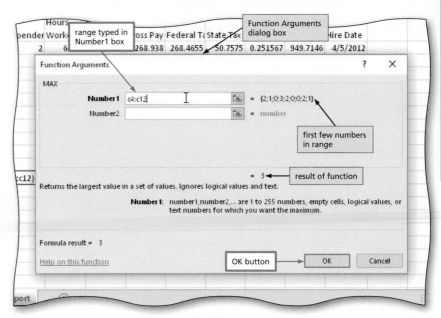

Figure 2–18

3

- Click the OK button (Function Arguments dialog box) to display the highest value in the chosen range in cell C14 (Figure 2–19).

Q&A Why should I not just enter the highest value that I see in the range C4:C12 in cell C14?
In this example, rather than entering the MAX function, you could examine the range C4:C12, determine that the highest number of dependents is 3, and manually enter the number 3 as a constant in cell C14. Excel would display the number similar to how it appears in Figure 2–19. However, because C14 would then contain a constant, Excel would continue to display 3 in cell C14 even if the values in the range change. If you use the MAX function, Excel will recalculate the highest value in the range each time a new value is entered.

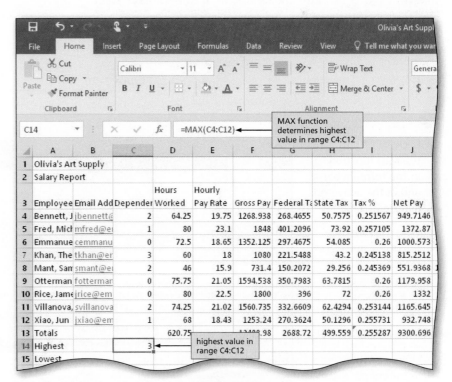

Figure 2–19

Other Ways

1. Click Sum arrow (Home tab | Editing group), click Max

2. Click Sum arrow (Formulas tab | Function Library group), click Max

3. Type **=MAX (** in cell, specify range, type **)**

To Determine the Lowest Number in a Range of Numbers Using the Sum Menu

1 ENTER FORMULAS | 2 ENTER FUNCTIONS | 3 VERIFY FORMULAS
4 FORMAT WORKSHEET | 5 CHECK SPELLING | 6 PRINT WORKSHEET

The next step is to enter the **MIN function** in cell C15 to determine the lowest (minimum) number in the range C4:C12. Although you can enter the MIN function using the method used to enter the MAX function, the following steps illustrate an alternative method using the Sum button (Home tab | Editing group). *Why? Using the Sum menu allows you quick access to five commonly used functions, without having to memorize their names or required arguments.*

1

- Select cell C15 and then click the Sum arrow (Home tab | Editing group) to display the Sum menu (Figure 2–20).

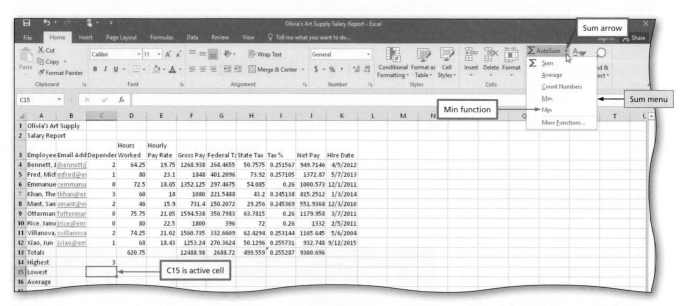

Figure 2–20

2

- Click Min to display the MIN function in the formula bar and in the active cell (Figure 2–21).

Q&A Why does Excel select the incorrect range?
The range selected by Excel is not always the right one. Excel attempts to guess which cells you want to include in the function by looking for ranges containing numeric data that are adjacent to the selected cell.

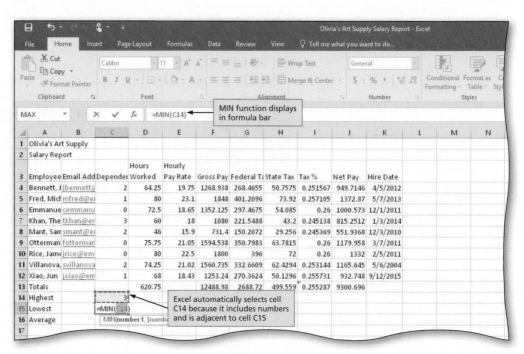

Figure 2–21

3

- Click cell C4 and then drag through cell C12 to update the function with the new range (Figure 2–22).

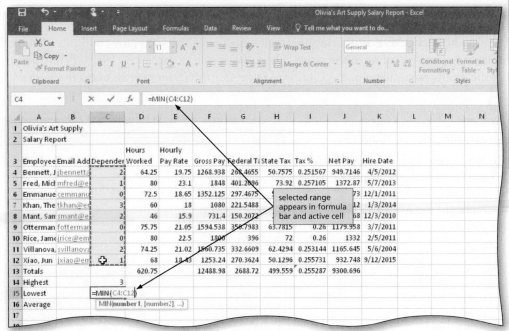

Figure 2–22

4

- Click the Enter button to determine the lowest value in the range C4:C12 and display the result in cell C15 (Figure 2–23).

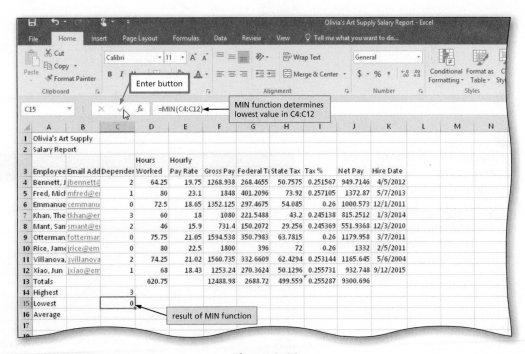

Figure 2–23

Other Ways

1. Click Insert Function button in formula bar, select Statistical category if necessary, click MIN, specify arguments

2. Click Sum arrow (Formulas tab | Function Library group), click Min

3. Type `=MIN(` in cell, fill in arguments, type)

To Determine the Average of a Range
of Numbers Using the Keyboard

The **AVERAGE function** sums the numbers in a specified range and then divides the sum by the number of cells with numeric values in the range. The following steps use the AVERAGE function to determine the average of the numbers in the range C4:C12. **Why?** *The AVERAGE function calculates the average of a range of numbers.*

1

- Select the cell to contain the average, cell C16 in this case.

- Type **=av** in the cell to display the Formula AutoComplete list. Press the DOWN ARROW key to highlight the AVERAGE function (Figure 2–24).

Q&A What is happening as I type?
As you type the equal sign followed by the characters in the name of a function, Excel displays the Formula AutoComplete list. This list contains those functions whose names match the letters you have typed.

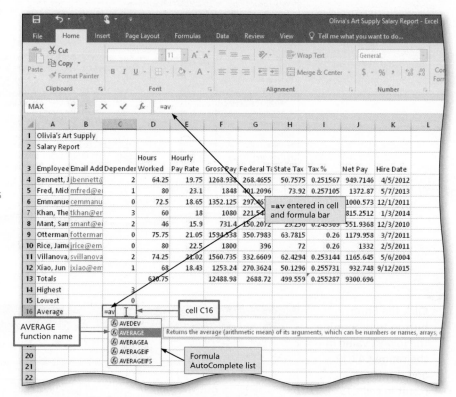

Figure 2–24

2

- Double-click AVERAGE in the Formula AutoComplete list to select the function.

- Select the range to be averaged, C4:C12 in this case, to insert the range as the argument to the function (Figure 2–25).

Q&A As I drag, why does the function in cell C16 change?
When you click cell C4, Excel surrounds cell C4 with a marquee and appends C4 to the left parenthesis in the formula bar. When you begin dragging, Excel appends to the argument a colon (:) and the cell reference of the cell where the pointer is located.

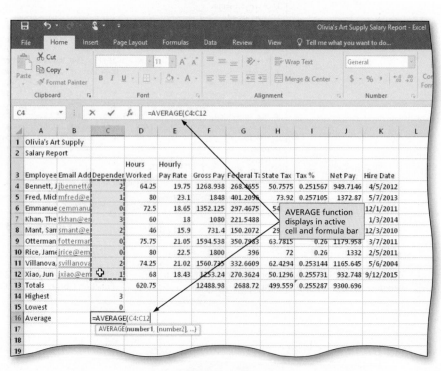

Figure 2–25

3

- Click the Enter button to compute the average of the numbers in the selected range and display the result in the selected cell (Figure 2–26).

Q&A Can I use the arrow keys to complete the entry instead?

No. While in Point mode, the arrow keys change the selected cell reference in the range you are selecting instead of completing the entry.

What is the purpose of the parentheses in the function?

Most Excel functions require that the argument (in this case, the range C4:C12) be included within parentheses following the function name. In this case, Excel appended the right parenthesis to complete the AVERAGE function when you clicked the Enter button.

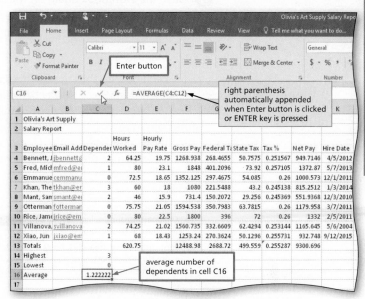

Figure 2–26

To Copy a Range of Cells across Columns to an Adjacent Range Using the Fill Handle

The next step is to copy the AVERAGE, MAX, and MIN functions in the range C14:C16 to the adjacent range D14:J16. The following steps use the fill handle to copy the functions.

1 Select the source range from which to copy the functions, in this case C14:C16.

2 Drag the fill handle in the lower-right corner of the selected range through cell J16 to copy the three functions to the selected range.

3 Select cell I16 and then press the DELETE key to delete the average of the Tax % (Figure 2–27).

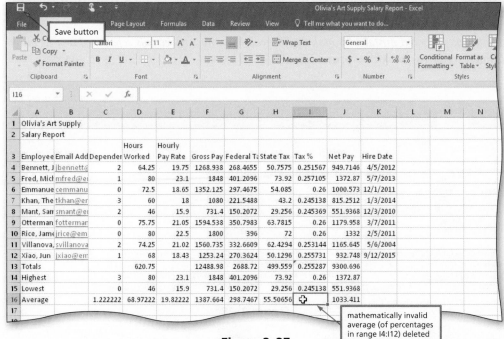

Figure 2–27

④ Save the workbook again on the same storage location with the same file name.

Q&A

Why delete the formula in cell I16?
You deleted the average in cell I16 because averaging this type of percentage is mathematically invalid.

How can I be sure that the function arguments are correct for the cells in range D14:J16?
Remember that Excel adjusts the cell references in the copied functions so that each function refers to the range of numbers above it in the same column. Review the functions in rows 14 through 16 by clicking on individual cells and examining the function as it appears in the formula bar. You should see that the functions in each column reference the appropriate ranges.

Other Ways

1. Select source area, click Copy button (Home tab | Clipboard group), select destination area, click Paste button (Home tab | Clipboard group)

2. Right-click source area, click Copy on shortcut menu; right-click destination area, click Paste icon on shortcut menu

3. Select source area and then point to border of range; while holding down CTRL, drag source area to destination area

4. Select source area, press CTRL+C, select destination area, press CTRL+V

Break Point: If you wish to take a break, this is a good place to do so. You can exit Excel now. To resume at a later time, run Excel, open the file called Olivia's Art Supply Salary Report, and continue following the steps from this location forward.

Verifying Formulas Using Range Finder

One of the more common mistakes made with Excel is to include an incorrect cell reference in a formula. An easy way to verify that a formula references the cells you want it to reference is to use Range Finder. **Range Finder** checks which cells are referenced in the formula assigned to the active cell.

To use Range Finder to verify that a formula contains the intended cell references, double-click the cell with the formula you want to check. Excel responds by highlighting the cells referenced in the formula so that you can verify that the cell references are correct.

To Verify a Formula Using Range Finder

1 ENTER FORMULAS | 2 ENTER FUNCTIONS | 3 **VERIFY FORMULAS**
4 FORMAT WORKSHEET | 5 CHECK SPELLING | 6 PRINT WORKSHEET

Why? *Range Finder allows you to correct mistakes by making immediate changes to the cells referenced in a formula.* The following steps use Range Finder to check the formula in cell I4.

1

• Double-click cell I4 to activate Range Finder (Figure 2–28).

2

• Press the ESC key to quit Range Finder and then click anywhere in the worksheet, such as cell A18, to deselect the current cell.

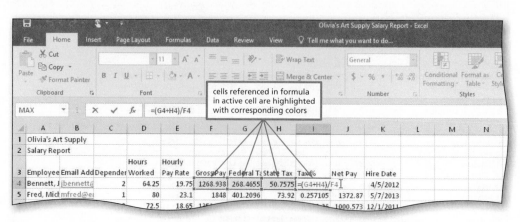

Figure 2–28

Formatting the Worksheet

Although the worksheet contains the appropriate data, formulas, and functions, the text and numbers need to be formatted to improve their appearance and readability.

In Module 1, cell styles were used to format much of the worksheet. This section describes how to change the unformatted worksheet in Figure 2–29a to the formatted worksheet in Figure 2–29b using a theme and other commands on the ribbon. A **theme** formats a worksheet by applying a collection of fonts, font styles, colors, and effects to give it a consistent appearance.

(a) Unformatted Worksheet

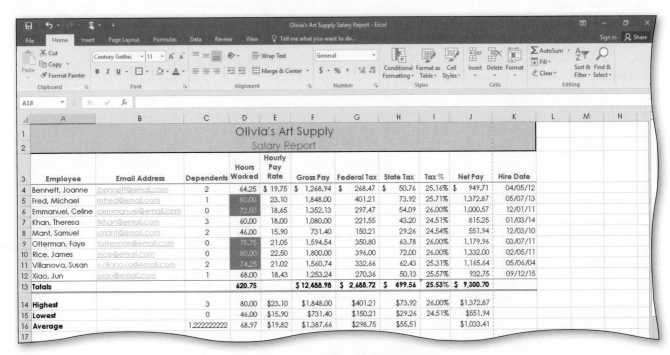

(b) Formatted Worksheet

Figure 2–29

To Change the Workbook Theme

Why? *A company or department may choose a specific theme as their standard theme so that all of their documents have a similar appearance. Similarly, you may want to have a theme that sets your work apart from the work of others. Other Office programs, such as Word and PowerPoint, include the same themes so that all of your Microsoft Office documents can share a common look.* The following steps change the workbook theme to the Ion theme.

1

- Click Page Layout to display the Page Layout tab.
- Click the Themes button (Page Layout tab | Themes group) to display the Themes gallery (Figure 2–30).

🔍 **Experiment**

- Point to several themes in the Themes gallery to preview the themes.

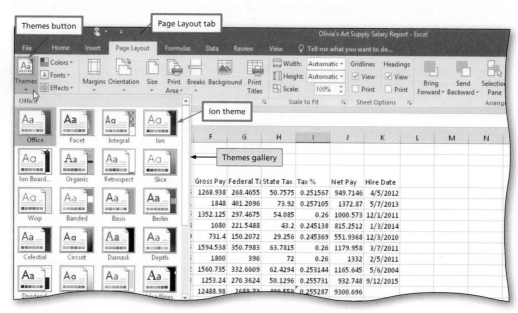

Figure 2–30

2

- Click Ion in the Themes gallery to change the workbook theme (Figure 2–31).

Q&A Why did the cells in the worksheet change?
Originally, the cells in the worksheet were formatted with the default font of the default Office theme. The Ion theme has a different default font than the Office theme, so when you changed the theme, the font changed. If you had modified the font for any cells, those cells would not have changed to the default font of the Ion theme.

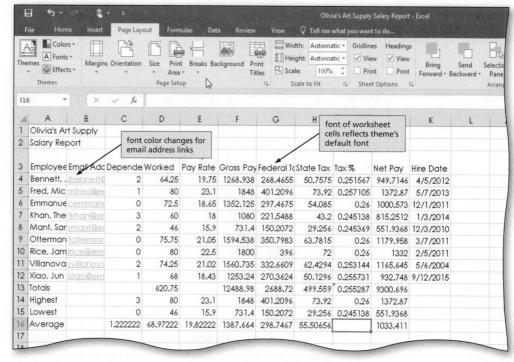

Figure 2–31

To Format the Worksheet Titles

The following steps merge and center the worksheet titles, apply the Title cells style to the worksheet titles, and decrease the font of the worksheet subtitle.

1 Display the Home tab.

2 Select the range to be merged, A1:K1 in this case, and then click the 'Merge & Center' button (Home tab | Alignment group) to merge and center the text in the selected range.

3 Select the range A2:K2 and then click the 'Merge & Center' button (Home tab | Alignment group) to merge and center the text.

4 Select the range to contain the Title cell style, in this case A1:A2, click the Cell Styles button (Home tab | Styles group) to display the Cell Styles gallery, and then click the Title cell style in the Cell Styles gallery to apply the Title cell style to the selected range.

5 Select cell A2 and then click the 'Decrease Font Size' button (Home tab | Font group) to decrease the font size of the selected cell to the next lower font size (Figure 2–32).

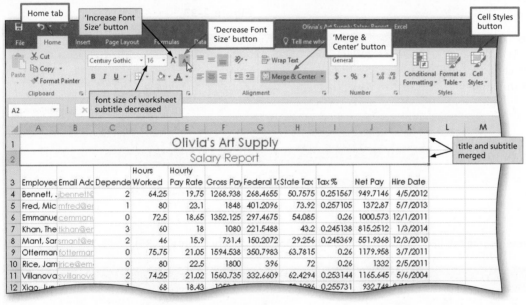

Figure 2–32

Q&A What happens when I click the 'Decrease Font Size' button?

When you click the 'Decrease Font Size' button, Excel assigns the next smaller font size in the Font Size gallery to the selected range. The 'Increase Font Size' button works in a similar manner, assigning the next larger font size in the Font Size gallery to the selected range.

Which colors work best when formatting your worksheet?

Knowing how people perceive colors can help you focus attention on parts of your worksheet. Warmer colors (red and orange) tend to reach toward the reader. Cooler colors (blue, green, and violet) tend to pull away from the reader.

To Change the Background Color and Apply a Box Border to the Worksheet Title and Subtitle

Why? *A background color and border can draw attention to the title of a worksheet.* The final formats assigned to the worksheet title and subtitle are the blue-gray background color and thick outside border. The following steps complete the formatting of the worksheet titles.

1

- Select the range A1:A2 and then click the Fill Color arrow (Home tab | Font group) to display the Fill Color gallery (Figure 2–33).

🔍 **Experiment**

- Point to a variety of colors in the Fill Color gallery to preview the selected colors in the range A1:A2.

Figure 2–33

2

- Click Blue-Gray, Accent 5, Lighter 60% (column 9, row 3) in the Theme Colors area to change the background color of the range of cells (Figure 2–34).

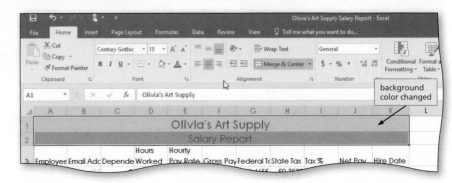

Figure 2–34

3

- Click the Borders arrow (Home tab | Font group) to display the Borders gallery (Figure 2–35).

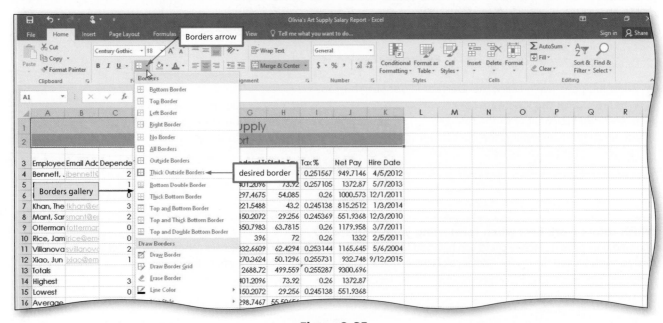

Figure 2–35

④

- Click 'Thick Outside Borders' in the Borders gallery to create a thick outside border around the selected range.

- Click anywhere in the worksheet, such as cell A18, to deselect the current range (Figure 2–36).

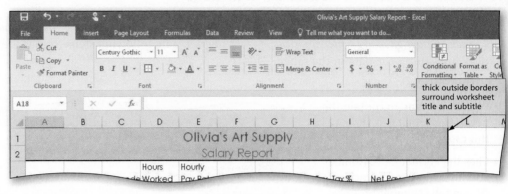

Figure 2–36

Other Ways

1. Click Font Settings Dialog Box Launcher (Home tab | Font group), click Fill tab (Format Cells dialog box), click desired fill, click OK button

2. Right-click range, click Format Cells on shortcut menu, click Fill tab (Format Cells dialog box), click desired fill, click OK button

3. Press CTRL+1, click Fill tab (Format Cells dialog box), click desired fill, click OK button

To Apply a Cell Style to the Column Headings and Format the Total Rows

As shown in Figure 2–29b, the column titles (row 3) should have the Heading 3 cell style and the totals row (row 13) should have the Total cell style. The headings in the range A14:A16 should be bold. The following steps assign these styles and formats to row 3, row 13, and the range A14:A16.

① Select the range to be formatted, cells A3:K3 in this case.

② Use the Cell Styles gallery to apply the Heading 3 cell style to the range A3:K3.

③ Click the Center button (Home tab | Alignment group) to center the column headings.

④ Apply the Total cell style to the range A13:K13.

⑤ Bold the range A14:A16 (Figure 2–37).

BTW

Color Selection
Bright colors jump out of a dark background and are easiest to see. White or yellow text on a dark blue, green, purple, or black background is ideal for highlighting.

BTW

Background Colors
The most popular background color is blue. Research shows that the color blue is used most often because this color connotes serenity, reflection, and proficiency. Use color in spreadsheets to highlight data or to format worksheet elements such as titles. In most cases, colors should not be used for data presentation.

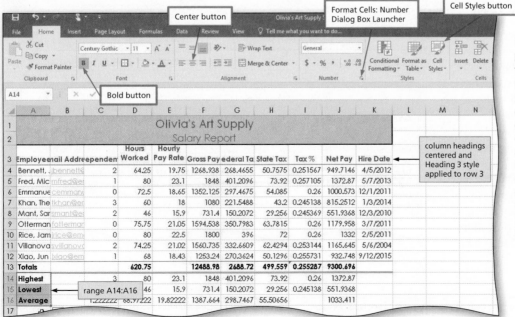

Figure 2–37

To Format Dates and Center Data in Cells

Why? *You may want to change the format of the dates to better suit your needs. In addition, numbers that are not used in calculations often are centered instead of right-aligned.* The following steps format the dates in the range K4:K12 and center the data in the range C4:C16.

1

- Select the range to contain the new date format, cells K4:K12 in this case.

- Click the Format Cells: Number Format Dialog Box Launcher (Home tab | Number group) (shown in Figure 2–37) to display the Format Cells dialog box.

- If necessary, click the Number tab (Format Cells dialog box), click Date in the Category list, and then click 03/14/12 in the Type list to choose the format for the selected range (Figure 2–38).

2

- Click the OK button (Format Cells dialog box) to format the dates in the current column using the selected date format style.

Figure 2–38

3

- Select the range C4:C16 and then click the Center button (Home tab | Alignment group) to center the data in the selected range.

- Select cell E4 to deselect the selected range (Figure 2–39).

Q&A How can I format an entire column at once?
Instead of selecting the range C4:C16 in Step 3, you could have clicked the column C heading immediately above cell C1, and then clicked the Center button (Home tab | Alignment group). In this case, all cells in column C down to the last cell in the worksheet would have been formatted to use center alignment. This same procedure could have been used to format the dates in column K.

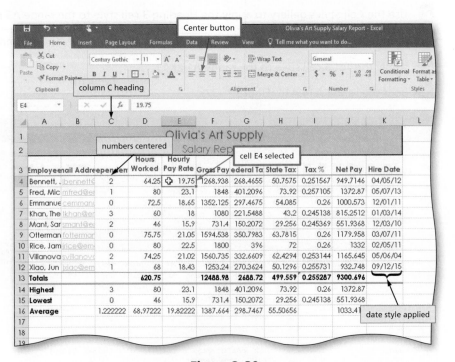

Figure 2–39

Other Ways

1. Right-click range, click Format Cells on shortcut menu, click Number tab (Format Cells dialog box), click desired number format, click OK button

2. Press CTRL+1, click Number tab (Format Cells dialog box), click desired number format, click OK button

To Apply an Accounting Number Format and Comma Style Format Using the Ribbon

As shown in Figure 2–29b, the worksheet is formatted to resemble an accounting report. In columns E through H and J, the numbers in the first row (row 4), the totals row (row 13), and the rows below the totals (rows 14 through 16) have dollar signs, while the remaining numbers (rows 5 through 12) in columns E through H and column J do not. The following steps assign formats using the 'Accounting Number Format' button and the Comma Style button. **Why?** *This gives the worksheet a more professional look.*

1 Select the range to contain the accounting number format, cells E4:H4 in this case.

2 While holding down the CTRL key, select cell J4, the range F13:H13, and cell J13 to select the nonadjacent ranges and cells.

3 Click the 'Accounting Number Format' button (Home tab | Number group) to apply the accounting number format with fixed dollar signs to the selected nonadjacent ranges.

Q&A What is the effect of applying the accounting number format?

The 'Accounting Number Format' button assigns a fixed dollar sign to the numbers in the ranges and rounds the figure to the nearest 100th. A fixed dollar sign is one that appears to the far left of the cell, with multiple spaces between it and the first digit in the cell.

4 Select the ranges to contain the comma style format, cells E5:H12 and J5:J12 in this case.

5 Click the Comma Style button (Home tab | Number group) to assign the comma style format to the selected ranges.

6 Select the range D4:D16 and then click the Comma Style button (Home tab | Number group) to assign the comma style format to the selected range (Figure 2–40).

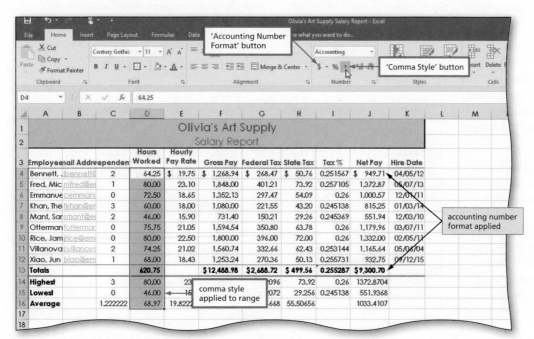

Figure 2–40

To Apply a Currency Style Format with a Floating Dollar Sign Using the Format Cells Dialog Box

1 ENTER FORMULAS | 2 ENTER FUNCTIONS | 3 VERIFY FORMULAS
4 FORMAT WORKSHEET | **5 CHECK SPELLING** | 6 PRINT WORKSHEET

Why? *The Currency format places dollar signs immediately to the left of the number (known as floating dollar signs, as they change position depending on the number of digits in the cell) and displays a zero for cells that have a value of zero.* The following steps use the Format Cells dialog box to apply the currency style format with a floating dollar sign to the numbers in the ranges E14:H16 and J14:J16.

1

- Select the ranges (E14:H16 and J14:J16) and then click the Number Format Dialog Box Launcher (Home tab | Number group) to display the Format Cells dialog box.

- If necessary, click the Number tab to display the Number sheet (Format Cells dialog box).

- Click Currency in the Category list to select the necessary number format category and then click the third style ($1,234.10) in the Negative numbers list to select the desired currency format for negative numbers (Figure 2–41).

Q&A How do I decide which number format to use?

Excel offers many ways to format numbers. Once you select a number category, you can select the number of decimal places, whether to include a dollar sign (or a symbol of another currency), and how negative numbers should appear. Selecting the appropriate negative numbers format is important, because some formats add a space to the right of the number in order to align numbers in the worksheet on the decimal points and some do not.

Figure 2–41

2

- Click the OK button (Format Cells dialog box) to assign the currency style format with a floating dollar sign to the selected ranges (Figure 2–42).

Q&A What is the difference between using the accounting number style and currency style?

When using the currency style, recall that a floating dollar sign always appears immediately to the left of the first digit. With the accounting number style, the fixed dollar sign always appears on the left side of the cell.

Figure 2–42

Other Ways

1. Press CTRL+1, click Number tab (Format Cells dialog box), click Currency in Category list, select format, click OK button

2. Press CTRL+SHIFT+DOLLAR SIGN ($)

To Apply a Percent Style Format and Use the Increase Decimal Button

The next step is to format the tax percentage in column I. **Why?** *Currently, Excel displays the numbers as decimal fractions when they should appear as percentages.* The following steps format the range I4:I15 to the percent style format with two decimal places.

1

- Select the range to format, cells I4:I15 in this case.

- Click the Percent Style button (Home tab | Number group) to display the numbers in the selected range as a rounded whole percent.

Q&A | What is the result of clicking the Percent Style button?
The Percent Style button instructs Excel to display a value as a percentage, which is determined by multiplying the cell entry by 100, rounding the result to the nearest percentage, and adding a percent sign. For example, when cell I4 is formatted using the Percent Style buttons, Excel displays the actual value 0.251567 as 25%.

2

- Click the Increase Decimal button (Home tab | Number group) two times to display the numbers in the selected range with two decimal places (Figure 2–43).

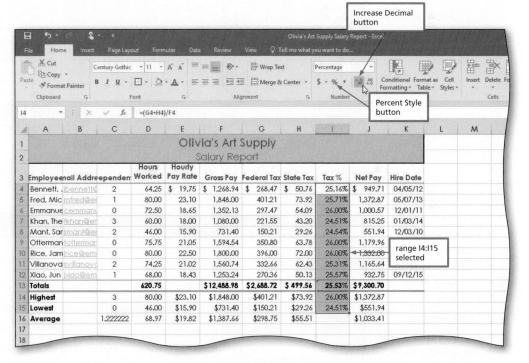

Figure 2–43

Other Ways

1. Right-click selected range, click Format Cells on shortcut menu, click Number tab (Format Cells dialog box), click Percentage in Category list, select format, click OK button

2. Press CTRL+1, click Number tab (Format Cells dialog box), click Percentage in Category list, select format, click OK button

3. Press CTRL+SHIFT+PERCENT SIGN (%)

Conditional Formatting

Conditional formatting offers you the ability to automatically change how a cell appears — the font, font color, background fill, and other options — based on the value in the cell. Excel offers a variety of commonly used conditional formatting rules, along with the ability to create your own custom rules and formatting. The next step is to emphasize the values greater than 72 in column D by formatting them to appear with a blue background and white font color (Figure 2–44).

BTW

Conditional Formatting
You can assign any format to a cell, a range of cells, a worksheet, or an entire workbook conditionally. If the value of the cell changes and no longer meets the specified condition, Excel suppresses the conditional formatting.

To Apply Conditional Formatting

The following steps assign conditional formatting to the range D4:D12. **Why?** *After formatting, any cell with a value greater than 72 in column D will appear with a blue background and a white font.*

1

- Select the range D4:D12.

- Click the Conditional Formatting button (Home tab | Styles group) to display the Conditional Formatting menu (Figure 2–44).

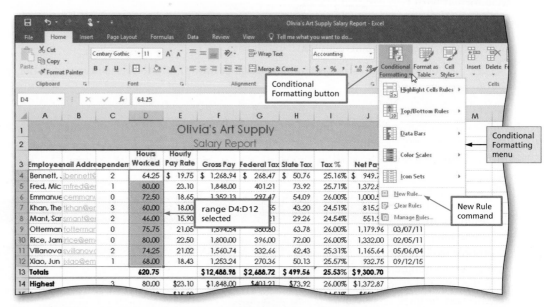

Figure 2–44

2

- Click New Rule on the Conditional Formatting menu to display the New Formatting Rule dialog box.

- Click 'Format only cells that contain' in the Select a Rule Type area (New Formatting Rule dialog box) to change the Edit the Rule Description area.

- In the Edit the Rule Description area, click the arrow in the relational operator box (second box) to display a list of relational operators, and then select greater than to select the desired operator.

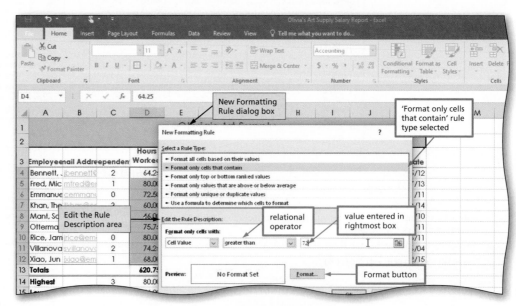

Figure 2–45

- Select the rightmost box, and then type   72   to enter the value of the rule description (Figure 2–45).

Q&A

What do the changes in the Edit the Rule Description area indicate?

The Edit the Rule Description area allows you to view and edit the rules for the conditional format. In this case, the rule indicates that Excel should format only those cells with cell values greater than 72.

3

- Click the Format button (New Formatting Rule dialog box) to display the Format Cells dialog box.

- If necessary, click the Font tab (Format Cells dialog box) to display the Font sheet. Click the Color arrow to display the Color gallery and then click White, Background 1 (column 1, row 1) in the Color gallery to select the font color (Figure 2–46).

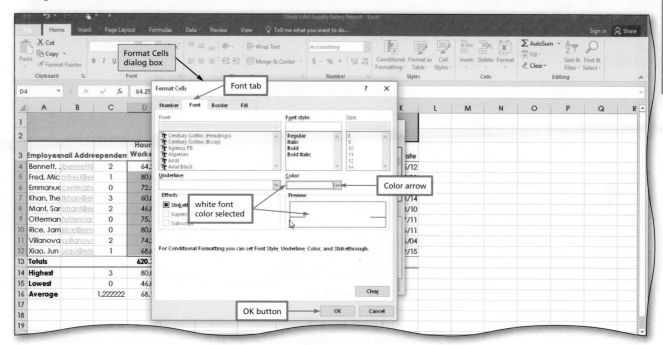

Figure 2–46

4

- Click the Fill tab (Format Cells dialog box) to display the Fill sheet and then click the blue color in column 9, row 1 to select the background color (Figure 2–47).

Figure 2–47

• Click the OK button (Format Cells dialog box) to close the Format Cells dialog box and display the New Formatting Rule dialog box with the desired font and background colors displayed in the Preview area (Figure 2–48).

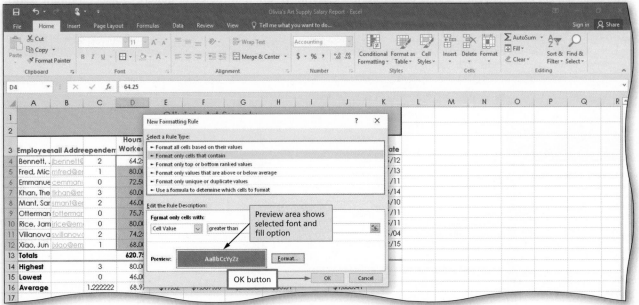

Figure 2–48

• Click the OK button (New Formatting Rule dialog box) to assign the conditional format to the selected range.

• Click anywhere in the worksheet, such as cell A18, to deselect the current range (Figure 2–49).

Q&A What should I do if I make a mistake setting up a rule?
If after you have applied the conditional formatting you realize you made a mistake when creating a rule, select the cell(s) with the rule you want to edit, click the Conditional Formatting button (Home tab | Styles group), select the rule you want to edit, and then click either the Edit Rule button (to edit the selected rule) or the Delete Rule button (to delete the selected rule).

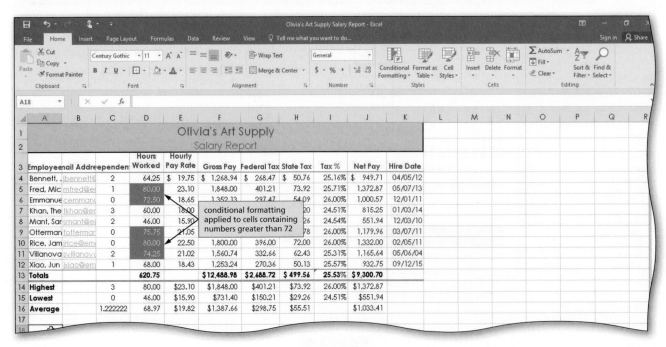

Figure 2–49

Conditional Formatting Operators

As shown in the New Formatting Rule dialog box, when the selected rule type is "Format only the cells that contain," the second text box in the Edit the Rule Description area allows you to select a relational operator, such as greater than, to use in the condition. The eight different relational operators from which you can choose for conditional formatting are summarized in Table 2–5.

Table 2–5 Summary of Conditional Formatting Relational Operators	
Relational Operator	**Formatting will be applied if...**
between	cell value is between two numbers
not between	cell value is not between two numbers
equal to	cell value is equal to a number
not equal to	cell value is not equal to a number
greater than	cell value is greater than a number
less than	cell value is less than a number
greater than or equal to	cell value is greater than or equal to a number
less than or equal to	cell value is less than or equal to a number

Changing Column Width and Row Height

You can change the width of the columns or height of the rows at any time to make the worksheet easier to read or to ensure that an entry fits properly in a cell. By default, all of the columns in a blank worksheet have a width of 8.43 characters, or 64 pixels. This value may change depending on the theme applied to the workbook. For example, when the Ion theme was applied to the workbook in this module, the default width of the columns changed to 8.38 characters. A **character** is defined as a letter, number, symbol, or punctuation mark. An average of 8.43 characters in 11-point Calibri font (the default font used by Excel) will fit in a cell.

The default row height in a blank worksheet is 15 points (or 20 pixels), which easily fits the 11-point default font. Recall from Module 1 that a point is equal to 1/72 of an inch. Thus, 15 points is equal to about 1/5 of an inch.

Another measure of the height and width of cells is pixels. A **pixel**, which is short for picture element, is a dot on the screen that contains a color. The size of the dot is based on your screen's resolution. At the resolution of 1366 × 768 used in this book, 1366 pixels appear across the screen and 768 pixels appear down the screen for a total of 1,049,088 pixels. It is these 1,049,088 pixels that form the font and other items you see on the screen.

To Change Column Width

1 ENTER FORMULAS | 2 ENTER FUNCTIONS | 3 VERIFY FORMULAS
4 FORMAT WORKSHEET | 5 CHECK SPELLING | 6 PRINT WORKSHEET

When changing the column width, you can set the width manually or you can instruct Excel to size the column to best fit. **Best fit** means that the width of the column will be increased or decreased so that the widest entry will fit in the column. *Why? Sometimes, you may prefer more or less white space in a column than best fit provides. To change the white space, Excel allows you to change column widths manually.*

When the format you assign to a cell causes the entry to exceed the width of a column, Excel changes the column width to best fit. If you do not assign a format to a cell or cells in a column, the column width will remain 8.43 characters. Recall from Module 1 that to set a column width to best fit, double-click the right boundary of the column heading above row 1. The following steps change the column widths.

1

- Drag through column headings A, B, and C above row 1 to select the columns.

- Point to the boundary on the right side of column heading C to cause the pointer to become a split double arrow (Figure 2–50).

Q&A

What if I want to make a large change to the column width?
If you want to increase or decrease column width significantly, you can right-click a column heading and then use the Column Width command on the shortcut menu to change the column's width. To use this command, however, you must select one or more entire columns.

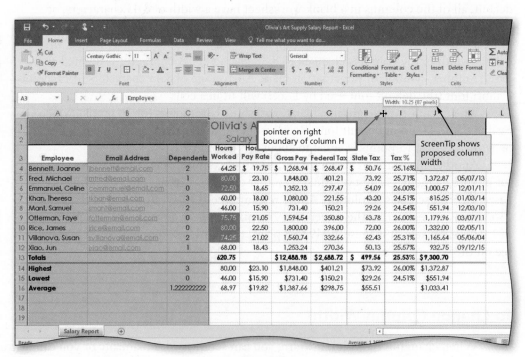

Figure 2–50

2

- Double-click the right boundary of column heading C to change the width of the selected columns to best fit.

- Point to the right boundary of the column H heading above row 1.

- When the pointer changes to a split double arrow, drag until the ScreenTip indicates Width: 10.25 (87 pixels). Do not release the mouse button (Figure 2–51).

Q&A

What happens if I change the column width to zero (0)?
If you decrease the column width to 0, the column is hidden. Hiding cells is a technique you can use to hide data that might not be relevant to a particular report. To instruct Excel to display a hidden column, position the mouse pointer to the right of the column heading boundary where the hidden column is located and then drag to the right.

Figure 2–51

3

- Release the mouse button to change the column width.

- Click the column D heading above row 1 to select the column.

- While holding down the CTRL key, click the column E heading and then the column I heading above row 1 so that nonadjacent columns are selected.

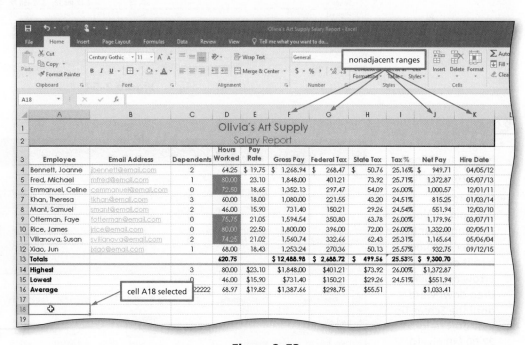

- Point to the boundary on the right side of the column I heading above row 1.

- Drag until the ScreenTip indicates Width: 7.50 (65 pixels). Do not release the mouse button (Figure 2–52).

Figure 2–52

4

- Release the mouse button to change the column widths.

- Click the column F heading and drag to select the column G heading.

- While holding down the CTRL key, click the column J heading and drag to select the column K heading above row 1 so that nonadjacent columns are selected.

- Drag the right boundary of column G until the ScreenTip indicates Width: 11.00 (93 pixels). Release the mouse button to change the column widths.

- Click anywhere in the worksheet, such as cell A18, to deselect the columns (Figure 2–53).

Figure 2–53

Other Ways

1. Click column heading or drag through multiple column headings, right-click selected column, click Column Width on shortcut menu, enter desired column width, click OK button

To Change Row Height

Why? *You also can increase or decrease the height of a row manually to improve the appearance of the worksheet.* When you increase the font size of a cell entry, such as the title in cell A1, Excel increases the row height to best fit so that it can display the characters properly. Recall that Excel did this earlier when multiple lines were entered in a cell in row 3, and when the cell style of the worksheet title and subtitle was changed. The following steps improve the appearance of the worksheet by increasing the height of row 3 to 48.00 points and increasing the height of row 14 to 27.00 points.

1

- Point to the boundary below row heading 3 until the pointer becomes a split double arrow.

- Drag down until the ScreenTip indicates Height: 48.00 (64 pixels). Do not release the mouse button (Figure 2–54).

Figure 2–54

2

- Release the mouse button to change the row height.

- Point to the boundary below row heading 14 until the pointer becomes a split double arrow and then drag downward until the ScreenTip indicates Height: 27.00 (36 pixels). Do not release the mouse button (Figure 2–55).

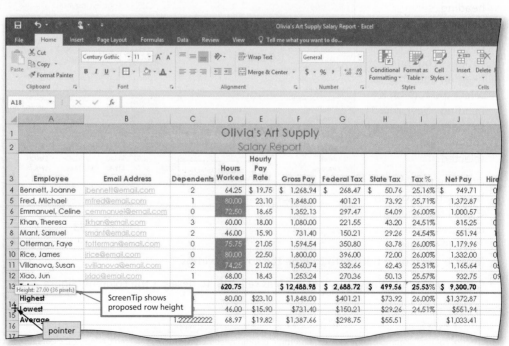

Figure 2–55

❸

- Release the mouse button to change the row height.

- Click anywhere in the worksheet, such as cell A18, to deselect the current cell (Figure 2–56).

Q&A Can I hide a row?
Yes. As with column widths, when you decrease the row height to 0, the row is hidden. To instruct Excel to display a hidden row, position the pointer just below the row heading boundary where the row is hidden and then drag downward. To set a row height to best fit, double-click the bottom boundary of the row heading. You also can hide and unhide rows by right-clicking the row or column heading and selecting the option to hide or unhide the cells.

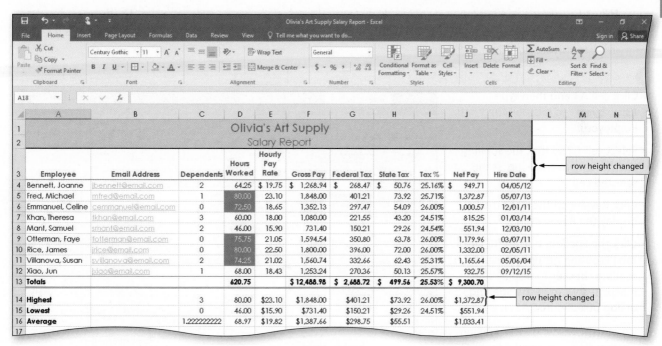

Figure 2–56

Other Ways

1. Right-click row heading or drag through multiple row headings, right-click selected heading, click Row Height on shortcut menu, enter desired row height, click OK button

Break Point: If you wish to take a break, this is a good place to do so. Be sure to save the Olivia's Art Supply Salary Report file again and then you can exit Excel. To resume at a later time, run Excel, open the file called Olivia's Art Supply Salary Report, and continue following the steps from this location forward.

Checking Spelling

Excel includes a **spelling checker** you can use to check a worksheet for spelling errors. The spelling checker looks for spelling errors by comparing words on the worksheet against words contained in its standard dictionary. If you often use specialized terms that are not in the standard dictionary, you may want to add them to a custom dictionary using the Spelling dialog box. When the spelling checker finds a word that is not in either dictionary, it displays the word in the Spelling dialog box. You then can correct it if it is misspelled.

BTW
Spell Checking
While Excel's spell checker is a valuable tool, it is not infallible. You should proofread your workbook carefully by pointing to each word and saying it aloud as you point to it. Be mindful of misused words such as its and it's, through and though, and to and too. Nothing undermines a good impression more than a professional looking report with misspelled words.

Does the spelling checker catch all spelling mistakes?

While Excel's spelling checker is a valuable tool, it is not infallible. You should proofread your workbook carefully by pointing to each word and saying it aloud as you point to it. Be mindful of misused words such as its and it's, through and though, your and you're, and to and too. Nothing undermines a good impression more than a professional report with misspelled words.

To Check Spelling on the Worksheet

1 ENTER FORMULAS | 2 ENTER FUNCTIONS | 3 VERIFY FORMULAS
4 FORMAT WORKSHEET | 5 CHECK SPELLING | 6 PRINT WORKSHEET

Why? *Everything in a worksheet should be checked to make sure there are no spelling errors.* To illustrate how Excel responds to a misspelled word, the following steps purposely misspell the word, Employee, in cell A3 as the word, Empolyee, as shown in Figure 2–57.

1

- Click cell A3 and then type **Empolyee** to misspell the word, Employee.

- Select cell A2 so that the spelling checker begins checking at the selected cell.

- Click Review on the ribbon to display the Review tab.

- Click the Spelling button (Review tab | Proofing group) to use the spelling checker to display the misspelled word in the Spelling dialog box (Figure 2–57).

What happens when the spelling checker finds a misspelled word?
When the spelling checker identifies that a cell contains a word not in its standard or custom dictionary, it selects that cell as the active cell and displays the Spelling dialog box. The Spelling dialog box displays the word that was not found in the dictionary and offers a list of suggested corrections (Figure 2–58).

Figure 2–57

2

- Verify that the word highlighted in the Suggestion area is correct.

- Click the Change button (Spelling dialog box) to change the misspelled word to the correct word (Figure 2–58).

- Click the Close button to close the Spelling dialog box.

- If a Microsoft Excel dialog box is displayed, click the OK button.

Figure 2–58

3

- Click anywhere in the worksheet, such as cell A18, to deselect the current cell.

- Display the Home tab.

- Save the workbook again on the same storage location with the same file name.

Q&A | What other actions can I take in the Spelling dialog box?
If one of the words in the Suggestions list is correct, select it and then click the Change button. If none of the suggested words are correct, type the correct word in the 'Not in Dictionary' text box and then click the Change button. To change the word throughout the worksheet, click the Change All button instead of the Change button. To skip correcting the word, click the Ignore Once button. To have Excel ignore the word for the remainder of the worksheet, click the Ignore All button.

Other Ways

1. Press F7

Additional Spelling Checker Considerations

Consider these additional guidelines when using the spelling checker:
- To check the spelling of the text in a single cell, double-click the cell to make the formula bar active and then click the Spelling button (Review tab | Proofing group).

- If you select a single cell so that the formula bar is not active and then start the spelling checker, Excel checks the remainder of the worksheet, including notes and embedded charts.

- If you select a cell other than cell A1 before you start the spelling checker, Excel will display a dialog box when the spelling checker reaches the end of the worksheet, asking if you want to continue checking at the beginning.

- If you select a range of cells before starting the spelling checker, Excel checks the spelling of the words only in the selected range.

- To check the spelling of all the sheets in a workbook, right-click any sheet tab, click 'Select All Sheets' on the sheet tab shortcut menu, and then start the spelling checker.

- To add words to the dictionary, such as your last name, click the 'Add to Dictionary' button in the Spelling dialog box (shown in Figure 2–58) when Excel flags the word as not being in the dictionary.

- Click the AutoCorrect button (shown in Figure 2–58) to add the misspelled word and the correct version of the word to the AutoCorrect list. For example, suppose that you misspell the word, do, as the word, dox. When the spelling checker displays the Spelling dialog box with the correct word, do, in the Suggestions list, click the AutoCorrect button. Then, anytime in the future that you type the word, dox, Excel will change it to the word, do.

Printing the Worksheet

Excel allows for a great deal of customization in how a worksheet appears when printed. For example, the margins on the page can be adjusted. A header or footer can be added to each printed page as well. A **header** is text and graphics that print at the

BTW

Error Checking
Always take the time to check the formulas of a worksheet before submitting it to your supervisor. You can check formulas by clicking the Error Checking button (Formulas tab | Formula Auditing group). You also should test the formulas by employing data that tests the limits of formulas. Experienced spreadsheet specialists spend as much time testing a workbook as they do creating it, and they do so before placing the workbook into production.

BTW

Distributing a Workbook
Instead of printing and distributing a hard copy of a workbook, you can distribute the workbook electronically. Options include sending the workbook via email; posting it on cloud storage (such as OneDrive) and sharing the file with others; posting it on social media, a blog, or other website; and sharing a link associated with an online location of the workbook. You also can create and share a PDF or XPS image of the workbook, so that users can view the file in Acrobat Reader or XPS Viewer instead of in Excel.

top of each page. Similarly, a **footer** is text and graphics that print at the bottom of each page. Excel also has the capability to alter the worksheet in Page Layout view. Page Layout view allows you to create or modify a worksheet while viewing how it will look in printed format. The default view that you have worked in up until this point in the book is called Normal view.

To Change the Worksheet's Margins, Header, and Orientation in Page Layout View

1 ENTER FORMULAS | 2 ENTER FUNCTIONS | 3 VERIFY FORMULAS
4 FORMAT WORKSHEET | 5 CHECK SPELLING | 6 PRINT WORKSHEET

The following steps change to Page Layout view, narrow the margins of the worksheet, change the header of the worksheet, and set the orientation of the worksheet to landscape. *Why? You may want the printed worksheet to fit on one page. You can do that by reducing the page margins and changing the page orientation to fit wider printouts across a sheet of paper. You can use the header to identify the content on each page.* **Margins** are those portions of a printed page outside the main body of the printed document and always are blank when printed. The current worksheet is too wide for a single page and requires landscape orientation to fit on one page in a readable manner.

1

● Click the Page Layout button on the status bar to view the worksheet in Page Layout view (Figure 2–59).

Q&A What are the features of Page Layout view?
Page Layout view shows the worksheet divided into pages. A gray background separates each page. The white areas surrounding each page indicate the print margins. The top of each page includes a Header area, and the bottom of each page includes a Footer area. Page Layout view also includes rulers at the top and left margin of the page that assists you in placing objects on the page, such as charts and pictures.

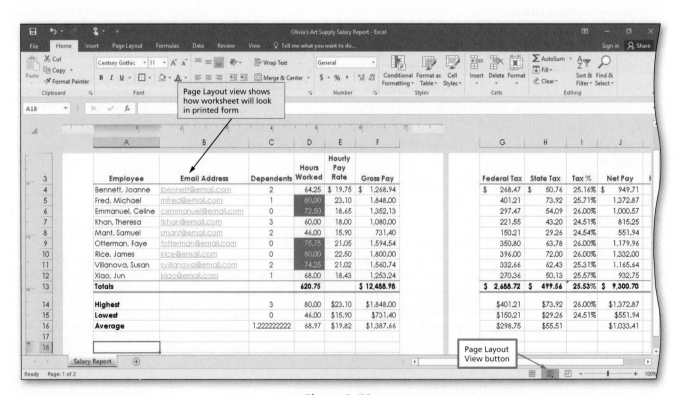

Figure 2–59

2

- Display the Page Layout tab.

- Click the Adjust Margins button (Page Layout tab | Page Setup group) to display the Margins gallery (Figure 2–60).

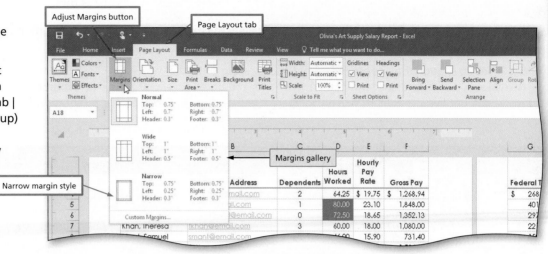

Figure 2–60

3

- Click Narrow in the Margins gallery to change the worksheet margins to the Narrow margin style.

- Click the center of the Header area above the worksheet title.

- Type **Jayne Smith** and then press the ENTER key. Type **Chief Financial Officer** to complete the worksheet header (Figure 2–61).

- If requested by your instructor, type your name instead of Jayne Smith.

- Select cell A6 to deselect the header.

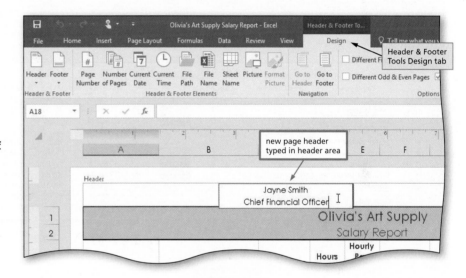

Figure 2–61

Q&A What else can I place in a header?

You can add additional text, page number information, date and time information, the file path of the workbook, the file name of the workbook, the sheet name of the workbook, and pictures to a header.

4

- Display the Page Layout tab.

- Click the 'Change Page Orientation' button (Page Layout tab | Page Setup group) to display the Change Page Orientation gallery (Figure 2–62).

Figure 2–62

5

- Click Landscape in the Change Page Orientation gallery to change the worksheet's orientation to landscape (Figure 2–63).

Q&A

Do I need to change the orientation every time I want to print the worksheet?

No. Once you change the orientation and save the workbook, Excel will save the orientation setting for that workbook until you change it. When you open a new workbook, Excel sets the orientation to portrait.

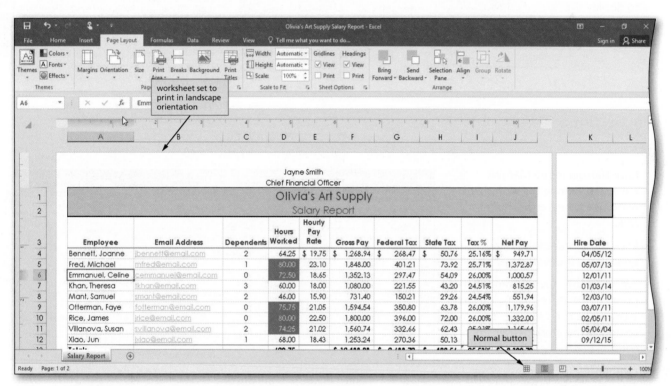

Figure 2–63

Other Ways

1. Click Page Setup Dialog Box Launcher (Page Layout tab | Page Setup group), click Page tab (Page Setup dialog box), click Portrait or Landscape, click OK button

To Print a Worksheet

Excel provides multiple options for printing a worksheet. In the following sections, you first print the worksheet and then print a section of the worksheet. The following steps print the worksheet.

1 Click File on the ribbon to open the Backstage view.

2 Click the Print tab in the Backstage view to display the Print gallery.

3 If necessary, click the Printer Status button in the Print gallery to display a list of available Printer options and then click the desired printer to change the currently selected printer.

4 Click the No Scaling button and then select 'Fit Sheet on One Page' to select it.

5 Click the Print button in the Print gallery to print the worksheet in landscape orientation on the currently selected printer.

6 When the printer stops, retrieve the hard copy (Figure 2–64).

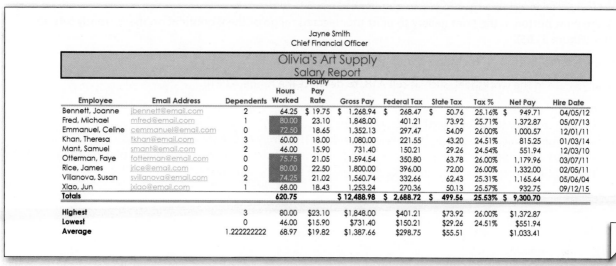

Employee	Email Address	Dependents	Hours Worked	Hourly Pay Rate	Gross Pay	Federal Tax	State Tax	Tax %	Net Pay	Hire Date
Bennett, Joanne	jbennett@email.com	2	64.25	$ 19.75	$ 1,268.94	$ 268.47	$ 50.76	25.16%	$ 949.71	04/05/12
Fred, Michael	mfred@email.com	1	80.00	23.10	1,848.00	401.21	73.92	25.71%	1,372.87	05/07/13
Emmanuel, Celine	cemmanuel@email.com	0	72.50	18.65	1,352.13	297.47	54.09	26.00%	1,000.57	12/01/11
Khan, Theresa	tkhan@email.com	3	60.00	18.00	1,080.00	221.55	43.20	24.51%	815.25	01/03/14
Mant, Samuel	smant@email.com	2	46.00	15.90	731.40	150.21	29.26	24.54%	551.94	12/03/10
Otterman, Faye	fotterman@email.com	0	75.75	21.05	1,594.54	350.80	63.78	26.00%	1,179.96	03/07/11
Rice, James	jrice@email.com	0	80.00	22.50	1,800.00	396.00	72.00	26.00%	1,332.00	02/05/11
Villanova, Susan	svillanova@email.com	2	74.25	21.02	1,560.74	332.66	62.43	25.31%	1,165.64	05/06/04
Xiao, Jun	jxiao@email.com	1	68.00	18.43	1,253.24	270.36	50.13	25.57%	932.75	09/12/15
Totals			620.75		$ 12,488.98	$ 2,688.72	$ 499.56	25.53%	$ 9,300.70	
Highest		3	80.00	$23.10	$1,848.00	$401.21	$73.92	26.00%	$1,372.87	
Lowest		0	46.00	$15.90	$731.40	$150.21	$29.26	24.51%	$551.94	
Average		1.222222222	68.97	$19.82	$1,387.66	$298.75	$55.51		$1,033.41	

Jayne Smith
Chief Financial Officer

Olivia's Art Supply
Salary Report

Figure 2–64

To Print a Section of the Worksheet

1 ENTER FORMULAS | 2 ENTER FUNCTIONS | 3 VERIFY FORMULAS
4 FORMAT WORKSHEET | 5 CHECK SPELLING | 6 PRINT WORKSHEET

You can print portions of the worksheet by selecting the range of cells to print and then clicking the Selection option button in the Print what area in the Print dialog box. *Why? To save paper, you only want to print the portion of the worksheet you need, instead of printing the entire worksheet.* The following steps print the range A3:F16.

1

- Select the range to print, cells A3:F16 in this case.
- Click File on the ribbon to open the Backstage view.
- Click the Print tab to display the Print gallery.
- Click 'Print Active Sheets' in the Settings area (Print tab | Print gallery) to display a list of options that determine what Excel should print (Figure 2–65).

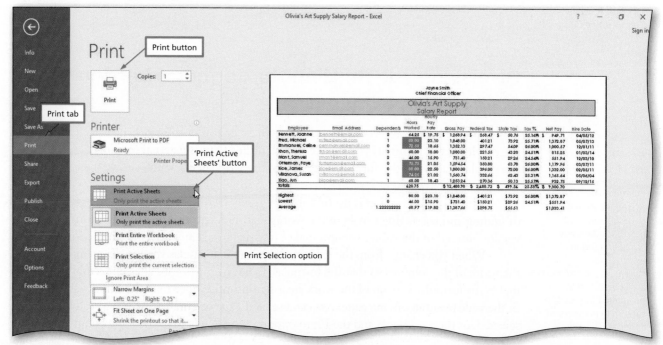

Figure 2–65

2

- Click Print Selection to instruct Excel to print only the selected range.

- Click the Print button in the Print gallery to print the selected range of the worksheet on the currently selected printer (Figure 2–66).

- Click the Normal button on the status bar to return to Normal view.

- Click anywhere in the worksheet, such as cell A18, to deselect the range A3:F16.

Q&A

What can I print?

Excel includes three options for selecting what to print (Figure 2–65). As shown in the previous steps, the Print Selection option instructs Excel to print the selected range. The 'Print Active Sheets' option instructs Excel to print the active worksheet (the worksheet currently on the screen) or selected worksheets. Finally, the 'Print Entire Workbook' option instructs Excel to print all of the worksheets in the workbook.

Jayne Smith
Chief Financial Officer

Employee	Email Address	Dependents	Hours Worked	Hourly Pay Rate	Gross Pay
Bennett, Joanne	jbennett@email.com	2	64.25	$ 19.75	$ 1,268.94
Fred, Michael	mfred@email.com	1	80.00	23.10	1,848.00
Emmanuel, Celine	cemmanuel@email.com	0	72.50	18.65	1,352.13
Khan, Theresa	tkhan@email.com	3	60.00	18.00	1,080.00
Mant, Samuel	smant@email.com	2	46.00	15.90	731.40
Otterman, Faye	fotterman@email.com	0	75.75	21.05	1,594.54
Rice, James	jrice@email.com	0	80.00	22.50	1,800.00
Villanova, Susan	svillanova@email.com	2	74.25	21.02	1,560.74
Xiao, Jun	jxiao@email.com	1	68.00	18.43	1,253.24
Totals			**620.75**		**$ 12,488.98**
Highest		3	80.00	$23.10	$1,848.00
Lowest		0	46.00	$15.90	$731.40
Average		1.222222222	68.97	$19.82	$1,387.66

Figure 2–66

Other Ways

1. Select range, click Print Area button (Page Layout tab | Page Setup group), click 'Set Print Area', click File tab to open Backstage view, click Print tab, click Print button

Displaying and Printing the Formulas Version of the Worksheet

BTW

Values versus Formulas

When completing class assignments, do not enter numbers in cells that require formulas. Most instructors will check both the values version and formulas version of your worksheets. The formulas version verifies that you entered formulas, rather than numbers, in formula-based cells.

Thus far, you have been working with the values version of the worksheet, which shows the results of the formulas you have entered, rather than the actual formulas. Excel also can display and print the formulas version of the worksheet, which shows the actual formulas you have entered, rather than the resulting values.

The formulas version is useful for debugging a worksheet. **Debugging** is the process of finding and correcting errors in the worksheet. Viewing and printing the formulas version instead of the values version makes it easier to see any mistakes in the formulas.

When you change from the values version to the formulas version, Excel increases the width of the columns so that the formulas do not overflow into adjacent cells, which makes the formulas version of the worksheet significantly wider than the values version. To fit the wide printout on one page, you can use landscape orientation, which already has been selected for the workbook, and the Fit to option in the Page tab in the Page Setup dialog box.

To Display the Formulas in the Worksheet and Fit the Printout on One Page

The following steps change the view of the worksheet from the values version to the formulas version of the worksheet and then print the formulas version on one page. *Why? Printing the formulas in the worksheet can help you verify that your formulas are correct and that the worksheet displays the correct calculations.*

1

• Press CTRL+ACCENT MARK (`) to display the worksheet with formulas.

• Click the right horizontal scroll arrow until column K appears (Figure 2–67).

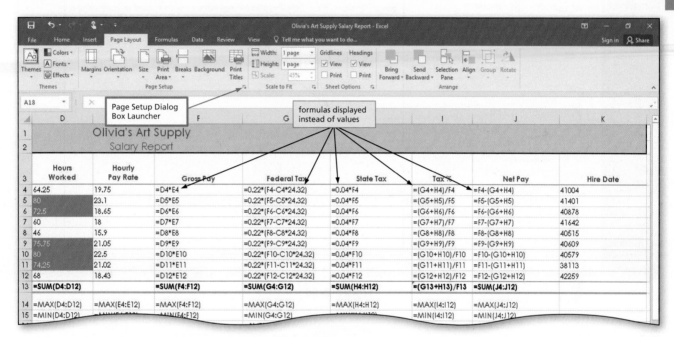

Figure 2–67

2

• Click the Page Setup Dialog Box Launcher (Page Layout tab | Page Setup group) to display the Page Setup dialog box (Figure 2–68).

• If necessary, click Landscape in the Orientation area in the Page tab to select it.

• If necessary, click the Fit to option button in the Scaling area to select it.

Figure 2–68

3

- Click the Print button (Page Setup dialog box) to open the Print tab in the Backstage view. In the Backstage view, select the Print Active Sheets option in the Settings area of the Print gallery (Figure 2–69).
- Click the Print button to print the worksheet.

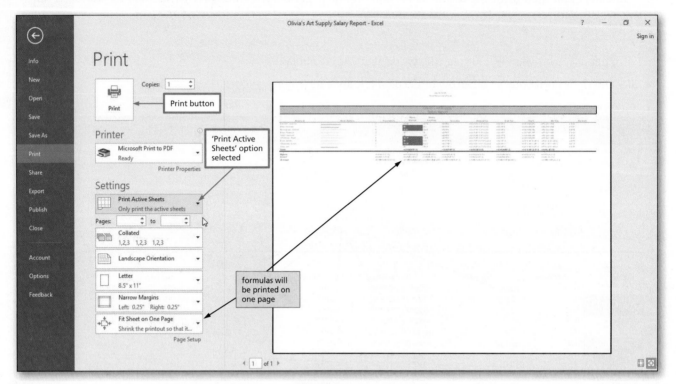

Figure 2–69

4

- After viewing and printing the formulas version, press CTRL+ACCENT MARK (`) to instruct Excel to display the values version.
- Click the left horizontal scroll arrow until column A appears.

To Change the Print Scaling Option Back to 100%

Depending on your printer, you may have to change the Print Scaling option back to 100% after using the Fit to option. Doing so will cause the worksheet to print at the default print scaling of 100%. The following steps reset the Print Scaling option so that future worksheets print at 100%, instead of being resized to print on one page.

1 If necessary, display the Page Layout tab and then click the Page Setup Dialog Box Launcher (Page Layout tab | Page Setup group) to display the Page Setup dialog box.

2 Click the Adjust to option button in the Scaling area to select the Adjust to setting.

3 If necessary, type 100 in the Adjust to box to adjust the print scaling to 100%.

4 Click the OK button (Page Setup dialog box) to set the print scaling to normal.

5 Display the Home tab.

6 Save the workbook again on the same storage location with the same file name.

7 If desired, sign out of your Microsoft account.

8 Exit Excel.

Q&A What is the purpose of the Adjust to box in the Page Setup dialog box?
The Adjust to box allows you to specify the percentage of reduction or enlargement in the printout of a worksheet. The default percentage is 100%. When you click the Fit to option button, this percentage changes to the percentage required to fit the printout on one page.

Summary

In this module you have learned how to enter formulas, calculate an average, find the highest and lowest numbers in a range, verify formulas using Range Finder, add borders, align text, format numbers, change column widths and row heights, and add conditional formatting to a range of numbers. In addition, you learned how to use the spelling checker to identify misspelled words in a worksheet, print a section of a worksheet, and display and print the formulas version of the worksheet using the Fit to option.

What decisions will you need to make when creating workbooks in the future?

1. Determine the workbook structure.

a) Determine the formulas and functions you will need for your workbook.

b) Sketch a layout of your data and functions.

2. Create the worksheet.

a) Enter the titles, subtitles, and headings.

b) Enter the data, desired functions, and formulas.

3. Format the worksheet.

a) Determine the theme for the worksheet.

b) Format the titles, subtitles, and headings using styles.

c) Format the totals, minimums, maximums, and averages.

d) Format the numbers and text.

e) Resize columns and rows.

CONSIDER THIS: PLAN AHEAD

Apply Your Knowledge

Reinforce the skills and apply the concepts you learned in this module.

Cost Analysis Worksheet

Note: To complete this assignment, you will be required to use the Data Files. Please contact your instructor for information about accessing the required files.

Instructions: Run Excel. Open the workbook Apply 2-1 Proximity Bus. You will enter and copy formulas and functions and apply formatting to the worksheet in order to analyze the costs associated with a bus company's fleet of vehicles, as shown in Figure 2–70.

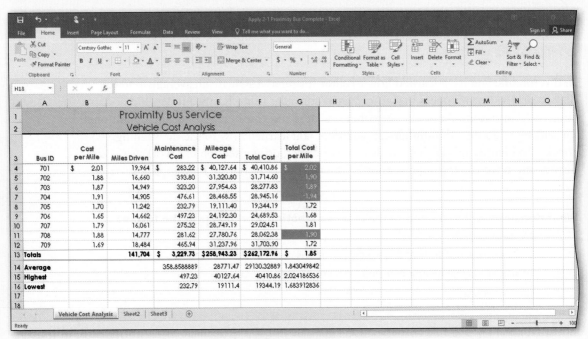

Figure 2–70

Perform the following tasks:

1. Use the following formulas in cells E4, F4, and G4:
   Mileage Cost (cell E4) = Cost per Mile * Miles Driven or = B4 * C4
   Total Cost (cell F4) = Maintenance Cost + Mileage Cost or = D4 + E4
   Total Cost per Mile (cell G4) = Total Cost / Miles Driven or = F4 / C4
   Use the fill handle to copy the three formulas in the range E4:G4 to the range E5:G12.

2. Determine totals for the miles driven, maintenance cost, mileage cost, and total cost in row 13. Copy the formula in cell G12 to G13 to assign the formula in cell G12 to G13 in the total line. If necessary, reapply the Total cell style to cell G13.

3. In the range D14:D16, determine the average value, highest value, and lowest value, respectively, for the values in the range D4:D12. Use the fill handle to copy the three functions to the range E14:G16.

4. Format the worksheet as follows:
   a. Change the workbook theme to Vapor Trail by using the Themes button (Page Layout tab | Themes group)
   b. Cell A1 — change to Title cell style
   c. Cell A2 — change to a font size of 16
   d. Cells A1:A2 — Red, Accent 1, Lighter 60% fill color and a thick outside borders
   e. Cells B4, D4:G4, and D13:G13 — accounting number format with two decimal places and fixed dollar signs by using the 'Accounting Number Format' button (Home tab | Number group)

   f. Cells B5:B12, and D5:G12 — comma style format with two decimal places by using the Comma Style button (Home tab | Number group)

   g. Cells C4:C13 — comma style format with no decimal places.

   h. Cells G4:G12 — apply conditional formatting so that cells with a value greater than 1.85 appear with a red background color and white font

5. If necessary increase the size of any columns that do not properly display data.

6. Switch to Page Layout view. Enter your name, course, laboratory assignment number, and any other information, as specified by your instructor, in the Header area.

7. Preview and print the worksheet in landscape orientation. Save the workbook using the file name, Apply 2-1 Proximity Bus Complete.

8. Use Range Finder to verify the formula in cell G13.

9. Print the range A3:D16. Press CTRL+ACCENT MARK (`) to change the display from the values version of the worksheet to the formulas version. Print the formulas version in landscape orientation on one page by using the Fit to option in the Page tab in the Page Setup dialog box. Press CTRL+ACCENT MARK (`) to change the display of the worksheet back to the values version. Close the workbook without saving it.

10. ✸ Besides adding a header to your document, can you think of anything else that could be added when printing the worksheet?

11. Submit the workbook as specified by your instructor.

Extend Your Knowledge

Extend the skills you learned in this module and experiment with new skills. You may need to use Help to complete the assignment.

Creating a Customer Tracking Worksheet for Jonee's Animal Supply

Note: To complete this assignment, you will be required to use the Data Files. Please contact your instructor for information about accessing the required files.

Instructions: Run Excel. Open the workbook Extend 2–1 Jonee's Animal Supply. You are to apply Flash Fill and four types of conditional formatting to cells in a worksheet (Figure 2–71).

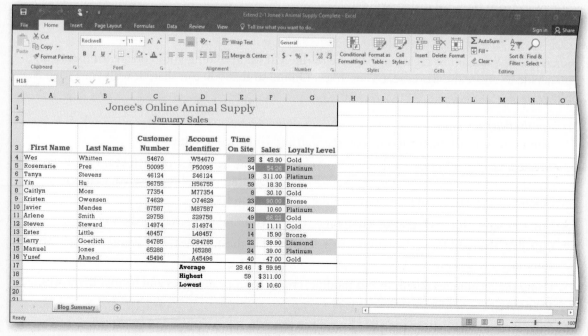

Figure 2–71

Continued >

Extend Your Knowledge *continued*

Perform the following tasks:

1. Add the account identifiers to the cells in the range D4:D16. The account identifier is determined by taking the first initial of the customer's last name followed by the entire customer number. For example, the account identifier for Wes Whitten is W54670. Continue entering two or three account identifiers, then use Flash Fill to complete the remaining cells. If necessary, add the thick bottom border back to cell D16.

2. Select the range E4:E16. Click the Conditional Formatting button (Home tab | Styles group) and then click New Rule on the Conditional Formatting menu. Select 'Format only top or bottom ranked values' in the Select a Rule Type area (New Formatting Rule dialog box).

3. If requested by your instructor, enter any value between 10 and 30 in the text box, (otherwise enter 20) in the Edit the Rule Description (New Formatting Rule dialog box) area, and then click the '% of the selected range' check box to select it.

4. Click the Format button, and choose a light purple background in the Fill sheet to assign this conditional format. Click the OK button in each dialog box and view the worksheet.

5. With range E4:E16 selected, apply a conditional format to the range that uses a yellow background color to highlight cells with scores that are below average. *Hint:* Explore some of the preset conditional rules to assist with formatting this range of cells.

6. With range F4:F16 selected, apply a conditional format to the range that uses a white font and green background to highlight cells that contain a value between 50 and 150.

7. With range G4:G16 selected, apply a conditional format to the range that uses a light gray background color to highlight cells that contain Platinum or Diamond. (*Hint:* You need to apply two separate formats, one for Platinum and one for Diamond.)

8. ✸ When might you want to look for values above the average in a worksheet?

9. Save the workbook using the file name, Extend 2–1 Jonee's Animal Supply Complete. Submit the revised workbook as specified by your instructor.

Expand Your World

Create a solution that uses cloud or web technologies by learning and investigating on your own from general guidance.

Four-Year College Cost Calculator

Instructions: You want to create an estimate of the cost for attending your college for four years. You decide to create the worksheet using Excel Online so that you can share it with your friends online.

Perform the following tasks:

1. Sign in to your Microsoft account on the web and run Excel Online.

2. Create a blank workbook. In the first worksheet, use row headings for each year of college (Freshman, Sophomore, Junior, and Senior). For the column headings, use your current expenses (such as car payment, rent, utilities, tuition, and food).

3. Enter expenses for each year based upon estimates you find by searching the web.

4. Calculate the total for each column. Also determine highest, lowest, and average values for each column.

5. Using the techniques taught in this module, create appropriate titles and format the worksheet accordingly.

6. Submit the assignment as specified by your instructor.

In the Labs

Design, create, modify, and/or use a workbook following the guidelines, concepts, and skills presented in this module. Labs 1 and 2, which increase in difficulty, require you to create solutions based on what you learned in the module; Lab 3 requires you to apply your creative thinking and problem-solving skills to design and implement a solution.

Lab 1: Insurance Premium Worksheet

Problem: You are a part-time assistant in the accounting department at Aylin Insurance, an Orlando-based insurance company. You have been asked to use Excel to generate a report that summarizes the existing balances on annual premiums, similar to the one shown in Figure 2–72. Include the three columns of customer data in Table 2-6 in the report, plus two additional columns to compute a monthly fee and a current balance for each customer. Assume no negative unpaid monthly balances.

Perform the following tasks:

1. Enter and format the worksheet title **Aylin Insurance** and worksheet subtitle **Premium Analysis** in cells A1 and A2. Change the theme of the worksheet to the Berlin theme. Apply the Title cell style to cells A1 and A2. Change the font size in cell A1 to 26 points, and change the font size in cell A2 to 18 points. Merge and center the worksheet title and subtitle across columns A through E. Draw a thick outside border around the range A1:A2.

2. Change the width of column A to 20.00 points. Change the widths of columns B through E to 14.00 points. Change the heights of row 3 to 36.00 points and row 14 to 25.50 points.

Table 2–6 Aylin Insurance Premium Data

Customer	Previous Balance	Payments
Albasco, Robin	1600.72	72.15
Deon, Jade	1518.62	382.3
Goodman, Brad	679.29	80.69
Hill, Raine	1060.42	107.6
Klonde, Albert	1178.83	125.63
Lang, Rose	1280.2	79.85
Moore, Jeffrey	1253.88	389.79
Piper, Taylor	477.11	278.52
Sothens, Mary	821.31	153.14

© 2015 Cengage Learning

Figure 2–72

Continued >

In the Labs *continued*

3. Enter the column titles in row 3 and row titles in the range A13:A16, as shown in Figure 2–72. Center the column titles in the range A3:E3. Apply the Heading 4 cell style to the range A3:E3. Apply the Total cell style to the range A13:E13. Bold the titles in the range A13:A16. Change the font size in the range A3:E16 to 12 points.

4. Enter the data in Table 2-6 in the range A4:C12.

5. Use the following formulas to determine the installment fee in column D and the current balance in column E for the first customer. Copy the two formulas down through the remaining customers.

   a. Installment Fee (cell D4) = 1% * Previous Balance

   b. Current Balance (E4) = Previous Balance – Payments + Installment Fee

6. Determine the totals in row 13.

7. Determine the average, minimum, and maximum values in cells B14:B16 for the range B4:B12, and then copy the range B14:B16 to C14:E16.

8. Format the numbers as follows: (a) assign the currency style with a floating dollar sign to the cells containing numeric data in the ranges B4:E4 and B13:E16, and (b) assign a number style with two decimal places and a thousand's separator (currency with no dollar sign) to the range B5:E12.

9. Use conditional formatting to change the formatting to white font on an orange background in any cell in the range D4:D12 that contains a value greater than 10.

10. Change the worksheet name from Sheet1 to Loan Balance and the sheet tab color to the Orange standard color.

11. Change the worksheet header with your name, course number, and other information as specified by your instructor.

12. Use the spelling checker to check the spelling in the worksheet. Preview and then print the worksheet in landscape orientation. Save the workbook using the file name, Lab 2-1 Aylin Insurance Premium Analysis.

13. ✸ When you created the formula for the installment fee, you used 1%. What would you have to do if the rate changed today to 2% to update the formulas?

Lab 2: **Sales Summary Worksheet**

Problem: You have been asked to build a worksheet for International Moving Company that analyzes the financing needs for the company's first year in business. The company plans to begin operations in January with an initial investment of $750,000.00. The expected revenue and costs for the company's first year are shown in Table 2–7. The desired worksheet is shown in Figure 2–73. The initial investment is shown as the starting balance for January (cell B4). The amount of financing required by the company is shown as the lowest ending balance (cell F18).

Table 2–7 International Moving Company Financing Needs Data		
Month	**Incomes**	**Expenses**
January	1209081	1262911
February	1163811	1381881
March	1300660	1250143
April	1229207	1209498
May	1248369	1355232
June	1196118	1260888
July	1162970	1242599
August	1195824	1368955
September	1305669	1235604
October	1224741	1383254
November	1159644	1411768
December	1210000	1540000

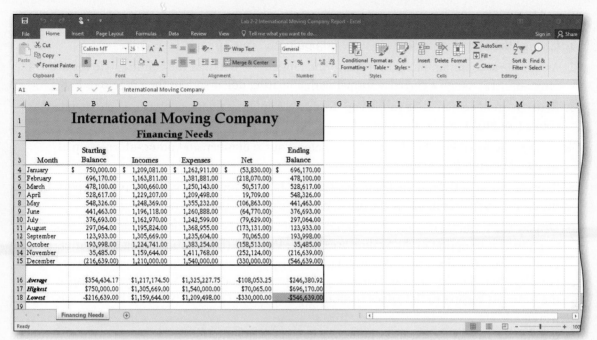

Figure 2–73

Perform the following tasks:

1. Apply the Slate theme to a new workbook.

2. Increase the width of column A to 12.00 and the width of columns B through F to 14.50.

3. Enter the worksheet title `International Moving Company` in cell A1 and the worksheet subtitle `Financing Needs` in cell A2. Enter the column titles in row 3, as shown in Figure 2–74. In row 3, use ALT+ENTER to start a new line in a cell.

4. Enter the financing needs data described in Table 2-7 in columns A, C, and D in rows 4 through 15. Enter the initial starting balance (cell B4) of 750000.00. Enter the row titles in the range A16:A18, as shown in Figure 2–73.

5. For the months of February through December, the starting balance is equal to the previous month's ending balance. Obtain the starting balance for February by setting the starting balance of February to the ending balance of January. Use a cell reference rather than typing in the data. Copy the formula for February to the remaining months.

6. Obtain the net amounts in column E by subtracting the expenses in column D from the incomes in column C. Enter the formula in cell E4 and copy it to the range E5:E15. Obtain the ending balance amounts in column F by adding the starting balance in column B to the net in column E. Enter the formula in cell F4 and copy it to the range F5:F15.

7. In the range B16:B18, use the AVERAGE, MAX, and MIN functions to determine the average value, highest value, and lowest value in the range B4:B15. Copy the range B16:B18 to the range C16:F18.

8. One at a time, merge and center the worksheet title and subtitle across columns A through F. Select cells A1 and A2 and change the background color to Tan, Accent 2 from the theme colors (column 6, row 1). Apply the Title cell style to cells A1 and A2. Change the worksheet title in cell A1 to 26-point. Bold both the title and subtitle. Draw a thick outside border around the range A1:A2.

9. Center the titles in row 3, columns A through F. Apply the Heading 2 cell style to the range A3:F3. Italicize and bold the row titles in the range A16:A18.

10. Draw a thick outside border around the range A16:F18. Change the background color for cell F18 to the same colors applied to the worksheet title in Step 8.

Continued >

In the Labs *continued*

11. Change the row heights of row 3 to 42.00 points and row 16 to 33.00 points.

12. Assign the accounting number format to the range B4:F4. Assign the comma style format to the range B5:F15. Assign a currency format with a floating dollar sign to the range B16:F18.

13. Rename the sheet tab as **Financing Needs**. Apply the Orange color from the standard colors (column 3) to the sheet tab.

14. Change the worksheet header with your name, course number, and other information as specified by your instructor.

15. Save the workbook using the file name, Lab 2-2 International Moving Company Report. Print the entire worksheet in landscape orientation. Next, print only the range A3:B15.

16. Display the formulas version by pressing CTRL+ACCENT MARK (`). Print the formulas version using the Fit to option in the Scaling area in the Page tab (Page Setup dialog box). After printing the worksheet, reset the Scaling option by selecting the Adjust to option in the Page tab (Page Setup dialog box) and changing the percent value to 100%. Change the display from the formulas version to the values version by pressing CTRL+ACCENT MARK (`). Do not save the workbook.

17. Submit the revised workbook as requested by your instructor.

18. ✳ In reviewing the worksheet you created, how do you think the company could obtain a positive result without increasing income or decreasing expenses?

Lab 3: **Consider This: Your Turn**

Apply your creative thinking and problem-solving skills to design and implement a solution.

Internet Service Summary

Instructions Part 1: You and your friends have decided to subscribe to a new Internet service provider. You would like to maximize services while keeping costs low. Research and find three Internet service providers in your area. If you cannot find three service providers in your area, you can research three service providers in another area of your choosing. For each company, find the best service package as well as the basic service package. Using the cost figures you find, calculate the cost per month for each service for a year. Include totals, minimum, maximum, and average values. Use the concepts and techniques presented in this module to create and format the worksheet.

Instructions Part 2: Which companies did you choose for your report? Which services offered the best deals that you would be willing to use?

PrattLast Associates : Database- C:\Users\Owner\Documents\CIS

Microsoft Access 2016

File   Home   Create   External Data   Database Tools   ♀ Tell me what you want to do...

1 Databases and Database Objects: An Introduction

Objectives

You will have mastered the material in this module when you can:

- Describe the features of the Access window
- Create a database
- Create tables in Datasheet and Design views
- Add records to a table
- Close a database
- Open a database
- Print the contents of a table
- Import data
- Create and use a query
- Create and use a form
- Create and print custom reports
- Modify a report in Layout view
- Perform special database operations
- Design a database to satisfy a collection of requirements

Introduction

The term **database** describes a collection of data organized in a manner that allows access, retrieval, and use of that data. Microsoft Access 2016, usually referred to as simply Access, is a database management system. A **database management system** is software that allows you to use a computer to create a database; add, change, and delete data in the database; ask and answer questions concerning the data; and create forms and reports using the data.

Project — Database Creation

PrattLast Associates is a human resources outsourcing company that provides HR services, such as payroll, hiring, training, and employee benefits management to small and medium-size businesses in the Midwest. Organizations might outsource only one function, such as payroll, or might outsource several functions. While there are many different ways to charge customers, PrattLast charges a set amount per employee per month. The amount varies based on number and type of functions outsourced.

Microsoft Access 2016

File   Home   Create   External Data   Database Tools   ♀ Tell me what you want to do...

PrattLast Associates : Database- C:\Users\Owner\Documents\CIS

Account managers serve their respective client companies by providing HR solutions and understanding the businesses for which they are responsible. The PrattLast account managers can earn bonuses if their client companies elect to outsource additional HR functions. For example, if the business currently outsources only payroll but is convinced by the account manager to add hiring to the outsourced functions, the account manager receives a bonus.

To ensure that operations run smoothly, PrattLast organizes data on its accounts and account managers in a database managed by Access. In this way, PrattLast keeps its data current and accurate and can analyze it for trends; PrattLast can also create a variety of useful reports.

In a **relational database** such as those maintained by Access, a database consists of a collection of tables, each of which contains information on a specific subject. Figure 1–1 shows the database for PrattLast Associates. It consists of two tables: the Account table (Figure 1–1a) contains information about PrattLast accounts, and the Account Manager table (Figure 1–1b) contains information about the account managers to whom these accounts are assigned.

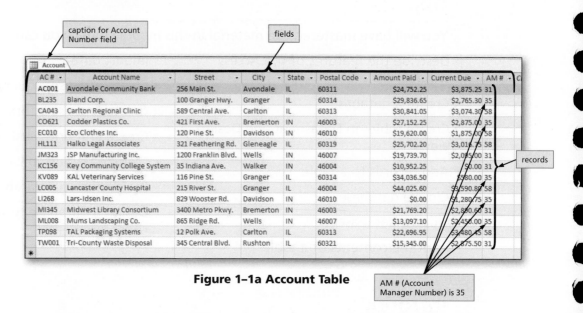

caption for Account Number field

fields

AC #	Account Name	Street	City	State	Postal Code	Amount Paid	Current Due	AM #	C
AC001	Avondale Community Bank	256 Main St.	Avondale	IL	60311	$24,752.25	$3,875.25	31	
BL235	Bland Corp.	100 Granger Hwy.	Granger	IL	60314	$29,836.65	$2,765.30	35	
CA043	Carlton Regional Clinic	589 Central Ave.	Carlton	IL	60313	$30,841.05	$3,074.30	58	
CO621	Codder Plastics Co.	421 First Ave.	Bremerton	IN	46003	$27,152.25	$2,875.00	35	
EC010	Eco Clothes Inc.	120 Pine St.	Davidson	IN	46010	$19,620.00	$1,875.00	58	
HL111	Halko Legal Associates	321 Feathering Rd.	Gleneagle	IL	60319	$25,702.20	$3,016.75	58	
JM323	JSP Manufacturing Inc.	1200 Franklin Blvd.	Wells	IN	46007	$19,739.70	$2,095.00	31	
KC156	Key Community College System	35 Indiana Ave.	Walker	IN	46004	$10,952.25	$0.00	31	
KV089	KAL Veterinary Services	116 Pine St.	Granger	IL	60314	$34,036.50	$580.00	35	
LC005	Lancaster County Hospital	215 River St.	Granger	IL	46004	$44,025.60	$3,590.80	58	
LI268	Lars-Idsen Inc.	829 Wooster Rd.	Davidson	IN	46010	$0.00	$1,280.75	35	
MI345	Midwest Library Consortium	3400 Metro Pkwy.	Bremerton	IN	46003	$21,769.20	$2,890.60	31	
ML008	Mums Landscaping Co.	865 Ridge Rd.	Wells	IN	46007	$13,097.10	$2,450.00	35	
TP098	TAL Packaging Systems	12 Polk Ave.	Carlton	IL	60313	$22,696.95	$3,480.45	58	
TW001	Tri-County Waste Disposal	345 Central Blvd.	Rushton	IL	60321	$15,345.00	$2,875.50	31	

records

Figure 1–1a Account Table

AM # (Account Manager Number) is 35

AM #	Last Name	First Name	Street	City	State	Postal Code	Start Date	Salary	Bonus Rate	C
31	Rivera	Haydee	325 Twiddy St.	Avondale	IL	60311	6/3/2013	$48,750.00	0.15	
35	Simson	Mark	1467 Hartwell St.	Walker	IN	46004	5/19/2014	$40,500.00	0.12	
42	Lu	Peter	5624 Murray Ave.	Davidson	IN	46007	8/3/2015	$36,750.00	0.09	
58	Murowski	Karen	168 Truesdale Dr.	Carlton	IL	60313	11/9/2016	$24,000.00	0.08	

Figure 1–1b Account Manager Table

AM # (Account Manager Number) for Mark Simson is 35

The rows in the tables are called **records**. A record contains information about a given person, product, or event. A row in the Account table, for example, contains information about a specific account, such as the account's name, address information, and other data.

PrattLast Associates : Database- C:\Users\Owner\Documents\CIS

Microsoft Access 2016

File   Home   Create   External Data   Database Tools   ○ Tell me what you want to do...

The columns in the tables are called fields. A **field** contains a specific piece of information within a record. In the Account table, for example, the fourth field, City, contains the name of the city where the account is located.

The first field in the Account table is AC #, which is an abbreviation for Account Number. PrattLast Associates assigns each account a number; the PrattLast account numbers consist of two uppercase letters followed by a three-digit number.

The account numbers are unique; that is, no two accounts have the same number. Such a field is a **unique identifier**. A unique identifier, as its name suggests, is a way of uniquely identifying each record in the database. A given account number will appear only in a single record in the table. Only one record exists, for example, in which the account number is JM323. A unique identifier is also called a **primary key**. Thus, the Account Number field is the primary key for the Account table. This means the Account Number field can be used to uniquely identify a record in the table. No two records can have the same value in the Account Number field.

The next seven fields in the Account table are Account Name, Street, City, State, Postal Code, Amount Paid, and Current Due. The Amount Paid column contains the amount that the account has paid PrattLast Associates year to date (YTD) prior to the current period. The Current Due column contains the amount due to PrattLast for the current period. For example, account JM323 is JSP Manufacturing Inc. The address is 1200 Franklin Blvd., in Wells, Indiana. The postal code is 46007. The amount paid is $19,739.70 and the current due amount is $2,095.00.

PrattLast assigns a single account manager to work with each account. The last column in the Account table, AM # (an abbreviation for Account Manager Number) gives the number of the account's account manager. The account manager number for JSP Manufacturing is 31.

The first field in the Account Manager table is also AM #, for Account Manager Number. The account manager numbers are unique, so the Account Manager Number field is the primary key of the Account Manager table.

The other fields in the Account Manager table are Last Name, First Name, Street, City, State, Postal Code, Start Date, Salary, and Bonus Rate. The Start Date field gives the date the account manager began working for PrattLast. The Salary field gives the salary paid to the account manager thus far this year. The Bonus Rate gives the potential bonus percentage based on personal performance. The bonus rate applies when the account manager either brings in new business or recommends productivity improvements. For example, account manager 31 is Haydee Rivera. Her address is 325 Twiddy St., in Avondale, Illinois. Her postal code is 60311. Haydee started working for PrattLast on June 3, 2013. So far this year, she has been paid $48,750.00 in salary. Her bonus rate is 0.15 (15%).

The account manager number appears in both the Account table and the Account Manager table, and relates accounts and account managers. Account manager 42, Peter Lu, was recently promoted to account manager and has not yet been assigned any accounts. His account manager number, therefore, does not appear on any row in the Account table.

BTW
Naming Fields
Access 2016 has a number of reserved words, words that have a special meaning to Access. You cannot use these reserved words as field names. For example, Name is a reserved word and could not be used in the Account table to describe an account's name. For a complete list of reserved words in Access 2016, consult Access Help.

How would you find the name of the account manager for Midwest Library Consortium?

In the Account table, you see that the account manager number for account Midwest Library Consortium is 31. To find the name of this account manager, look for the row in the Account Manager table that contains 31 in the AM # column. After you have found it, you know that the account manager for Midwest Library Consortium is Haydee Rivera.

CONSIDER THIS

How would you find all the accounts assigned to Haydee Rivera?
First, look in the Account Manager table to find that her number is 31. You would then look through the Account table for all the accounts that contain 31 in the AM # column. Haydee's accounts are AC001 (Avondale Community Bank), JM323 (JSP Manufacturing Inc.), KC156 (Key Community College System), MI345 (Midwest Library Consortium), and TW001 (Tri-County Waste Disposal).

For an introduction to Windows and instructions about how to perform basic Windows tasks, read the Office and Windows module at the beginning of this book, where you can learn how to resize windows, change screen resolution, create folders, move and rename files, use Windows Help, and much more.

In this module, you will learn how to create and use the database shown in Figure 1–1. The following roadmap identifies general activities you will perform as you progress through this module:

1. CREATE the FIRST TABLE, Account Manager, using Datasheet view.
2. ADD RECORDS to the Account Manager table.
3. PRINT the CONTENTS of the Account Manager table.
4. IMPORT RECORDS into the second table, Account.
5. MODIFY the SECOND TABLE using Design view.
6. CREATE a QUERY for the Account table.
7. CREATE a FORM for the Account table.
8. CREATE a REPORT for the Account table.

Creating a Database

For an introduction to Office and instructions about how to perform basic tasks in Office apps, read the Office and Windows module at the beginning of this book, where you can learn how to run an application, use the ribbon, save a file, open a file, print a file, exit an application, use Help, and much more.

In Access, all the tables, reports, forms, and queries that you create are stored in a single file called a database. A database is a structure that can store information about multiple types of objects, the properties of those objects, and the relationships among the objects. The first step is to create the database that will hold your tables, reports, forms, and queries. You can use either the Blank desktop database option or a template to create a new database. If you already know the tables and fields you want in your database, you would use the Blank desktop database option. If not, you can use a template. Templates can guide you by suggesting some commonly used databases.

To Create a Database

Because you already know the tables and fields you want in the PrattLast Associates database, you would use the Blank desktop database option rather than using a template. The following steps create the database.

1 Run Access.

2 Using the steps in the "To Create an Access Database" section in the Office and Windows module, create the database on your hard disk, OneDrive, or other storage location using PrattLast Associates as the file name (Figure 1–2).

◀ | The title bar for my Navigation Pane contains All Tables rather than All Access Objects,
Q&A | as in the figure. Is that a problem?
It is not a problem. The title bar indicates how the Navigation Pane is organized. You can carry out the steps in the text with either organization. To make your screens match the ones in the text, click the Navigation Pane arrow and then click Object Type.

I do not have the Search bar that appears in the figure. Is that a problem?
It is not a problem. If your Navigation Pane does not display a Search bar and you want your screens to match the ones in the text, right-click the Navigation Pane title bar arrow to display a shortcut menu, and then click Search Bar.

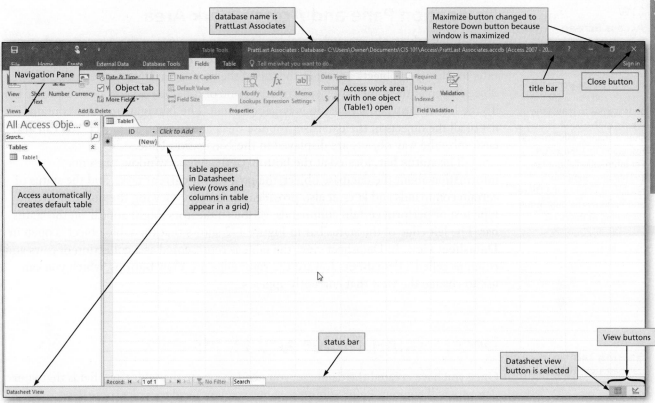

Figure 1–2

To Create a Database Using a Template

Ideally, you will design your own database, create a blank database, and then create the tables you have determined that your database should contain. If you are not sure what database design you will need, you could use a template. Templates can guide you by suggesting some commonly used databases. To create a database using a template, you would use the following steps.

1 If you have another database open, close it without exiting Access by clicking File on the ribbon to open the Backstage view and then clicking Close.

2 If you do not see a template that you want, you can search Microsoft Office online for additional templates.

3 Click the template you want to use. Be sure you have selected one that indicates it is for a desktop database.

4 Enter a file name and select a location for the database.

5 Click the Create button to create the database.

The Access Window

The Access window consists of a variety of components to make your work more efficient. These include the Navigation Pane, Access work area, ribbon, shortcut menus, and Quick Access Toolbar. Some of these components are common to other Microsoft Office apps; others are unique to Access.

BTW

Available Templates
The templates gallery includes both desktop and web-based templates. If you are creating an Access database for your own use, select a desktop template. Web-based templates allow you to create databases that you can publish to a SharePoint server.

BTW

Organizing Files and Folders
You should organize and store files in folders so that you easily can find the files later. For example, if you are taking an introductory computer class called CIS 101, a good practice would be to save all Access files in an Access folder in a CIS 101 folder. For a discussion of folders and detailed examples of creating folders, refer to the Office and Windows module at the beginning of this book.

BTW
Access Screen Resolution
If you are using a computer or mobile device to step through the project in this module and you want your screens to match the figures in this book, you should change your screen's resolution to 1366 x 768. For information about how to change a computer's resolution, refer to the Office and Windows module at the beginning of this book.

Navigation Pane and Access Work Area

You work on objects such as tables, forms, and reports in the **Access work area**. In the work area in Figure 1–2, a single table, Table1, is open in the work area. **Object tabs** for the open objects appear at the top of the work area. If you have multiple objects open at the same time, you can select one of the open objects by clicking its tab. To the left of the work area is the Navigation Pane. The **Navigation Pane** contains a list of all the objects in the database. You use this pane to open an object. You can also customize the way objects are displayed in the Navigation Pane.

The **status bar**, located at the bottom of the Access window, presents information about the database object, the progress of current tasks, and the status of certain commands and keys; it also provides controls for viewing the object. As you type text or perform certain commands, various indicators might appear on the status bar. The left edge of the status bar in Figure 1–2 shows that the table object is open in **Datasheet view**. In Datasheet view, the table is represented as a collection of rows and columns called a **datasheet**. Toward the right edge are View buttons, which you can use to change the view that currently appears.

BTW
Naming Tables
Database users typically have their own guidelines for naming tables. Some use the singular version of the object being described while others use the prefix tbl with a table name. This book uses the singular version of the object (Account, Account Manager).

Determining Tables and Fields

Once you have created the database, you need to create the tables and fields that your database will contain. Before doing so, however, you need to make some decisions regarding the tables and fields.

Naming Tables and Fields

In creating your database, you must name tables, fields, and other objects. Before beginning the design process, you must understand the rules Access applies to table and field names. These rules are:

1. Names can be up to 64 characters in length.
2. Names can contain letters, digits, and spaces, as well as most of the punctuation symbols.
3. Names cannot contain periods (.), exclamation points (!), accent graves (`), or square brackets ([ ]).
4. Each field in a table must have a unique name.

BTW
Multiple-Word Names
There are several ways to handle multiple word names. You can omit the space (AccountNumber) or use an underscore in place of the space (Account_Number). Another option is to use an underscore in place of a space, but use the same case for all letters (ACCOUNT_NUMBER or account_number).

The approach to naming tables and fields used in this text is to begin the names with an uppercase letter and to use lowercase for the other letters. In multiple-word names, each word begins with an uppercase letter, and there is a space between words (for example, Account Number).

Determining the Primary Key

For each table, you need to determine the primary key, the unique identifier. In many cases, you will have obvious choices, such as Account Number or Account Manager Number. If you do not have an obvious choice, you can use the primary key that Access creates automatically. It is a field called ID. It is an **autonumber field**, which means that Access will assign the value 1 to the first record, 2 to the second record, and so on.

Determining Data Types for the Fields

For each field in your database, you must determine the field's **data type**, that is, the type of data that can be stored in the field. Four of the most commonly used data types in Access are:

1. **Short Text** — The field can contain any characters. A maximum number of 255 characters is allowed in a field whose data type is Short Text.
2. **Number** — The field can contain only numbers. The numbers can be either positive or negative. Fields assigned this type can be used in arithmetic operations. You usually assign fields that contain numbers but will not be used for arithmetic operations (such as postal codes) a data type of Short Text.
3. **Currency** — The field can contain only monetary data. The values will appear with currency symbols, such as dollar signs, commas, and decimal points, and with two digits following the decimal point. Like numeric fields, you can use currency fields in arithmetic operations. Access assigns a size to currency fields automatically.
4. **Date & Time** — The field can contain dates and/or times.

Table 1–1 shows the other data types that are available in Access.

BTW
Data Types
Different database management systems have different available data types. Even data types that are essentially the same can have different names. The Currency data type in Access, for example, is referred to as Money in SQL Server.

BTW
AutoNumber Fields
AutoNumber fields also are called AutoIncrement fields. In Design view, the New Values field property allows you to increment the field sequentially (Sequential) or randomly (Random). The default is sequential.

Table 1-1 Additional Data Types	
Data Type	**Description**
Long Text	Field can store a variable amount of text or combinations of text and numbers where the total number of characters may exceed 255.
AutoNumber	Field can store a unique sequential number that Access assigns to a record. Access will increment the number by 1 as each new record is added.
Yes/No	Field can store only one of two values. The choices are Yes/No, True/False, or On/Off.
OLE Object	Field can store an OLE object, which is an object linked to or embedded in the table.
Hyperlink	Field can store text that can be used as a hyperlink address.
Attachment	Field can contain an attached file. Images, spreadsheets, documents, charts, and other elements can be attached to this field in a record in the database. You can view and edit the attached file.
Calculated	Field specified as a calculation based on other fields. The value is not actually stored.

In the Account table, because the Account Number, Account Name, Street, City, and State can all contain letters, their data types should be Short Text. The data type for Postal Code is Short Text instead of Number because you typically do not use postal codes in arithmetic operations; you do not add postal codes or find an average postal code, for example. The Amount Paid and Current Due fields contain monetary data, so their data types should be Currency. The Account Manager Number field contains numbers, but you will not use these numbers in arithmetic operations, so its data type should be Short Text.

Similarly, in the Account Manager table, the data type for the Account Manager Number, Last Name, First Name, Street, City, State, and Postal Code fields should all be Short Text. The Start Date field should have a data type of Date & Time. The Salary field contains monetary amounts, so its data type should be Currency. The Bonus Rate field contains numbers that are not dollar amounts, so its data type should be Number.

For fields whose data type is Short Text, you can change the field size, that is, the maximum number of characters that can be entered in the field. If you set the field size

BTW
Currency Symbols
To show the symbol for the Euro (€) instead of the dollar sign, change the Format property for the field whose data type is currency. To change the default symbols for currency, change the settings in Windows.

for the State field to 2, for example, Access will not allow the user to enter more than two characters in the field. On the other hand, fields whose data type is Number often require you to change the field size, which is the storage space assigned to the field by Access. Table 1–2 shows the possible field sizes for Number fields.

Table 1-2 Field Sizes for Number Fields	
Field Size	**Description**
Byte	Integer value in the range of 0 to 255
Integer	Integer value in the range of -32,768 to 32,767
Long Integer	Integer value in the range of -2,147,483,648 to 2,147,483,647
Single	Numeric values with decimal places to seven significant digits—requires 4 bytes of storage
Double	Numeric values with decimal places to more accuracy than Single—requires 8 bytes of storage
Replication ID	Special identifier required for replication
Decimal	Numeric values with decimal places to more accuracy than Single or Double—requires 12 bytes of storage.

CONSIDER THIS

What is the appropriate size for the Bonus Rate field?
If the size were Byte, Integer, or Long Integer, only integers could be stored. If you try to store a value that has decimal places, such as 0.18, in fields of these sizes, the portion to the right of the decimal point would be removed, giving a result of 0. To address this problem, the bonus rate should have a size of Single, Double, or Decimal. With such small numbers involved, Single, which requires the least storage of the three, is the appropriate choice.

BTW
Naming Files
The following characters cannot be used in a file name: question mark (?), quotation mark ("), slash (/), backslash (\ ), colon (:), asterisk (*), vertical bar (|), greater than symbol (>), and less than symbol (<).

Creating a Table

To create a table in Access, you must define its structure. That is, you must define all the fields that make up the table and their characteristics. You must also indicate the primary key.

In Access, you can use two different views to create a table: Datasheet view and Design view. In **Datasheet view**, the data in the table is presented in rows and columns, similar to a spreadsheet. Although the main reason to use Datasheet view is to add or update records in a table, you can also use it to create a table or to later modify its structure. The other view, **Design view**, is only used to create a table or to modify the structure of a table.

As you might expect, Design view has more functionality for creating a table than Datasheet view. That is, there are certain actions that can only be performed in Design view. One such action is assigning Single as the field size for the Bonus Rate field. In this module, you will create the first table, the Account Manager table, in Datasheet view. Once you have created the table in Datasheet view, you will use Design view to change the field size.

Whichever view you choose to use, before creating the table, you need to know the names and data types of the fields that will make up the table. You can also decide to enter a description for a particular field to explain important details about the field. When you select this field, this description will appear on the status bar. You might also choose to assign a **caption** to a particular field. If you assign a caption, Access will display the value you assign, rather than the field name, in datasheets and in forms. If you do not assign a caption, Access will display the field name.

CONSIDER THIS

When would you want to use a caption?

You would use a caption whenever you want something other than the field name displayed. One common example is when the field name is relatively long and the data in the field is relatively short. In the Account Manager table, the name of the first field is Account Manager Number, but the field contains data that is only two characters long. You will change the caption for this field to AM #, which is much shorter than Account Manager Number yet still describes the field. Doing so will enable you to greatly reduce the width of the column.

The results of these decisions for the fields in the Account Manager table are shown in Table 1–3. The table also shows the data types and field sizes of the fields as well as any special properties that need to be changed. The Account Manager Number field has a caption of AM #, enabling the width of the Account Manager Number column to be reduced in the datasheet.

Table 1-3 Structure of Account Manager Table			
Field Name	**Data Type**	**Field Size**	**Description**
Account Manager Number	Short Text	2	Primary Key **Description:** Unique identifier of account manager **Caption:** AM #
Last Name	Short Text	15	
First Name	Short Text	15	
Street	Short Text	20	
City	Short Text	20	
State	Short Text	2	
Postal Code	Short Text	5	
Start Date	Date/Time	(This appears as Date & Time on the menu of available data types)	
Salary	Currency		
Bonus Rate	Number	Single	Format: Fixed Decimal Places: 2

CONSIDER THIS

How do you determine the field size?

You need to determine the maximum number of characters that can be entered in the field. In some cases, it is obvious. Field sizes of 2 for the State field and 5 for the Postal Code field are certainly the appropriate choices. In other cases, you need to determine how many characters you want to allow. In the list shown in Table 1–3, PrattLast decided allowing 15 characters was sufficient for last names. This field size can be changed later if it proves to be insufficient.

CONSIDER THIS

What is the purpose of the Format and Decimal Places properties?

The format guarantees that bonus rates will be displayed with a fixed number of decimal places. Setting the decimal places property to 2 guarantees that the rates will be displayed with precisely two decimal places. Thus, a bonus rate of 0.2 will be displayed as 0.20.

To Modify the Primary Key

When you first create your database, Access automatically creates a table for you. You can immediately begin defining the fields. If, for any reason, you do not have this table or inadvertently delete it, you can create the table by clicking Create on the ribbon and then clicking the Table button (Create tab | Tables group). In either case, you are ready to define the fields.

The following steps change the name, data type, and other properties of the first field to match the Account Manager Number field in Table 1–3, which is the primary key. *Why? Access has already created the first field as the primary key field, which it has named ID. Account Manager Number is a more appropriate choice.*

❶

- Right-click the column heading for the ID field to display a shortcut menu (Figure 1–3).

Q&A Why does my shortcut menu look different?
You displayed a shortcut menu for the column instead of the column heading. Be sure you right-click the column heading.

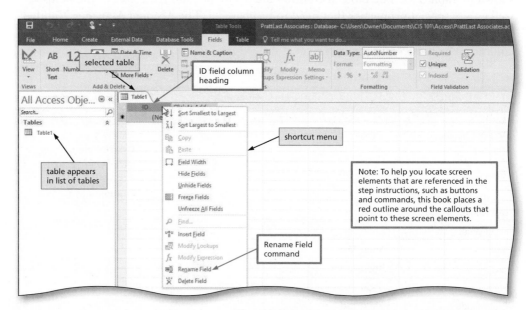

Figure 1–3

❷

- Click Rename Field on the shortcut menu to highlight the current name.

- Type `Account Manager Number` to assign a name to the new field.

- Click the white space immediately below the field name to complete the addition of the field (Figure 1–4).

Figure 1–4

Q&A Why does the full name of the field not appear?
The default column size is not large enough for Account Manager Number to be displayed in its entirety. You will address this issue in later steps.

❸

- Because the data type needs to be changed from AutoNumber to Short Text, click the Data Type arrow (Table Tools Fields tab | Formatting group) to display a menu of available data types (Figure 1–5).

Figure 1–5

- Click Short Text to select the data type for the field (Figure 1–6).

Figure 1–6

- Click the Field Size text box (Table Tools Fields tab | Properties group) to select the current field size, use either the DELETE or BACKSPACE keys to erase the current field size, if necessary, and then type 2 as the new field size.

- Click the Name & Caption button (Table Tools Fields tab | Properties group) to display the Enter Field Properties dialog box.

- Click the Caption text box (Enter Field Properties dialog box), and then type AM # as the caption.

- Click the Description text box, and then type **Unique identifier of account manager** as the description (Figure 1–7).

Figure 1–7

- Click the OK button (Enter Field Properties dialog box) to change the caption and description (Figure 1–8).

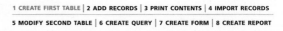

Figure 1–8

To Define the Remaining Fields in a Table

1 CREATE FIRST TABLE | 2 ADD RECORDS | 3 PRINT CONTENTS | 4 IMPORT RECORDS
5 MODIFY SECOND TABLE | 6 CREATE QUERY | 7 CREATE FORM | 8 CREATE REPORT

To define an additional field, you click the 'Click to Add' column heading, select the data type, and then type the field name. This is different from the process you used to modify the ID field. The following steps define the remaining fields shown in Table 1–3. These steps do not change the field size of the Bonus Rate field, however. **Why?** *You can only change the field size of a Number field in Design view. Later, you will use Design view to change this field size and change the format and number of decimal places.*

- Click the 'Click to Add' column heading to display a menu of available data types (Figure 1–9).

Figure 1–9

2

- Click Short Text in the menu of available data types to select the Short Text data type.

- Type `Last Name` to enter a field name.

- Click the blank space below the field name to complete the change of the name. Click the blank space a second time to select the field (Figure 1–10).

Figure 1–10

Q&A

After entering the field name, I realized that I selected the wrong data type. How can I correct it?
Click the Data Type arrow, and then select the correct type.

I inadvertently clicked the blank space before entering the field name. How can I correct the name?
Right-click the field name, click Rename Field on the shortcut menu, and then type the new name.

3

- Change the field size to 15 just as you changed the field size of the Account Manager Number field.

- Using the same technique, add the remaining fields in the Account Manager

Figure 1–11

table. For the First Name, Street, City, State, and Postal Code fields, use the Short Text data type, but change the field sizes to match Table 1–3. For the Start Date field, change the data type to Date/Time. For the Salary field, change the data type to Currency. For the Bonus Rate field, change the data type to Number (Figure 1–11).

Q&A

I have an extra row between the row containing the field names and the row that begins with the asterisk. What happened? Is this a problem? If so, how do I fix it?
You inadvertently added a record to the table by pressing a key. Even pressing the SPACEBAR would add a record. You now have an unwanted record. To fix it, press the ESC key or click the Undo button to undo the action. You may need to do this more than once.

When I try to move on to specify another field, I get an error message indicating that the primary key cannot contain a null value. How do I correct this?
First, click the OK button to remove the error message. Next, press the ESC key or click the Undo button to undo the action. You may need to do this more than once.

BTW
Touch Screen
Differences
The Office and Windows interfaces may vary if you are using a touch screen. For this reason, you might notice that the function or appearance of your touch screen differs slightly from this module's presentation.

Making Changes to the Structure

When creating a table, check the entries carefully to ensure they are correct. If you discover a mistake while still typing the entry, you can correct the error by repeatedly pressing the BACKSPACE key until the incorrect characters are removed. Then, type the correct characters. If you do not discover a mistake until later, you can use the following techniques to make the necessary changes to the structure:

- To undo your most recent change, click the Undo button on the Quick Access Toolbar. If there is nothing that Access can undo, this button will be dim, and clicking it will have no effect.

- To delete a field, right-click the column heading for the field (the position containing the field name), and then click Delete Field on the shortcut menu.

- To change the name of a field, right-click the column heading for the field, click Rename Field on the shortcut menu, and then type the desired field name.

- To insert a field as the last field, click the 'Click to Add' column heading, click the appropriate data type on the menu of available data types, type the desired field name, and, if necessary, change the field size.

- To insert a field between existing fields, right-click the column heading for the field that will follow the new field, and then click Insert Field on the shortcut menu. Right-click the column heading for the field, click Rename Field on the shortcut menu, and then type the desired field name.

- To move a field, click the column heading for the field to be moved to select the field, and then drag the field to the desired position.

As an alternative to these steps, you might want to start over. To do so, click the Close button for the table, and then click the No button in the Microsoft Access dialog box. Click Create on the ribbon, and then click the Table button to create a table. You then can repeat the process you used earlier to define the fields in the table.

To Save a Table

1 CREATE FIRST TABLE | 2 ADD RECORDS | 3 PRINT CONTENTS | 4 IMPORT RECORDS
5 MODIFY SECOND TABLE | 6 CREATE QUERY | 7 CREATE FORM | 8 CREATE REPORT

The Account Manager table structure is complete. The final step is to save the table within the database. As part of the process, you will give the table a name. The following steps save the table, giving it the name Account Manager. **Why?** *PrattLast has decided that Account Manager is an appropriate name for the table.*

1

- Click the **Save** button on the Quick Access Toolbar to display the Save As dialog box (Figure 1–12).

Figure 1–12

2

- Type `Account Manager` to change the name assigned to the table.

- Click the OK button (Save As dialog box) to save the table (Figure 1–13).

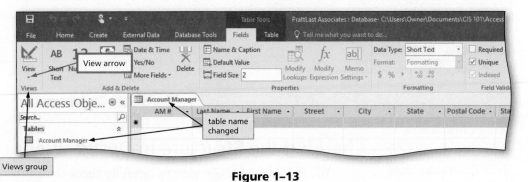

Figure 1–13

Other Ways

1. Click File on the ribbon, click Save in the Backstage view
2. Right-click tab for table, click Save on shortcut menu

3. Press CTRL+S

To View the Table in Design View

Even when creating a table in Datasheet view, Design view can be helpful. **Why?** *You easily can view the fields, data types, and properties to ensure you have entered them correctly. It is also easier to determine the primary key in Design view.* The following steps display the structure of the Account Manager table in Design view so that you can verify the design is correct.

1

• Click the View arrow (Table Tools Fields tab | Views group) to display the View menu (Figure 1–14).

Q&A

Could I just click the View button rather than the arrow?
Yes. Clicking the button is equivalent to clicking the command represented by the icon currently appearing on the button. Because the icon on the button in Figure 1–14 is for Design view, clicking the button would display the table in Design view. If you are uncertain, you can always click the arrow and select from the menu.

Figure 1–14

2

• Click Design View on the View menu to view the table in Design view (Figure 1–15).

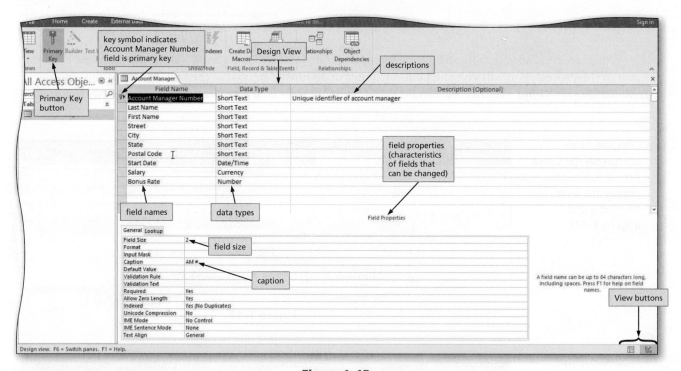

Figure 1–15

Other Ways

1. Click Design View button on status bar

BTW

The Ribbon and Screen Resolution
Access may change how the groups and buttons within the groups appear on the ribbon, depending on the computer or mobile device's screen resolution. Thus, your ribbon may look different from the ones in this book if you are using a screen resolution other than 1366 x 768.

Checking the Structure in Design View

You should use Design view to carefully check the entries you have made. In Figure 1–15, for example, you can see that the Account Manager Number field is the primary key of the Account Manager table by the key symbol in front of the field name. If your table does not have a key symbol, you can click the Primary Key button (Table Tools Design tab | Tools group) to designate a field as the primary key. You can also check that the data type, description, field size, and caption are all correct.

For the other fields, you can see the field name, data type, and description without taking any special action. To see the field size and/or caption for a field, click the field's **row selector**, the small box to the left of the field. Clicking the row selector for the Last Name field, for example, displays the properties for that field. You then can check to see that the field size is correct. In addition, if the field has a caption, you can check to see if that is correct. If you find any mistakes, you can make the necessary corrections on this screen. When you have finished, click the Save button to save your changes.

To Change a Field Size in Design View

1 CREATE FIRST TABLE | 2 ADD RECORDS | 3 PRINT CONTENTS | 4 IMPORT RECORDS
5 MODIFY SECOND TABLE | 6 CREATE QUERY | 7 CREATE FORM | 8 CREATE REPORT

Most field size changes can be made in either Datasheet view or Design view. However, changing the field size for Number fields, such as the Bonus Rate field, can only be done in Design view. Because the values in the Bonus Rate field have decimal places, only Single, Double, or Decimal are possible choices for the field size. The difference between these choices concerns the amount of accuracy, that is, the number of decimal places to which the number is accurate. Double is more accurate than Single, for example, but requires more storage space. Because the rates are only two decimal places, Single is an acceptable choice.

The following steps change the field size of the Bonus Rate field to Single, the format to Fixed, and the number of decimal places to 2. **Why change the format and number of decimal places?** *Changing the format and number ensures that each value will appear with precisely two decimal places.*

1

- If necessary, click the vertical scroll bar to display the Bonus Rate field. Click the row selector for the Bonus Rate field to select the field (Figure 1–16).

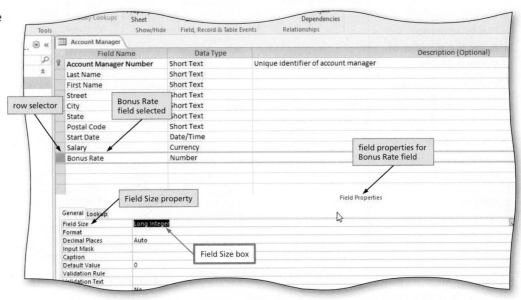

Figure 1–16

2

- Click the Field Size box to display the Field Size arrow.

- Click the Field Size arrow to display the Field Size menu (Figure 1–17).

Q&A What would happen if I left the field size set to Long Integer?

Figure 1–17

If the field size is Long Integer, Integer, or Byte, no decimal places can be stored. For example, a value of .10 would be stored as 0. If you enter rates and the values all appear as 0, chances are you did not change the field size property.

❸

- Click Single to select single precision as the field size.

- Click the Format box to display the Format arrow (Figure 1-18).

Figure 1–18

❹

- Click the Format arrow to display the Format menu.

- Click Fixed to select fixed as the format.

- Click the Decimal Places box to display the Decimal Places arrow.

- Click the Decimal Places arrow to enter the number of decimal places.

- Click 2 to assign the number of decimal places.

- Click the Save button to save your changes (Figure 1–19).

Q&A Why did the 'Property Update Options' button appear?

You changed the number of decimal places. The 'Property

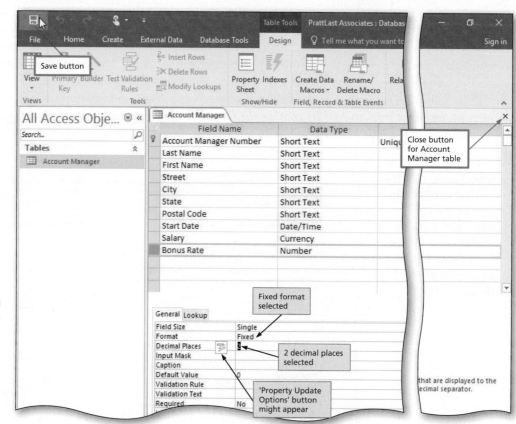

Figure 1–19

Update Options' button offers a quick way of making the same change everywhere Bonus Rate appears. So far, you have not added any data or created any forms or reports that use the Bonus Rate field, so no such changes are necessary.

To Close the Table

Once you are sure that your entries are correct and you have saved your changes, you can close the table. The following step closes the table.

❶   Click the Close button for the Account Manager table to close the table.

Other Ways

1. Right-click tab for table, click Close on shortcut menu

To Add Records to a Table

Creating a table by building the structure and saving the table is the first step in the two-step process of using a table in a database. The second step is to add records to the table. To add records to a table, the table must be open. When making changes to tables, you work in Datasheet view.

You often add records in phases. ***Why?*** *You might not have enough time to add all the records in one session, or you might not have all the records currently available.* The following steps open the Account Manager table in Datasheet view and then add the first two records in the Account Manager table (Figure 1–20).

AM #	Last Name	First Name	Street	City	State	Postal Code	Start Date	Salary	Bonus Rate
42	Lu	Peter	5624 Murray Ave.	Davidson	IN	46007	8/3/2015	$36,750.00	0.09
31	Rivera	Haydee	325 Twiddy St.	Avondale	IL	60311	6/3/2013	$48,750.00	0.15

Figure 1–20

1

- Right-click the Account Manager table in the Navigation Pane to display the shortcut menu (Figure 1–21).

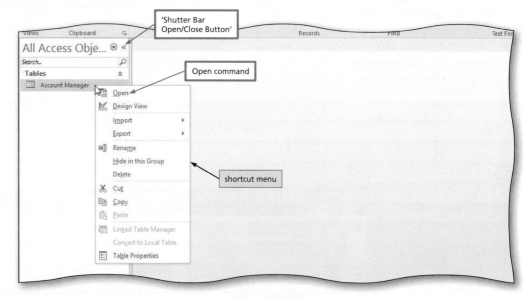

Figure 1–21

2

- Click Open on the shortcut menu to open the table in Datasheet view.
- Click the 'Shutter Bar Open/Close Button' to close the Navigation Pane (Figure 1–22).

Figure 1–22

3

- Click the first row in the AM # field if necessary to display an insertion point, and type 42 to enter the first account manager number (Figure 1–23).

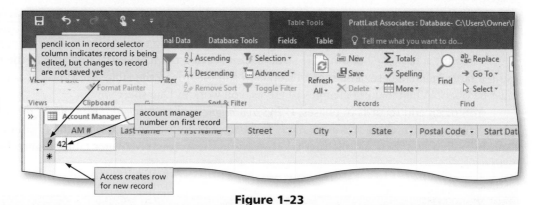

Figure 1–23

4

- Press the TAB key to move to the next field.

- Enter the last name, first name, street, city, state, and postal code by typing the following entries, pressing the TAB key after each one: Lu as the last name, Peter as the first name, 5624 Murray Ave. as the street, Davidson as the city, IN as the state, and 46007 as the postal code.

Figure 1–24

- If requested by your instructor, enter your address instead of 5624 Murray Ave. as the street. If your address is longer than 20 characters, enter the first 20 characters.

- Type 8/3/2015 in the Start Date field (Figure 1–24).

5

- Press the TAB key and then type 36750 in the Salary field.

Q&A Do I need to type a dollar sign?
You do not need to type dollar signs or commas. In addition, because the digits to the right of the decimal point are both zeros, you do not need to type either the decimal point or the zeros.

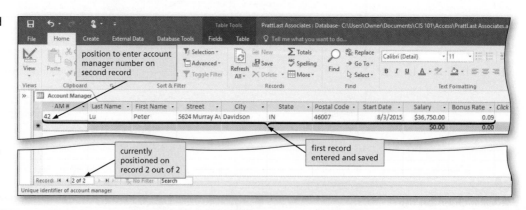

Figure 1–25

- Press the TAB key to complete the entry for the Salary field.

- Type 0.09 in the Bonus Rate field, and then press the TAB key to complete the entry of the first record (Figure 1–25).

Q&A Do I need to type the leading zero for the Bonus Rate?
Typing the leading zero is not necessary. You could type .09 if you prefer. In addition, you would not have to type any final zeros. For example, if you needed to enter 0.20, you could simply type .2 as your entry.

How and when do I save the record?
As soon as you have entered or modified a record and moved to another record, Access saves the original record. This is different from other applications. The rows entered in an Excel worksheet, for example, are not saved until the entire worksheet is saved.

6

- Use the techniques shown in Steps 3 through 5 to enter the data for the second record (Figure 1–26).

Q&A Does it matter that I entered account manager 31 after I entered account manager 42? Should the account manager numbers be in order?

The order in which you enter the records is not important. When you close and later reopen the table, the records will be in account manager number order, because the Account Manager Number field is the primary key.

Experiment

- Click the Salary field on either of the records. Be sure the Table Tools Fields tab is selected. Click the Format arrow, and then click each of the formats in the Format box menu to see the effect on the values in the Salary field. When finished, click Currency in the Format box menu.

Q&A I made a mistake in entering the data. When should I fix it?

It is a good idea to fix it now, although you can fix it later as well. In any case, the following section gives you the techniques you can use to make any necessary corrections. If you want to fix it now, read that section and make your corrections before proceeding to the next step.

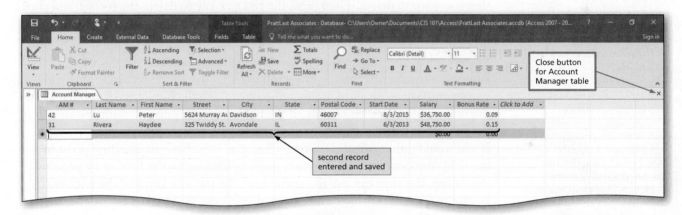

Figure 1–26

7

- Click the Close button for the Account Manager table, shown in Figure 1–26, to close the table (Figure 1–27).

- Exit Access.

Q&A Is it necessary for me to exit Access at this point?

No. The step is here for two reasons.

First, you will often not be able to add all the records you need to add in one sitting. In such a case, you will add some records, and then exit Access. When you are ready to resume adding the records, you will run Access, open the table, and then continue the addition process. Second, there is a break point coming up in the module. If you want to take advantage of that break, you need to first exit Access.

Figure 1–27

Making Changes to the Data

As you enter data, check your entries carefully to ensure they are correct. If you make a mistake and discover it before you press the TAB key, correct it by pressing the BACKSPACE key until the incorrect characters are removed, and then type the correct characters. If you do not discover a mistake until later, you can use the following techniques to make the necessary corrections to the data:

BTW
AutoCorrect Feature
The AutoCorrect feature of Access corrects common data entry errors. AutoCorrect corrects two capital letters by changing the second letter to lowercase and capitalizes the first letter in the names of days. It also corrects more than 400 commonly misspelled words.

BTW
Other AutoCorrect Options
Using the Office AutoCorrect feature, you can create entries that will replace abbreviations with spelled-out names and phrases automatically. To specify AutoCorrect rules, click File on the ribbon to open the Backstage view, click Options, and then click Proofing in the Access Options dialog box.

- To undo your most recent change, click the Undo button on the Quick Access Toolbar. If there is nothing that Access can undo, this button will be dimmed, and clicking it will have no effect.

- To add a record, click the 'New (blank) record' button, click the position for the Account Manager Number field on the first open record, and then add the record. Do not worry about it being in the correct position in the table. Access will reposition the record based on the primary key, in this case, the Account Manager Number.

- To delete a record, click the record selector, shown in Figure 1–22, for the record that you want to delete. Then press the DELETE key to delete the record, and click the Yes button when Access asks you to verify that you want to delete the record.

- To change the contents of one or more fields in a record, the record must be on the screen. If it is not, use any appropriate technique, such as the UP ARROW and DOWN ARROW keys or the vertical scroll bar, to move to the record. If the field you want to correct is not visible on the screen, use the horizontal scroll bar along the bottom of the screen to shift all the fields until the one you want appears. If the value in the field is currently highlighted, you can simply type the new value. If you would rather edit the existing value, you must have an insertion point in the field. You can place the insertion point by clicking in the field or by pressing the F2 key. You then can use the arrow keys, the DELETE key, and the BACKSPACE key for making the correction. You can also use the INSERT key to switch between Insert and Overtype mode. When you have made the change, press the TAB key to move to the next field.

If you cannot determine how to correct the data, you may find that you are "stuck" on the record, in which case Access neither allows you to move to another record nor allows you to close the table until you have made the correction. If you encounter this situation, simply press the ESC key. Pressing the ESC key will remove from the screen the record you are trying to add. You then can move to any other record, close the table, or take any other action you desire.

Break Point: If you wish to take a break, this is a good place to do so. You can exit Access now. To resume at a later time, run Access, open the database called PrattLast Associates, and continue following the steps from this location forward.

To Add Records to a Table that Contains Data

1 CREATE FIRST TABLE | 2 ADD RECORDS | 3 PRINT CONTENTS | 4 IMPORT RECORDS
5 MODIFY SECOND TABLE | 6 CREATE QUERY | 7 CREATE FORM | 8 CREATE REPORT

You can add records to a table that already contains data using a process almost identical to that used to add records to an empty table. The only difference is that you place the insertion point after the last record before you enter the additional data. To position the insertion point after the last record, you can use the **Navigation buttons**, which are buttons used to move within a table, found near the lower-left corner of the screen when a table is open. *Why not just click the Account Manager Number (AM #) on the first open record? You could click the first open record, but it is a good habit to use the 'New (blank) record' button. Once a table contains more records than will fit on the screen, it is easier to click the 'New (blank) record' button.* The purpose of each Navigation button is described in Table 1–4.

Table 1–4 Navigation Buttons in Datasheet View	
Button	**Purpose**
First record	Moves to the first record in the table
Previous record	Moves to the previous record
Next record	Moves to the next record
Last record	Moves to the last record in the table
New (blank) record	Moves to the end of the table to a position for entering a new record

BTW
Enabling Content
If the database is one that you created, or if it comes from a trusted source, you can enable the content. You should disable the content of a database if you suspect that your database might contain harmful content or damaging macros.

The following steps add the remaining records (Figure 1–28) to the Account Manager table.

AM #	Last Name	First Name	Street	City	State	Postal Code	Start Date	Salary	Bonus Rate
58	Murowski	Karen	168 Truesdale Dr.	Carlton	IL	60313	11/9/2016	$24,000.00	0.08
35	Simson	Mark	1467 Hartwell St.	Walker	IN	46004	5/19/2014	$40,500.00	0.12

Figure 1–28

1

• Run Access, unless it is already running.

• Open the PrattLast Associates database from your hard disk, OneDrive, or other storage location (Figure 1-29).

• If a Security Warning appears, click the Enable Content button.

Figure 1–29

2

• If the Navigation Pane is closed, click the 'Shutter Bar Open/Close Button', shown in Figure 1–27, to open the Navigation Pane (Figure 1–30).

Figure 1–30

③

- Right-click the Account Manager table in the Navigation Pane to display a shortcut menu.

- Click Open on the shortcut menu to open the table in Datasheet view.

Q&A Why do the records appear in a different order than the order in which I entered them?
When you open the table, they are sorted in the order of the primary key. In this case, that means they will appear in Account Manager Number order.

- Close the Navigation Pane by clicking the 'Shutter Bar Open/ Close Button' (Figure 1–31).

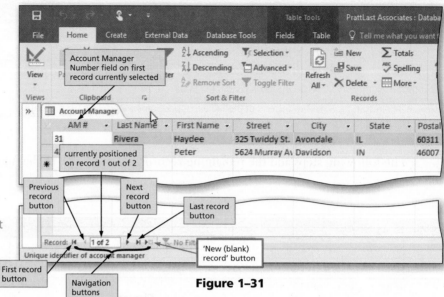

Figure 1–31

④

- Click the 'New (blank) record' button to move to a position to enter a new record (Figure 1–32).

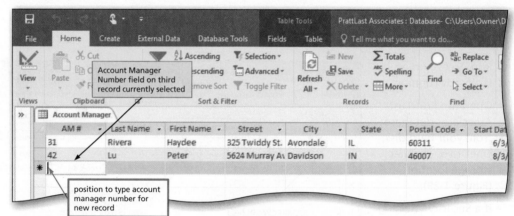

Figure 1–32

⑤

- Add the records shown in Figure 1–28 using the same techniques you used to add the first two records (Figure 1–33).

⑥

- Close the table.

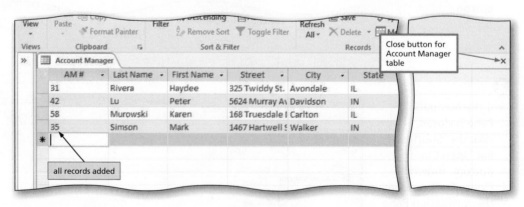

Figure 1–33

Other Ways

1. Click New button (Home tab | Records group)   2. Press CTRL+PLUS SIGN (+)

To Resize Columns in a Datasheet

Access assigns default column sizes, which do not always provide space to display all the data in the field. In some cases, the data might appear but the entire field name will not. You can correct this problem by resizing the column (changing its size) in the datasheet. In some instances, you may want to reduce the size of a column. *Why? Some fields, such as the State field, are short enough that they do not require all the space on the screen that is allotted to them.* Changing a column width changes the layout, or design, of a table. The following steps resize the columns in the Account Manager table and save the changes to the layout.

1

- Open the Navigation Pane if it is not already open.

- Open the Account Manager table and then close the Navigation Pane.

- Point to the right boundary of the field selector for the Account Manager Number (AM #) field (Figure 1–34) so that the pointer becomes a two-headed arrow.

Q&A I am using touch and I cannot see the pointer. Is this a problem?
It is not a problem. Remember that if you are using your finger on a touch screen, you will not see the pointer.

Figure 1–34

2

- Double-click the right boundary of the field selector to resize the field so that it best fits the data.

- Use the same technique to resize all the other fields to best fit the data.

- Save the changes to the layout by clicking the Save button on the Quick Access Toolbar (Figure 1–35).

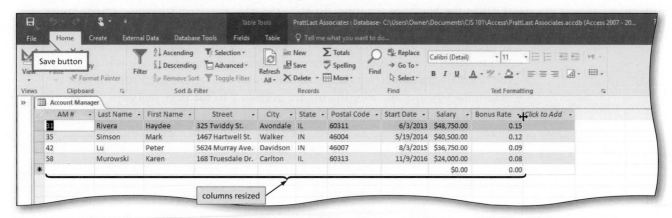

Figure 1–35

3

- Click the table's Close button (shown in Figure 1–33) to close the table.

Q&A What if I closed the table without saving the layout changes?
You would be asked if you want to save the changes.

Other Ways
1. Right-click field name, click Field Width

CONSIDER THIS

What is the best method for distributing database objects?

The traditional method of distributing database objects such as tables, reports, and forms uses a printer to produce a hard copy. A hard copy or printout is information that exists on a physical medium such as paper. Hard copies can be useful for the following reasons:

- Some people prefer proofreading a hard copy of a document rather than viewing it on the screen to check for errors and readability.

- Hard copies can serve as a backup reference if your storage medium is lost or becomes corrupted and you need to recreate the document. Instead of distributing a hard copy, users can distribute the document as an electronic image that mirrors the original document's appearance. The electronic image of the document can be emailed, posted on a website, or copied to a portable storage medium such as a USB flash drive. Two popular electronic image formats, sometimes called fixed formats, are PDF by Adobe Systems and XPS by Microsoft.

In Access, you can create electronic image files through the External Data tab on the ribbon. Electronic images of documents, such as PDF and XPS, can be useful for the following reasons:

- Users can view electronic images of documents without the software that created the original document (e.g., Access). Specifically, to view a PDF file, you use a program called Adobe Reader, which can be downloaded free from Adobe's website. Similarly, to view an XPS file, you use a program called XPS Viewer, which is included in the latest versions of Windows and Edge.

- Sending electronic documents saves paper and printer supplies. Society encourages users to contribute to **green computing**, which involves reducing the electricity consumed and environmental waste generated when using computers, mobile devices, and related technologies.

BTW

Changing Printers
To change the default printer that appears in the Print dialog box, click File on the ribbon, click the Print tab in the Backstage view, click Print in the Print gallery, then click the Name arrow and select the desired printer.

Previewing and Printing the Contents of a Table

When working with a database, you will often need to print a copy of the table contents. Figure 1–36 shows a printed copy of the contents of the Account Manager table. (Yours might look slightly different, depending on your printer.) Because the Account Manager table is substantially wider than the screen, it will also be wider than the normal printed page in portrait orientation. **Portrait orientation** means the printout is across the width of the page. **Landscape orientation** means the printout is across the height of the page. To print the wide database table, you might prefer to use landscape orientation. A convenient way to change to landscape orientation is to preview what the printed copy will look like by using Print Preview. This allows you to determine whether landscape orientation is necessary and, if it is, to change the orientation easily to landscape. In addition, you can also use Print Preview to determine whether any adjustments are necessary to the page margins.

Account Manager   9/12/2017

AM #	Last Name	First Name	Street	City	State	Postal Code	Start Date	Salary	Bonus Rate
31	Rivera	Haydee	325 Twiddy St.	Avondale	IL	60311	6/3/2013	$48,750.00	0.15
35	Simson	Mark	1467 Hartwell St.	Walker	IN	46004	5/19/2014	$40,500.00	0.12
42	Lu	Peter	5624 Murray Ave.	Davidson	IN	46007	8/3/2015	$36,750.00	0.09
58	Murowski	Karen	168 Truesdale Dr.	Carlton	IL	60313	11/9/2016	$24,000.00	0.08

Figure 1–36

To Preview and Print the Contents of a Table

The following steps use Print Preview to preview and then print the contents of the Account Manager table. *Why? By previewing the contents of the table in Print Preview, you can make any necessary adjustments to the orientation or to the margins before printing the contents.*

1

- If the Navigation Pane is closed, open the Navigation Pane by clicking the 'Shutter Bar Open/ Close Button'.

- Be sure the Account Manager table is selected.

Q&A Why do I have to be sure the Account Manager table is selected? It is the only object in the database.

When the database contains only one object, you do not have to worry about selecting the object. Ensuring that the correct object is selected is a good habit to form, however, to make sure that the object you print is the one you want.

- Click File on the ribbon to open the Backstage view.

- Click the Print tab in the Backstage view to display the Print gallery (Figure 1–37).

Figure 1–37

2

- Click the Print Preview button in the Print gallery to display a preview of what the table will look like when printed (Figure 1–38).

Q&A I cannot read the table. Can I magnify a portion of the table?

Yes. Point the pointer, whose shape will change to a magnifying glass, at the portion of the table that you want to magnify, and then click. You can return to the original view of the table by clicking a second time.

Figure 1–38

3

- Click the pointer in the position shown in Figure 1–38 to magnify the upper-right section of the table (Figure 1–39).

Q&A My table was already magnified in a different area. How can I see the area shown in the figure? One way is to use the scroll bars to move to the desired portion of the table. You can also click the pointer anywhere in the table to produce a screen like the one shown in Figure 1–38, and then click in the location shown in the figure.

When I magnify the upper-right section, my table moves to the right of the screen and there is a lot of white space. Is that a problem?
No, use the horizontal scroll bar to move the table to the left and reduce the size of the white space.

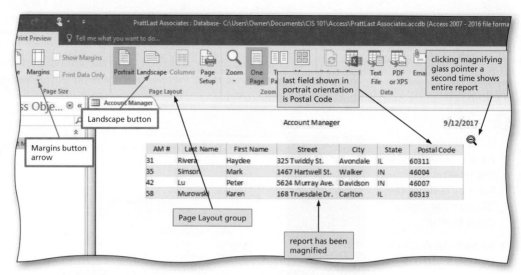

Figure 1–39

4

- Click the Landscape button (Print Preview tab | Page Layout group) to change to landscape orientation.

- Click the Margins button arrow (Print Preview tab | Page Size group) and then click Normal, if necessary, to display all the fields (Figure 1–40).

5

- Click the Print button (Print Preview tab | Print group) to display the Print dialog box.

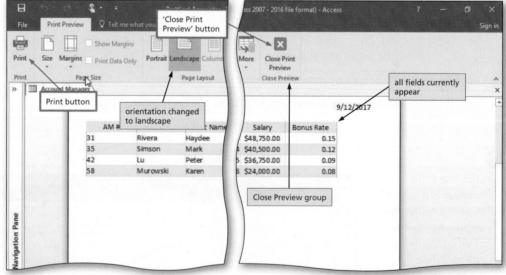

Figure 1–40

- Click the OK button (Print dialog box) to print the table.

- When the printer stops, retrieve the hard copy of the Account Manager table.

- Click the 'Close Print Preview' button (Print Preview tab | Close Preview group) to close the Print Preview window.

Q&A Do I have to select Print Preview before printing the table?
No. If you want to print without previewing, you would select either Print or Quick Print rather than Print Preview.

Other Ways

1. Press CTRL+P, click OK button in Print dialog box

Importing or Linking Data From Other Applications to Access

If your data for a table is stored in an Excel worksheet, you can **import** the data, which means to make a copy of the data as a table in the Access database. In this case, any changes to the data made in Access would not be reflected in the Excel worksheet.

Figure 1–41, which contains the Account data, is an example of the type of worksheet that can be imported. In this type of worksheet, the data is stored as a **list**, that is, a collection of rows and columns in which all the entries in a column represent the same type of data. In this type of list, the first row contains **column headings**, that is, descriptions of the contents of the column, rather than data. In the worksheet in Figure 1–41, for example, the entry in the first column of the first row is Account Number. This indicates that all the other values in this column are account numbers. The fact that the entry in the second column of the first row is Account Name indicates that all the other values in the second column are account names.

BTW

Linking Versus Importing
When you link to the data in the worksheet, the data appears as a table in the Access database but it is maintained in its original form in Excel. Any changes to the Excel data are reflected when the linked table is viewed in Access. In this arrangement, Access would typically be used as a vehicle for querying and presenting the data, with actual updates being made in Excel.

BTW

Importing Data in Other Formats
You can import data into a table from Excel workbooks, Access databases, XML files, ODBC databases such as SQL Server, text files, HTML documents, Outlook folders, and SharePoint lists.

Figure 1–41

Access Module 1

CONSIDER THIS

Does it matter how the data in the Excel workbook is formatted? If so, how can you be sure the Excel data is formatted in such a way that you can import it?
The format of data in an Excel workbook is important when you want to import it into Access. To ensure the data is in an appropriate format:

1. Make sure the data is in the form of a list; a collection of rows and columns in which all the entries in a column represent the same type of data.

2. Make sure there are no blank rows within the list. If there are, remove them prior to importing or linking.

3. Make sure there are no blank columns within the list. If there are, remove them prior to importing or linking.

4. Determine whether the first row contains column headings that will make appropriate field names in the resulting table. If not, you should consider adding such a row. In general, the process is simpler if the first row in the worksheet contains appropriate column headings.

The Import process will create a table. In this table, the column headings in the first row of the worksheet become the field names. The rows of the worksheet, other than the first row, become the records in the table. In the process, each field will be assigned the data type that seems the most reasonable, given the data currently in the worksheet. When the Import process is finished, you can use Datasheet view or Design view to modify these data types or to make any other changes to the structure you feel are necessary.

To Import an Excel Worksheet

1 CREATE FIRST TABLE | 2 ADD RECORDS | 3 PRINT CONTENTS | 4 IMPORT RECORDS
5 MODIFY SECOND TABLE | 6 CREATE QUERY | 7 CREATE FORM | 8 CREATE REPORT

You import a worksheet by using the Import Spreadsheet Wizard. In the process, you will indicate that the first row in the worksheet contains the column headings. *Why? You are indicating that Access is to use those column headings as the field names in the Access table.* In addition, you will indicate the primary key for the table. As part of the process, you could, if appropriate, choose not to include all the fields from the worksheet in the resulting table.

The following steps import the Account worksheet.

1

- Click External Data on the ribbon to display the External Data tab (Figure 1–42).

Figure 1–42

2

- Click the Excel button (External Data tab | Import & Link group) to display the Get External Data - Excel Spreadsheet dialog box.

- Click the Browse button in the Get External Data - Excel Spreadsheet dialog box.

- Navigate to the location containing the workbook (for example, the Access folder in the CIS 101 folder). For a detailed example of this procedure, refer to the Office and Windows module at the beginning of this book.

- Click the Account workbook, and then click the Open button to select the workbook (Figure 1–43).

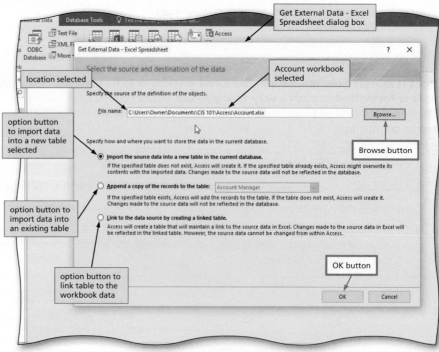

Figure 1–43

3

- With the option button to import the source data to a new table selected, click the OK button to display the Import Spreadsheet Wizard dialog box (Figure 1–44).

Q&A What happens if I select the option button to append records to an existing table?
Instead of the records being placed in a new table, they will be added to an existing table that you specify, provided the value in the primary key field does not duplicate that of an existing record.

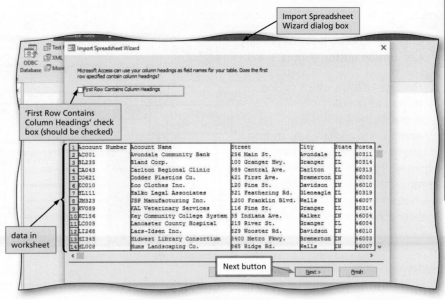

Figure 1–44

4

- Be sure the 'First Row Contains Column Headings' check box is selected. If it is not, click the 'First Row Contains Column Headings' check box to select it.

- Click the Next button (Figure 1–45).

Q&A When would I use the Field Options on the Import Spreadsheet Wizard?
You would use these options if you wanted to change properties for one or more fields. You can change the name, the data type, and whether the field is indexed. You can also indicate that some fields should not be imported.

Figure 1–45

5

- Because the Field Options need not be specified, click the Next button (Figure 1–46).

Figure 1–46

6

- Click the 'Choose my own primary key' option button (Figure 1–47).

Q&A How do I decide which option button to select?
If one of the fields is an appropriate primary key, choose your own primary key from the list of fields. If you are sure you do not want a primary key, choose 'No primary key'. Otherwise, let Access add the primary key.

Figure 1–47

7

- Because the Account Number field, which is the correct field, is already selected as the primary key, click the Next button.

- Use the DELETE or BACKSPACE keys as necessary to erase the current entry, and then type **Account** in the Import to Table text box.

- Click the Finish button to import the data (Figure 1–48).

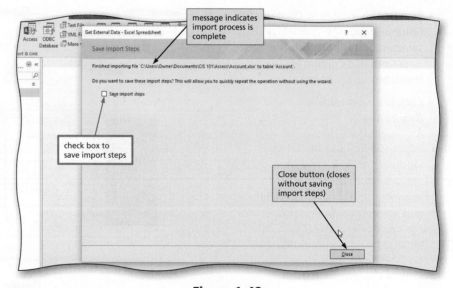

Figure 1–48

8

- Click the 'Save import steps' check box to display the Save import steps options.

- If necessary, type **Import-Account** in the Save as text box.

- Type **Import data from Account workbook into Account table** in the Description text box (Figure 1–49).

Q&A When would I create an Outlook task?
If the import operation is one you will repeat on a regular basis, you can create and schedule the import process just as you can schedule any other Outlook task.

Figure 1–49

9

- Click the Save Import button to save the import steps (Figure 1–50).

Q&A I saved the table as Account Data. How can I change the name?
Right-click the table name in the Navigation Pane. Click Rename on the shortcut menu and change the table name to Account.

Figure 1–50

Modifying the Table

The import process has created the Account table. The table has the correct fields and records. There are some details the process cannot handle, however. These include field sizes, descriptions, and captions. You will use Design view to make the necessary changes. The information you need is shown in Table 1–5.

Table 1–5 Structure of Account Table			
Field Name	**Data Type**	**Field Size**	**Notes**
Account Number	Short Text	5	Primary Key **Description:** Account Number (two uppercase letters followed by 3-digit number) **Caption:** AC #
Account Name	Short Text	30	
Street	Short Text	20	
City	Short Text	20	
State	Short Text	2	
Postal Code	Short Text	5	
Amount Paid	Currency		
Current Due	Currency		
Account Manager Number	Short Text	2	**Description:** Account Manager Number (number of account manager for account) **Caption:** AM #

BTW

Creating a Table in Design View
To create a table in Design view, display the Create tab, and then click the Table Design button (Create tab | Tables group). You will then see the same screen as in Figure 1–51, except that there will be no entries. Make all the necessary entries for the fields in your table, save the table, and assign the table a name.

To Modify a Table in Design View

1 CREATE FIRST TABLE | 2 ADD RECORDS | 3 PRINT CONTENTS | 4 IMPORT RECORDS
5 MODIFY SECOND TABLE | 6 CREATE QUERY | 7 CREATE FORM | 8 CREATE REPORT

You will usually need to modify the design of a table created during the import process. *Why? Some properties of a table are not specified during the import process, such as descriptions, captions, and field sizes. You might also need to change a data type.* The following steps make the necessary modifications to the design of the Account table.

1

- Open the Navigation Pane, if necessary.

- Right-click the Account table in the Navigation Pane to display the shortcut menu, and then click Design View on the shortcut menu to open the table in Design view (Figure 1–51).

Figure 1–51

2

- Click the Description (Optional) box for the Account Number field, and then type **Account Number (two uppercase letters followed by a 3-digit number)** as the description.

- With the Account Number field selected, click the Field Size box, erase the current field size, and type **5** as the new field size.

Figure 1–52

- Click the Caption box, and type **AC #** as the caption (Figure 1–52).

Q&A | What does the @ symbol represent in the Format box?
The @ symbol is a default format added by Access when the table was imported from Excel.

3

- Make the other changes shown in Table 1–5. To select a field to be changed, click the field's row selector. For most fields, you only need to change the field size. For the Account Manager Number field, you also need to change the description and caption.

- Click the Save button on the Quick Access Toolbar to save your changes.

- Because you know the data will satisfy the new field sizes, click the Yes button when given a message about the possibility of data loss.

Other Ways

1. Press F6 to move between upper and lower panes in Table Design window

Correcting Errors in the Structure

Whenever you create or modify a table in Design view, you should check the entries carefully to ensure they are correct. If you make a mistake and discover it before you press the TAB key, you can correct the error by repeatedly pressing the BACKSPACE key until the incorrect characters are removed. Then, type the correct characters. If you do not discover a mistake until later, you can click the entry, type the correct value, and then press the ENTER key. You can use the following techniques to make changes to the structure:

- If you accidentally add an extra field to the structure, select the field by clicking the row selector (the leftmost column on the row that contains the field to be deleted). Once you have selected the field, press the DELETE key. This will remove the field from the structure.

- If you forget to include a field, select the field that will follow the one you want to add by clicking the row selector, and then press the INSERT key. The remaining fields move down one row, making room for the missing field. Make the entries for the new field in the usual manner.

- If you made the wrong field a primary key field, click the correct primary key entry for the field and then click the Primary Key button (Table Tools Design tab | Tools group).

- To move a field, click the row selector for the field to be moved to select the field, and then drag the field to the desired position.

As an alternative to these steps, you might want to start over. To do so, click the Close button for the window containing the table, and then click the No button in the Microsoft Access dialog box. You then can repeat the process you used earlier to define the fields in the table.

BTW

Importing Data to an Existing Table
When you create a new table in Design view, you can import data from other sources into the table using the External Data tab.

To Close the Table

Now that you have completed and saved the Account table, you can close it. The following step closes the table.

1 Click the Close button for the Account table (see Figure 1–52) to close the table.

To Resize Columns in a Datasheet

You can resize the columns in the datasheet for the Account table just as you resized the columns in the datasheet for the Account Manager table. The following steps resize the columns in the Account table to best fit the data.

1 Open the Account table in Datasheet view.

2 Double-click the right boundary of the field selectors of each of the fields to resize the columns so that they best fit the data.

3 Save the changes to the layout by clicking the Save button on the Quick Access Toolbar.

4 Close the table.

BTW

Resizing Columns
To resize all columns in a datasheet to best fit simultaneously, select the column heading for the first column, hold down the SHIFT key and select the last column in the datasheet. Then, double-click the right boundary of any field selector.

Break Point: If you wish to take a break, this is a good place to do so. You can exit Access now. To resume at a later time, run Access, open the database called PrattLast Associates, and continue following the steps from this location forward.

Additional Database Objects

A database contains many types of objects. Tables are the objects you use to store and manipulate data. Access supports other important types of objects as well; each object has a specific purpose that helps maximize the benefits of a database. Through queries (questions), Access makes it possible to ask complex questions concerning the data in the database and then receive instant answers. Access also allows the user to produce attractive and useful forms for viewing and updating data. Additionally, Access includes report creation tools that make it easy to produce sophisticated reports for presenting data.

BTW

Creating Queries
Although the Simple Query Wizard is a convenient way to create straightforward queries, you will find that many of the queries you create require more control than the wizard provides. In Module 2, you will use Design view to create customized queries.

Creating Queries

Queries are simply questions, the answers to which are in the database. Access contains a powerful query feature that helps you find the answers to a wide variety of questions. Once you have examined the question you want to ask to determine the fields involved in the question, you can begin creating the query. If the query involves no special sort order, restrictions, or calculations, you can use the Simple Query Wizard.

To Use the Simple Query Wizard to Create a Query

1 CREATE FIRST TABLE | 2 ADD RECORDS | 3 PRINT CONTENTS | 4 IMPORT RECORDS
5 MODIFY SECOND TABLE | 6 CREATE QUERY | 7 CREATE FORM | 8 CREATE REPORT

The following steps use the Simple Query Wizard to create a query that PrattLast Associates might use to obtain financial information on its accounts. *Why? The Simple Query Wizard is the quickest and easiest way to create a query.* This query displays the number, name, amount paid, current due, and account manager number of all accounts.

1

- If the Navigation Pane is closed, click the 'Shutter Bar Open/Close Button' to open the Navigation Pane.

- Be sure the Account table is selected.

- Click Create on the ribbon to display the Create tab.

- Click the Query Wizard button (Create tab | Queries group) to display the New Query dialog box (Figure 1–53).

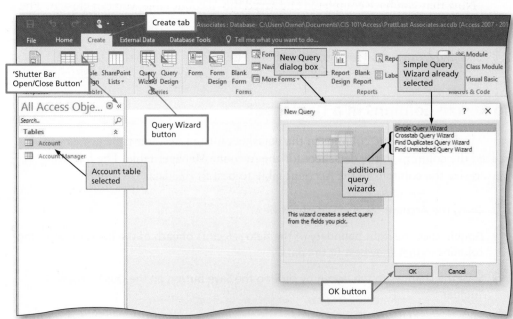

Figure 1–53

2

- Be sure Simple Query Wizard is selected, and then click the OK button (New Query dialog box) to display the Simple Query Wizard dialog box (Figure 1–54).

Q&A What would happen if the Account Manager table were selected instead of the Account table?

The list of available fields would contain fields from the Account Manager table rather than the Account table.

If the list contained Account Manager table fields, how could I make it contain Account table fields?

Click the arrow in the Tables/Queries box, and then click the Account table in the list that appears.

Figure 1–54

3

- With the Account Number field selected, click the Add Field button to add the field to the query.

- With the Account Name field selected, click the Add Field button a second time to add the field.

- Click the Amount Paid field, and then click the Add Field button to add the field.

- In a similar fashion, add the Current Due and Account Manager Number fields (Figure 1–55).

Figure 1–55

4

- Click the Next button to move to the next screen.

- Ensure that the 'Detail (shows every field of every record)' option button is selected (Figure 1–56).

Q&A What is the difference between Detail and Summary?

Detail shows all the records and fields. Summary only shows computations (for example, the total amount paid).

Figure 1–56

- Click the Next button to move to the next screen.

- Confirm that the title of the query is Account Query (Figure 1–57).

Q&A What should I do if the title is incorrect?
Click the box containing the title to produce an insertion point. Erase the current title and then type Account Query.

Figure 1–57

6

- Click the Finish button to create the query (Figure 1–58).

- Click the Close button for the Account Query to remove the query results from the screen.

Q&A If I want to use this query in the future, do I need to save the query?
Normally you would. The one exception is a query created by the wizard. The wizard automatically saves the query it creates.

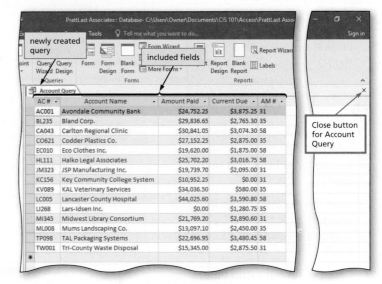

Figure 1–58

Using Queries

After you have created and saved a query, Access stores it as a database object and makes it available for use in a variety of ways:

- If you want to change the design of the query, right-click the query in the Navigation Pane and then click Design View on the shortcut menu to open the query in Design view.

- To view the results of the query from Design view, click the Run button to instruct Access to **run** the query, that is, to perform the necessary actions to produce and display the results in Datasheet view.

- To view the results of the query from the Navigation Pane, open it by right-clicking the query and clicking Open on the shortcut menu. Access automatically runs the query and displays the results in Datasheet view.

- To print the results with the query open in either Design view or Datasheet view, click File on the ribbon, click the Print tab, and then click either Print or Quick Print.

- To print the query without first opening it, be sure the query is selected in the Navigation Pane and click File on the ribbon, click the Print tab, and then click either Print or Quick Print.

You can switch between views of a query using the View button (Home tab | Views group). Clicking the arrow in the bottom of the button produces the View button menu. You then click the desired view in the menu. The two query views you will use in this module are Datasheet view (which displays the query results) and Design view (for changing the query design). You can also click the top part of the View button, in which case you will switch to the view identified by the icon on the button. For the most part, the icon on the button represents the view you want, so you can usually simply click the button.

To Use a Criterion in a Query

1 CREATE FIRST TABLE | 2 ADD RECORDS | 3 PRINT CONTENTS | 4 IMPORT RECORDS
5 MODIFY SECOND TABLE | 6 CREATE QUERY | 7 CREATE FORM | 8 CREATE REPORT

After you have determined the fields to be included in a query, you will determine whether you need to further restrict the results of the query. For example, you might want to include only those accounts managed by account manager 35, Mark Simson. In such a case, you need to enter the number 35 as a criterion for the account manager field. *Why? A criterion is a condition that the records must satisfy in order to be included in the query results.* To do so, you will open the query in Design view, enter the criterion below the appropriate field, and then view the results of the query. The following steps enter a criterion to include only the accounts of account manager 35 and then view the query results.

1

- Right-click the Account Query in the Navigation Pane to produce a shortcut menu (Figure 1–59).

Figure 1–59

2

- Click Design View on the shortcut menu to open the query in Design view (Figure 1–60).

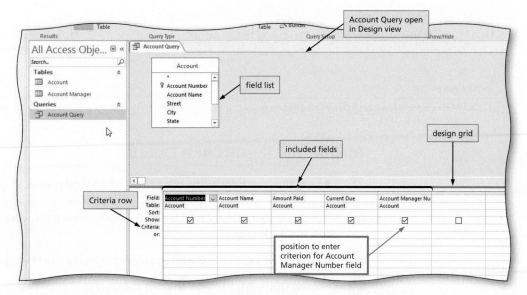

Figure 1–60

3

- Click the Criteria row in the Account Manager Number column of the grid, and then type 35 as the criterion (Figure 1–61).

Q&A The Account Manager Number field is a text field. Do I need to enclose the value for a text field in quotation marks?

You could, but it is not necessary because Access inserts the quotation marks for you automatically.

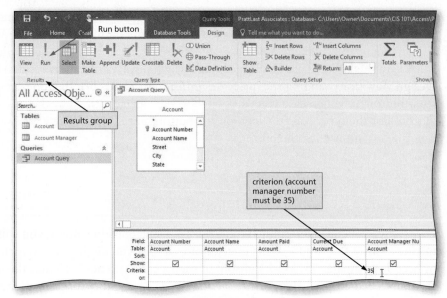

Figure 1–61

4

- Click the Run button (Query Tools Design tab | Results group) to run the query and display the results in Datasheet view (Figure 1–62).

Figure 1–62

5

- Click the Close button for the Account Query to close the query.
- When asked if you want to save your changes, click the No button.

Q&A If I saved the query, what would happen the next time I ran the query?

You would see only accounts of account manager 35.

Could I save a query with another name?

Yes. To save a query with a different name, click File on the ribbon, click the Save As tab, click Save Object As, click the Save As button, enter a new file name in the Save As dialog box, and then click the OK button (Save As dialog box).

Other Ways

1. Click View button (Query Tools Design tab | Results group)   2. Click Datasheet View button on status bar

To Print the Results of a Query

The following steps print the results of a saved query.

1 With the Account Query selected in the Navigation Pane, click File on the ribbon to open the Backstage view.

2 Click the Print tab in the Backstage view to display the Print gallery.

3 Click the Quick Print button to print the query.

Creating Forms

In Datasheet view, you can view many records at once. If there are many fields, however, only some of the fields in each record might be visible at a time. In **Form view**, where data is displayed in a form on the screen, you can usually see all the fields, but only for one record.

To Create a Form

1 CREATE FIRST TABLE | 2 ADD RECORDS | 3 PRINT CONTENTS | 4 IMPORT RECORDS
5 MODIFY SECOND TABLE | 6 CREATE QUERY | 7 CREATE FORM | 8 CREATE REPORT

Like a paper form, a **form** in a database is a formatted document with fields that contain data. Forms allow you to view and maintain data. Forms can also be used to print data, but reports are more commonly used for that purpose. The simplest type of form in Access is one that includes all the fields in a table stacked one above the other. The following steps use the Form button to create a form. *Why? Using the Form button is the simplest way to create this type of form. The steps use the form to view records and then save the form.*

1

- Select the Account table in the Navigation Pane.

- If necessary, click Create on the ribbon to display the Create tab (Figure 1–63).

Figure 1–63

2

- Click the Form button (Create tab | Forms group) to create a simple form (Figure 1–64).

Q&A
A Field list appeared on my screen. What should I do?
Click the 'Add Existing Fields' button (Form Layout Tools Design tab | Tools group) to remove the Field list from the screen.

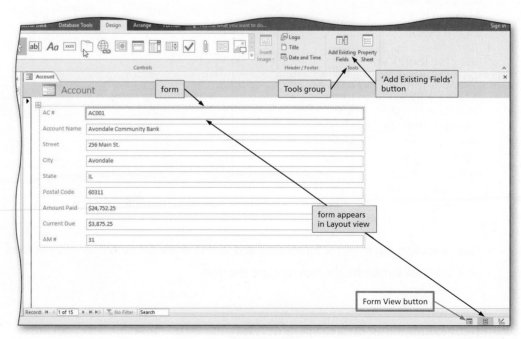

Figure 1–64

3

- Click the Form View button on the Access status bar to display the form in Form view rather than Layout view.

Q&A What is the difference between Layout view and Form view?
Layout view allows you to make changes to the look of the form. Form view is the view you use to examine or make changes to the data.

How can I tell when I am in Layout view?
Access identifies Layout view in three ways. The left side of the status bar will contain the words, Layout View; shading will appear around the outside of the selected field in the form; and the Layout View button will be selected on the right side of the status bar.

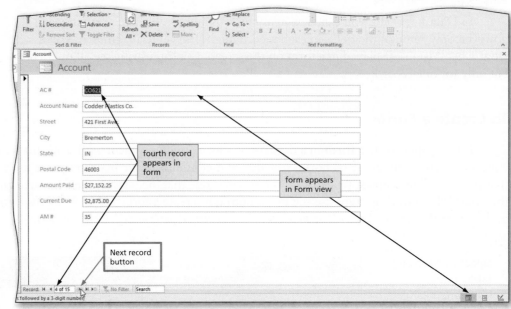

Figure 1–65

- Click the Next record button three times to move to record 4 (Figure 1–65).

4

- Click the Save button on the Quick Access Toolbar to display the Save As dialog box (Figure 1–66).

Q&A Do I have to click the Next record button before saving?
No. The only reason you were asked to click the button was so that you could experience navigation within the form.

Figure 1–66

5

- Type **Account Form** as the form name, and then click the OK button to save the form.
- Click the Close button for the form to close the form.

Other Ways

1. Click View button (Form Layout Tools Design tab | Views group)

Using a Form

After you have saved a form, you can use it at any time by right-clicking the form in the Navigation Pane and then clicking Open on the shortcut menu. In addition to viewing data in the form, you can also use it to enter or update data, a process that is very similar to updating data using a datasheet. If you plan to use the form to enter or revise data, you must ensure you are viewing the form in Form view.

Break Point: If you wish to take a break, this is a good place to do so. You can exit Access now. To resume at a later time, run Access, open the database called PrattLast Associates, and continue following the steps from this location forward.

Creating and Printing Reports

PrattLast Associates wants to be able to present account financial data in a useful format. To do so, they will create the Account Financial Report shown in Figure 1–67. To create this report, you will first create a simple report containing all records. Then, you will modify the report to match the one shown in Figure 1–67.

Account Number	Account Name	Amount Paid	Current Due	Account Manager Number
	Account Financial Report		Tuesday, September 12, 2017	7:54:24 PM
AC001	Avondale Community Bank	$24,752.25	$3,875.25	31
BL235	Bland Corp.	$29,836.65	$2,765.30	35
CA043	Carlton Regional Clinic	$30,841.05	$3,074.30	58
CO621	Codder Plastics Co.	$27,152.25	$2,875.00	35
EC010	Eco Clothes Inc.	$19,620.00	$1,875.00	58
HL111	Halko Legal Associates	$25,702.20	$3,016.75	58
JM323	JSP Manufacturing Inc.	$19,739.70	$2,095.00	31
KV089	KAL Veterinary Services	$34,036.50	$580.00	35
KC156	Key Community College System	$10,952.25	$0.00	31
LC005	Lancaster County Hospital	$44,025.60	$3,590.80	58
LI268	Lars-Idsen Inc.	$0.00	$1,280.75	35
MI345	Midwest Library Consortium	$21,769.20	$2,890.60	31
ML008	Mums Landscaping Co.	$13,097.10	$2,450.00	35
TP098	TAL Packaging Systems	$22,696.95	$3,480.45	58
TW001	Tri-County Waste Disposal	$15,345.00	$2,875.50	31
		$339,566.70	$36,724.70	

Figure 1–67

To Create a Report

1 CREATE FIRST TABLE | 2 ADD RECORDS | 3 PRINT CONTENTS | 4 IMPORT RECORDS | 5 MODIFY SECOND TABLE | 6 CREATE QUERY | 7 CREATE FORM | **8 CREATE REPORT**

You will first create a report containing all fields. *Why? It is easiest to create a report with all the fields and then delete the fields you do not want.* The following steps create and save the initial report. They also modify the report title.

1

- Be sure the Account table is selected in the Navigation Pane.

- Click Create on the ribbon to display the Create tab (Figure 1–68).

Q&A
Do I need to select the Account table prior to clicking Create on the ribbon?
You do not need to select the table at that point. You do need to select a table prior to clicking the Report button, because Access will include all the fields in whichever table or query is currently selected.

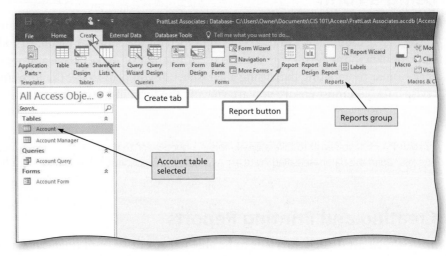

Figure 1–68

2

- Click the Report button (Create tab | Reports group) to create the report (Figure 1–69).

Q&A
Why is the report title Account?
Access automatically assigns the name of the table or query as the title of the report. It also automatically includes the date and time. You can change either of these later.

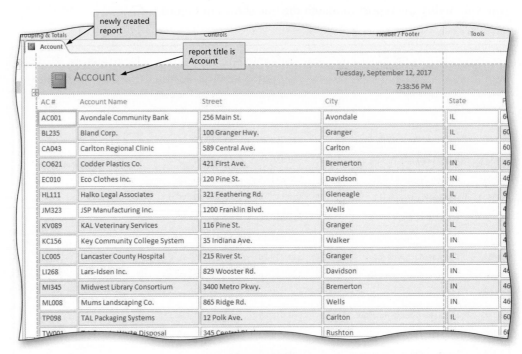

Figure 1–69

3

- Click the Save button on the Quick Access Toolbar to display the Save As dialog box, and then type Account Financial Report as the name of the report (Figure 1–70).

Figure 1–70

4

- Click the OK button (Save As dialog box) to save the report (Figure 1–71).

Q&A The name of the report changed. Why did the report title not change? The report title is assigned the same name as the report by default. Changing the name of the report does not change the report title. You can change the title at any time to anything you like.

Figure 1–71

5

- Close the report by clicking its Close button.

Using Layout View in a Report

Access has four different ways to view reports: Report view, Print Preview, Layout view, and Design view. Report view shows the report on the screen. Print Preview shows the report as it will appear when printed. Layout view is similar to Report view in that it shows the report on the screen, but it also allows you to make changes to the report. Layout view is usually the easiest way to make such changes. Design view also allows you to make changes, but does not show you the actual report. Design view is most useful when the changes you need to make are especially complex. In this module, you will use Layout view to modify the report.

BTW

Report Navigation
When previewing a report, you can use the Navigation buttons on the status bar to move from one page to another.

To Modify Report Column Headings and Resize Columns

1 CREATE FIRST TABLE | 2 ADD RECORDS | 3 PRINT CONTENTS | 4 IMPORT RECORDS
5 MODIFY SECOND TABLE | 6 CREATE QUERY | 7 CREATE FORM | **8 CREATE REPORT**

To make the report match the one shown in Figure 1–67, you need to change the title, remove some columns, modify the column headings, and also resize the columns. The following steps use Layout view to make the necessary modifications to the report. *Why? Working in Layout view gives you all the tools you need to make the desired modifications. You can view the results of the modifications immediately.*

1

- Right-click Account Financial Report in the Navigation Pane, and then click Layout View on the shortcut menu to open the report in Layout view.

- If a Field list appears, click the 'Add Existing Fields' button (Report Layout Tools Design tab | Tools group) to remove the Field list from the screen.

- Close the Navigation Pane.

- Click the report title once to select it.

- Click the report title a second time to produce an insertion point (Figure 1–72).

Figure 1–72

Q&A My insertion point is in the middle of Account. How do I produce an insertion point at the position shown in the figure? You can use the RIGHT ARROW key to move the insertion point to the position in the figure, or you can click the desired position.

2

- Press the SPACEBAR to insert a space, and then type **Financial Report** to complete the title.

- Click the column heading for the Street field to select it.

- Press and hold the CTRL key and then click the column headings for the City, State, and Postal Code fields to select multiple column headings.

Q&A What happens if I do not hold down the CTRL key?

When you click another column heading, it will be the only one that is selected. To select multiple objects, you need to hold the CTRL key down for every object after the first selection.

I selected the wrong collection of objects. What should I do?

You can click somewhere else on the report so that the objects you want are not selected, and then begin the process again. Alternatively, you can repeatedly click the Undo button on the Quick Access Toolbar to undo your selections. Once you have done so, you can select the objects you want.

- Click Arrange on the ribbon to display the Report Layout Tools Arrange tab (Figure 1–73).

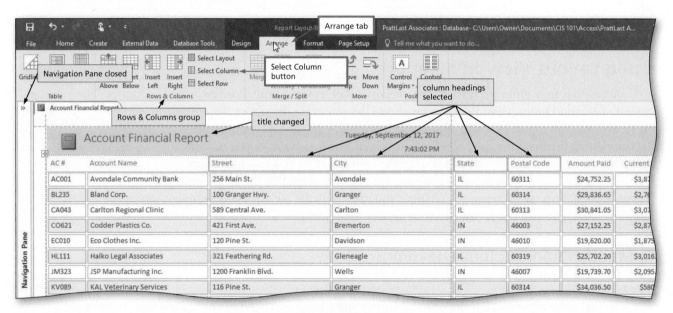

Figure 1–73

3

- Click the Select Column button (Report Layout Tools Arrange tab | Rows & Columns group) to select the entire columns corresponding to the column headings you selected in the previous step.

- Press the DELETE key to delete the selected columns.

- Click the column heading for the Account Number field twice, once to select it and the second time to produce an insertion point (Figure 1–74).

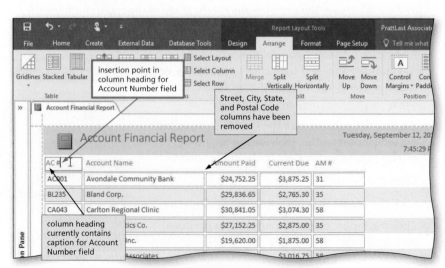

Figure 1–74

Q&A I selected the wrong field. What should I do?

Click somewhere outside the various fields to deselect the one you have selected. Then, click the Account Number field twice.

4

- Use the DELETE or BACKSPACE keys as necessary to erase the current entry, and then type **Account Number** as the new entry.

- Click the heading for the Account Manager Number field twice, erase the current entry, and then type **Account Manager Number** as the new entry.

- Click the Account Number field heading to select it, point to the lower boundary of the heading for the Account Number field so that the pointer changes to a two-headed arrow, and then drag the

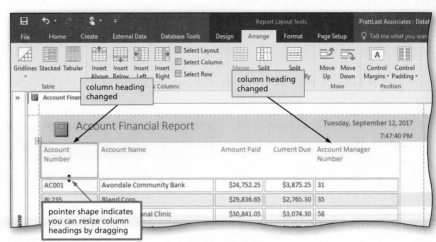

Figure 1–75

lower boundary to the approximate position shown in Figure 1–75 to expand the column headings.

Q&A I did something wrong when I dragged and now my report looks strange. What should I do?
Click the Undo button on the Quick Access Toolbar to undo the change. Depending on the specific action you took, you might need to click it more than once.

My screen displays Account Manager Number on one line, not two. Is this a problem?
No. You will adjust the column heading in a later step.

5

- Point to the right boundary of the heading for the Account Number field so that the pointer changes to a two-headed arrow, and then drag the right boundary to the approximate position shown in Figure 1–76 to reduce the width of the column.

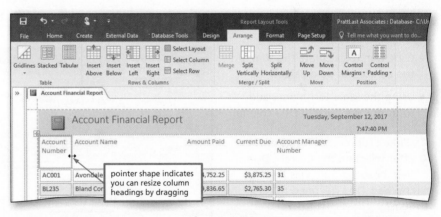

Figure 1–76

6

- Using the same technique, resize the other columns to the sizes shown in Figure 1–77.

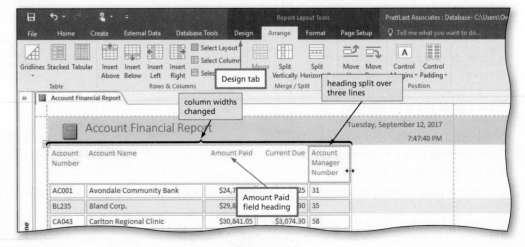

Figure 1–77

To Add Totals to a Report

The report in Figure 1–67 contains totals for the Amount Paid and Current Due columns. You can use Layout view to add these totals. Once you have added the totals, Access will calculate the appropriate values whenever you display or print the report. The following steps use Layout view to include totals for these three columns. *Why? In Layout view you can click a single button to add totals. This button sums all the values in the field.*

❶

- Click the Amount Paid field heading (shown in Figure 1–77) to select the field.

Q&A Do I have to click the heading? Could I click the field on one of the records?
You do not have to click the heading. You also could click the Amount Paid field on any record.

- Click Design on the ribbon to display the Design tab.

- Click the Totals button (Report Layout Tools Design tab | Grouping & Totals group) to display the Totals menu containing a list of available calculations (Figure 1–78).

Figure 1–78

❷

- Click Sum to calculate the sum of the amount of paid values.

- Using the same technique, add totals for the Current Due column.

Q&A When I clicked the Totals button after selecting the Current Due field heading, Sum was already checked. Do I still need to click Sum?
No. In fact, if you do click it, you will remove the check mark, which will remove the total from the column.

- Scroll down to the bottom of the report to verify that the totals are included. If necessary, expand the size of the total controls so they appear completely by dragging the lower boundary of the controls to the approximate position shown in Figure 1–79.

Figure 1–79

- Click the page number to select it, and then drag it to the approximate position shown in Figure 1–79.

Q&A Why did I need to move the page number?
The dotted line near the right-hand edge of the screen indicates the right-hand border of the available space on the printed page, based on whatever margins and orientation are currently selected. A portion of the page number extends beyond this border. By moving the page number, it no longer extends beyond the border.

③

- Click the Save button on the Quick Access Toolbar to save your changes to the report layout.

- Close the report.

To Print a Report

The following steps print the report.

① Open the Navigation Pane, if necessary, confirm that the Account Financial Report is selected, and then click File on the ribbon to open the Backstage view.

② Click the Print tab in the Backstage view to display the Print gallery.

③ Click the Quick Print button to print the report.

Q&A When I print the report, I have pound signs (####) rather than numbers where the totals should be for the Amount Paid and Current Due columns. The report looked fine on the screen. How can I correct it?
The columns are not wide enough to display the complete number. Open the report in Layout view and slightly increase the width of the Amount Paid and Current Due columns by dragging the right boundary of the column headings.

How can I print multiple copies of my report?
Click File on the ribbon to open the Backstage view. Click the Print tab, click Print in the Print gallery to display the Print dialog box, increase the number in the Number of Copies box, and then click the OK button .

How can I print a range of pages rather than printing the whole report?
Click File on the ribbon to open the Backstage view. Click the Print tab, click Print in the Print gallery to display the Print dialog box, click the Pages option button in the Print Range area, enter the desired page range, and then click the OK button (Print dialog box).

Database Properties

Access helps you organize and identify your databases by using **database properties,** which are the details about a file. Database properties, also known as **metadata,** can include such information as the project author, title, or subject. **Keywords** are words or phrases that further describe the database. For example, a class name or database topic can describe the file's purpose or content.

Five different types of database properties exist, but the more common ones used in this book are standard and automatically updated properties. **Standard properties** are associated with all Microsoft Office documents and include author, title, and subject. **Automatically updated properties** include file system properties, such as the date you create or change a file, and statistics, such as the file size.

BTW

Distributing a Document
Instead of printing and distributing a hard copy of a document, you can distribute the document electronically. Options include sending the document via email; posting it on cloud storage (such as OneDrive) and sharing the file with others; posting it on social media, a blog, or other website; and sharing a link associated with an online location of the document. You also can create and share a PDF or XPS image of the document, so that users can view the file in Acrobat Reader or XPS Viewer instead of in Access.

BTW

Exporting a Report as a PDF or XPS File
To export a report as a PDF or XPS file, display the External Data tab, and then click the PDF or XPS button (External Data tab | Export group). Enter the appropriate information in the Publish to PDF or XPS dialog box and click the Publish button.

CONSIDER THIS

Why would you want to assign database properties to a database?
Database properties are valuable for a variety of reasons:

- Users can save time locating a particular file because they can view a file's database properties without opening the database.

- By creating consistent properties for files having similar content, users can better organize their databases.

- Some organizations require Access users to add database properties so that other employees can view details about these files.

To Change Database Properties

To change database properties, you would follow these steps.

1 Click File on the ribbon to open the Backstage view and then, if necessary, click the Info tab in the Backstage view to display the Info gallery.

2 Click the 'View and edit database properties' link in the right pane of the Info gallery to display the PrattLast Associates Properties dialog box.

Q&A Why are some of the database properties already filled in?
The person who installed Office 2016 on your computer or network might have set or customized the properties.

3 If the property you want to change is displayed in the Properties dialog box, click the text box for the property and make the desired change. Skip the remaining steps.

4 If the property you want to change is not displayed in the Properties dialog box, click the appropriate tab so the property is displayed and then make the desired change.

5 Click the OK button in the Properties dialog box to save your changes and remove the dialog box from the screen.

BTW

Tabbed Documents Versus Overlapping Windows
By default, Access 2016 displays database objects in tabbed documents instead of in overlapping windows. If your database is in overlapping windows mode, click File on the ribbon, click Options in the Backstage view, click Current Database in the Access Options dialog box, and select the 'Display Document Tabs' check box and the Tabbed Documents option button.

Special Database Operations

Additional operations involved in maintaining a database are backup, recovery, compacting, and repairing.

Backup and Recovery

It is possible to damage or destroy a database. Users can enter data that is incorrect; programs that are updating the database can end abnormally during an update; a hardware problem can occur; and so on. After any such event has occurred, the database may contain invalid data or it might be totally destroyed.

Obviously, you cannot allow a situation in which data has been damaged or destroyed to go uncorrected. You must somehow return the database to a correct state. This process is called recovery; that is, you **recover** the database.

The simplest approach to recovery involves periodically making a copy of the database (called a **backup copy** or a **save copy**). This is referred to as **backing up** the database. If a problem occurs, you correct the problem by overwriting the actual database — often referred to as the **live database** — with the backup copy.

To back up the database that is currently open, you use the Back Up Database command on the Save As tab in the Backstage view. In the process, Access suggests a name that is a combination of the database name and the current date. For example, if you back up the PrattLast Associates database on October 20, 2017, Access will suggest the name, PrattLast Associates_2017-10-20. You can change this name if you desire, although it is a good idea to use this name. By doing so, it will be easy to distinguish between all the backup copies you have made to determine which is the most recent. In addition, if you discover that a critical problem occurred on October 18, 2017, you may want to go back to the most recent backup before October 18. If, for example, the database was not backed up on October 17 but was backed up on October 16, you would use PrattLast Associates_2017-10-16.

TO BACK UP A DATABASE

You would use the following steps to back up a database to a file on a hard disk, high-capacity removable disk, or other storage location.

1. Open the database to be backed up.
2. Click File on the ribbon to open the Backstage view, and then click the Save As tab.
3. With Save Database As selected in the File Types area, click 'Back Up Database' in the Save Database As area, and then click the Save As button.
4. Navigate to the desired location in the Save As box. If you do not want the name Access has suggested, enter the desired name in the File name text box.
5. Click the Save button to back up the database.

Access creates a backup copy with the desired name in the desired location. Should you ever need to recover the database using this backup copy, you can simply copy it over the live version.

Compacting and Repairing a Database

As you add more data to a database, it naturally grows larger. When you delete an object (records, tables, forms, or queries), the space previously occupied by the object does not become available for additional objects. Instead, the additional objects are given new space; that is, space that was not already allocated. To remove this empty space from the database, you must **compact** the database. The same option that compacts the database also repairs problems that might have occurred in the database.

TO COMPACT AND REPAIR A DATABASE

You would use the following steps to compact and repair a database.

1. Open the database to be compacted.
2. Click File on the ribbon to open the Backstage view, and then, if necessary, select the Info tab.
3. Click the 'Compact & Repair Database' button in the Info gallery to compact and repair the database.

The database now is the compacted form of the original.

Additional Operations

Additional special operations include opening another database, closing a database without exiting Access, and saving a database with another name. They also include deleting a table (or other object) as well as renaming an object.

When you are working in a database and you open another database, Access will automatically close the database that was previously open. Before deleting or renaming an object, you should ensure that the object has no dependent objects; that is, other objects that depend on the object you want to delete.

TO CLOSE A DATABASE WITHOUT EXITING ACCESS

You would use the following steps to close a database without exiting Access.

1. Click File on the ribbon to open the Backstage view.
2. Click Close.

To Save a Database with Another Name

To save a database with another name, you would use the following steps.

1. Click File on the ribbon to open the Backstage view, and then select the Save As tab.

2. With Save Database As selected in the File Types area and Access Database selected in the Save Database As area, click the Save As button.

3. Enter a name and select a location for the new version.

4. Click the Save button.

CONSIDER THIS

If you want to make a backup, could you just save the database with another name?
You could certainly do that. Using the backup procedure discussed earlier is useful because doing so automatically includes the current database name and the date in the name of the file it creates.

To Delete a Table or Other Object in the Database

You would use the following steps to delete a database object.

1. Right-click the object in the Navigation Pane.

2. Click Delete on the shortcut menu.

3. Click the Yes button in the Microsoft Access dialog box.

To Rename an Object in the Database

You would use the following steps to rename a database object.

1. Right-click the object in the Navigation Pane.

2. Click Rename on the shortcut menu.

3. Type the new name and press the ENTER key.

BTW
Access Help
At any time while using Access, you can find answers to questions and display information about various topics through Access Help. Used properly, this form of assistance can increase your productivity and reduce your frustrations by minimizing the time you spend learning how to use Access. For instructions about Access Help and exercises that will help you gain confidence in using it, read the Office and Windows module at the beginning of this book.

To Exit Access

All the steps in this module are now complete.

1 If desired, sign out of your Microsoft account.

2 Exit Access.

BTW
Determining Database Requirements
The determination of database requirements is part of a process known as systems analysis. A systems analyst examines existing and proposed documents, and examines organizational policies to determine exactly the type of data needs the database must support.

Database Design

This section illustrates the **database design** process, that is, the process of determining the tables and fields that make up the database. It does so by showing how you would design the database for PrattLast Associates from a set of requirements. In this section, you will use commonly accepted shorthand to represent the tables and fields that make up the database as well as the primary keys for the tables. For each table, you give the name of the table followed by a set of parentheses. Within the parentheses is a list of the fields in the table separated by commas. You underline the primary key. For example,

Product (Product Code, Description, On Hand, Price)

represents a table called Product. The Product table contains four fields: Product Code, Description, On Hand, and Price. The Product Code field is the primary key.

Database Requirements

The PrattLast Associates database must maintain information on both accounts and account managers. The business currently keeps this data in two Word tables and two Excel workbooks, as shown in Figure 1–80. They use Word tables for address information and Excel workbooks for financial information.

- For accounts, PrattLast needs to maintain address data. It currently keeps this data in a Word table (Figure 1–80a).

- PrattLast also maintains financial data for each account. This includes the amount paid and current amount due for the account. It keeps these amounts, along with the account name and number, in the Excel worksheet shown in Figure 1–80b.

- PrattLast keeps account manager address data in a Word table, as shown in Figure 1–80c.

- Just as with accounts, it keeps financial data for account managers, including their start date, salary, and bonus rate, in a separate Excel worksheet, as shown in Figure 1–80d.

Finally, PrattLast keeps track of which accounts are assigned to which account managers. Each account is assigned to a single account manager, but each account manager might be assigned many accounts. Currently, for example, accounts AC001 (Avondale Community Bank), JM323 (JSP Manufacturing Inc.), KC156 (Key Community College System), MI345 (Midwest Library Consortium), and TW001 (Tri-County Waste Disposal) are assigned to account manager 31 (Haydee Rivera). Accounts BL235 (Bland Corp.), CO621 (Codder Plastics Co.), KV089 (KAL Veterinary Services), LI268 (Lars-Idsen Inc.), and ML008 (Mums Landscaping Co.) are assigned to account manager 35 (Mark Simson). Accounts CA043 (Carlton Regional Clinic), EC010 (Eco Clothes Inc.), HL111 (Halko Legal Associates), LC005 (Lancaster County Hospital), and TP098 (TAL Packaging Systems) are assigned to account manager 58 (Karen Murowski). PrattLast has an additional account manager, Peter Lu, whose number has been assigned as 42, but who has not yet been assigned any accounts.

BTW

Additional Data for PrattLast Associates

PrattLast could include other types of data in the database. The Account table could include data on a contact person at each organization, such as name, telephone number, and email address. The Account Manager table could include the mobile telephone number, email address, and emergency contact information for the account manager.

Account Number	Account Name	Street	City	State	Postal Code
AC001	Avondale Community Bank	256 Main St.	Avondale	IL	60311
BL235	Bland Corp.	100 Granger Hwy.	Granger	IL	60314
CA043	Carlton Regional Clinic	589 Central Ave.	Carlton	IL	60313
CO621	Codder Plastics Co.	421 First Ave.	Bremerton	IN	46003
EC010	Eco Clothes Inc.	120 Pine St.	Davidson	IN	46010
HL111	Halko Legal Associates	321 Feathering Rd.	Gleneagle	IL	60319
JM323	JSP Manufacturing Inc.	1200 Franklin Blvd.	Wells	IN	46007
KC156	Key Community College System	35 Indiana Ave.	Walker	IN	46004
KV089	KAL Veterinary Services	116 Pine St.	Granger	IL	60314
LC005	Lancaster County Hospital	215 River St.	Granger	IL	46004
LI268	Lars-Idsen Inc.	829 Wooster Rd.	Davidson	IN	46010
MI345	Midwest Library Consortium	3400 Metro Pkwy.	Bremerton	IN	46003
ML008	Mums Landscaping Co.	865 Ridge Rd.	Wells	IN	46007
TP098	TAL Packaging Systems	12 Polk Ave.	Carlton	IL	60313
TW001	Tri-County Waste Disposal	345 Central Blvd.	Rushton	IL	60321

Figure 1–80a Account Addresses

A1	▾	⋮	✕	✓	*fx*	Account Number				

	A	B	C	D	E	F	G	H	I	J
1	Account Number	Account Name	Amount Paid	Current Due						
2	AC001	Avondale Community Bank	24,752.25	3,875.25						
3	BL235	Bland Corp.	29,836.65	2,765.30						
4	CA043	Carlton Regional Clinic	30,841.05	3,074.30						
5	CO621	Codder Plastics Co.	27,152.25	2,875.00						
6	EC010	Eco Clothes Inc.	19,620.00	1,875.00						
7	HL111	Halko Legal Associates	25,702.20	3,016.75						
8	JM323	JSP Manufacturing Inc.	19,739.70	2,095.00						
9	KV089	KAL Veterinary Services	34,036.50	580.00						
10	KC156	Key Community College System	10,952.25	0.00						
11	LC005	Lancaster County Hospital	44,025.60	3,590.80						
12	LI268	Lars-Idsen Inc.	0.00	1,280.75						
13	MI345	Midwest Library Consortium	21,769.20	2,890.60						
14	ML008	Mums Landscaping Co.	13,097.10	2,450.00						
15	TP098	TAL Packaging Systems	22,696.95	3,480.45						
16	TW001	Tri-County Waste Disposal	15,345.00	2,875.50						

Figure 1–80b Account Financial Data

Account Manager Number	Last Name	First Name	Street	City	State	Postal Code
31	Rivera	Haydee	325 Twiddy St.	Avondale	IL	60311
35	Simson	Mark	1467 Hartwell St.	Walker	IN	46004
42	Lu	Peter	5624 Murray Ave.	Davidson	IN	46007
58	Murowski	Karen	168 Truesdale Dr.	Carlton	IL	60313

Figure 1–80c Account Manager Addresses

	A	B	C	D	E	F	G	H	I
1	Account Manager Number	Last Name	First Name	Start Date	Salary	Bonus Rate			
2	31	Rivera	Haydee	6/3/2013	48,750.00	0.15			
3	35	Simson	Mark	5/19/2014	40,500.00	0.12			
4	42	Lu	Peter	8/3/2015	36,750.00	0.09			
5	58	Murowski	Karen	11/9/2016	24,000.00	0.08			
6									

Figure 1–80d Account Manager Financial Data

Database Design Process

The database design process involves several steps.

CONSIDER THIS

What is the first step in the process?
Identify the tables. Examine the requirements for the database to identify the main objects that are involved. There will be a table for each object you identify.

In a database for one organization, for example, the main objects might be departments and employees. This would require two tables: one for departments and the other for employees. In the database for another organization, the main objects might be accounts and account managers. In this case, there also would be two tables: one for accounts and the other for account managers. In still another organization's database, the main objects might be books, publishers, and authors. This database would require three tables: one for books, a second for publishers, and a third for authors.

Identifying the Tables

For the PrattLast Associates database, the main objects are accounts and account managers. This leads to two tables, which you must name. Reasonable names for these two tables are:

Account

Account Manager

CONSIDER THIS

After identifying the tables, what is the second step in the database design process?
Determine the primary keys. Recall that the primary key is the unique identifier for records in the table. For each table, determine the unique identifier. In a Department table, for example, the unique identifier might be the Department Code. For a Book table, the unique identifier might be the ISBN (International Standard Book Number).

Determining the Primary Keys

The next step is to identify the fields that will be the unique identifiers, or primary keys. Account numbers uniquely identify accounts, and account manager numbers uniquely identify account managers. Thus, the primary key for the Account table is the account number, and the primary key for the Account Manager table is the account manager number. Reasonable names for these fields would be Account Number and Account Manager Number, respectively. Adding these primary keys to the tables gives:

Account (<u>Account Number</u>)

Account Manager (<u>Account Manager Number</u>)

CONSIDER THIS

What is the third step in the database design process after determining the primary keys?
Determine the additional fields. The primary key will be a field or combination of fields in a table. A table will typically contain many additional fields, each of which contains a type of data. Examine the project requirements to determine these additional fields. For example, in an Employee table, additional fields might include Employee Name, Street Address, City, State, Postal Code, Date Hired, and Salary.

Determining Additional Fields

After identifying the primary keys, you need to determine and name the additional fields. In addition to the account number, the Account Address Information shown in Figure 1–80a contains the account name, street, city, state, and postal code. These would be fields in the Account table. The Account Financial Information shown in Figure 1–80b also contains the account number and account name, which are already included in the Account table. The financial information also contains the amount paid and current due. Adding the amount paid and current due fields to those already identified in the Account table and assigning reasonable names gives:

Account (<u>Account Number</u>, Account Name, Street, City, State, Postal Code, Amount Paid, Current Due)

Similarly, examining the Account Manager Address Information in Figure 1–80c adds the last name, first name, street, city, state, and postal code fields to the Account Manager table. In addition to the account manager number, last name, and first name, the Account Manager Financial Information in Figure 1–80d would add the start date, salary, and bonus rate. Adding these fields to the Account Manager table and assigning reasonable names gives:

Account Manager (<u>Account Manager Number</u>, Last Name, First Name, Street, City, State, Postal Code, Start Date, Salary, Bonus Rate)

BTW
Database Design Language (DBDL)
Database Design Language (DBDL) is a commonly accepted shorthand representation for showing the structure of a relational database. You write the name of the table and then within parentheses you list all the columns in the table. If the columns continue beyond one line, indent the subsequent lines.

What happens as the fourth step, after determining additional fields?

Determine relationships between the tables. A relationship is an association between objects. In a database containing information about departments and employees, there is an association between the departments and the employees. A department is associated with all the employees in the department, and an employee is associated with the department to which he or she is assigned. Technically, you say that a department is related to all the employees in the department, and an employee is related to his or her department.

The relationship between department and employees is an example of a **one-to-many relationship** because one employee is associated with one department, but each department can be associated with many employees. The Department table would be the "one" table in the relationship. The Employee table would be the "many" table in the relationship.

When you have determined that two tables are related, follow these general guidelines:

• Identify the "one" table.

• Identify the "many" table.

• Include the primary key from the "one" table as a field in the "many" table.

Determining and Implementing Relationships between the Tables

According to the requirements, each account has one account manager, but each account manager can have many accounts. Thus, the Account Manager table is the "one" table, and the Account table is the "many" table. To implement this one-to-many relationship between account managers and accounts, add the Account Manager Number field (the primary key of the Account Manager table) to the Account table. This produces:

Account (<u>Account Number</u>, Account Name, Street, City, State, Postal Code, Amount Paid, Current Due, Account Manager Number)

Account Manager (<u>Account Manager Number</u>, Last Name, First Name, Street, City, State, Postal Code, Start Date, Salary, Bonus Rate)

After creating relationships between tables, what is the fifth step in the database design process?

Determine data types for the fields, that is, the type of data that can be stored in the field.

Assigning Data Types to the Fields

See the earlier section Determing Data Types for the Fields for a discussion of the available data types and their use in the PrattLast Associates database. That section also discusses other properties that can be assigned, such as captions, field size, and the number of decimal places.

Identifying and Removing Redundancy

Redundancy means storing the same fact in more than one place. It usually results from placing too many fields in a table — fields that really belong in separate tables — and often causes serious problems. If you had not realized there were two objects, such as accounts and account managers, you might have placed all the data in a single Account table. Figure 1–81 shows an example of a table that includes both account and account manager information. Notice that the data for a given account manager (number, name, address, and so on) occurs on more than one record. The data for rep 35, Mark Simson, is repeated in the figure. Storing this data on multiple records is an example of redundancy.

Account table

Account Number	Account Name	Street	...	Account Manager Number	Last Name	First Name
AC001	Avondale Community Bank	256 Main St.	...	31	Rivera	Haydee
BL235	Bland Corp.	100 Granger Hwy.	...	35	Simson	Mark
CA043	Carlton Regional Clinic	589 Central Ave.	...	58	Murowski	Karen
CO621	Codder Plastics Co.	421 First Ave.	...	35	Simson	Mark
EC010	Eco Clothes Inc.	120 Pine St.	...	58	Murowski	Karen
...	...	...	...	...	...	...
...	...	...	...	...	...	...

Account Manager numbers are 35

name of Account Manager 35 appears more than once

Figure 1–81

What problems does this redundancy cause?

Redundancy results in several problems, including:

1. Wasted storage space. The name of account manager 35, Mark Simson, for example, should be stored only once. Storing this information several times is wasteful.

2. More complex database updates. If, for example, Mark Simson's name is spelled incorrectly and needs to be changed in the database, his name would need to be changed in several different places.

3. Possible inconsistent data. Nothing prohibits the account manager's last name from being Simson on account BL235's record and Stimson on account CO621's record. The data would be inconsistent. In both cases, the account manager number is 35, but the last names are different.

How do you eliminate redundancy?

The solution to the problem is to place the redundant data in a separate table, one in which the data will no longer be redundant. If, for example, you place the data for account managers in a separate table (Figure 1–82), the data for each account manager will appear only once.

Account table

Account Number	Account Name	Street	...	Account Manager Number
AC001	Avondale Community Bank	256 Main St.	...	31
BL235	Bland Corp.	100 Granger Hwy.	...	35
CA043	Carlton Regional Clinic	589 Central Ave.	...	58
CO621	Codder Plastics Co.	421 First Ave.	...	35
EC010	Eco Clothes Inc.	120 Pine St.	...	58
...	...	...	...	...
...	...	...	...	...

Account Manager numbers are 35

Account Manager Table

Account Manager Number	Last Name	First Name	...
31	Rivera	Haydee	...
35	Simson	Mark	...
42	Lu	Peter	...
58	Murowski	Karen	...

name of Account Manager 35 appears only once

Figure 1–82

Notice that you need to have the account manager number in both tables. Without it, there would be no way to tell which account manager is associated with which account. The remaining account manager data, however, was removed from the Account table and placed in the Account Manager table. This new arrangement corrects the problems of redundancy in the following ways:

• Because the data for each account manager is stored only once, space is not wasted.

• Changing the name of an account manager is easy. You need to change only one row in the Account Manager table.

• Because the data for an account manager is stored only once, inconsistent data cannot occur.

Designing to omit redundancy will help you to produce good and valid database designs. You should always examine your design to see if it contains redundancy. If it does, you should decide whether you need to remove the redundancy by creating a separate table.

If you examine your design, you will see that there is one area of redundancy (see the data in Figure 1–1). Cities and states are both repeated. Every account whose postal code is 60314, for example, has Granger as the city and IL as the state. To remove this redundancy, you would create a table with the primary key Postal Code and City and State as additional fields. City and State would be removed from the Account table. Having City, State, and Postal Code in a table is very common, however, and usually you would not take such action. No other redundancy exists in your tables.

Summary

In this module you have learned to create an Access database, create tables and add records to a database, print the contents of tables, import data, create queries, create forms, create reports, and change database properties. You have also learned how to design a database.

What decisions will you need to make when creating your next database?
Use these guidelines as you complete the assignments in this module and create your own databases outside of this class.

1. Identify the tables that will be included in the database.

2. Determine the primary keys for each of the tables.

3. Determine the additional fields that should be included in each of the tables.

4. Determine relationships between the tables.

    a) Identify the "one" table.

    b) Identify the "many" table.

    c) Include the primary key of the "one" table as a field in the "many" table.

5. Determine data types for the fields in the tables.

6. Determine additional properties for fields.

    a) Determine if a caption is warranted.

    b) Determine if a description of the field is warranted.

    c) Determine field sizes.

    d) Determine formats.

7. Identify and remove any unwanted redundancy.

8. Determine a storage location for the database.

9. Determine the best method for distributing the database objects.

CONSIDER THIS

How should you submit solutions to questions in the assignments identified with a symbol?

Every assignment in this book contains one or more questions identified with a symbol. These questions require you to think beyond the assigned database. Present your solutions to the questions in the format required by your instructor. Possible formats may include one or more of these options: write the answer; create a document that contains the answer; present your answer to the class; discuss your answer in a group; record the answer as audio or video using a webcam, smartphone, or portable media player; or post answers on a blog, wiki, or website.

Apply Your Knowledge

Reinforce the skills and apply the concepts you learned in this module.

Adding a Caption, Changing a Data Type, and Creating a Query, Form, and Report

Note: To complete this assignment, you will be required to use the Data Files. Please contact your instructor for information about accessing the Data Files.

Instructions: Friendly Janitorial Services provides janitorial services to local businesses. The company uses a team-based approach and each team has a team leader or supervisor. Friendly Janitorial Services has a database that keeps track of its supervisors and its clients. Each client is assigned to a single supervisor; each supervisor may be assigned many clients. The database has two tables. The Client table contains data on the clients who use Friendly Janitorial Services. The Supervisor table contains data on the supervisors. You will add a caption, change a data type, and create a query, a form, and a report, as shown in Figure 1–83.

Perform the following tasks:

1. Run Access, open the Apply Friendly Janitorial Services database from the Data Files, and enable the content.

2. Open the Supervisor table in Datasheet view, add SU # as the caption for the Supervisor Number field, and resize all columns to best fit the data. Save the changes to the layout of the table and close the table.

3. Open the Client table in Design view and change the data type for the Supervisor Number field to Short Text. Change the field size for the field to 3 and add SU # as the caption for the Supervisor Number field. Save the changes to the table and close the table. Then, open the Client table in Datasheet view and resize all columns to best fit the data. Save the changes to the layout of the table and close the table.

4. Use the Simple Query Wizard to create a query for the Client table that contains the Client Number, Client Name, Amount Paid, Current Due, and Supervisor Number. The query is a detail query. Use the name Client Query for the query and close the query.

5. Create a simple form for the Supervisor table. Save the form and use the name Supervisor for the form. Close the form.

6. Create the report shown in Figure 1–83 for the Client table. The report includes totals for both the Amount Paid and Current Due fields. Be sure the totals appear completely. You might need to expand the size of the total controls. Move the page number so that it is within the margins. Save the report as Client Financial Report.

7. If requested by your instructor, add your last name to the title of the report, that is, change the title to Client Financial Report LastName where LastName is your actual last name.

8. Compact and repair the database.

9. Submit the revised database in the format specified by your instructor.

10. ✳ How would you change the field name of the Street field in the Client table to Address?

Continued >

Apply Your Knowledge *continued*

Client Financial Report				Tuesday, September 12, 2017
				6:19:45 PM
Client Number	Client Name	Amount Paid	Current Due	Supervisor Number
AT13	Atlas Repair	$5,400.00	$600.00	103
AZ01	AZ Auto	$9,250.00	$975.00	110
BB35	Babbage Bookkeeping	$8,820.00	$980.00	110
BL24	Blanton Shoes	$1,850.75	$210.25	120
MM01	Moss Manufacturing	$10,456.25	$1,125.00	114
PL03	Prime Legal Associates	$19,905.00	$2,245.00	110
PS67	PRIM Staffing	$4,500.00	$500.00	114
TE15	Telton-Edwards	$0.00	$700.00	120
		$129,979.20	$14,542.55	

Figure 1–83

Extend Your Knowledge

Extend the skills you learned in this module and experiment with new skills. You may need to use Help to complete the assignment.

Using a Database Template to Create an Events Database

Instructions: Access includes both desktop database templates and web-based templates. You can use a template to create a beginning database that can be modified to meet your specific needs. You will use a template to create an Events database. The database template includes sample tables, queries, forms, and reports. You will modify the database and create the Events Query shown in Figure 1–84.

Perform the following tasks:
1. Run Access.
2. Select the Desktop event management template in the template gallery and create a new database with the file name Extend Events.
3. Enable the content and close the Event List form.
4. Open the Navigation Pane and change the organization to Object Type.
5. Open the Events table in Datasheet view and delete the Attachments field in the table. The Attachments field has a paperclip as the column heading.
6. Add the Event Type field to the end of the table. Assign the Short Text data type with a field size of 15.
7. Save the changes to the Events table and close the table.
8. Use the Simple Query Wizard to create the Events Query shown in Figure 1–84. Close the query.

Figure 1–84

9. Open the Current Events report in Layout view. Delete the controls containing the current date and current time in the upper-right corner of the report. Change the title of the report to Current Events List.

10. Save the changes to the report.

11. If requested to do so by your instructor, add your first and last names to the end of the title and save the changes to the report.

12. Submit the revised database in the format specified by your instructor.

13. ✴ a. Why would you use a template instead of creating a database from scratch with just the fields you need?

    b. The Attachment data type allows you to attach files to a database record. If you were using this database to keep track of events for a 4th of July celebration in a small town, what specific documents might you attach to an Events record?

Expand Your World

Create a solution, which uses cloud and web technologies, by learning and investigating on your own from general guidance.

Problem: You and two friends recently started a business that provides temporary non-medical help to individuals and families in need of assistance. You want to be able to share query results and reports, so you have decided to store the items in the cloud. You are still learning Access, so you are going to create a sample query and the report shown in Figure 1–85, export the results, and save to a cloud storage location, such as Microsoft OneDrive, Dropbox, or Google Drive.

Note: To complete this assignment, you will be required to use the Data Files. Please contact your instructor for information about accessing the Data Files.

Instructions:
1. Open the Expand Temporary Help database from the Data Files and enable the content.

2. Use the Simple Query Wizard to create a query that includes the Client Number, First Name, Last Name, Balance, and Helper Number. Save the query as Client Query.

3. Export the Client Query as an XPS document to a cloud-based storage location of your choice.

4. Create the report shown in Figure 1–85. Save the report as Client Status Report.

Continued >

Expand Your World *continued*

Figure 1–85

5. Export the Client Status Report as a PDF document to a cloud-based storage location of your choice. You do not need to change any optimization or export settings. Do not save the export steps.

6. If requested to do so by your instructor, open the Helper table and change the last name and first name for helper 203 to your last name and your first name.

7. Submit the assignment in the format specified by your instructor.

8. ✷ Which cloud-based storage location did you use for this assignment? Why?

In the Labs

Design, create, modify, and/or use a database following the guidelines, concepts, and skills presented in this module. Labs are listed in order of increasing difficulty. Labs 1 and 2, which increase in difficulty, require you to create solutions based on what you learned in the module; Lab 3 requires you to apply your creative thinking and problem-solving skills to design and implement a solution.

Lab 1: Creating Objects for the Garden Naturally Database

Problem: Garden Naturally is a company that provides products for the organic gardening community. Sales representatives are responsible for selling to distributors, nurseries, and retail stores. The company recently decided to store its customer and sales rep data in a database. Each customer is assigned to a single sales rep, but each sales rep may be assigned many customers. The database and the Sales Rep table have been created, but the Salary YTD field needs to be added to the table. The records shown in Table 1–6 must be added to the Sales Rep table. The company plans to import the Customer table from the Excel worksheet shown in Figure 1–86. Garden Naturally would like to finish storing this data in a database and has asked you to help.

Note: To complete this assignment, you will be required to use the Data Files. Please contact your instructor for information about accessing the Data Files.

Instructions: Perform the following tasks:

1. Run Access, open the Lab 1 Garden Naturally database from the Data Files, and enable the content.

2. Open the Sales Rep table in Datasheet view and add the Salary YTD field to the end of the table. The field has the Currency data type. Assign the caption SR # to the Sales Rep Number field.

3. Add the records shown in Table 1–6.

Table 1–6 Data for Sales Rep Table

Sales Rep Number	Last Name	First Name	Street	City	State	Postal Code	Start Date	Commission Rate	Salary YTD
32	Ortiz	Gloria	982 Victoria Ln.	Chesnee	NJ	07053	9/12/2015	.05	$32,555.65
35	Sinson	Mike	45 Elm St.	Quaker	DE	19719	8/28/2017	.04	$1,500.00
29	Gupta	Rufus	678 Hillcrest Rd.	Gossett	PA	19157	6/1/2015	.06	$35,075.30
26	Jones	Pat	43 Third St.	Greer	PA	19158	5/16/2016	.05	$33,100.50

4. Resize the columns to best fit the data. Save the changes to the layout of the table.

5. Import the Lab 1–1 Customer workbook shown in Figure 1–86 into the database. The first row of the workbook contains the column headings. Customer Number is the primary key for the new table. Assign the name Customer to the table. Save the Import steps, and assign the name Import-Customer Workbook to the steps. Assign Import Customer Workbook as the description.

	A	B	C	D	E	F	G	H	I
1	Customer Number	Customer Name	Address	City	State	Postal Code	Amount Paid	Balance Due	Sales Rep Number
2	AA30	All About Gardens	47 Berton St.	Greer	PA	19158	$1,190.00	$365.00	26
3	CT02	Christmas Tree Farm	483 Cantor Rd.	Pleasantburg	NJ	07025	$2,285.50	$825.35	29
4	GG01	Garden Gnome	10 Main St.	Gossett	PA	19157	$1,300.00	$297.50	29
5	GT34	Green Thumb Growers	26 Jefferson Hwy.	Pleasantburg	NJ	07025	$3,325.45	$865.50	32
6	LH15	Lawn & Home Store	33 Maple St.	Chambers	NJ	07037	$895.00	$515.00	26
7	ML25	Mum's Landscaping	196 Lincoln Ave.	Quaker	DE	19719	$0.00	$1,805.00	29
8	OA45	Outside Architects	234 Magnolia Rd.	Gaston	DE	19723	$4,205.50	$945.00	32
9	PL10	Pat's Landscaping	22 Main St.	Chesnee	NJ	07053	$1,165.00	$180.00	26
10	PN18	Pyke Nurseries	10 Grant Blvd.	Adelphia	PA	19159	$2,465.00	$530.00	32
11	SL25	Summit Lawn Service	345 Oaktree Rd.	Chesnee	NJ	07053	$3,225.45	$675.50	26
12	TG38	TriState Growers	24 Main St.	Gaston	DE	19723	$1,075.00	$0.00	29
13	TW34	TAL Wholesalers	234 Cantor Rd.	Pleasantburg	NJ	07025	$4,125.00	$350.00	26
14	TY03	TLC Yard Care	24 Berton St.	Greer	PA	19158	$1,845.00	$689.45	29
15	YS04	Yard Shoppe	124 Elm St.	Quaker	DE	19719	$445.00	$575.00	32
16	YW01	Young's Wholesalers	5239 Lancaster Hwy.	Adelphia	PA	19156	$1,785.50	$345.60	32
17									
18									
19									
20									
21									

Figure 1–86

Continued >

In the Labs *continued*

6. Open the Customer table in Design view and make the following changes:

   a. Change the field size for the Customer Number field to 4. Change the field size for the Customer Name field to 30. Change the field size for the Address field to 25 and the field size for the City field to 20. Change the field size for the State field to 2 and the field size for the Postal Code field to 5. Change the field size for the Sales Rep Number field to 2.

   b. Add the caption CU # to the Customer Number field.

   c. Add the caption SR # to the Sales Rep Number field.

7. Save the changes to the Customer table. If a Microsoft Access dialog box appears with the 'Some data may be lost' message, click the Yes button.

8. Open the Customer table in Datasheet view and resize all columns to best fit the data. Save the changes to the layout of the table.

9. Create a query using the Simple Query Wizard for the Customer table that displays the Customer Number, Customer Name, Amount Paid, Balance Due, and Sales Rep Number. Save the query as Customer Query.

Customer Financial Report

Tuesday, September 12, 2017
6:25:09 PM

Customer Number	Customer Name	Amount Paid	Balance Due	Sales Rep Number
AA30	All About Gardens	$1,190.00	$365.00	26
CT02	Christmas Tree Farm	$2,285.50	$825.35	29
TG38	TriState Growers	$1,075.00	$0.00	29
TW34	TAL Wholesalers	$4,125.00	$350.00	26
TY03	TLC Yard Care	$1,845.00	$689.45	29
YS04	Yard Shoppe	$445.00	$575.00	32
YW01	Young's Wholesalers	$1,785.50	$345.60	32
		$29,332.40	$8,963.90	

Figure 1–87

10. Create the report shown in Figure 1–87 for the Customer table. The report should include the Customer Number, Customer Name, Amount Paid, Balance Due, and Sales Rep Number fields. Include totals for the Amount Paid and Balance Due fields. Be sure to change the column headings to those shown in Figure 1–87. Save the report as Customer Financial Report.

11. If requested to do so by your instructor, change the address for Pat Jones in the Sales Rep table to your address. If your address is longer than 20 characters, simply enter as much as you can.

12. Submit the revised database in the format specified by your instructor.

13. ✳ The Commission Rate field has a field size of Single. If you changed the field size to Integer, what values would appear in the Commission Rate column? Why?

Lab 2: **Creating the Museum Gift Shop Database**

Problem: The local science museum operates a gift shop that sells science-related items. The gift shop purchases the items from vendors that deal in science-related games, toys, and other merchandise. Currently, the information about the items and the vendors is stored in two Excel workbooks. Each item is assigned to a single vendor, but each vendor may be assigned many items. You are to create a database that will store the item and vendor information. You have already determined that you need two tables, a Vendor table and an Item table, in which to store the information.

Note: To complete this assignment, you will be required to use the Data Files. Please contact your instructor for information about accessing the Data Files.

Instructions: Perform the following tasks:
1. Use the Blank desktop database option to create a new database in which to store all objects related to the items for sale. Call the database Lab 2 Museum Gift Shop.

2. Import the Lab 1–2 Vendor Data Excel workbook into the database. The first row of the workbook contains the column headings. Vendor Code is the primary key for the new table. Assign the name Vendor to the table. Do not save the Import steps.

3. Open the Vendor table in Datasheet view. Change the field size for the Vendor Code field to 2; the field size for the Vendor Name field to 25; and the field size for the Telephone Number field to 12. Assign the caption VC to the Vendor Code field.

4. Import the Lab 1–2 Item Data Excel workbook into the database. The first row of the workbook contains the column headings. Item Number is the primary key for this table. Assign the name Item to the table. Do not save the Import steps.

5. Open the Item table in Design view. Change the field size for the Item Number field to 4. Change the field size for the Description field to 28. Add the caption Wholesale for the Wholesale Cost field, the caption Retail for the Retail Price field, and the caption VC for the vendor code. The On Hand field should be an Integer field. Be sure that the field size for the Vendor Code in the Item table is identical to the field size for the Vendor Code in the Vendor table. Save the changes to the table and close the table.

6. Open the Item table in Datasheet view and resize the columns to best fit the data. Save the changes to the layout of the table and close the table.

7. Create a query for the Item table. Include the Item Number, Description, Wholesale Cost, Retail Price, and Vendor Code. Save the query as Item Query.

8. Create a simple form for the Item table. Use the name Item for the form.

9. Create the report shown in Figure 1–88 for the Item table. Do not add any totals. Save the report as Item Status Report.

Item Status Report			Tuesday, September 12, 2017 6:26:31 PM
Item Number	Description	On Hand	Wholesale Price
3663	Agate Bookends	4	$16.25
3673	Amazing Science Fun	8	$13.50
4553	Cosmos Uncovered	9	$8.95
4573	Crystal Growing Kit	7	$6.75
4583	Dinosaur Egg Ornament	12	$7.50

Figure 1–88

Continued >

In the Labs *continued*

10. If requested to do so by your instructor, change the telephone number for Atherton Wholesalers to your telephone number.

11. Submit the database in the format specified by your instructor.

12. ✳ If you had designed this database, could you have used the field name, Name, for the Vendor Name field name? If not, why not?

Lab 3: **Consider This: Your Turn**

Apply your creative thinking and problem solving skills to design and implement a solution.

Creating the Camshay Marketing Database

Note: To complete this assignment, you will be required to use the Data Files. Please contact your instructor for information about accessing the Data Files.

Part 1: Camshay Marketing Associates is a small company that specializes in data mining for marketing research and analysis. The company focuses on the service, nonprofit, and retail sectors. Camshay uses marketing analysts to work collaboratively with clients. Marketing analysts are paid a base salary and can earn incentive pay for maintaining and expanding client relationships. Based on the information in the Lab 1–3 Camshay Marketing workbook, use the concepts and techniques presented in this module to design and create a database to store the Camshay Marketing data. Change data types and field sizes as necessary. Add captions where appropriate. Create a form for the Client table and a report for the Client table similar to the Account Financial Report shown in Figure 1-67. Use the simple query wizard to create a query for the Client table that includes the Client Number, Client Name, Current Due and Marketing Analyst Number. Open the query and add a criterion to the query results to find only those clients whose amount due is $0.00 and save this modified query with a different name. Submit your assignment in the format specified by your instructor.

Part 2: You made several decisions while determining the table structures and adding data to the tables in this assignment. What method did you use to add the data to each table? Are there any other methods that would also have worked?

PrattLast Associates : Database- C:\Users\Owner\Documents\CIS

Microsoft Access 2016

File   Home   Create   External Data   Database Tools   ♀ Tell me what you want to do...

2 | Querying a Database

Objectives

You will have mastered the material in this module when you can:

- Create queries using Design view
- Include fields in the design grid
- Use text and numeric data in criteria
- Save a query and use the saved query
- Create and use parameter queries
- Use compound criteria in queries
- Sort data in queries

- Join tables in queries
- Create a report and a form from a query
- Export data from a query to another application
- Perform calculations and calculate statistics in queries
- Create crosstab queries
- Customize the Navigation Pane

Introduction

One of the primary benefits of using a database management system such as Access is having the ability to find answers to questions related to data stored in the database. When you pose a question to Access, or any other database management system, the question is called a query. A **query** is simply a question presented in a way that Access can process.

To find the answer to a question, you first create a corresponding query using the techniques illustrated in this module. After you have created the query, you instruct Access to run the query, that is, to perform the steps necessary to obtain the answer. Access then displays the answer in Datasheet view.

For an introduction to Windows and instructions about how to perform basic Windows tasks, read the Office and Windows module at the beginning of this book, where you can learn how to resize windows, change screen resolution, create folders, move and rename files, use Windows Help, and much more

Project — Querying a Database

Examples of questions related to the data in the PrattLast Associates database are shown in Figure 2–1.

In addition to these questions, PrattLast managers need to find information about accounts located in a specific city, but they want to enter a different city each time they ask the question. The company can use a parameter query to accomplish this task. PrattLast managers also want to summarize data in a specific way, which might involve performing calculations, and they can use a crosstab query to present the data in the desired form.

Microsoft Access 2016
File   Home   Create   External Data   Database Tools   Tell me what you want to do...

PrattLast Associates : Database- C:\Users\Owner\Documents\CIS

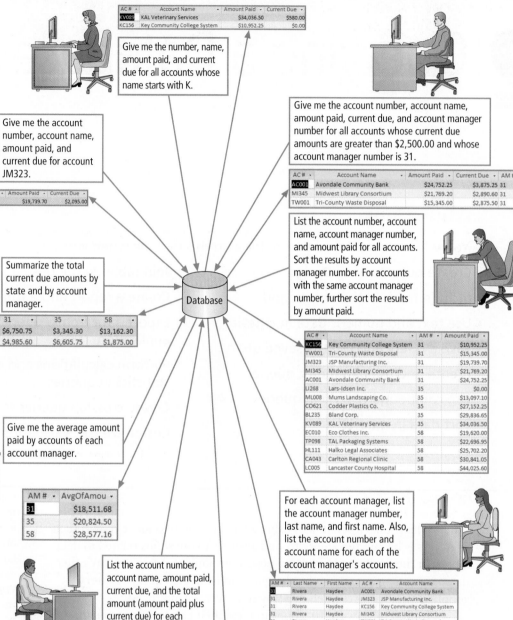

Give me the number, name, amount paid, and current due for all accounts whose name starts with K.

AC #	Account Name	Amount Paid	Current Due
KV089	KAL Veterinary Services	$34,036.50	$580.00
KC156	Key Community College System	$10,952.25	$0.00

Give me the account number, account name, amount paid, and current due for account JM323.

AC #	Account Name	Amount Paid	Current Due
JM323	JSP Manufacturing Inc.	$19,739.70	$2,095.00

Give me the account number, account name, amount paid, current due, and account manager number for all accounts whose current due amounts are greater than $2,500.00 and whose account manager number is 31.

AC #	Account Name	Amount Paid	Current Due	AM #
AC001	Avondale Community Bank	$24,752.25	$3,875.25	31
MI345	Midwest Library Consortium	$21,769.20	$2,890.60	31
TW001	Tri-County Waste Disposal	$15,345.00	$2,875.50	31

Summarize the total current due amounts by state and by account manager.

State	Total Of Curr	31	35	58
IL	$23,258.35	$6,750.75	$3,345.30	$13,162.30
IN	$13,466.35	$4,985.60	$6,605.75	$1,875.00

List the account number, account name, account manager number, and amount paid for all accounts. Sort the results by account manager number. For accounts with the same account manager number, further sort the results by amount paid.

AC #	Account Name	AM #	Amount Paid
KC156	Key Community College System	31	$10,952.25
TW001	Tri-County Waste Disposal	31	$15,345.00
JM323	JSP Manufacturing Inc.	31	$19,739.70
MI345	Midwest Library Consortium	31	$21,769.20
AC001	Avondale Community Bank	31	$24,752.25
LI268	Lars-Idsen Inc.	35	$0.00
ML008	Mums Landscaping Co.	35	$13,097.10
CO621	Codder Plastics Co.	35	$27,152.25
BL235	Bland Corp.	35	$29,836.65
KV089	KAL Veterinary Services	35	$34,036.50
EC010	Eco Clothes Inc.	58	$19,620.00
TP098	TAL Packaging Systems	58	$22,696.95
HL111	Halko Legal Associates	58	$25,702.20
CA043	Carlton Regional Clinic	58	$30,841.05
LC005	Lancaster County Hospital	58	$44,025.60

Give me the average amount paid by accounts of each account manager.

AM #	AvgOfAmou
31	$18,511.68
35	$20,824.50
58	$28,577.16

For each account manager, list the account manager number, last name, and first name. Also, list the account number and account name for each of the account manager's accounts.

AM #	Last Name	First Name	AC #	Account Name
31	Rivera	Haydee	AC001	Avondale Community Bank
31	Rivera	Haydee	JM323	JSP Manufacturing Inc.
31	Rivera	Haydee	KC156	Key Community College System
31	Rivera	Haydee	MI345	Midwest Library Consortium
31	Rivera	Haydee	TW001	Tri-County Waste Disposal
35	Simson	Mark	BL235	Bland Corp.
35	Simson	Mark	CO621	Codder Plastics Co.
35	Simson	Mark	KV089	KAL Veterinary Services
35	Simson	Mark	LI268	Lars-Idsen Inc.
35	Simson	Mark	ML008	Mums Landscaping Co.
42	Lu	Peter		
58	Murowski	Karen	CA043	Carlton Regional Clinic
58	Murowski	Karen	EC010	Eco Clothes Inc.
58	Murowski	Karen	HL111	Halko Legal Associates
58	Murowski	Karen	LC005	Lancaster County Hospital
58	Murowski	Karen	TP098	TAL Packaging Systems

List the account number, account name, amount paid, current due, and the total amount (amount paid plus current due) for each account.

AC #	Account Name	Amount Paid	Current Due	Total Amour
AC001	Avondale Community Bank	$24,752.25	$3,875.25	$28,627.50
BL235	Bland Corp.	$29,836.65	$2,765.30	$32,601.95
CA043	Carlton Regional Clinic	$30,841.05	$3,074.30	$33,915.35
CO621	Codder Plastics Co.	$27,152.25	$2,875.00	$30,027.25
EC010	Eco Clothes Inc.	$19,620.00	$1,875.00	$21,495.00
HL111	Halko Legal Associates	$25,702.20	$3,016.75	$28,718.95
JM323	JSP Manufacturing Inc.	$19,739.70	$2,095.00	$21,834.70
KC156	Key Community College System	$10,952.25	$0.00	$10,952.25
KV089	KAL Veterinary Services	$34,036.50	$580.00	$34,616.50
LC005	Lancaster County Hospital	$44,025.60	$3,590.80	$47,616.40
LI268	Lars-Idsen Inc.	$0.00	$1,280.75	$1,280.75
MI345	Midwest Library Consortium	$21,769.20	$2,890.60	$24,659.80
ML008	Mums Landscaping Co.	$13,097.10	$2,450.00	$15,547.10
TP098	TAL Packaging Systems	$22,696.95	$3,480.45	$26,177.40
TW001	Tri-County Waste Disposal	$15,345.00	$2,875.50	$18,220.50

Database

Figure 2–1

In this module, you will learn how to create and use the queries shown in Figure 2–1. The following roadmap identifies general activities you will perform as you progress through this module:

1. **CREATE QUERIES** in Design view.
2. **USE CRITERIA** in queries.
3. **SORT DATA** in queries.
4. **JOIN TABLES** in queries.
5. **EXPORT** query **RESULTS**.
6. **PERFORM CALCULATIONS** in queries.
7. **CREATE** a **CROSSTAB** query.
8. **CUSTOMIZE** the **NAVIGATION PANE**.

Creating Queries

As you learned in Module 1, you can use queries in Access to find answers to questions about the data contained in the database. *Note:* In this module, you will save each query example. When you use a query for another task, such as to create a form or report, you will assign a specific name to a query, for example, Manager-Account Query. In situations in which you will not use the query again, you will assign a name using a convention that includes the module number and a query number, for example, m02q01. Queries are numbered consecutively.

BTW
Select Queries
The queries you create in this module are select queries. In a select query, you retrieve data from one or more tables using criteria that you specify and display the data in a datasheet.

To Create a Query in Design View

1 CREATE QUERIES | 2 USE CRITERIA | 3 SORT DATA | 4 JOIN TABLES | 5 EXPORT RESULTS
6 PERFORM CALCULATIONS | 7 CREATE CROSSTAB | 8 CUSTOMIZE NAVIGATION PANE

In Module 1, you used the Simple Query Wizard to create a query. Most of the time, however, you will use Design view, which is the primary option for creating queries. *Why? Once you have created a new query in Design view, you have more options than with the wizard and can specify fields, criteria, sorting, calculations, and so on.* The following steps create a new query in Design view.

1
• Run Access and open the database named PrattLast Associates from your hard disk, OneDrive, or other storage location.

• Click the 'Shutter Bar Open/Close Button' to close the Navigation Pane.

• Click Create on the ribbon to display the Create tab (Figure 2–2).

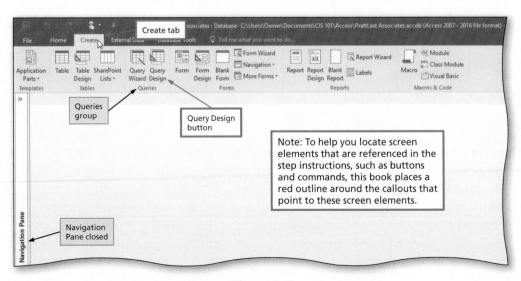

Figure 2–2

2

- Click the Query Design button (Create tab | Queries group) to create a new query (Figure 2–3).

Q&A Is it necessary to close the Navigation Pane?

No. Closing the pane gives you more room for the query, however, so it is usually a good practice.

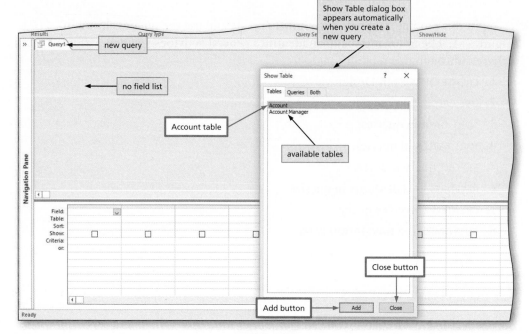

Figure 2–3

3

- Ensure the Account table (Show Table dialog box) is selected. If it is not, click the Account table to select it.
- Click the Add button to add the selected table to the query.
- Click the Close button to remove the dialog box from the screen.

Q&A What if I inadvertently add the wrong table?

Right-click the table that you added in error and click Remove Table on the shortcut menu. You also can just close the query, indicate that you do not want to save it, and then start over.

- Drag the lower edge of the field list down far enough so all fields in the table appear (Figure 2–4).

Q&A Is it essential that I resize the field list?

No. You can always scroll through the list of fields using the scroll bar. Resizing the field list so that all fields appear is usually more convenient.

Figure 2–4

To Add Fields to the Design Grid

Once you have a new query displayed in Design view, you are ready to make entries in the **design grid**, the portion of the window where you specify fields and criteria for the query. The design grid is located in the lower pane of the window. You add the fields you want included in the query to the Field row in the grid. *Why add fields to the grid? Only the fields that appear in the design grid are included in the query results.* The following step begins creating a query that PrattLast Associates might use to obtain the account number, account name, amount paid, and current due for a particular account.

1

- Double-click the Account Number field in the field list to add the field to the query.

Q&A What if I add the wrong field? Click just above the field name in the design grid to select the column and then press the DELETE key to remove the field.

- Double-click the Account Name field in the field list to add the field to the query.

- Add the Amount Paid field to the query.

- Add the Current Due field to the query (Figure 2–5).

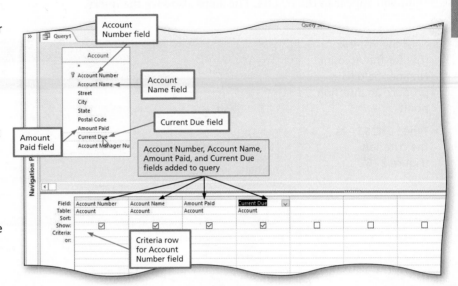

Figure 2–5

Q&A What if I want to include all fields? Do I have to add each field individually?
No. Instead of adding individual fields, you can double-click the asterisk (*) to add the asterisk to the design grid. The asterisk is a shortcut indicating all fields are to be included.

Determining Criteria

When you use queries, usually you are looking for those records that satisfy some criterion. In the simple query you created in the previous module, for example, you entered a criterion to restrict the records to those with the account manager number 35. In another query, you might want the name, amount paid, and current due amounts for the account whose number is JM323, for example, or for those accounts whose names start with the letters, La. You enter criteria in the Criteria row in the design grid below the field name to which the criterion applies. For example, to indicate that the account number must be JM323, you first must add the Account Number field to the design grid. You then would type JM323 in the Criteria row below the Account Number field.

Running the Query

After adding the appropriate fields and defining the query's criteria, you must run the query to get the results. To view the results of the query from Design view, click the Run button to instruct Access to run the query, that is, to perform the necessary actions to produce and display the results in Datasheet view.

BTW
Touch Screen Differences
The Office and Windows interfaces may vary if you are using a touch screen. For this reason, you might notice that the function or appearance of your touch screen differs slightly from this module's presentation.

BTW
Access Screen Resolution
If you are using a computer or mobile device to step through the project in this module and you want your screens to match the figures in this book, you should change your screen's resolution to 1366 x 768. For information about how to change a computer's resolution, refer to the Office and Windows module at the beginning of this book.

To Use Text Data in a Criterion

To use **text data** (data in a field whose data type is Short Text) in criteria, simply type the text in the Criteria row below the corresponding field name, just as you did in Module 1. In Access, you do not need to enclose text data in quotation marks as you do in many other database management systems. *Why? Access will enter the quotation marks automatically, so you can simply type the desired text.* The following steps finish creating a query that PrattLast Associates might use to obtain the account number, account name, amount paid, and current due amount of account JM323. These steps add the appropriate criterion so that only the desired account will appear in the results. The steps also save the query.

1

- Click the Criteria row for the Account Number field to produce an insertion point.

- Type JM323 as the criterion (Figure 2–6).

Figure 2–6

2

- Click the Run button (Query Tools Design tab | Results group) to run the query (Figure 2–7).

Q&A Can I also use the View button in the Results group to run the query?

Yes. You can click the View button to view the query results in Datasheet view.

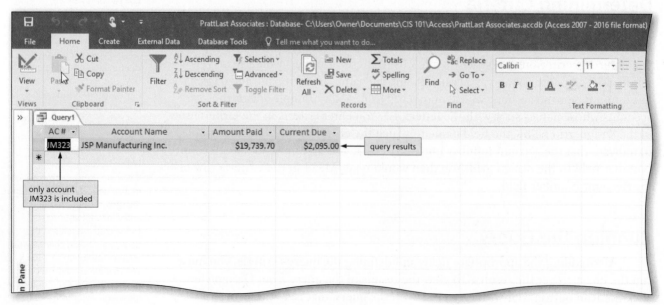

Figure 2–7

3

- Click the Save button on the Quick Access Toolbar to display the Save As dialog box.

- Type **m02q01** as the name of the query (Figure 2–8).

Q&A Can I also save from Design view?
Yes. You can save the query when you view it in Design view just as you can save it when you view query results in Datasheet view.

Figure 2–8

4

- Click the OK button (Save As dialog box) to save the query (Figure 2–9).

Figure 2–9

Other Ways

1. Right-click query tab, click Save on shortcut menu

2. Press CTRL+S

Using Saved Queries

After you have created and saved a query, you can use it in a variety of ways:

- To view the results of a query that is not currently open, open it by right-clicking the query in the Navigation Pane and clicking Open on the shortcut menu.

- If you want to change the design of a query that is already open, return to Design view and make the changes.

- If you want to change the design of a query that is not currently open, right-click the query in the Navigation Pane and then click Design View on the shortcut menu to open the query in Design view.

- To print the results with a query open, click File on the ribbon, click the Print tab in the Backstage view, and then click Quick Print.

BTW

The Ribbon and Screen Resolution
Access may change how the groups and buttons within the groups appear on the ribbon, depending on the computer or mobile device's screen resolution. Thus, your ribbon may look different from the ones in this book if you are using a screen resolution other than 1366 x 768.

BTW
Organizing Files and Folders
You should organize and store files in folders so that you easily can find the files later. For example, if you are taking an introductory computer class called CIS 101, a good practice would be to save all Access files in an Access folder in a CIS 101 folder. For a discussion of folders and detailed examples of creating folders, refer to the Office and Windows module at the beginning of this book.

- To print a query without first opening it, be sure the query is selected in the Navigation Pane and click File on the ribbon, click the Print tab in the Backstage view, and then click Quick Print.

- You can switch between views of a query using the View button (Home tab | Views group). Clicking the arrow at the bottom of the button produces the View button menu. You then click the desired view in the menu. The two query views you use in this module are Datasheet view (to see the results) and Design view (to change the design). You can also click the top part of the View button, in which case you will switch to the view identified by the icon on the button. In Figure 2–9, the View button displays the icon for Design view, so clicking the button would change to Design view. For the most part, the icon on the button represents the view you want, so you can usually simply click the button.

Wildcards

Microsoft Access supports wildcards. **Wildcards** are symbols that represent any character or combination of characters. One common wildcard, the **asterisk** (*), represents any collection of characters. Another wildcard symbol is the **question mark (?)**, which represents any individual character.

What does S* represent? What does T?m represent?

S* represents the letter, S, followed by any collection of characters. A search for S* might return System, So, or Superlative. T?m represents the letter, T, followed by any single character, followed by the letter, m. A search for T?m might return the names Tim or Tom.

To Use a Wildcard

1 CREATE QUERIES | 2 USE CRITERIA | 3 SORT DATA | 4 JOIN TABLES | 5 EXPORT RESULTS
6 PERFORM CALCULATIONS | 7 CREATE CROSSTAB | 8 CUSTOMIZE NAVIGATION PANE

The following steps modify the previous query to use the asterisk wildcard so that PrattLast Associates can select only those accounts whose names begin with K. *Why? Because you do not know how many characters will follow the K, the asterisk wildcard symbol is appropriate.* The steps also save the query with a new name using the Save As command.

- Click the View button (Home tab | Views group), shown in Figure 2–9, to return to Design view.

- If necessary, click the Criteria row below the Account Number field to produce an insertion point.

Q&A The text I entered now has quotation marks surrounding it. What happened?
Criteria for text data needs to be enclosed in quotation marks. You do not have to type the quotation marks; Access adds them automatically.

- Use the DELETE or BACKSPACE key as necessary to delete the current entry.

- Click the Criteria row below the Account Name field to produce an insertion point.

- Type **K*** as the criterion (Figure 2–10).

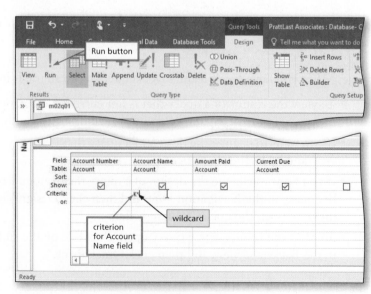

Figure 2–10

2

- Run the query by clicking the Run button (Query Tools Design tab | Results group) (Figure 2–11).

Experiment

- Change the letter K to lowercase in the criterion and run the query to determine whether case makes a difference when entering a wildcard.

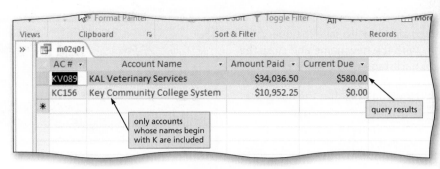

Figure 2–11

3

- Click File on the ribbon to open the Backstage view.

- Click the Save As tab in the Backstage view to display the Save As gallery.

- Click 'Save Object As' in the File Types area (Figure 2–12).

Q&A Can I just click the Save button on the Quick Access Toolbar as I did when saving the previous query?
If you clicked the Save button, you would replace the previous query with the version you just created. Because you want to save both the previous query and the new one, you need to save the new version with a different name. To do so, you must use Save Object As, which is available through the Backstage view.

Figure 2–12

4

- With Save Object As selected in the File Types gallery, click the Save As button to display the Save As dialog box.

- Erase the name of the current query and type m02q02 as the name for the saved query (Figure 2–13).

Q&A The current entry in the As text box is Query. Could I save the query as some other type of object?
Although you usually would want to save the query as another query, you can also save it as a form or report by changing the entry in the As text box. If you do, Access would create either a simple form or a simple report for the query.

Figure 2–13

5

- Click the OK button (Save As dialog box) to save the query with the new name and close the Backstage view (Figure 2–14).

Q&A How can I tell that the query was saved with the new name?
The new name will appear on the tab.

Figure 2–14

Other Ways

1. Click Design View button on status bar

To Use Criteria for a Field Not Included in the Results

1 CREATE QUERIES | 2 USE CRITERIA | 3 SORT DATA | 4 JOIN TABLES | 5 EXPORT RESULTS
6 PERFORM CALCULATIONS | 7 CREATE CROSSTAB | 8 CUSTOMIZE NAVIGATION PANE

In some cases, you might require criteria for a particular field that should not appear in the results of the query. For example, you may want to see the account number, account name, amount paid, and current due for all accounts located in Granger. The criteria involve the City field, but you do not want to include the City field in the results.

To enter a criterion for the City field, it must be included in the design grid. Normally, it would then appear in the results. To prevent this from happening, remove the check mark from its check box in the Show row of the grid. **Why?** *A check mark in the Show check box instructs Access to show the field in the result. If you remove the check mark, you can use the field in the query without displaying it in the query results.*

The following steps modify the previous query so that PrattLast Associates can select only those accounts located in Granger. PrattLast does not want the city to appear in the results, however. The steps also save the query with a new name.

1

- Click the View button (Home tab | Views group), shown in Figure 2–14, to return to Design view.

Q&A The text I entered is now preceded by the word, Like. What happened?
Criteria that include wildcards need to be preceded by the word, Like. However, you do not have to type it; Access adds the word automatically to any criterion involving a wildcard.

- Erase the criterion in the Criteria row of the Account Name field.

- Add the City field to the query.

- Type **Granger** as the criterion for the City field (Figure 2–15).

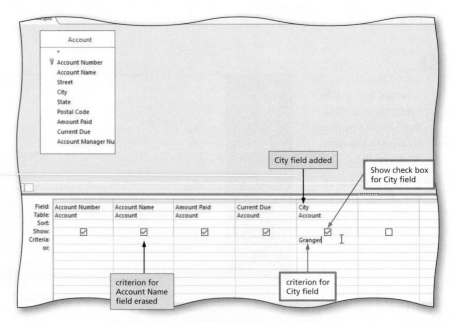

Figure 2–15

2

- Click the Show check box for the City field to remove the check mark (Figure 2–16).

Q&A
Could I have removed the check mark before entering the criterion?
Yes. The order in which you perform the two operations does not matter.

Figure 2–16

3

- Run the query (Figure 2–17).

Experiment

- Click the View button to return to Design view, enter a different city name as the criterion, and run the query. Repeat this process with additional city names, including at least one city name that is not in the database. When finished, change the criterion back to Granger.

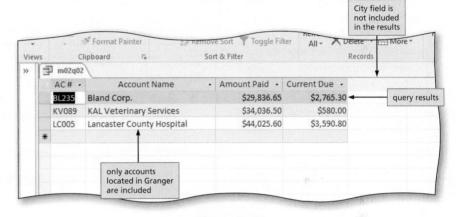

Figure 2–17

Creating a Parameter Query

If you wanted to find accounts located in Wells instead of Granger, you would either have to create a new query or modify the existing query by replacing Granger with Wells as the criterion. Rather than giving a specific criterion when you first create the query, occasionally you may want to be able to enter part of the criterion when you run the query and then have the appropriate results appear. For example, you might want a query to return the account number, account name, amount paid, and current due for all accounts in a specific city, specifying a different city each time you run the query. A user could run the query, enter Wells as the city, and then see all the accounts in Wells. Later, the user could use the same query but enter Granger as the city, and then see all the accounts in Granger.

To enable this flexibility, you create a **parameter query**, which is a query that prompts for input whenever it is used. You enter a parameter (the prompt for the user) rather than a specific value as the criterion. You create the parameter by enclosing the criterion value in square brackets. It is important that the value in the brackets does not match the name of any field. If you enter a field name in square brackets, Access assumes you want that particular field and does not prompt the user for input. To prompt the user to enter the city name as the input, you could place [Enter City] as the criterion in the City field.

BTW

Designing Queries
Before creating queries, examine the contents of the tables involved. You need to know the data type for each field and how the data for the field is stored. If a query includes a state, for example, you need to know whether state is stored as the two-character abbreviation or as the full state name.

To Create and View a Parameter Query

The following steps create a parameter query. *Why? The parameter query will give users at PrattLast the ability to enter a different city each time they run the query rather than having a specific city as part of the criterion in the query.* The steps also save the query with a new name.

1

- Return to Design view.
- Erase the current criterion in the City column, and then type `[Enter City]` as the new criterion (Figure 2–18).

Q&A What is the purpose of the square brackets?

The square brackets indicate that the text entered is not text that the value in the column must match. Without the brackets, Access would search for records in which the city is Enter City.

What if I typed a field name in the square brackets?

Access would simply use the value in that field. To create a parameter query, you must not use a field name in the square brackets.

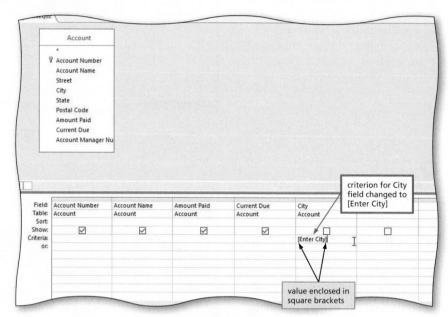

Figure 2–18

2

- Click the Run button (Query Tools Design tab | Results group) to display the Enter Parameter Value dialog box (Figure 2–19).

Figure 2–19

3

- Type `Wells` as the parameter value in the Enter City text box, and then click the OK button (Enter Parameter Value dialog box) to close the dialog box and view the query (Figure 2–20).

Experiment

- Try using other characters between the square brackets. In each case, run the query. When finished, change the characters between the square brackets back to Enter City.

Figure 2–20

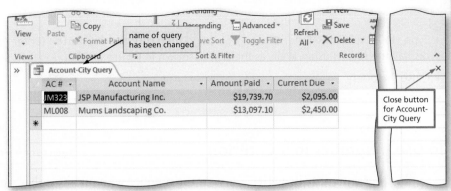

Figure 2–21

④
- Click File on the ribbon to open the Backstage view.
- Click the Save As tab in the Backstage view to display the Save As gallery.
- Click 'Save Object As' in the File Types area.
- With Save Object As selected in the File Types area, click the Save As button to display the Save As dialog box.
- Type `Account-City Query` as the name for the saved query.
- Click the OK button (Save As dialog box) to save the query with the new name and close the Backstage view (Figure 2–21).

⑤
- Click the Close button for the Account-City Query to close the query.

Break Point: If you wish to take a break, this is a good place to do so. You can exit Access now. To resume later, run Access, open the database called PrattLast Associates, and continue following the steps from this location forward.

To Use a Parameter Query

1 CREATE QUERIES | 2 USE CRITERIA | 3 SORT DATA | 4 JOIN TABLES | 5 EXPORT RESULTS
6 PERFORM CALCULATIONS | 7 CREATE CROSSTAB | 8 CUSTOMIZE NAVIGATION PANE

You use a parameter query like any other saved query. You can open it or you can print the query results. In either case, Access prompts you to supply a value for the parameter each time you use the query. If changes have been made to the data since the last time you ran the query, the results of the query may be different, even if you enter the same value for the parameter. *Why? In addition to the ability to enter different field values each time the parameter query is run, the query always uses the data that is currently in the table.* The following steps use the parameter query named Account-City Query.

①
- Open the Navigation Pane.
- Right-click the Account-City Query to produce a shortcut menu.
- Click Open on the shortcut menu to open the query and display the Enter Parameter Value dialog box (Figure 2–22).

Q&A
The title bar for my Navigation Pane contains Tables and Related Views rather than All Access Objects as it did in Module 1. What should I do?
Click the Navigation Pane arrow and then click 'All Access Objects'.

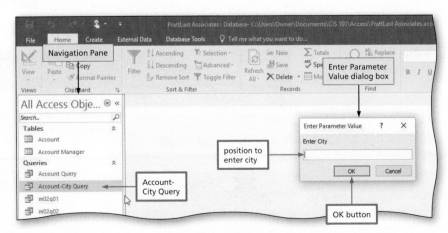

Figure 2–22

I do not have the Search bar at the top of the Navigation Pane that I had in Module 1. What should I do?
Right-click the Navigation Pane title bar arrow to display a shortcut menu, and then click Search Bar.

②

- Type **Wells** in the Enter City text box, and then click the OK button (Enter Parameter Value dialog box) to display the results using Wells as the city, as shown in Figure 2–21.

- Close the query.

To Use a Number in a Criterion

1 CREATE QUERIES | 2 USE CRITERIA | 3 SORT DATA | 4 JOIN TABLES | 5 EXPORT RESULTS
6 PERFORM CALCULATIONS | 7 CREATE CROSSTAB | 8 CUSTOMIZE NAVIGATION PANE

To enter a number in a criterion, type the number without any dollar signs or commas. *Why? If you enter a dollar sign, Access assumes you are entering text. If you enter a comma, Access considers the criterion invalid.* The following steps create a query that PrattLast Associates might use to display all accounts whose current due amount is $0. The steps also save the query with a new name.

①

- Close the Navigation Pane.

- Click Create on the ribbon to display the Create tab.

- Click the Query Design button (Create tab | Queries group) to create a new query.

- If necessary, click the Account table (Show Table dialog box) to select the table.

- Click the Add button to add the selected table to the query.

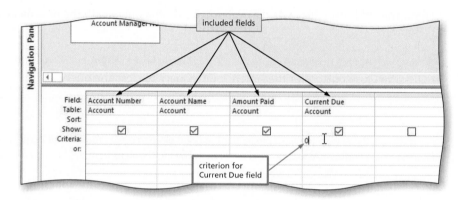

Figure 2–23

- Click the Close button to remove the dialog box from the screen.

- Drag the lower edge of the field list down far enough so all fields in the list are displayed.

- Include the Account Number, Account Name, Amount Paid, and Current Due fields in the query.

- Type **0** as the criterion for the Current Due field (Figure 2–23).

Q&A Do I need to enter a dollar sign and decimal point?
No. Access will interpret 0 as $0 because the data type for the Current Due field is currency.

②

- Run the query (Figure 2–24).

Q&A Why did Access display the results as $0.00 when I only entered 0?
Access uses the format for the field to determine how to display the result. In this case, the format indicated that Access should include the dollar sign, decimal point, and two decimal places.

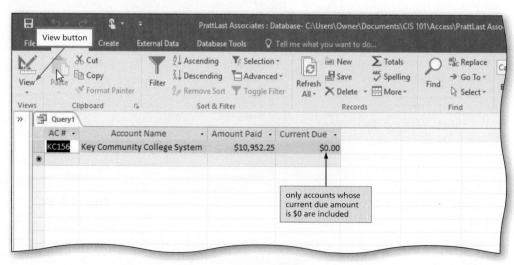

Figure 2–24

3

- Save the query as m02q03.

Q&A How do I know when to use the Save button to save a query or use the Backstage view to perform a Save As?
If you are saving a new query, the simplest way is to use the Save button on the Quick Access Toolbar. If you are saving changes to a previously saved query but do not want to change the name, use the Save button. If you want to save a previously saved query with a new name, you must use the Backstage view and perform a Save Object As.

- Close the query.

Comparison Operators

Unless you specify otherwise, Access assumes that the criteria you enter involve equality (exact matches). In the last query, for example, you were requesting those accounts whose current due amount is equal to 0 (zero). In other situations, you might want to find a range of results; for example, you could request accounts whose current due is greater than $1,000.00. If you want a query to return something other than an exact match, you must enter the appropriate **comparison operator**. The comparison operators are > (greater than), < (less than), >= (greater than or equal to), <= (less than or equal to), and NOT (not equal to).

To Use a Comparison Operator in a Criterion

1 CREATE QUERIES | 2 USE CRITERIA | 3 SORT DATA | 4 JOIN TABLES | 5 EXPORT RESULTS
6 PERFORM CALCULATIONS | 7 CREATE CROSSTAB | 8 CUSTOMIZE NAVIGATION PANE

The following steps use the > operator to create a query that PrattLast Associates might use to find all account managers whose start date is after 1/1/2015. **Why?** *A date greater than 1/1/2015 means the date comes after 1/1/2015.* The steps also save the query with a new name.

1

- Start a new query using the Account Manager table.

- Include the Account Manager Number, Last Name, First Name, and Start Date fields.

- Type **>1/01/2015** as the criterion for the Start Date field (Figure 2–25).

Q&A Why did I not have to type the leading zero in the Month portion of the date?
It is fine as you typed it. You also could have typed 01/1/2015. Some people often type the day using two digits, such as 1/01/2015. You also could have typed a leading zero for both the month and the day: 01/01/2015.

Figure 2–25

2

- Run the query (Figure 2–26).

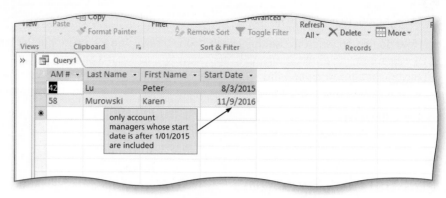

Figure 2–26

Experiment

- Return to Design view. Try a different criterion involving a comparison operator in the Start Date field and run the query. When finished, return to Design view, enter the original criterion (>1/01/2015) in the Start Date field, and run the query.

Q&A

I returned to Design view and noticed that Access changed 1/01/2015 to #1/01/2015#. Why does the date now have number signs around it?
This is the date format in Access. You usually do not have to enter the number signs because in most cases Access will insert them automatically.

My records are in a different order. Is this a problem?
No. The important thing is which records are included in the results. You will see later in this module how you can specify the specific order you want for cases when the order is important.

Can I use the same comparison operators with text data?
Yes. Comparison operators function the same whether you use them with number fields, currency fields, date fields, or text fields. With a text field, comparison operators use alphabetical order in making the determination.

3

- Save the query as m02q04.

- Close the query.

BTW
Queries:
Query-by-Example
Query-By-Example, often referred to as QBE, was a query language first proposed in the mid-1970s. In this approach, users asked questions by filling in a table on the screen. The Access approach to queries is based on Query-By-Example.

Using Compound Criteria

Often your search data must satisfy more than one criterion. This type of criterion is called a **compound criterion** and is created using the words AND or OR.

In an **AND criterion**, each individual criterion must be true in order for the compound criterion to be true. For example, an AND criterion would allow you to find accounts that have current due amounts greater than $2,500.00 and whose account manager is manager 31.

An **OR criterion** is true if either individual criterion is true. An OR criterion would allow you to find accounts that have current due amounts greater than $2,500.00 as well as accounts whose account manager is account manager 31. In this case, any account who has a current due amount greater than $2,500.00 would be included in the answer, regardless of whether the account's account manager is account manager 31. Likewise, any account whose account manager is account manager 31 would be included, regardless of whether the account has a current due amount greater than $2,500.00.

To Use a Compound Criterion Involving AND

1 CREATE QUERIES | 2 USE CRITERIA | 3 SORT DATA | 4 JOIN TABLES | 5 EXPORT RESULTS
6 PERFORM CALCULATIONS | 7 CREATE CROSSTAB | 8 CUSTOMIZE NAVIGATION PANE

To combine criteria with AND, place the criteria on the same row of the design grid. **Why?** *Placing the criteria in the same row indicates that both criteria must be true in Access.* The following steps use an AND criterion to enable PrattLast to find those accounts who have a current due amount greater than $2,500.00 and whose account manager is manager 31. The steps also save the query.

①

- Start a new query using the Account table.

- Include the Account Number, Account Name, Amount Paid, Current Due, and Account Manager Number fields.

- Type **>2500** as the criterion for the Current Due field.

- Type **31** as the criterion for the Account Manager Number field (Figure 2–27).

Figure 2–27

②

- Run the query (Figure 2–28).

③

- Save the query as m02q05.

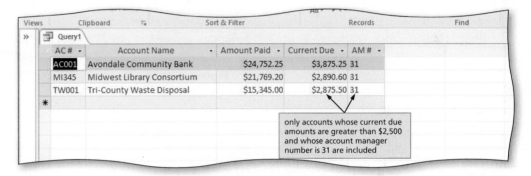

Figure 2–28

To Use a Compound Criterion Involving OR

1 CREATE QUERIES | 2 USE CRITERIA | 3 SORT DATA | 4 JOIN TABLES | 5 EXPORT RESULTS
6 PERFORM CALCULATIONS | 7 CREATE CROSSTAB | 8 CUSTOMIZE NAVIGATION PANE

To combine criteria with OR, each criterion must go on separate rows in the Criteria area of the grid. **Why?** *Placing criteria on separate rows indicates at least one criterion must be true in Access.* The following steps use an OR criterion to enable PrattLast to find those accounts who have a current due amount greater than $2,500.00 or whose account manager is manager 31 (or both). The steps also save the query with a new name.

①

- Return to Design view.

- If necessary, click the Criteria entry for the Account Manager Number field and then use the BACKSPACE key or the DELETE key to erase the entry ("31").

- Click the or row (the row below the Criteria row) for the Account Manager Number field, and then type **31** as the entry (Figure 2–29).

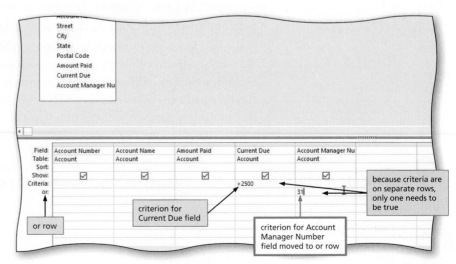

Figure 2–29

2
- Run the query (Figure 2-30).

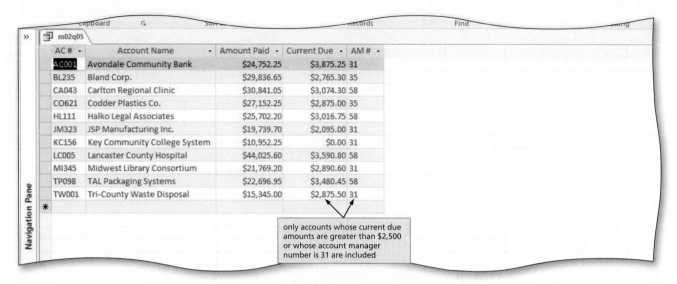

only accounts whose current due amounts are greater than $2,500 or whose account manager number is 31 are included

Figure 2-30

3
- Save the query as m02q06.

Special Criteria

You can use three special criteria in queries:

BTW
Rearranging Fields in a Query
To move a field in the design grid, click the column selector for the field to select the field and drag it to the appropriate location.

1. If you want to create a criterion involving a range of values in a single field, you can use the **AND operator**. You place the word AND between the individual conditions. For example, if you wanted to find all accounts whose amount paid is greater than or equal to $20,000.00 and less than or equal to $40,000.00, you would enter >= 20000 AND <= 40000 as the criterion in the Amount Paid column.

2. You can select values in a given range by using the **BETWEEN operator**. This is often an alternative to the AND operator. For example, to find all accounts whose amount paid is between $20,000.00 and $40,000.00, inclusive, you would enter BETWEEN 20000 AND 40000 as the criterion in the Amount Paid column. This is equivalent to entering >=20000 and <=40000.

3. You can select a list of values by using the **IN operator**. You follow the word IN with the list of values in parentheses. For example, to find accounts whose account manager number is 31 and accounts whose account manager is 35 using the IN operator, you would enter IN ("31","35") on the Criteria row in the Account Manager Number column. Unlike when you enter a simple criterion, you must enclose text values in quotation marks.

CONSIDER THIS

How would you find accounts whose account manager number is 31 or 35 without using the IN operator?
Place the number 31 in the Criteria row of the Account Manager Number column. Place the number 35 in the or row of the Account Manager Number column.

Sorting

In some queries, the order in which the records appear is irrelevant. All you need to be concerned about are the records that appear in the results. It does not matter which one is first or which one is last.

In other queries, however, the order can be very important. You may want to see the cities in which accounts are located and would like them arranged alphabetically. Perhaps you want to see the accounts listed by account manager number. Further, within all the accounts of any given account manager, you might want them to be listed by amount paid from largest amount to smallest.

To order the records in a query result in a particular way, you **sort** the records. The field or fields on which the records are sorted is called the **sort key**. If you are sorting on more than one field (such as sorting by amount paid within account manager number), the more important field (Account Manager Number) is called the **major key** (also called the **primary sort key**) and the less important field (Amount Paid) is called the **minor key** (also called the **secondary sort key**).

To sort in Microsoft Access, specify the sort order in the Sort row of the design grid below the field that is the sort key. If you specify more than one sort key, the sort key on the left will be the major sort key, and the one on the right will be the minor key.

BTW
Sorting Data in a Query
When sorting data in a query, the records in the underlying tables (the tables on which the query is based) are not actually rearranged. Instead, the DBMS determines the most efficient method of simply displaying the records in the requested order. The records in the underlying tables remain in their original order.

BTW
Clearing the Design Grid
You can also clear the design grid using the ribbon. To do so, click the Home tab, click the Advanced button to display the Advanced menu, and then click Clear Grid on the Advanced menu.

To Clear the Design Grid

1 CREATE QUERIES | 2 USE CRITERIA | 3 SORT DATA | 4 JOIN TABLES | 5 EXPORT RESULTS
6 PERFORM CALCULATIONS | 7 CREATE CROSSTAB | 8 CUSTOMIZE NAVIGATION PANE

Why? *If the fields you want to include in the next query are different from those in the previous query, it is usually simpler to start with a clear grid, that is, one with no fields already in the design grid.* You always can clear the entries in the design grid by closing the query and then starting over. A simpler approach to clearing the entries is to select all the entries and then press the DELETE key. The following steps return to Design view and clear the design grid.

1
- Return to Design view.
- Click just above the Account Number column heading in the grid to select the column.

Q&A I clicked above the column heading, but the column is not selected. What should I do?
You did not point to the correct location. Be sure the pointer changes into a down-pointing arrow and then click again.

Figure 2–31

- Hold the SHIFT key down and click just above the Account Manager Number column heading to select all the columns (Figure 2–31).

2
- Press the DELETE key to clear the design grid.

To Sort Data in a Query

If you determine that the query results should be sorted, you will need to specify the sort key. The following steps sort the cities in the Account table by indicating that the City field is to be sorted. The steps specify Ascending sort order. *Why? When sorting text data, Ascending sort order arranges the results in alphabetical order.*

1

- Include the City field in the design grid.

- Click the Sort row in the City field column, and then click the Sort arrow to display a menu of possible sort orders (Figure 2–32).

Figure 2–32

2

- Click Ascending to select the sort order (Figure 2–33).

Figure 2–33

3

- Run the query (Figure 2–34).

🔎 **Experiment**

- Return to Design view and change the sort order to Descending. Run the query. Return to Design view and change the sort order back to Ascending. Run the query.

Q&A Why do some cities appear more than once?
More than one account is located in those cities.

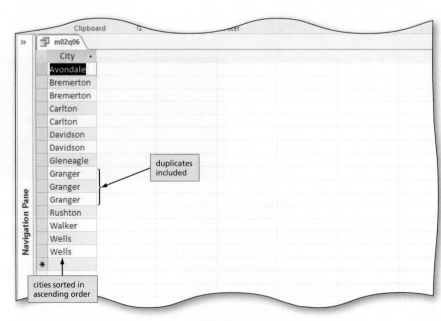

Figure 2–34

To Omit Duplicates

When you sort data, duplicates normally are included. In the query shown in Figure 2–34, for example, Bremerton appears twice. Several other cities appear multiple times as well. You eliminate duplicates using the query's property sheet. A **property sheet** is a window containing the various properties of the object. To omit duplicates, you will use the property sheet to change the Unique Values property from No to Yes.

The following steps create a query that PrattLast Associates might use to obtain a sorted list of the cities in the Account table in which each city is listed only once. *Why? Unless you wanted to know how many accounts were located in each city, the duplicates typically do not add any value.* The steps also save the query with a new name.

1
- Return to Design view.
- Click the second field (the empty field to the right of City) in the design grid to produce an insertion point.
- If necessary, click Design on the ribbon to display the Design tab.
- Click the Property Sheet button (Query Tools Design tab | Show/Hide group) to display the property sheet (Figure 2–35).

Q&A My property sheet looks different. What should I do?
If your sheet looks different, close the property sheet and repeat this step.

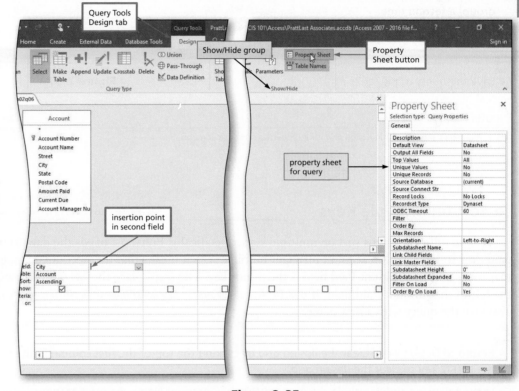

Figure 2–35

2
- Click the Unique Values property box, and then click the arrow that appears to display a list of available choices (Figure 2–36).

Figure 2–36

- Click Yes to indicate that the query will return unique values, which means that each value will appear only once in the query results.

- Close the Query Properties property sheet by clicking the Property Sheet button (Query Tools Design tab | Show/Hide group) a second time.

- Run the query (Figure 2–37).

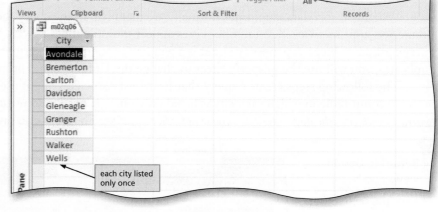

each city listed only once

Figure 2–37

- Save the query as m02q07.

Other Ways

1. Right-click second field in design grid, click Properties on shortcut menu

To Sort on Multiple Keys

1 CREATE QUERIES | 2 USE CRITERIA | 3 SORT DATA | 4 JOIN TABLES | 5 EXPORT RESULTS
6 PERFORM CALCULATIONS | 7 CREATE CROSSTAB | 8 CUSTOMIZE NAVIGATION PANE

The following steps sort on multiple keys. Specifically, PrattLast needs the data to be sorted by amount paid (low to high) within account manager number, which means that the Account Manager Number field is the major key and the Amount Paid field is the minor key. The steps place the Account Manager Number field to the left of the Amount Paid field. *Why? In Access, the major key must appear to the left of the minor key.* The steps also save the query with a new name.

1

- Return to Design view. Clear the design grid by clicking the top of the first column in the grid, and then pressing the DELETE key to clear the design grid.

- In the following order, include the Account Number, Account Name, Account Manager Number, and Amount Paid fields in the query.

- Select Ascending as the sort order for both the Account Manager Number field and the Amount Paid field (Figure 2–38).

Figure 2–38

2

• Run the query (Figure 2–39).

 Experiment

• Return to Design view and try other sort combinations for the Account Manager Number and Amount Paid fields, such as Ascending for Account Manager Number and Descending for Amount Paid. In each case, run the query to see the effect of the changes. When finished, select Ascending as the sort order for both fields.

Q&A

What if the Amount Paid field is to the left of the Account Manager Number field?

It is important to remember that the major sort key must appear to the left of the minor sort key in the design grid. If you attempted to sort by amount paid within account manager number, but placed the Amount Paid field to the left of the Account Manager Number field, your results would not accurately represent the intended sort.

AC # ▾	Account Name ▾	AM # ▾	Amount Paid ▾
KC156	Key Community College System	31	$10,952.25
TW001	Tri-County Waste Disposal	31	$15,345.00
JM323	JSP Manufacturing Inc.	31	$19,739.70
MI345	Midwest Library Consortium	31	$21,769.20
AC001	Avondale Community Bank	31	$24,752.25
LI268	Lars-Idsen Inc.	35	$0.00
ML008	Mums Landscaping Co.	35	$13,097.10
CO621	Codder Plastics Co.	35	$27,152.25
BL235	Bland Corp.	35	$29,836.65
KV089	KAL Veterinary Services	35	$34,036.50
EC010	Eco Clothes Inc.	58	$19,620.00
TP098	TAL Packaging Systems	58	$22,696.95
HL111	Halko Legal Associates	58	$25,702.20
CA043	Carlton Regional Clinic	58	$30,841.05
LC005	Lancaster County Hospital	58	$44,025.60

within group of accounts with the same account manager number, rows are sorted by amount paid in ascending order

overall order is by account manager number in ascending order

Figure 2–39

3

• Save the query as m02q08.

Is there any way to sort the records in this same order, but have the Amount Paid field appear to the left of the Account Manager Number field in the query results?

Yes. Remove the check mark from the Account Manager Number field, and then add an additional Account Manager Number field at the end of the query. The first Account Manager Number field will be used for sorting but will not appear in the results. The second will appear in the results, but will not be involved in the sorting process.

How do you approach the creation of a query that might involve sorting?

Examine the query or request to see if it contains words such as *order* or *sort*. Such words imply that the order of the query results is important. If so, you need to sort the query.

• If sorting is required, identify the field or fields on which the results are to be sorted. In the request, look for language such as *ordered by* or *sort the results by*, both of which would indicate that the specified field is a sort key.

• If using multiple sort keys, determine the major and minor keys. If you are using two sort keys, determine which one is the more important, or the major key. Look for language such as *sort by amount paid within account manager number*, which implies that the overall order is by account manager number. In this case, the Account Manager Number field would be the major sort key and the Amount Paid field would be the minor sort key.

• Determine sort order. Words such as *increasing*, *ascending*, or *low-to-high* imply Ascending order. Words such as *decreasing*, *descending*, or *high-to-low* imply Descending order. Sorting in *alphabetical order* implies Ascending order. If there were no words to imply a particular order, you would typically use Ascending.

• Examine the query or request to see if there are any special restrictions. One common restriction is to exclude duplicates. Another common restriction is to list only a certain number of records, such as the first five records.

To Create a Top-Values Query

Rather than show all the results of a query, you may want to show only a specified number of records or a percentage of records. ***Why?*** *You might not need to see all the records, just enough to get a general idea of the results.* Creating a **top-values query** allows you to restrict the number of records that appear. When you sort records, you can limit results to those records having the highest (descending sort) or lowest (ascending sort) values. To do so, first create a query that sorts the data in the desired order. Next, use the Return box on the Design tab to change the number of records to be included from All to the desired number or percentage.

The following steps create a query for PrattLast Associates that shows only the first five records that were included in the results of the previous query. The steps also save the resulting query with a new name.

①

- Return to Design view.

- If necessary, click Design on the ribbon to display the Design tab.

- Click the Return arrow (Query Tools Design tab | Query Setup group) to display the Return menu (Figure 2–40).

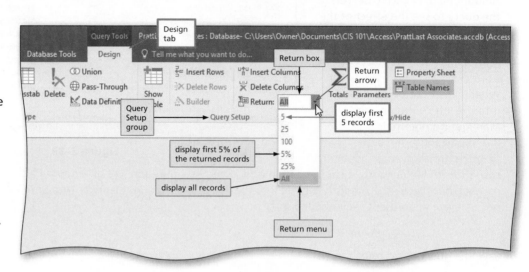

Figure 2–40

②

- Click 5 in the Return menu to specify that the query results should contain the first five rows.

Q&A Could I have typed the 5? What about other numbers that do not appear in the list?
Yes, you could have typed the 5. For numbers not appearing in the list, you must type the number.

- Run the query (Figure 2–41).

③

- Save the query as m02q09.

- Close the query.

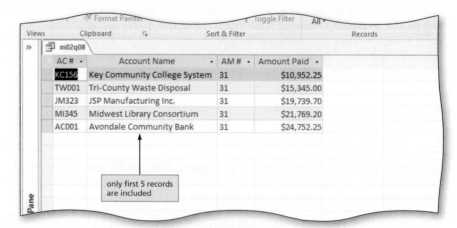

Figure 2–41

Q&A Do I need to close the query before creating my next query?
Not necessarily. When you use a top-values query, however, it is important to change the value in the Return box back to All. If you do not change the Return value back to All, the previous value will remain in effect. Consequently, you might not get all the records you should in the next query. A good practice whenever you use a top-values query is to close the query as soon as you are done. That way, you will begin your next query from scratch, which ensures that the value is reset to All.

Joining Tables

In designing a query, you need to determine whether more than one table is required. For example, if the question being asked involves data from both the Account and Account Manager tables, then both tables are required for the query. For example, you might want a query that gives the number and name of each account (from the Account table) along with the number and name of the account's account manager (from the Account Manager table). Both the Account and Account Manager tables are required for this query. You need to **join** the tables to find records in the two tables that have identical values in matching fields (Figure 2–42). In this example, you need to find records in the Account table and the Account Manager table that have the same value in the Account Manager Number fields.

BTW

Ad Hoc Relationships

When you join tables in a query, you are creating an ad hoc relationship, that is, a relationship between tables created for a specific purpose. In Module 3, you will create general-purpose relationships using the Relationships window.

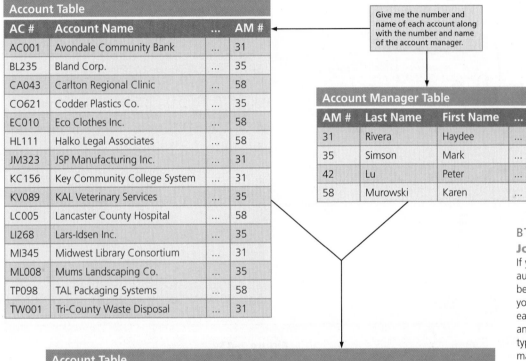

Figure 2–42

BTW

Join Line

If you do not get a join line automatically, there may be a problem with one of your table designs. Open each table in Design view and make sure that the data types are the same for the matching field in both tables and that one of the matching fields is the primary key in a table. Correct these errors and create the query again.

BTW

Join Types

The type of join that finds records from both tables that have identical values in matching fields is called an inner join. An inner join is the default join in Access. Outer joins are used to show all the records in one table as well as the common records; that is, the records that share the same value in the join field. In a left outer join, all rows from the table on the left are included. In a right outer join, all rows from the table on the right are included.

To Join Tables

If you have determined that you need to join tables, you first will bring field lists for both tables to the upper pane of the Query window while working in Design view. Access will draw a line, called a **join line**, between matching fields in the two tables, indicating that the tables are related. You then can select fields from either table. Access joins the tables automatically.

The first step is to create a new query and add the Account Manager table to the query. Then, add the Account table to the query. A join line should appear, connecting the Account Manager Number fields in the two field lists. *Why might the join line not appear? If the names of the matching fields differ from one table to the other, Access will not insert the line. You can insert it manually, however, by clicking one of the two matching fields and dragging the pointer to the other matching field.*

The following steps create a query to display information from both the Account table and the Account Manager table.

1

- Click Create on the ribbon to display the Create tab.

- Click the Query Design button (Create tab | Queries group) to create a new query.

- If necessary, click the Account Manager table (Show Table dialog box) to select the table.

- Click the Add button (Show Table dialog box) to add a field list for the Account Manager Table to the query (Figure 2–43).

Figure 2–43

2

- Click the Account table (Show Table dialog box).

- Click the Add button (Show Table dialog box) to add a field list for the Account table.

- Close the Show Table dialog box by clicking the Close button.

- Expand the size of the two field lists so all the fields in the Account Manager and Account tables appear (Figure 2–44).

Q&A
I did not get a join line. What should I do?
Ensure that the names of the matching fields are the same, the data types are the same, and the matching field is the primary key in one of the two tables. If all of these factors are true and you still do not have a join line, you can produce one by pointing to a matching field and dragging to the other matching field.

Figure 2–44

3

- In the design grid, include the Account Manager Number, Last Name, and First Name fields from the Account Manager Table as well as the Account Number and Account Name fields from the Account table.
- Select Ascending as the sort order for both the Account Manager Number field and the Account Number field (Figure 2–45).

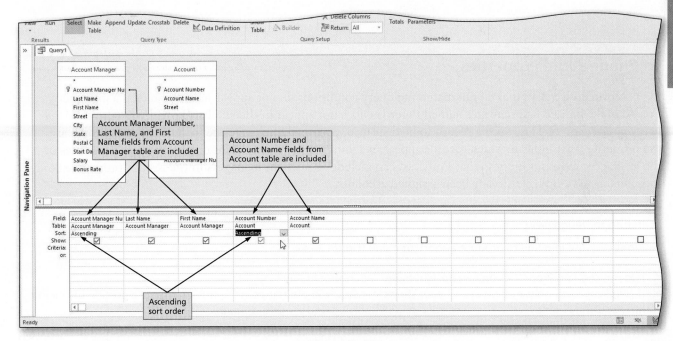

Figure 2–45

4

- Run the query (Figure 2–46).

Figure 2–46

5

- Click the Save button on the Quick Access Toolbar to display the Save As dialog box.

- Type **Manager-Account Query** as the query name.

- Click the OK button (Save As dialog box) to save the query.

To Change Join Properties

Normally, records that do not match the query conditions do not appear in the results of a join query. For example, the account manager named Peter Lu does not appear in the results. ***Why?*** *He currently does not have any accounts.* To cause such a record to be displayed, you need to change the **join properties**, which are the properties that indicate which records appear in a join. The following steps change the join properties of the Manager-Account Query so that PrattLast can include all account managers in the results, rather than only those managers who have already been assigned accounts.

1

- Return to Design view.

- Right-click the join line to produce a shortcut menu (Figure 2–47).

Q&A | I do not see Join Properties on my shortcut menu. What should I do?
If Join Properties does not appear on your shortcut menu, you did not point to the appropriate portion of the join line. You will need to point to the correct (middle) portion and right-click again.

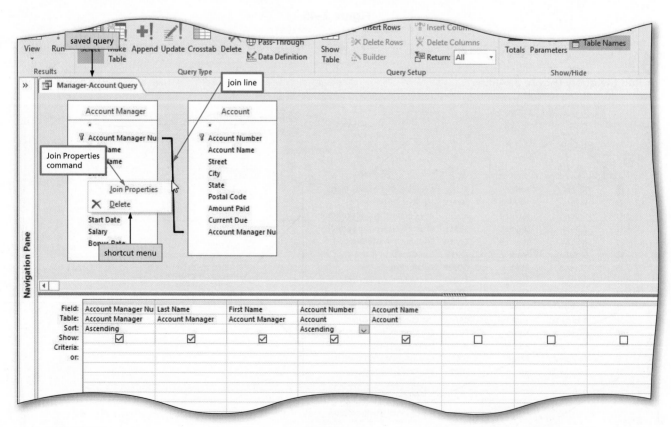

Figure 2–47

2

- Click Join Properties on the shortcut menu to display the Join Properties dialog box (Figure 2–48).

Figure 2–48

3

- Click option button 2 (Join Properties dialog box) to include all records from the Account Manager Table regardless of whether they match any accounts.

- Click the OK button (Join Properties dialog box) to modify the join properties.

- Run the query (Figure 2–49).

Experiment

- Return to Design view, change the Join properties, and select option button 3. Run the query to see the effect of this option. When done, return to Design view, change the join properties, and once again select option button 2.

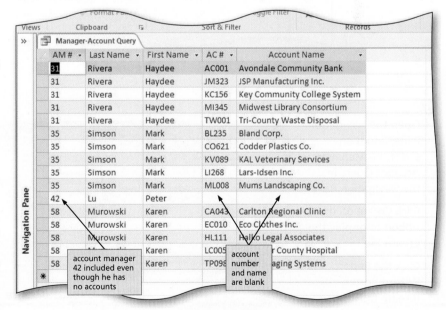

Figure 2–49

4

- Click the Save button on the Quick Access Toolbar to save the changes to the query.

- Close the Manager-Account Query.

Q&A | I see a dialog box that asks if I want to save the query. What should I do?
Click the OK button to save the query.

To Create a Report from a Query

You can use queries in the creation of reports. The report in Figure 2–50 involves data from more than one table. *Why? The Last Name and First Name fields are in the Account Manager table. The Account Number and Account Name fields are in the Account table. The Account Manager Number field is in both tables.* The easiest way to create such a report is to base it on a query that joins the two tables. The following steps use the Report Wizard and the Manager-Account Query to create the report.

Manager-Account Report

AM #	Last Name	First Name	AC #	Account Name
31	Rivera	Haydee	AC001	Avondale Community Bank
31	Rivera	Haydee	JM323	JSP Manufacturing Inc.
31	Rivera	Haydee	KC156	Key Community College System
31	Rivera	Haydee	MI345	Midwest Library Consortium
31	Rivera	Haydee	TW001	Tri-County Waste Disposal
35	Simson	Mark	BL235	Bland Corp.
35	Simson	Mark	CO621	Codder Plastics Co.
35	Simson	Mark	KV089	KAL Veterinary Services
35	Simson	Mark	LI268	Lars-Idsen Inc.
35	Simson	Mark	ML008	Mums Landscaping Co.
42	Lu	Peter		
58	Murowski	Karen	CA043	Carlton Regional Clinic
58	Murowski	Karen	EC010	Eco Clothes Inc.
58	Murowski	Karen	HL111	Halko Legal Associates
58	Murowski	Karen	LC005	Lancaster County Hospital
58	Murowski	Karen	TP098	TAL Packaging Systems

Figure 2–50

1

- Open the Navigation Pane, and then select the Manager-Account Query in the Navigation Pane.

- Click Create on the ribbon to display the Create tab.

- Click the Report Wizard button (Create tab | Reports group) to display the Report Wizard dialog box (Figure 2–51).

Figure 2–51

2

- Click the 'Add
All Fields' button
(Report Wizard
dialog box) to add
all the fields in the
Manager-Account
Query.

- Click the Next
button to display the
next Report Wizard
screen (Figure 2–52).

Figure 2–52

3

- Because you will not specify any
grouping, click the Next button
in the Report Wizard dialog box
to display the next Report Wizard
screen.

- Because you already specified the
sort order in the query, click the
Next button again to display the
next Report Wizard screen.

- Make sure that Tabular is selected
as the Layout and Portrait is
selected as the Orientation.

- Click the Next button to display
the next Report Wizard screen.

- Erase the current title, and then
type **Manager-Account
Report** as the new title.

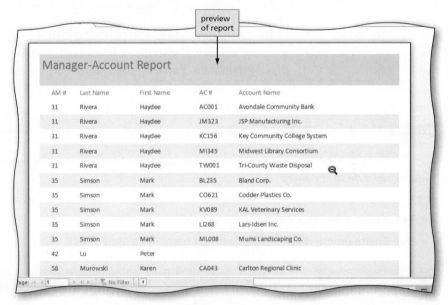

Figure 2–53

- Click the Finish button to produce the report (Figure 2–53).

Q&A | My report is very small and does not look like the one in the figure. What should I do?
     | Click the pointer, which should look like a magnifying glass, anywhere in the report to magnify the report.

- Close the Manager-Account Report.

To Print a Report

The following steps print a hard copy of the report.

1 With the Manager-Account Report selected in the Navigation Pane, click File on the
ribbon to open the Backstage view.

2 Click the Print tab in the Backstage view to display the Print gallery.

3 Click the Quick Print button to print the report.

How would you approach the creation of a query that might involve multiple tables?

• Examine the request to see if all the fields involved in the request are in one table. If the fields are in two (or more) tables, you need to join the tables.

• If joining is required, identify within the two tables the matching fields that have identical values. Look for the same column name in the two tables or for column names that are similar.

• Determine whether sorting is required. Queries that join tables often are used as the basis for a report. If this is the case, it may be necessary to sort the results. For example, the Manager-Account Report is based on a query that joins the Account Manager and Account tables. The query is sorted by account manager number and account number.

• Examine the request to see if there are any special restrictions. For example, the user may only want accounts whose current due amount is $0.00.

• Examine the request to see if you only want records from both tables that have identical values in matching fields. If you want to see records in one of the tables that do not have identical values in the other table, then you need to change the join properties.

Creating a Form for a Query

In the previous module, you created a form for the Account table. You can also create a form for a query. Recall that a **form** in a database is a formatted document with fields that contain data. Forms allow you to view and maintain data.

To Create a Form for a Query

1 CREATE QUERIES | 2 USE CRITERIA | 3 SORT DATA | 4 JOIN TABLES | 5 EXPORT RESULTS
6 PERFORM CALCULATIONS | 7 CREATE CROSSTAB | 8 CUSTOMIZE NAVIGATION PANE

The following steps create a form, then save the form. *Why? The form will be available for future use in viewing the data in the query.*

• If necessary, select the Manager-Account Query in the Navigation Pane.

• Click Create on the ribbon to display the Create tab (Figure 2–54).

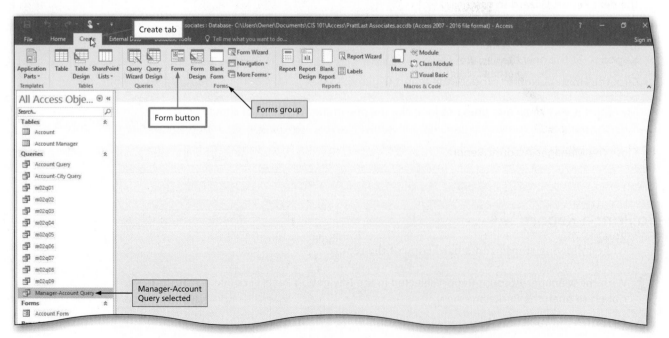

Figure 2–54

2

● Click the Form button (Create tab | Forms group) to create a simple form (Figure 2–55).

◄ | I see a field list also. What should I do?
Q&A | Click the Close button for the Field List.

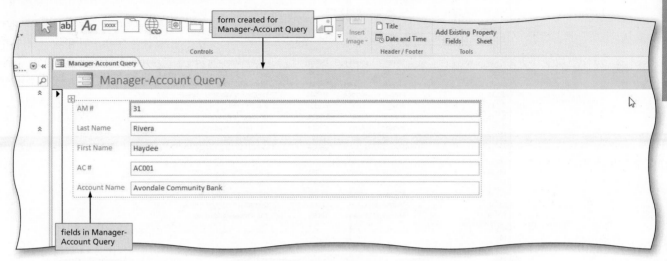

Figure 2–55

3

● Click the Save button on the Quick Access Toolbar to display the Save As dialog box.

● Type **Manager-Account Form** as the form name.

● Click the OK button to save the form.

● Click the Close button for the form to close the form.

Using a Form

After you have saved a form, you can use it at any time by right-clicking the form in the Navigation Pane and then clicking Open on the shortcut menu. If you plan to use the form to enter data, you must ensure you are viewing the form in Form view.

Break Point: If you wish to take a break, this is a good place to do so. You can exit Access now. To resume later, run Access, open the database called PrattLast Associates, and continue following the steps from this location forward.

Exporting Data From Access to Other Applications

You can **export**, or copy, tables or queries from an Access database so that another application (for example, Excel or Word) can use the data. The application that will receive the data determines the export process to be used. You can export to text files in a variety of formats. For applications to which you cannot directly export data, you often can export an appropriately formatted text file that the other application can import. Figure 2–56 shows the workbook produced by exporting the Manager-Account Query to Excel. The columns in the workbook have been resized to best fit the data.

BTW

Exporting Data
You frequently need to export data so that it can be used in other applications and by other users in an organization. For example, the Accounting department might require financial data in an Excel format to perform certain financial functions. Marketing might require a list of account names and addresses in Word or RTF format for marketing campaigns.

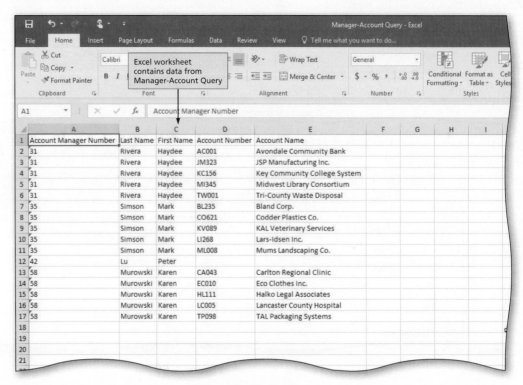

Figure 2–56

1 CREATE QUERIES | 2 USE CRITERIA | 3 SORT DATA | 4 JOIN TABLES | **5 EXPORT RESULTS**
6 PERFORM CALCULATIONS | 7 CREATE CROSSTAB | 8 CUSTOMIZE NAVIGATION PANE

To Export Data to Excel

For PrattLast Associates to make the Manager-Account Query available to Excel users, it needs to export the data. To export data to Excel, select the table or query to be exported and then click the Excel button in the Export group on the External Data tab. The following steps export the Manager-Account Query to Excel and save the export steps. *Why save the export steps? By saving the export steps, you could easily repeat the export process whenever you like without going through all the steps.* You would use the saved steps to export data in the future by clicking the Saved Exports button (External Data tab | Export group) and then selecting the steps you saved.

1

- If necessary, click the Manager-Account Query in the Navigation Pane to select it.

- Click External Data on the ribbon to display the External Data tab (Figure 2–57).

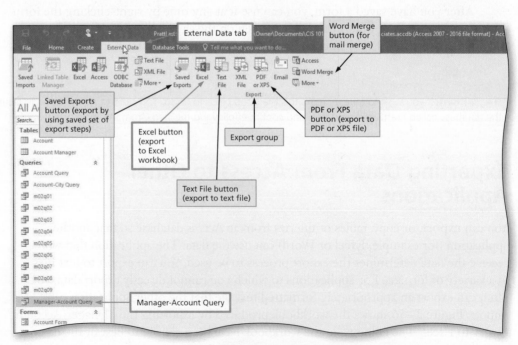

Figure 2–57

2

- Click the Excel button (External Data tab | Export group) to display the Export-Excel Spreadsheet dialog box.

- Click the Browse button (Export-Excel Spreadsheet dialog box), and then navigate to the location where you want to export the query (your hard disk, OneDrive, or other storage location).

- Confirm that the file format is Excel Workbook (*.xlsx), and the file name is Manager-Account Query, and then click the Save button (File Save dialog box) to select the file name and location (Figure 2–58).

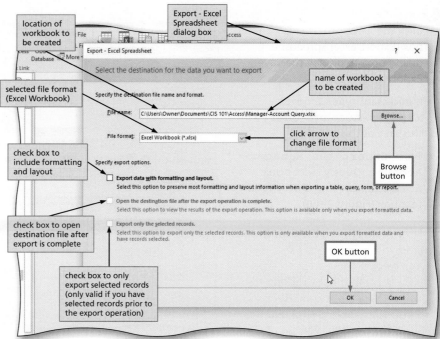

Figure 2–58

Q&A

Did I need to browse?
No. You could type the appropriate file location.

Could I change the name of the file?
You could change it. Simply replace the current file name with the one you want.

What if the file I want to export already exists?
Access will indicate that the file already exists and ask if you want to replace it. If you click the Yes button, the file you export will replace the old file. If you click the No button, you must either change the name of the export file or cancel the process.

- Click the OK button (Export-Excel Spreadsheet dialog box) to export the data (Figure 2–59).

Figure 2–59

3

- Click the 'Save export steps' check box (Export-Excel Spreadsheet dialog box) to display the Save Export Steps options.

- If necessary, type **Export-Manager-Account Query** in the Save as text box.

- Type **Export the Manager-Account Query without formatting** in the Description text box (Figure 2–60).

How could I re-use the export steps?

You can use these steps to export data in the future by clicking the Saved Exports button (External Data tab | Export group) and then selecting the steps you saved.

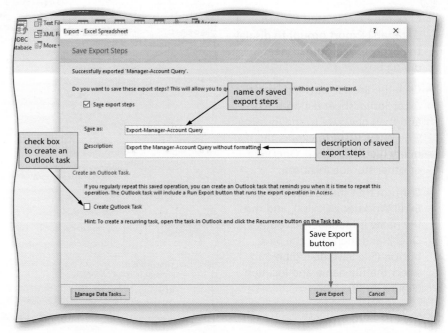

Figure 2–60

4

- Click the Save Export button (Export-Excel Spreadsheet dialog box) to save the export steps.

Other Ways
1. Right-click database object in Navigation Pane, click Export.

BTW

Saving Export Steps

Because query results are based on the data in the underlying tables, a change to an underlying table would result in a new query answer. For example, if the last name for account manager 35 changed from Simson to Smith, the change would be made in the Account Manager table. If you run the Manager-Account Query again and export the query using the saved export steps, the Excel workbook would show the changed name.

TO EXPORT DATA TO WORD

It is not possible to export data from Access to the standard Word format. It is possible, however, to export the data as a rich text format (RTF) file, which Word can use. To export data from a query or table to an RTF file, you would use the following steps.

1. With the query or table to be exported selected in the Navigation Pane, click the More button (External Data tab | Export group) and then click Word on the More menu to display the Export-RTF File dialog box.

2. Navigate to the location in which to save the file and assign a file name.

3. Click the Save button, and then click the OK button to export the data.

4. Save the export steps if you want, or simply click the Close button in the Export-RTF File dialog box to close the dialog box without saving the export steps.

Text Files

You can also export Access data to text files, which can be used for a variety of purposes. Text files contain unformatted characters, including alphanumeric characters, and some special characters, such as tabs, carriage returns, and line feeds.

In **delimited files**, each record is on a separate line and the fields are separated by a special character, called the **delimiter**. Common delimiters are tabs, semicolons, commas, and spaces. You can also choose any other value that does not appear within the field contents as the delimiter. The comma-separated values (CSV) file often used in Excel is an example of a delimited file.

In **fixed-width files**, the width of any field is the same on every record. For example, if the width of the first field on the first record is 12 characters, the width of the first field on every other record must also be 12 characters.

TO EXPORT DATA TO A TEXT FILE

When exporting data to a text file, you can choose to export the data with formatting and layout. This option preserves much of the formatting and layout in tables, queries, forms, and reports. For forms and reports, this is the only option for exporting to a text file.

If you do not need to preserve the formatting, you can choose either delimited or fixed-width as the format for the exported file. The most common option, especially if formatting is not an issue, is delimited. You can choose the delimiter. You can also choose whether to include field names on the first row. In many cases, delimiting with a comma and including the field names is a good choice.

To export data from a table or query to a comma-delimited file in which the first row contains the column headings, you would use the following steps.

1. With the query or table to be exported selected in the Navigation Pane, click the Text File button (External Data tab | Export group) to display the Export-Text File dialog box.
2. Select the name and location for the file to be created.
3. If you need to preserve formatting and layout, be sure the 'Export data with formatting and layout' check box is checked. If you do not need to preserve formatting and layout, make sure the check box is not checked. Once you have made your selection, click the OK button in the Export-Text File dialog box.
4. To create a delimited file, be sure the Delimited option button is selected in the Export Text Wizard dialog box. To create a fixed-width file, be sure the Fixed Width option button is selected. Once you have made your selection, click the Next button.
5. a. If you are exporting to a delimited file, choose the delimiter that you want to separate your fields, such as a comma. Decide whether to include field names on the first row and, if so, click the 'Include Field Names on First Row' check box. If you want to select a text qualifier, select it in the Text Qualifier list. When you have made your selections, click the Next button.
   b. If you are exporting to a fixed-width file, review the position of the vertical lines that separate your fields. If any lines are not positioned correctly, follow the directions on the screen to reposition them. When you have finished, click the Next button.
6. Click the Finish button to export the data.
7. Save the export steps if you want, or simply click the Close button in the Export-Text File dialog box to close the dialog box without saving the export steps.

Adding Criteria to a Join Query

Sometimes you will want to join tables, but you will not want to include all possible records. For example, you would like to create a report showing only those accounts whose amount paid is greater than $20,000.00. In this case, you would relate the tables and include fields just as you did before. You will also include criteria. To include only those accounts whose amount paid is more than $20,000.00, you will include >20000 as a criterion for the Amount Paid field.

BTW
Distributing a Document
Instead of printing and distributing a hard copy of a document, you can distribute the document electronically. Options include sending the document via email; posting it on cloud storage (such as OneDrive) and sharing the file with others; posting it on social media, a blog, or other website; and sharing a link associated with an online location of the document. You also can create and share a PDF or XPS image of the document, so that users can view the file in Acrobat Reader or XPS Viewer instead of in Access.

To Restrict the Records in a Join

The following steps modify the Manager-Account Query so that the results for PrattLast Associates include a criterion. *Why? PrattLast wants to include only those accounts whose amount paid is more than $20,000.00.*

1

- Open the Navigation Pane, if necessary, and then right-click the Manager-Account Query to produce a shortcut menu.

- Click Design View on the shortcut menu to open the Manager-Account Query in Design view.

- Close the Navigation Pane.

- Add the Amount Paid field to the query.

- Type **>20000** as the criterion for the Amount Paid field (Figure 2–61).

Figure 2–61

2

- Run the query (Figure 2–62).

3

- Close the query.

- When asked if you want to save your changes, click the No button.

Q&A
What would happen if I saved the changes?
The next time you used this query, you would only see accounts whose amount paid is more than $20,000.00.

Figure 2–62

BTW
Expression Builder
Access includes a tool to help you create complex expressions. If you click Build on the shortcut menu (see Figure 2–63), Access displays the Expression Builder dialog box, which includes an expression box, operator buttons, and expression elements. You can type parts of the expression directly and paste operator buttons and expression elements into the box. You also can use functions in expressions.

Calculations

If a special calculation is required for a query, you need to determine whether the calculation is an **individual record calculation** (for example, adding the values in two fields for one record) or a **group calculation** (for example, finding the total of the values in a particular field on all the records).

PrattLast Associates might want to know the total amount (amount paid and current due) for each account. This would seem to pose a problem because the Account table does not include a field for total amount. You can calculate it, however, because the total amount is equal to the amount paid plus the current due. A field that can be computed from other fields is called a **calculated field** or a **computed field** and is not usually included in the table. Including it introduces the possibility for errors in the table. If the value in the field does not happen to match the results of the calculation, the data is inconsistent. A calculated field is an individual record calculation because each calculation only involves fields in a single record.

PrattLast might also want to calculate the average amount paid for the accounts of each account manager. That is, they may want the average for accounts of account manager 31, the average for accounts of account manager 35, and so on. This type of calculation is called a **group calculation** because each calculation involves groups of records. In this example, the accounts of account manager 31 would form one group, the accounts of account manager 35 would be a second group, and the accounts of account manager 58 would form a third group.

To Use a Calculated Field in a Query

1 CREATE QUERIES | 2 USE CRITERIA | 3 SORT DATA | 4 JOIN TABLES | 5 EXPORT RESULTS
6 PERFORM CALCULATIONS | 7 CREATE CROSSTAB | 8 CUSTOMIZE NAVIGATION PANE

If you need a calculated field in a query, you enter a name, or alias, for the calculated field, a colon, and then the calculation in one of the columns in the Field row of the design grid for the query. Any fields included in the expression must be enclosed in square brackets ([ ]). For example, for the total amount, you will type Total Amount:[Amount Paid]+[Current Due] as the expression.

You can type the expression directly into the Field row in Design view. The preferred method, however, is to select the column in the Field row and then use the Zoom command on its shortcut menu. When Access displays the Zoom dialog box, you can enter the expression. *Why use the Zoom command? You will not be able to see the entire entry in the Field row, because the space available is not large enough.*

You can use addition (+), subtraction (-), multiplication (*), or division (/) in calculations. If you have multiple calculations in an expression, you can include parentheses to indicate which calculations should be done first.

The following steps create a query that PrattLast Associates might use to obtain financial information on its accounts, including the total amount (amount paid + current due), which is a calculated field.

1

- Create a query with a field list for the Account table.

- Add the Account Number, Account Name, Amount Paid, and Current Due fields to the query.

- Right-click the Field row in the first open column in the design grid to display a shortcut menu (Figure 2–63).

Figure 2–63

2

- Click Zoom on the shortcut menu to display the Zoom dialog box.

- Type **Total Amount:[Amount Paid]+[Current Due]** in the Zoom dialog box (Figure 2–64).

Q&A Do I always need to put square brackets around field names?
If the field name does not contain spaces, square brackets are technically not required. It is a good practice, however, to get in the habit of using the brackets in field calculations.

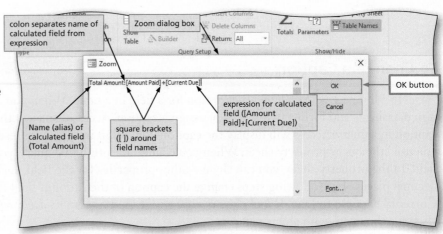

Figure 2–64

3

- Click the OK button (Zoom dialog box) to enter the expression (Figure 2–65).

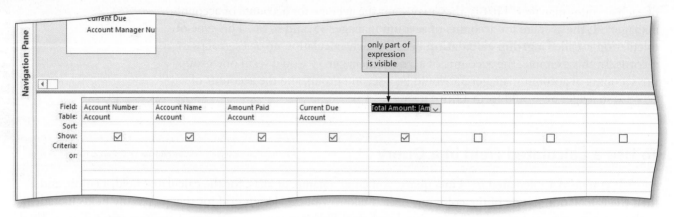

Figure 2–65

4

- Run the query (Figure 2–66).

Experiment

- Return to Design view and try other expressions. In at least one case, omit the Total Amount and the colon. In at least one case, intentionally misspell a field name. In each case, run the query to see the effect of your changes. When finished, reenter the original expression.

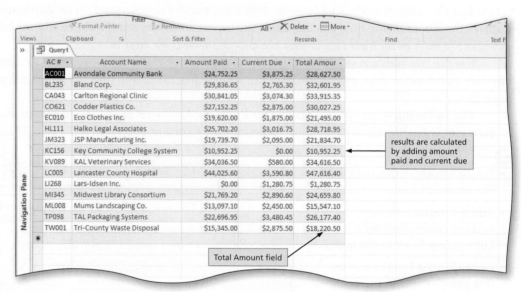

Figure 2–66

Other Ways

1. Press SHIFT+F2

To Change a Caption

1 CREATE QUERIES | 2 USE CRITERIA | 3 SORT DATA | 4 JOIN TABLES | 5 EXPORT RESULTS
6 PERFORM CALCULATIONS | 7 CREATE CROSSTAB | 8 CUSTOMIZE NAVIGATION PANE

In Module 1, you changed the caption for a field in a table. When you assigned a caption, Access displayed it in datasheets and forms. If you did not assign a caption, Access displayed the field name. You can also change a caption in a query. Access will display the caption you assign in the query results. When you omitted duplicates, you used the query property sheet. When you change a caption in a query, you use the property sheet for the field. In the property sheet, you can change other properties for the field, such as the format and number of decimal places. The following steps change the caption of the Amount Paid field to Paid and the caption of the Current Due field to Due. *Why? These changes give shorter, yet very readable, column headings for the fields.* The steps also save the query with a new name.

1

- Return to Design view.

- If necessary, click Design on the ribbon to display the Query Tools Design tab.

- Click the Amount Paid field in the design grid, and then click the Property Sheet button (Query Tools Design tab | Show/Hide group) to display the properties for the Amount Paid field.

- Click the Caption box, and then type **Paid** as the caption (Figure 2–67).

Q&A | My property sheet looks different. What should I do?
Close the property sheet and repeat this step.

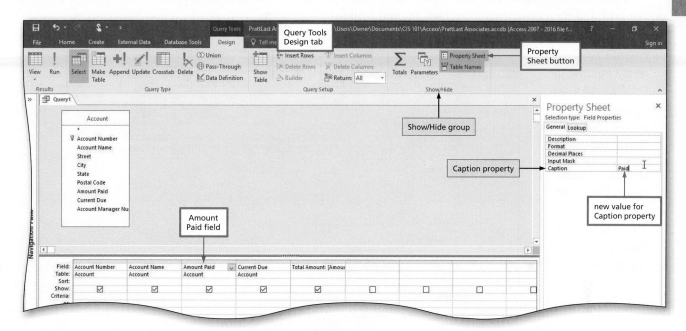

Figure 2–67

2

- Click the Current Due field in the design grid to view its properties in the Property Sheet.

- Click the Caption box, and then type **Due** as the caption.

- Close the Property Sheet by clicking the Property Sheet button a second time.

- Run the query (Figure 2–68).

3

- Save the query as m02q10.

- Close the query.

AC #	Account Name	Paid	Due	Total Amour
AC001	Avondale Community Bank	$24,752.25	$3,875.25	$28,627.50
BL235	Bland Corp.	$29,836.65	$2,765.30	$32,601.95
CA043	Carlton Regional Clinic	$30,841.05	$3,074.30	$33,915.35
CO621	Codder Plastics Co.	$27,152.25	$2,875.00	$30,027.25
EC010	Eco Clothes Inc.	$19,620.00	$1,875.00	$21,495.00
HL111	Halko Legal Associates	$25,702.20	$3,016.75	$28,718.95
JM323	JSP Manufacturing Inc.	$19,739.70	$2,095.00	$21,834.70
KC156	Key Community College System	$10,952.25	$0.00	$10,952.25
KV089	KAL Veterinary Services	$34,036.50	$580.00	$34,616.50
LC005	Lancaster County Hospital	$44,025.60	$3,590.80	$47,616.40
LI268	Lars-Idsen Inc.	$0.00	$1,280.75	$1,280.75
MI345	Midwest Library Consortium	$21,769.20	$2,890.60	$24,659.80
ML008	Mums Landscaping Co.	$13,097.10	$2,450.00	$15,547.10
TP098	TAL Packaging Systems	$22,696.95	$3,480.45	$26,177.40
TW001	Tri-County Waste Disposal	$15,345.00	$2,875.50	$18,220.50

Figure 2–68

Other Ways

1. Right-click field in design grid, click Properties on shortcut menu

To Calculate Statistics

For group calculations, Microsoft Access supports several built-in statistics: COUNT (count of the number of records), SUM (total), AVG (average), MAX (largest value), MIN (smallest value), STDEV (standard deviation), VAR (variance), FIRST (first value), and LAST (last value). These statistics are called aggregate functions. An **aggregate function** is a function that performs some mathematical function against a group of records. To use an aggregate function in a query, you include it in the Total row in the design grid. In order to do so, you must first include the Total row by clicking the Totals button on the Design tab. *Why? The Total row usually does not appear in the grid.*

The following steps create a new query for the Account table. The steps include the Total row in the design grid, and then calculate the average amount paid for all accounts.

❶

- Create a new query with a field list for the Account table.
- Click the Totals button (Query Tools Design tab | Show/Hide group) to include the Total row in the design grid.
- Add the Amount Paid field to the query (Figure 2–69).

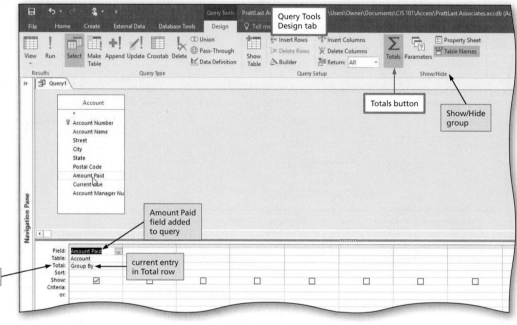

Figure 2–69

❷

- Click the Total row in the Amount Paid column to display the Total arrow.
- Click the Total arrow to display the Total list (Figure 2–70).

Figure 2–70

❸

- Click Avg to select the calculation that Access is to perform (Figure 2–71).

Figure 2–71

4

- Run the query (Figure 2–72).

  Experiment

- Return to Design view and try other aggregate functions. In each case, run the query to see the effect of your selection. When finished, select Avg once again.

Figure 2–72

To Use Criteria in Calculating Statistics

1 CREATE QUERIES | 2 USE CRITERIA | 3 SORT DATA | 4 JOIN TABLES | 5 EXPORT RESULTS
6 PERFORM CALCULATIONS | 7 CREATE CROSSTAB | 8 CUSTOMIZE NAVIGATION PANE

Why? Sometimes calculating statistics for all the records in the table is appropriate. In other cases, however, you will need to calculate the statistics for only those records that satisfy certain criteria. To enter a criterion in a field, first you select Where as the entry in the Total row for the field, and then enter the criterion in the Criteria row. Access uses the word, Where, to indicate that you will enter a criterion. The following steps use this technique to calculate the average amount paid for accounts of account manager 31. The steps also save the query with a new name.

1

- Return to Design view.

- Include the Account Manager Number field in the design grid.

- Click the Total row in the Account Manager Number column.

- Click the Total arrow in the Account Manager Number column to produce a Total list (Figure 2–73).

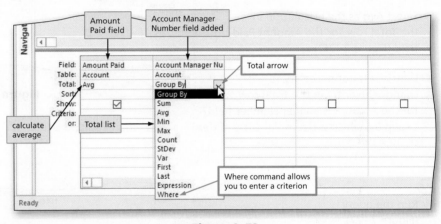

Figure 2–73

2

- Click Where to be able to enter a criterion.

- Type 31 as the criterion for the Account Manager Number field (Figure 2–74).

Figure 2–74

3

- Run the query (Figure 2–75).

4

- Save the query as m02q11.

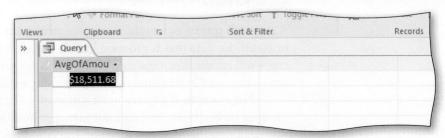

Figure 2–75

To Use Grouping

Why? *Statistics are often used in combination with grouping; that is, statistics are calculated for groups of records. For example, PrattLast could calculate the average amount paid for the accounts of each account manager, which would require the average for the accounts of account manager 31, account manager 35, and so on.* **Grouping** means creating groups of records that share some common characteristic. In grouping by Account Manager Number, for example, the accounts of account manager 31 would form one group, the accounts of account manager 35 would form a second, and the accounts of account manager 58 would form a third group. The calculations are then made for each group. To indicate grouping in Access, select Group By as the entry in the Total row for the field to be used for grouping.

The following steps create a query that calculates the average amount paid for the accounts of each account manager at PrattLast Associates. The steps also save the query with a new name.

①

- Return to Design view and clear the design grid.

- Include the Account Manager Number field in the query.

- Include the Amount Paid field in the query.

- Select Avg as the calculation in the Total row for the Amount Paid field (Figure 2–76).

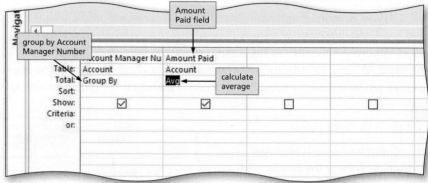

Q&A
Why was it not necessary to change the entry in the Total row for the Account Manager Number field?
Group By, which is the initial entry in the Total row when you add a field, is correct. Thus, you did not need to change the entry.

Figure 2–76

②

- Run the query (Figure 2–77).

③

- Save the query as m02q12.

- Close the query.

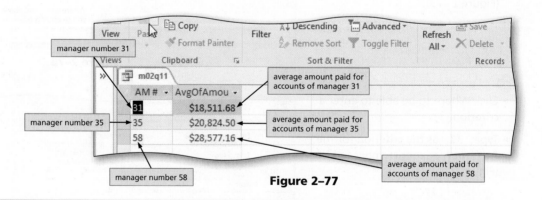

Figure 2–77

Crosstab Queries

A **crosstab query**, or simply, crosstab, calculates a statistic (for example, sum, average, or count) for data that is grouped by two different types of information. One of the types will appear down the side of the resulting datasheet, and the other will appear across the top. Crosstab queries are useful for summarizing data by category or group.

For example, if a query must summarize the sum of the current due amounts grouped by both state and account manager number, you could have states as the row headings, that is, down the side. You could have account manager numbers as the column headings, that is, across the top. The entries within the datasheet represent the total of the current due amounts. Figure 2–78 shows a crosstab in which the total of current due amounts is grouped by both state and account manager number, with states down the left side and account manager numbers across the top. For example, the entry in the row labeled IL and in the column labeled 31 represents the total of the current due amounts by all accounts of account manager 31 who are located in Illinois.

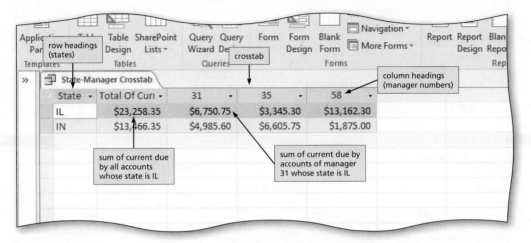

Figure 2–78

How do you know when to use a crosstab query?

If data is to be grouped by two different types of information, you can use a crosstab query. You will need to identify the two types of information. One of the types will form the row headings and the other will form the column headings in the query results.

To Create a Crosstab Query

1 CREATE QUERIES | 2 USE CRITERIA | 3 SORT DATA | 4 JOIN TABLES | 5 EXPORT RESULTS
6 PERFORM CALCULATIONS | 7 CREATE CROSSTAB | 8 CUSTOMIZE NAVIGATION PANE

The following steps use the Crosstab Query Wizard to create a crosstab query. *Why? PrattLast Associates wants to group data on current due amounts by two types of information: state and account manager.*

1

- Click Create on the ribbon to display the Create tab.

- Click the Query Wizard button (Create tab | Queries group) to display the New Query dialog box (Figure 2–79).

Figure 2–79

2

- Click Crosstab Query Wizard (New Query dialog box).

- Click the OK button to display the Crosstab Query Wizard dialog box (Figure 2–80).

Figure 2–80

3

- With the Tables option button selected, click Table: Account to select the Account table, and then click the Next button to display the next Crosstab Query Wizard screen.

- Click the State field, and then click the Add Field button to select the State field for row headings (Figure 2–81).

Figure 2–81

4

- Click the Next button to display the next Crosstab Query Wizard screen.

- Click the Account Manager Number field to select the field for column headings (Figure 2–82).

Figure 2–82

5

- Click the Next button to display the next Crosstab Query Wizard screen.

- Click the Current Due field to select the field for calculations.

🔎 **Experiment**

- Click other fields. For each field, examine the list of calculations that are available. When finished, click the Current Due field again.

- Click Sum to select the calculation to be performed (Figure 2–83).

Figure 2–83

Q&A My list of functions is different. What did I do wrong?

Either you clicked the wrong field, or the Current Due field has the wrong data type. For example, if you mistakenly assigned it the Short Text data type, you would not see Sum in the list of available calculations.

6

- Click the Next button to display the next Crosstab Query Wizard screen.

- Erase the text in the name text box and type **State-Manager Crosstab** as the name of the query (Figure 2–84).

7

- If requested to do so by your instructor, name the crosstab query as FirstName LastName Crosstab where FirstName and LastName are your first and last names.

- Click the Finish button to produce the crosstab shown in Figure 2–78.

- Close the query.

Figure 2–84

Customizing the Navigation Pane

Currently, the entries in the Navigation Pane are organized by object type. That is, all the tables are together, all the queries are together, and so on. You might want to change the way the information is organized. For example, you might want to have the Navigation Pane organized by table, with all the queries, forms, and reports associated with a particular table appearing after the name of the table. You can also use the Search bar to restrict the objects that appear to only those that have a certain collection of characters in their name. For example, if you entered the letters, Ma, only those objects containing Ma somewhere within the name will be included.

BTW

Access Help

At any time while using Access, you can find answers to questions and display information about various topics through Access Help. Used properly, this form of assistance can increase your productivity and reduce your frustrations by minimizing the time you spend learning how to use Access. For instructions about Access Help and exercises that will help you gain confidence in using it, read the Office and Windows module at the beginning of this book.

To Customize the Navigation Pane

The following steps change the organization of the Navigation Pane. They also use the Search bar to restrict the objects that appear. *Why? Using the Search bar, you can reduce the number of objects that appear in the Navigation Pane and just show the ones in which you are interested.*

1
- If necessary, click the 'Shutter Bar Open/ Close Button' to open the Navigation Pane.
- Click the Navigation Pane arrow to produce the Navigation Pane menu (Figure 2–85).

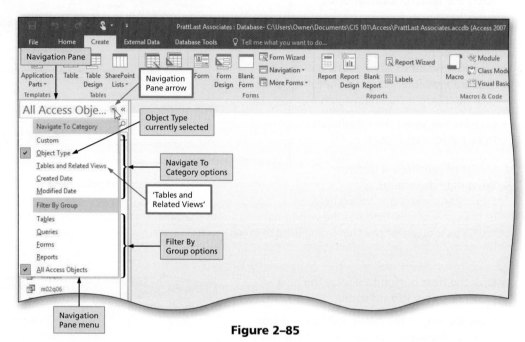

Figure 2–85

2
- Click 'Tables and Related Views' to organize the Navigation Pane by table rather than by the type of object (Figure 2–86).

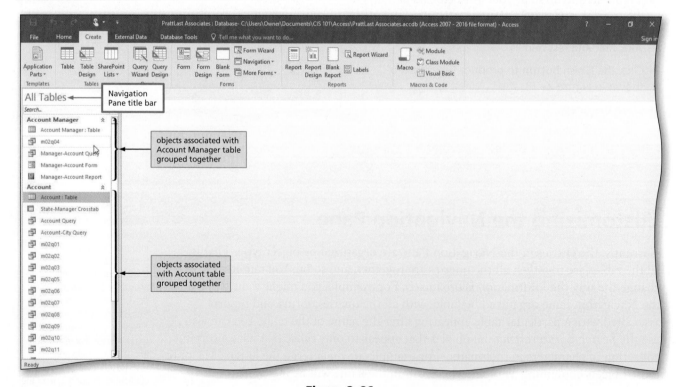

Figure 2–86

③

- Click the Navigation Pane arrow to produce the Navigation Pane menu.
- Click Object Type to once again organize the Navigation Pane by object type.

🔍 Experiment

- Select different Navigate To Category options to see the effect of the option. With each option you select, select different Filter By Group options to see the effect of the filtering. When you have finished experimenting, select the 'Object Type Navigate To Category' option and the 'All Access Objects Filter By Group' option.
- If the Search bar does not appear, right-click the Navigation Pane and click Search Bar on the shortcut menu.
- Click in the Search box to produce an insertion point.
- Type **Ma** as the search string to restrict the objects displayed to only those containing the desired string (Figure 2–87).

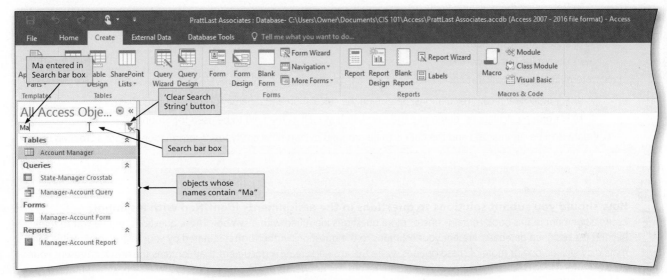

Figure 2–87

④

- Click the 'Clear Search String' button to remove the search string and redisplay all objects.

Q&A | Did I have to click the button to redisplay all objects? Could I simply have erased the current string to achieve the same result?
You did not have to click the button. You could have used the DELETE or BACKSPACE keys to erase the current search string.

- If desired, sign out of your Microsoft account.
- Exit Access.

Summary

In this module you have learned to create queries, enter fields, enter criteria, use text and numeric data in queries, use wildcards, use compound criteria, create parameter queries, sort data in queries, join tables in queries, perform calculations in queries, and create crosstab queries. You also learned to create a report and a form that used a query, to export a query, and to customize the Navigation Pane.

CONSIDER THIS

What decisions will you need to make when creating queries?

Use these guidelines as you complete the assignments in this module and create your own queries outside of this class.

1. Identify the fields by examining the question or request to determine which fields from the tables in the database are involved.

2. Identify restrictions or the conditions that records must satisfy to be included in the results.

3. Determine whether special order is required.

   a) Determine the sort key(s).

   b) If using two sort keys, determine the major and minor key.

   c) Determine sort order. If there are no words to imply a particular order, you would typically use Ascending.

   d) Determine restrictions, such as excluding duplicates.

4. Determine whether more than one table is required.

   a) Determine which tables to include.

   b) Determine the matching fields.

   c) Determine whether sorting is required.

   d) Determine restrictions.

   e) Determine join properties.

5. Determine whether calculations are required.

   a) For individual record calculations, determine the calculation and a name for the calculated field.

   b) For group calculations, determine the calculation as well as the field to be used for grouping.

6. If data is to be summarized and the data is to be grouped by two different types of information, create a crosstab query.

CONSIDER THIS

How should you submit solutions to questions in the assignments identified with a symbol?

Every assignment in this book contains one or more questions identified with a symbol. These questions require you to think beyond the assigned database. Present your solutions to the questions in the format required by your instructor. Possible formats may include one or more of these options: write the answer; create a document that contains the answer; present your answer to the class; discuss your answer in a group; record the answer as audio or video using a webcam, smartphone, or portable media player; or post answers on a blog, wiki, or website.

Apply Your Knowledge

Reinforce the skills and apply the concepts you learned in this module.

Using Wildcards in a Query, Creating a Parameter Query, Joining Tables, and Creating a Report

Instructions: Run Access. Open the Apply Friendly Janitorial Services database that you modified in Apply Your Knowledge in Module 1. (If you did not complete the exercise, see your instructor for a copy of the modified database.)

Perform the following tasks:

1. Create a query for the Client table and add the Client Number, Client Name, Amount Paid, and Current Due fields to the design grid. Add a criterion to find all clients whose names start with the letter B. Run the query and then save it as Apply 2 Step 1 Query.

2. Create a query for the Client table and add the Client Number, Client Name, Amount Paid, and Supervisor Number fields to the design grid. Sort the records in descending order by Amount Paid. Add a criterion for the Supervisor Number field that allows the user to enter a different supervisor each time the query is run. Run the query and enter 114 as the supervisor number to test the query. Save the query as Apply 2 Step 2 Query.

3. Create a query for the Client table and add the Client Number, Client Name, and Current Due fields to the design grid. Add a criterion to find all clients whose current due amount is less than $500.00. Run the query and then save it as Apply 2 Step 3 Query.

4. Create a query that joins the Supervisor and Client tables. Add the Supervisor Number, Last Name, and First Name fields from the Supervisor table and the Client Number and Client Name fields from the Client table to the design grid. Sort the records in ascending order by Client Number within Supervisor Number. Run the query and save it as Supervisor-Client Query.

5. Create the report shown in Figure 2–88. The report uses the Supervisor-Client Query.

Supervisor-Client Report

SU #	Last Name	First Name	CL #	Client Name
103	Estevez	Enrique	AT13	Atlas Repair
103	Estevez	Enrique	CP03	Calder Plastics
103	Estevez	Enrique	HC17	Hill Crafts
103	Estevez	Enrique	KD15	Klean n Dri
110	Hillsdale	Rachel	AZ01	AZ Auto
110	Hillsdale	Rachel	BB35	Babbage Bookkeeping
110	Hillsdale	Rachel	CJ45	C Joe Diner
110	Hillsdale	Rachel	HN23	Hurley National Bank
110	Hillsdale	Rachel	PL03	Prime Legal Associates
114	Liu	Chou	CC25	Cramden Co.
114	Liu	Chou	MM01	Moss Manufacturing
114	Liu	Chou	PS67	PRIM Staffing
120	Short	Chris	BL24	Blanton Shoes
120	Short	Chris	KC12	Kady Regional Clinic
120	Short	Chris	TE15	Telton-Edwards

Figure 2–88

6. If requested to do so by your instructor, rename the Supervisor-Client Report in the Navigation Pane as LastName-Client Report where LastName is your last name.

7. Submit the revised database in the format specified by your instructor.

8. ✳ What criteria would you enter in the Street field if you wanted to find all clients whose businesses were on Beard?

Extend Your Knowledge

Extend the skills you learned in this module and experiment with new skills. You may need to use Help to complete the assignment.

Creating Crosstab Queries Using Criteria and Exporting a Query

Note: To complete this assignment, you will be required to use the Data Files. Please contact your instructor for information about accessing the Data Files.

Continued >

Extend Your Knowledge *continued*

Instructions: Run Access. Open the Extend TAL Maintenance database, which is located in the Data Files. TAL Maintenance is a small business that provides various outdoor maintenance services, such as painting, lawn maintenance, and parking lot re-paving, to commercial customers. The owner has created an Access database in which to store information about the customers the company serves and team leaders working for the company. You will create the crosstab query shown in Figure 2–89. You will also query the database using specified criteria and export a query.

Perform the following tasks:

1. Create the crosstab query shown in Figure 2–89. The crosstab groups the total of customers' balance by city and team leader number.

2. Create a query to find all customers who are not located in Rock Hill. Include the Customer Number, Customer Name, and Balance fields in the query results. Save the query as Extend 2 Step 2 Query.

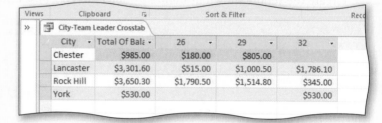

Figure 2–89

3. Create a query to find all team leaders whose first name is either Alex or Alix. Include the Team Leader Number, First Name, and Last Name in the query results. Save the query as Extend 2 Step 3 Query.

4. Create a query to find all customers where the team leader number is either 29 or 32 and the balance is greater than $550.00. Include the Customer Number, Customer Name, Balance, and Team Leader Number fields in the design grid in that order. Use the IN operator in your query design. Sort the results by customer number within team leader number. Save the query as Extend 2 Step 4 Query.

5. Export the City-Team Leader Crosstab as a Word file with the name City-Team Leader Crosstab.rtf and save the export steps.

6. Open the Customer table and change the balance for account C04 to $1,000.50.

7. If requested to do so by your instructor, change the customer name of customer K10 from Kathy's Books to Last Name Books where Last Name is your last name.

8. Use the saved export steps to export the City-Team Leader Crosstab again. When asked if you want to replace the existing file, click Yes.

9. Submit the revised database and the exported RTF file in the format specified by your instructor.

10. ✳ How would you create the query in Step 4 without using the IN operator?

Expand Your World

Create a solution, which uses cloud and web technologies, by learning and investigating on your own from general guidance.

Problem: You are taking a general science course and the instructor would like you to gather some weather statistics and query the statistics as part of the unit on climate change.

Instructions:
1. Examine a website that contains historical weather data, such as accuweather.com or weatherunderground.com. Select weather data for the city in which you were born for the month of January, 2014. If you cannot find your city, then select a large city near your current location.

2. Create a database that contains one table and has the following fields: Day of the month (1 through 31), Day of the week, high temperature for the day, and low temperature for the day. (*Hint:* Use the autonumber data type to record the day of the month.)

3. Create queries that do the following:
   a. Display the five days with the highest high temperature.
   b. Display the five days with lowest low temperature.
   c. Display the average high and low temperature for the entire month.
   d. Calculate the difference between the high and low temperatures for each day.
   e. Display the high and low temperatures for each day in both Fahrenheit and Celsius. (*Hint:* Use the Internet to find the conversion formula.)

4. Submit the revised database in the format specified by your instructor.

5. Use an Internet search engine to find the historical average high and low temperatures in January for your city.

6. ✺ Which websites did you use to gather data and search for the historical averages? How does the query result in Step 3c differ from the historical average?

In the Labs

Design, create, modify, and/or use a database following the guidelines, concepts, and skills presented in this module. Labs are listed in order of increasing difficulty. Labs 1 and 2, which increase in difficulty, require you to create solutions based on what you learned in the module; Lab 3 requires you to apply your creative thinking and problem solving skills to design and implement a solution.

Lab 1: Querying the Garden Naturally Database

Problem: The management of Garden Naturally has determined a number of questions it wants the database management system to answer. You must obtain the answers to these questions.

Note: Use the database modified in Lab 1 of Module 1 for this assignment, or see your instructor for information on accessing the required files.

Instructions: Perform the following tasks:
1. Run Access. Open the Lab 1 Garden Naturally database you modified in Module 1 and create a new query for the Customer table. Add the Customer Number, Customer Name, Amount Paid, Balance Due, and Sales Rep Number fields to the design grid, and restrict the query results to only those customers where the sales rep number is 29. Save the query as Lab 2-1 Step 1 Query.

2. Create a query for the Customer table that includes the Customer Number, Customer Name, and Balance Due fields for all customers located in Delaware (DE) with a balance due greater than $1,000.00. Save the query as Lab 2-1 Step 2 Query.

3. Create a query for the Customer table that includes the Customer Number, Customer Name, Address, City, and State fields for all customers located in cities that begin with Ch. Save the query as Lab 2-1 Step 3 Query.

Continued >

In the Labs *continued*

4. Create a query for the Customer table that lists all states in ascending order. Each state should appear only once. Save the query as Lab 2-1 Step 4 Query.

5. Create a query for the Customer table that allows the user to type the name of the desired city when the query is run. The query results should display the Customer Number, Customer Name, Balance Due, and Amount Paid fields in that order. Test the query by searching for those records where the customer is located in Quaker. Save the query as Lab 2-1 Step 5 Query.

6. Create a query for the Sales Rep table that includes the First Name, Last Name, and Start Date for all sales reps who started after June 1, 2015. Save the query as Lab 2-1 Step 6 Query.

7. Create a query that joins the Sales Rep and Customer tables. Include the Sales Rep Number, Last Name, and First Name from the Sales Rep table. Include the Customer Number, Customer Name, and Amount Paid from the Customer table. Sort the records in ascending order by sales rep's last name and then by customer name. All sales reps should appear in the result even if they currently have no customers. Save the query as Lab 2-1 Step 7 Query.

8. Open the Lab 2-1 Step 7 Query in Design view and remove the Sales Rep table from the query. Add the Balance Due field to the design grid. Calculate the total of the balance and amount paid amounts. Assign the alias Total Amount to the calculated field. Change the caption for the Amount Paid field to Paid and the caption for the Balance Due field to Owed. Save the query as Lab 2-1 Step 8 Query.

9. Create a query for the Customer table to display the total amount paid for sales rep 26. Save the query as Lab 2-1 Step 9 Query.

10. Create a query for the Customer table to display the average balance due for each sales rep. Save the query as Lab 2-1 Step 10 Query.

11. Create the crosstab query shown in Figure 2–90. The crosstab groups the average of customers' amount paid by state and sales rep number. Save the crosstab as State-Sales Rep Crosstab.

State	Total Of Am	26	29	32
DE	$1,431.38		$537.50	$2,325.25
NJ	$2,503.57	$2,352.61	$2,285.50	$3,325.45
PA	$1,717.10	$1,190.00	$1,572.50	$2,125.25

Figure 2–90

12. If requested to do so by your instructor, open the Lab 2-1 Step 1 query and change the caption for the Sales Rep Number field to your last name.

13. Submit the revised database in the format specified by your instructor.

14. ✷ How would you modify the query in Step 7 to include only sales reps that currently have customers?

Lab 2: Querying the Museum Gift Shop Database

Problem: The manager of the Museum gift shop has determined a number of questions she wants the database management system to answer. You must obtain answers to these questions.

Note: Use the database created in Lab 2 of Module 1 for this assignment or see your instructor for information on accessing the required files.

Instructions: Perform the following tasks:

1. Run Access. Open the Lab 2 Museum Gift Shop database and create a query for the Item table that includes all fields and all records in the Item table. Name the query Lab 2-2 Step 1 Query.

2. Create a query for the Item table that includes the Item Number, Description, Wholesale Cost, and Vendor Code fields for all records where the vendor code is AW. Save the query as Lab 2-2 Step 2 Query.

3. Create a query for the Item table that includes the Item Number and Description fields for all items where the description starts with G. Save the query as Lab 2-2 Step 3 Query.

4. Create a query for the Item table that includes the Item Number and Description for all items with a Wholesale Cost greater than $15.00. Save the query as Lab 2-2 Step 4 Query.

5. Create a query for the Item table that includes the Item Number, Description, and Wholesale Cost fields for all items with a Wholesale Cost between $5.00 and $10.00. Save the query as Lab 2-2 Step 5 Query.

6. Create a query for the Item table that includes the Item Number, Description, On Hand, and Wholesale Cost fields for all items where the number on hand is less than 5 and the wholesale cost is less than $15.00. Save the query as Lab 2-2 Step 6 Query.

7. Create a query for the Item table that includes the Item Number, Description, Wholesale Cost, and Vendor Code for all items that have a Wholesale Cost greater than $20.00 or a Supplier Code of SD. Save the query as Lab 2-2 Step 7 Query.

8. Create a query that joins the Vendor and the Item tables. Include the Vendor Code and Vendor Name from the Vendor table and the Item Number, Description, Wholesale Cost, and Retail Price fields from the Item table. Sort the query in ascending order by Description within Vendor Code. Save the query as Vendor-Item Query.

9. Create a form for the Vendor-Item Query. Save the form as Vendor-Item Form.

10. If requested to do so by your instructor, rename the form in the Navigation Pane as LastName-Item Form where LastName is your last name.

11. Create the report shown in Figure 2–91. The report uses the Vendor-Item Query but does not use all the fields in the query.

Vendor-Item Report

Vendor Name	Description	Wholesale	Retail
Atherton Wholesalers	Amazing Science Fun	$13.50	$24.99
Atherton Wholesalers	Crystal Growing Kit	$6.75	$12.97
Atherton Wholesalers	Discovery Dinosaurs	$12.35	$19.95
Atherton Wholesalers	Gem Nature Guide	$9.50	$14.95
Atherton Wholesalers	Onyx Jar	$7.50	$13.97
Gift Specialties	Agate Bookends	$16.25	$27.97
Gift Specialties	Dinosaur Egg Ornament	$7.50	$14.99
Gift Specialties	Fibonacci Necklace	$16.75	$29.99
Gift Specialties	Gyrobot	$27.99	$49.99
Gift Specialties	Molecule Necklace	$16.25	$29.95
Smith Distributors	Cosmos Uncovered	$8.95	$15.00
Smith Distributors	Fun with Math	$12.95	$24.95
Smith Distributors	Geek Toys Guide	$5.10	$9.99
Smith Distributors	Paper Planes	$7.10	$13.99
Smith Distributors	Slime Time	$15.35	$24.99

Figure 2–91

Continued >

12. Create a query for the Item table that includes the Item Number, Description, Wholesale Cost, and Retail Price. Calculate the difference between Retail Price and Wholesale Cost (Retail Price – Wholesale Cost). Assign the alias Mark Up to the calculated field. Save the query as Lab 2-2 Step 12 Query.

13. Create a query for the Item table that displays the average Wholesale Cost and the average Retail Price of all items. Save the query as Lab 2-2 Step 13 Query.

14. Create a query for the Item table that displays the Item Number, Description, On Hand, and Retail Price for the 5 items with the lowest retail price. Save the query as Lab 2-2 Step 14 Query.

15. Submit the revised database in the format specified by your instructor.

16. ✸ How could you modify the query in step 2 to find all vendors where the vendor code is AW or GS? If there is more than one way to perform this query, list all ways.

Lab 3: **Consider This: Your Turn**

Querying the Camshay Marketing Database

Instructions: Open the Lab 3 Camshay Marketing database you created in Module 1. If you did not create this database, contact your instructor for information about accessing the required files.

Part 1:   Use the concepts and techniques presented in this module to create queries for the following. Save each query.
   a.   Find all marketing analysts who started between June 1, 2015 and September 30, 2015. Show the marketing analyst's first name, last name, salary YTD, and incentive YTD.
   b.   Find the client name and street address of all clients located in a city that starts with Bu.
   c.   Find the client number, client name, amount paid and current due of all clients whose amount paid is $0.00 or whose current due is $0.00.
   d.   Find the client number, client name, amount paid, current due, and total amount for all clients located in North Carolina (NC).
   e.   Create a parameter query for the Client table that will allow the user to enter a different city each time the query is run. The user should see all fields in the query result.
   f.   Create a crosstab query that groups the amount paid total by city and marketing analyst.
   g.   Find the marketing analyst for each client. List the marketing analyst number, first name, last name, client number, client name, and current due. Sort the results by client number within marketing analyst number.
   h.   Open the query you created in Step g above and restrict retrieval to only those clients whose current due amount is greater than $5,000.00.
   i.   Change the organization of the Navigation Pane so that all objects associated with the Client table are grouped together and all objects associated with the Marketing Analyst are grouped together.

Submit your assignment in the format specified by your instructor.

Part 2:   You made several decisions while creating the queries in this assignment, including the parameter query in Step e. What was the rationale behind your decisions? There are two ways to create the query in step e. What are they? Which one did you use?

Index

3-D pie chart, EX 35–36
@ symbol (Format box), AC 32

A

Access, **OFF 8**, **OFF 59**,
    OFF 59–60, AC 1
  to applications, exporting data,
    AC 97–101
  AutoCorrect feature of, AC 20
  closing database without exiting,
    AC 49
  creating databases, OFF 61–62
  data types, AC 7
  exiting, AC 50
  Help, AC 50, AC 111
  importing/linking data from,
    AC 27–33
  running, OFF 59–60
  screen resolution, AC 6, AC 69
  unique elements in, OFF 60–63
  window, AC 5–6
Access work area, **OFF 60**, **AC 6**
  and Navigation Pane, AC 6
account, signing in, OFF 6–7
account manager in library,
    finding, AC 3
Account table, AC 31
'Accounting Number Format'
    button, EX 85
accounting number style, EX 85
  and currency style, EX 86
active cell, **OFF 57**
active tab, **OFF 16**
ad hoc relationships, AC 89
add-in, **PA-10**
additions (changes to documents),
    WD 43
address bar, **OFF 27**
Adjust to box, purpose, EX 105
Adobe Reader, OFF 23, EX 41,
    AC 24
aggregate function, **AC 106**
American Psychological
    Association (APA), **WD 58**
  appendix, WD 58
  documentation style, WD 58
AND criterion, **AC 80**
  compound criterion with,
    AC 80–81

AND operator, **AC 82**
animation emphasis effects, **PA-8**
app(s), **OFF 2**
  exiting Office, OFF 41–42,
    OFF 53, OFF 59, OFF 63
  Office Mix, PA-12
  running and using. *See* running
    apps
  switching between, OFF 30–31
Apply to All button *vs.* Apply
    button, PPT 99
area charts, EX 34
arithmetic operations, EX 66
asterisk (*), **AC 72**
augmented reality with Office Mix,
    teaching, PA-13
'Auto Fill Options' button, EX 15
AutoCalculate area, **EX 43**,
    EX 43–45
  to determine maximum total,
    EX 44–45
  Status Bar commands, EX 43
AutoCorrect dialog box,
    WD 77–78
AutoCorrect entry, creating,
    WD 75–76
AutoCorrect feature, **WD 74**,
    EX 7, EX 7–9
  of Access, AC 20
  options, AC 20
  types of corrections, EX 7
AutoCorrect Options button,
    WD 75
AutoIncrement fields, AC 7
automatic corrections, WD 77
automatic page breaks, **WD 91**,
    WD 91–94
automatic recalculation, EX 66
automatic spelling correction,
    WD 8, PPT 17
automatically updated properties,
    WD 42, **PPT 44**, **EX 40**,
    AC 47
autonumber field, **AC 6**, AC 7
AVERAGE function, **EX 76**,
    EX 76–77

B

background color, EX 83
  to worksheet titles, EX 82–83
background repagination, **WD 91**
backgrounds, slide

formatting background picture fill
    transparency, PPT 88
  inserting picture to create,
    PPT 87–88
  in specific order, PPT 86
backing up, **AC 48**
  database, AC 49
BACKSPACE key
  clear cell entries using, EX 48
  error correction, OFF 21,
    WD 4
Backstage view, **OFF 22**
  closing, OFF 31
  closing Office using, OFF 52
  creating new documents from,
    OFF 50–51
  Info tab in, OFF 50
  opening recent files using,
    OFF 52–53
backup copy, **AC 48**
Berlin theme, PPT 4–5, PPT 9
best fit, **EX 91**
BETWEEN operator, **AC 82**
bevel effects, PPT 71
bibliographical list, **WD 96**
  creating, WD 96–97
bibliography, **WD 95**
  changing style, WD 78–79
  field to regular text, WD 100
  style, WD 78
  updating field, WD 99–100
black slide, **PPT 37**
blank line, inserting, WD 5–6
blank space between paragraph,
    OFF 21, WD 4
blinking bar, OFF 21
blue wavy underline (Word flags),
    WD 8
body copy, **WD 10**
body text in Word, WD 1
bold characters, **WD 27**
border, adding page, WD 39–40
box & whisker chart, EX 34
brightness (picture), **PPT 66**
bulleted list, **WD 21**, WD 21–22,
    PPT 13
  adding text slide with,
    PPT 12–13
  creating text slide with multilevel,
    PPT 13–19
  deleting bullets on slide, PPT 16
  presentation with pictures and,
    PPT 2–3

removing extra, PPT 17
bulleted paragraph, WD 12

C

calculated field, **AC 102**
  in query, AC 103–104
calculations for query, AC 102–108
  calculated field in, AC 103–104
  changing caption, AC 104–105
  grouping, AC 108
  statistics, AC 106–107
caption, **AC 8**, AC 9
  changing, AC 104–105
card, **PA-6**
cell(s), **OFF 56**
  applying body style to, EX 23–24
  clearing cell or range of,
    EX 47–48
  copying to adjacent cells in row,
    EX 14–15, EX 19
  correcting errors after entering
    data into, EX 45–46
  correcting errors while entering
    data into, EX 45
cell entries
  centering across columns,
    EX 26–27
  changing font color, EX 25–26
  clearing and formatting using
    Clear button, EX 48
  clearing using BACKSPACE key,
    EX 48
  clearing using fill handle, EX 47
  clearing using shortcut menu,
    EX 48
  increasing font size of, EX 24–25
  undoing last, EX 46–47
cell reference, **OFF 57**
cell reference C6, OFF 57
cell style, **EX 21**
  changing, EX 21–22
  formatting rows using, EX 27–29
Cell Styles button, clear formatting
    using, EX 48
centered (headline), **WD 13**
characters, WD 11, **EX 91**
  font change, WD 12
  increasing font size of, WD 12
  inserting special, PPT 71
  width, WD 12
characters formatting, **WD 11**
  bold text, WD 27–28

changing case of selected text,
    WD 17
font change of selected text,
    WD 16–17
font size of selected text,
    WD 15, WD 20–21
keyboard shortcuts, WD 71
  in presentation, PPT 9–12
selecting line, WD 14
selecting multiple lines, WD 20
single *vs.* multiple, WD 14–30
text effects to selected text,
    WD 18
underlined text, WD 27
undo and redo actions,
    WD 22–23
chart sheet, **EX 34**
charts, **OFF 53**, **EX 1**
  applying style to, EX 36–37
  column, EX 34
  creating, EX 49
  moving to new sheet, EX 38
  personal budget, EX 1–3
circular reference, **EX 65**
citations in Word, WD 78–82
  changing bibliography style, WD
    78–79
  editing, WD 88–89
  inserting placeholder,
    WD 83–84, WD 91
  inserting sources and,
    WD 79–81
  process for adding, WD 78
Clear button, clear cell entries and
    formatting using, EX 48
Click and Type feature, **WD 70**
clip, **PA-11**
color, **PPT 9**
color scheme, **WD 29**
color selection, EX 83
column chart, EX 34
column headings, **OFF 56**, **AC 27**
  modifying, AC 43–45
columns, worksheets
  adjusting width, EX 31–32
  cell style to column headings,
    EX 83
  changing width, EX 91–93
  hidden rows and, EX 91
  titles, entering, EX 7–8, EX 61
columns in datasheet, resizing,
    AC 23, AC 33, AC 43–45
combo chart, EX 34

Comma Style button, EX 85
command, **OFF 9**
compacting database, **AC 49**
comparison operator, **AC 79**
  in criterion, AC 79–80
compound criterion, **AC 80**
  with AND criterion, AC 80–81
  with OR criterion, AC 81–82
computed field, **AC 102**
conditional formatting, EX 87–90
  applying, EX 88–90
  operators, EX 91
'Connect to Internet' button,
    OFF 6
contents
  enabling, AC 21
  of tables, AC 24–26
contextual tabs, OFF 14
contrast (picture), **PPT 66**
copy area, **EX 13**
copying (Office Clipboard),
    WD 101, WD 102
Cortana, **OFF 74**, **PA-14**
  in Microsoft Edge, PA-14–16
Creative Commons license, **PA-7**
criteria/criterion
  adding to join query,
    AC 101–102
  in calculating statistics, AC 107
  compound, AC 80–82
  determining, AC 69
  for field, AC 74–75
  in query, AC 37–38, AC 82
  using comparison operator in,
    AC 79–80
  using number in, AC 78–79
  using text data in, AC 70–71
crosstab query, **AC 108**,
    AC 108–111
  creating, AC 109–111
  using, AC 109
currency (data type), **AC 7**
currency style format, EX 86
currency symbols, AC 7
custom dictionary, WD 107–111,
    PPT 97
  setting default, WD 108
  viewing/modifying entries in,
    WD 108
custom layout, **PPT 19**
cutting (Office Clipboard),
    WD 101
cylinder chart, EX 34

D

data, making changes to, AC 20–23
data series, **EX 35**
data type, **AC 7**
  for fields, AC 7–8, AC 54
database(s), **OFF 59**, **AC 1**, AC 4
  backing up, AC 49
  closing without exiting Access, AC 49
  compacting and repairing, AC 49
  creating Access, OFF 61–62
  creation, AC 1–5
  deleting table or object in, AC 50
  distributing database objects, AC 24
  objects, AC 34–47
  querying, AC 65–66
  renaming object in, AC 50
  requirements, AC 50–52
  saving, AC 50
  special operations, AC 48–50
  using template, creating, AC 5
database design, **AC 50**, AC 50–56
  data types to fields, AC 54
  determining additional fields, AC 53
  determining primary keys, AC 53
  identifying and removing redundancy, AC 54–56
  identifying tables, AC 52–53
  process, AC 52
  relationships between tables, AC 54
Database Design Language (DBDL), AC 53
database management system, **OFF 59**, **AC 1**
database properties, **AC 47**
  changing, AC 48
  purpose of, AC 47
datasheet, **AC 6**
  resizing columns in, AC 23, AC 33
Datasheet view, **AC 6**, **AC 8**
date formats, WD 69
dates and/or times (field's data type), **AC 7**
debugging process, **EX 102**
decimal places properties, AC 9
deck, **PPT 1**
'Decrease Font Size' button, EX 81

deletions (changes to documents), **WD 43**
delimited files, **AC 100**
delimiter, **AC 100**
demoting text, **PPT 15**
design grid, **AC 69**
  clearing, AC 83
Design view, **AC 8**
  changing field size in, AC 15–16
  checking structure in, AC 14–19
  creating queries in, AC 67–68
  creating table in, AC 31
  modifying table in, AC 31–32
  viewing table in, AC 14
desktop (Windows 10), OFF 7
destination area, **EX 13**
destination range, **EX 69**
dialog box(es)
  navigating in, **OFF 34**, OFF 34–37
  replacing, PPT 94–97
Dialog Box Launcher, **OFF 15**
direct circular reference, **EX 65**
Docs.com, Microsoft, **PA-8**
document(s)
  changing settings, WD 60–64
  choosing colors when creating, WD 29
  correcting errors and revising, WD 42–47
  distributing, WD 46, PPT 102, AC 47, AC 101
  electronic image of, OFF 24
  graphic file to use in, WD 31
  inserting blank line, WD 5–6
  inserting text in existing, WD 43–44
  method for distributing, OFF 23
  navigating, WD 10–11
  opening, WD 43
  overlapping windows *vs.* tabbed, AC 48
  printing, OFF 23–24, WD 45–46, WD 111
  saving, WD 42, WD 45–46, WD 111
  specify settings, WD 43
  text entry in, OFF 21
  types of changes, WD 43
  zooming, WD 33–34
document properties, **OFF 22**, **WD 42**, **PPT 44**, PPT 44–45, **EX 40**

  changing, OFF 22, WD 42, PPT 44–45, EX 40
  printing, WD 42, PPT 44, PPT102
  purpose, OFF 22, EX 40
document window, **OFF 12**
double-space, **WD 62**
download, **WD 31**
drag-and-drop editing, **WD 44**, WD 45, **PPT 39**
drawing canvas, **PA-3**
Drawing Tools Format tab, PPT 89

E

'Ease of access' button, OFF 6
Edit mode, **EX 45**
Edit the Rule Description area, EX 88
effect, picture, **PPT 89**
email, **OFF 64**
endnote, **WD 82**
  location, WD 89
  working with, WD 89–91
equal sign (=), **EX 65**
Error Checking button, EX 97
errors correction, EX 45–48
  BACKSPACE key, OFF 21, WD 4
  clearing cell or range of cells, EX 47–48
  clearing entire worksheet, EX 48
  in structure, AC 33
  undoing last cell entry, EX 46–47
  while entering data into cell, EX 45–46
Excel, **OFF 8**, **OFF 53**, OFF 53–56
  charts, OFF 53
  creating new documents from File Explorer, OFF 54–55
  entering worksheet titles, OFF 57–58
  exiting, OFF 59
  exporting data to, AC 98–100
  formula bar, **OFF 57**
  formulas, EX 66, EX 67
  Help, EX 34, EX 91
  option buttons in, EX 70
  ribbon, OFF 57
  running from File Explorer, OFF 55–56

saving files, OFF 58–59
screen resolution, EX 5
selecting cell in, EX 33
tables, OFF 54
unique features of, OFF 56–59
web support, OFF 54
workbook, **OFF 53**
worksheet functions, EX 60
worksheets, **OFF 53**, OFF 56–57
exploded pie chart, EX 37
exporting data, **AC 97**
  from Access to applications,
    AC 97–101
  to Excel, AC 98–100
  saving steps, AC 100
  to text file, AC 101
  to Word, AC 100
expression builder, AC 102

F

fields, **AC 3**
  adding to design grid, AC 69
  autonumber, AC 7
  changing size in Design view,
    AC 15–16
  data types for, AC 7–8, AC 54
  determining, AC 6–8, AC 53
  naming, AC 3, AC 6
  rearranging in queries, AC 82
  size, AC 8–9
  in tables, AC 11–12
file(s), **OFF 7**, OFF 23
  closing, OFF 62
  deleting, OFF 69
  moving, OFF 68–69
  naming, AC 8
  opening existing, OFF 63
  organizing, OFF 25, WD 10,
    WD 94, PPT 12, PPT 63,
    EX 19, EX 64, AC 5, AC 72
  renaming, OFF 68
  saving, OFF 31–34, OFF 49–52
  type, OFF 23, WD 13, PPT 14
File Explorer
  creating new documents from,
    OFF 54–55
  running apps from, OFF 55–56
  window, OFF 27
file management, **OFF 67**
file names, **OFF 23**
  saving existing files with same file
    name, OFF 58

saving with new file name,
    OFF 59
File tab, OFF 36
fill (background), **PPT 83–84**
fill handle, **EX 14**
  clear cell entries using, EX 47
  to copy cell to adjacent cells,
    EX 13–19
  to copy formulas, EX 69
  to copy functions, EX 77–78
Find and Replace dialog box,
    WD 105–107
'First Line Indent' marker, **WD 72**
first-line indent paragraph,
    WD 72, WD 72–74
Fit to option, EX 103–104
fixed formats, OFF 23, EX 41,
    AC 24
fixed-width files, **AC 101**
flags (Word), WD 8
Flash Fill, **EX 62**, EX 62–64
  entering row titles, EX 64
  sheet tab name and color,
    changing, EX 64
  using, EX 63
flyers
  creating, WD 47
  formats to use in, WD 12
  organizing text in, WD 10
  with pictures, WD 1–2
  positioning graphic on, WD 33
folder(s), **OFF 9**
  collapsing, OFF 29–30
  copying to OneDrive,
    OFF 42–43
  creating, OFF 26–28
  expanding, OFF 29–30
  within folders, creating, OFF 28
  OneNote, **OFF 67**
  organizing, OFF 25, WD 10,
    WD 94, PPT 12, PPT 63,
    EX 19, EX 64, AC 5, AC 72
  saving files, OFF 31–34,
    OFF 49–52
  scrolling through contents,
    OFF 29–30
folder windows, **OFF 27**,
    OFF 27–34
font, **WD 12**, **PPT 9**, **EX 21**
  change of characters, WD 12
  changing, PPT 78–79, EX 22–23
  and font styles, PPT 9–12
  of selected text, WD 16–17

selecting orange color, PPT 12
Font Color button, WD 24
Font Color gallery, EX 25
font colors, **EX 21**, EX 21–33
  of cell entry, EX 25–26
font size, **WD 12**, **EX 21**,
    EX 21–33
  of cell entry, EX 24–25
  of characters, WD 12
  increasing, PPT 10, PPT 18–19
  of selected text, WD 15,
    WD 20–21
Font Size arrow, WD 15
font styles, PPT 9–12, **EX 21**,
    EX 21–33
footer, **WD 64**, WD 66, **EX 98**
footnote, **WD 82**, WD 82–84
  entering text, WD 83
  inserting citation placeholder,
    WD 83–84
  inserting reference mark,
    WD 82–83
  location, WD 89
  working with, WD 89–91
Footnote Text style, WD 84–89
  modifying using shortcut menu,
    WD 84–86
Form view, **AC 39**
  Layout view and, AC 40
Format Cells dialog box, EX 86
Format Painter, PPT 80–83
formats, **WD 11**, **PPT 9**, **EX 19**,
    AC 9
  importing data in other, AC 27
  to use in flyer, WD 12
formatting mark, **WD 5**, WD 20
  displaying, WD 5
formatting worksheets, EX 19–33,
    EX 59–60, EX 64, EX 79–95
  adjusting column width,
    EX 31–32
  applying body style to cell,
    EX 23–24
  background color and border,
    EX 82–83
  cell style to column headings,
    EX 83
  center data in cells, EX 84
  changing cell style, EX 21–22
  changing column width,
    EX 91–93
  changing font, EX 22–23
  changing row height, EX 94–95

changing workbook theme,
EX 80
colors, EX 81
conditional formatting,
EX 87–91
dates, EX 84
Name box to select cell,
EX 32–33
numbers in, EX 29–31
percent style format, EX 87
steps to consider, EX 19
titles, EX 81
total rows, EX 83
using 'Accounting Number
Format' button, EX 85
using Comma Style button,
EX 85
using Format Cells dialog box,
EX 86
forms, **AC 39**, **AC 96**
creating, AC 39–40
for queries, AC 96–97
using, AC 41, AC 97
formula bar, **OFF 57**
appearance, EX 6
formulas, **EX 65**
copy using fill handle, EX 69
enter using Point mode,
EX 67–69
entering, EX 18, EX 65–69
Excel, EX 66, EX 67
troubling, EX 66
using keyboard, enter,
EX 65–66
values *vs.*, EX 102
verifying using Range Finder,
EX 78
version of worksheets,
EX 102–105
worksheets with, EX 58–60
free-response quiz, **PA-12**
Full Screen mode, **OFF 17**
functions, **EX 12**
AVERAGE function, **EX 76**,
EX 76–77
fill handle to copy, EX 77–78
MAX function, **EX 72**,
EX 72–73
MIN function, **EX 74**,
EX 74–75
PRODUCT function, **EX 65**
statistical, EX 72
worksheets with, EX 58–60

G

gallery, **OFF 14**
gesture, **OFF 3**
gradient fill, **PPT 84**, **PPT 86**
inserting, PPT 86–87
graphic (picture)
positioning on flyer, WD 33
resizing, WD 34–35
symbols, WD 33
using in document, WD 31
gray text box, deleting, PPT 66
green computing, **OFF 23**, **EX 41**,
AC 24
green wavy underline (Word flags),
WD 8
gridlines, **OFF 57**
group (ribbon), **OFF 14**
group calculation, **AC 102**,
AC 103
group of words, selecting, WD 26
grouping, **AC 108**

H

handouts, presentation, PPT 100
hanging indent, **WD 98**
Hanging Indent marker, **WD 98**
hard copy, **OFF 23**, **EX 41**
hard page break, **WD 95**
header, **WD 64**, **EX 97–98**
changing worksheet's, EX 98–100
closing, WD 68
creating, WD 64–68
inserting page number,
WD 66–67
switching to, WD 65
headline, **WD 10**
hiding cells, EX 92
histogram chart, EX 34
horizontal ruler, **WD 72**
Hub, **PA-14**

I

illustration, resizing, PPT 34–35
importing data, **AC 27**
from applications to Access,
AC 27–33
to existing table, AC 33
linking *vs.*, AC 27
in other formats, AC 27
in-cell editing, **EX 45**, EX 46

IN operator, **AC 82**
Increase Decimal button, EX 87
indirect circular reference, **EX 65**
individual record calculation,
AC 102
Info tab in Backstage view, OFF 50
initial cap, WD 17
ink, conserving, WD 46, WD 98,
PPT 47, PPT 102
Ink to Text button, **PA-3**
inked handwriting, **PA-3**
Inking toolbar, **PA-15**, PA-16
Insert Function dialog box,
EX 72–73
insert mode, **WD 44**, **EX 46**
Insert Picture dialog box, **PPT 28**
insertion point, OFF 21, WD 4
moving with keyboard, WD 11
italic text, **WD 23**, **PPT 10**

J

join line, AC 89, **AC 90**
join properties, **AC 92**
changing, AC 92–93
joining tables, **AC 89**, AC 89–95
creating queries in, AC 96
steps to, AC 90–92
type of, AC 89

K

keyboard shortcuts, **OFF 5**,
WD 71, WD 71–76
for formatting characters, WD 71
for formatting paragraphs,
WD 71
formatting text using, WD 71
keyboards
AVERAGE function using,
EX 76–77
entering formulas using, EX 18,
EX 65–66
moving insertion point with,
WD 11
KeyTips, **OFF 16**
keywords, **AC 47**

L

landscape orientation, **OFF 48**,
PPT 5, **EX 41**, **AC 24**

preview and print worksheet in, EX 41–43
worksheet's, EX 98–100
layout, slide, **PPT 19**
layout gallery, **PPT 19**
Layout Options button, WD 33
Layout view and Form view, AC 40
layouts, **OFF 48**
lecture in OneNote, recording, PA-4
left-aligned document, **WD 12**
left-aligned text, EX 9
Left Indent marker, **WD 72**
level, paragraph, **PPT 7**
line chart, EX 34
line spacing, **WD 62**
  changing, WD 62–63
line width, PPT 69, PPT 93
linking data, AC 27–33
list, **AC 27**
live database, **AC 48**
live preview, **OFF 14**
lock screen, **OFF 5**
look up information, WD 108–109

M

main dictionary, WD 107–111
major key, **AC 83**
manual page break, **WD 95**
margins, **EX 98**
  changing worksheet's, EX 98–100
MAX function, **EX 72**, EX 72–73
maximizing windows, **OFF 11**, OFF 11–12
menu, **OFF 9**
merging cells, **EX 26**
  centering cell entries across columns by, EX 26–27
metadata, **AC 47**
Microsoft Access 2016. See Access
Microsoft accounts
  area, OFF 16
  signing out of, OFF 37
Microsoft Clip Organizer, PPT 28
Microsoft Edge, PA-14
  annotating webpages, PA-15
  browsing web with, PA-14
  Inking with, PA-16
  locating information with Cortana, PA-14–15, PA-16
  online news with Reading view, PA-16

tools, PA-14
Microsoft Excel 2016. See Excel
Microsoft Office 365, **OFF 8**
Microsoft Office 2016, **OFF 7**
  apps. See Office apps
  Help window, OFF 70–74
  suites, OFF 8
Microsoft Office Online, **OFF 8**
Microsoft OneNote 2016. See OneNote 2016
Microsoft OneNote Mobile app, **PA-2**
Microsoft Outlook 2016. See Outlook
Microsoft PowerPoint 2016. See PowerPoint
Microsoft Publisher 2016. See Publisher
Microsoft Sway. See Sway
Microsoft Word 2016. See Word
MIN function, **EX 74**, EX 74–75
mini toolbar, **OFF 15**
  to format text, WD 25–26
  turning off, OFF 16
minimized window, **OFF 34**, OFF 34–35
minor key, **AC 83**
Modern Language Association of America (MLA), **WD 58**
  documentation style, WD 58–60
modifications (changes to documents), **WD 43**
Money in SQL Server, AC 7
mouse operations, OFF 4
multilevel bulleted list slide, **PPT 14**
  typing, PPT 15–17
multiple word names, AC 6

N

n. pag. entry (Pages text box), WD 80
Name box, **OFF 57**
  to select cell, EX 32–33
navigating a document, WD 10–11
navigating in dialog boxes, **OFF 34**, OFF 34–37
Navigation buttons, **AC 20**
Navigation Pane, **OFF 28**, WD 101, **AC 6**
  and Access work area, AC 6
  Backboard, PPT 64

customizing, AC 111–113
n.d. in first work, WD 97
nonadjacent items, selecting, WD 30
Normal style, **WD 3**, **WD 60**
Normal view, **PPT 26**
  moving to another slide in, PPT 26–27
note reference mark, **WD 82**
note text, **WD 82**
notebook, OneNote, **OFF 67**
notes pages, **PPT 95**
  adding notes, PPT 95–96
  print speaker, PPT 101–102
Notes pane, **PPT 26**, **PPT 95**
  formatting text, PPT 97
Number fields, **AC 7**
  field sizes for, AC 8
numbers, **EX 9**
  AVERAGE function, EX 76–77
  in criterion, AC 78–79
  entering, EX 9–11, EX 60–62
  formatting in worksheet, EX 29–31
  MAX function, EX 72–73
  MIN function, EX 74–75
  in range, EX 65
  right-aligned, EX 11
  summing column of, EX 12–13

O

object tabs, **OFF 60**, **AC 6**
Office apps, OFF 7–8, OFF 45–63
  exiting, OFF 41–42, OFF 53, OFF 59, OFF 63
  Help in, OFF 73–74
  opening Help window, OFF 70
Office Clipboard, **WD 101**
Office Help
  opening window, OFF 70
  using Search text box, OFF 72–73
  using Tell Me box, OFF 74
  while working in apps, OFF 73–74
Office Mix, PA-10
  adding to PowerPoint, PA-10
  capturing video clips, PA-11
  inserting quizzes, live webpages, and apps, PA-12
  marketing travel destination with, PA-13

sharing presentation, PA-12
teaching augmented reality with,
	PA-13
tutorial for OneNote, PA-13
offset, **PPT 84**
on-screen keyboard, OFF 7
one-to-many relationship, **AC 54**
OneDrive, **OFF 8**
 account, unlinking, OFF 44–45
 copying folder to, OFF 42–43
 saving on, OFF 32, OFF 35–36
OneNote 2016, **OFF 8**, **OFF 66**,
	OFF 66–67
 career planning, PA-5
 converting handwriting to text,
	PA-3–4
 creating notebook, PA-2
 Office Mix tutorial for, PA-13
 organizing research paper, PA-5
 recording lecture, PA-4
 syncing notebook to cloud,
	PA-2–3
 taking notes, PA-3, PA-5
 window, OFF 67
online Sway newsletter, creating,
	PA-9
online theme, downloading,
	PPT 59–60
operating system (OS), **OFF 2**
option buttons, EX 70–71
 in Excel, EX 70
 importance of, EX 70
OR criterion, **AC 80**
 compound criterion with,
	AC 81–82
order of operations, **EX 66**,
	EX 66–69
 arithmetic operations, EX 66
 Excel formulas, EX 66, EX 67
orphan (paragraph), **WD 91**
Outlook, **OFF 8**, **OFF 64**
 window, OFF 64–65
Overtype mode, **EX 46**

P

page(s)
 adding border, WD 39–40
 centering page contents, WD
	41–42
 changing paragraph spacing,
	WD 40–41
 enhancing, WD 38–42

OneNote, **OFF 67**
 using Navigation Pane, WD 101
 width, zooming, WD 6–7,
	WD 30
 zooming multiple, WD 109–110
 zooming single, WD 28, WD 40
page break
 locations, WD 91
 manual, WD 95
Page Layout view
 changing worksheet, EX 98–100
 features of, EX 98
paragraph spacing, **WD 62**
paragraphs, **PPT 7**
 blank space between, OFF 21,
	WD 4
 entering presentation subtitle,
	PPT 7–8
 first-line indent, WD 72–74
 removing space after, WD 63–64
 to right-align, WD 66
 selecting, PPT 9
paragraphs formatting, **WD 11**
 alignment, WD 12
 bulleted list, WD 21–22
 centering, WD 13, WD 31
 change spacing, WD 40–41
 with hanging indent, WD 98
 italic text, WD 23
 keyboard shortcuts, WD 71
 selecting line, WD 14
 selecting multiple lines, WD 20
 shading, WD 19
 single *vs.* multiple, WD 14–30
 undo and redo actions,
	WD 22–23
parameter query, **AC 75**,
	AC 75–79
 creating and viewing, AC 76–77
 using, AC 77–78
parentheses, EX 67
 purpose of, EX 77
parenthetical references, **WD 58**
password, **OFF 5**
paste area, **EX 13**
Paste Options button, WD 45,
	WD 103, EX 70
pasting (Office Clipboard),
	WD 101, WD 102
path, **OFF 25**
pattern fill, **PPT 84**
PDF, report as, AC 47
percent style format, EX 87

picture(s)
 adding picture border,
	PPT 68–69
 applying effects, WD 37–38,
	PPT 70–71
 applying styles, WD 36–37,
	PPT 67–68
 changing, PPT 65–66
 correcting, PPT 66–67
 double-clicking to insert,
	PPT 29–30
 flyers with, WD 1–2
 inserting and formatting in Word,
	WD 31–38
 moving, PPT 35–36
 nonproportionally resizing,
	PPT 33–34
 picture border color, PPT 69–70
 presentation with, PPT 57–58
 presentation with bulleted list
	and, PPT 2–3
 proportionally resizing,
	PPT 32–33
 removing effects from, PPT 67
 resizing graphic, WD 34–35
 rotating, PPT 36–37
 wrapping text around, PPT 29
picture fill, **PPT 84**
Picture Tools Format tab, OFF 14,
	WD 40, PPT 34, PPT 68,
	PPT 70
pie chart, EX 34
 3-D, EX 35–36
 exploding, EX 37
 to worksheet, EX 33–37
pixels, **EX 91**
placeholders, **OFF 48**, **PPT 5**
 deleting text in, PPT 40–41
 inserting citation, WD 83–84,
	WD 91
 inserting picture into content,
	PPT 30–31
 inserting picture into slide
	without content, PPT 29,
	PPT 31, PPT 63–64
 selecting text, PPT 15
 selecting text before typing in,
	PPT 61
 white box with arrow, PPT 21
plagiarize, **WD 69**
Point mode, **EX 67**
 formulas using, EX 67–69
point size, **EX 21**

pointer (touch screen), OFF 4

points, **WD 12**, **PPT 9**, EX 21

portrait orientation, **EX 41**, **AC 24**

postal codes, AC 54

PowerPoint, **OFF 8**, OFF 46–48

adding to Office Mix, PA-10

closing using Backstage view, OFF 52

creating new documents from Backstage view, OFF 50–51

entering content in title slides, OFF 49, OFF 51

exiting, OFF 53

opening recent files using Backstage view, OFF 52–53

saving files in folders, OFF 49–50

window and ribbon, OFF 48–53

presentation (PowerPoint), **OFF 46**, **PPT 1**

adding new slide to, PPT 12–13

assigning document properties to, PPT 44

bulleted list and pictures, PPT 2–3

creating Sway, PA-6-7

entering presentation title, PPT 6

formatting characters in, PPT 9–12

handouts, PPT 100

help, PPT 45, PPT 99

inserting and formatting pictures, PPT 63–71

saving and printing, PPT 47, PPT 102

screen resolution, PPT 5, PPT 61

sharing Office Mix, PA-12

technology (Sway), PA-9

views, PPT 26–27

Welcome back, PPT 26

window, PPT 3, PPT 46

Previous Locations arrow, **OFF 27**

primary key, **AC 3**

determining, AC 6, AC 53

modifying, AC 10–11

primary sort key, **AC 83**

Print Layout view, **OFF 12**, **WD 3**

switching to, WD 46–47

Print Scaling option, EX 104–105

printers, changing, AC 24

printout, **OFF 23**, **EX 41**

PRODUCT function, **EX 65**

Product table, AC 50

promoting text, **PPT 15**

proofreading, **WD 98**

property sheet, **AC 85**

'Property Update Options' button, AC 16

publication types, **OFF 65**

Publisher, **OFF 8**, **OFF 65**

running, OFF 65

window, OFF 65–66

Q

queries, **AC 34**, **AC 65**

adding criteria to join, AC 101–102

calculations for. *See* calculations for query

creating, AC 34–36, AC 67–82

creating in joining tables, AC 96

creating parameter, AC 75–79

creating top-values query, **AC 88**

creation in sorting, AC 87

database, AC 65–66

in Design view, creating, AC 67–68

designing, AC 75

determining criteria, AC 69

form for, AC 96–97

printing results of, AC 38

rearranging fields in, AC 82

reports from, AC 94–95

running, AC 69–71

selecting, AC 67

Simple Query Wizard to create, AC 34–36

sorting data in, AC 83–84

special criteria in, AC 82

using, AC 36–38

using criterion, AC 37–38

using saved, AC 71–72

Query-By-Example (QBE), AC 80

question mark (?), **AC 72**

Quick Access area, **OFF 28**

Quick Access Toolbar, **OFF 16**

customizing, OFF 20–21

relocating, OFF 19–20

R

radar chart, EX 34

range, **EX 12**

selection, EX 70

Range Finder, **EX 78**

verifying formulas using, EX 78

Read mode, **WD 46**

changing color, WD 110–111

switching to, WD 46

readability statistics, WD 108

Reading view, **PA-14**

viewing online news with, PA-16

records, **AC 2**

to tables, AC 17–22

recover, **AC 48**

Recycle Bin, **OFF 7**

red wavy underline (Word flags), WD 8

redo actions, WD 22–23

Redo button, EX 47

redundancy, **AC 54**

eliminating, AC 55–56

problems, AC 55

Refresh button, **OFF 27**

relational database, **AC 2**

relative cell references, **EX 14**, **EX 69**

Replace All button, WD 105

reports

adding totals to, AC 46

creating, AC 41–43

creating from query, AC 94–95

exporting, AC 47

modifying column headings, AC 43–45

navigation, AC 43

printing, AC 41–43, AC 47, AC 95

resizing columns, AC 43–45

using Layout view in, AC 43–47

research paper, **WD 57**, WD 57–58

AutoCorrect dialog box, WD 77–78

automatic page breaks, WD 91–94

citations, WD 78–82

creating, WD 111

entering name and course information, WD 69

first draft of, WD 68–69

Footnote Text style, WD 84–89

footnotes, WD 82–84

keyboard shortcuts, WD 71–76

proofreading and revising, WD 98–111

typing text of, WD 68–94

working with footnotes and endnotes, WD 89–91

Reset Picture button, WD 38

resizing graphic (picture), **WD 34**, WD 34–35, **PPT 32**
  columns in datasheet, AC 23, AC 33
  illustration, PPT 34–35
  nonproportionally, PPT 33–34
  photos and illustrations, PPT 32–37
  proportionally, PPT 32–33
  shapes, PPT 73–74
responsive design, **PA-6**
Restart command, OFF 6
restoring windows, OFF 34–35
ribbon, OFF 12–15, **OFF 28**
  Access, OFF 61
  collapsing and expanding, OFF 17–19
  customizing, OFF 57
  displaying tabs, OFF 16–17
  Excel, OFF 57
  formatting worksheets, EX 85
  in PowerPoint, OFF 48
  and screen resolution, WD 14, WD 64, PPT 13, PPT 62, EX 7, EX 62, AC 14, AC 71
right-aligned numbers, EX 11
right-aligned paragraph, **WD 66**
rotation handle, **WD 36**, **PPT 36**
row heading, **OFF 56**
row selector, **AC 15**
rows, worksheets
  changing height, EX 94–95
  copying cell to adjacent cells in, EX 14–15, EX 19
  entering titles, EX 9, EX 64
  formatting using cell style, EX 27–29
  hidden columns and, EX 91
ruler, **WD 72**
  displaying, WD 72
running apps, OFF 9–21
  Access, OFF 59–60
  from File Explorer, OFF 55–56
  using Search box, OFF 47–48
  using Start menu, OFF 9–11
running query, **AC 36**

S

salary data in Excel, EX 62
sandbox, **PA-15**
save copy, **AC 48**
saving files

existing files with same file name, OFF 58
  in folders, OFF 31–34, OFF 49–52
  naming, OFF 32
  with new file name, OFF 59
  on OneDrive, OFF 32, OFF 35–36
  purpose, OFF 34
scatter charts, EX 34
screen clipping, PA-15
screen recording, **PA-11**
screen resolution, **OFF 38**, OFF 38–45, EX 61
  Access, AC 6, AC 69
  changing, OFF 39–41
  Excel, EX 5
  ribbon and, WD 14, WD 64, PPT 13, PPT 62, EX 7, EX 62, AC 14, AC 71
ScreenTip, **OFF 14**
scroll, **WD 10**
scroll arrows, **OFF 4**, **PPT 26**
scroll bar, **OFF 4**, OFF 12, **PPT 26**
  to scroll vertically with mouse, WD 11
scroll boxes, **OFF 4**, **PPT 26**
search box, **OFF 27**
  running apps using, OFF 47–48
  Windows, OFF 74
Search text box, Office Help using, OFF 72–73
secondary sort key, **AC 83**
sections, OneNote, **OFF 67**
selected text
  changing case of, WD 17
  changing font of, WD 16–17
  changing font size of, WD 15, WD 20–21
  text effects to, WD 18
selecting cell, **EX 4**
  in Excel, EX 33
  using Name box to, EX 32–33
  ways to, EX 33
selecting nonadjacent text, PPT 40
selection handle (small circle), WD 20
selection rectangle, **WD 33**, **PPT 32**
shade text, **WD 19**
shapes
  adding, PPT 72–73

  adding other, PPT 74–75
  adding text to, PPT 78
  applying style, PPT 75–77, PPT 77
  changing WordArt, PPT 90–91
  copying and pasting, PPT 81–83
  deleting, PPT 77
  pointer change, PPT 73, PPT 80
  presentation with, PPT 57–58
  pressing SHIFT key, PPT
  resizing, PPT 73–74
  text in, PPT 79
sheet tab, **OFF 56**
sheet tab names
  changing, EX 37–40, EX 64
  maximum length for, EX 39
  moving chart to new sheet, EX 38
Short Text, **AC 7**
shortcut keys, WD 71–76
shortcut menu, **OFF 19**
  clear cell entries using, EX 48
  commands, displaying, OFF 39
  modifying Footnote Text style using, WD 84–86
  Status Bar commands, EX 43
Shut down command, OFF 6
sign-in screen, **OFF 5**
signature line, **WD 10**
signing out of Microsoft accounts, OFF 37
Simple Query Wizard, AC 34–36
size, **PPT 9**
sizing handles, **WD 33**, **PPT 32**
Sleep command, OFF 6
slide(s), **OFF 48**
  adding transition between, PPT 100
  black and white preview, PPT 101
  creating first text, PPT 62
  creating second text, PPT 63
  creating title, PPT 61–62
  deleting, PPT 60–61
  inserting number, PPT 99
  layout, customizing, PPT 19
  selecting consecutive, PPT 60
slide backgrounds
  formatting background picture fill transparency, PPT 88
  inserting picture to create, PPT 87–88
slide indicator, **PPT 26**
Slide Notes, **PA-11**

Slide pane, **PPT 26**
slide recording, **PA-11**
slide show, **OFF 46**, **PPT 1**
  ending with closing slide,
    PPT 37–39
  moving manually through slides
    in, PPT 46–47
Slide Show view, **PPT 45**
  'Start From Beginning' button,
    PPT 45–46
  starting, PPT 45–46
slide transition, **PPT 42**
Slides tab, **PPT 26**
  star appearing in, PPT 43
Smart Guides, PowerPoint,
    PPT 35, PPT 35–36
soft page breaks, **WD 91**
solid fill, **PPT 84**
solid state drive (SSD), OFF 23
sort key, **AC 83**
sort/sorting, **AC 83**, AC 83–88
  creation of query, AC 87
  data in query, AC 83–84
  on multiple keys, AC 86–87
  omitting duplicates, AC 85–86
source, citation
  editing, WD 86–88, WD 93–94
  inserting, WD 79–81
  modifying, WD 99
  requirements, WD 79
source area, **EX 13**
source range, **EX 69**
spacing after punctuation, WD 77
speaker notes, printing, PPT
    101–102
spelling and grammar check,
    WD 106–107, PPT 97–99
Spelling and Grammar Check icon,
    WD 4, WD 8–10
spelling checker, **EX 95**, EX 95–97
  considerations, EX 97
  purpose, EX 96
  on worksheet, EX 96–97
spelling errors, detecting, PPT 98
Spelling Pane buttons and actions,
    PPT 98
splitting cells, **EX 27**
square brackets, purpose, AC 76
standard properties, **WD 42**,
    PPT 44, **EX 40**, **AC 47**
Start button, **OFF 9**
'Start From Beginning' button,
    PPT 45–46

Start menu, **OFF 9**
  running apps using, OFF 9–11
starting Windows, OFF 5–7
statistical charts, EX 34
statistical functions, EX 72
statistics, calculations, AC 106–107
  using criterion in, AC 107
status bar, **OFF 12**, **AC 6**
Status Bar commands, EX 43
storage medium, OFF 23
Storyline, **PA-6**
style(s), **WD 36**, **WD 60**,
    WD 60–62, **PPT 9**
  applying, WD 96
  applying picture, WD 36–37
  formats, WD 60
  modifying, WD 61–62
  picture, **PPT 67**, PPT 67–68
  updating, WD 64
suite, **OFF 8**
Sum arrow, EX 13
Sum button
  determine totals using,
    EX 70–71
  MIN function using, EX 74–75
SUM function, **EX 12**
  calculating, EX 12–13
  calculating multiple totals,
    EX 16–17
  column of numbers, EX 12–13
  entries, EX 14
sunburst chart, EX 34
surface chart, EX 34
Sway
  adding content to build story,
    PA-7
  creating presentation, PA-6–7
  creating resume, PA-9
  designing, PA-8
  online newsletter, creating, PA-9
  presentation on technology, PA-9
  publishing, PA-8
  sharing, PA-8
Sway site, **PA-6**
syncing, **PA-2**
synonym, **WD 105**, **PPT 94**
  finding and inserting,
    WD 105–106, PPT 94–95
  locating for multiple words, PPT
    95
Synonyms submenu, PPT 95
systems analysis, AC 50

T

tab (ribbon), **OFF 14**
tab color, changing, EX 64
table(s), **OFF 54**
  Account, AC 31
  Account Manager, AC 9
  adding records to, AC 17–22
  closing, AC 16, AC 33
  creating, AC 8–24
  creating in Design view, AC 31
  deleting in database, AC 50
  determining, AC 6–8
  fields in, AC 11–12
  identifying, AC 52–53
  importing data to existing,
    AC 33
  make changes to structure,
    AC 12–14
  modifying, AC 31–32
  modifying in Design view,
    AC 31–32
  naming, AC 6
  previewing and printing contents
    of, AC 24–26
  relationships between, AC 54
  saving, AC 13
  viewing in Design view, AC 14
task pane, **OFF 15**
tax percentage, totals, EX 71
Tell Me box, **OFF 15**
  Office Help in, OFF 74
templates
  available, AC 5
  creating database using, AC 5
  online themes and, PPT 59
text, **OFF 57**, **EX 4**
  adding text to shape, PPT 78
  bold, WD 27–28, PPT 18
  box, OFF 6
  centering, WD 94
  changing color of, PPT 11–12
  coloring, WD 24
  copy text wordwraps, WD 7
  deleting, WD 44, PPT 40–41
  difficulties of reading, EX 7
  effects to selected text, WD 18
  field to regular, WD 100
  finding, WD 103–104
  finding and replacing, PPT 94,
    PPT 96–97
  formatting, PPT 79
  italicizing, WD 23
  layouts for, PPT 19

left-aligned, EX 9
mini toolbar to format,
    WD 25–26
moving, WD 44–45
organizing in flyer, WD 10
replacing, WD 104–105
selecting, WD 30
selecting nonadjacent, PPT 40
shadowing, PPT 80
in shape, PPT 79
typing, WD 4
underlined, **WD 27**
undo text formatting changes,
    PPT 84
using Format Painter to format,
    PPT 80–81
using keyboard shortcut to format,
    WD 71
wrapping, EX 61
text data, **AC 70**
in criterion, AC 70–71
text entry, WD 3–11, WD 66,
    EX 4–9
in documents, OFF 21
entering more, WD 9–10,
    WD 77–78, WD 81–82,
    WD 90–91, WD 94
text files, AC 100–101
exporting data to, AC 101
texture fill, **PPT 84**
formatting transparency, PPT 86
inserting, PPT 84–85
theme, **WD 12, PPT 3**
Berlin theme, PPT 4–5, PPT 9
change, PPT 23–24
changing colors, WD 29
choosing document, PPT 3–5
download online, PPT 59–60
previews of other, PPT 4
previews of slides in, PPT 60
theme formats, **EX 79**
changing workbook, EX 80
thesaurus, **WD 105, PPT 94**
tiling option, **PPT 84**
title bar, **OFF 11**
Title Only layout, PPT 21–22
Title Slide layout, **OFF 48, PPT 5**
adding new slide and entering,
    PPT 19–21
adding transition between, PPT
    42–44
arrange, PPT 39
choosing words for, PPT 6

creating, PPT 5–8, PPT 61–62
duplicating, PPT 38
entering, PPT 14, PPT 23
entering contents in, OFF 49,
    OFF 51
inserting picture into,
    PPT 28–29
replacing text in existing,
    PPT 40
toner, WD 46, WD 98
conserving, PPT 47, PPT 102
tool tabs, **OFF 14**
top-values query, **AC 88**
totals, determining
tax percentage, EX 71
using Sum button, EX 70–71
Touch Keyboard button, OFF 12
touch mode, OFF 15
touch screens, OFF 3–4
differences, WD 38, WD 82,
    PPT 7, PPT 62, EX 4, EX 60,
    AC 12, AC 69
finding synonym, PPT 95
gestures, **OFF 3**
maintaining Oval shape's
    proportion, PPT 75
pointer, OFF 4
using touch keyboard, WD 5,
    PPT 7
transition, adding, PPT 42–45
transparency, **PPT 84**
Transparency slider, **PPT 86**
treemap chart, EX 34
two-digit year value, EX 62
typing, correcting mistakes when,
    PPT 7

U

underlined text, **WD 27**
undo actions, WD 22–23
Undo button, EX 46–47
unique identifier, **AC 3**
user account, **OFF 5**
user icon, **OFF 5**, OFF6
user name, **OFF 5**

V

variants, **PPT 3**
changing, PPT 25
choosing document theme and,
    PPT 3–5

vertical ruler, **WD 72**
view, **PPT 26**
virus, **WD 31**

W

waterfall chart, EX 34
Web Note, **PA-15**
web support, Excel, **OFF 54**
weight, WordArt, **PPT 92**
white space, hiding, WD 92–93
widow (paragraph), **WD 91**
wildcards, **AC 72**, AC 72–75
criteria for field, AC 74–75
using, AC 72–74
windows, **OFF 11**
dragging to move, OFF 70–71
dragging to resize, OFF 71
maximizing, **OFF 11**,
    OFF 11–12
minimizing, OFF **34**,
    OFF 34–35
OneNote, OFF 67
Outlook, OFF 64–65
PowerPoint, OFF 48–53
Publisher, OFF 65–66
restoring, OFF 34–35
Word, WD 3
worksheet size and, OFF 56
Windows 10, **OFF 2**
desktop, OFF 7
keyboard shortcuts, OFF 5
overview, OFF 2
scrolling, OFF 4
search box, OFF 74
starting, OFF 5–7
touch screen and mouse,
    OFF 3–4
Word, **OFF 7**, OFF 9–12
body text in, WD 1
citations in, WD 78–82
exiting, WD 42, WD 111
exporting data to, AC 100
flags, WD 8
Help, WD 43, WD 78
running, WD 3, WD 43,
    WD 60
window, WD 3
WordArt, **PPT 88**
changing shape of, PPT 90–91
inserting, PPT 89
presentation with, PPT 57–58
WordArt fill, **PPT 89**

applying, PPT 91–92
WordArt outline, **PPT 89**
  changing color of, PPT 93–94
  changing weight of, PPT 92–93
words
  choosing for slide, PPT 6
  counting, WD 90–91
  selecting, PPT 11
  selecting group of, WD 26,
    PPT 17–18
wordwrap, **WD 7**
  text, WD 7
workbook, **OFF 53**
  changing theme formats, EX 80
  creating, EX 49
  distributing, EX 43, EX 97
  method for distributing, EX 41
works cited page, **WD 60**, **WD 95**
  creating alphabetical, WD 95–98
worksheet titles, OFF 57–58,
    EX 4–5
  background color to, EX 82–83
  entering, EX 5–6

and numbers, EX 60–62
worksheets, **OFF 53**, OFF 56–57
  adding pie chart to, EX 33–37
  changing Page Layout view,
    EX 98–100
  clearing entire, EX 48
  column titles, EX 61
  creating, EX 105
  Fit to option, EX 103–104
  formatting. *See* formatting
    worksheets
  formatting numbers in,
    EX 29–31
  with formulas and functions,
    EX 58–60
  formulas version of, EX 102–105
  function of Excel, EX 60
  importance of, EX 3
  importing Excel, AC 28–31
  personal budget, EX 1–3
  Print Scaling option,
    EX 104–105
  printing, EX 41–43, EX 100–102

salary data, EX 62
size and window, OFF 56
spelling check on, EX 96–97
subtitle, EX 61
wrapping text, EX 61

X

X Y (scatter) chart, EX 34
XPS file, report as, AC 47
XPS Viewer, EX 41, AC 24

Z

Zoom dialog box, WD 7
zooming, WD 7, **PPT 8**
  document, WD 33–34
  multiple pages, WD 109–110
  page width, WD 6–7
  screen to 100%, WD 35–36
  single page, WD 28, WD 40
  slide, PPT 8